PUBLICATION No. 159: PATTERSON SMITH REPRINT SERIES IN CRIMINOLOGY, LAW ENFORCEMENT, AND SOCIAL PROBLEMS

An Experiment in the

PREVENTION

of DELINQUENCY

The CAMBRIDGE-SOMERVILLE
YOUTH STUDY

by EDWIN POWERS and HELEN WITMER

with a Foreword by GORDON W. ALLPORT

MONTCLAIR, NEW JERSEY

PATTERSON SMITH

1972

First published 1951 by Columbia University Press
Copyright 1951 by Columbia University Press
Reprinted 1972, with permission, by
Patterson Smith Publishing Corporation
Montclair, New Jersey 07042

Library of Congress Cataloging in Publication Data

Powers, Edwin.
     An experiment in the prevention of delinquency.

     (Patterson Smith reprint series in criminology, law
enforcement, and social problems, publication no. 159)
     Reprint of the 1951 ed.
     Bibliography: p.
     1. Cambridge-Somerville Youth Study.   2. Juvenile
delinquency—Cambridge, Mass.   3. Juvenile delinquency—
Somerville, Mass.   I. Witmer, Helen Leland, joint author.
II. Title.   III. Title: Prevention of delinquency.

HV9106.C33P67 1972   364.36′3′097444   70-172573
ISBN 0-87585-159-2

An Experiment in the

PREVENTION OF DELINQUENCY

PATTERSON SMITH REPRINT SERIES IN
CRIMINOLOGY, LAW ENFORCEMENT, AND SOCIAL PROBLEMS

A listing of publications in the SERIES *will be found at rear of volume*

FOREWORD

THE ACTION-RESEARCH REPORTED IN THIS VOLUME HAMMERS AWAY at one of the resistant frontiers of social science. It formulates a program of crime prevention and boldly seeks to evaluate the success of this program in practice.

The origin of this audacious enterprise can be traced back twenty years to an important Foreword that Dr. Richard Clarke Cabot wrote to an important book. In it he assessed the dispiriting findings that the authors, Sheldon and Eleanor T. Glueck, presented in their study of *500 Criminal Careers*. Reformatories, they discovered, did not reform. Nor did any of the current methods for dealing with criminals seem to any appreciable degree to impede their antisocial course of conduct. Lines for delinquent careers, it turned out, are laid early in life, but the causative factors are so little understood that preventive and remedial social policies are largely ineffectual. Summing up the bleak evidence Dr. Cabot concluded that the problem is "too difficult for any wisdom yet existent."

But at the close of his Foreword he added a challenge. "Doubtless there are many persons," he wrote, "who believe they know the remedy so much needed for these men. I hope that the failures pointed out in this book will lead such persons to bring forward their remedies and to give us all the benefit of them." While he was writing this challenge he had in the back of his own mind a definite hunch concerning the remedy needed. Granted that genuine reformation of criminals is a rare phenomenon, he had none the less observed that in all cases known to him, "there has been at least one necessary condition: *that someone should come to know and to understand the man in so intimate and friendly a way that he comes to a better understanding of himself and to a truer comprehension of the world he lives in.*" The personal factor is the indispensable factor. Friendly understanding—implying an ingredient of love—is the basis of all therapy.

This affiliative relationship, of course, should be established early in life before bad habits and an antisocial outlook become too firmly rooted. A youngster, even in a dismal home and given to defensive and rebellious conduct, may conceivably be steered away from a delinquent career and toward useful citizenship if a devoted individual outside his own family gives him consistent emotional support, friendship, and timely guidance.

Such was Dr. Cabot's opinion based on long experience in medicine, teaching, and social service. But he knew it to be merely a hunch—an hypothesis needing verification. He was a scientist as well as a physician and moralist: he wished to put his ethical propositions to a test. The hardheaded empiricism of the Gluecks' study had impressed him. The pretensions of an important social agency —a reformatory—had been put to a test and found wanting. Why should not other social agencies, schools, meliorative programs of all sorts, be submitted to an equally rigorous test? In his presidential address to the National Conference of Social Work in 1931 he admonished professional social workers to take stock: "Measure, evaluate, estimate, appraise your results in some form," he urged, "in any terms that rest on something beyond faith, assertion, and illustrative cases." Too often an expensive social or educational service drifts along on the prestige of its sponsors. No one really knows whether the expenditure of money and effort is worth while.

Dr. Cabot's hypothesis that delinquency can be prevented by establishing a sustained friendly ego-ideal for boys in trouble, and his desire to test the hypothesis in a rigorous fashion, led him to establish the Cambridge-Somerville Youth Study whose history and findings are presented to the reader in this volume.

About the time of his retirement from teaching at Harvard (1934) the plan for the research took form in Dr. Cabot's mind. After considerable consultation with interested colleagues he drew the basic design for the experiment, engaged an initial staff of workers, and himself gave medical examinations to several hundred boys destined for inclusion in the Study. Likewise he made financial and legal provisions for the continuance of the investigation for a period of ten years. Before the program had come into full swing Dr. Cabot died, on May 7, 1939. Had he lived, the course of the experiment might have altered its form, and the outcome might have been different. Yet those who were entrusted with the project—both the staff and the members of the Ella Lyman Cabot Foundation which he established as a corporate board before his death—continued the plan essentially as he had conceived it.

THE RESEARCH DESIGN

The experimental design is simple and scientifically correct. Two groups of 325 boys each, carefully matched, were formed out of a much larger number of referrals. Each group had the same number of "problem boys" judged by teachers and by a team of experts to be "pre-delinquents." One group was to be let alone, thus serving as a "control" to the other, experimental or "treated" group. This latter group was to receive all the aid that a resourceful counselor, backed by the Study, the school, and community agencies, could possibly give.

It was immediately recognized that the "control" boys would not lack services similar in many respects to those given to the "treatment" boys. In a modern community it would not be possible to find a matched group of boys, many of them with known tendencies toward delinquency, who would be wholly neglected. Thus the C-group was only in a limited sense a control. At most it can be said that the boys in this group presumably lacked the special service given to the T-group: sustained, friendly counseling whether or not an acute problem was momentarily active.

The original plan called for a ten-year period of work with the T-boys, starting at as early an age as possible. (Actually the median age at the start of treatment was 10½ years.) Ideally each boy should have one and only one counselor throughout this entire period. At the conclusion of the ten-year treatment an evaluation of the conduct (and character) of the T-boys should be made in comparison with the conduct (and character) of their "twins," the C-boys.

Such a design is unexceptionable from the scientific point of view. If carried through with fidelity it should yield the answer Dr. Cabot sought. But, alas, strict fidelity to such an ambitious research design is impossible to achieve with shifting human material over a period of years, especially war years. Some shrinkage in cases, and some changes in staff, were of course anticipated. But what could not be foreseen was the disruption caused by World War II. Most of the counselors were of military age or else their skills were in demand by the Red Cross or other war services. The resulting turnover in personnel made it difficult indeed to test the essential hypothesis, viz., that the influence of skilled and directed friendship on the part of a continuously available counselor may succeed in preventing delinquency in boys. Technically stated, the independent variable in the experiment (whose force we wished to measure) was badly tampered with. Furthermore, many of the boys reached the age of 17 after only five or six years of treatment, and were swallowed up by the armed services or by war industries so that contact with them was lost. Thus the Study was forced to restrict its period of operation and to reduce the number of boys in the treatment group. No boy received more than eight years of treatment, the median period being about five years.

In view of these necessary deviations from the design I find it difficult to decide whether or not the hypothesis has received a fair test. I am inclined to believe that, although the results are not as definitive and conclusive as we should like, still the trends and indications that emerge are probably "in the right direction." If they cannot be accepted with finality, yet they are unquestionably instructive, in many respects a better guide to social policy and psychological theory in the field of delinquency than we have previously had.

THE TREATMENT METHOD

"To these boys," said Dr. Cabot, "we plan to give personal advice and guidance through the services of paid visitors, both men and women, who will come to know the boys intimately, to see them frequently, and to influence their conduct." The counselor's behavior constitutes the independent variable in the research.

Now a lively dispute runs through the pages of this volume, as indeed it did throughout the course of the Study. Is this conception of treatment to be equated with the practice and policy of modern social work? Most debaters of this issue say no. Directed friendship, as conceived by Dr. Cabot, and as applied in this research, differs in two essential respects from the accepted practice of social work. In the first place, it took the initiative in seeking out "clients." Neither the boy nor his parents asked for help. They were wooed and won to the Study, led into accepting its services. In the second place, the relationship was sustained whether or not there was an acute problem to be met or a specific service to render. No case was closed simply because its presenting problem, if indeed it had one, was "solved." To state the case as harshly as possible: the Study intruded itself into a home and school situation without invitation or a well-defined function to fulfill. It remained on the job as long as it found it convenient to do so, being guided more by the research needs than by the human needs. Yet in spite of this seeming impertinence, the fact is clearly established in this volume that in less than 10 percent of the cases did the workers fail to achieve a working basis with the boy and his family.

This factor of "intrusion" (seeking out the client) seems to me to be of little long-run consequence in the research or its evaluation; nor does it afford a significant difference between Youth Study services and social work services. For once good contact is established, human needs readily come to light. Ere long neither the boy nor his parents (nor indeed the worker) recalls who made the first overtures. If they do recall, they no longer care.

More central to the dispute is the issue of "friendship" versus the "human engineering" skills of professional social service. That the distinction existed, at least in some cases, is shown by the remarks made by certain boys after the treatment program had terminated. Speaking of his own counselors one boy remarked, "They weren't regular social workers—they were friendly." In the same vein another said, "It was like social work—only friendly."

It would be invidious to let the matter rest here. Not even the most professionally austere social worker would deny her clients the benefits of a friendly approach. Yet it is true, as Dr. Witmer points out in her chapters, that many professional workers would regard Dr. Cabot's conception of the treatment program as somewhat old-fashioned ("big brotherly"). The dispute grows warmer. Is big-brotherliness merely an old-fashioned, pre-professional conception of social service, or is it perchance an eternally valid formula lost to view in current fads of a human engineering? Dr.

Cabot has asked, "What is it that keeps any of us straight unless it is the contagion of the highest personalities whom we have known?" Can the contagion of personality ever be adequately replaced by the skill-applied-to-specific-need that is the ideal of much modern social work?

The research design hoped to find out the answer. Presumably the C-boys had the benefits of much ordinary social service, while the T-boys had the extra benefit of "sustained and directed friendship." The issue is of potential importance, not only for the interpretation of this specific research, but for the science of human relations generally. Suppose it should turn out that the Youth Study treatment program failed in its purposes, would the negative conclusion cast a shadow of suspicion over all social work designed to prevent delinquency? Social workers would, under such circumstances, be quick to say, "Not at all. You simply have not been using modern case-work techniques. Your failure does not involve us." Conversely, a report of success would not be taken as a victory of social work generally, but only for the method of directed friendship.

Though fascinating and theoretically important, this whole issue seems to grow increasingly irrelevant as I read the pages of the report. Unless I am greatly mistaken all counselors did to some degree employ approved techniques of case work—meeting specific needs, cooperating with other agencies. Furthermore, the majority of counselors did in fact have social work training; and, for the greater part of the treatment period, case-work supervision was available to all the counselors, a supervision with a definitely psychiatric slant. Much emphasis was placed on health, tutoring, camping—common practices in any child welfare agency. True, "group therapy" (reeducation of the gang) was not used to any appreciable degree; but neither is it yet a prevailing practice in social work agencies.

So, all in all, I am inclined to say that the findings do not enable us to choose between "directed friendship" and "case work." The two are inextricably blended in this program. There is, however, one bit of evidence that, so far as it goes, may indicate the superiority of the "friendly" over the "professional" approach. In Chapter XXX we read that the most successful single counselor (that is, the one having the largest percentage of cases judged by an independent evaluator to have benefited from the treatment) was a nurse without formal training in social work. She was the only counselor who retained virtually her entire case load throughout the whole term of the Study. Not only were her contacts with her cases (many of them tough ones) firm and enduring, but of the 19 counselors employed she most obviously carried through the Cabotian ideals of treatment. She was "motherly" in her approach— and like many mothers she was sometimes indulgent and sometimes authoritarian—but always she was outgoing and profoundly sincere in her relations with the boy and his family. She troubled herself not at all with alleged standards of "good" social work, and undoubtedly violated some of them—but most of her cases came through with flying colors. We must not overweight this bit of evidence; but neither should we disregard its possible significance. It may mean that a warm-hearted unprofessional approach—consistently maintained for a long period of time—will in fact accomplish more than a professional approach lacking equal warmth. Or it may mean that we are here dealing with a genius in human relationships—"heaven born and seldom seen"—whose native gifts are rare and not reducible to any formula.

THE INTERPLAY OF PERSONALITIES

The basic principles involved in building character are not known. If they were, it might have been possible to standardize the treatment program and therewith the variable whose effect the Study desired to measure. Actually, of course, there were 19 styles of approach—one for each counselor—and probably more because counselors in their perplexity varied their own procedures. The workers enjoyed wide freedom in their efforts to arouse in the boy a sense of socially sound values. The initial hypothesis was a broad one: that the impact of personality upon personality, guided by good will and maturity of judgment, would have beneficial results.

Although this hypothesis is certainly worth the testing, it is clear that, even if established, the bare statistics of success would not tell us *how* or *why* the change came about. The dynamics of the influence would have to be sought from an analysis of the case records—from a *post factum* reconstruction of the interplay of the two personalities at each stage of the relationship. To state the matter more technically: the hypothesis itself states a phenotypic relationship (merely that an undefined "impact" has a gross effect). To discover the how and why of the change, that is, the genotypic relationship, a deeper study of cause and effect would be needed. And this study would have to focus upon single cases because only in single cases can the factors producing the change be identified.

Diversity in the counselors was matched by diversity in the boys. Even when a counselor held his style of approach constant (or relatively so) boys perceived and responded to his efforts in sharply contrasting ways. Two Negro brothers, for example, were assigned to the same counselor who, of course, offered her friendship impartially to both lads. The responsiveness of one contrasts with the indifference of the other. At the termination of the treatment period, the first (now 18 years of age) said:

I had that roving spirit. I needed someone to keep me in harness. I was a problem child. I got expelled and suspended from school. I got fresh with the teachers. I ran away from home. I was going through that period they all do. I was restless and had to get rid of that extra energy. Then Miss A. came down. She was really quite a wonderful person. It was her job to lend a helping hand over the rough spots. She was an all around help. It was her pep talks that really did the most good. She talked about all kinds of things, but mostly to get an education—and how to keep life attractive and interesting. When a person is really interested in you and tries to help—it helps. When anything came up I could always go to Miss A. and get it straightened out. They also had a psychiatrist down there who could psychoanalyze you. He was really pretty good. He had a different way of talking to you so he could find out what was on your mind—things you didn't mean to tell him. Then he'd tell Miss A. and she'd talk it over with me and that's how they tried to solve my problems. There's a wall that has to be broken down. The whole purpose of the place to me was to get to the boys who were acting bad and show them that they did have good qualities. There's a certain amount of inferiority complex in them; they get to feeling sorry for themselves and get to act bad. You had to bring out the good in them instead of them hiding it.

The brother of this writer, aged 17, gave a more negative evaluation of the Study and of this same counselor's efforts:

She got me a job cleaning up the place on Washington Avenue—putting books away and stuff. I just did my job and left. She said she

wanted to train me to be some sort of a leader and a benefit to my race.
I don't know what she was supposed to do. She just sort of entertained
me. Nothing was very important to me. I wanted to be an engineer. So
she'd call me out of school and introduce me to some guy and say,
"Here, meet Jim, he wants to be an engineer." But nothing would ever
happen. For a while I kept thinking it would lead to something—but
it never did. Most of the time she came to see me. I had no choice. I
never did anything for her but apparently she likes going around doing
favors for people.

The same warmth that wins one lad repels his brother. The counselor to both these boys is the nurse whose array of successes is so
impressive. But even she failed to reach through to the cynical lad.[1]

Such subtleties of interaction between boy and counselor
should, and did, provide a separate subject for the Study's investigation. Many cause and effect relationships are depicted in the
pages of this volume, and in the final chapter Dr. Witmer does a
notable job in deriving certain generalizations (genotypic principles) from the massive records of individual cases. But the Study's
chief effort to throw light upon the dyadic relationships of counselor and boy is not yet ready for publication. It is planned to
issue a separate volume dealing with this basic problem.

One finding may be divulged in advance. The counselor and the
boy often have markedly different views of their relationship. The
worker may believe that the rapport between them is excellent, but
the boy's own story shows that such a judgment is sometimes merely
a pleasant delusion on the counselor's part. Conversely, a worker
may feel discouraged by his failure to "get at" the boy, and yet the
boy's report shows unsuspected receptivity. Effects are sometimes
obtained when least expected. Some boys respond well to the psychiatric services offered by the Study; others do not. One lad said,
"I was burning inside; but most of the things that bothered me I
never told him. That's just like me." Other lads seemed to grasp
sooner or later the whole design of the Study and to enter enthusiastically into its purposes. At the close of the Study one boy described himself with blunt eloquence: "He [the counselor] helped
make me a character. I was shy, then I was wild, now I'm medium."

[1] A recent unsolicited communication from the "cynical lad" (now 21 years old)
speaks in highest terms of Miss A.'s influence upon his life. The reversal in his
evaluation points up sharply a basic issue: *when* in the course of an individual's
life shall we assess the effects of character-building influences? It takes many years
for some seeds to germinate.

I have called attention to the problem of interplay of personalities, for it is, of course, the pivot of the entire Study. We shall be disappointed if we look for a simple one-to-one correspondence between the worker's effort and its reception by the boy. Even if it turns out that the average impact of the counselor's work is good, we shall not be able to understand or apply this result without analyzing the dynamics involved in successful dyadic relationships, and they differ in baffling ways from case to case. The problem is obviously too vast for any single study to solve; indeed it extends far beyond the limits of any science of human relationships existing today. Yet this volume, and its sequel on the counselor-boy dyad, provide, I believe, a notable contribution to the topic.

CASE RECORDS

A closely related issue is the status and scientific significance of case records. The total accumulation of single-spaced recordings of visits, interviews, activities centering about the lives of the T-boys amounts to approximately 22,000 pages. A social scientist beholds this bulk with consternation. Was it necessary to record so much? How should a case report be written for maximum yield and efficiency? What to do with this mountain of material now that it exists? I suspect that no social (or research) agency has ever found satisfactory answers. Early in its course the Youth Study hoped that an important by-product of its work might be discoveries concerning the best means of keeping and analyzing case records. This hope was not realized in spite of various attempts to make periodic summaries and the invention of variegated record blanks. The files of the Study do not differ greatly in appearance from those of any hard-working busy agency. They contain many more personal pronouns and more reflections on the part of workers. But they are still too voluminous.

For many years the problems of case records perplexed Dr. Cabot. To his mind the inexcusable sin of case reports was their dullness —and therefore, he adds—their falsity. In his Foreword to *Children Astray* by Drucker and Hexter (1923) he wrote:

Now it seems to me obvious that one cannot give a true picture of any episode in the life of a family or an individual and yet make it dull to read. The facts are never dull. It is only our catalogue that makes them so. If truth to life is our intention, we must, I think, realize that we are doomed to attempt literature. No modest confession of incompetence excuses us. The comedy, the tragedy, the poignant unexpectedness which emerge in almost every day of case work, cannot truthfully be left out of a record. But if we try to put them in, we are trying to write good literature and can escape neither its privileges nor its trials.

The heaps and heaps of fragments that comprise the dossier on a single case are not interesting—and therefore, as Dr. Cabot says, are not true. Unlike human lives they lack vitality, sequence, structure. Whether the solution lies in imitating the art of literature, as Dr. Cabot proposes, or in discovering new scientific ways to designate the component elements and relationships of personality, I cannot say. All I am sure of at the moment is that experimentation along both lines is greatly needed to improve our methods of case recording and case writing.

The Study has used its case material in various ways. The records, of course, provide the source material for all the analyses contained in the present volume, also for many illustrative passages in the text. The bibliography presented in the Appendix shows that a few of the cases have been used for special types of analysis. In one particular instance the Study engaged the services of a professional writer—socially sensitive but not a social worker—for a period of two months to recast one of its longest and most vivid case records into a consecutive and readable form. The result proved especially successful in fashioning good teaching material out of a forbidding dossier. The issue of the technical journal containing the published study was promptly sold out. In the interests of maintaining the disguise of the case (a vital consideration, of course, in the printing of case records) I shall not here identify the report in question. I mention the matter merely to show that the Youth Study has been aware of its obligation to experiment in making the fullest use of its rich material. I personally regret that the collaboration between the Study and professional writers did not extend further than it did.

THE PROBLEM OF EVALUATION

The unique feature of the Study was its determination from the beginning to measure its own success or failure. Perhaps never before in history has a social agency been created for the purpose of assessing its own work.

Now when we attempt to measure our progress toward a goal we must know what our goal is. In social science this elementary requirement is remarkably hard to fulfill, for it is always hard to achieve clarity or specificity respecting social values. Occasionally, of course, the task is not difficult, for example in market research where evaluation is extensively practiced. In this field the investigators can quickly agree that increased purchase of a given commodity is "good." Sales are the goal. It is relatively easy then to determine whether this or that advertising campaign brought "good" results and to precisely what degree.

But in measuring the effects of a summer camp, of a liberal education, of training for citizenship, of a program for delinquency-prevention, the task is not so simple. Just what change does a summer camp wish to effect in its campers? What are the objectives of a liberal education? What are the specific products and by-products that training for citizenship should achieve?

At first glance the goal of "delinquency-prevention" seems clearer. But even here the operational definition of the goal is elusive. Arrests, adjudications, commitments are, as Chapter XIV shows, far from reliable indicators of antisocial conduct. The vast majority of legally delinquent acts never result in arrest, adjudication, or commitment. The administration of justice is sometimes capricious, and often varies in efficiency and severity over a period of time. Even so, the Study makes extensive use of official records of delinquency, and it is a bit distressing to have to admit that these fallible criteria are probably the most "objective" and most convincing available criteria for evaluation.

But the Study aimed at more than keeping boys out of trouble. The recriprocal of delinquency-prevention is the building of character. All meliorative social policy aims at the strengthening of character, at "socialization." Dr. Cabot designated the goal as "growth." While in ordinary discourse we assume we know what these objectives mean, we find ourselves baffled if we try to specify the measurable equivalents of "strong character," "socialized behavior," or of "growth."

In facing this problem, Dr. Witmer, in Chapter XXIV, attempts to assess the general "adjustment" of the boy from the total evidence contained in his voluminous case record. She rated both T- and C-boys (although, of course, less information was available on the latter group). Using this procedure she finds that the two groups did not differ significantly in *initial* adjustment before the treatment program began. (This fact indicates that the boys were well matched.) But she finds further that Ts and Cs did not differ significantly in *terminal* adjustment when the program ended. (Taken by itself, this indicates that the treatment efforts were futile.)

The question, however, arises, whether "adjustment" (as determined by over-all ratings) did in fact represent the goal of the Study, or one of its goals. One can readily understand why Dr. Witmer used this criterion: for one thing, society wants "well-adjusted" citizens; for another, social work has from long experience evolved standards that an experienced worker can apply in gauging adjustment, even if the final judgment remains somewhat impressionistic. But—and I repeat the question—should "adjustment" be regarded as one of the goals of this (or any other) social agency? Are not animals well adjusted to their environments and creative human beings seldom so? Objectives couched in terms of "strength of character" or "growth" seem ethically superior. Dr. Cabot himself deplored the concept of adjustment. To him it implied merely a *status quo*. For him "growth" was the highest good, and the success of the treatment program, therefore, should be gauged in terms of its contributions to the boy's spiritual growth.

But how are we to measure growth (since mere physical and mental development are not the issue)? Here is a noble ethics, but we cannot yet specify the concrete activities in the course of a boy's life that would unambiguously demonstrate growth—and hence we cannot measure his progress. Although I have criticized Dr. Witmer's use of the concept of adjustment, yet I will readily admit that a better alternative is hard to find.

Thus, when we set out to evaluate the Study we run head foremost into the basic and unsolved issue of concrete purpose to be achieved. Yet a beginning must be made somewhere, and the efforts of the Study to experiment with various criteria and methods of evaluation constitute one of its principal contributions to social science. Four major methods were tried:

1. A Battery of Attitude Scales and Personality Tests. In part these measures were based on standard instruments; in part they were *ad hoc,* devised by the research staff of the Study. As reported in Chapter XIX they were used only in two interim surveys conducted in 1941–42 and in 1943. Their yield did not seem to justify their use again at the completion of the program, especially since the war and the shrinkage of cases made it impracticable to find the large number of T- and C-boys required to make significant comparisons.

2. Statistics of Delinquency. Though in principle some record of overt conduct is ideal for evaluative purposes, yet in fact we know that police and court actions are a fallible criterion. In Chapter XX we find a careful attempt to make the most of such records, and to estimate both the frequency and seriousness of delinquent acts engaged in by T- and by C-boys and to determine whether significant differences exist between them.

3. Ratings on Adjustment. As I have pointed out, Dr. Witmer —the impartial research social worker engaged by the Study specifically for the evaluation work—made a judgment of the terminal adjustment of both T- and C-boys. Chapter XXIV describes her procedures and sets forth her conclusions.

4. Case Analyses. The dossiers of all 254 T-boys who had received an appreciable amount of service from the Study were analyzed from various points of view to determine how many had benefited, or failed to benefit, from the treatment, and what factors were associated with such benefit (Chapters XXVI–XXIX).

In addition to these four major evaluative procedures, various minor methods are tried. The grades in school of T- and C-boys are compared, without significant differences being found. The boys' own evaluations of the Study are available (Chapter XIII) and prove to be enlightening, especially when used in conjunction with the evaluator's own estimates (Chapter XXV). From time to time during the course of the Study the counselors' assessments of their own successes and failures were obtained. Since these minor methods shed only supplementary light let us concentrate our attention upon the findings obtained in the four principal evaluative attempts.

FINDINGS

The most general conclusion seems to be that none of the evaluative methods employed indicates any great degree of success for the treatment program. Certainly we cannot say that the initial hypothesis selected for testing has been satisfactorily established.

Why not? Is it because the hypothesis is in fact intrinsically unsound and therefore disproved? Is it that the treatment efforts were defective and not worthy of the hypothesis itself? Is the hypothesis perhaps not so much wrong as coarse and undifferentiated, stating a sweeping phenotypic generalization that obscures the types of instances where, in a revised form, the hypothesis might still prove to be valid? Or, are the evaluative procedures employed just too crude to determine subtle gains in character and growth? Finally, may it be that we are attempting to assess the results too soon? Perhaps the same boys studied ten years hence may reflect delayed gains from the treatment program. All of these possibilities are present, and all of them together may be conspiring to produce the somewhat negative results that confront us.

The Study does not, therefore, yield a categorical answer to the question, "Can delinquency be prevented by the treatment methods employed?" But, scratching as we are at the frontiers of social science, we have no right to expect categorical answers. Our duty is to examine the detailed results yielded by each of the four major evaluative methods, and to infer, as best we can, their probable meaning.

1. Both *interim surveys,* employing schedules, scales, ratings, tests, show a slight but persistent trend favoring the T-boys on the majority of measures used. True, scarcely any single T-C comparison is of statistical significance, and the measures employed for the most part have low reliabilities. Yet the impressive fact remains that a large majority of measures give a slight edge to the T-boys. There is probably no statistical device that could give us an adequate estimate of the probabilities involved in this finding, where measures are unreliable and, taken individually, non-significant. The Study offers no such estimate, but the trend remains.

I regret that this method was not employed at the conclusion of the Study. No one believes that pencil-and-paper or rating devices are adequate means for assessing growth in character. Yet at the present stage of progress we should not abandon the attempt to employ and improve such pioneer instruments as we have, even the brittle tests of personality.

To me a reasonable interpretation of this finding would be as follows: In midstream the counselors were, on the average, making slight gains. In order to confirm this indication later tests should have been given. As time went on the divergences between T- and C-boys would increase if the treatment program was in fact effective. But, since the final and conclusive step in the use of this method was not tried, we must table the whole matter.

2. The evidence from delinquency statistics, in spite of its fallibility, is perhaps the most convincing evidence we have. In brief, there seems to be no significant difference between T- and C-boys in the frequency of their appearances before the Crime Prevention Bureau, before the courts, or in the number of commitments to correctional institutions. If anything the T-boys come off somewhat worse, but for reasons probably not significantly related to the treatment program.

Yet in the analysis presented in Chapter XX a light of considerable promise shines through. At the time of the last reckoning T-boys were *less* frequently found among the serious offenders, among those committed to the Commonwealth's correctional institutions for older offenders. It is vital that this finding be rechecked in future years, for if the ratio is maintained, a discovery of considerable importance has been made.

The discovery—if I may call it such, pending confirmation— tells us a great deal about the probable course of character formation—or of "social learning." It tells us that treatment efforts of the type employed here will probably not prevent a boy, beset by poor home and neighborhood—and headed in an antisocial direction—from drifting into delinquency. But the counselor's efforts may take effect after the boy has been burned. The boy must learn, in part, from hard experience. *He then learns more surely if he has had the benefit of friendly precept and example.*

I am reminded here of Judd's classic experiment in psychology wherein an experimental and control group of boys were used. The former group learned verbally, without practice, the principles of refraction under water. The control group had no such instruction. All the boys were then invited to throw darts at an underwater target. The "trained" boys at first made just as many and as bad errors as the C-boys; *but soon* the teaching given the first group took effect. They understood their mistakes and corrected them. But first they had to *make* them. May it not be that the effect of the Study's treatment efforts are analogous? Only a follow-up investigation after several years will tell us the answer for sure.

3. The only evaluative procedure to yield wholly negative results is the method of over-all ratings on the terminal social adjustment of 148 T- and 148 C-boys. After a careful reading of the records of T-boys, and of such information as could be obtained on C-boys, Dr. Witmer gave each case a rating on the following scale: good adjustment, fairly good, rather poor, very poor, delinquent, neurotic. In none of these categories did she find a significant difference between the percentage of T- and of C-boys. Nor did she find that the first group excelled the second in improvement over the prognostic scores assigned each boy at the outset of the Study.

I have already raised the question whether "adjustment" as defined by Dr. Witmer was in fact a central objective of the Study. I did so not in order to undermine her negative findings. Indeed I am inclined to accept her experienced judgment of the cases in this respect, and to admit that the criterion of adjustment has at least "something to do" with the objectives of the Study, and that so far as this is true the negative findings must be given weight.

4. The final, and most subtle, of the evaluative procedures is based on clinical (intuitive) analysis of all the T-cases where any considerable amount of work was done. Some would say that one-person judgments of this sort are subject to the operation of deep, perhaps unconscious, biases on the part of the analyst. From the beginning the Study was aware of this danger, but likewise knew that no final evaluation would be complete unless it contained the seasoned judgment of an experienced case analyst. Not all of the "objective" tests available in the world today can perceive relations, synthesize the evidence, and cluster data in new ways to enhance our understanding of human personality. I feel certain that the Study could not have chosen a more competent or experienced evaluator than Dr. Witmer. Its only failure, I think, was in neg-

lecting to study evaluator-reliability. Would another analyst agree with Dr. Witmer? This defect from the scientific point of view is regrettable, but in view of the immense amount of time required to get the "feel" of the individual cases, is entirely understandable. Dr. Witmer analyzes the cases with inexhaustible patience. She looks at them from many points of view, combines and recombines them to discover important syndromes and possible generalizations of value.

On the whole, she concludes, at least one-fifth of the T-boys derived substantial and identifiable benefit from the efforts of their counselors. By including additional cases where the gains were un-questioned but less marked, the proportion benefited rises to ap-proximately one-third. The boys themselves, as reported in Chapter XIII, are somewhat more generous in their evaluation, fully half claiming benefits and expressing enthusiasm for their counselors' efforts. But it is well to take Dr. Witmer's more conservative esti-mate, and to note with satisfaction that in a large proportion of cases her own evaluation checks well with that made by the boys themselves.

We perceive a contradiction between this conclusion that one-third benefited from the treatment and the finding reported pre-viously that the terminal adjustment of T- and of C-boys did not differ. The contradiction is especially troublesome in view of the fact that in the 30 cases of T-boys who benefit most, their gains over their matched twins was significantly high. In Chapter XXIX the reader finds several alternative explanations for the paradox. For example, the possibility is explored that while some boys were helped, an equivalent number were harmed—leaving the *average* adjustment equal for Ts and Cs. But this possibility is not sustained by the analysis: at most eight cases turn up where the relationship with the counselor (or an abrupt severing of the relationship) may have damaged the boy—a negligible fraction of the 254 cases examined.

Dr. Witmer offers still other possible explanations for the con-tradiction. To her list I would add the following observation. The subjective error involved in classifying the grade of adjustment attained by 148 T- and 148 C-boys must necessarily be large; so too the error in determining the number of T-boys for whom treatment

was beneficial. It would not take a very large error favoring the
C-boys in the first case and the T-boys in the second to account
for the discrepancy.

In 42 percent of the cases Dr. Witmer judges the counselors'
efforts to be "clearly ineffectual." She analyzes the reasons for these
relative failures at length. Briefly, it seems that the counselors were
wasting their efforts with cases where either the boy or the parents
were resistant to the Study or disinterested in its efforts. They
missed fire, too, in certain cases where they failed to diagnose correctly the principal needs of the boy or, in certain other cases, where
errors of judgment ruined the plans for treatment. Still more clear-
cut were the failures that could be traced to a wretched emotional
situation in the home, so evil in its impact upon the boy that an
outside friend could not offset its ravages. In these cases it is questionable whether any known form of counseling or social service
could have succeeded. It is particularly from the latter group that
persistent delinquency comes, heavily freighted with neurotic com-
plications. Dr. Witmer is of the opinion that confirmed delinquency
is usually a problem of a serious psychiatric order, and as such it is
too severe to be handled by the type of treatment the Study offered.
Perhaps the only solution for cases of this type is commitment to
hostels of a graded and varied type, on the order of the Approved
Schools in Britain. Here children who require more or less discipline, more or less psychiatric treatment, and are ready for more
or less responsibility, find the environment they need. One hopes
that they find likewise a fair substitute for the parental love that
they crave.

Turning to the successful cases, it appears that a necessary condition for success lies in the warm acceptance of the counselor by
boy and by parent: "In record after record of boys definitely aided
it is stated that the boy and his parents seemed very fond of the
counselor and eager to have his help." This necessary condition of
help is not, however, in itself sufficient. Successful cases showed, in
addition, that the boy's problem was seldom of an extreme or
pathological type. Counselors seem effective especially with youngsters whose emotional conflicts are not severe, and who are capable
of handling them in an "internal" manner, and are not hardened
in the habit of acting them out in open rebellion against society.

Further, the successful cases showed that the counselor was usually adroit in spotting a tangible need and meeting it (tutoring in a school subject, improving the teacher's understanding of the boy and his problems, correcting a physical handicap). Finally, the successful cases included several wherein the counselor was able to serve as a kind of cultural ideal for the lad whose own parents, however warm and dependable, lacked sufficient acquaintance with current American standards. For a second-generation American, especially, the counselor can often represent a cultural ideal which the parents cannot supply.

It is important to note that in very few cases was a counselor able to provide full and sufficient emotional anchorage for a boy whose own parents rejected him. Every youngster, at least until the age of adolescence, needs a rooted sense of security and love in his home. Neither the school nor the social agency can supply the lack nor fully repair the ravages if this condition is missing. When a basic security in the home exists, then, it is found, counselors can do much to make up for other, less serious, parental inadequacies.

CAUSES OF JUVENILE DELINQUENCY

Although the research was not focused primarily upon etiological factors, certain revealing insights emerge. The most impressive lesson, I think, is the one to which I have just alluded. Emotionally inadequate homes engender deep conflict in the child. This conflict often expresses itself in neurotic disorder and in delinquency. It is not the homes that are substandard in plumbing, cleanliness, or recreational opportunities that engender delinquency—not if security in the home and wholesome example are provided. Nor do "delinquency areas" automatically produce criminals. Most boys from these areas grow up to be law-abiding citizens. The differentiating condition is almost always the emotional tone of the home.

Although this discovery is not new, the finding as presented in Chapters XVI, XXII, and XXIV, sheds new light upon the matter. Often, for example, we hear that delinquency is highly correlated with "broken homes." If a broken home is defined merely in terms of the absence of one or both parents, we find very few cases of this order. *It is the home emotionally broken in an irreparable manner that predisposes to crime.* This finding fortifies social psychologists in their claim that all sources of moral ideals pale in comparison with parental influence. Children absorb both their ethical and their religious ideals from parents wherever a basis for emotional identification with the parent exists. If this basis for identification is lacking, or if the parent himself is an antisocial model, the child can rarely become a good citizen. If I am interpreting the evidence aright, all causes of delinquency, other than parental attitude, fade in importance.

Looking at the boy himself, instead of at the home, we find that persistent delinquents generally develop unwholesome, often neurotic, defenses against their home situation. Half-conscious of their misery they take to illegal adventure. The boys themselves are unable to surmount their handicap, not even with the aid of counselors who would gladly serve them as parent-surrogates. If most persistent delinquents are, as Dr. Witmer asserts, "seriously neurotic youngsters from homes that are very unsatisfying emotionally," we can only conclude that the prevention of delinquency requires the establishment and maintenance of better homes under the control of better parents. Would attitude therapy for deficient parents help matters? Theoretically yes, but the case analysis reveals few instances where counselors were successful in such attempts. In many cases they were dealing with native and constitutional defects in parents, and in others with lives hopelessly warped in early years.

Would preventive efforts started in still younger years yield better results? One of the T-boys, when asked whether the Study had helped him, called attention to the tardiness of the effort. Said he, "Well, usually it was too late. Before they tell you what not to do, you've already done it." Dr. Cabot, it will be recalled, urgently desired that the work start with children as young as possible. But to spot pre-delinquents before the school age seems virtually impossible, and methods for working preventively with small children are not well understood. Perhaps, in time, play therapy, and other devices employed by child analysts, will develop to help offset the immense handicap of emotionally inadequate homes. Somewhere the vicious circle must be broken. If parents are the decisive influence, then better parents must be trained.

The boys themselves were asked what they regarded as the causes of delinquency (Chapter XVII). To my mind the most remarkable

finding here is the fact that virtually no boy mentions the importance of parental attitudes. Some of the boys may have been sensitive about admitting in an interview that emotionally unsatisfying
parents lay at the root of their difficulty. More likely, I suspect,
young people are simply unable to perceive the effect that the
emotional atmosphere of their home is having upon them. Parents
are the very ground of their lives. Grounds, psychologists know, are
seldom perceived unless the individual is trained to look at them.

One type of theory holds that delinquency comes entirely from
disorders in our social system. Capitalism, it is said, breeds crime;
or our commercial culture, with its overweighting of competition
and meretricious recreation, is to blame. The Study does not extend
its analysis to this "ultimate" level of causation, and therefore it
sheds no light directly upon the issue. Yet I cannot escape the conviction that unless a reformed social system results in better parents
we are unlikely to prevent delinquency merely by adopting one
form or another of political or social change.

IMPLICATIONS FOR SOCIAL WORK

One of the by-products of the Study, it was hoped, would be discoveries that might benefit social work, either by indicating possible
improvements in its methods or by indicating types of cases where
expensive and time-consuming efforts are merely wasted. I am not
competent to interpret the results from this point of view. Dr.
Witmer, in the concluding chapter of this volume, undertakes the
task, and I trust that the reader will follow her guidance in the
matter rather than mine. I shall, however, venture to plagiarize
some of her points that strike me as especially important, and shall
dare to add one or two thoughts of my own on this subject.

It is clear to me now that neither the enthusiasm nor the rep-
utable sponsorship of a social agency is in itself a sufficient guarantee of the value of its service. I am persuaded that only a critical
and arduous evaluation of results can yield a satisfactory justification for an agency's existence. This volume makes us fully aware of
the difficulties that lie along this road, but also of the fact that the
obligation cannot be evaded. Perhaps the trauma of World War II
has shocked us out of our complacency concerning our social policies. At any rate, for some reason it is now evident that social work,

camps, schools, courts of law, government bureaus—all the civic and private paraphernalia we have developed—are gradually being forced to submit themselves to the critical scrutiny of social science evaluation.

But here a word of caution is in order. Should it turn out in an evaluation program that little or no desirable accomplishment is apparent, one may not impulsively conclude that social service—confining ourselves to this particular topic—is in vain. Before such a conclusion can be reached one would also have to demonstrate that without this service conditions (or cases) would have deteriorated. What I have in mind is the very real possibility that in a period of social disruption, such as we are living in, it may take all the combined efforts of all agencies simply to "hold the line." Maybe for the time being we dare not expect improvement, but may only hope to prevent disastrous collapse.

I am struck by Dr. Witmer's finding that relatively few of the families failed to enter willingly into the program, and that few showed resistance or hostility during the course of treatment. To my mind this finding suggests that social agencies need not wait for clients to knock at their doors with acute "felt needs." So far as I can see an agency is justified in going out into the highways and byways to seek individuals whom it thinks it can serve. But I put this heretical view aside.

Professional social work seems to be right in its emphasis upon the removal of specific handicaps and the meeting of concrete problems as they arise. Diffuse good will is not by itself effective. The Study counselors, Dr. Witmer finds, were most successful when health, school, home problems could be identified, attacked, and solved. Yet behind this skill in human engineering must lie the warm sense of mutual trust between the boy, his family, and the worker. It seems to me that this combined condition for success essentially vindicates the conception of social work *both* as a skilled profession and as an application of directed and sustained friendship.

Of far reaching significance is the indication, emerging from this Study, that unless it possesses unlimited resources an agency would do well to refuse cases for which the probability of successful work is slight. Specifically, an agency like the Youth Study would do well to concentrate on children not extremely handicapped by neurotic disorders or by parents resistant to the agency or themselves hopelessly inadequate in emotional balance. (Other types of agencies, employing more drastic policies, may, of course, be somewhat more successful with these "hopeless" cases. We do not yet know.)

One curious finding, presented in Chapter XVIII, seems to me to hold a lesson for all of us. The young people involved in this Study —both Ts and Cs—turn out considerably better than experts had predicted. Both the teachers and the "selection committee" grossly overpredicted potential delinquency. To be sure, they picked out future delinquents with surprising accuracy, but they picked out too many boys who in fact turned out well. The moral, I think, is, Don't expect the worst to happen to your problem children; it probably won't.

Finally, to repeat an earlier point, social work needs continually to examine, reformulate, and define in concrete terms its own goals and objectives. Evaluation cannot proceed until objectives are specified. Adjustment by itself is probably not a worthy goal. The concept of "spiritual growth" raises our sights and satisfies a more exacting ethics. But this (or any other) abstract concept requires specification in terms of personal traits, personal change, personal conduct, and interpersonal relations. Closer cooperation between social work, ethics, and psychology will be required before the needed progress in defining goals can be achieved.

IMPLICATIONS FOR SOCIAL SCIENCE

The account contained in this volume is marked by scrupulous honesty. There is no self-laudation, no special pleading. The product is a model of objective reporting. In this respect it should be imitated by investigators who are both participants in, and observers of, the course of any social program.

The attempt to match two groups of boys for experimental and for control purposes seems to me the most ambitious effort of the sort that has been made to date. Although future investigators will undoubtedly invent improvements in this essential tool of action-research they will do so more surely if they are guided by the experience described in Chapter VI.

There have been perhaps a dozen or more major researches of the "longitudinal" variety where children are followed carefully through a number of successive years of growth and social development. Such investigations are exceedingly expensive to conduct. Up to now, their yield has been disappointing, chiefly because clearcut hypotheses were not devised at the outset and critically tested. Faulty as it is in some respects, this Study, I believe, conforms more closely than has any other longitudinal research to the scientific ideal of hypothesis-testing. As such it deserves to be carefully examined by all investigators who conduct such researches in the future. Many helpful do's and cautionary don't's emerge from a close inspection of these pages. It would be unforgivable to overlook the hard-won experience here recorded.

In yet another respect I regard this research as successfully pioneer. It takes a bold plunge into the sea of values. Almost every social scientist has come to realize that social science cannot possibly remain indifferent to ethics. There are value-assumptions, and ethical consequences, in every step the social scientist takes. His skills are needed for the preservation and improvement of society; and his own research and writing, whether he likes it or not, are bound to reflect his own value-assumptions. It was during the tragic experience of the Second World War that most social scientists began to think clearly about this issue. The Youth Study, however, some years previous to the war had accepted the logical marriage of science and ethics. It assumed that to prevent delinquency and to foster spiritual growth were worthy ends. But it knew that starting with such assumptions the tools of science (even awkwardly applied at the beginning) might be counted on to hasten the achievement of these goals, or might (as has happened) demand that the goals be better defined. In the long run, social science working hand in hand with ethics can help mankind evolve a clearer, sounder, and more viable statement of its own moral objectives.

At long last I bring my preview to a close. I know the reader of the following chapters is likely to question some of my interpretations. He may find some of the evidence blurred where I think it clear, or clear where I think it blurred. But I shall be surprised if he fails to agree with me that here is a bold and significant conception of social research, faithfully executed in spite of many obstacles, rich in conclusions, and foreshadowing future developments of greater importance both for social science and for social policy.

GORDON W. ALLPORT

CAMBRIDGE, MASSACHUSETTS

JANUARY, 1950

ACKNOWLEDGMENTS

THE TWO AUTHORS OF THIS REPORT WERE NOT COLLABORATORS IN THE usual sense, for each wrote independently of the other. Edwin Powers, one of the original ten counselors, and since 1941 the Director of the Study, wrote Part I (Chapters I–XX). Part II (Chapters XXI–XXX) is the work of Dr. Helen L. Witmer who was invited by the Study to evaluate as an "outsider," the accomplishments of the counselors. Her interpretations are her own, based upon a thorough study of the counselors' records and all other available data.

The basic material from which this book was written represents the contributions of many individuals. The story of referrals, classification and selection of cases (Chapters III–V) is based on an unpublished manuscript written by Dr. P. S. de Q. Cabot, the Co-director of the Study with Dr. Richard C. Cabot, until the latter's death in May, 1939, and from that time until the fall of 1940 the Director of the Study. Much of the early organization, including the development of the procedures and policies of the Study, was developed by the staff under his direction.

The description of the two interim evaluation surveys (Chapter XIX) was drawn from extensive statistical material prepared by Dr. William D. Turner of the research staff, who devised and carried through the first evaluation survey, and by Dr. George W. Hartmann who planned and directed the second. The interpretations of the data are the responsibility of the author of Part I. Dr. Hartmann also prepared the basic material for the description of the two cities and their school systems which appears in Chapter II. We also acknowledge the assistance of Dr. Hans-Lukas Teuber, who worked on these interim evaluations, set up the post-treatment interview plan, and made other valuable contributions. We are indebted to Mr. Henry C. Patey and to Dr. Edward A. Lincoln not only for their creation of the matching plan, described in Chapter VI, but for devising many of the forms and procedures used during the early days of the Study and for assisting in the research planning. Our thanks are also due to Professor Leo J. Postman for statistical advice on the problems of prediction discussed in Chapter XVIII, and to Jeanne Adams for the statistical compilations and the preparation of many tables.

Although these various colleagues made important contributions to the research none is to be held responsible for the final form of the material or the conclusions presented in this volume.

In a project of such magnitude it is quite impossible to mention the separate contributions of the many staff members who played a significant role in the development of the Study. A list of all who were at some time engaged in this project between 1935 and 1945, some 84 altogether, appears in the Appendix.

Without the help of the many public and private agencies it would have been impossible to carry on an experiment of this nature. We are heavily indebted to the school systems, both public and parochial. In Cambridge, the late Mr. Michael E. Fitzgerald, Superintendent of Schools, and later his successor, Mr. John M. Tobin, and in Somerville, Superintendent Everett W. Ireland, worked in close harmony with our counselors and placed the facilities of the schools at the service of the Study. We wish to record particularly the indispensable aid given by the late Miss Gertrude B. Duffy, for many years the Supervisor of the Department of Tests and Measurements in the Cambridge schools, who took a personal interest in the Study and served as a valued advisor and intermediary. Her assistant, Dr. Ruth Boland, also gave generously of her time over a ten-year period. The close working relationship between the Study and the schools is perhaps unparalleled in delinquency research. The teachers welcomed the visits of the counselors and were always willing to give their own time, often during the noon lunch hour, to the problems of the boys in which the Study was interested. They showed inexhaustible patience in meeting the demands of countless forms and questionnaires. We should particularly like to mention the support and interest of Monsignor Augustine F. Hickey who presented our aims to the Cambridge parochial school teachers and thus assisted in the conduct of our research.

To the courts and law-enforcement authorities the Study must at first have seemed like a strange creation, combining as it did the methods of treatment with the aims of research. Once they understood our purposes they gave generously of their time and made available to us the official records. Captain Thomas J. Stokes of the Crime Prevention Bureau of the Cambridge Police Department and his staff were ready at all times to listen to the problems of our counselors and to help us in working out the plans of treatment. In Somerville, Inspector Edward G. Forrestal and his fellow-officers of the Somerville Police Department gave us similar aid. We are also indebted to the officials of the state training schools for delinquent boys who frequently discussed problems with us and permitted our counselors to visit boys committed to their care.

Our thanks also go to Miss Laura G. Woodbury, Director of the Social Service Exchange of Boston, who enabled us to clear all of our cases through her agency; to Mr. Albert C. Carter, Commissioner of the Massachusetts Board of Probation, who was ever willing to give us the information we needed; to the Cambridge Young Men's Christian Association for permitting our boys to use their facilities and allowing us to occupy space in their building for several years while we were conducting the follow-up study.

In its early years the Study had an imposing list of Advisors consisting of the following specialists: Gordon W. Allport, Edith M. H. Baylor, William Boyd, Augusta F. Bronner, Hadley Cantril, Stanley Cobb, William Healy, Earnest A. Hooton, Cheney C. Jones, Theodore A. Lothrop, Donald J. MacPherson, Henry A. Murray, Jr., Jean Piaget, Eli C. Romberg, Philip J. Rulon, A. Warren Stearns, William Stern, Douglas A. Thom, and Alfred F. Whitman. In succeeding years this group was depleted by deaths and resignations. During the war particularly it was difficult to call upon them for active service. Nevertheless, especially in the early days of the Study, valuable advice was secured from many of these individuals. We regret that our profitable contacts were not consistently maintained. The original design upon which the Study was based owed much to the advice of Sheldon and Eleanor T. Glueck. Inasmuch as we were not able to keep contact with our Advisors throughout the entire period of treatment we must absolve them individually and collectively from responsibility for the course of the research in its later years and for the interpretations offered in this volume.

The Ella Lyman Cabot Foundation subsidized the Study and its Directors had ultimate responsibility for the conduct of its affairs. The Directors were Gordon W. Allport, President, Alice G. O'Gorman, Clerk, Burton A. Miller, Treasurer, George A. Macomber, Assistant Treasurer, P. S. de Q. Cabot, Richard B. O'R. Hocking, David R. Hunter, Cheney C. Jones, Marcus Morton, Jr., and Eleanor C. Slater. The last two resigned before the completion of the research. The manuscript of this volume was read by most of the Directors, and their criticisms have been taken into account in the present report.

An editorial committee consisting of Gordon W. Allport, Alice O'Gorman, Luberta H. McCabe, and Edwin Powers made the final decisions in the preparation of the manuscript for publication. Special thanks are due Louise E. Fouhy, Secretary of the Study, for her expert assistance and loyalty to the end.

CONTENTS

FIGURES

TABLES

PART I. THE STUDY

By Edwin Powers

CHAPTER I

AN IDEA BECOMES
A REALITY

IN ANY CITY AT ANY GIVEN TIME THERE ARE A NUMBER OF INNOCENT-looking small boys who are not acquiring the social attitudes and moral values they will need for successful living. Instead they are developing habits and outlooks that will lead them into antisocial channels, perhaps into criminal careers. May it not be possible, Dr. Richard C. Cabot asked, to discover who these boys are, then to submit them to a program deliberately designed to prevent the ripening of their delinquent tendencies, and finally to evaluate the results of this effort? *Can* delinquency be prevented?

The plan soon took definite form in his mind. Eventually formalized and known as the Cambridge-Somerville Youth Study the project involved two main objectives throughout:

1. The prevention of delinquency by the employment of friendly counselors who would deal with a selected group of boys over a long period of time.

2. The measurement of the effectiveness of this work by comparing the treatment group with a substantially similar control group that received no help or guidance from the Study.

OUTLINE OF THE PLAN

To reach these objectives Dr. Cabot established the following criteria:

1. Only *boys* were to be chosen—those who were at the time attending the public and parochial schools in Cambridge, Massachusetts.[1]

2. Treatment would be restricted to a group of probable pre-delinquents of the age of six or seven years. It was believed that the

---

[1] In 1937 the public schools of Somerville, Massachusetts, were brought into the plan.

upper age limit should be no greater than seven because treatment becomes progressively more difficult as habits and attitudes become more fixed. On the other hand, it seemed impractical, no matter how desirable, to select boys younger than six because it would be difficult and discouragingly time-consuming for a small staff to learn very much about a large number of boys of pre-school age. Adequate treatment depended to a considerable degree on information supplied by the schools. These age limitations, however, were flexible and were necessarily shifted upward for reasons stated in subsequent chapters.

3. Treatment would be whatever was best for the boy and would be personally administered by well-equipped counselors. In writing of the reformation of criminals, apropos of the Glueck research, Dr. Cabot said,

So far as I have seen such reforms or heard of them from others, there has been at least one necessary condition: *That someone should come to know and to understand the man in so intimate and friendly a way that he comes to a better understanding of himself and to a truer comprehension of the world he lives in.*[2]

A boy, he thought, should be early supplied with an ideal. It might be possible to find this ideal in the living personality of a counselor. Certainly it would be worth a try. Treatment, then, would be focused upon the individual child, directed toward discovering his potentialities for growth spiritually, intellectually, physically, and socially.

4. The program would, ideally, extend over a period of ten years, making it possible to observe the child's development and to note his responses to varying types of treatment. (Later events caused the shortening of this ten-year term.)

5. The school would be the focal point not only for initial information concerning the boy but for the planning of the treatment program, although all local agencies of a religious, social, educational, or recreational nature would be asked to assist.

ORGANIZATION OF THE PROJECT

To put into practical operation a ten-year social service plan as a private venture without official or community financial support,

[2] Sheldon Glueck and Eleanor T. Glueck, *500 Criminal Careers* (New York, Alfred A. Knopf, 1930), p. ix.

Dr. Richard C. Cabot felt the need of a supporting organization to handle finances and to guide him in planning the work. Accordingly, in July, 1935, he created a charitable corporation under the laws of the Commonwealth of Massachusetts, known as the Ella Lyman Cabot Foundation, in memory of his wife who had died in 1934 and who was known for her interest and activities in character education and social welfare.

It cannot be said that the project had its beginning on any specific day. The first presentation of the program to the public schools in Cambridge was made on June 3, 1935, just prior to the incorporation of the Foundation. At this meeting it was explained to the principals and teachers of the lower grades of the elementary schools that Dr. Cabot wished to inaugurate a practical treatment project as an experiment, one that would be original and bold and yet "carefully constructed." "A scientific effort to determine the causes of crime and the treatment of juvenile delinquency" would be made, provided the schools were willing to give the necessary help by referring boys who showed early signs of problem behavior.

In the fall of 1935 several organization meetings were convened at Dr. Richard C. Cabot's home in Cambridge, attended by Dr. P. S. de Q. Cabot, a psychologist, Miss Gertrude B. Duffy, Supervisor of the Department of Measurement and Adjustment in the Cambridge Schools, the Right Reverend Augustine F. Hickey, the parish priest of St. Paul's church in Cambridge, and Professor and Mrs. Sheldon Glueck of the Harvard Law School.[3] These authorities suggested possible research methods and weighed the advantages and limitations involved in carrying out a project of such complexity.

Many other specialists and citizens were consulted and their interest and support elicited. The directors set up an advisory committee to meet with them and the staff to work out policies and procedures.

During the fall of 1935 and the following winter the preliminary work of the Study was actually begun. Dr. P. S. de Q. Cabot was appointed co-director and the executive head of the staff. The respon-

---

[3] The Gluecks did not continue their affiliation with the Study beyond the early period of discussion and exploration of the problems.

sibility for planning, developing, and executing the program in the first few years was essentially his. Plans were necessarily revised many times before the clear outlines of the project appeared.

By December, 1935, the confidence and cooperation of the Cambridge school authorities had been obtained and the names of 150 boys had been submitted. Preliminary investigations and gathering of data consumed the time and energies of the staff for many months. It was not until the fall of 1937 that conditions were set for the actual commencement of work with a few of the selected boys and not until May, 1939, that the last of the 325 boys selected was entered in the treatment program.

Assisting them in this early period, the two directors had a staff consisting of a registered nurse, two psychologists, and a secretary. Miss Gertrude B. Duffy, Supervisor of the Department of Measurement and Adjustment in the public schools of Cambridge, served as liaison between the Study and the School Department.

There follows a summary of the essential steps in the development of the project between the years 1935–1945:

NINE STEPS IN THE DEVELOPMENT OF THE PROJECT

Step One: Finding the Boys. The first problem was to obtain the names and addresses of boys who might be selected as subjects. The schools were asked to submit names of boys who were difficult and also the names of boys who, in contrast, were not considered difficult or troublesome in any way—referred to for convenience as average boys.[4] An intensive effort was made to discover all of the so-called bad boys or potential criminals in Cambridge and Somerville. Therefore, the search did not stop with the school referral. The court records were searched, social agencies most likely to know such boys were asked to submit names, probation officers and police officers were interviewed and many other supplementary sources of information were tapped. Ultimately nearly 2,000 names were obtained.

Step Two: Investigation. Many months were spent in collecting data concerning each boy, including mental and physical tests, home visits, questionnaires, teacher interviews and reports, and

[4] The reason for inclusion of average boys is more fully explained in Chap. III.

official records not only of the schools but of the courts and of other public and private agencies, together with delinquency surveys of the two cities.

Step Three: Pre-selection. Only 650 boys were needed to make up the total population of the Study—325 in each of the two groups. As almost three times that number of names had been submitted, a process of screening was necessary. The boys who, in the time intervening between referral and investigation, had passed their twelfth birthdays were automatically rejected along with boys who could not be found or who had in the meantime moved out of town.

Step Four: Classification. The names still remaining after the pre-selection process were referred to a committee of three experts (called the Selection Committee) who were not members of the staff. They examined the data and estimated the probabilities of each boy's becoming or not becoming a delinquent. They rated each boy on an 11-point scale, ranging from plus five (minimum probability of later delinquency), through zero to minus five (maximum probability of later delinquency). Seven hundred and eighty-two boys were classified, the entire process extending over a period of 15 months.

Step Five: Matching. The 782 cases were turned over to two psychologists for the purpose of matching one boy with another so that two equated groups could be set up. A matching procedure was developed from a combination of statistical devices and clinical syndromes. After two boys were paired, a coin was tossed to determine which one would fall into the treatment group and which into the control group. Ultimately 650 boys were thus divided into two groups of 325 each.

Step Six: Assignment. Before the matching process was completed, the directors had assembled the original treatment staff of ten workers. Each worker, or counselor as he or she was called, was assigned a few boys at a time as rapidly as the boys were matched and allocated to the treatment group. The assignment process began in November, 1937, and was completed in May, 1939.

Step Seven: Treatment. By treatment was meant the effort of the counselor to carry out the objectives of the Study in relation to the boys assigned to him.

Step Eight: Reclassification. In 1941, when it was realized that a case load of 33 to 35 boys per worker was too high, a process was undertaken to *retire* "high-average" boys who did not particularly need the services that the Study could provide. The remaining group of 260 was further reduced by death and by the necessity of *dropping* boys who had moved to areas outside of Cambridge and Somerville. (It was a time of gasoline shortage.) The reduction of staff because of war demands necessitated the dropping of additional cases. As the war continued and the shortages in personnel remained acute, the Foundation decided to *terminate* treatment of 72 boys as they reached the age of 17, particularly since most of them were, in any case, leaving town for war work in other cities or to join the Armed Forces or the Merchant Marine. The remaining 75 boys were carried to the end of the treatment period—December 31, 1945. The retiring, dropping, and terminating of cases led to a progressive reduction of the population of boys, and curtailed the treatment program.

TABLE 1

Length of Treatment Period

Number of Boys	Average Period of Treatment
65 (retired)	2 years, 6 months
113 (dropped)	4 years, 2 months
72 (terminated)	5 years, 11 months
75 (carried to end)	6 years, 9 months
Average for group of 325	4 years, 10 months
Maximum period	8 years, 1 month

NOTE: Twelve boys were in treatment for 7 years or more, and four for 8 years or more.

Step Nine: Close of the Study. By 1945 so many of the boys had joined the Armed Forces or had left the local area that it was decided to close treatment for all cases at the end of that year. This date, therefore, marked the end of the treatment period three or four years sooner than anticipated.

CHAPTER II

THE SOCIAL SETTING

IN ANY EXTENSIVE PLAN FOR DELINQUENCY-PREVENTION OR CHARAC-
ter development, the nature of the social setting is of major importance. The development of the present study was governed in many
respects by its location in two large, industrialized, urban communities in one of the oldest parts of the United States—the adjoining
cities of Cambridge and Somerville in the greater Boston area.

Cambridge and Somerville lie in Middlesex County, roughly
north and west of the seaport and capital city of Boston proper.
Both communities were settled within the decade after the landing
at Plymouth Rock and are particularly rich in the history of the
early phases of the Revolutionary War.

CAMBRIDGE

The narrow, winding Charles River separates Cambridge from
Boston on the south and east; a jagged street boundary divides Cambridge from Somerville on the north. The less crowded, residential
suburb of Belmont borders Cambridge on the west; Arlington
abuts on its northwestern edge and Watertown stretches toward the
southwest. Most of Cambridge's land surface is flat, much of the
ground near the river having been reclaimed from marshes.

Save for the Common, the 21 playgrounds, 18 city parks and the
ribbons of lawn near public buildings, the six square miles of Cambridge have little space that is not the site of some structure. Cambridge was the seventh most densely populated community in the
United States in 1930, having 17,390 inhabitants per square mile;
the neighboring city of Somerville was actually the first in population density with 24,623 residents per square mile. (Jersey City was
second with a density of 24,363, New York standing third with
23,179.) The 1940 federal census reported a Cambridge population
of 110,879—a drop from 113,643 in 1930. There were 28,717 oc-

cupied dwellings with an average population of 3.86 per dwelling (1940 census).

Even the casual eye discerns the fact that there are in reality at least two Cambridges. The smaller or "more cultivated," centering about the Harvard University buildings and stretching generally westward to the city limits, is a middle-class residential district containing a few famous mansions identified with notable literary figures active during the "Flowering of New England." The larger Cambridge, focusing on Central Square and stretching to the south and northeast, is largely a retail and industrial area.

The marked difference in physical appearance is matched by an equally profound social cleavage between the University area and other sections of the city. However unified the city may be by common higher loyalties to the State and nation, it is sharply divided internally on local issues by a variety of cultural antagonisms—a feature which limits efforts at reforms dependent upon increased intercommunication between groups. Symbolic of the situation is the literal proximity of old and depressing housing accommodations to the dormitories and research laboratories of two such outstanding institutions as Harvard and Massachusetts Institute of Technology. The large amount of tax-exempt college property has not made for amicable relations between town and gown.

Cambridge is the second industrial city in Massachusetts, with over 400 manufacturing plants, 1,500 merchandising outlets and over nine miles of store frontings. From its varied industrial plants soap, candy, bakery products, rubber goods, glass instruments, electrical machinery and apparatus, wire cable, foundry products, boxes and chemicals are shipped to all parts of the world. Two regional railroads, the Boston and Maine and the Boston and Albany, have substantial properties within the city limits. Local trolleys, buses, and subways are an integral part of the Boston transportation system.

Its residents speak of their city as "the foremost educational center in America," pointing with pride to the renowned institutions of higher learning—Harvard University, Radcliffe College, Massachusetts Institute of Technology, and the Episcopal Theological School. Contributing also to its intellectual reputation are some forty less well-known private schools, colleges, and academies.

Within the city there are about seventy church edifices of many different denominations, a number of which are rich in historical tradition.

Although at the time the Study was organized there was no public or private agency concerned exclusively with delinquency-prevention, Cambridge had numerous social service facilities. In addition to a large and active YMCA and YWCA, scout troops, and church young people's societies, the city is well supplied with welfare, recreational, health, social, and fraternal organizations. Since 1938 a Community Council, administered by a professional executive, has coordinated the social agencies, both public and private. Numerous committees on youth problems have been formed from time to time, and the total number of individuals in the city, professionally and otherwise interested in the welfare of boys, has been large.[1] In 1938 a "delinquency squad" consisting of three police officers was appointed within the City Police Department. Known as the Crime Prevention Bureau or the Juvenile Aid Bureau, it is particularly concerned with juvenile offenders and in advising and counseling the boys and their parents who are brought to their attention. This official group was cooperative with the Study in working out problems of mutual concern.

During the entire treatment period there was no psychiatric child guidance clinic in the cities of Cambridge or Somerville, but limited psychiatric services were available in the out-patient departments of the hospitals. The well-known Judge Baker Guidance Center of Boston was also used as a resource for children in need of psychiatric guidance.

Cambridge is served by three large hospitals, one public and two private, as well as by five or six small private hospitals and a large, well-equipped, municipal tuberculosis sanatorium. A visiting nurse organization also provides nursing care and public health education. One hundred and thirty-nine physicians resided in the city in 1940. In addition to the various family and other social agencies

[1] This social consciousness is important to note in respect to the Study's control group, for it is unlikely that a family living in Cambridge would be in dire need for any length of time before some organized social group would become aware of it and make some attempt to offer treatment. It would be artificial, therefore, to consider the control group, either in Cambridge or Somerville, as one that was not receiving treatment of any kind.

there are numerous groups interested in child welfare, such as an art center for children, a camping association offering summer camping facilities for children who cannot afford to pay the total costs, a community center for colored children, a child-placing agency and three neighborhood or settlement houses. Though there is no juvenile court, as such, the district courts of the county, both in Cambridge and in Somerville, hold juvenile sessions once a week and support two or more probation officers.

The 1940 census showed a heterogeneous population. Almost one-fourth of the residents of Cambridge were foreign-born. Slightly more than half of the parents of students in the Cambridge High and Latin School were born outside the United States. The dominant religion was Roman Catholic. Politically the city could be considered Democratic, for that party outnumbered the registered Republicans almost three to one. The Negro population comprised about 4.5 percent of the total. Canadians were the most populous foreign-born group, the Irish and Italians holding second and third place, respectively.

Small well-defined areas within the city, particularly in the eastern portion, could be marked off as predominantly Italian, Lithuanian, Polish, or Portuguese, while in North Cambridge there was a large French-Canadian settlement and in the area just south and southwest of Central Square a concentration of Negroes.

SOMERVILLE

Somerville, contiguous all along its southern border to the city of Cambridge, is slightly smaller in population (102,177 in 1940, a slight drop from 103,908 in 1930) and gives a much more homogeneous impression.

Somerville occupies a hilly terrain. "Ten Hills Farm" was the appropriate name Governor John Winthrop gave to the original settlement in 1630. Its boundaries are defined by Cambridge to the south, the Charlestown section of Boston to the east, Arlington to the west, and Medford and the Mystic River to the north. As in Cambridge, the principal traffic arteries run along the east-west axis, a transportation peculiarity which makes intercourse between the two communities of this Study more difficult, and therefore less frequent than their apparent "togetherness" would lead one to expect.

It has a considerably smaller area than Cambridge. It consists of 4.2 square miles compared to Cambridge's 6.2. Its foreign-born population is about the same as that of Cambridge, constituting 23.4 percent. In spite of its population density it claims to have a larger area of parks and playgrounds than Cambridge, though in some sections of the city where they are particularly needed these facilities are inadequate. East Somerville with its many industries and its old and deteriorated dwellings is in sharp contrast to the western section of the city including the residential area adjacent to Tufts College, most of whose properties lie just across the line in Medford.

The more "local" character of Somerville's economic life is seen in the predominance of consumer goods among its odds and ends of manufactures: paper products, caskets, vinegar, ladders and woodenware, spraying equipment, kitchen furniture, metal stamps, tools, dies, novelties, ornamental iron, suitcases and bags, wagon and truck bodies, piano tuners' supplies, children's and dolls' dresses, elastic specialties, brooms, etc.

The inhabitants often refer to their city as the "bedroom of Boston" because so many commute to work in the larger center. This sense of being an annex or satellite also appears in Cambridge but is much less pronounced. In Somerville there is no town and gown division. There is marked community morale and community pride and cohesiveness.

The interesting pioneer effort of Thorndike to score American communities according to a "General Goodness of Life" gave to Cambridge a score of 735 and to Somerville one of 680. This index is merely a composite of quantitative census data taken to imply degrees of social excellence such as the local infant death rate, percentage of home ownership, per capita public expenditures for schools, circulation of public library books, and other selected factors. (The scale runs from a score of 330 for Augusta and Columbus, both of Georgia; Meridian, Mississippi; High Point, North Carolina; and Charleston, South Carolina, at the low extreme to a high score of 1,020 to 1,110 for Pasadena, California—the highest—

Montclair, New Jersey, and Cleveland Heights, Ohio.) Cambridge is slightly above and Somerville slightly below the median of cities of over 30,000 population in 1930.[2] Such averages, of course, reveal little about the various components which enter into them, but insofar as any combined figure can be meaningfully used, it appears that Somerville stands at about the same civic level as Bridgeport, Jersey City, Newark, and Cincinnati, and that Cambridge is on the same plane occupied by Washington, Omaha, Worcester, Toledo, and Salt Lake City.

Somerville is less highly organized than Cambridge in respect to social services, and yet with the outstanding program of its Recreation Commission and its numerous church and social groups interested in the problem of youth it offers many facilities for character-building. It has a large YMCA and many active boy scout troops. Boys living in the eastern section of Somerville have easy access to the appealing and well-equipped Boys' Club building of Charlestown. (In 1942, 384 Somerville boys joined this club.) Somerville boys are served by the many child welfare organizations in Boston.

During most of the treatment period there was no delinquency bureau within the Police Department in Somerville though such a unit was formed in 1943, some five years after this method of dealing with delinquents had been tried out in Cambridge. This unit was much less active than the Crime Prevention Bureau in Cambridge, due in part to the fact that there was less delinquency in Somerville.

THE SCHOOLS OF CAMBRIDGE AND SOMERVILLE

The school, charged with the almost daily responsibility of supervising a child during his formative years, is in the best position to make adequate observations of his early development. It has been found consistently in studies of delinquents that early signs of delinquent behavior, notably truancy, appear long before any overt antisocial act is committed. It was appropriate, therefore, that the public schools should be not only an agency of treatment but the main source of referrals.

A brief statement about the public school systems in both cities is pertinent to our story. Like all cities in Massachusetts these systems

[2] E. L. Thorndike, *Your City* (New York, Harcourt, Brace, 1940).

operate under the school committee form of government. The committees, consisting of seven members in Cambridge and nine in Somerville, elected for two-year terms, are given by the legislature very broad discretionary powers on matters of vital concern to the pupils.

The Committee in Cambridge operated during the time of the Study's program on a budget of about two million dollars; Somerville on a budget of approximately one and one-half million dollars. In each city there were some 26 or 27 different school buildings valued at approximately five million dollars. In Cambridge the elementary schools carry the pupil through the eighth grade, from which he can graduate to a technical high school or a classical high school. In Somerville the pupils advance through six grades and then transfer to one of three junior high schools. A senior high school is also provided. In both cities there are special classes for the mentally retarded, the hard-of-hearing, and for those with defective vision, while home instruction is provided for the physically handicapped. There are also health classes, vocational schools, prevocational classes, trade schools, evening and continuation schools.

A few statistics are necessary to give an adequate idea of the school population from which the Study cases were drawn. The 1936 registered population of the public day schools in Cambridge totaled approximately 17,500 boys and girls, in Somerville approximately 18,000. In the elementary public schools in Cambridge up through the fifth grade there were some 3,700 boys, in Somerville 3,800. If we add to these figures about 1,000 boys in the lower grades of the parochial schools that were cooperating with the Study we find a group of about 8,500 boys from both cities from which referrals might have been drawn. About one out of every five of these boys was in fact referred. One out of every 13 was placed in the treatment or the control group, and one out of every 26 was assigned to a counselor for treatment.

In Cambridge, the Department of Measurement and Adjustment deals with problems of guidance, measurement, and special education. This department was headed by the late Gertrude B. Duffy, a psychologist whose experience as a teacher in all grades equipped her for dealing with children's problems. She was assisted by two psychologists. Although there was no psychiatrist on the staff, the school referred cases to the psychiatric clinics of the local hospitals, with whom a cooperative relationship existed. It was Miss Duffy's generosity and vision that enabled the Study to work so harmoniously with the Cambridge schools. One of the advisors of the Study in its early development, she remained one of its most loyal supporters, contributing practical aid in establishing a smooth working relationship between the Study and the schools.

In Somerville, Everett W. Ireland, Superintendent of Schools, served a similar function in acting as liaison between the Study and the various schoolmasters under his charge. With his help and that of Miss Duffy in Cambridge the Study operated in close harmony with the two school departments.

DELINQUENCY IN CAMBRIDGE AND SOMERVILLE

The choice of Cambridge and Somerville as the field of operations was not based on the incidence of delinquency, as neither city was outstanding in that respect. Locating the Study in Cambridge was principally a matter of convenience. Somerville was included in 1937 when it became evident that the desired number of predelinquent referrals could not be obtained in Cambridge alone.

It was believed that it would be helpful at the outset to acquire at least the basic official figures pertaining to delinquency in both cities. A survey was undertaken to show the incidence of delinquency and the location of "delinquency areas." This information was essential in classifying and later matching the treatment with the control group and in revealing those school districts from which the Study might expect to obtain the greatest number of predelinquents. The survey also aided the search for new cases and disclosed other facts relating to delinquency which were of later use to the counselors.

It was at first thought that surveys made from time to time, and particularly at the end of the treatment period, might reflect the effectiveness or ineffectiveness of the treatment program, by showing the presence or absence of any subtle carry-over to the larger community. This hypothesis rested on the assumption that during the long period of treatment the major factors would remain constant. Such was not the case. The war brought with it an increase in delinquency materially affecting the rate for the entire community while treatment was in progress. Offsetting this to an unknown extent was the work of the Crime Prevention Bureaus of the Police Departments which were set up in both cities after the treatment program was commenced. Such bureaus sifted out many of the less serious delinquents who might otherwise have been brought to court. Repeated surveys, therefore, would not have been comparable or meaningful.

Much time was spent in the early days of the Study in trying to arrive at a satisfactory non-legal definition of delinquency. In this preliminary survey of the two cities the problem was by-passed by dealing only with those boys who were charged with being delinquent and officially recorded in the court dockets. The shortcomings of delinquency statistics based solely on the official records were nevertheless readily admitted. It was understood, for example, that differences between the serious offender and the less serious could not be considered in this preliminary survey; that many boys commit delinquent acts without being apprehended; that many who are apprehended are not officially recorded in the office of the Clerk of Court; that a few who are recorded as delinquent may not actually have committed the acts charged, and so on. "The boy who is a disturbing element on the street, in playgrounds and in other public places; who is careless, destructive, noisy, perhaps a 'gang' leader, perhaps a loafer, may get into the juvenile court, *but more often he does not,* even though his type contributes almost one-third of the boys' cases handled by the court," the U.S. Children's Bureau reports. "Only a very small proportion of the school children who present problems of personality and behavior come to the juvenile court. . . . In a western city 1,430 cases involving such problems as truancy, morals and insubordination were investigated by the school department during a period of four months, and only 116 (8 percent) were referred to the juvenile court." [3]

The staff made a special study at the conclusion of the treatment program of unrecorded delinquencies.[4] This study made clear the unsatisfactory nature of official delinquency records. A tabulation was made of the number of violations of laws and city ordinances

[3] U.S. Children's Bureau, *Facts about Juvenile Delinquency* (Publication No. 215, 1932), pp. 4–5.
[4] Fred J. Murphy, Mary M. Shirley, and Helen L. Witmer, "The Incidence of Hidden Delinquency," *American Journal of Orthopsychiatry*, XVI (1946), 686–696.

of 114 boys who were members of the treatment group during their eleventh to sixteenth years. It was found that 95 violations committed by these boys had become a matter of official court complaint, but it was conservatively estimated that these same boys had committed a minimum of 6,416 infractions of the law during that five-year period. "In other words," the authors stated, "the authorities took official action in less than 1½ percent of the infractions" (p. 688). In short, the official records alone would not give an adequate picture of the number of delinquent boys in the city. Nevertheless, for the purpose of comparing Cambridge with Somerville and for locating the so-called "delinquency areas" the data were reasonably satisfactory.

The only source of information used in this survey was the official record. The docket and files in the offices of the clerks of the various courts gave the name, age, address, and alleged offense of each child charged with delinquency. With the court's permission these records were searched and data extracted covering a four-year period from October 1, 1933, to October 1, 1937. A four-year period was necessary to insure enough data to clarify the "delinquency areas" on the city maps. As all boys referred to the Study at that time were under 11 years of age on October 1, 1937, the survey would also reveal the names of any of these boys who had been delinquent during the four-year period when they were between the ages of seven and eleven.

The following courts supplied the data:

1. The Third District Court of Eastern Middlesex County, located in Cambridge, having jurisdiction over offenses committed in Cambridge, Belmont and Arlington. (Supplied names of 847 boys and 96 girls living in Cambridge or Somerville.)

2. The District Court of Somerville, having jurisdiction over Somerville offenses only. (Supplied names of 350 boys and 24 girls living in Cambridge or Somerville.)

3. The Municipal Court of the Charlestown District of the City of Boston, having jurisdiction over offenses committed in Charlestown. The survey was interested in the records of this court only to the extent that they revealed delinquencies committed in Charlestown by boys residing in Cambridge or Somerville. (Supplied names of 19 boys, no girls living in Cambridge or Somerville.)

4. The Boston Juvenile Court, having jurisdiction over part of the city of Boston. The survey was interested in the records of this court respecting only those Cambridge and Somerville children who had committed delinquent acts within the area presided over by this court. (Supplied names of 82 boys, 9 girls living in Cambridge or Somerville.)

The information gathered from these records revealed the following facts:

The General Distribution of Delinquents' Homes. Two large maps, one of Cambridge and one of Somerville, were "spotted" with small red dots placed exactly at the home address of each delinquent whose name appeared in the official records of the courts listed above. A small dot represented the unit of the identification system; large dots, two or more delinquents or delinquencies at the same address. When completed, the maps showed graphically the general city-wide distribution of the homes of the delinquents. The counselors, who, incidentally, prior to their employment were not residents of either Cambridge or Somerville, found the maps useful in affording a quick orientation to the so-called "bad" neighborhoods.

In Cambridge there were a total of 933 "delinquency units," approximately 90 percent of which represented boys; in Somerville there were 467 such units, about 93 percent of which represented boys. The fact that Somerville, almost as populous as Cambridge, had just half the number of units found in Cambridge was of considerable sociological interest.[5]

In Cambridge fairly obvious delinquency areas appeared in the eastern and southeastern sections of the city. Scattered minor areas could be seen in the North Cambridge district, though 84.2 percent of the units were to be found east of Harvard Square, Wards 1 and 2 in East Cambridge accounting for more than half the total number in the city's 11 wards. The greatest concentration was in areas adjacent to railroads and industrial plants where the cheapest and most unlivable residences were found, a fact already known to sociologists.[6] Somerville showed a wider scatter, with some concentra-

---

[5] For every 100 residents of Cambridge there were 92 residents of Somerville (1940 census).

[6] References to studies on delinquency areas are given in Chap. XVI.

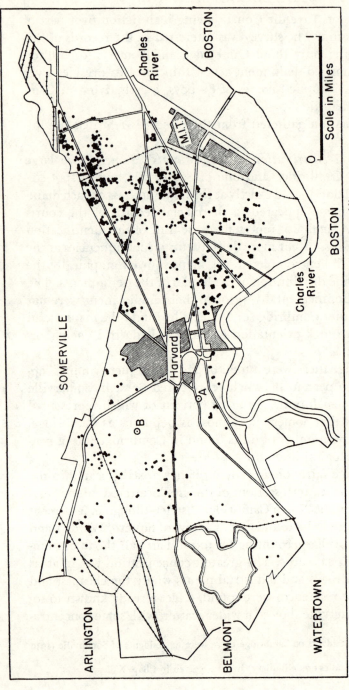

⊙A Location of Dr. Cabot's home and first Study office.
⊙B Location of Study headquarters 1940 and later.

MAP 1. DELINQUENCY SPOT MAP OF CAMBRIDGE, MASSACHUSETTS

On this map a small dot marks the home of each boy between the ages of 7 and 16 inclusive who, charged with delinquency, was recorded officially in the office of the clerk of the various courts named, within the four-year period ending October 1, 1937, and who was living in Cambridge at the time. The delinquencies of these boys may have occurred in Cambridge, Somerville, Belmont, Arlington, or certain sections of Boston.

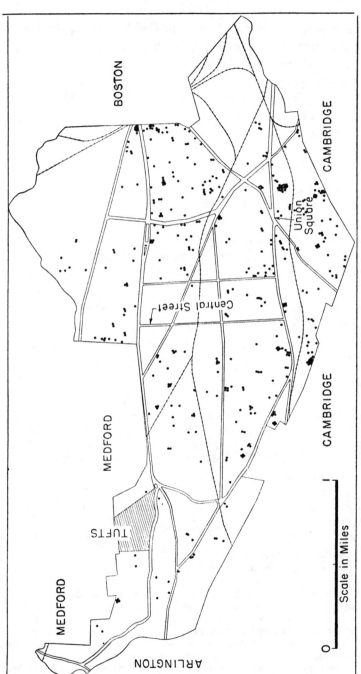

MAP 2. DELINQUENCY SPOT MAP OF SOMERVILLE, MASSACHUSETTS

On this map a small dot marks the home of each boy between the ages of 7 and 16 inclusive, who, charged with delinquency, was recorded officially in the office of the clerk of the various courts named, within the four-year period ending October 1, 1937, and who was living in Somerville at the time. The delinquencies of these boys may have occurred in Cambridge, Somerville, Belmont, Arlington, or certain sections of Boston.

tion in the crowded sections adjacent to Cambridge on the south and the Charlestown section of Boston on the east. Two-thirds of the Somerville delinquent units were found east of a line, running generally north and south, drawn through Central Street in the mid-section of the city. In Cambridge, areas closest to Boston had the greatest concentration of delinquency. The accompanying maps, redrawn from the originals (but dealing only with boys), illustrate these points.

Delinquency and School Zones. It was possible to show the delinquent character of the various zones served by the elementary public schools in the two cities by counting the number of delinquency units appearing in the respective zones. Also, by comparing the school population in each case with the number of units in the area served by that school, a comparative ranking of the schools was established.[7]

The Annual Incidence of Delinquency. In neither city was official delinquency on the increase when the Study commenced operations. In fact, in both cities there were fewer cases before the juvenile sessions of these courts in 1936 and 1937 than in 1933 and 1934, as shown by Table 2. Frequently the same boys were charged with

TABLE 2

Comparative Number of Annual Court Charges
(From October 1 to September 30)

Year	Cambridge (847 Boys) [a]	Somerville (350 Boys) [b]
1933–34	268	121
1934–35	364	87
1935–36	288	81
1936–37	255	81
Total	1,175	370

a Only 591 of these boys lived in Cambridge.
b Only 244 of these boys lived in Somerville.

7 By such methods it was found that in Cambridge, for example, Roberts, Thorndike, and Houghton schools, and, in Somerville, Hanscom-Edgerly-Prescott, and the Baxter-Perry-Knapp schools were located in the areas where the homes of the delinquents were most frequently found. It was more useful to the Study, however, to know the incidence of delinquency relative to school populations. It was found that of the 20 elementary Cambridge schools those located in areas of little delinquency relative to school population were, in this order: Haggerty, Agassiz, Russell, and Peabody; while Roberts, Thorndike, Fletcher, and Houghton showed the greatest number

several offenses at different times during the four-year period. In Cambridge the 1,175 cases represented 847 boys; in Somerville the 370 cases represented 350 boys. There were evidently considerably more repeaters in the Cambridge court than in the Somerville court.

The Delinquency Rate. A delinquency rate is ordinarily determined by computing the relationship between two factors: (a) the number of boys who committed one or more delinquent acts within a given period and territory, and (b) the number of boys of delinquent age living within that period and territory. Simply stated, the question is: "What proportion of boys who *could* have committed delinquency did so?" It is not possible to find the exact figures for either of these two factors. No one, of course, knows the number of boys who commit delinquent acts in any given period of time, for most delinquencies go undetected. As previously pointed out, the official records are not entirely comparable, since the methods of recording differ from one political jurisdiction to another, the practice of the court varies from time to time, and so on. However, there was available nothing but the official count which, for purposes of comparing Cambridge with Somerville, was reasonably adequate.

The second quantity, the number of boys of delinquent age (from seven to 16 inclusive) who were residing in Cambridge or Somerville during the period in question, could not be directly determined for they were not officially recorded as such. We could find, however, the number of registered minors in both cities, including those in public schools, private schools, special schools and institutions, and those not in school at all. From the school reports it was possible by certain computations, the details of which need not be given here, to approximate the number of boys within the registered minor group who were within the delinquent age range. From the delinquency survey data the number of boys in each city

of delinquent units relative to school population. It was learned later that Roberts School, which was located in the worst delinquency area in either city, absolutely or relatively, actually referred more boys who were later characterized as minus boys by the Selection Committee. In Somerville, among the 23 elementary public schools, the school zones where delinquency, relative to school populations, was most infrequently found were in this order: Lowe-Highland, Cutler, Hodgkins, Glines. Somerville schools located in dense delinquency areas, relative to school populations, were: Durrell, Baxter-Knapp-Perry, Pope, and Burns. School maps based on these factors furnished definite leads to the location of probable pre-delinquent boys.

officially charged with delinquency during the four years could be closely estimated.

The average number of these boys in Cambridge in 1933 to 1937 is estimated at 9,608. The Cambridge court records list the names of 591 boys who lived in Cambridge, the Somerville court 45, the Boston Juvenile Court 51, and the Municipal Court of Charlestown 2. How many Cambridge boys were on the court records of other cities we do not know, but it would seem reasonable to assume that there were at least ten such cases, giving an estimated total of 699 Cambridge boys for the four-year period, or an average of 175 boys per year. The delinquency rate, based on the boy population (9,608) and the number of delinqent boys (175) was found to be 1.82 per hundred.

In Somerville, by a similar method, it was estimated that for an average year during this period there were 9,108 boys between the ages of seven and 16 inclusive. Our survey indicated that there were 244 Somerville boys listed in the Somerville court, 52 in the Cambridge court, 31 in the Boston court, and 17 in the Charlestown court. We might assume also that there were approximately ten Somerville boys listed in courts outside of these cities, thus giving us a total of 354 boys or an average of 89 per year for the period. The delinquency rate for Somerville was thus estimated to be 89 per 9,108 or .98 per hundred.

About two out of every 100 Cambridge boys of delinquent age were involved each year in some form of delinquency resulting in a court appearance. The rate for Somerville was somewhat lower— approximately one out of every 100 boys of delinquent age. It is difficult to compare Cambridge and Somerville with other cities in this respect for the basis for determining the rate varies widely from place to place. Some cities base calculations on the number of offenses rather than on the number of individuals; some may not include non-resident delinquents; some may include delinquents of different age range than that provided by law in this state, while most delinquency statistics include both boys and girls. Nevertheless, it is of interest to note that in neither Cambridge nor Somerville was the rate unusually high. The U.S. Children's Bureau reported "approximately one child in every hundred of juvenile-court age comes before the courts as delinqent in the course of a year." This conclusion was based upon statistics gathered from many courts and evidently included both boys and girls.[8] The delinquency rate (for boys only) for different cities throughout the country in 1933 showed wide variations: San Francisco with .79 per hundred, New York City with 1.15; Bridgeport (Conn.) with 2.16; Baltimore (Md.) with 3.48; Hartford (Conn.) with 4.09.[9]

Age Distribution. Though it is well known that boys frequently commit delinquent acts long before they are brought to court, the survey revealed only the age when the boy was officially charged. By "age" is meant the age stated in the court files. Generally the date of birth was not given (or when given was not verified) but the age of the boy in terms of years was given and this presumably was the age at his *last* birthday. There were 21 cases where the age was omitted or questioned. Of the 350 boys listed in the Somerville court docket, five were of unspecified age. In Somerville "age" meant age at the birthday nearest to the time of recording. Thus a boy 16 years and 7 months old might be listed in Cambridge as 16 and in Somerville as 17. Nevertheless, it is apparent that in both cities 15–17 are the most frequently recorded ages. Relatively few boys under 11 years of age (that is, within the age limits for Study referrals at that time) were found listed in the court dockets.

TABLE 3

Age Distribution of Delinquent Boys in Cambridge and Somerville Courts

	CAMBRIDGE COURT		SOMERVILLE COURT	
Age	*Number of Cases*	*Percent*	*Number of Cases*	*Percent*
7	3	.4	—	—
8	10	1.2	1	.3
9	33	4.0	2	.6
10	35	4.2	9	2.6
11	54	6.5	14	4.1
12	85	10.3	16	4.6
13	109	13.2	34	9.9
14	123	14.9	59	17.1
15	160	19.4	75	21.7
16	214	25.9	91	26.4
17	...	...	44	12.7
	826	100.0	345	100.0

[8] U.S. Children's Bureau, *Facts about Juvenile Delinquency: Its Prevention and Treatment* (Publication No. 215, 1932), p. 4.

[9] *Ibid., Juvenile Court Statistics and Federal Juvenile Offenders* (Publication No. 232, 1933), p. 8.

Nature of the Offenses. Tables 4 and 5 show the incidence of the various offenses entered in the official dockets. Fifty-five percent of the offenses charged against boys in Cambridge were for larceny and/or breaking and entering, compared to 64 percent in Somerville.

TABLE 4

Offense Distribution of Delinquent Boys (Cambridge Court)

Offenses	Frequency	Approximate Percent
Larceny	327	30
Breaking and entering and/or larceny	275	25
Motor vehicle law violations	97	9
Trespass	68	6
Breaking glass	50	4
Assault and battery	49	5
Stubborn child	38	4
Injury to property	32	3
Evasion of fare	31	3
Sex offenses	21	2
Metropolitan District Commission violations	14	1
Runaway	14	1
Robbery (armed)	10	x [a]
Disturbing peace	9	x
Selling, peddling (no license)	9	x
Carrying weapon	8	x
Violation city ordinance	7	x
School offenses	6	x
False fire alarm	6	x
Assault with dangerous weapon	5	x
Drunkenness	5	x
Robbery	4	x
Idle and disorderly	4	x
Dice on Sunday	3	x
Tampering with railroad appliances	2	x
Wayward child	2	x
Miscellaneous	9	x
Total	1,095	100

[a] x = less than 1 percent.

Seasonal Differences. All cases were tabulated in terms of the month of the year in which the charge against the child was recorded. It was found that the warmer half of the year—April

TABLE 5

Offense Distribution of Delinquent Boys (Somerville Court)

Offenses	Frequency	Approximate Percent
Breaking and entering and/or larceny	130	33
Larceny	124	31
Trespass	46	12
Motor vehicle law	19	5
Stubborn child	16	4
Assault and battery	14	4
Injury to property	14	4
Violation of city ordinance	11	3
Riding on street and freight cars	11	3
Sex offenses	3	x [a]
School offenders	3	x
Runaway	1	x
Miscellaneous	6	2
Total	398	100

[a] x = less than 1 percent.

NOTE: The total number of offenses listed in Tables 4 and 5 differs slightly from the totals given in Table 2 because sometimes a delinquency record comprises two or more counts, each listed as a separate offense. At other times two counts are listed as one offense.

through September—accounted for 56 percent of the cases. More cases (165) were recorded in August than in any other month. The smallest number (72) fell in December.

Geographical Distribution of Delinquent Boys. Approximately 30 percent of the boys charged in the District Court of Cambridge resided outside of Cambridge, but it should be kept in mind that this court also had jurisdiction over offenses committed in Belmont and Arlington. The same percentage in respect to non-residents was true of cases brought into the District Court in Somerville. Approximately 6 percent of the boys in the Cambridge court resided in Somerville, whereas about 13 percent of the boys in the Somerville court came from Cambridge. About 9 percent of the boys in the Cambridge court lived in Boston. Bostonians in the Somerville court likewise made up 9 percent of the total.

The survey revealed the names of 28 delinquent boys who by October, 1937, were not yet 11 years old and hence might be considered possible subjects for the Study, but most of these boys could not be located before they reached the age of 11 or for some other reason could not be accepted. A few referral possibilities were listed among the younger brothers of delinquents.

The survey proved to be valuable in selecting and classifying referrals from delinquent and non-delinquent school zones and neighborhoods, and in setting up two comparable groups—one for treatment and one as a control. The counselors, too, who later had to take into consideration the character of the neighborhood in which the boy lived, found the data useful in planning their programs.

CHAPTER III

THE SEARCH FOR
TOMORROW'S
DELINQUENTS

ALTHOUGH THE SURVEY SUPPLIED US WITH THE NAMES OF MANY official delinquents, all but a few were past the upper age limit for the Study or reached it before they could be visited. Furthermore, the Study was seeking potential delinquents not yet known to the authorities. Who were these youngsters and where did they live— these little boys who today might be found playing innocently in the streets or peering from behind a book at their desks in the first or second grades? Who could give us the names of these boys who now were innocent of wrongdoing but who might later comprise part of our prison population?

REFERRALS FROM THE SCHOOLS

The school presumably was in an advantageous position to select boys who seemed most likely to be well on the road toward a delinquent career, and yet teachers could not be expected to make infallible judgments, nor were they always willing to reveal the names of boys who seemed to them most likely to become delinquent. The Study could not ask the schools to list the names of all suspected predelinquents. Few teachers would care to burden a child with that label; nor could it be made clear to teachers—nor, in fact, to anyone, exactly what "pre-delinquent" meant.

From a survey of the current literature, a list of behavior manifestations commonly associated with actual delinquents was prepared and submitted to the Cambridge public school officials in June, 1935, at the first meeting where the program of the Study was publicly presented. The principals and the teachers from the kindergartens and the first, second, and third grades were asked to nominate boys below the age of ten who showed some of the following traits or habits to the extent that they might be considered difficult boys: [1]

Persistent truancy	School retardation
Aggressiveness	Lack of emotional control
Persistent breaking of rules	Smoking
Stealing	Petty pilfering
Sex delinquencies	Lying
Excessive lying	Daydreaming
Repeated disobedience and defiance of authority	Persistent disobedience
	Destructiveness
Extreme timidity	Extreme jealousy
Temper tantrums	Cruelty
Bullying	Obscenity
Revengefulness	Reading difficulties
Undesirable companions	Undesirable gang activities
Begging	Cheating
Continual tardiness	Breaking into and entering premises

Until they understood the nature of the project, the teachers were slow to refer names of boys. The directors and some of the staff met with small groups of teachers and principals at the schools to clarify the objectives of the Study. After a number of such conferences the number of referrals markedly increased.

During the following school year (1936–37) an important change was made in the experimental design of the Study: non-difficult boys were now to be included. It was soon realized that if the treatment group comprised only selected pre-delinquents or "bad" boys, unhappy public relations might result. All boys recognized as Study boys might be stigmatized by friends and the general public as delinquents. Some confusion resulted when this necessary change was made. Quite a few teachers continued to think of the Study exclusively in terms of delinquents. For example, a teacher of the first grade in one of the schools wrote on the record card of Jimmy, who was originally referred by another agency, "James is a very good boy; I don't know why he is in the Study." Throughout

[1] Though at this time names were desired of as many boys as possible from the six- and seven-year-old group, the difficulty of obtaining an adequate number was realized and the age limit was extended to ten. Later, for practical reasons, this age was extended to 11, and then to 12.

the life of the Study the original impression, that the Study was interested only in the pre-delinquent, was hard to overcome. As boys advanced to higher grades their teachers were less well-informed about the purposes of the Study and sometimes embarrassed the boy (and his counselor, too) by expressing surprise that "this child" who was "such a good boy" should belong in a group of "problem boys." Italo, for example, after a chance meeting with the school nurse, developed some anxiety about his selection. After the Study terminated, he reflected

I thought it [the Study] was all right and then one day I went down to see the school nurse and I happened to say something about Mr. N. [his counselor] and she said, "Do you know Mr. N.?" and I said "Yes." She said, "You must be in the Cambridge-Somerville Youth Study then." I said, "Yes, I was." She said, "Well, what's wrong with you?" Jeez, I didn't know what she meant and I said, "What do you mean—what's wrong with me?" She said, "Well, what are you in the Study for then?" Well, I got worried then and so I went and asked Mr. N. I couldn't figure out what she meant. I began to wonder if there was something wrong with me. Mr. N. said she was just misinformed. He said they just picked out a bunch of boys to study and see that they grew all right and helped them out if they had any trouble but the way that nurse looked at me, well, I could tell she did think there was something wrong with me. I don't know where she got that idea but she was wrong.

Non-difficult boys, for convenience, were called average boys, a term having no statistical connotation but representing the general run-of-the-mine boy who showed no present signs of future delinquency, without, on the positive side, being necessarily a paragon of virtue. A rapid increase in the number of names was immediately noted. The teachers found it much easier, and no doubt pleasanter, to refer names of so-called good boys. As three research groups were then contemplated, teachers were asked to refer two average boys for every difficult one. The three groups were to comprise one of 200 difficult, one of 200 average boys, both to be treated, and one of 200 average boys for comparison. The final research design, however, consisted of one treatment group of 325 boys, difficult and average, and one control group similarly made up, thus automatically creating a surplus of average boys. Still later, even when it was evident that a sufficient total number of names had been referred, it was necessary to request further referrals of difficult boys because the proportion of difficult to average was less than the desired ratio of approximately two difficult to one average.

SOMERVILLE SCHOOLS INCLUDED

In the fall of 1937 the public schools of Somerville were included as an integral part of the experiment. The parochial schools in Somerville were reluctant to be included, and hence referred no names, although later when the treatment program was under way, they cooperated in planning treatment programs for boys transferred from the public schools to their own classrooms. The parochial schools in Cambridge were interested but relatively cautious, referring fewer names than was expected from an examination of the areas in which these schools were located as disclosed by the delinquency "spot maps." By January, 1937, the number of referrals was still behind expectations. Three Cambridge public schools and seven in Somerville had not yet submitted any names. During the ensuing months the referral process was facilitated by a further clarification of the Study's objectives, by furnishing the teachers with a definition of difficult and average, and by the development of questionnaires and check lists that enabled the teachers to make fairly clear-cut decisions. The teacher's characterization of a boy as difficult or average was considered tentative, to await a more exact classification by the Selection Committee (see Chapter V). Hundreds of visits were made by staff personnel to the schools, for the purpose of giving psychological and physical examinations to boys already referred and of carrying through an extensive program of teacher interviews. By January, 1938, 1,096 names had been referred by the schools, or by others and cleared through the schools. Schools that had by 1938 referred less than the proportion of predelinquents one would expect, after an examination of the delinquency "spot maps," were especially urged to submit further names. (A correlation of +.74 was later found between the rank order of Cambridge schools in terms of the number of delinquency units in the respective school areas and the rank order of these schools in the proportion of boys referred who later were rated minus, that is, predelinquent, by the Selection Committee. In Somerville, where there were fewer areas of heavy concentration of delinquency, a correlation, obtained in a similar manner, was no greater than a +.12.)

When the referral period ended in 1938, it was found that, in general, Cambridge teachers, and to a less degree those in Somerville, were able to locate the pre-delinquent as that term was understood by the Selection Committee. In other words, the teachers, as a general rule, tended to nominate as difficult those boys who were later rated minus by the Selection Committee, but many exceptions were noted. To what extent the Committee's judgment, in turn, was determined by the teacher's characterization of the boy is not known.

It was natural that a few teachers should experience some reluctance to refer names to the Study. Some said they did not know their boys intimately enough, particularly if the request was made at the beginning of the school year. Some thought it was presumptuous on the part of anyone to predict that a first- or second-grade child would be a future troublemaker. Others believed that it was unkind, if not unethical, for a teacher to point a finger at a child and say, "This boy will be a criminal." Some teachers, too, feared that if they referred a large number of difficult boys from their own classrooms, they might be considered inept as disciplinarians. One, in fact, said, "There are no 'difficult' boys in my room. I don't permit any misbehavior. I'm very strict with my boys. Not one of them is a bad child." As a result no boys were referred as difficult from that classroom although the school was located in a zone where many delinquents lived. Others at first suspected the motives of the Study and were afraid that publicity harmful to the boy might result or that the teacher herself might later be accused by irate parents of having created a prejudice against the child. It was not surprising, therefore, that the referral process could not be completed in a few months' time. After the teachers had become better acquainted with the purposes and needs of the project and were assured that the Study was concerned only with the child's best interests, that no child would be stigmatized as a delinquent or predelinquent and that the project would not in any sense be a "guinea pig experiment," they cooperated wholeheartedly. Every one of the grade schools in the public schools of both cities eventually submitted names. From Table 6, showing the source of referrals, it is evident that (a) no referrals were made from grades beyond the fifth; (b) more than three-fourths of all school referrals were

from the third grade and below; (c) about two-thirds of the boys
were from Cambridge, one-third from Somerville; (d) only 11 percent were parochial school boys.

TABLE 6

Distribution of School Referrals by Grades

Grade When Referred	RATING OF BOYS			PERCENT OF REFERRALS		
	Diffi-cult	*Aver-age*	*Total*	*Cambridge Public*	*Somerville Public*	*Cambridge Parochial*
Kindergarten	49	51	100	63	37	..
I	178	186	364	47	41	12
II	168	211	379	56	34	10
III	136	184	320	53	33	14
IV	82	150	232	53	34	13
V	30	37	67	58	30	12
Pre-Vocational	1	3	4	100		
Nursery	2	1	3	100		
Special Class	18	1	19	84	16	
Unclassified	5	4	9	45	22	33
Total	669	828	1,497	54 (808) [a]	35 (524) [a]	11 (165) [a]

[a] Figures in parentheses represent the number of boys from the indicated source.

REFERRALS FROM OTHER SOURCES

Only 77 percent of all referrals came directly from the teachers
or schoolmasters. Other sources had to be tapped to bring in the
names of substantially all Cambridge and Somerville boys (with the
exception of Somerville parochial school boys or boys attending
private schools) who might have been considered pre-delinquent.
The directors therefore called together the representatives of community organizations; staff members personally visited police sta-
tions or talked to policemen on their beats; occasionally, a home
visitor from the Study heard indirectly of some boy known as a
"nuisance" in the community. Playground supervisors were consulted during the summer months, social agencies were visited,
youth leaders interviewed; in short, no possible source of information was overlooked in the search for the "worst boys" in the community. Of the 337 names thus gathered, 19 percent were found to
be too old for the Study, 12 percent were in parochial schools which
had not yet cooperated with the Study, 5 percent had moved out of
town and 7 percent could not be found. About 15 percent had al-

ready been referred by more than one agency or individual. Eventually 110 of the 337 referrals became members of the treatment or control group.

Names of boys referred by agencies other than schools were forwarded to the appropriate schools for verification and for further information and ratings by the teachers.

Table 7 shows the sources and numbers of supplementary referrals. Table 8 shows the sources from which all referrals were drawn.

TABLE 7

Source and Number of Supplementary Referrals

Source	Number	Totals
Cambridge:		
1. A Family Welfare Agency	46	
2. Police Department	36	
3. An Episcopal Church	14	
4. A neighborhood house	13	
5. A community center	10	
6. A health association	8	
7. X Settlement House	7	
8. Y Settlement House	6	
9. Playground Supervisors	5	
10. Boy Scouts	1	
Total		146
Somerville:		
1. Probation Officers	51	
2. Police Department	15	
3. Visiting teachers	10	
4. The "A" Family Welfare Agency	3	
5. The "B" Family Welfare Agency	2	
6. YMCA	1	
7. Red Cross	1	
Total		83
Court Records: (from Cambridge and Somerville)		
1. Delinquent boys	28	
2. Boys whose older brothers were delinquent	78	
3. Boys whose parents were charged with neglect	2	
Total		108
Grand total		337

TABLE 8

Distribution of Cases Referred from All Sources

Referring Groups	Number	Percent
Cambridge Public Schools	808	41.4
Somerville Public Schools	524	26.8
Social Agencies and others	337	17.3
Cambridge Parochial Schools	165	8.5
Miscellaneous [a]	119	6.0
Total	1,953	100.0

[a] This category includes names picked up indirectly or referred by individuals, but it also unavoidably included some names received from two or more different sources. Likewise there was some duplication of names from social agencies. Eliminating all duplications there remained approximately 1,800 referrals.

CHAPTER IV

THE INITIAL STUDY
OF THE BOYS
AND THEIR
FAMILIES

SHORTLY AFTER THE FIRST CASES WERE REFERRED, THE STAFF SET about the search for the facts considered essential in planning a research and treatment program of this nature. There was no precedent to follow; the staff was not large; the assignments were heavy. Throughout 1937 and 1938 there was increasing pressure to accelerate the process, for it was realized that until these data were collected, recorded, and passed on to the Selection Committee for classification and thence to the matchers, no treatment could be commenced.[1] In the meantime some cases had to be rejected, for some of the older boys had passed the upper age limit for inclusion in the treatment program before all of the information concerning them had been collected.

BASIC INFORMATION

The forms or schedules of information used can be briefly described:

1. The Home Visitor Schedule.[2] This schedule provided the most valuable single source of information. The comprehensive and detailed reports of the home visitors were used by the Selection Committee when they were faced with the task of weighing the de-

---

[1] It should be noted that in about a dozen cases the special problem was of such an emergency nature that treatment was initiated at once in spite of the research demand for prior classification and matching. Some of the emergency cases were treated as "good will" cases rather than official Study cases; a few were later classified, matched, and arbitrarily placed in the treatment group.

[2] For a copy of this schedule see Appendix C.

linquency probabilities of each boy. One member of this committee stated:

The quality of the home visitor reports was quite consistently superior to any with which I have been acquainted among the thousands of agency reports reviewed in my previous work in the correctional field. Because of the degree of objectivity which the home visitors maintained and their increasing skill in capturing the total family situation, the prognostic value of the data was great.

The many items of this schedule were filled in by social workers who visited the homes of 839 boys, spending one hour to several hours in each home talking in a friendly manner with the mother or whoever was in charge of the boy at that time, sometimes returning many times in order to complete the interview. The completed schedule included the developmental history of the boy and gave information, as a rule from the mother's point of view, of the boy's habits, his recreation, his attitudes toward school, his religion, and his personality. This schedule also furnished the Study with information concerning the parents' education, personality, employment history, and methods of discipline, the neighborhood and home conditions, and facts regarding the boy's siblings. It concluded with a statement of the total situation as it impressed the visitor.

The Selection Committee suggested certain items in the schedule (which was revised from time to time) and thus was able in a limited way to direct the gathering of information particularly pertinent to its own deliberations.

There were three home visitors working full time and two on part-time, all of them women. Two of the full-time and one of the part-time visitors were social workers; one of the full-time visitors was a registered nurse. The task confronting them at the outset seemed little short of appalling. To go, unsolicited and unannounced, to homes in a community in which they were not well acquainted, while the housewife was likely to be preoccupied with cooking or bathing the baby; to ask for an hour's interview in surroundings that were anything but conducive to reflection, and then to ply this puzzled stranger with numerous personal questions, was a task that few investigators would relish. And yet the visitor was usually able to bring back a vivid picture of the home as it appeared on her unheralded call. In the Smith family, for example, the parents of seven young children were an irresponsible father and a distraught mother who, for obvious reasons, had not been cordial to officials or inquisitive strangers. The visitor from the Study reported:

Family lives on the first floor of four-story brick tenements about midway in the block. They have five rooms and separate toilet for nine people. Place so dark that a light has to be on in kitchen all day. Entries very dark and cluttered with boxes and refuse. Ventilation very poor and quarters extremely ill-smelling. Furniture inadequate, falling apart. Soiled clothing, dirty dishes, refuse, puddles of urine on floor, and general dirt and disorder told a story of long-time neglect and deterioration.

Mother had heard us asking a neighbor where to find her and we got the impression that she was on the point of trying to sneak out without seeing us. She had a coat half on and looked as though she had been caught doing something she shouldn't. However, she made no attempt to excuse herself and rather helplessly backed into the kitchen again and said she realized things were in an awful mess; explained that after the kids had gone to school that she had gone back to bed and so hadn't gotten her work done. All the time we were talking she proceeded to try to clean things up. She did this in a most disorganized fashion, apparently forgetting from time to time what she had started and rather frantically attacking whatever her eye lit on. In appearance she was a short, pudgy woman with stringy yellow hair and staring blue eyes. Some of her front teeth were gone and others broken which affected her speech and appearance. Her cheeks were flushed and her manner distracted. She wore a ragged cotton dress that had not been ironed and was put on wrong side out. Her whole manner and looks spoke of an individual who had long ceased to care very much what others' opinion of her was or to have any hope for the future. The only exception to this was her account of her struggle the previous Sunday to look presentable for church; said that someone had given her a nice looking silk dress [the only other one she owns] and that it turned out to be too tight for her. She put on corsets and pulled herself in all she could and went out feeling as though she looked fine but that she might burst apart any minute.

At first mother believed our interest in Billy meant that we wanted to take him away because of the trouble he had been causing in school. Apparently she did not intend to dispute our right to do this. Said later that she really didn't want to put him away " 'cause he's my child." We reassured her on this point and told her that no matter how bad he was we would be interested in him because we wanted to know more about all kinds of boys. Later on when we explained the possibility of our coming back and inviting him to share in the advantages we had to offer she said that "anything that would help my Billy would be okay with me." Actually we would expect a rather submissive type of cooperation with occasional flare-ups of suspicion and defensiveness on the part of both parents. Anything that we could do to relieve them of the burden of responsibility for this child would probably be welcome to them as they are very worried about his future and felt keenly the judge's remark at the time of his court appearance to the effect that if they had been decent parents the boy wouldn't have gotten into trouble. [Mother believes that the father stopped drinking on account of this. Whether he actually did or not is a question, as we were aware of a strong smell of liquor in the house.]

We had occasion to observe the mother in her attempts to handle the younger boys who came into the house during our visit. At first she took no notice of them, simply remarked to us that having the kids underfoot drove her crazy. Then one of them began to scratch his head. She dove after him and began to look for nits. A minute later she grabbed the youngest one and very roughly wiped his face with the same wet cloth that she had used to wipe up the table and wash the dishes. Then for our benefit she began to ask him who God was and where he lived. After getting the proper answers, she picked him up and began to hug and kiss him. Not long afterwards she told them all to get outdoors in a hurry. Two of them started to go but Bob sat there stubbornly as though to defy her to do her worst; she then began to hit him and pull him towards the door; gave this up and threatened him with all sorts of things saying that she would kill him, that she would have the nurse take him away. When this did not work she told him that the next penny she got would be his if he would go out and he promptly left. Her six-months-old baby [a very pale sickly looking child] slept quietly in his carriage in the middle of the room during all this.

The discipline is not at all clear at this point. Mother said that the reasons for punishing Billy were mainly for lying, stubbornness, "sassing back," and staying out late nights. She and father are mainly concerned about the last and are dreading the summer months when they expect to spend most of their time looking for him. Told of how in the last stages of pregnancy she spent half the night searching for him and finally had to give up because the pains were so bad. All summer the neighbors tell her of one boy that has been drowned and another that has been hit by an auto and she is always sure it must be Billy. When it gets bad enough, father licks him but he continues to stay out just the same. She knows very little about his present associates or activities and one gets the impression that she feels well rid of him when he is out of the house and simply hopes that he won't get them all into trouble. His appearance in court in 1936 alarmed them a great deal; caused them to move away from the neighborhood where he was running around with "desperate characters," and the father to give him a beating. However, it apparently had little effect on Billy as mother said that it was impossible to scare him or shame him and that he was just as bold and daring as ever; does not even seem to be afraid of the cops.

When he first started school this last fall he truanted a number of times and his father also beat him for this. Mother thinks that Billy has stopped on this account. She knows that he is a problem to the teacher and at times believes that he deserves all that he gets in school. However, there have been times when she resented his having been punished and hit by the teacher and she proceeded to write "insulting notes." On one occasion she regretted having done a thing of this kind and went to the principal to apologize. For the most part she says that the father's bark is worse than his bite and cited an instance when he started to make Billy go to bed without his supper for having been out late and then backed down saying he couldn't bear to make any child do without food. However, father has recently told Billy that for every licking he gets in the school he will give him one ten times worse.

Subsequently, in spite of the efforts of the counselor assigned to work with Billy, the boy developed a propensity for delinquent behavior and was institutionalized several times.

In all the homes visited the investigators made a rating on the following items: [3]

A. Standard of living in the home (a rating from "least able" to "most able" to "maintain health and decency").
B. The home as a place likely or unlikely to produce delinquency.
C. The nature of the discipline by the parent ("opposed discipline," "inert," "well-balanced," "severe").
D. The mother's personality ("conscientious," "talkative," "domineering," etc.).
E. The boy's personality ("quiet," "fresh," "immature," etc.).
F. The cooperativeness of the family, indicating the likelihood or unlikelihood that the family would cooperate with the Study in a treatment program.

Of the 839 families visited there were only eight that definitely refused to be interviewed. From a few others genuine cooperation was lacking at first, but subsequent visits by another or the same

---

[3] The first two items as they related to the homes of boys who later became delinquent are compared with ratings of the non-delinquents' homes in Chap. XVI.

visitor yielded adequate results. The visitors recorded their judgments as to the probable degree of cooperation to be expected from
the family in the coming years, as indicated in Table 9.

TABLE 9

Degree of Expected Cooperativeness as Rated by Home Visitors

Degree of Cooperativeness	Frequency	Percent
1. Least	38	5.0
2. Slight	168	22.1
3. Active (meaning to an average degree)	349	45.9
4. Slightly more than average	142	18.7
5. Most	63	8.3
	760	100.0

NOTE: Although 839 different homes were visited, the cooperativeness scale was checked in only 760 cases. When the first visits were made in 1936, this scale had not been developed. There is no reason to believe that any significant change in the percentages would have occurred had all cases been so rated.

After reviewing the evidence, the visitor rated the boy on the
same 11-point scale used by the Selection Committee, estimating
the probabilities of a delinquent career.

People with chronic anxieties, it was found, generally liked to
talk out their worries with a sympathetic listener. Joseph's mother
was typical of the group that felt the need to reach out for some
confirmation of their worst fears or for some assurance that they
were doing all they could as parents in the face of overwhelming
odds. She complained that no one ever came to her home to express
an interest in Joseph, who was "worrying her sick," unless it was
an officer of the law who always reminded Joseph that bad boys
should be "put away." A visit by the Study representative stood out
as a bright spot in this mother's memories for years to come. Now
someone in the city was, at last, interested in her son, "who was not
really a bad boy" but just "picked on" by everyone.

How shall we account for the success of these first contacts with
the boys' families? The personality of the visitor was probably the
most important factor. Her procedure was quite simple. She arrived
at the home generally during school hours so that the interview
could be held in the absence of the boy. She introduced herself as a
person interested in boys and particularly in the boy of this family
who had already been seen by the Study physician and the nurse

at school.[4] The association of the Study with the school made a good impression. The visitor pointed out that the work was being carried on with the permission of the school and with the cooperation of the boy's teacher and principal. Many parents would probably not have understood the purpose of an organization completely unknown in the community unless it were affiliated with a socially acceptable institution. The visitor before making her call was well supplied with information obtained from the school and if there was any special school problem involved, she familiarized herself with it. It was thus not difficult to convince the parents of her interest in the child. Unfortunately, she could not promise the mother that the boy would be helped, for at that time it was not known whether the boy would become a treatment or control boy. (There turned out to be about one chance in 2.6 that the boy would be included in the treatment group.) If any problem encountered was of an emergency nature, the visitor usually referred the case to another agency.

Intuitive skill and sympathetic interest were needed to inspire the parents' confidence. The lack of education of the mother or her inability to speak English clearly was at times an obstacle. Suspicion and resistance were sometimes met with, especially where guilt feelings centered around the criminal history of some member of the family. In a few cases a generalized attitude of suspicion was characteristic. It was reported, for example, that Nova Scotians and British West Indians were more reluctant on the first visit to divulge personal information than the Irish and the Italians. In some instances the parents became particularly alarmed because of a suspicion that the child must have been involved in serious trouble at school. Such fears were usually dissipated when the visitor informed the parents that many hundreds of boys had been referred and that their boy was simply one of a large group made up of "all kinds of boys" in whom the Study was interested. A second or third interview was sometimes required before the parents would feel comfortable about responding to the questions.

2. *Trait Record Card.* The most valuable information concerning the behavior of a child outside his home was obtained from the schoolteachers. The staff prepared a check list of antisocial or unde-

---

[4] See p. 46 for a description of the physical examinations made in the schools.

sirable symptoms or characteristics and presented it to that teacher who presumably knew the boy best in the school in which he was registered. This list was an elaboration of the original list of traits of difficult boys submitted to the teachers when referrals were sought (see p. 30). It comprised no "good" or socially approved characteristics but left blanks that the teacher could fill in if she so desired.[5] It dealt with the following areas of behavior, seven to 15 items being listed under each division: [6]

A. Troublemaking behavior, such as refusing to cooperate, blaming others for difficulties, and the like.
B. Neurotic behavior, such as worrying, being fearful, restless, nervous.
C. "Show-off" behavior, such as seeking the limelight, or acting silly.
D. Retiring or shy behavior, such as daydreaming or being easily embarrassed.
E. Aggressive reactions, such as quarreling, fighting, teasing.
F. Submissive behavior, such as keeping to himself, feeling that he is being "picked on."
G. Antisocial acts of a more overt sort, such as truanting, stealing, and destruction of property.
H. Undesirable habits, such as poor work habits, nail biting, masturbation.

The teachers were also asked to give a thumbnail sketch of the personality of the boy. Some were too brief or general to be of use, but most of these little sketches gave adequate and colorful descriptions.[7]

3. Descriptive Rating Scale.[8] In addition to the Trait Record Card, each teacher filled out a scale modeled after the Haggerty-Olson-Wickman Schedule.[9] Approximately 100 specialists in child psychology, psychiatry, sociology, juvenile delinquency and social

[5] The first card contained 68 items; the fourth and final revision contained 93. For a copy of this card see Appendix C.
[6] The contrast between the "most delinquent" boys and those who were less delinquent in respect to these traits is shown in Chap. XVII.
[7] Illustrations are given in Chap. XVII.
[8] See Appendix C.
[9] M. E. Haggerty, W. C. Olson, and E. K. Wickman, *Haggerty-Olson-Wickman Behavior Rating Schedules* (Yonkers, N.Y., World Book Company, 1930).

work were asked to list the qualities that seemed to them to characterize the behavior of a typical pre-delinquent boy. The 26 items
most frequently mentioned, or appearing most frequently in constellations (possibly yielding nothing more than a sort of delinquent stereotype of an extreme nature) were chosen as the basis
for the scale. The teacher checked one of five degrees in each item.
For example, a teacher, asked to rate a boy in terms of restlessness,
would place a check in the parenthesis over the most appropriate
descriptive phrase:

Is he restless?

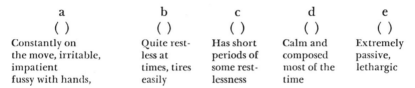

a	b	c	d	e
( )	( )	( )	( )	( )
Constantly on the move, irritable, impatient fussy with hands,	Quite restless at times, tires easily	Has short periods of some restlessness	Calm and composed most of the time	Extremely passive, lethargic

4. Psychological Tests. Approximately 100 of the boys who were
among the early referrals were given individual psychometric tests
by two psychologists using the 1937 Revision of the Stanford-Binet
test and the Grace Arthur Performance Scale. It was impossible to
continue the individual testing program when the referrals began
to come in at a more rapid rate. Group testing in the schools was
then resorted to, the Kuhlmann-Anderson test being used. All boys
were tested before selection and matching. In most cases the
Stanford Achievement test was given at the same time. In a few
cases some of the boys who were three years mentally retarded had
been tested by the State Clinic (using the 1916 revision of the
Stanford-Binet).

5. Teacher Interviews. Teachers were sometimes reluctant to
express opinions in writing about a child for fear of some repercus-
sions from the boy or his family but were willing to talk frankly and
freely to someone with a legitimate reason for making an inquiry.
Two members of the staff interviewed the teachers of 961 referred
boys. In most cases the comments of the teacher were recorded in
shorthand. The interviewers were particularly interested in knowing whether the boy caused trouble in school; whether he was a
leader; whether he was cruel to other children, impulsive, restless,

destructive; whether he made friends easily, was easily teased, was regular in school attendance, orderly and neat; what attitude he took toward his school work and so on.[10]

The interviewing afforded an opportunity for representatives of the Study to explain the program more fully. Confidence and rapport were built up in this way, and teachers were encouraged to suggest further names at a time when the Study had an insufficient number of difficult boys.

6. Physical Examinations. A physical examination, even though relatively superficial, was considered essential. Arrangements were made to examine each child at the school. In the first two years Dr. Richard C. Cabot personally examined about a thousand boys. He traveled from school to school, week after week, thumping chests, listening to heart beats, and talking in a friendly way with each boy until his own physical condition prevented him from carrying the work further.[11] Altogether, approximately 1,100 boys were examined. Assisting the doctors was a trained nurse who later became one of the home visitors and still later one of the counselors in the treatment program.

The physician's schedule consisted of two parts.[12] One contained the numerous items of the kind usually included in a physical examination that does not involve X-rays or other elaborate equipment. The second part consisted of the general impression made by the child while he was being examined and his answers to the doctor's questions concerning his health, appetite, sleep, school, how he liked certain playmates, how often he went to the movies, what his three wishes were, what he did at home, what he was afraid of, and so on. The doctor rated the boy in terms of general behavior, checking some sixteen personality or behavior items or as many of these as seemed to apply. A brief personality sketch was included. The nurse who assisted at each examination gave an independent impression of the boy and her ratings on the same items. These examinations helped to establish rapport with the family later, particularly when it was possible to give the parents advice as to the

[10] Illustrations of these interviews are given in Chap. XVII

[11] Dr. Donald Gates was employed in the fall of 1938 to complete the few remaining examinations.

[12] For a copy of the form used in recording the results of the physical examination see Appendix C.

boy's physical needs. The appropriate authorities were notified if some chronic or acute health need was discovered. If the condition was not in need of immediate attention, the doctor made a notation of it to be read by the person who might later become the boy's counselor.

7. *Prognosis Sheet.*[13] All of the prognostic ratings on the 11-point scale were collated and transferred to a prognostic sheet. At least five independent ratings were entered for each of the 782 boys—by the home visitor, the psychologist, the teacher-interviewer, the physician, and the nurse or others on the staff (see Table 10). Here also were recorded the various personality sketches of the boy.

TABLE 10

The Predictive Rating Scale Used throughout the Study

Average (plus boys)	$\begin{cases} +5 \\ +4 \\ +3 \\ +2 \\ +1 \end{cases}$	Markedly not difficult or non-pre-delinquent. (Extreme probability of no delinquent career.)
	0	Uncertain or equal probability of development toward or away from delinquency.
Difficult (minus boys)	$\begin{cases} -1 \\ -2 \\ -3 \\ -4 \\ -5 \end{cases}$	Markedly difficult or pre-delinquent. (Extreme probability of a delinquent career.)

8. The Board of Probation Records. Records were obtained, through the courtesy of the State Commissioner of Probation, of any existing official court records of the boy or any member of his family or immediate relatives.

9. Social Service Index Records. These records listed the social welfare agencies in the local area, both public and private, which had known the boys' families. A field worker from the Study visited most of these agencies making a note of pertinent information ap-

[13] See Appendix C.

pearing in their records. (Boys who later became treatment boys were re-registered with the Index when treatment started, and subsequently from time to time.)

10. Delinquency Spot Maps.[14] From the delinquency "spot maps" previously described it was possible to answer the following questions concerning each boy: (1) Did he come from an area where delinquency was relatively common? (2) If so, how does this area compare with others?

11. Delinquency Rating of the Neighborhood. Two special investigators inspected the immediate neighborhood in which the boy lived. Using the same 11-point scale they rated this location in terms of its probable good or bad influences on the boy. They took into consideration the incidence of delinquency in that particular locality as indicated by the delinquency maps and also observed the presence or absence of recreational facilities, railroad yards, taverns, poor housing and so on.[15]

12. Overnight Camps. In the summer of 1937 two staff psychologists conducted a series of seven overnight camping trips. On each trip a group of seven or eight of the older boys who had been referred to the Study (but not yet assigned to the treatment or control group) was taken to the country. Unfortunately only 47 boys were included, a mere 2½ percent of the total group referred. The purpose of these outings was to obtain by direct observation diagnostically valuable information. For that reason there were practically no formal camp rules or regulations that one usually finds in a boys' camp, although limits had to be placed on acts that were dangerous or annoying to others. Boys, for example, could go to bed at any time they wished or, if they preferred (which incidentally none did), they could stay up all night. They could play ball, tramp through the woods or simply sit around and do nothing. With a minimum of disciplinary supervision there was a maximum of opportunity for display of free behavior. When given this freedom the boys at first were incredulous. Most of them later said they had never before had so much fun at camp. Echoes of these outings were heard for years afterwards from the boys who became members of

14 See Maps 1 and 2 in Chap. II.
15 A comparison of delinquents' and non-delinquents' homes in respect to these neighborhoods appears in Chap. XVI.

the treatment group. Notes of their behavior with personality descriptions were taken independently by the two camp leaders. Photographs of each boy were also filed with each case. Henry, who later became a serious delinquent, was described by the two leaders in the following words:

Camp Leader A. A tough, mischievous, very active boy, not to be trusted. He is an habitual liar, is thoroughly spoiled and must have his own way or he gets very abusive. When accused of doing something he was told not to do, he immediately rationalizes, puts the blame on others and "tells tales" on them. Went out with another boy in the night with a flashlight but was frightened by a shadow and came screaming back to his tent. He likes to scare others. When told not to put firewood on the fire, he watches his chance and throws it on when he thinks he is not being watched. In cooperative undertakings he is poor, gets "sore" when playing baseball, and resorts to shouting and swearing. Likes to tell of his escapades with the cops. If there is any clear-cut pre-delinquent in this group of 47 boys, Henry is the one.

Camp Leader B. Usually he is talkative. He is never lacking in something to do or say; usually there is something quite clever in the way he behaves, almost quite annoying. He has the other boys cowed, they don't dare to jibe him or to squeal, to "butt into my business" which "is everything." He plays many pranks, such as holding a boy's head under water, destroying trees, burning up kindling, throwing away dishwater, all of which seems to be due partly to overactivity and partly to intention. He is an unscrupulous liar. Every three minutes he is disobedient. He likes to talk and easily could become a leader of a gang. Already he has one boy in the group under his "influence." He tells of having set fires on the railroad tracks. The cops and Scouts put it out and he tells with evident relish of his escapes from the cops.

13. Photographs of Boys. In almost every case a small snapshot of a boy was obtained from the school where such photos were taken each year.

14. Miscellaneous Information. Not infrequently additional information was secured; for example, statements from police officers or neighbors of boys or statements by boys about other boys.

SUMMARY

The fourteen items yielded a comprehensive picture of the boy and the environment in which he was living. The staff was able to obtain this picture of more than 800 boys. The portfolio of information on each boy thus covered the following items:

1. His Family. An impressionistic picture of the personality of one or both parents, together with information concerning their background, education, work history, religion, their attitudes toward their children and the kind of discipline they said they used in the home; vital statistics concerning the family group, contacts with social agencies or with law-enforcement authorities. Comments about the family from school officials, neighbors or other sources within the community were generally included.

2. The Boy Himself. A brief sketch of the developmental history of the boy as told by the parent or parents was given with records of the boy's progress in school, his general attitudes and his personality from the teacher's viewpoint; undesirable traits checked by his teachers; the mother's impressions of the boy and her own attitude toward him made known through the home visitor's report; psychometric tests, school reports, and various rating scales indicating the impression he made upon his teacher, home visitor, physician and others; official records from the State Board of Probation and the courts, if any, and reports from other agencies, as well as a variety of miscellaneous sources giving a general picture of the boy's reputation in the community. In every case the boy himself was seen by two to six members of the staff, each of whom talked with him and gave a report and a prognostic rating. A general description of the boy's state of health, his physical coordination and structural development was given with reports of childhood diseases and illnesses as recalled by the mother. If the boy had been in a hospital, the hospital records were studied. Usually a photograph was filed with the school data.

3. The Boy's Environment. The neighborhood in which the boy lived was described by the home visitor and by two special investigators.

This information was sufficient to warrant classification by the Selection Committee; to permit the matching of one boy with another in setting up a treatment and a control group; to serve as a basis for a prediction study, and to afford a counselor adequate material for initiating a treatment plan.

CHAPTER V

WHO SHALL BE CHOSEN?

ALTHOUGH DURING THE EARLY MONTHS THE STAFF HAD SOME DOUBTS that the required number of boys could be found, eventually far more cases were referred than the Study could include in the treatment and control groups. By the spring of 1938 the files bulged with almost two thousand names, whereas the working program called for only 650 (half of them to be treated, half to be placed in a control group). Most of the referred cases, however, were presumably average boys, making it doubtful that the required proportion of difficult to average could be established.[1] The Study was thus confronted with two questions: (1) Which cases should be selected? and (2) Which of these boys could be characterized as pre-delinquent?

To answer these questions it was necessary to call in a small group of experts who became known as the Selection Committee (referred to in this chapter as "the committee"), whose function it was to examine all of the information obtained for each boy referred to it and to classify all cases in terms of apparent trends toward or away from delinquency.

PRE-SELECTION

It soon became obvious that a preliminary screening process would make it possible to discard a large number of surplus cases quickly without asking the committee to undertake an intensive and time-consuming study of the total group. When the intake of

---

[1] Originally there was to be one large group comprising only difficult boys and two of equal size made up entirely of average boys; later (as stated in Chap. III) it was decided to have only two groups—each to contain *both* difficult and average boys in the proportion of two difficult for every one average. This shift in the design after many cases had already been referred caused an ultimate disproportion that was never fully corrected.

referrals was closed Dr. P. S. de Q. Cabot set up a pre-selection technique that involved the consideration of more than one thousand cases. Many boys could be immediately rejected because they were beyond the age limit, as could others who represented a surplus of older boys within the age limit. It was not always easy to forecast the ultimate fate of the boy in the hands of the committee; that is, one could not be sure that a boy who appeared to a teacher, for example, to be difficult would be so classified by the committee, which had available more information than the teacher possessed and probably a different frame of reference. By studying the committee's judgments for the first few months one could get some idea of what kind of a boy was usually judged difficult by them. It could be determined within reasonable limits, for example, that boys with certain constellations of traits would probably be labeled difficult by the committee. Probabilities worked out on the basis of such constellations were checked against the performance of the committee, thus furnishing clues for pre-selection. In this way it was possible to control to some extent the ratio of average to difficult and of older to younger boys. No attempt was made to see that the group ultimately selected would be a cross section of the population of the two cities. On the contrary, it was hoped that the group would contain far more pre-delinquents than a true cross section would yield.

The 1,953 cases referred to the Study were finally disposed of as follows:

1. Two hundred and twenty-one cases had already been considered and classified by the committee before the pre-selection process had been set up.

2. Six hundred and thirty-three were rejected as of little or no use to the Study. Over one-half of them were now too old, or had moved out of town or could not be located, while on at least one-third there was insufficient evidence upon which to base a judgment. A small number were rejected for miscellaneous reasons such as death, lack of cooperation, and duplication of names.

3. Five hundred and thirty-eight cases, after study by the pre-selector, were rejected, generally in accordance with the probabilities that had been determined.

4. The remaining 561 cases were retained by the pre-selector and passed on to the committee for its consideration.

As the screening process developed it became evident that the function of selecting cases for the Study was carried out by the pre-selector rather than by the committee. The latter turned out to be a classification body, describing and classifying all of the 782 cases passing through its hands, rejecting none.

Later comparisons of the pre-selector's "guesses" as to the ratings to be made by the committee showed that approximately 80 percent of the cases considered average by the pre-selector were later so rated by the committee while approximately 61 percent of the pre-selected difficult cases remained in that category after the committee passed judgment upon them. The committee was unaware of the characterization made by the pre-selector. As a general rule there was greater agreement between the pre-selector and the committee in dealing with the older boys for whom more information was available.

Pre-selection was successful in cutting down the time spent by the committee and in assuring the Study of the maximum number of pre-delinquents when the treatment and control groups were finally organized. *No boy who showed obvious pre-delinquent trends was excluded, provided he met the other necessary requirements of age, residence, and school attendance.*

PROGNOSIS AND CLASSIFICATION

The value of the treatment program naturally depended to a great extent upon the kind of boy the counselor would have to deal with. One would also have to know the delinquency prognosis in order that the boy might be matched with another boy. The committee, therefore, occupied a peculiarly central position in the whole plan of the Study.

A committee of three was chosen. Each member had special competence and experience in his own field and had had no previous association with the Study. As all three had been professional students of criminology with practical experience with criminals, it was believed that they would be in a favorable position to make delinquency prognostications on the basis of the early life histories of these young boys.[2]

[2] The three members were: (1) Dr. Bryant E. Moulton, practicing psychiatrist, formerly with the Judge Baker Guidance Center, Boston. He had served as Assistant Physician, State Psychopathic Hospital, Ann Arbor, Michigan; Assistant Superin-

The committee was organized in the fall of 1937 and held many preliminary meetings to discuss functions, definitions, and methods of operation. Its members were able, by and large, to devote only evenings to the task. They began the actual classification of cases in November, 1937, and did not complete their work until January, 1939. By that time they had classified 782 cases, which seemed to be a sufficient number, for it gave the matchers a surplus of 132 cases beyond the limit determined—325 for the treatment group and 325 for the control group.

In classifying a boy the committee used the 11-point scale previously described. The scale was, in effect, a prognostic indicator of the probabilities of good or bad behavior. Not knowing whether a boy under consideration would fall into the treatment or control group, the committee's prognostications were based on the assumption that the boy would not receive special preventive treatment. The committee drew up definitions of the terms—difficult, zero, and average—which corresponded to the —, o, and + ratings respectively.[3]

What Is a Difficult Boy? The judges were asked to define their own understanding of "difficult." One judge defined a difficult boy as one "whose habits, attitudes and behavior gave evidence of an incipient or actual antisocial career whether or not he had as yet come into open conflict with the law." A second judge also expressed the opinion that court appearance was not a necessary criterion of delinquency. He emphasized the observed disorganization of the personality. The third judge expressed his opinion of a difficult boy by stating that he had in mind "one who in the face of a

---

tendent, Hospital for Criminal Insane, Ionia, Michigan; and Assistant Superintendent, Wayne County Training School, Northville, Michigan. (2) Wilbur C. Irving, Director of Case Work, Massachusetts Reformatory, was engaged in social investigation, the preparation of case histories, the classification of inmates, and the supervision of staff workers. He was formerly on the staff of the State Prison engaged in prison case work. (3) Richard S. Winslow, Head Social Worker of the Division of Classification of the State Department of Correction. served for several years as supervisor, teacher, and coordinator of case work at the State Prison, the Massachusetts Reformatory, and the Norfolk (Mass.) Prison Colony; after October, 1938, he was a settlement house director at the South End House, Boston.

[3] It will be recalled that the words difficult, pre-delinquent, and minus boys were used synonymously; likewise, average, non-pre-delinquent, and plus boys were different expressions of the idea that the boy in question was not developing in the direction of a delinquent career.

normal amount of deterrence gets into difficulty with society. He may not be actually delinquent, but he either shows evidence of a lack of personality adjustment sufficient to cope with the average environment or the environmental influences are such that the average boy would not be able to resist them persistently and would turn to some antisocial conduct as a solution." He also would not base his judgment on a legal definition nor would he claim that delinquency was *necessarily* the result of a disorganized personality. In fact, he believed that delinquency might be the normal result of adverse environmental influences. A disorganized personality, he maintained, is not necessarily antisocial. These views showed some diversity and yet there was enough fundamental agreement so that the same scale could be used by all three judges with a reasonable amount of common understanding. Each had avoided the pitfalls inherent in holding to the concept of a difficult boy as one with an *official record* of delinquency.

What Is an Average Boy? The average boy was harder to define. The first judge described him as a boy "who is physically, mentally and morally capable of conducting himself in accordance with the generally accepted standards of behavior in the broader community (that is, not merely the immediate neighborhood)." The second judge did not hold to a strict definition of the average boy but considered him broadly as one who could adjust in a changing situation to the problems of his age level without impairment of personality. The third judge also refused to see the average boy in terms of any particular typology. He might even be an abnormal personality, but as long as he did not respond to stress with disturbing *conduct,* he might still be considered average. He was considered to be one who has "built up a stable sense of values and ethical standards which would act as a deterrent to antisocial acts." Acceptable social conduct rather than a well-integrated personality was the chief characteristic of the average boy as interpreted by the judges.

When the judges attempted a definition or description of what they meant by the zero classification it was evident that some confusion had crept in. Logically a zero classification should mean that the probabilities of future delinquency and of future non-delinquency are equal; it becomes then the midpoint between difficult and average. The point at which two contrary probabilities come together is virtually a point of indecision or uncertainty. Boys whose future seemed completely uncertain were thus rated zero. Frequently the judges also placed in this group boys upon whom they had insufficient information. This category also included some who were too young to have developed easily recognized social attitudes outside of the home. During the early part of the selecting process confusion arose as to how to classify the boy who had personality deviations. Such boys were sometimes tentatively placed in the zero group and remained there for lack of further clarification. This group was thus considered a weak category for it could not be thought of as invariably representing a midpoint on a scale constituted of equal gradations from plus to minus.

How Judgments Were Made. For 91 percent of the cases each of the three judges independently made a prognostic judgment. A rating was accepted as final if at least two of the judges had independently agreed and the third member did not disagree by more than two points on the scale. If this was not the case, a discussion was held until a perfect agreement was reached. This agreed rating then became the final one. In the remaining 9 percent of the cases two of the judges made independent preliminary judgments. If they agreed, the rating was considered final. If they did not, the third judge was called in for a joint discussion which resulted in a final agreed judgment.

A few representative samples of the descriptions given by the raters as the basis for their judgments follow:

Example A. In this case the boy gave the appearance of a predelinquent. The committee members rated him —3 or —4 with a final rating of —3 (a high delinquency rating, for the extreme —5 rating was seldom used). This boy, later placed in the treatment group, did *not* become delinquent at least up to the age of 18.

Judge 1:—3. A highly neurotic boy emulating the neurotic behavior of the mother by whom he is defended on every occasion. A serious behavior problem at school, where he is recognized by several teachers as a potential source of continued difficulty, which may be expressed in several types of delinquency (truancy to escape unpleasantness, fighting as immediate reaction to any restraint, and so on). Several siblings neurotic. One brother has court record for assault and battery. There are now charges pending against boy for assault on teacher. Boy undisciplined and out of control in home. Home situated on margin of one of principal delinquency areas, and home during previous five years located in one of worst delinquency areas. Some of the outward appearance of disorder in home situation must be discounted because it is due to an habitual excess of emotionality in facing all situations. Boy may be expected to encounter greater difficulty as he meets responsibility of increasing age.

Judge 2:—3. Poor pattern in both parents. Mother distinctly neurotic and children are taking on her self-excusing impulsive traits with physical symptoms. Father is obviously evading. Boy undisciplined and shielded by mother. On the streets much in delinquency area. Is acquisitive and "cashing in" on an attractive, glib personality in the easiest way. Can't stand discipline.

Judge 3:—4. A thoroughly undisciplined youngster, son of a highly neurotic, aggressive mother who speaks little English. One brother already on probation for assault and battery. Boy a problem in home and school. Recently assaulted teacher who tried to restrain him. Mother also attacked teachers. Is handsome and spoiled. Few, if any, assets and many liabilities.

Example B. This boy, in spite of treatment, became a very serious delinquent and was finally sentenced to state prison for a term of five to eight years for armed robbery when he was 18 years, 8 months old. Each member of the committee independently rated him on the delinquent side at —2 on the scale.

Judge 1:—2. An unsupervised boy in a home broken by separation of parents. Boy a frequent truant and is developing anti-authoritarian attitude at school where he is leader, mischievous, lies, suspected of stealing; bold, impudent. Good neighborhood and home furnished well, but little security offered by home. No criminality.

Judge 2:—2. Colored boy long without supervision at home and resents authority. Has built up poor work habits and evasive methods. Already truants much—possibly steals. Is aggressive enough to get into trouble. Mother, while well-meaning, works and will gradually lose control. Father's influence in the broken family too far removed.

Judge 3:—2. Negro, age 11, the youngest of four children in a home broken by separation of parents (no details) and further handicapped by need of mother working out, and hence inadequate supervision. Fair district, though one case of delinquency in same house or next, and a sister may have had illegitimate child. Boy has average intelligence and is in Grade V. Bright but not interested in anything but manual training. Has truanted at least 20 times this year and is leader of clique of four Negroes; a fighter and liar.

Example C. This boy, later placed in the treatment group, seemed to show the conventional signs of future delinquency and was so rated. Final rating —2. As a matter of fact, he adjusted fairly well in the following nine years and was not delinquent officially or unofficially so far as the Study knows.

Judge 1:—2. A retarded boy (three years in Grade I, now failing Grade II) who is one of 12 children in a home broken by death of father three years ago. Economic stress, poor health of mother who feels inadequate to cope with the problems of so large a family and a decidedly poor neighborhood environment are striking liabilities. One brother has court record, another brother recently expelled from school, several younger siblings are retarded at school, one being in a special class. Boy shows aggressive and troublesome traits at times, but under control in schoolroom.

Judge 2:—2. Boy is dull and accomplishes little. Rickets earlier. At present is compliant and inadequate in reaction but has temper and shows evidence of aggressive ideas (toughness). Mother feels inadequate and apprehensive of trouble; restricts boy. Later boy will recognize mother's inadequacy and follow own desire for recognition, probably in delinquent companionship.

Judge 3:—3. Aged 9, in Grade II, two years retarded and may repeat this year. The youngest of 12 children (one dead and two married) in a home broken by father's death three years ago. Has inferior intelligence on tests. Two brothers have been in juvenile court. Mother not well and on relief. A congested and delinquent area. Is docile and tries to please in school.

The judgments of the committee members were not arrived at by mathematical computations of weighted variables. From the testimony of the judges themselves there is little doubt but that the judgments were configurational or impressionistic, the determining elements of which could not well be separated.

Just how predictions of delinquency were made by our experts is in itself a fascinating problem. Dr. Donald W. Taylor has reported a special study of this matter.[4] Although the configurational trend dominates the picture, still by analyzing the "conscious" reasons each judge gave for his own prediction, a revealing comparison of the judges with one another can be made. Taylor's findings, here abbreviated, are as follows:

1. The over-all agreement in the prediction of delinquency, de-

---

[4] See Donald W. Taylor, "An Analysis of Predictions of Delinquency Based on Case Studies," *Journal of Abnormal and Social Psychology,* XLII (1947), 45–56.

termined by product-moment correlation of the ratings, was for each pair of judges over +.80

2. The most frequently mentioned reasons given by all the judges for their predictions were adequacy of the home, quality of the neighborhood, and intelligence of the boy.

3. Yet the variety of items mentioned by judges to justify their prediction differed greatly. What impressed one judge as a valid indicator was often omitted by another judge entirely. Even when the three judges agreed on the ratings they never listed exactly the same items as grounds for their judgments. The mean indices of agreement on the items mentioned by the judges showed correlations of only +.41, +.43 and +.32.

The interesting psychological fact that emerges from Taylor's study is that the *reliability of prediction* is far greater than the *reliability of reasons for the prediction*. Later in this report it will be shown that the validity of the predictions of the judges was also fairly high (see Chapter XVIII). One can only infer that much of the prediction process is "global" or "intuitive" in character, and that experts are not able fully to verbalize the grounds for their diagnoses and prognoses.

The committee believed that in spite of the great variety of available data on each boy, two important sectors of information were missing that are highly relevant in making prognoses. First, no interviews of the boy by the judges themselves were possible. Judgments had to be based solely on information submitted by the investigators. The psychiatrist member of the committee stated: "The lack of any psychiatric interview with the subject did lessen tremendously the accuracy of the work. . . . This, in my opinion, is the most valuable prognostic aid that there is." This restriction, however, was dictated by the limitations of time. Secondly, in all but a relatively small number of cases the father was not seen by any of the investigators. Information about the father was found in official records, if any, or obtained by the home visitor from an interview with the mother or boy. Reports of the father's personality and his attitude toward the boy were generally believed to be less valid than information concerning the mother.

Distribution of Prognostic Ratings. The final distribution of the committee ratings is shown in Table 11, revealing an obvious bimodality. The committee apparently refrained from extreme ratings. Their conservative trend was evidenced by the absence of any plus fives and the inclusion of only two minus fives in the entire series of 782 cases. The plus twos and the minus ones were the steps in the scale most frequently used. About three-fourths of the total group was placed in the minus two, minus one, plus one, or plus two categories, compared with a hypothetical 36 percent if the boys had been equally distributed over the 11-point scale.

TABLE 11

Distribution of the 782 Prognostic Ratings

Ratings	Boys	Percent
−5	2	.3
−4	9	1.2
−3	44	5.6
−2	145	18.5
−1	161	20.6
0	87	11.1
+1	119	15.2
+2	149	19.1
+3	55	7.0
+4	11	1.4
+5	0	0.0
	782	100.0

SUMMARY

The Selection Committee turned over 782 cases to the matchers for distribution into two equal groups. Each case had been thoroughly studied and given a prognostic rating indicating the degree of probability of a delinquent career, in the absence of special preventive treatment. The largest group, consisting of 361 (or 46 percent), were thought by the committee to show varying degrees of probability of delinquency, compared to 334 (or 43 percent) who were believed to show a tendency in the opposite direction. As to the remaining 87 (or 11 percent), who were rated zero, there was considerable doubt. Of the minus cases 248 were Cambridge boys, 112 were from Somerville (address of one uncertain). This ratio of about two to one between Cambridge and Somerville boys reflected the incidence of delinquency in these two cities as already reported in Chapter II. This ratio also held in the distribution of referrals from the two cities and in the final selection of cases for treatment.

CHAPTER VI

THE TWO MATCHED
GROUPS: TREATMENT
AND CONTROL

THIS CHAPTER HAS BEEN PREPARED ESPECIALLY FOR READERS WHO
are interested in the technical problems of matching.

An essential technique in sociological and medical research is the
employment of a control or comparison group. The Study adopted
this scientific model. Our assumption is that if the two groups, one·
treated and one not, were similar at the outset, then any significant
differences between them at the end of the ten-year program could
be attributed to the major variable in the picture—the counselors'
treatment. In what respects should these two groups be similar and
how could similar groups be found in view of the unquestioned
uniqueness of the boys' personalities?

POSSIBLE MATCHING PLANS

It would be possible, of course, to divide 650 boys into two
equally large groups, without any thought of matching them, by
simply distributing them alphabetically, or in some other way
randomizing the sample. Chance would give some sort of rough
group equating, but the two groups could not be "proved" similar
enough to afford a convincing basis for final evaluation. A treatment program so elaborate and so prolonged seemed to deserve a
more systematic control.

The original plan was to create two groups by placing the names
of the boys on cards and distributing them in two equal piles, holding one or two variables constant, such as age and predictions of
probable delinquency, and letting chance take care of the remaining variables. It was believed, however, that two variables, no mat-

ter what two were chosen, were not enough to guarantee good matches. The treatment program warranted a more careful matching, for upon it the evaluation of the accomplishments of the Study would hinge. What was desired was (a) a large number of variables, and (b) a system based upon careful individual (clinical) matching. Two members of the staff undertook the development of a matching procedure adapted to the research needs of the Study.[1]

It seemed desirable to draw into the matching process at least a dozen variables, all discovered to be important in earlier research on character formation and delinquency. Yet all statisticians know that the difficulty of matching increases to an alarming degree in proportion to the number of variables chosen. For one thing it would require a very large pool of cases upon which to draw, in order to get a relatively small group of boys well matched in respect to even five or six different factors. The matchers, therefore, were faced with a dilemma, for the number of cases from which they could select potential matches was limited.[2]

The usual matching method of equating isolated factors was abandoned, not so much because of the restricted number of available cases, but because a more dynamic interpretation of the personality was desired. A unique plan was determined upon; one that would combine a clinical approach with a statistical treatment of the more relevant variables.

BASIC PROCEDURE

The cardinal principle of the matching procedure was that each personality would be studied both statistically and configuration-

[1] Henry C. Patey and Dr. Edward A. Lincoln, staff psychologists, were assigned this task. The basic design of the plan was Mr. Patey's contribution. Much of the preparation of forms, charting, plotting, and statistical groundwork was done by Mrs. Henry C. Patey.

[2] The reader will recall that 782 cases were classified by the Selection Committee and made available for matching. This group was reduced to approximately 750. As 650 boys had to be paired and split into two groups of 325 each there was a dispensable margin of only 100. The matchers therefore were not free to adopt a plan that would require a pool of disproportionate size from which to choose their matched pairs. On the other hand, the large number of minus boys (as rated by the Selection Committee) presented in some respects a fairly homogeneous group from which it was not too difficult to draw matchable pairs. A like homogeneity characterized the plus group. In other words, large sub-groups of boys had come from fairly similar cultural backgrounds, making it possible to match boys more readily than if the group had consisted, for example, of a cross section of the boy population of the United States with all the sociological diversity that that implies.

ally. The emphasis was upon the relationship of the variables, upon the profile or contour of the personality. The disadvantage of a configurational approach lies in the fact that no method has ever been developed for discovering and standardizing the interrelationships that comprise a total configuration. It was clear that the procedure ultimately was in large part subjective, and yet the matchers believed that sound clinical judgment based partly on subjective factors and partly on quantitative measures would succeed in striking at the essentials. They attempted to see the clinical implications in a study of each case without losing sight of the statistical formulations.

SELECTION OF VARIABLES

Though the method was partly clinical it rested on selected variables and their computed interrelationships. The first step was to choose appropriate variables.

The rich source material that was used by the Selection Committee was made available to the matchers. A preliminary sample of 80 of the oldest boys (11 years and 5 months old when the matching started) was intensively studied. This group included the 47 boys who had been taken on an overnight camping trip and in relation to whom a great deal of information had been gathered (see Chapter IV). Mr. Patey himself was one of the observers on these camping trips; hence he knew these boys personally.[3]

After studying the data the matchers concluded that approximately 142 variables in each case were available and relevant to the objectives of the Study. What constituted relevancy cannot be precisely stated. Factors that were considered important in published studies on delinquency were, of course, included. Other variables were added because of their manifest bearing on personality. All these variables were grouped into six categories or divisions:

1. Physical health
2. The intelligence and educational quotients
3. Personality (emotional adjustment)

[3] In some 300 other cases both Mr. Patey and Dr. Lincoln had some superficial acquaintance with boys whom they had tested in the schools prior to matching, but the actual pairing of boys was done with the aid of matching charts on which boys' names did not appear. Aside from the 47 campers, the matching was done for the most part on the basis of ratings and interpretations of data gathered by others rather than on the matchers' personal and direct knowledge of the boy.

4. Delinquency prognoses
5. Factors relating to primary social groups (home)
6. Factors relating to secondary social groups (neighborhood)

Later it was found possible to reduce each of these divisions to a single quantitative rating,[4] and to plot on a single graph the profiles

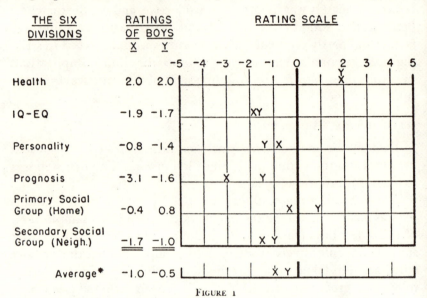

THE SIX DIVISIONS	RATINGS OF BOYS		RATING SCALE
	X	Y	
Health	2.0	2.0	
IQ-EQ	-1.9	-1.7	
Personality	-0.8	-1.4	
Prognosis	-3.1	-1.6	
Primary Social Group (Home)	-0.4	0.8	
Secondary Social Group (Neigh.)	-1.7	-1.0	
Average*	-1.0	-0.5	

FIGURE 1

PLOTTING THE SCORES ON EACH OF THE SIX DIVISIONS FOR
TWO INDIVIDUALS, X AND Y

* Average rating for X is —5.9/6 or —1.0; average rating for Y is —2.9/6 or
—0.5. The difference between the average ratings for X and Y is 0.5.

NOTE: The scores or ratings of the two boys are indicated on the graph by
an X and Y at the appropriate scale points. Differences between the X and Y
averages were held to 0.4 as a general rule. Differences greater than this might
not prevent a pairing of X and Y if additional evidence for similarity existed.

of the two members of the potentially matched pair in order that
a quick comparison could be made. Figure 1 illustrates how this
was done. In reality, of course, each division (with the exception of
health) was the composite of several variables.

A brief discussion as to how a selection was made of the most

---

[4] Quantities were always represented by a point on the 11-point scale running from
plus five through zero to minus five. Values that were considered desirable or good
were always at the plus end of the scale. I.Q.'s were converted to points on the scale
by considering .50 or below a —5, .60 a —4, and so on up to 1.50 a +5 with 1.00 at
the zero point on the scale.

appropriate or meaningful variables within the six divisions is essential to an understanding of the process.

Using the same 80 cases that had been intensively studied, slotted cards were prepared similar in principle to the Hollerith Card. In these cards holes were punched out at certain designated places corresponding to each of the 142 variables with their quantitative or qualitative sub-divisions. These cards were then placed in a file and with the aid of a long needle thrust through the holes it was possible to separate out of the pile those having the most similar contours or profiles in respect to each variable. The matchers found that there were six variables that, if held constant, nearly always located cards with similar total profiles. Or, to state it another way, boys who most resembled each other in terms of these 142 scattered variables of unknown values and weights seemed to resemble each other most consistently in terms of the six variables which thereafter were called starred variables. The starred variables became an essential part of every match and no boys were considered well-matched if they showed a wide discrepancy on the scores representing these six factors.

THE SIX STARRED VARIABLES

1. Physical Health. This measure was derived from the physical examination (as described in Chapter IV) and supplementary medical information in the record. The condition of the boy's health, as reported by the doctor, was indicated on the same 11-point scale reflecting the varying degrees of excellence or poorness of health.

2. I.Q. This quotient was obtained for the most part from the Kuhlmann-Anderson Group Intelligence Test. In about 12 percent of the cases a Stanford-Binet test score was also available. If the quotients of two boys did not differ by more than ten points the match was considered a good one in this respect, though in approximately 5 percent of the cases the matchers had to depart from this ideal.

3. Ratio of Emotional Outlets and Tension. This measure was an attempt to express the relationship between the desirability of emotional outlets that a boy seemed to have and that boy's degree of personality tension. (The word "tension" is used in a neutral sense to express a boy's drive.) This measure was an interpretative score derived from a rating given by the schoolteachers on the Descriptive Rating Scale (described in Chapter IV). The two psychologists assigned values to each item on the 11-point scale that pertained to these two factors. These factors seemed to have interesting interrelationships. A boy, for example, who had a strong drive for expression differed considerably from another boy similarly characterized by his teacher if the former sought less desirable outlets for his expression than the latter. This difference could be taken into account by noting the relationships as expresesd in the quotient found by dividing the D value (desirability of emotional outlets) by the T value (tension). Using a quadrille graph the D–T values for two boys could be readily compared. An example is given in Figure 2.

4. *The Selection Committee Rating.* This measure, of course, was one of the most important variables, representing the boy's probable development toward, or away from, a delinquent career. An attempt was made to match boys closely in respect to this rating. Table 12 indicates the degree to which this was accomplished.

TABLE 12

Similarity of Matched Pairs in Prognostic Ratings by Three Judges

Scale Point Differences in Ratings	Number of Matched Pairs	Percent
None (ratings were identical)	158	48.6
One	138	42.5
Two	25	7.7
Three	4	1.2
	325	100.0

5. *The Boy's Home as a Place Likely to Produce Delinquency.* This variable, representing the primary social group listed in the six divisions, was directly derived from the ratings on the 11-point scale made by the home visitors (as described in Chapter IV).

6. *Neighborhood.* This variable represented the secondary social group listed in the six divisions. It was a rating of the neighborhood (as described in Chapter IV) as a place likely or unlikely to produce delinquency.

Each of these six variables was assessed on an 11-point scale. The matching chart showed graphically how any two boys might compare in respect to these basic variables.

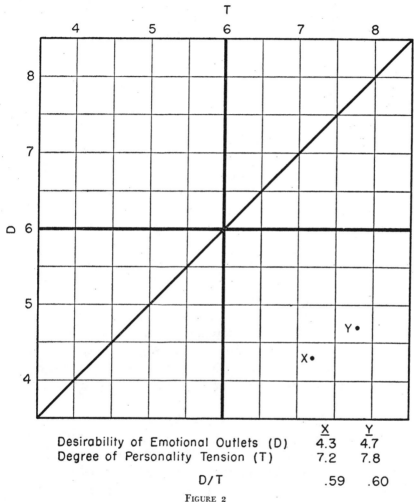

	X	Y
Desirability of Emotional Outlets (D)	4.3	4.7
Degree of Personality Tension (T)	7.2	7.8
D/T	.59	.60

FIGURE 2

PLOTTING THE D/T RATIO OF TWO POTENTIAL MEMBERS OF
A PAIR, X AND Y

THE TWENTY VARIABLES

The matchers were now convinced that by holding to the clinical-statistical viewpoint it would be possible to bring in more than these six primary variables. It was not known at this point which of the remaining variables were most relevant and measurable. It was therefore necessary to carry further the process of trial sorting the slotted cards as was done in the search for the first six. By this method 13 additional variables were identified that seemed psychologically important and readily accessible, thus giving 19 that were considered by close observation or inspection to be the most diagnostic in producing similar contours. The matchers at this point arbitrarily decided that the Selection Committee rating in itself was so directly related to the objectives of the Study that it should receive a double weight and hence it was counted again, giving 20 variables. In each potential match the quantitative scores for all 20 were averaged and compared. There follow the additional 13 variables, numbered from 7 to 19:

One was a test score obtained by using the Stanford Achievement Test and the chronological age, namely (7) an *Educational Quotient.*

One was a rating made directly in the first instance by a home visitor, namely (8) the *Standard of Living* (Chapter IV).

Two of the ratings were deductions made from data in the record. They were (9) *Occupation of the Father,* and (10) *School Occupation Level.* In the former the matchers had adapted the Rulon revision of the Minnesota Occupations Status Classification and converted the scores to the same 11-point scale. The latter was an invention of the matchers by which they sampled the occupational levels in each public school and were thus able to assign a social status level to that school.

Two were synthetic prognostic ratings supplementing the Selection Committee ratings: One (11) called the *TZV* was based on (a) the original referral of the boy by the teacher as average or difficult, (b) the home visitor's rating of the boy's personality, and (c) a judgment by two psychologists of the boy's chances of developing a delinquent career as they could see that reflected in the Trait Record Card and the Descriptive Rating Scale. This formula was derived by a multiple correlation technique. The other (12), called the *TZF,* was also a composite rating similar to the *TZV,* with the exception that the home visitors' rating of the home as a place likely or unlikely to produce delinquency displaced the home visitor's rating of the boy's personality.

The remaining variables were interpretative judgments made by the two matchers or by Mr. Patey and a staff psychologist. The first three were interpretations based solely on the teachers' Descriptive Rating Scale and the teachers' Trait Record Card: [5] (13) *Mental Health* as seen in teachers' ratings on items pertaining to freedom from mental conflict and maladjustment and evidence of expressions of a wholesome personality; (14) *Social Adjustment,* the boy's ability to maintain satisfying and normal relationships with his fellows; (15) *Social Aggressiveness* was also used in a neutral sense in that the degree of social assertiveness rather than the desirability or undesirability of the trait was kept in mind; (16) *Acceptance of Authority* based on teachers' reports. The following three ratings were interpretative judgments made by one of the psychologists: (17) *The Goodness of Discipline* was based upon the home visitor's reports concerning the discipline of the home as related to the visitor by the mother (see Chapter IV), supplemented by the schoolteacher's or schoolmaster's comments that may have been made in some cases concerning this topic; (18) *Delinquency in the Home* was based upon the official court records relating to delinquency or criminality in other members of the family; (19) *Disruption of the Home* was based, in the main, on information gathered by the home visitor concerning divorce, separation, death of one or both parents, family quarrels, parent-child relationships.

It will be evident at this point that in quantifying these factors the matchers relied heavily on their own judgments and clinical interpretations in order to avoid a purely mechanical approach. They took advantage of clinical impressions concerning patterns and pure hunches and utilized qualitative description. Yet, they cross-checked these items against each other, finding quantitative equivalents for as many of the mental processes as possible and utilizing these as reference points and reference patterns for the higher order of clinical judgment. Throughout, the matchers emphasized the fact that the individuals to be matched must have likenesses similar in psychological configurations of growth and style of living. They should then be "prognostic twins."

[5] See Chap. IV for a description and Appendix C for examples of these two instruments.

RATIOS AND PATTERNS AS VARIABLES

Consistent with this configurational approach the matchers devised several new variables which were combinations of variables previously mentioned. Syndromes of comparable design in each member of a pair were generally preferred to a series of equated averages in scores on separate variables. These new combinations were called ratios or patterns and consisted of the following:

1. The Pattern of Social Adjustment. By comparing scores on three variables—Mental Health (No. 13), Amenability to or Acceptance of Authority (No. 16), and Social Aggressiveness (No. 15) —with the Selection Committee prognoses (No. 4) the matchers discovered a complex interrelationship which they believed to be particularly meaningful. For example, high social aggressiveness may make for poor social adjustment in some combinations and for good social adjustment in other combinations—a leader or a bully. The matchers believed it to be "incorrect either in statistics or in clinical interpretation to think of a given rating as having one and only one constant meaning." This example helps to make clear the way in which the matchers attempted to apply the clinical viewpoint to statistical data.

2. Ratio of Mental Health to Overtness of Behavior. These two variables were derived by interpretation from the Teachers' Rating Card and the Descriptive Rating Scale. The ratio was then obtained. Overtness of behavior like the concept of tension was regarded as a neutral trait. Mental health was the qualitative term in the ratio. Of two boys, for example, rated poor in mental health, one might be also rated low in overtness of behavior, giving us a picture of a boy who is withdrawn, retiring, and ineffectual. The other boy with equally poor mental health might be high in overtness of behavior and definitely antisocial. On the other hand, a boy with good mental health and high overtness might become a good leader. Other combinations are conceivable, showing the importance of the interrelationships. A quadrille graph was used to plot the ratios of two members of a potential match in the same way as was done in the case of the D-T Ratio (see Figure 3). This graph was relied on to show the type of adjustment the individual was making in respect to these two variables, a fact not obvious in the ratio itself.

3. Ratio of Social Adjustment to Social Aggressiveness. In the some vein the matchers believed that a high positive score on social aggressiveness may have had quite a different meaning for a boy with a low score on social adjustment than for a boy with a high score on this item. The ratio, therefore, was considered important and this value was likewise plotted on a similar quadrille graph in order that a qualitative comparison might be made by inspection.

4. The Environmental Pattern. This measure resulted from a technique that combined various environmental factors expected to have some prognostic value in relation to future delinquency. Four variables were considered—Discipline (No. 17), Delinquency in the Home (No. 18), Disruption (or Security) of the Home (No. 19), and Neighborhood Rating (No. 6). The interrelationships of these four variables were considered relevant to possible delinquent behavior. A boy, for example, might live in a minus neighborhood but not be a delinquent himself because the other three factors were positive. Another boy might be delinquent though not living in a minus neighborhood if there was disruption and poor discipline in the home. A single measure was thus eventually derived from transmuted values which were related to delinquency.

PLOTTING OF VALUES FOR EACH VARIABLE

Figure 3, taken from a typical matching chart, shows how the 20 variables were plotted and how their differences and the average of the differences were recorded. Each of the six divisions are represented by a graph upon which are plotted the scores of two matched boys, represented by an "X" and a "Y." The 20 variables are listed and numbered, the starred variables being indicated by asterisks. It can be seen that there is a single starred variable in each of the six divisions. The boy's rating on each of the 20 variables is assessed in terms of a point on the 11-point scale. It is recorded under the columns "X" and "Y" and plotted on the graph. For example, in the division Primary Social Group, the home as a place likely to produce or not produce delinquency is rated a minus three in the case of "X" and a plus one in the case of "Y." The algebraic difference in rating is thus four, and the plotting on the graph makes this difference immediately obvious. The other four variables in this division are similarly recorded and plotted. At the bottom of the figure the plus and minus ratings for both "X" and "Y" on each of the 20 variables are added algebraically and averaged. It was discovered that the most satisfying matches were obtained when the average differences on each of the six divisions as well as on the total of the 20 variables were less than 1.3. Differences greater than this generally meant differences of three or more scale points on several separate variables which in itself would suggest a poor match.

ACCESSORY FACTORS

In addition to the 20 variables and the four composite variables expressing ratios or patterns, the matchers decided to consider five accessory factors that could not be reduced to an 11-point scale. These five factors were considered relevant but were not included with the original 20, partly because no one of the five could be reduced to comparable terms on the scale and partly because each one was considered more nearly a constant than a variable and served as a "lead" to the comparison of the variables already mentioned. There follows a list of these five:

1. Dominant Stock. Wherever possible, boys of Irish ancestry were paired, Negro was matched with Negro, and so on. This variable was disregarded only when the cultural pattern of the home was considered of greater significance than parental nativity.

2. Religion. The religious affiliation of the parents (Catholic, Protestant, or other) was noted on the matching chart. It was usually, but not always, observed in the matchings.

3. Public or Parochial School. School affiliation was also noted on the matching chart but was not a determinative factor in the matching.

4. Types of Interests. The Descriptive Rating Scale was so devised that one could tell by an examination of the form whether the boy's interests, as seen by the teacher, were predominantly social, physical, manual, or academic, or some combination of these. Each of these four aspects of interests was rated by the teacher on a five-point scale. These ratings were then plotted on a graph on the

RATINGS -5 -4 -3 -2 -1 0 1 2 3 4 5

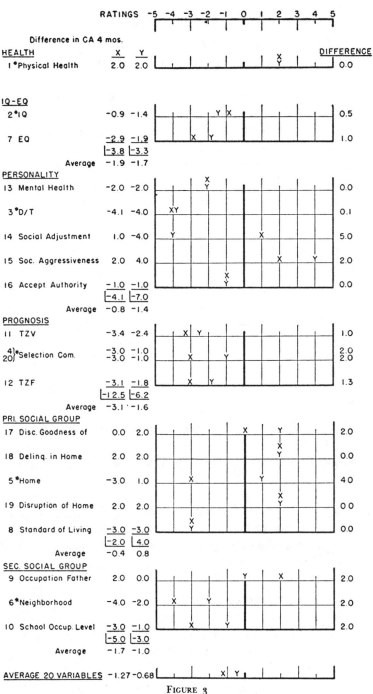

Difference in CA 4 mos.

	X	Y		DIFFERENCE
HEALTH				
1 *Physical Health	2.0	2.0		0.0
IQ-EQ				
2 *IQ	-0.9	-1.4		0.5
7 EQ	-2.9	-1.9		1.0
	-3.8	-3.3		
Average	-1.9	-1.7		
PERSONALITY				
13 Mental Health	-2.0	-2.0		0.0
3 *D/T	-4.1	-4.0		0.1
14 Social Adjustment	1.0	-4.0		5.0
15 Soc. Aggressiveness	2.0	4.0		2.0
16 Accept. Authority	-1.0	-1.0		0.0
	-4.1	-7.0		
Average	-0.8	-1.4		
PROGNOSIS				
11 TZV	-3.4	-2.4		1.0
4) 20) *Selection Com.	-3.0 -3.0	-1.0 -1.0		2.0 2.0
12 TZF	-3.1	-1.8		1.3
	-12.5	-6.2		
Average	-3.1	-1.6		
PRI. SOCIAL GROUP				
17 Disc. Goodness of	0.0	2.0		2.0
18 Delinq. in Home	2.0	2.0		0.0
5 *Home	-3.0	1.0		4.0
19 Disruption of Home	2.0	2.0		0.0
8 Standard of Living	-3.0	-3.0		0.0
	-2.0	4.0		
Average	-0.4	0.8		
SEC. SOCIAL GROUP				
9 Occupation Father	2.0	0.0		2.0
6 *Neighborhood	-4.0	-2.0		2.0
10 School Occup. Level	-3.0	-1.0		2.0
	-5.0	-3.0		
Average	-1.7	-1.0		
AVERAGE 20 VARIABLES	-1.27	-0.68		

FIGURE 3

PLOTTING THE TWENTY MATCHING VARIABLES

NOTE: Asterisks represent the starred variables.

matching chart for each boy of a potential pair, such graph contributing to the total impression gathered by an inspection of the chart.

5. *Cooperativeness of the Home with the Study*. Even though two boys seemed to be fairly well equated in terms of most of the variables, they could not fairly be matched if the parents of one were uncooperative, and of the other cooperative, with the Study or with other agencies that might wish to be of help to the boy. Each matching chart, therefore, had a notation of the cooperativeness of the home as seen by the home visitor prior to treatment (see Chapter IV).

ONE "SPECIAL CONSTANT"

One "special constant" was the boy's age at the time of the matching. This consideration was primary and determinative. The younger boys could not be adequately paired with the older no matter how closely they seemed to resemble each other, either from a statistical or clinical point of view. This restriction, naturally, greatly narrowed the choices for matching any given boy with another. A variation in age of no greater than six months was considered the desirable limit and was observed in 57.2 percent of the matches. In 16 percent, a greater than 12 months discrepancy was permitted because of the limited number of available boys, and in a few cases (6.2 percent) boys were paired who differed in age by 19 to 25 months. Age differences in matched pairs are shown in Table 13.

THE MATCHING CHART

Each matching chart thus contained the ratings of all of the variables listed for each of the two boys of a potential match. In addition, all available data on the boys were read and the essentials thereof transcribed in two-color type on the sheets accompanying the graphs. In this way the remaining 100 to 110 variables (of the original 142) were not necessarily lost sight of. The descriptive statements pointed out all similarities and differences between the two boys. This complete summary was made on the first 50 pairs; subsequently an abbreviated form was developed to serve the same purpose.

TABLE 13

Age Difference between the T-Boy and His Matched Control [a]

Difference in Months	Number of Pairs
0	24
1–2	66
3–4	53
5–6	43
7–8	35
9–10	28
11–12	24
13–14	15
15–16	9
17–18	8
19–20	11
21–22	6
25	3
	325

[a] The mean difference for the 325 pairs is 6.8 months.

LIMITATIONS IN NUMBER OF AVAILABLE CASES FOR MATCHING

Unfortunately the entire pool of 750 cases was not made available to the matchers at any one time. For five and a half of the eight months of the matching procedure, the Selection Committee was simultaneously deliberating on the prognoses, turning over only 25 to 35 cases (generally of the same age group) from which the matchers had to select "good" pairs. It was highly desirable from a methodological point of view (but obviously impractical) for the matchers to wait until all of the 782 cases had been selected and classified. The treatment staff was waiting breathlessly for cases to be assigned and the pressure on the matchers for speeding-up the process was continuous. In any event, pairs had to be drawn from relatively small sub-groups. The implications of this limitation cannot be overlooked. For example, as indicated above, older boys could not be matched with those who were much younger. The possibilities of finding two similar profiles was further limited by the necessity of holding the Selection Committee ratings within a narrow range of variability. For example, "plus threes" could not be matched with "minus threes." A good match for the 55 "plus threes" therefore had to be drawn from a fairly limited number of "plus fours," "plus threes" or "plus twos" who were at the same time within the same general age group. Table 14 shows the age distribution of boys who had been classified by the Selection Committee. A subsequent rating of the "goodness" of the matches by a committee of three, including the two matchers, disclosed the fact that the poorest matches were among the youngest boys, due partly to the narrower range of choices and partly to the fact that there was less information concerning them.

TABLE 14

*Age Distribution of the 782 Selected Boys
at the Time of Matching*

Age	Number	Percent
6 and below	27	3.5
6–7	54	6.9
7–8	103	13.2
8–9	112	14.3
9–10	164	21.0
10–11	235	30.0
11–12	87	11.1
	782	100.0

HOW THE MATCHES WERE MADE

The steps in the matching process might be summarized as follows:

1. A case was selected at random and a search was made to find another boy (of approximately the same age and prognostic rating) who presented roughly the same profile. Perhaps three or four cases were drawn out of the pile as possibilities. If these were insufficient more were taken and if none could be found that seemed to appear reasonably similar in terms of the six basic variables this potential match was discarded and another case was selected.

2. When a potential pair was found by inspection, the scores on all the variables relating to both boys were entered on the matching chart, averages were determined, graphs were plotted, and so on, as described above. Thus, assuming the validity of data, one could get an immediate picture of the similarities and differences between these two tentative members of the pair.

3. When two boys were thus selected as possible matches and

their respective scores transcribed to the matching chart, it became a matter of clinical judgment to decide whether they were close enough to constitute a satisfactory match in terms of these many variables and ratios. No critical scores were considered binding upon the matchers although the critical points of representative averages and items were taken into consideration. A match could be arrived at, even though the statistical averages gave a contra-indication. The clinical picture was dominant, the emphasis being on the constellation of variables. Given a very large pool of cases and ample time for the matchers to perfect their techniques and to verify their methods, it might have been possible to set a critical score that would differentiate a "good" match from a "bad" one.

4. If a potential match showed, by inspection of the chart, too great a discrepancy one of the two cases was discarded and another drawn for a second trial match. If the second drawing proved unsatisfactory a third attempt was made, and so on, sometimes necessitating several replottings of the matching charts. Experience proved that by a rapid inspection of available potential matches time could be saved by screening out improbable matches.

SET MATCHING

5. After a number of individual matches had been decided upon, the matchers undertook to form sets or sub-groups of fairly homogeneous boys. One of the unique features of the matching plan was that in addition to a boy-for-boy matching there would be a matching of small groups of boys with each other. Set-matching was introduced to allow for and to minimize the extent of individual differences in paired matches. Sets were first developed by matching "foursomes," any two of which might be matched. The matchers believed that by so doing one could later evaluate the program by comparing the differential behavior of the sets. The chief purpose of matching by sets was to allow for a greater flexibility in the ultimate evaluation of the treatment program. One practical advantage was thought to be that if one member of a pair should die or for some other reason be removed from the Study, a substitute could immediately be called upon to stand for that missing member in any future comparison. For example, A could be matched with B, C with D, or E with F in such a way that A-D, A-F, C-B, C-F, E-B

and E-D might also be considered reasonably well matched. If B dropped out of the Study, D could be A's control "twin," and so on. Sets were not limited to three such pairs but generally involved eight or nine pairs and sometimes extended even to 25 pairs. The grouping of matched pairs into similar sets no doubt produced a better group matching, although the plans for set-evaluation had to be abandoned when so many boys were dropped from the program during the war years.

SEGREGATION OF THE TWO GROUPS

The next question was to determine whether any given boy should fall into the treatment or the control group. It was evident that an arbitrary decision might give rise to a constant error. The proper method of determining this question was, of course, by chance. Accordingly, a coin was flipped and the cases fell into the treatment or control groups in accordance with its fall. For the first 12 pairs the coin was flipped for each pair; thereafter for each set.[6] It was believed that, even if the measures used in the matching were not perfectly reliable, chance would tend to preserve, in groups as large as 325 each, an even balance of important factors.

THE VERIFICATION OF THE MATCHING

How well were these boys matched individually and as groups? The similarity of the two groups can be estimated by comparing their average scores on some of the variables.

1. As to Selection Committee Ratings. An inspection of Table 12 shows that the prognostic ratings for the members of each matched pair were either identical or differed by only one point on the scale in 91.1 percent of the matches. Although the total number of minus and plus cases were about equally distributed in the two groups, the

---

[6] Thus the coin was not tossed 325 times for that number of pairs, but rather about 45 times, for once cases had been placed into sets the fall of the coin had to determine the distribution of the entire set which could not be broken up. In other words, if the set consisted of 20 pairs, all one side of the pair, if they were represented in column formation, must fall into the treatment or control group, as the case may be. There is no reason to suppose that this had any distorting effect. It should also be mentioned that eight of the 325 matches were made before the matching technique was fully evolved. These were emergency cases where the boys in question were serious school problems. Treatment with them had to commence at once and subsequently control twins were found for them. There is no reason to believe that these eight pairs were not matched as well as the remaining 317.

distribution as to each point on the scale as shown in Table 15 was not quite equal.

TABLE 15

Distribution of Selection Committee Ratings
in the Treatment and Control Groups

Plus Boys	T	C
+5	0	0
+4	2	7
+3	24	26
+2	59	63
+1	52	39
Total	137	135
Zero Boys	25	25
Minus Boys		
−1	65	81
−2	71	64
−3	23	14
−4	4	4
−5	0	2
Total	163	165
Grand Total	325	325

An examination of the table shows that (a) of the very "bad" boys (those rated −5, −4, −3) the treatment group was overbalanced, having 27 compared to 20 in the control group, and (b) of the very "good" boys (+5, +4, +3) the treatment group was relatively deficient, having only 26 compared to 33 in the control group. Looking at it another way, one can determine the "plusness" or "minusness" of the treatment and control groups by multiplying the rating by the frequency and adding the products. We find, for example, that the treatment group had a "plusness" of 250 compared to 271 for the control group and a "minusness" of 292 compared to 277 for the control group. These differences are not statistically significant, the T minus boys having an average "minusness" of 1.79 compared to an average "minusness" of 1.68 for the C-boys.[7]

2. *As to Age.* As already shown in Table 13 matched pairs did

---

[7] T and C are used here, and in subsequent chapters, to refer to treatment and control boys.

not vary greatly in respect to age. As groups, the boys were also well matched in age, as shown in Table 16.

TABLE 16

Numbers of T- and C-Boys by Age Groups

Age (when matched)	T	C
Under 7	30	32
7 to 8½	57	55
8½ to 9	51	51
9 to 10½	59	61
10½ to 12	128	126
Total	325	325

3. *As to 19 Variables.* In Table 17 we compare the distribution of the averages of the ratings for both groups in respect to 19 variables. (The 20th variable is omitted from the table for it was merely the Selection Committee rating taken again.) Such distribution was computed on a sample of 264 pairs.[8]

TABLE 17

Distribution of Means of the Ratings on 19 Variables [a] in a Large Sample of the Treatment and Control Groups

1	2	3	4	5
Variable	Number of Boys	Arithmetic Means for Ts & Cs	Standard Deviation	Group Differences in Arithmetic Means
1. Health *	264 T	1.736	.710	.119
	264 C	1.855	.452	
2. I.Q. *	263 T	− .464	.977	.033
	262 C	− .431	1.003	
3. Desirability/	264 T	− .864	2.612	.057
Tension Ratio *	264 C	− .807	2.588	
4. Selection Commit-	264 T	− .504	1.728	.193
tee Rating *	264 C	− .311	1.803	
5. Home *	263 T	− .525	2.279	.158
	264 C	− .367	2.217	

[8] The original case load had been reduced to 324 by death of one boy and at the time the computation given in Table 17 was made 60 other cases had been retired from the treatment program as explained in Chap. XI, leaving 264. This reduction of the total number of matched cases would probably have no bearing on the representativeness of the remaining matches for the group dropped had been matched with the same technique as the group retained. Group differences in ratings, therefore, on this sample can be considered roughly equivalent to group differences for the entire 325 pairs.

I	2	3	4	5
Variable	Number of Boys	Arithmetic Means for Ts & Cs	Standard Deviation	Group Differences in Arithmetic Means
6. Neighborhood *	264 T	−1.864	2.277	.038
	264 C	−1.826	2.192	
7. Educational	184 T	−1.016	1.653	.108
Quotient	184 C	− .908	1.774	
8. Standard of	264 T	− .352	2.273	.182
Living	264 C	− .170	2.489	
9. Occupation of	253 T	−1.107	1.132	.025
Father	255 C	−1.082	1.129	
10. School Occupa-	244 T	−1.406	1.292	.029
tional Level	236 C	−1.377	1.192	
11. TZV (Delinquency	264 T	− .625	1.183	.061
Proneness)	264 C	− .564	1.757	
12. TZF (Delinquency	263 T	− .643	1.921	.029
Proneness)	264 C	− .614	1.841	
13. Mental Health	264 T	−1.337	2.128	.038
	264 C	−1.299	2.033	
14. Social	264 T	− .625	2.483	.326
Adjustment	264 C	− .299	2.381	
15. Social	264 T	1.886	2.149	.201
Aggressiveness	264 C	2.087	2.113	
16. Acceptance of	264 T	1.299	2.410	.072
Authority	264 C	1.227	2.360	
17. Goodness of	264 T	.152	1.998	.132
Discipline	264 C	.284	1.944	
18. Delinquency in	264 T	1.648	2.500	.015
the Home	264 C	1.663	2.444	
19. Disruption of	264 T	1.163	2.434	.060
the Home	264 C	1.223	2.429	

a The first six are the "starred variables."

Each variable as it applied to each boy was quantified by reducing it to a score on the 11-point scale previously described. The arithmetic means of the scale points as they applied to the treatment and control groups were then found for each variable. The group differences of course would be small if the groups were well matched, although a small group difference is no guarantee of good individual matches within the group. Table 17 shows small group differences on 19 variables as they pertained to the T- and C-boys. The group average of the 19 differences in arithmetic means is

.099. That is, on the average, the groups, as groups, differed by less than one-tenth of one scale point on the variables in question. The treatment group seemed to resemble the control group most closely in respect to the following four variables: (1) Delinquency in the Home, (2) Occupation of the Father, (3) School Occupational Level, and (4) the TZF formula relating to delinquency-proneness. The average differences in respect to these four variables was less than three one-hundredths of a point on the 11-point scale. In no case did the treatment and control groups differ by more than one-third of one scale point in respect to any of the remaining variables.

The close similarity of the two groups is thus revealed in the above tables. Subsequently, whenever large unselected sub-groups of T- and C-boys were compared during the course of treatment in respect to any important factor the results were consistent with the above tabulations.

This account of the matching process, unavoidably complex, brings to light the difficulties of achieving adequate experimental controls in investigations of therapeutic methods; indeed, in any investigation that concerns itself with personalities or social behavior. For the purpose of this Study, however, it was vital to attempt as sound an equating as possible.

CHAPTER VII

ASSIGNMENT OF BOYS
TO COUNSELORS

AFTER TWO BOYS HAD BEEN MATCHED AND CHANCE HAD DETERMINED into which group each should fall, the treatment case was assigned to a counselor. Rarely was it explained to the treatment boy that another young boy matched with him had been placed in a control group as an evaluation technique. Counselors were free to explain this fact, or not, as they saw fit. One counselor, toward the end of the treatment program, discussed with a few of her boys the purposes to be served by a control group. Some twenty-one months after the close of the program one of her boys said to an investigator who inquired about his knowledge of the Study, "They have somebody who looks like me. I know he leads the same kind of a life— has family troubles and all sorts of things. We're very much alike and the idea is to see which one of us turns out better. It's like a race. Well, I know this Miss A. won this race because I turned out better than he did." It might have been defensible to have given each of the boys in the treatment program some motivation based on the idea of competing with an unknown but very real control boy. Yet to do so would introduce into our treatment program an element of unknown force, one not available to other programs of delinquency-prevention.

The cases were not all assigned at the same time, the process being staggered from November, 1937, to May, 1939, overlapping the selection and matching procedures. By May 30, 1939, all 325 boys had been assigned.

PLANNED ASSIGNMENTS

The assignment of cases was not left to chance. The co-director of the Study, Dr. P. S. de Q. Cabot, had asked each of the ten available counselors to submit a statement of preferences and prejudices respecting cases, if any existed. Some counselors stated that they preferred to work with Italians rather than Portuguese; some preferred younger boys to older; nearly all expressed a strong preference for difficult cases, the male counselors being more insistent in respect to this preference. Insofar as consistent with the requirements of case load, these wishes were respected. It was necessary to see that no one had such an undue proportion of difficult cases that it would be impossible for him to attend to their many needs, and that no one was given too many cases of the kind that ranked low on his list of preferences. The case load also had to be well balanced in numbers, each of the nine full-time counselors receiving 34 or 35 cases, while the counselor working half-time received 18.

Other special considerations entered into the assignment. A few of these are of interest: (a) A counselor who had been a home visitor and had already developed some practical familiarity with the special problem of a particular family frequently requested that that case be assigned to her. Forty cases were so assigned. (b) Sometimes a boy was an intimate friend of another boy who had already been assigned. It was believed that it would make for greater efficiency if both cases were assigned to the same person. (c) There was a tendency to assign to the oldest male counselors boys whose fathers were not living or were unable to provide adequate affection and guidance to their sons. (d) Boys with serious physical handicaps were often referred to the counselor who had been trained as a nurse. (e) Frequently where the difficulties centered around specific family problems the boys were assigned to the two women counselors who had had more experience in family case work. (f) Generally the director assigning the cases looked for factors in the personalities of the boy and the counselor that he believed would make for a good relationship. (g) The older boys were, as a rule, assigned to the men counselors.

Many were trial assignments with the understanding that if a good working relationship did not develop, a reassignment could later be made. This transfer of cases was not easily accomplished, because of a hesitancy to take on an additional case or a reluctance to admit failure by requesting that one's case be reassigned to someone who might be more successful.

The following tables show how case loads differed in certain respects. No attempt was made to equate them in any exact sense, but if this had been done the relative effectiveness of the various counselors could have been compared. Such a theoretically desirable plan had to give way to practical considerations, not the least of which was the possibility that such a scheme would set up an unhealthy rivalry among the counselors.

DISTRIBUTIONS OF PLUS, ZERO, AND MINUS ASSIGNMENTS

Table 18 which shows the number of plus, zero, and minus cases assigned to each of the first ten counselors demonstrates a fairly even distribution.

TABLE 18

*Distribution of Plus, Zero, and Minus Cases
among the Ten Original Counselors*

Counselors	Minus	Zero	Plus	Totals
A	17	2	15	34
B	18	3	14	35
C	17	3	14	34
D	18	1	15	34
E	17	3	14	34
F	17	3	14	34
G	18	1	15	34
H	17	3	14	34
I	17	3	14	34
J [a]	7	3	8	18
Totals	163	25	137	325

[a] Counselor on part-time schedule.

By adding the plus and minus ratings in each counselor's case load one obtains a rough measure of the plusness or minusness of the group with which he had to deal. Table 19 shows how plusness and minusness were distributed in the assignment of cases to the first ten counselors.

It is evident from this table that the distribution was not exactly equal. The minus cases listed in Table 18 were not all of the same degree of minusness nor were the plus cases all of the same degree of plusness. One counselor, for example, had been assigned seven boys who were markedly difficult boys (they had been rated —3 or

TABLE 19

The Minusness and Plusness of the Ten Original Case Loads

(*Average of the Arithmetic Sum of Plus, Minus, and Zero Ratings*)

Counselors	Minusness or Plusness	Average Rating
A	−13	−.38
D	−10	−.29
I	− 8	−.24
C	− 5	−.17
F	− 5	−.15
B	− 5	−.14
E	0	0
H	+ 1	+.03
J	+ 1	+.06
G	+ 2	+.06

−4) while another counselor, though having one more minus boy, had only two in these categories.

Table 19 shows that six of the counselors had a slightly minus case load, three a slightly plus case load, while one had a group of boys whose average was neither minus nor plus, but zero. The average rating for the 325 boys was − .12.

DISTRIBUTION OF ASSIGNMENTS OF YOUNGER AND OLDER BOYS

The average age of the boys in each counselor's case load showed a much wider variation than the distribution of plusness and minusness. The average age of boys assigned to women counselors was 10 years, 5 months; to men counselors, 11 years, 5 months; while the average for the 325 boys was 11 years, 1 month, as of May 30, 1939, which marked the end of the period of assignment and the beginning of treatment for the last boys assigned.

DISTRIBUTION OF ASSIGNMENTS IN TERMS OF RELIGIOUS FAITH

The religious faith of the boys was not a vital factor in the assignment of cases to the counselors, six of whom were Protestant, three Catholic, and one Jewish.

Of the boys assigned to the Catholic counselors, for example, 62.7 percent were Catholics, compared to 60.5 percent of the boys assigned to non-Catholic workers; 61.2 percent of the total case load were Catholics.

FREQUENCY OF REASSIGNMENT

The original plan called for a ten-year period of treatment by counselors who would stay with the Study for long periods of time, thus minimizing the necessity of frequent reassignments. As counselors were later drawn into the war service or for other reasons left the Study, cases had to be reassigned to those remaining or to newly appointed counselors. Such reassignments were largely a matter of expediency, the chief consideration being the availability of the remaining counselors, who were generally already complaining of large case loads, or the possibility of engaging new counselors who would be assigned whatever cases were left without counselors. Nine new counselors joined the staff during the course of treatment. As a rule, no boy was assigned to more than one counselor at any one time, though there were three or four exceptions to this rule for brief periods when a boy needed a male advisor in addition to the woman counselor assigned to him, or where it was believed more effective for one counselor to deal with the boy and another with the boy's mother.[1]

In approximately one-third of the cases, a boy was assigned to one counselor only. The 75 boys carried through the entire treatment period experienced more reassignments than the group as a whole, for about one-third of them had been assigned to four or five different counselors. These facts are shown in Table 20.

TABLE 20

Number and Percentage of Boys Having One or More Counselors

Number of Counselors	TOTAL GROUP (325)		75 BOYS IN PROGRAM TO THE END	
	Number of Boys	Percent	Number of Boys	Percent
1	118	36.3	10	13.3
2	103	31.7	14	18.7
3	58	17.8	24	32.0
4	39	12.0	23	30.7
5	6	1.8	4	5.3
6	1	.3	0	0.0
	325	99.9	75	100.0

[1] The effect of the many reassignments on the counselor-boy relationship is discussed in Chap. XII.

NATURE OF THE
TREATMENT
PROGRAM

IT IS ESSENTIAL THAT WE HAVE A CLEAR PICTURE OF THE STUDY AS IT
appeared at the very outset of the treatment program.

THE BOYS

Age. The age of the boys on June 1, 1939, ranged from that of
Dickie, who was then five years and three months old and in the
kindergarten in one of the public schools, to that of Ernest, who was
then twelve years and eight months old and in the sixth grade.[1] The
median age was approximately eleven years.

The age of the boy at the time treatment started was a significant
factor in his treatment. As it was later necessary to terminate all
treatment before the expiration of the proposed ten years, the
younger group was not treated during the difficult late adolescent
years. Figure 4 shows the distribution of the ages of the boys at the
time treatment started with them. Fifty-eight percent of the boys
had passed their tenth birthdays before the counselors' work began.

Intelligence Quotient. A study of the intelligence quotients of
the total group was made before the selection and matching procedures were undertaken. The Kuhlmann-Anderson group test was administered to all but five of the 325 boys. The mean intelligence
quotient for the group was 96.6. Ten percent achieved a quotient of

---

[1] The date June 1, 1939, was selected because not until then had initial visits been
made by the counselors to *all* 325 boys. Some of the boys at that time had been in
treatment for over a year, but each boy was under 12 when he (or his family) first
met his counselor.

110 or over, while 19 percent scored 89 or lower. A few years after the treatment program started, 251 of the boys were retested by the Binet test (Form L). Their scores ranged from a low of 53 to a high of 149. The median and the mean intelligence quotient was 92.

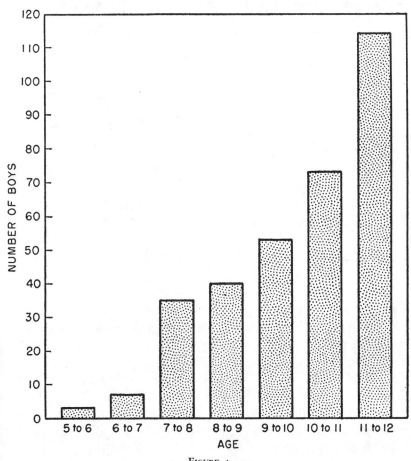

FIGURE 4

AGE DISTRIBUTION AT THE TIME TREATMENT BEGAN

The retested group comprised only 77 percent of the total group and may have been slightly unrepresentative. Most of the boys who were not given the Binet test were those who were retired from the program (as described in Chapter XI) and who had a slightly higher quotient than the remaining group. It would be reasonable to assume that the mean intelligence quotient for the 325 boys was between 92 and 96.[2]

TABLE 21

Distribution of Kuhlmann-Anderson Group Intelligence-Test Scores [a]

Scores	Number of Boys	Percent of Total
Under 70	2	.6
70–79	5	1.5
80–89	54	16.9
90–99	167	52.2
100–109	60	18.8
110–119	28	8.8
Over 119	4	1.2
	320	100.0

[a] Range: 45–133; mean 96.6.

Nativity of Parents. In only about one-third (117) of the 325 cases were both parents born in the United States. In 124 cases both parents were born outside the United States: Italy, 44; Canada, 21; Portugal, 21; British West Indies, 13; Poland, 6; other countries, 10; unknown, 9.

Negroes. Of the 325 boys 27 were Negroes, a ratio of one Negro to every 11 non-Negroes. This proportion was higher than that for the two cities as a whole. In the Cambridge population (1940 census) there was one Negro to every 22 non-Negroes; in Somerville one Negro to every 389 non-Negroes.

School Location. While 191 boys were attending the Cambridge public day schools, 29 were in the Cambridge parochial day schools, 97 in the Somerville public day schools and two in the Somerville parochial day schools. Between the time of referral and of assignment three boys transferred to schools of neighboring towns. One boy was at a county training school, one at a convalescent home,

[2] Using the first 100 cases in which both the Kuhlmann-Anderson and the Binet tests were administered a coefficient of correlation between the scores on these two tests was found to be .76. The Binet scores had a slightly wider range. The highest Binet score, for example, was 149, whereas the Kuhlmann-Anderson score for the same boy was 133. Similarly, the lowest Binet score was 53, the Kuhlmann-Anderson score 72, for the same boy. The Binet scores showed a greater average deviation, though the means for the two series were close—95.9 for the Kuhlmann-Anderson and 94.1 for the Binet.

and one had been removed from school because of mental deficiency, although all three were in the public day school at the time of referral.

Delinquency. It was originally intended to exclude from the program the boys who had already been adjudged delinquent; yet it would have been impractical to have done so, inasmuch as the setting-up of the research consumed such a long time that a number of boys who were not known to be delinquent when referred may have become delinquent somewhere along the line. An examination of the records shows that seven boys (or 2.2 percent) had been recorded in the district courts for some delinquency prior to treatment and probably many times this number were already known to the police but not officially recorded by the courts, or had committed delinquent acts unknown to the police. In short, it could not be said that all T-boys were either average (non-delinquent) or *pre*-delinquent. Many of the T-boys in this "prevention" program had already progressed a considerable distance along the road to serious delinquent behavior before their first meeting with the counselors. As someone put it, "probably two dozen T-boys already had one foot in Lyman School [for delinquents] before the counselor made his first visit to the home!" Presumably these facts were substantially true of the C-boys of comparable age. There were five C-boys who appeared in court prior to the date on which treatment began for their matched twins.

Before treatment started, the Selection Committee had rated the 325 boys as: 50 percent, difficult; 42 percent, average; 8 percent, zero (midway between difficult and average). There were, then, 163 T-boys who showed obvious delinquent behavior or indications of delinquent probabilities in the years ahead. (See Table 15 in Chapter VI).

Other Social Factors. (a) There were 13 boys who had lost their mothers before treatment started; 29 boys whose mothers were living but whose fathers had died or had disappeared; and three boys, both of whose parents were dead or whose whereabouts were unknown. There were thus about 45 boys (14 percent) from homes in which one or both parents were missing. (b) Twenty-six boys were considered fairly serious enuretics. (c) In 45 of the cases the mother or father was alcoholic or at least had been recorded as addicted to alcohol over a considerable time, although the evidence in some cases was inconclusive. (d) Seventeen boys were either known to be illegitimate or there was some question concerning their parentage. (e) Sixty boys were living in homes that were notorious for the neglect of the child or for cruelty or desertion, or homes where one or both parents were guilty of immorality or criminal behavior. (f) The mothers or fathers, or both, of 13 of these boys were known to have had a venereal disease at one time or another. It is probable that there were other cases where the facts were not available.

Such was the nature of the group for which this research had been set up.

THE STAFF

Who was to carry forward the treatment program? In 1935 the directors began a search for men and women of good character, intelligence, and tact, who had had professional experience in dealing with people. They wanted only those who had a lively faith in the value of the project, willing to give their time and strength to an untried venture.

A social worker, no matter how well trained, was not to be preferred to a warm, outgoing person who had that vital spark so essential in human relationships, but who had not had the benefit of formal social work education. In fact, of the first four candidates chosen for the treatment program, only one had had such formal training, though subsequent selections were drawn, as a rule, from the professional social work group.

Altogether over 250 individuals were considered for the ten staff positions as counselors. Although all of the subjects of the experiment were boys, women, it was thought, would be of special value in dealing with the younger boys and with their families; accordingly, of the ten original counselors four were women. It will be recalled that the average age of the boys assigned to the women counselors was one year less than that of the boys assigned to the men. In subsequent years three of the women counselors left the Study, their charges being reassigned to male counselors. The one remaining woman counselor retained most of her case load of young boys but did shift some of the older boys to the men. Of the number of treatment months throughout the entire program 69 percent were male-counselor months.

By February, 1939, the ten counselors who were to initiate the treatment program were chosen. Before the termination of the program a total of 19 different counselors were employed—15 men and four women, but at no time were there more than ten working simultaneously. Of the 19 counselors, eight were professional social workers, six had completed part of the academic requirements for a degree in social work, two were experienced boys' workers, one was a trained nurse, and two were psychologists. The counselors represented a wide distribution of ages, with an average of approximately 31 years. Three of them were about the same age as the boys' parents; nine were under 30.

When treatment started there was no pediatrician or psychiatrist on the staff. Boys in need of such treatment were taken to near-by public or private clinics. The counselor who had had extensive clinical experience as a nurse became an advisor on some of the medical problems, particularly relating to diseases of the skin. Thus, the treatment program was launched with a staff consisting of the two co-directors, ten counselors, three psychologists, one research assistant, and four secretaries. There were also available for consultation 19 advisors well known in social work, psychology, medicine, and allied fields, who were called upon in group meetings and in individual group conferences for advice and suggestions. Other professional people were added to the staff from time to time.

During the course of the ensuing years many staff changes occurred.[3] Some staff members were employed specifically for treatment and some specifically for research, although there was some overlapping in these two functions. Altogether, from the inception of the Study to the end of the treatment period, 84 people were employed by the Foundation. About 60 percent of this number were giving their entire time to the work.

THE FUNCTION AND POLICIES OF THE STUDY

Emphasis on the Importance of the Friendly Relationship. Given the 325 subjects and a competent staff, how were the objectives of

[3] See Appendix B, for list of staff members.

the Study to be achieved? The founder believed that "moral suasion" would play a large part in effecting a change in the boy's character and that the example of a person of good character might be a deciding factor in the boy's development, provided the worker could win and retain his confidence and friendship. "What is it that keeps any of us straight," Dr. Richard C. Cabot asked, "unless it is the contagion of the highest personalities whom we have known?" [4]

Dr. Cabot had also emphasized the importance of religion in a program based upon growth. "The first fact about our growth," he pointed out in a talk to the staff, "is our dependence on God." He made clear to the counselors how spiritual growth would become an essential focus of treatment:

> Before and beyond any special kind of treatment or influence which we should try to bring to bear upon any child in our Study, is our desire that he come face to face with the two greatest realities which concern him, God and his own soul; that is, the material, mental and spiritual resources of creation which God and man offer to him but which he must freely appropriate and assimilate to the needs of his individual growth.
>
> We believe that religion and the spiritual life are not one among many other human interests, but are the center of all special interests of man. Unless the resources of creation which can be drawn into the individual's life are recognized by him, unless he gets himself into the moving current of creation—physically by proper nutrition and hygiene,—mentally by an enlightening education, and spiritually by the recognition of his dependence on God, the individual's free will cannot be effectively used to promote his own growth. It will run into perversions and conflicts whereby his growth will be arrested or destroyed.

Obviously there is no rule of thumb for the development of character. "The bulk of our work," he pointed out, "will be accomplished through the personal intimacy of our workers with the individual boy and with his family. To make him understand himself and the world that he lives in, so that he can find satisfaction in his life without harming himself or others, will be the chief effort of our workers."

The initiative and resources of each counselor were deeply challenged. One accustomed to working in a social agency where the functions were well charted felt at a loss in an organization offering

---

[4] In an address called "The Consecration of Affections," given before The American Social Hygiene Association, 1911.

such a diversified program. One counselor, for example, after several years with the Study, wrote:

I feel strongly that our work in the past, and to a lesser degree even now, has been hampered because the Study lacked one of the important features common to a so-called orthodox social case work agency—that of an interpretative function. *Being unable to fully explain this function, in a manner satisfying to parents and boys,* without the long process of continued relationship with families, had made early progress very slow.

Instead of being predetermined, as in other social work agencies, the Study function was gradually forged in the fires of treatment itself. Furthermore, it was not the plan of the Study to close cases after specific problems were satisfactorily met, as is the usual practice in social work agencies.

To some, the idea of giving free services to all kinds of boys who had not specifically expressed any need for them harked back to the early days of social work when environmental manipulation was supplemented by intellectual exhortation and moral suasion. Indeed, the sponsors of the plan believed that the modern trend of social work had often, by striving to be objective and straining to use scientific terminology, placed considerable distance between the worker and the client.

The counselor was to bring to his job a real enthusiasm and a zeal for helping others. He was to be a friend (in as realistic a sense as possible for one who was being paid for cultivating friendship), not hesitating to invite the boy to his home. He was to fight for and alongside the boy, if he felt the boy was being unjustly and helplessly submerged by powerful forces, though he was not, of course, to oppose the orderly and legal processes of society, nor to seek special privileges which were not warranted. In short, the counselor might, on occasion, "identify" with the boy; he was not to be afraid of this taboo in social work. Furthermore, the counselor was to be a constant source of inspiration. In speaking of the relation between ethics and the medical profession Dr. Cabot wrote: "In medical men, as in all men, the strongest force for ethical advance has been, in my experience, the intimate contact with other medical men better than ourselves, whereby by 'osmosis' nobler habits of thought and action seep across from teacher to pupil, from chief to intern, from colleague to colleague without a word spoken on the subject." [5] And yet, in spite of this seemingly old-fashioned and paternalistic slant, the counselors were permitted and encouraged to utilize any of the modern techniques of social work with which they were familiar. The friendly relationship was to be a means of encouraging the boy's own development, enabling him to muster his own inner resources. Thus the boy could be encouraged to utilize those forces that would lead to the best development from within.

Since no counselor was discouraged from following the most modern developments of social work some of them considered the job to be that of a social case worker. Others did not. None felt that he was limited in his operations to any particular school of thought. Although each counselor might use a wide variety of techniques, certain limitations of function had to be faced. These conditions will be described as they existed on June 1, 1939.

Is It Advisable to Offer Help to Those Who Are Not Asking for It? A fact of which all the counselors were keenly, and at times, painfully aware was that none of the boys had asked to be included in the Study. It was imperative, therefore, that the boy's confidence and that of his parents be obtained before any plan of treatment could be put into operation. The Study could not fall back on official standing in the community; it must rest solely on confidence and mutual trust. The fact that the Study was unique in this respect was understood by most of the boys. After the Study ended Douglas expressed the difference between the Study and the Y in this way: "The Study is in its own class. You didn't have to pay anything. If you wanted to go—you could—if you didn't you didn't have to. They had the right idea. Let the boy decide. Mr. B. used to come down here and he'd say, 'You can either talk to me or play with the other fellows'—there was no rule that I had to talk to them—that I had to stay; but I did. I don't think anyone would want to have left; they all would want to stay and talk." And yet, just how case work could get started when neither the boy nor his family was asking help was a question not infrequently raised. As one counselor put it,

[5] R. C. Cabot, *The Adventures on the Borderlands of Ethics* (New York, Harper and Brothers, 1926).

case work "cannot artificially be imposed on the client like a blanket or a mustard plaster."

Under such circumstances some counselors were inhibited in discussing freely the function of the Study with the families. They feared that they might "lose the case" (which would be unfortunate, after the tedious selection and matching procedures) if they gave the family a free choice as to whether they wished to accept or reject the services offered. On the other hand, they did not feel that they could impose upon the unwilling their friendly offers of help. Other members of the staff, generally those without formal social work training, were not particularly concerned about this. It seemed to be true, furthermore, that after a good relationship was established, the work proceeded along lines basically similar to social case work. In some cases, indeed, the situation did not differ greatly from that found in a child guidance clinic to which a boy had been taken unwillingly by someone in authority, although in clinic cases the patient is usually aware that something is amiss. In dealing with his boys the counselor had to give some reason, explicitly or implicitly, for his presence. Sometimes the boy was cooperative but retained lingering suspicions that he never dared voice. Douglas said at the end of the program, "Ya, when you look back on it, when I come to think about it, I don't know why they did anything for me. I didn't know them—always seemed like there was a catch to it but there wasn't. It seemed funny their doing this just for nothing. But," he concluded, "it helped a great many of them."

Frequently it was found that after a friendly relationship had been established the boy discussed his problems with the counselor who could then proceed as naturally as though the boy had originally come to the Study for help. The greatest difficulties occurred when the family and the boy, while not openly hostile, offered merely passive cooperation or remained indifferent, and the actual needs were not pressing.

One incidental result of selecting boys on the basis of research needs was that quite often a boy would be singled out of a large family when his brothers or sisters were in greater need of help. As the father of one boy said on the counselor's initial visit, "You should have taken Freddie instead of Mario." Freddie was not taken because he was one year too old for the Study, but he was an active delinquent, whereas Mario was a well-behaved child. In many cases the counselor had to turn his attention to other members of the family. It happened on occasion that the child selected already was the favored one in a group of jealous siblings. Further attention, to the neglect of the others, was not apt to improve family harmony nor was it easy for the counselor to explain to the family or to the boy his preferential attentions.

The Study, obviously, had not narrowed the range of help to cases that were most in need or even to those who would most profit from the services or were most amenable to treatment. The selection was more research-centered than treatment-centered.

The fact that the Study was committed to a program of giving unsolicited help caused endless staff discussions. Many informal arguments and several staff seminars revealed an issue between those who believed themselves to be strictly social case workers and those who adopted a more informal or eclectic approach. One counselor, a recent graduate of a school of social work, stated that he could see in the Study program two general methods of treatment: one he called social case work, the other simply a friendly relationship. To him the difference in theory was fundamental, for the social case workers must relate their treatment efforts

to the individual's own want to do something about it—without that want no case work is possible. [He feared that those who were pursuing the strictly friendly relationship approach took over the task of] initiating, organizing or producing the changes necessary for the boy to achieve this goal [the boy's proper growth and adjustment]. . . . Treatment efforts may or may not be in accord with the individual's felt wants . . . the individual boy is the subject, the worker the builder. The responsibility for change is the agency's and not the individual's.

This approach, the worker sincerely believed, was wrong. But as time went on these differences became more academic and less real. The problem of giving unsolicited help grew dimmer and less important in the later years when boys least eager for help were dropped from the list and the case load was cut down to a smaller group, which for the most part desired and actively sought the counselors' advice.

Should Environmental Changes or Group Work Be Attempted?

NATURE OF THE TREATMENT PROGRAM 99

Although the counselor had great freedom of choice in drawing up his plan for character development, he had to refrain from any radical alteration of the larger environment in which the boy lived. Counselors, for example, were instructed that they were not to initiate community projects such as the building of new playgrounds or the organization of boys' clubs that might affect all of the residents of the neighborhood including the controls who happened to reside there. The aim of the Study was to determine just how much or how little could be done within the prevailing socioeconomic framework. It would have seemed to some advisors more productive to suggest that a bolder attack on delinquency be made through slum clearance or some political reform that could get at "basic causes." Dr. Cabot was aware of the fundamental social ills but in this particular project he chose to focus attention on the treatment of the individual.

How Many Boys Could Each Counselor Befriend? When the research program was first established, the number of cases to be assigned to each worker was undetermined, and before treatment started, there was considerable discussion about this optimum number. Only three-fourths of the boys would need close attention, it was thought, because of the presence in the group of so many average boys. The size of the case load was, of course, directly related to the budget. Practically all counselors believed that their case loads (34 or 35 for each full-time counselor) were too high, considering the nature of the work and the research demands constantly made on the counselor's time. It was held that one could not be a real friend to so many boys.

How Frequently Should Counselors See the Boys? No definite rule or restricting policy was adopted. There were boys who had no apparent need of treatment and there were boys who were already known to the court and police for their antisocial behavior for which preventive work was in the nature of emergency treatment. The frequency of interviews was determined by the boys' need and the counselors' industriousness and skill but was in reality limited by the boys' availability and the extent of the counselors' case load. There would be, of course, wide variations from case to case. In general, the number of visits was largely discretionary with the counselors (see Chapter IX).

Because the boys were to be seen in their own homes or at school, no place was provided for interviewing at the office, which served merely as staff headquarters and as a place for the writing and keeping of records.[6] It was supposed that the boy would look upon the counselor as one who had come from "some organization interested in boys" and who was rather closely, though not officially, affiliated with the schools. There was an initial fear, probably exaggerated, that the suspicion or hostility of the boy or his parents might be aroused if they believed that the counselor was sent by a *research* organization interested in studying them, or if it were known that the counselor was directly seeking to prevent delinquency. Thus, the counselor did not always feel free to present a comprehensive statement to the families, though of course no deception, expressed or implied, was practiced. The "whole story," the directors believed, need not be told these families unless they asked. Of course, if they asked direct questions, the counselors were to tell them the truth. In retrospect, some counselors believed that the policy of partial concealment was not wise and that some cases were less effectively dealt with because of consequent suspicion. Brian, for example, an unusually sensitive boy, resented being asked personal questions. He soon developed a fear that his counselor and the staff had some ulterior purpose in questioning him and offering him help he had not asked for. "They would do something for you," he said later, "and then wanted to see what progress they made. They were more interested in progress. That's what I didn't like about it. I don't like to be a guinea pig!" Fortunately, this reaction was shared by only a few boys in the Study.

Should Financial Aid Be Given to the Boy? There were, of course, financial limitations. Although the plan called for "whatever is best for the boy," it was not intended that the Study would meet the boys' material needs except in unusual circumstances. The counselors could not assume financial responsibility for families. The staff was understandably annoyed when one of the local newspapers reported the experiment as one that would provide "lush opportunities and support" to these children, to whom it would give "every imaginable care in the way of nutrition, educational training, ex-

---

[6] This policy was changed when the Study moved to new quarters in the summer of 1939 (see Chap. XI).

ercises, medical attention, recreation, the best schooling, the best summer camps, the most intelligent tutoring. The cream of civilization in the most modern and enlightened forms is put at their feet." The staff was also aware of the dangers of "bribing" the boys or of creating a feeling of financial dependence. Needy cases were to be referred to private or public welfare agencies. The aim was to see what could be done for the boys without recourse to expensive and drastic measures that could not be duplicated elsewhere.

Should Boys Be Removed to Foster Homes? It was urged by some that, as most delinquency can be traced to the home, the Study might best prevent the development of delinquent careers by sending boys from inadequate homes to private schools, or by placing them on farms or in foster homes at the very beginning. This suggestion obviously was not in line with the essential purpose of the Study. The counselor was, therefore, to encourage the boy to get all that he could from his home, his church, his school, and from the other character-building agencies available to him. Except in rare and specific cases the Study did not intend to advise the boy's removal from his own home. It thus became a policy of the Study to consider a foster home placement as a last resort, particularly when the counselor personally would be unable to keep in close touch with the boy.

Relationship with Other Social Agencies. Although not at first considered a social agency in the usual sense, for it did not take on new cases or limit its case load to those in need, the Study worked cooperatively with other agencies in the community interested in similar problems and was on the same footing with them. It would not ask other agencies to give special consideration to its cases nor to serve its cases to the neglect of their own. Its position was, in this respect, like that of a private citizen calling upon local agencies to aid a particular boy or family. Its policy was to cooperate with all existing agencies working toward the same end.[7]

[7] Many writers in this field have stressed the importance of community cooperation in delinquency prevention. See Lowell J. Carr, *Delinquency Control* (New York, Harper and Brothers, 1940).

CHAPTER IX

THE COUNSELOR
MEETS THE BOY

TREATMENT STARTED WITH A VISIT TO ONE BOY IN NOVEMBER AND four in December, 1937. Other cases were taken on gradually as they passed through the hands of the Selection Committee and the matchers. In 1938, 71 new cases were started. During the first four months of 1939, 91 additional boys were seen by their counselors. The balance of 158 cases were added to the program in May, 1939. By that time the treatment staff had been increased to ten and no further cases were taken on.

THE PROBLEM OF "BREAKING THE ICE"

The treatment staff was faced with many puzzling questions. How were boys to be notified that they had been selected for treatment? How was their consent and that of the families to be obtained? What explanation of the Study could be given them? These questions were discussed in staff meetings but answers had to be found by actual trial and error in terms of each counselor's resourcefulness. The approach, therefore, became individualized: no standardized treatment was planned—or possible.

For each case that was assigned to him the counselor was given a folder containing all of the data described in Chapter IV but not including the Selection Committee ratings. He was asked to read and summarize this material, writing a digest of it in the form of a "pre-treatment summary." [1] He thus had a fairly adequate picture of the boy and the family with whom he was soon to become acquainted. He was provided with a map of the city showing the location of the various schools and the delinquency areas. [2] He was then

[1] For a typical Pre-treatment Summary see Appendix C.
[2] None of the ten counselors was a resident of Cambridge or Somerville prior to commencement of the work. Seven out of ten of them came from other states.

told, in effect, "Here is our information about the case. Now go find your boy and get acquainted! He probably isn't expecting you, so be tactful. Establish to the best of your ability a personal, friendly relationship that might have some meaning for the boy, that might endure for a considerable period of time and result in the boy's constructive growth. Your special concern is with preventing him from developing a delinquent career."

THE COUNSELOR'S EXPLANATION

The counselor's explanation of the Study was not a completely new story, for in every case, it will be recalled, each home had been previously visited by a representative of the Study for the purpose of obtaining information prior to classification. There had also been a visit to the school by a psychologist, who tested the boy, and by an investigator, who interviewed the teacher. Each boy had also been examined at the school by a doctor from the Study. Some of the families, even though they did not recall the home visit, may have heard about the Study from the boys' reports of these experiences or from school officials. Eighteen of the 325 boys had been taken on overnight camping trips in the summer of 1937 (before the treatment program started) by two members of the staff, one of whom later became a counselor (see Chapter IV). Most of these camp boys retained vivid memories of the Study as a "camping organization." The counselor could, therefore, on his first visit refer to associations with parent, school, or camp and thus lay a foundation for building up the confidence of the family.

In practically every case on his first visit to the home the counselor, by way of explanation, reminded the parent of the prior interview with the home visitor.[3] In only a few cases, however, had these visits been made within two or three months of the initial visit of the counselor. On the average, at least a year had elapsed; in many cases two, and in one case three years had gone by before the counselor arrived on the scene. In introducing himself the counselor would frequently say, "You may remember a visit by Miss A. last year. Perhaps you recall that she was interested in your boy and spoke to you about our organization." In about 70 percent of the cases the mother or father recalled the visit; in about two-thirds of

3 See Chap. IV for a description of these home visits.

these cases the recall was a pleasant one and produced an acceptable mental state for the establishment of a new relationship.

Most of the homes were in the middle or lower economic groups. Those in need seemed eager to receive the worker, once they understood that he was offering help. On the other hand, many of the poorer families had no doorbells and few facilities conducive to privacy. The counselor sometimes felt like an intruder, arriving unannounced, often interrupting a meal or finding the mother busy with household duties and in no condition to receive a stranger. Tact was needed when a counselor suddenly walked into a home to present his message to a surprised mother. Language was an occasional barrier. Words like "relationship," "growth and development," "objectives of our Study" were, of course, inappropriate in families where English was scarcely understood. Those born abroad who had not acquired facility with our language or knowledge of our institutions could not easily accept the fact that we wished to come into their homes unsolicited, to offer assistance without seeking to collect a fee, to sell something, or to "send the boy away."

MEN AND WOMEN COUNSELORS: ADVANTAGES OF HAVING BOTH

It will be recalled that the home visitors had rated the father or the mother in terms of potential expected cooperation.[4] Only 5 percent of the families were rated as least cooperative, 22 percent as slightly uncooperative. In this way the counselor was given advance warning. He knew in which families to expect a hostile attitude although by the time he made his visit conditions might have changed and the expected hostility might have evaporated. Evidently in most cases, the personality of the home visitor or the counselor was the important factor in arousing hostility or in winning the friendship of the families. The counselor had some advantage over the home visitor in that he could offer the family some prospects of service; this the home visitor could not do, not knowing whether the family in question would later fall into the treatment or the control group.[5] On the whole, the reception of the counselors was good.

It was anticipated that the six men counselors would have a nat-

---

[4] See Chap. IV.
[5] Only 39 percent of the homes visited later became homes of T-boys.

ural advantage over the four women in building up a friendly relationship with the boy and, if accepted by the boy, would find it easier to get the confidence of the parents. On the other hand, certain advantages accrued to the women. A woman visiting a home in the morning was not apt to arouse the suspicions of the parents or be considered a detective, a truant officer, a probation officer, or a saleswoman. In one case the grandmother who was in charge of the boy thought the counselor (a man) was selling encyclopedias. When he talked about the boy's reading difficulties that he had heard about from the school, she was further convinced that there was some mercenary motive back of his explanation and that he would probably later try to sell her some sort of a book on how to make boys study. It took the counselor several weeks to dispel this suspicion.

A mother could talk more freely to another woman, and as most of these visits were made in the day time the mother, not the father, was seen on the first visit. One of the women counselors was a nurse and on most of her initial visits wore a nurse's uniform. She was accepted as a person having a professional interest in the health of the boy in question. Certainly the knack of carrying on a discussion of the everyday problems of housekeeping was an advantage in the women's favor, and yet there were not a few cases where the mother welcomed a chance to talk to a man visitor.

In 12 percent of the cases the counselor happened to be the same person who had originally made the first home visit so that the explanation of the Study to the parent at the time treatment commenced was made more smoothly.

FIRST VISITS TO SCHOOL

In about two-thirds of the cases the counselor first went to the school. There he spoke to the boy's teacher and was introduced to the boy. When a visit to the home was subsequently made, the counselor found that his explanation to the mother was readily accepted for he could say to her, "I have just been to the Graham School and have talked with Joe's teacher, Miss Jones. She tells me that Joe is doing pretty well but needs help in reading." The mother was thus assured that this visitor was a responsible person who was accepted by the schools. The boy's progress in school—a subject of great interest to the mother—was then made the focus of the interview and the counselor, if skillful, could go on from there, suggesting possible plans for help.

FIRST VISITS TO HOMES

In about one-third of the cases the counselor's first move was a visit to the home. There were, however, several cases where the counselor preferred to meet the boy in a casual way on the street before visiting his school or home. Such a procedure was more or less experimental and was not generally adopted, for it was found that the cooperation of the parents—so essential in this kind of work—could best be obtained by going directly to them before seeing the boy.

In some cases little explanation was given and none was asked for. The family needed help and they accepted most casually the counselor's introductory remarks. In three or four cases the mother was seen for some months before the boy himself was visited. In none of the explanations to the parents was the word "research" emphasized. The essence of the explanations was simply this: "We are interested in boys"; "We are working with the schools"; "We would like to get acquainted with your boy"; but the explanation of course had to be adapted to the response. The counselors were, on the whole, surprised to find that only a few parents asked further questions and few boys seemed to question the intent of the counselor. Most of the boys, like Ross, took the program more or less as a matter of course. When later he was asked how he happened to get acquainted with the Study, Ross said, "I didn't get acquainted with the Study—it got acquainted. Here's how it happened. One of the men from the organization came over to my house just as I was getting out of school one day. He was describing all of the wonderful things the Study was doing. He was really a swell fellow to go on picnics with. I would say that their job was to keep boys out of trouble and show them a swell time."

WHAT DID THE BOYS THINK?

After the close of the program many boys were asked by non-staff interviewers how they happened to be included in the Study.[6]

[6] See Chap. XIII for a description of the interviewing methods and an analysis of the interviews.

Forty-four percent of the sample of 118 boys interviewed definitely associated the Study with the public schools, believing that the counselor selected them because they were not doing well in their school work (19 percent); or that the counselors had come down to see them because they had heard their school conduct was bad (9 percent); or that the school had given all the pupils in their classrooms certain tests and the Study had selected boys on the basis of test scores (5 percent); or that the schoolteacher had picked them out for some special reason unknown to them (11 percent).

Other explanations given by the boys were: the Study had previously become acquainted with their families or their friends (20 percent); they never knew why they had been selected (14 percent); they were not in good health (9 percent); or they had been in trouble in the neighborhood and some person whom they later knew as a counselor had come down to talk to them about it (6 percent). Three percent accepted the counselor casually without reflecting upon his motivations, simply saying, "Oh, a man just came down to see me," or "Miss C. just came and took me riding." The remaining 4 percent gave a variety of other reasons.

SUMMARY OF RESPONSES TO THE INITIAL INTERVIEW

A rough classification of the kinds of responses to the counselors' first visits, with illustrations from the records, follows.

1. An Eagerness to Be Included in the Study (about 33 percent of the cases).

"Will Jeffrey be accepted by the Study?" his mother asked anxiously. The counselor explained that Jeffrey had already been selected. She almost screamed with delight and called the boy into the room. She said how glad she was that it was really true. (The boy's father was dead; the mother was working and trying to support her own mother and father as well as this boy who was then only 12.) She said she felt the need of having some man take an interest in her son. "What is the first thing you are going to do?" she asked eagerly. The counselor had in mind helping the boy with his studies, as he had been having difficulty in school. The mother, going beyond the counselor's aspirations, said to the boy, hugging him to her side, "Just think, Jeff, they will help you in your schoolwork and when you grow up, they will send you to college!"

2. *An Interest in the General Idea and a Willingness to Hear More about It* (comprising about 25 percent of the cases). Visiting Maurice's home for the first time the counselor met a rather incredulous woman. The record states:

She shuffled to the door in her slippers and what looked like a nightgown. She had light red hair, looked very pale and ill, and her manner was not cordial. I introduced myself and asked if she could conveniently give me a few minutes time to tell her about the Study and that Maurice had been invited to be one of the 325 boys to join. Ungraciously she said, "I don't know what more information I can give you. . . ." (Evidently referring to the first home visit and the questions asked then.) She added she had been sick in bed. I tried to persuade her to let me return another time when she felt better and more like talking. Somewhat mollified she said, "Now that you're here you may as well say what you want." I explained then that we were interested in boys and wanted to have a chance to know a few specially selected ones, whose parents were interested. We thought it was going to be a good deal of fun and expected that there might be some situations in which we might be able to help a boy develop his own special ability. She seemed to relax and become more and more pleased. She raised the question of what it would cost, saying she couldn't pay *anything.* She added that she had had to stop another son's music lessons, so certainly couldn't afford to spare any additional expense for Maurice.

Shortly the mother was talking about her own ill health. She said, "I have bronchial asthma and it has been wearing me out for nine years." The counselor then discussed *her* problem. She became more interested. Several interviews followed and the counselor became acquainted with the boy. The mother called upon the counselor for help many times during the ensuing years and a great deal of time was spent with the boy.

3. *An Attitude of Indifference* (about 16 percent of the cases). Lester's father was home when the counselor made his first call. "It is okay with me," he said, returning to his newspaper and showing no further interest or curiosity concerning the counselor's plans.

4. *A Suspiciousness about the Purpose of the Study* (about 25 percent of the cases). The counselor stated in Hank's record:

Mr. F. answered the door. He is a short, thin, wrinkled man with seamed face. He speaks broken English and seems quite suspicious of me. He impresses me as shrewd, sly, taciturn and reserved—he glared suspiciously at me. I started to explain my interest in Hank and the reason for my visit. He listened a bit and then said he had been out of work all year and didn't want anything to do with it. He called in another son, who was 24 years old. The young man asked suspiciously what it was that we wanted to do. I explained this in terms of various interests that the boys might have and in terms of our connection with the schools, etc. He said quite frankly that it sounded screwy to him. "Listen, Buddy, I've been around a hell of a lot but never heard anything like this. Just tell me one thing you can do for Hank!"

The suspicion lingered for some time until the counselor was able to show the family that he was sincere in his attempt to be helpful and that the program would not involve any cost.

5. *A Rejection or Unwillingness to Hear More about It* (about 1 percent of the cases). On the first visit to Rudolph's home the mother questioned the value of the Study. She kept interrupting the explanation of the counselor by asking why the counselor assumed that there must be something wrong with Rudolph. If he had to be examined by a doctor, she reasoned, he must be in poor health. Why did he have a mental test if we did not think there was something peculiar about him? She went to the school to inquire why the Study was interested in her boy. She rejected the explanation of the master of the school who tried to reassure her of the counselor's sincere interest. She felt that the counselor was hiding something. She concluded that she did not want her boy "to serve as a guinea pig." The counselor then talked to the father who shared the suspicions of the mother. The father said, "There's no reason for you to be interested in my boy, especially as there are so many boys needing special attention." The father became belligerent in his attitude and said, "Every time one of you people come around the boy's mother is a nervous wreck afterwards. I want to get at the bottom of it." He said he would see the school superintendent. (The parents got in touch with the school and with the help of the teachers some cooperation was obtained, although the case never became an active one.)

OVERCOMING RESISTANCE

Most of the initial resistance was overcome by repeated visits that generally convinced the family of the good intent and practical helpfulness of the counselor. On a number of occasions the counselor appealed to the school officials, who were generous in giving their time to the problems of the Study and who were usually able to explain the Study satisfactorily to the parents. Only one of the 325 cases had to be written off as a loss at the very outset due to a definite refusal to participate.

Acceptance by the families was greater than expected. Relatively few families asked for complete explanations and the boys themselves rarely questioned the purpose of the counselors' visits. The families most in need were, on the whole, more responsive to the initial visits. The key to acceptance of the Study seemed to be the ability to win the confidence of the parents, but it was the counselors' opinion that without the backing and the prestige of the public and parochial schools such success would have been practically impossible.

CHAPTER X

THE FIRST FEW YEARS
OF THE PROGRAM

TREATMENT PLANNING

After introducing themselves to the boys and their families, the counselors were faced with the necessity of planning and operating a long-range project. Before treatment began the directors had requested that some plan be drawn up for each boy. Every three or six months the counselor was to write down again his plans for the immediate future. It was anticipated that many revisions would have to be made, once the counselor became familiar with the problems. Where the need was specifically described in the home visitor's report, the counselor could make definite plans, as in Cornelius' case, where it was known the boy had suffered from rheumatic fever. The counselor, before commencing work with Cornelius, wrote:

It is important to find out as quickly as possible the amount of heart damage and the amount of restricted activity that will be necessary; (a) if the child is still under the care of the local doctor to seek his cooperation; (b) if not, get him into Children's Heart Clinic at Cambridge Hospital. One must act slowly in this family as mother wasn't overly cooperative on first contact (home visit). It is likewise very important that teacher no longer treat him so completely as an invalid and make him continuously conscious of his handicap; to try to get family to appreciate that boy has need of companionship of boys of his own age and the dangers inherent in so much overprotection; to find out what his real educational abilities or handicaps are at the present time.

Likewise, in the case of Oliver the counselor could plan specifically because the boy was already known to the police. The counselor made the following "pre-treatment" plans, most of which were later carried out:

(1) To keep Oliver away from his brother who was a serious delinquent and was at that time at Lyman School but about to be returned; (2) to

consider the possibility of a foster home for Oliver; (3) to give him intensive attention at the very beginning, planning for two or three visits a week at first; (4) to give some attention to the boy's school difficulties, plan tutoring for him and possibly obtain a scholarship at a university clinic.

Sometimes the initial plans could not, for practical reasons, be carried through. One difficulty, for example, was that the plan was based upon information obtained by a home visit made one or two years earlier, so that the counselor was unaware of the most recent developments.

The directors were not so much concerned about the failure to carry through the original plan as they were interested to see that the counselor did some serious thinking about his treatment of the boy. They asked each counselor to state frankly in the running record, under the heading of "Reflections," what he thought about his own performance and his hopes for the case. He was thus encouraged to reflect upon his own failures and to change his plan whenever he thought he could improve it.

THE PROBLEM OF DIAGNOSIS

A review of the 325 treatment plans reveals the fact that seldom was a plan tied closely to a specific diagnosis. There was a great deal of information available in each case, certainly as much as is ordinarily available to agencies in making a social diagnosis of the client's needs. And yet the philosophy of the Study tended away from a strict diagnostic procedure for reasons that are brilliantly stated in Dr. Cabot's presidential address to the National Conference of Social Work in 1931. In this significant speech he said, in part:

The working principles of social endeavor have been warped by medical analogies. Since Miss Richmond's epoch-making book on Social Diagnosis, we are living in the epoch which that book made—convinced that before we can rightly attempt to help anyone we must know what is the matter with him. As our splendid Massachusetts Commissioner of Correction has recently said: "A hypothesis has been set up, namely, that the proper way to handle the problems of human beings is first of all to find out what is the matter with them." [1]

I challenge that hypothesis. Note that it is made to apply to all human beings. It is not a way but "the proper way" to handle not certain prob-

[1] Dr. A. Warren Stearns, in *Proceedings of the National Conference of Social Work* (Chicago, University of Chicago Press, 1931), p. 99.

lems but all problems. Moreover, the diagnosis is to come "first of all." But on the contrary it is often better I believe, to find out, first of all, what-is-not-the-matter, what is sound, what the client can build on—his assets. Often—if not always—this should come first of all. Later we shall almost inevitably find out what is the matter, so far as we ever can. But until we make further trial of the "assets-first" sort of "diagnosis" and compare our results with the medical way—which starts with what is wrong, not with what is right—we cannot be sure that the medical way is best in our field.

I do not find that "diagnosis first" is always best even in the medical problems of a hospital. We do not always believe in pushing our diagnostic procedures to their limit before we start treatment. . . . Accurate and early diagnosis is sometimes essential, often desirable, usually helpful, but even in medicine, sometimes unnecessary. Many a patient recovers without the luxury of a diagnosis. Even when there are evidences of an emergency demanding prompt and specific treatment (if we had it), it is often best to see if the *vis medicatrix naturae* will not pull the patient out of his trouble without the bother and exhaustion attendant on the search—sometimes fruitless search—for a modern scientific diagnosis.

In social work this is far more often the case. . . . Even in medicine—but still more in social work—a diagnosis (or some of the facts pointing toward one) may be reached at an expense to the patient and to our relationship that is dangerous to our ultimate success in helping him.

This is made clearer if we scrutinize another medical analogy which I think often misleads us in social work. I mean the search for "the cause" of a person's troubles. In medicine we rightly search for the cause of a fever. Is it the tubercle bacillus, is it sunstroke, is it cancer of the liver? Recognizing that many other influences may favor the action of the main cause at a certain time, we yet know that we should search for "the cause"—that is, for something the removal or neutralization of which will cure the disease. But the attempt at causal diagnosis in social work is, I think, particularly apt to upset treatment. There is no cause for individuality in any part of nature. Hence, if we succeed in getting into relation with the most individual parts of his character, we shall not be dealing there with a "cause" for his actions. His purely habitual actions are often the fruit of one or more causes. But when he is most himself, when he acts most characteristically, he is himself the "cause" and there is no use in looking elsewhere for it. Medical and psychoanalytical fashions in social work are now doing harm by making us look for any "causes" for a person's behavior except the total character of the person in the environment which he faces.

The success of our social treatment is endangered, then, first, by the effort to put a unique individual into a class (diagnosis) and, secondly, by the fruitless attempt to make out that he is merely a mechanism subject to causes the removal of which will set him right; in short, by the attempt to treat him like a disease. . . . To look for the "cause" of what is most characteristic in a person's life, his opinions, his total behavior, is as much a wild goose chase as to look for perpetual motion. It is also an insult and, therefore, a bad way to start a relationship which is friendly or else a failure.[2]

WHAT THE COUNSELOR ATTEMPTED TO DO

Though written plans, on the whole, evidenced a high order of aspiration, their success or failure naturally depended on actual accomplishments. The original diagnosis could be wrong or unimportant. The important fact for the boy was what the counselor actually did. In January, 1940, at a time when our boys had been in treatment about nine months (on the average), an analysis was made of what the counselors believed they were trying to accomplish.[3] In reply to written questionnaires the ten counselors answered that their general aims were: "establishing friendly relationships," "developing personality and character," or "helping boys to solve problems." In reply to the question, "What are you trying to do?" the following answers were representative:

To lead a boy from one stage of development to another by helping him meet his problems in the best way.

To focus, utilize and interpret the community resources when one cannot carry out the aims alone.

To be a person to whom the boy will turn for service that he believes is important to him.

To help a boy see and understand his own assets and liabilities, develop his potentialities to the fullest extent.

To supply a "masculine ideal."

To be available to the boy and family when needed.

To discuss family problems and work out plans with some continuity.

These statements might, of course, be mere theoretical formulations. No empirical study could be made at that time, but the records of each counselor were examined to see, at least, what he claimed he had actually accomplished in specific ways in furthering his general objectives. The following might be considered fairly

[2] In *Proceedings of the National Conference of Social Work* (Chicago, University of Chicago Press, 1931), pp. 3–7.

[3] Here the account of the counselors' activities is in his own words. In Chaps. XXIII–XXIX Dr. Helen L. Witmer evaluates the work of the counselors and describes their services as seen by an "outsider."

representative of the current practices during the first two years of the program:

Arranging for physical examinations, interpreting to family, and so on.
Attempting to establish helpful relationship with family.
Taking boy on educational trips to "see things."
Arranging for camp and farm placements, and, in a few cases, foster homes.
Finding employment for boy and family.
Advising and counseling family in respect to boy's problems (sex, discipline, and the like).
Giving specific tutorial help in school subjects.
Giving specific attention to analysis and correction of reading disability.
Arranging for intelligence and achievement tests.
Referring to other agencies for specific help.
Procuring legal advice for family.
Carrying out "play therapy."
Inviting the boy to spend day at counselor's home.
Getting much-needed clothes for the boy.
Procuring psychiatric advice and treatment for the boy or family.
Interpreting the boy to the teacher.
Encouraging recreation by engaging in sports with the boy.
Placing family in contact with priests.
Teaching or encouraging hobbies.
Getting more information—through the boy's friends, other agencies, and the like.

TREATMENT EMPHASIS

When asked what was their *emphasis* in treatment, some mentioned the use of psychological techniques, some pointed out the importance of physical development. Four counselors believed that they were focusing a good deal of attention on family problems. Three said they were not conscious of any particular emphasis. School adjustment and religious training were also mentioned as areas of special attention. Some pointed out the value of close working relationships with other social agencies.

It was obvious from this survey that the counselors were not following any set pattern or procedure; a great variety of problems came within their jurisdiction. The report stated that the counselors were "not social revolutionists, nor policemen, nor jailors, nor fairy godmothers, nor candidates for mayor." It seemed obvious at this point that in spite of inevitable diversities in theoretical orientation they were operating as guides, friends, and counselors to the boys and, probably to a lesser degree, as professional social case workers.

The spirit of friendliness was apparent to most of the boys who accepted the program and who were more intensively dealt with. Many referred to their counselors as "my friend" or "my pal." Spencer wrote a lengthy letter to his counselor from the Pacific battlefield. He summed up what the Study had meant to him as follows, "Friendship really had everything to do with it." To Bruce the counselor "was a good egg. He was just like one of us. He was just like a pal—everybody liked him. Why, if he came through the door right now I'd be awfully glad to see him. He was more our age." (This counselor had children of his own about the same age as the Study boys.)

In many cases where the work commenced in the spring (63 percent of the cases were started in March, April, or May, 1939), the counselor was able to offer the boy the opportunity of a camping experience, if such a plan seemed suitable, thus giving the family assurance of some actual gain resulting from the boy "joining" the Study. Also, counselors took boys on trips to the airport, museums, the zoo, and other places of interest where the boy had never been.[4] These trips served the purpose of establishing a friendly basis of operations and gave the counselor an excellent opportunity of knowing the boy better and, where trips were made in small groups, of observing his behavior when in the company of other boys.

SPECIFIC AREAS OF TREATMENT

In terms of specific areas of treatment we find from the records that the counselors most frequently devoted time and attention to the following areas and in this order:

The Boys' School Adjustment. This approach was the most natural

[4] In nearly every case a boy was taken on one or more of these trips during the first year of treatment. Most of the boys seemed to enjoy them but one of the more articulate boys did not see how these trips could prevent boys from getting into trouble. He said, "Anybody with half a brain wouldn't want it. You feel like they're wasting their time—an occasional ride in the country or up to see a few animals or something like that or going to some ancient library to see some prehistoric animals isn't what a young kid wants to do. A fellow would like to go and see the World Series, go to New York, take a trip in the summertime, go to the beach, have beach parties—dances. Teach kids how to dance, football, basketball games—such things like that."

one as most of these boys were originally referred by the schools. The counselor talked with the teachers and the masters in order to find out the nature of the difficulties. He was then in a position to offer definite services, such as special tutorial help.

Physical Condition. Of the 325 boys, 14 had a brain injury (or some suggestion of one); one was post-encephalitic; two had suspected or incipient tuberculosis; ten, heart damage; ten, congenital syphilis; and many were suffering from minor ailments or general poor health. Here was an area where the counselor could acquire a feeling of definite accomplishment by taking the boy to a hospital clinic and following through on the recommendations of the doctors. This service also gave some positive assurance to the parents of the counselor's genuine interest in the boy. During the first year of treatment a great amount of time was consumed in taking boys to medical, dental, and psychiatric clinics or to specialists of one kind or another. The ten counselors in the first six months made 385 visits to clinics and hospitals. One might have assumed that the parents themselves would have taken advantage of the many clinics in the Greater Boston area, but evidently many parents were neglectful, due to ignorance or indifference, or simply to the fact that they were too burdened with other duties. Minor illnesses or physical deficiencies were not always spotted by the school doctor or nurse, or if they were noted, the boy or family frequently failed to carry out recommendations of the school officials. Many times all that was needed was the additional "push" that a counselor could give.

Summer Camping. A third area of treatment was summer camping. Although the Study had no camp of its own, it could refer boys to the many facilities in the Boston area. When it was believed that two or more weeks at some well-managed summer camp would benefit a boy, the Study sent a special application to the local camping organization, underwriting the necessary expenses. The counselors adopted the policy of encouraging the boy or his family to share these expenses if they were able to do so. With small groups of interested boys overnight camping trips also became a common practice.[5]

---

[5] Over a period of seven years 204 different boys went to camp for a total of 802 weeks. For the statistics of the camping program see Appendix D.

Problems of the Family. In addition to dealing directly with the boy the counselor was necessarily concerned with the problems of the family. The women counselors more often dealt with the family problems, although these were not altogether neglected by the men counselors. Help was offered in respect to employment or illness and in referring families to the appropriate public and private agencies. Excepting in rare emergencies the Study did not offer the families financial aid. In a few cases clothing was furnished to those in special need, and Christmas and Thanksgiving baskets were distributed to some families during the first two or three years. Occasionally money was furnished for medical supplies where such could not be obtained at the hospital clinics.

Foster Home Placement. During the first few years of treatment there was some attention to the problem of foster home placement. It soon became obvious that in a few cases the home was so inadequate that nothing could be accomplished without removing the boy from its influence. Altogether, 24 boys were placed in foster homes on the counselors' initiative.

Other Services. There were, of course, many other forms of service. Especially common were talks with the parents, particularly the mother, as the father was generally not home during the day and could be seen only on special evening calls. There were, of course, innumerable talks with the boys alone. Some counselors were frankly moralistic in such talks, some were not.

THE PURPOSE OF THE STUDY AS THE BOY SAW IT

When questioned as to the general purpose of the Study, the boys presented some diversity in viewpoint. In their younger years they were neither articulate nor reflective about it, but as they grew older, they saw their relationship to the Study in clearer focus and began to inquire about its purpose and its special interest in them.

After the termination of the program, when most of the boys were between the ages of 18 and 20, a large sample of the treatment group was interviewed.[6] Non-staff investigators asked them to give their own explanations of what the Study was about. The difficult boy was naturally more aware of the "keeping-me-out-of-trouble"

---

[6] A description of the methods used in the post-treatment interviews is given in Chap. XIII.

purpose of the Study than the average boy. The following viewpoints were typical:

GROUP A (DELINQUENTS) [7]

1. When asked by the investigator if he recalled a group he used to belong to, Luke replied, "I was in the third grade in school. I wasn't doing so well and a Mrs. U. [staff tutor] came down. She used to see me to help me out. They thought my hearing was bad. They didn't know it was just my attitude, so that woman kind of learned me. I never took much interest in school. I wasn't stupid, of course. Mr. S. [counselor] used to come down and take me bowling. I used to see S. at night and then in the daytime if I called him. If I call up Mr. S. and say, 'I want to go bowling,' he'd say, 'Sure,' and I'd go bowling. But what if he didn't say sure? Suppose he told me he didn't want to go bowling, then I would go downstairs and I would start fooling around with cars. The next thing I know, I'm in trouble."

2. Peter said, "A case worker used to come down and talk to me. He tried to get me on the right track. He looked into the background—how you got started into trouble." (The case worker was unsuccessful in keeping Peter out of a number of serious crimes.)

3. Angelo explained that he happened to meet his counselor in school. "He tried to straighten me out. I would call them [the counselors] humanitarians. They tried to put into me what I was doing wrong. I don't know if that explains it too well. They were more like your own folks, looking after you and sometimes they would help you just like your own folks do."

4. Tony gave this version of how he happened to become one of the Study boys: "Well," he said, "when I was nine years old, I got St. Vitus. My mother knew this Mr. D. One day he came down and asked if it was all right to take me out to Dorchester. They had some convalescent home or something so I went out there for a while. Later on I got sick again. He sent me to Wellesley. Next time I got sick he sent me up to Vermont. I liked it up there. We used to pitch hay and eat and do nothing but get healthy."

[7] "Delinquent," as here used, means having been adjudicated delinquent by a court. All the boys in Group A were considered serious delinquents and were committed to an institution.

5. A delinquent from a poor neighborhood said, "It was a group that wanted to study boys and find out all about them. A lot of fellows used to ask me what it was all about but I couldn't tell them the guy [his counselor] was trying to do good, they'd think I was crazy and they wouldn't believe me or they might think he was a fruit."

6. Jack, when asked if he knew what the counselors were trying to do, replied quickly, "Yes, sure. I knew all along—to keep kids out of trouble."

7. Oliver, asked what he thought the idea of the Study was, said, "I don't know—I always used to wonder. I guess it was to help fellows out. You know—if some fellow wanted to play ball and wanted a football and didn't have any money he'd go and steal it. Well, here, it wasn't necessary to do that. The guys would go up to the place [the Study] and they'd get a football and play there—the fellows didn't have to steal the stuff. It started way back in 1938. I used to do a lot of little things—like, picking up things in stores, and then they caught me in a dormitory up at Harvard. I wasn't stealing anything but a lot of stuff had been stolen so they picked me up. Then Mr. D. started to come down and saw my brother. And then one day my brother said Mr. D. said he wanted to see me so I didn't come down when he was supposed to be there. The next time that they told me he was coming down I ran away and didn't come back until the next day. But about a week later he came down on a day he wasn't supposed to and got me there. He took me to different places to do things, go riding, go to the airport, ride around. Then every time I'd get into trouble he'd help me. They [the Study] get less fortunate kids and help them out and sort of give them somebody to lean on."

GROUP B (NON-DELINQUENTS) [8]

1. When asked what he thought the counselor's job was, Lloyd said, "To help, to lend a helping hand over the rough spots, something like that. To find out how I was doing in school, keep things attractive, keep me interested in things—that's the main thing. No

---

[8] Non-delinquent, as here used, means (1) that the boy committed no delinquent acts that led to court appearances, and (2) that in the opinion of the research staff, who knew them well, the boys were not otherwise seriously or frequently delinquent.

matter how thick-skulled you are, you're bound to get something out of it. There are a lot of problem children. That's what we all were, I guess, problem children. I never had heard of this organization till I saw Miss A. They all were socially trained up there. They all had some connection with youth work but I didn't have much to do with anybody except Miss A. She was my counselor."

2. Fred, a retarded child who was having difficulty in school, saw the purpose of the program as "helping me in school work. It seemed like they wanted to help the boys and girls a lot. If they needed help in school and weren't getting along with the teachers, they'd go and speak to them. They teach you how to get along with people." When asked if the counselors were like teachers, he said, "Sort of different. Weren't as strict. Liked them better. They just seemed to like to talk to you, to explain to you. They tell us to have an argument by talking not by fighting and don't lose your temper quickly."

3. Myron, an average boy who was considerably brighter than the others, not in need of intensive treatment said, "In all the years they came to me I didn't know what it was all about. To me it was like an observation. An observation for people to watch and study —nothing to really interest you there. Their [the counselors'] job was something like a roaming counselor. Like when you go to camp you have a counselor in charge of so many kids. I believe that they wanted all kinds of boys, you know, boys that studied a lot and those who didn't study quite as much and those that didn't study at all, guys that liked sports and guys that didn't. They wanted to get a sample. This way they could see how the program could help fellows—different fellows. It was more like a study place to me."

4. Carmen, who had spent three years in the second grade before he became acquainted with the counselor from the Study, thought the most important part of the program was to make him "more educated." "I wasn't interested in school," he admitted. "Too large a class. Teacher couldn't take care of everyone. If she [the counselor] hadn't come along, I would have graduated without knowing anything."

5. To Harold who was having difficulty in getting along with his aunt with whom he was living, in the absence from the home of his mother, the purpose of the counselor was to act "as a third person, to let you see the other person's point of view, to give me a chance to

talk over my troubles. He seemed like a second father, I guess, to me. He talked to us, tried to point out that everyone has to live his own life. You have to become good citizens for the country." He explained that the Study chose him "because I was a bad boy. They wanted to change me or I could have been any one of a dozen they picked. They had a lot of other fellows. It was run for ten years to help the boys. It is just temporary to find out what they could do, just a model. Dr. Cabot—he died—and he wanted to try this out to see if they could help them out before they got into juvenile court —to test—to see how much they could do. Now it has stopped—now they are looking up the fellows." The most important part of the program, Harold thought, was "talking things over with him [his counselor]. I think talking things over was the main idea of the whole thing. Not only that, but if you do things together like going to these things and places it helps to be more friendly. It isn't just meeting him in an office cold-blooded like. It isn't just to keep you off the street. It's to teach you to lead a better life. When a fellow thinks his family doesn't like him and he doesn't care, it is pretty easy for him to cross the line and become a crook. He needs someone to sway him."

6. Sydney, whose problems were mainly in the area of emotional adjustment, saw the Study as a group of social workers who were helping boys. "They make them see the right way to go and then help them on it. She [his counselor] would take me out every Wednesday and we'd go riding. I used to tell her problems I had. She'd help me out with them. Sometimes she'd tell me to do something about them and I wouldn't like it so I'd tell her and she'd suggest something else, so finally I would like what she said and I would do it. Or sometimes she would tell me what to do and if I didn't agree with it, she'd give me other examples and pretty soon I would see what it was all about." Later Sydney was assigned to a man counselor. "I could tell him problems that I couldn't tell Miss C.," he said. "You know how it is. There are some things you can't tell a woman." The objectives of the Study he explained in this way: "Oh, it started by some rich guy who had a lot of money and wanted to help out the boys, I guess, fellows who didn't have much, so that they didn't go wrong—keep them off the corner and away from bad company. That's what happened to me—I started to do that until Mr. R. got hold of me."

7. When asked how he happened to be chosen Donald recalled that "she [his counselor] went around to the different schools and chose different students to belong and I happened to be one of them. Maybe it was because a person could have a friend, have someone to talk to. She was always asking if we had any trouble and had any problems on our minds but she didn't pry into our personal affairs, but just let us talk if we felt like talking. They gave you physical examinations. If they found something wrong with you, they would have taken care of you. It was free. It seemed that the money was left by some woman who died."

8. Allen could not recall the name of the Study some two years after its close but he did recall the name of his last counselor. His explanation of the origin of the Study was as follows: "Well, it seems there was a doctor, I don't know his name, who had a lot of money when he died and he left it to help young people. They used all the money he left. When it ran out, they sold the house and the cars. They were just trying to help young fellows and I happened to be one of them who was lucky enough to be chosen. They gave a lot of tests and then in terms of those tests they were able to tell me what I was good at and what I wasn't good at. They found out that I was good at mechanical drawing and probably because of that I'm taking mechanical drawing this year but I think I'll probably wind up being a truck driver. I was never told why I was chosen but, you know, I was always in trouble while I was in school, in serious trouble. I was at the principal's office a good deal of the time so I suppose they got my name that way. They said if I ever had any trouble that they would be glad to help me out. I never got into any trouble except in school and that wasn't serious. Then there was another kind of thing they did—they took my tonsils out."

9. Leon, like many other boys, knew that the referrals came from the schools. "They got a gang of us together," he said. "I guess they got the devilish boys. Well, I suppose they called us that." When asked the purpose of the Study, as he recalled it, Leon said, "I don't know. I never found out."

10. Lloyd pointed out the difference between the Study and the schools. "In the schools they teach and that's all. If you foul up, they don't go into the details; all they do is just teach. Teachers just don't entertain the idea of looking into individual problems. With this kind of thing they really try to understand you. It shows initia-

tive. It's probably some individual [referring to how the Study was financed] that ran into the same difficulty when he was young."

11. Arnold's understanding: "My idea was that they were out to write a book. The Study has been going on for ten years to find out why kids don't grow any taller than they do [the boy was rather short] and to find out just what makes a kid start stealing."

12. Matthew explained it this way: "This doctor, a well-known doctor which I don't remember the name—I should—had an interest in young fellows and he had some money and he organized the Study. The way I got it he would take two boys and let one of them alone and take care of the other and see what would happen to the boys over a period of ten years."

13. Dexter had an immediate grasp of the founder's essential aim. He said, "The purpose of the counselor was to lead me on the right path like a father."

FREQUENCY OF VISITS

Inspection of the counselors' records gives us an approximate answer to the question, "How often did you see these boys?" A stratified sample of 60 cases shows that a composite T-boy was seen by his counselor during the first year of treatment approximately 11 times; four times alone and seven in the company of others. His family was seen 12 times, his school four times and other agencies on his behalf four times. In addition there were several office conferences relating to him. The second treatment year showed, on the average, slightly fewer visits but more time spent with the boy alone (see Table 22).

Not long after the treatment program started it was evident that workers had become highly selective in making their visits. Some boys were seen frequently and others relatively infrequently. For example, 10 percent of the boys were seen at least 26 times in the second year of treatment (14 times alone and 12 times in the company of others). On the other hand 10 percent of the boys were seen not more than once or twice a year (either alone or in the company of others) during the first or second years. Such boys were generally high plus boys. A division into two distinct groups in terms of the prognostic ratings of the Selection Committee (which were unknown to the counselor) makes this point clear. For the first group,

TABLE 22

Counselors' Visits in First Two Years of Treatment

(Computed on Sample of 60 Representative Cases)

Circumstances of Visit	NUMBER OF TIMES 1ST YEAR		NUMBER OF TIMES 2ND YEAR	
	Average	Maximum	Average	Maximum
Boy seen alone	4.1	19	5.5	50
Boy seen with others	6.6	21	5.4	23
Families visited	11.6	45	8.5	35
School officials interviewed	4.5	17	3.3	13
Other agencies interviewed	4.5	25	3.4	25
Office conferences (without boy)	2.4	11	2.8	12
Average number of conferences or visits for each boy in a year's period	33.7		28.9	

NOTE: The greatest number of visits or conferences for any one case in the first year of treatment was 91, while the minimum number of visits or conferences was nine. The greatest number of visits or conferences for any one case in the second year of treatment was 103, while the minimum number of visits or conferences was seven.

made up exclusively of minus cases, the total number of visits in the first two years of treatment averages about 73 per boy, whereas a similar computation made for the group consisting exclusively of plus cases showed only about 43 as the average number of visits (see Table 23).

TABLE 23

Visits to or on Behalf of Plus Boys and Minus Boys [a]

(Computed on a Sample of 60 Representative Cases)

Circumstances of Visit	NUMBER OF TIMES	
	Average for Plus Boys	Average for Minus Boys
Boy seen alone	5.6	12.0
Boy seen with others	9.2	12.9
Families visited	13.2	22.9
School officials interviewed	6.5	8.3
Other agencies interviewed	5.0	10.1
Office conferences (without boy)	3.4	6.4
	42.9	72.5

[a] Combining the first two years of treatment.

During 1939 and 1940 counselors were asked to keep a daily record of each visit. Taking 1940 as a sample year, a tabulation derived from the reports of ten counselors is reported in Table 24 (one of the counselors was working on a half-time schedule). There it is seen that a total of 8,804 visits or interviews were made on behalf of 322 boys in one year; an average of 27.3 per boy.

TABLE 24

Summary of Visits for a Typical Year (1940)

Goal of Visits	Number	Average per Counselor
Boy	3,247	325
Family	2,948	295
School	1,125	113
Hospital	559	56
Social agencies	536	54
Court and police	200	20
Settlements and churches	189	19
Total	8,804	882

NOTE: *In addition* there were 1,146 conferences during 1940 with the Director, or other staff members, 342 boy-trips to places of interest and 248 appointments relating to testing or tutoring. Monthly reports showed the peak of activity in April and May. July and August contacts were relatively few in 1940 due to: (a) vacations of one month per counselor and (b) the time taken by the counselor to make detailed reports to the Review Committee which was then visiting the Study (see Chap. XI).

Practically all counselors said that they would have liked to make more visits but they were necessarily limited by the size of the case load and the need for reserving time for recording. As time went on some cases became more intensive while others became less so to the point of relative inactivity. At the end of the first year's work, in only eight cases was there no cooperation or definite rejection of the services; in 14 cases the boy and/or his family were only mildly cooperative or passive in their attitude. The remaining seemed eager or at least willing to continue the relationship with the counselor, although in 50 cases (about 15 percent of the total group) the counselor was relatively inactive, as he or she could find no real needs to attend to.

CHANGE OF HEADQUARTERS

During the summer of 1939 an important event in the life of the Study took place. The portable house that had been set up at 101

Brattle Street, Cambridge, was splitting at the seams with records and activity, and could no longer contain the growing staff. A house of twelve spacious rooms, formerly a residence, located in another residential section of Cambridge about a half mile from the first office, was purchased by the Foundation. This became the home and office of the Study until the close of the treatment program on December 31, 1945.

CHAPTER XI

THE PROGRAM
EVOLVES

BY JUNE 1, 1940, ALL CASES HAD BEEN IN TREATMENT AT LEAST ONE year, and because the onset of treatment was staggered over a period of time, approximately half of the cases had been treated for a longer period.

While the work was in progress the objectives of the Study and the specific function of the agency were constantly reexamined. It was inevitable that a project unique in its objectives and methods of operation should, after a period of experimentation, be faced with theoretical and practical problems that could not have been anticipated. The Study became, if it had not already been, thoroughly introspective at this point. It asked: Is the staff carrying out the objectives of the Study as they were first conceived? Just what is the function of the agency? How far can a counselor go in attempting to remake the lives of those who are assigned to his care? How can he improve the quality of his treatment? Frequent staff discussions and seminars testified eloquently to the fact that when a social agency undertakes new functions it will be subjected from within and without to constant pressures for clarification.

THE PROGRAM REVIEWED

The Foundation, too, upon the death of its mentor in 1939, felt the need for evaluation of the project that it was supporting. Faced with the problem of ever increasing budgets that had already exceeded expectations, the Foundation appointed a small outside committee to review the work of the Study and to make recommendations concerning the expansion or curtailment of the work. Three individuals who up to this time had had no connection with or knowledge of the Study were selected.[1] After interviews with each member of the staff and the reading of records, the committee filed a report in the fall of 1940 making a number of recommendations as to treatment and research.

REORGANIZATION

At about this time Dr. P. S. de Q. Cabot, who had been the sole director of the Study since the death of Dr. Richard C. Cabot in May of the previous year, relinquished his administrative duties at the Study to become its research consultant and advisor and to enter into the private practice of psychological counseling. Edwin Powers, one of the original counselors, became the director on January 1, 1941.

Following the intensive study and report of the Review Committee the year 1941 became a year of reorganization and reorientation in all three of the functional divisions of the Study—administrative, treatment and research. The Foundation approved a number of significant changes in the program.

THE NEW EMPHASIS

An interview room was opened in the new building. Boys were invited to visit the counselor at his own office. A program of woodworking instruction was commenced in the spring of 1941 where boys were taught to make toys as well as useful articles. Classes were small, consisting of no more than two or three boys at a time, allowing for individual instruction. Those receiving instruction comprised only about 5 percent of the total case load. A boys' room was equipped in the basement of the building, affording a more attractive place for boys to play or to wait for their interviews. The large adjoining lawn of the house was used for informal outdoor games. There was much discussion as to whether or not the building should be further adapted for recreational activities. As the work was essentially case work and as the Study was not in any sense a youth center, the current facilities were not expanded. Nevertheless, a

[1] Constituting the Review Committee were: Sophia M. Robison, social worker and Executive Secretary of the National Council of Jewish Women, New York City; Thorsten Sellin, criminologist and Professor of Sociology, University of Pennsylvania; Father Paul Furfey, psychologist and Professor of Sociology, Catholic University of America.

trend developed toward working with small groups of boys rather than individually—a method that was not characteristic of the first year or two of treatment. Some of the counselors expressed the opinion that the program should be definitely altered to include a mixture of group work and case work. But to make a fair test of the theory underlying the Study it would not have been advisable to alter radically the original plan—case work with the individual boy.

To many boys the new building afforded the first opportunity for quiet talks with their counselors, removed from the eyes and ears of family, friends, or school officials. During the last few years of the program there were approximately 57 visits to the office per month, by boys or members of their families. Nevertheless, the most frequent meetings were still outside of the office, usually in the boy's home. Some of the counselors held their "interviews" in the Study's car. Sometimes the counselor would interview the boy on a more formal level. One of the counselors preferred the Rogers nondirective technique whenever possible—a technique usually less successful with boys below normal I.Q.[2] Miles, a hyperactive, distractible boy, commented upon the interviews at the termination of the program. When asked what he had talked about with his counselor he said, "Oh, he'd ask *me* what I wanted to talk about." "And what would you say?" "Oh, I'd ask him what *he* wanted to talk about, so nobody talked about anything. We just drove around and drove around [in the Study car]. Boy, did we burn up the gas! He didn't care though, it wasn't his gas."

On the other hand, there were a number of boys who were disappointed that the office was not converted into a recreational center or boys' club. Some did not enjoy coming a considerable distance to the office "just for an interview." They wanted some activity and they found the rather meager facilities at the office, such as reading books or playing around on the lawn, not particularly enticing. As Ambrose put it when interviewed after the Study closed, "They ought to make it more interesting. They ought to let the guys do what they want to do and make it a little less formal. The place was awful dark and dreary up there. Now, if the kids wanted to go swimming, why, they ought to organize beach parties and go swim-

2 Carl R. Rogers, *Counseling and Psychotherapy* (Boston, Houghton Mifflin, 1942), pp. 73–74.

ming or horseback riding. They could organize a club. It was too drab up there."

Sometimes boys brought to the office members of their own clubs or gangs seeking the counselor's help in organization and hoping to find an adequate clubhouse. Opportunities for dealing with the natural groupings of boys in the community presented themselves, but counselors seldom felt inclined to increase their circle of young friends, particularly where only one or two members of a gang or club happened to be Study boys. Given a choice, probably many boys would have preferred the group activities to the individual approach.

MEDICAL AND PSYCHIATRIC ADVICE

For necessary medical diagnosis and treatment during the first few years the counselors took the boys to the local hospital clinics. There was dissatisfaction with the limited medical service offered by these clinics. One could not expect a busy hospital to give routine physical examinations to boys who were presumably well. Accordingly, a pediatrician was appointed to the staff in March, 1941. He came to the Study one afternoon a week.[3]

The policy was adopted of examining most of the T-boys, whether or not they presented any special medical problem. Some boys did not wish to go through with such an examination, while others were receiving adequate medical attention elsewhere, either in hospital clinics or at the hands of their family physicians. Altogether about 170 boys were examined by the Study pediatricians, many of them three or four times at varying intervals.[4] It will be recalled that all boys (both T and C) had been seen by the doctor prior to treatment.

When the Study was established it was not thought necessary to appoint a staff psychiatrist, as psychiatric clinics in the local hospitals were available. After several years' experience the counselors

[3] Dr. Edward L. Tuohy, associated with the Children's Hospital, served as pediatrician from March, 1941, until he was called into active service with the Army in July of that year. Dr. Edward L. Cutter of the Boston Dispensary served for a period of three months, until called for active duty with the U.S. Public Health Service. Dr. Richard Wagner, associated with the Boston Dispensary and a Professor of Pediatrics at Tufts Medical School, served as pediatrician from 1942 to the end of the treatment program.

[4] See Appendix C for a copy of the schedule used in the examination.

agreed that it would save time to have a psychiatrist on the staff for consultation when difficult problems arose. Accordingly, a psychiatrist was appointed in April, 1941.[5] Most of his time was spent in diagnostic rather than therapeutic interviews in difficult cases. With the exception of the summer months this psychiatrist or his successor came to the Study one afternoon a week. Approximately 40 boys were interviewed, some of them regularly over a period of time, and in a few cases the parents of the boys were seen by the psychiatrist.

TUTORIAL SERVICES

One area of treatment that became prominent early in the program and further developed during the ensuing years was the special tutorial service for the retarded boy.

Teachers were asked at the very outset in 1937 and 1938 to rate the Study boys on a five-point scale indicating attitude toward gaining proficiency in schoolwork. The scale consisted of the following points: (a) negativistic toward learning, (b) amenable but negligent, (c) moderately interested, (d) gives enthusiastic responses, (e) completely absorbed.

When this scale was used by the teachers most of the boys were in the second or third grade. Ten years later a study was made of the boys who became our "most delinquent" boys and those who were our "least delinquent" boys. An analysis of the ratings showed that the boys who, in their early years in school, had the least motivation for schoolwork had become delinquent with greater frequency than those who were enthusiastic about their schoolwork. These findings are reported in Figure 5.

It was appropriate for a delinquency-prevention program to give particular attention to a child who was early showing signs of frustration in the school situation. A tutoring program was therefore instituted by the staff psychologist. As individual remedial reading work or tutoring was not available in the public schools between the years 1939 and 1941, permission was granted the Study to tutor any of the boys in need of special help, using schoolrooms and school hours for this purpose. At the outset, counselors not infrequently became the boys' tutors but as time went on this function

[5] Dr. William L. Woods, the first psychiatrist appointed by the Study, was succeeded in October, 1942, by Dr. Bryant E. Moulton, a practicing psychiatrist and a former member of the Study's Selection Committee.

was taken over entirely by a staff of trained educators. For the first year or two of treatment the staff employed, in addition to the psychologist, a professional teacher who was assisted by four volunteers for a short period of time. Two other professionally trained teachers

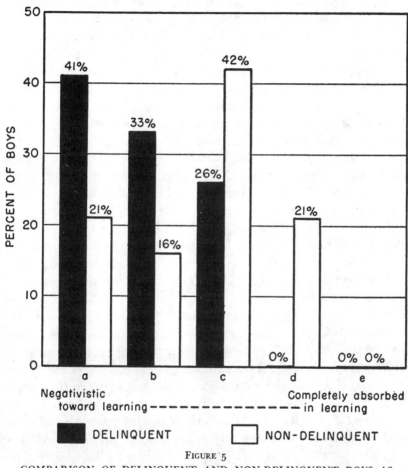

FIGURE 5

COMPARISON OF DELINQUENT AND NON-DELINQUENT BOYS AS
TO TEACHERS' RATINGS OF THEIR EARLY INTEREST

were employed from April, 1941, to June, 1943. During the last months of the Study, when so many boys had left school and the case load had been reduced, the tutoring staff was reduced to one tutor who continued until April, 1945. In the fall of 1945, the last year of the treatment program, a tutor, a former schoolteacher, was appointed to give special help in school subjects at the Study office to four or five boys who were still in need of this assistance.

Altogether, 93 individuals received tutoring help. The total number of sessions, or hours, was 5,218, or an average of 56.1 sessions per boy. Approximately half of the group was tutored for an average of 97.2 sessions per boy. The maximum number of sessions for any individual was 283. In addition to the special tutorial work given by the staff, several boys were referred to a clinic or a neighboring university, while 14 other boys were given special help by their own teachers under the supervision of the Study's psychologist.

During the entire period of treatment there were more boys who could have benefited by tutoring than could be fitted into the program. A selection of cases was not made solely on the ground that the boy seemed to be inclined toward delinquency (although two-thirds of the tutored boys had been rated on the minus side of the delinquency scale by the Selection Committee), but was based upon a thorough analysis of his case in which his ability to profit from tutoring was a prime factor. The boy's willingness to be tutored was often determinative, for boys in need of special help were not always willing to give the time to it or to do the assigned homework.

Reading was the subject in which deficiency was the greatest. Of the 93 boys who were tutored, 42 were tutored in reading alone, 22 in reading combined with some other subject. Arithmetic was next in importance. Other subjects were English, social studies, Latin, and French. About half of the boys being tutored were in the fourth, fifth, or sixth grade at the time tutoring began. Eleven of them were in special classes. Slightly more than half were between the ages of 11 and 13. Nearly two-thirds of the boys tutored were retarded one or two grades. The I.Q. distribution of the tutored group was slightly below the distribution for the total group of T-boys. The I.Q. scores for half of the group were between 80 and 100, the median for the total tutored group being 91.

In addition to the direct help to the boy in mastering his school subjects, tutoring was valuable in increasing the general feeling of good will between the boy and the boy's family and the Study, making the counselor's case work somewhat more effective. Furthermore, a great deal was learned about the boy's personality as well as his abilities and achievements in these informal tutoring sessions.

REFORMULATION OF OBJECTIVES

The objective of the Study had always been declared to be the prevention of delinquent careers in a group of young boys. A question frequently raised but never answered to the satisfaction of the counselors was: "If we are interested solely in the prevention of delinquency, what is our obligation toward boys who have problems but have no tendency toward delinquency?" Many illustrations could be given. Perhaps one will suffice. Tony was a neglected and deprived boy who was not "tending toward delinquency" but whose character, nevertheless, was not being built on a strong foundation. In terms of the prognostic scale he was rated $+4$ or $+5$ by his counselor, indicating a very strong probability of non-delinquency. The boy was more likely to express his reaction to frustration by neurotic behavior than by lawlessness. Should the counselor do anything in his case if the objective of the Study was solely the prevention of delinquency? The fact that he had real needs in the areas of health and education seemed at first glance irrelevant to the specific objective of the Study. Although the treatment objectives of the Study had been phrased in a negative form with emphasis on prevention, they were never narrowly construed. The fundamental purpose of the Study was to help the growth of character in children. Frequent delinquent behavior was considered symptomatic and could be treated only by resort to the larger problems of personality and culture. The focus of the counselors' work had, in fact, always been upon the concept of "growth." Hence the restatement of the objectives along broader lines more consistent with the spirit of the Study was recommended. A formulation prepared by the staff in 1941 received the approval of the Foundation.

The Cambridge-Somerville Youth Study is a project established by Dr. Richard C. Cabot to bring about and foster in a chosen group of boys, by intensive individual help and guidance, a continuing social, physical, intellectual and spiritual growth through which the boys will be assets to society and to themselves and, in particular, not sources of trouble or concern to others through behavior.

The Study is also to determine from time to time the extent to which the help it can give achieves its goal, and the ways in which it does so.

Originally no case work supervisor was provided to guide the individual counselor. There was little need to coordinate treatment of the various counselors as each one was encouraged to use his own approach and his own techniques. From 1938 to the summer of 1940 it was the custom of Dr. P. S. de Q. Cabot, the co-director, to meet once a month with each counselor to discuss with him the successes and failures encountered in his daily work and his specific plans for his boys. To assist him in working out the solution of difficult case work puzzles, which were naturally on the increase as boys approached adolescence, he appointed a social worker as consultant.[6] For about a year after Dr. P. S. de Q. Cabot gave up the direction of the Study there was no one on the staff to guide treatment. The staff asked for professional supervision, and in the fall of 1941 a clinical psychologist was appointed.[7]

Dr. Young insisted upon more frequent and more purposive interviews with the boys. Furthermore, a friendly relationship in itself, he maintained, did not solve problems in the more serious cases. "One may develop an excellent friendly relationship," he said, "but not know what to do with it. This is merely a tool by which good case work could be made possible." He pointed out that recreational activities with the boys might be valuable in building up a friendly relationship but he noted a tendency for certain counselors, blocked in other approaches, to let themselves be unduly guided by the boys' interests in airplanes, camping trips, and outings.

RETIREMENT OF CASES

The question of the optimum size of the counselor's case load was again raised: How could a counselor maintain real friendship

[6] Miss Elizabeth E. Bissell, General Secretary of the Children's Mission to Children, came to the Study on a consultant basis one day a week for a period of 68 weeks (1939–1941).

[7] Dr. Robert A. Young, the treatment supervisor, had had psychoanalytical training and ten years of experience in dealing with boys' problems as a staff member of the psychiatric clinic of the Massachusetts General Hospital. He also had had extensive experience as a camp director and had received his doctorate degree in the field of education. He was employed on a part-time schedule and remained with the Study until the close of the treatment program.

with 30 to 35 boys scattered throughout Cambridge, Somerville, and surrounding towns? [8] Although a case load of this size would not ordinarily be considered high in a social work agency, most counselors found it impossible to carry on intensive treatment of the kind demanded by the unique nature of the project and at the same time reserve sufficient hours for the necessary paper work demanded in a research organization.

To reduce each counselor's case load, and also to solve the troublesome problem of what to do with the average boy, the staff devised a plan of "retiring" 65 of the T-boys; 46 of them in the spring of 1941 and 19 in the summer of 1942. One counselor observed that "our greatest problems, from the point of view of treatment, were the boys with no problems." As has been pointed out, the so-called average boys were included largely in the interests of public relations. And yet it was evident that more average boys were placed in the treatment group than was necessary to achieve these purposes. (Forty-two percent of the entire group had been considered average by the Selection Committee but 59 percent had been rated as average by the counselors after a year's acquaintance with them.) Some advisors questioned whether the Study could carry out its program with both kinds of boys simultaneously. Would average boys resent being thrown together with difficult boys? This problem did not become an actual one, for since the treatment was on an individual basis, the boys saw each other, if at all, only in small groups. Nevertheless, a few of the average boys were aware of some class distinction. Jeremiah, a frail, rather timid, average boy, voiced his objections about the Study after it terminated: "I didn't fit with the class of boys there. Some were okay but some had records with the police. I never had a record with the police. There were a lot of rough guys. I didn't mix with them. Mr. N. [his counselor] told us he was a social worker. A social worker is a man who has something to do with poor people."

As time went on and good relationships were established with the difficult boy and his family, there was less and less need for a buffer group of average boys. The counselors were faced with the very practical question of how to be of help to the average boy. As one coun-

[8] By January 1, 1944, there were 28 boys still in the program who had moved to neighboring towns.

selor put it, "You cannot solve problems that do not exist." Another challenged this view by maintaining that "simply growing up is a problem and there are always things you can do to help an average boy." And yet the counselors tended to visit the average boy less and less frequently. Furthermore, most of them, particularly the *high* average boys ($+3$, $+4$, $+5$) were not asking for assistance; as a rule their parents were adequate to help them with their problems. The retirement process did not, however, eliminate all plus boys, for some presented special needs that the Study could meet. A number of average boys, for example, were not making adequate educational or social adjustments.

Retiring boys from the treatment program was not as radical a departure as it appeared to be. The original population of almost 1,900 referred boys had been cut down by a pre-selection process to 782 and by the matchers to 650. The proposed step, therefore, was simply one more process in getting a more significant group for research purposes. No difficult boys were retired.

The procedure was designed to insure the retirement of only the high plus boys who had relatively few needs. A staff committee passed upon all cases. No case was retired except upon the initiative of the counselors and unless it fulfilled these criteria set up by the committee: (1) The case had not been rated minus by the Selection Committee; (2) was not originally referred by the police, court officials, or attendance officers as a "problem"; (3) was not rated lower than a plus three by the counselor, at the time of his last summary; and (4) did not, in the opinion of the counselor or of the committee present any substantial need for the kind of service the Study was equipped to render. The committee held 79 hearings at which counselors presented reasons for retiring a case. Sixty-five of the 79 cases were retired. The reason for retaining a case was generally the existence of some problem that the committee thought the counselor could assist the boy in dealing with.

By the summer of 1942 the case load had been reduced to 257 cases. In addition to the 65 that were retired, two boys had died and one had moved out of the State.

CHAPTER XII

THE
WAR YEARS

REDUCTION OF STAFF

HOW LONG COULD THE STUDY RETAIN ITS STAFF? IT WOULD HAVE BEEN theoretically desirable at the outset to bind the staff by a contract to serve for a period of ten years. This, of course, could not be done. For one thing, it was difficult to determine a person's competence until he had been in the work for at least a year. Furthermore, it would have been almost impossible to find ambitious young people trained in this field who would be willing to stay with an organization for ten years with little advancement in status and with the knowledge that the Study had no future but must inevitably terminate at the end of a limited period of time. The Study retained intact its original treatment staff of ten counselors for a period of 30 months without a break.

The war struck the Study in its third year, calling into military service the younger members of the staff. A further reduction of the case load was inevitable, as it became more and more difficult to find staff replacements. Before the war ended, four of the counselors left to serve with the Army, two with the Navy, one with the Marine Corps, and two with the Red Cross.

In spite of staff shortages the work continued, though it proved impossible to maintain a full case load or to carry through for the entire ten-year period.

By November, 1944, the treatment staff became stabilized. Five counselors on full time, one on a part-time schedule, and the director, who was still carrying five or six active cases, constituted the counseling staff for the final 13 months of treatment. Throughout the history of the Study 19 different counselors were employed, though never more than ten at any one time (see Figure 6).

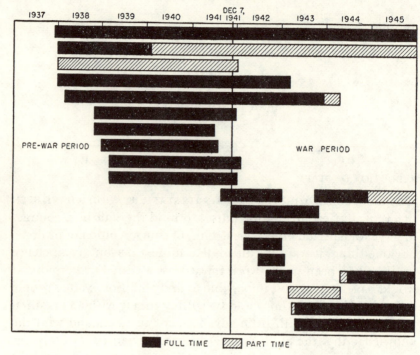

FIGURE 6

LENGTH OF TIME EACH OF 19 COUNSELORS SERVED

REASSIGNMENTS

As we learned in Chapter VII many cases had to be reassigned from one worker to another. The original hope was that the same counselors could carry through with very little transfer or break in the relationship during the treatment period. During the war sometimes six to twelve months elapsed before a new counselor could be found to replace one who was suddenly called into service. Each new counselor was required to read and summarize the entire record of cases assigned to him, and was invited to make a critical analysis of the previous work before stating his own plans. This task was time-consuming, particularly where the record had already exceeded 100 pages. Sometimes the delay in reassignment was so disrupting that the boy lost interest.[1]

[1] See Table 20 in Chap. VII showing the number of reassignments. About two-thirds of the cases were reassigned at least once.

Satisfactory reassignments could not always be made. The successor was often critical of his predecessor's techniques and sought to change the pattern of treatment. Sometimes he was more successful; sometimes less. Some boys were delighted to have a new and different "friend"; while others, shifted from one counselor to another, were not pleased by the change. Hank, for example, a pre-delinquent, was assigned to four different counselors. During the course of treatment he said to one of the research staff,

The first guy was the swellest I met in my life. I didn't mind that I didn't know what it was about. The other ones were not so hot. The next one—he was a sneak—no good. My father didn't like him. He says to me, "You keep away from him—that's a sneak!" I didn't listen. He was right though, but I had a good time with the first one. But then comes one after another and you get all these darn tests. Then comes another guy, a funny one. The next time that guy comes around we go down to the corner and he says, "Do you smoke?" I says, "Sure, want one?" He says, "You shouldn't smoke." I says, "The heck." I kept away from him ever since.

Angelo, one of our most persistent delinquents, interviewed after the termination of the treatment program, speaking of his first counselors said that they kept him active and that "they tried to straighten me out in school. After they left I lost all interest. Since then—since I haven't seen them—I got my neck caught." Speaking of the third counselor assigned to him he said, "He didn't know how to handle me. He lacked something. I don't know just what it was." Shortly after this reassignment Angelo was sent to a correctional school.

Oscar explained that he liked Mr. M. (his third counselor) "but then when Mr. S. [his fourth counselor] came along he wanted me to like him just as much so he took me out to the airport when I said I wanted to go out there." Many others showed a definite preference for their first counselors and experienced difficulty in adjusting to those who followed. Dexter, for example, said, "Mr. F. was a hell of a nice guy. He did more for me in two days than K. could have done in a thousand years." Ned (in a post-treatment interview) said of his first counselor, "He was quite sociable. I was awfully sorry when he left and I didn't want to continue with the organization." Of the second counselor he said, "I don't remember his name. He wasn't as sociable. He just took us places. He didn't talk much. If I hadn't gotten interested through Mr. G. [first counselor] I probably wouldn't have gone with this fellow." [2]

During the war years the counselors were still burdened with relatively large case loads just at the time when transportation difficulties increased, when boys with after-school and evening jobs were causing an additional strain on the visiting schedules, when research requirements became more demanding, and when the Supervisor of Treatment was calling for more frequent and more productive visits with boys who were now entering adolescence. The situation called for an increase in staff or a decrease in the case load. The latter was the only practical alternative.

THE DROPPING OF CASES

The dropping of cases was not originally contemplated, excepting for those boys who died or moved too far away. Each counselor was asked to consider carefully six factors in relation to each of his boys before recommending this special procedure.

1. Cooperativeness. (The boy's willingness to come to the office and his desire to continue the relationship.)

2. Capacity. (The boy's intellectual capacity to profit from treatment.)

3. Seriousness of the problem.

4. Extent of the effort already spent. (If a counselor had already done a great deal of work on a case, he was generally reluctant to drop it suddenly. Under such circumstances the relationship could not be abruptly terminated.)

5. Research needs. Although research considerations were not paramount, a few cases were retained simply because they offered good material for special study or were of particular interest to research. At this point the question arose: What effect will the dropping of cases have upon the final evaluation of the work? Obviously, sub-groups might not be as well matched as the parent groups from which they were drawn. Any evaluation, therefore, based upon a

[2] It is difficult to appraise the effect of these unexpected reassignments on the success of the program. Dr. Witmer (Chap. XXIX) compares the value of the program for a group of boys assigned throughout to only one counselor with its value for a group reassigned one or more times.

comparison of the T-boys with the C-boys would have to take this fact into consideration if the comparison dealt with less than the total population. In contrasting the T-boys and the C-boys in terms of police, court, and commitment records, for example, the total groups (650 boys) are considered, but in other evaluations where sub-groups are used as samples the nature of the sample must be described. The reduction of cases is therefore not necessarily fatal to any of the conclusions drawn from a comparison of sub-goups, but it does necessitate a discussion of the possible effects of reduction whenever such comparisons are made.

6. Distance. Boys who had moved too far from Cambridge or Somerville for frequent visits had to be dropped regardless of other criteria. The wartime restrictions on travel made such considerations necessary. Boys who still remained in an area not too inaccessible may or may not have been dropped, depending on other factors.

By July 1, 1943, 87 cases had been selected for discontinuance; subsequently the list was increased by 26, making a total of 113 dropped cases. Most of these were given up with considerable reluctance, and it was understood that if the war should terminate early and new counselors could be found, some of the cases would be reopened. (Only two cases were later taken back into the Study.) In general, the cases retained were those most in need of the counselors' services and those who were also most available, psychologically and geographically, and most able to profit from the treatment program.

Once a decision had been made to drop a case, the counselor usually made an effort to explain the reason to the boy. The boy did not always understand and in some cases seemed to resent the fact. One boy said, "They have a new group of devilish boys at the Study now; they're all through with us. I guess they think they've reformed us, that we're angels now. I guess we are until we get an idea to do something bad again."

Another put it this way, "Mr. N. came down and told me I couldn't be a member any more. They were too overworked—I really don't know what the point was or why they wanted to get rid of me. But I didn't care. I was getting too old for that sort of thing.

They should have had it through nineteen and twenty though, and had a club and dances and things—it would still have been good then."

Those retained were reclassified into intensive and less intensive cases. The resources of the Study were directed toward boys for whom it was believed the most effective work could be done. In a sense, the Study was now going back to the original plan of dealing with fewer cases and confining the work to difficult boys, presumably those who would need and want help.[3]

TERMINATION OF CASES

Not only was the staff depleted by the war, but the boys themselves began to respond one by one to the beat of the drums. By the middle of 1943 it was evident that most of the boys who were then 17 had joined the Navy or entered some other war work that took them beyond the reach of the treatment program. War jobs in Maine and Rhode Island attracted some of the older boys; the Merchant Marine was an inducement to others; and some boys even altered their birth certificates in order to get into the war in which their older brothers were fighting. In 1943 the staff decided to terminate all boys who had reached 17 unless there was some special reason for continuing with them. That age was a logical stopping place for treatment as it marked the upper end of the legal period of delinquency in Massachusetts (7 to 17). Furthermore, each boy who remained with the Study until he was 17 had had at least five years or more of treatment. Although this period was considerably shorter than the contemplated ten-year span, it was considered sufficiently extensive to test out the basic idea of the Study. Seven boys were thus terminated in 1943, 34 in 1944, and 31 in 1945, making a total of 72 boys whose treatment program closed on or near their 17th birthdays.

MORE INTENSIVE WORK WITH FEWER CASES

In July, 1943, the Supervisor inaugurated a new policy of holding weekly case conferences. Formerly, it will be recalled, each counselor operated more or less independently without group dis-

[3] It will be recalled that in the original plans for the Study no average boys were to be included in the treatment group.

cussion. Each counselor in turn was now given the opportunity of presenting one of his cases with his recommendations, plans, and requests for advice. This practice was continued until the close of the treatment period. Altogether 120 cases were presented. The review of the case, as well as the comments of each counselor, was made part of the record. The Supervisor also conducted group meetings for discussion of the nature of case work, rapport, correspondence with boys, sex education, and other topics of interest to all counselors. Staff meetings, seminars, and research discussions were frequent throughout the latter years of the Study.[4]

The counselors' records for the last two years of treatment showed an increasing attention to case-work techniques. The boys now constituted a more highly selected group, they were more mature and more aware of their relationship to the agency.

Group work gradually edged itself into the picture. Small groups of Study boys and their friends were taken by several counselors to the Cambridge "Y," where they were allowed the use of the swimming pool one evening a week for a period of two years. Although the groups were small, altogether the swimming parties included about 75 different boys. Some of the counselors took their boys on overnight camping trips in the spring, summer, and fall months.

THE RESEARCH PROGRAM

Research had always been an integral function of the Study and had naturally had some influence on the course of treatment.

In the first few years, accurate records were kept, but no definite plan for an ultimate evaluation of the program was decided upon until the program ended. Dr. William D. Turner, a research psychologist, was placed in charge of research.[5] He did not visit the C-boys or their families, but obtained annual records on each case from the schools. Later, two interim evaluational surveys were made, testing by questionnaires, interviews, and teachers' ratings the progress made in a sample of C-boys compared to their treatment "twins." These surveys are reported in Chapter XIX.

In the summer of 1942 Dr. George W. Hartmann, Professor of

4 One of the original counselors who had had training and experience in family case work served for several years in a consulting capacity on problems relating to the family.

5 Dr. Turner was appointed in June, 1939, remaining with the Study for four years.

Education, Teachers College, Columbia University, was appointed
to take charge of the research program. Hartmann commented that
the counselors' approach seemed too general; that they were trying
to develop a boy's character "in the abstract." "Here," he remarked,
"you are trying to improve this boy's all-around development but
you are doing nothing about teaching him politeness or about telling him that he should keep his face and hands clean or that he
should help his mother with the dishes." A bit of interesting conflict
developed between what Hartmann called "the educational approach" and the view of the Supervisor of Treatment that the objectives of the Study could best be realized by a case-work approach,
utilizing modern techniques. "In what specific ways," Hartmann
pointedly asked the counselors, "do you believe your group of boys
will eventually be better than or different from the corresponding
C-boys as a direct consequence of your work with them? Furthermore, what steps are you taking to produce these results?"

The contrast between the educational and the clinical approach
to treatment was evident in Dr. Young's talk to the staff in September, 1942. He said:

This discussion was prompted by the memoranda from the research
department which carried suggestions to the social workers regarding
their activities with the boys. . . . The memoranda suggest an *intellec-
tual-educational* approach. This approach is a worthy one, providing
education is the medium through which one wishes to approach character building. Certain stable children with adequate background can
take advantage of this type of program. But there are many children
who are too unstable emotionally to benefit from this intellectual approach. These children need personal, sympathetic understanding, an
opportunity to work out understandingly their emotional frustration
which may prevent them from making use of intellectual and educational opportunities and developing into well adjusted, useful adults.
It is this group of children which comprises the bulk of our case load.

To establish his point Hartmann drew up a list of specific departments of life in which the counselors acknowledged they were hoping to achieve definite improvement. The counselor was asked to
record on a rating scale the degree to which each of his boys had
achieved perfection in each area. Monthly records of progress could
thus be kept.[6] The areas to be considered were:

    [6] Such periodic records, Hartmann believed, might establish a basis for ultimate
evaluation, but illness prevented him from carrying this plan to a conclusion.

Physical condition	Personality appeal to others
Mentality	Ethical level
Family influences	Quality of recreation
Economic and cultural influences	Occupational competence
Social skills	Social sensitivity
Education-training-supervision	Citizenship and leadership
Self-insight	Harmony and balance of develop-
Poise and emotional stability	ment [7]

Actually, of course, the case-work emphasis and the didactic emphasis are not mutually exclusive. The amiable arguments between the treatment and research staffs resulted in a wholesome interchange of views and a clarification of the objectives of each department. The task of measuring change in character is at best alarming in its novelty and complexity; hence it is understandable that the research staff wished to reduce the problem to one of concrete operations. At the same time the case workers were right in insisting that a brittle reduction of character to a list of habits, factors, or specific activities was hazardous in principle and premature in practice.

How the issues of evaluation were solved will be told in subsequent chapters. Suffice it to say here that the two interim evaluation surveys focused upon relatively specific, measurable improvements in conduct, whereas the final evaluation included broader clinical estimates.

COMMUNITY RELATIONS

The Study was not set up as a continuing agency; it proposed to accomplish its objectives within a definitely limited span of time. Nor was it self-sufficient. It could not carry out its objectives without continuous dependence on the other social agencies in the local communities. The Study, for example, was not a child-placing agency. It had to call upon agencies whose specific function was placement, if that step in the treatment plan was indicated; nor was it a recreational club with facilities for group treatment; nor a health or psychiatric clinic or private school. In fact, most of the

[7] Many of these items were patterned after Dr. Carl Rogers' component factor analysis described in his book, *The Clinical Treatment of the Problem Child* (Boston, Houghton Mifflin Company, 1939). This list came to be known by the staff as the "Rogers-Hartmann Factor Analysis."

boys referred to the Study, particularly those designated as minus boys, were already known to one or more social agencies in the greater Boston area. As most of the agencies were more interested in the family than in the individual boy, they were agreeable to entrusting the care of the boy to the Study. In a number of cases, therefore, the Study and the other local agencies worked out cooperatively the treatment plan for the boy and his family.

It was not always easy to explain the function of the Study to other social agencies. At first they regarded it chiefly as a research project, but as time went on this emphasis was reversed in their minds as the Study came, more and more, to resemble a case-work agency. However, it was always distinguished from other agencies by the fact that after 1939 it refused new cases.

The dual aspect (treatment and research) caused additional misunderstandings. The Study, for example, had to keep more elaborate records than social workers usually do. It considered these records strictly confidential because of an agreement with the schools that "no publicity" would be given in respect to the boys referred by them. The schools had been reluctant to permit the Study to pass on to any other social agency information obtained from the teachers. After the first few years of treatment, however, a policy was worked out with the approval of the schools, allowing for the interchange of this information with other agencies when necessary to carry out treatment plans. Though looked upon at first as an odd combination of social service and research, the Study eventually was admitted to membership in the local Cambridge Council of Social Agencies and listed as a youth agency in the directory published by the Greater Boston Community Council.

On the whole, cooperation with other agencies was good. Many boys and their families were referred by the Study to hospitals, clinics, placement agencies, and family societies. In some cases the Study became a coordinating center bringing together the efforts of all interested agencies in working out the problem of a boy and his family.

In working with Joseph, for example, the counselor discovered that the boy was not well accepted in school or in the home. She endeavored to interpret Joseph's needs and personality to his parents, his teachers, and others in the community, with the result that there was a better appreciation of his assets and some allowance was made for his liabilities.[8]

In the early days of the Study some issues developed in the relationship between the staff and the local courts. Several counselors were evidently too zealous to "protect" their boys. Just how an enduring, friendly relationship could be developed without over-identification with the boy's own sentiments and emotions was a problem that not all of the counselors could handle successfully. It was difficult at times for the counselors to see that it was, as a rule, "best for the boy" to meet face to face the legal consequences of his own acts. The court, standing *in loco parentis* for "children in need of aid, encouragement and guidance" naturally resented interference and was understandably annoyed at the implication that the best interests of the boy would not be served by a court appearance. Some of the counselors, on the other hand, maintained that full cooperation with the police and the courts would risk a breakdown of the confidential counselor-boy relationship, particularly in cases where the boy convinced the counselor he had not been treated with justice by the court or the probation officer. If a boy mistook the counselor for a well-disguised special officer or plainclothesman would he be so willing to discuss with him his personal problems? A difficult balance had to be maintained between a friendly and confidential relationship with the boy on the one hand and a frank and honest spirit of cooperation with the law-enforcement authorities on the other. As time went on, the relations with the court improved and eventually complete cooperation was achieved. In the last few years of the Study the local court requested and received the help of the Study's professional staff in giving physical, psychiatric, and psychometric examinations to 44 boys in its care who were *not* Study boys.

The Crime Prevention Bureau of the Cambridge Police Department, established in 1938, was also helpful. Information was exchanged between the Bureau and the Study relating to boys in which the Study was interested, both in the treatment and control groups. A few of the counselors maintained (but without proof)

---

[8] Margaret G. Reilly, R.N., and Robert A. Young, Ed.D., "Agency-initiated Treatment of a Potentially Delinquent Boy," *American Journal of Orthopsychiatry*, XVI (1946), 697–706.

that more of the T-boys were brought to this police bureau and eventually to the court than would have been the case if the Bureau had not heard from the staff about these boys. On the other hand, the founder had frequently warned the counselors against considering the Study boy a "privileged boy," cautioning against too much dependence upon or protection by the Study that might excuse the boy from facing his normal obligations to the community. In furtherance of this policy a boy was not infrequently brought into court through the mediation of his own counselor when it was believed to be for the boy's best interests.

In a few cases a problem of "jurisdiction" in case work arose. When the counselor, for example, sought a foster home for one of his boys through a placement agency, the latter agreed to place the boy on the understanding that there would be no conflict in authority. This policy usually meant that the agency placing him would have exclusive control. It sent its own social worker to visit the foster home and to plan for the boy with the actual and the foster parents. Reports were received by the Study from time to time from the placement agency and the contact with the Study was resumed if the boy was subsequently returned to his home. In the meantime the Study did not ordinarily drop the case or lose interest in the boy, and yet a break in the case-work relationship was usually inevitable. Furthermore it was not possible to test or interview the boy while he was in the foster home. Thus from the research point of view this policy was usually disadvantageous.

The cooperation of the public schools in Cambridge, Somerville, and neighboring towns, and the parochial schools in Cambridge was indispensable to the success of the program. Not only did they supply most of the referrals but they cooperated throughout the entire treatment program.[9] Not more than two or three out of the hundreds of teachers of Study boys were found to be unsympathetic with the project. It will be recalled that the teachers were called upon originally to check the Trait Record Cards and other forms (see Chapter IV) and for the first three or four years they were asked to answer long questionnaires. Several thousand interviews with teachers were held during school hours. They took a genuine inter-

[9] By November, 1939, the school systems in 13 other cities and towns to which boys' families had moved were called on for assistance. By 1944 this number had increased to 18.

est in the Study boys and frequently telephoned concerning developments in a particular case that needed attention. The Study's relationship with the schools was so close that many boys mistook the counselors for official representatives of the school.

CLOSE OF THE STUDY

At the outset, the reader recalls, each boy was to be treated for ten years. It was our original intent that treatment should be undertaken only with boys who were approximately six or seven years old. They would thus be carried in treatment until 17, which was the upper age limit for delinquents in this state. When it became evident that a sufficient number of six- and seven-year-old boys were not being referred by the schools, the upper age limit was extended to 11 and then stretched to 12. The goal of a ten-year treatment period for each boy then became impractical. The usefulness of carrying on treatment with the 11- and 12-year-old boys through their 21st or 22nd years was questioned.

As war conditions made treatment increasingly difficult, the Foundation decided to close all cases still remaining in the Study at the end of the year 1945.[10] It was not easy to explain to the 75 boys still remaining in the Study why the program was coming to an end. Many of the boys expressed regrets over the coming event and urged a continuance of the work. Many of them were just reaching the crucial age during adolescence when they needed help and advice, but once the decision was made there was no turning back. Well over 50 of the boys continued to keep in touch with their counselors after the official close of the Study. Typical of such boys was Graham, who wrote, in anticipation of the Study's close, "My father, my mother and I appreciate all you have done for me. When the Study closes, I'll still want to see you—as friends only, remember that. I mean, just forget about my problems and keeping me out of trouble. Just plain good friends. . . . Nothing I could give you, tell you or do would show my appreciation for all you've done for me. I'm sorry you're not my social worker any more and I won't see you as much as I would like but we can still remain good friends."

A year or two later an investigator who talked with some of the

[10] In 1940 the committee appointed to review the Study (see Chap. XI) had advised that by 1945 a sufficient time would have elapsed to test out the basic ideas of the project.

boys sounded out their opinions of the Study (see Chapter XIII). A few of them mentioned the abrupt termination and had their own explanations for it. As one boy said, "There was one doctor there. He died and left a lot of money so kids wouldn't get into trouble but the money ran out. I remember when Mr. N. told us the place was closing up. Everybody tried to get it open. We felt pretty bad about it. A couple of kids started to cry but, of course, they were young. But Mr. B. and Mr. N. said the lease was up so they had to close down." Another boy, interrogated at age 20, said, "I don't see why they didn't keep it up. It was the best idea they ever had. I asked Mr. B. why the State didn't take it over."

Although the treatment period was considerably shorter than planned, it did provide each boy with at least five years of treatment if he were not previously retired or dropped. Table 25 gives in summary form the history of the original 325 T-boys.

TABLE 25

Disposition of the 325 Cases

Retired in 1940 and 1941		65
Dropped before the end of the program		113
A. Died during the treatment program	2	
B. Moved outside the field of operations	25	
C. Boy and/or family uncooperative	9	
D. Taken over completely by other agencies	2	
E. Mental retardation too great a handicap	4	
F. Following the reclassification during the war when the Study could not retain an adequate staff, it was necessary to drop cases that were relatively less able to profit from the treatment program	71	
Terminated: Most of the boys who had passed their 17th birthdays in 1944 and 1945		72
Closed: Carried through the entire treatment program		75
Total		325

SUMMARY OF THE TREATMENT PROGRAM

Starting with one boy in October, 1937, and building up the case load to a maximum of 325 carefully selected boys by May 1939, the Study sought "to bring about and foster . . . by intensive individual help and guidance a continuing social, physical, intellectual and spiritual growth through which the boys will be assets to society and to themselves and in particular not sources of trouble or concern to others through behavior." This broadly conceived objective became the goal of 15 men and four women counselors (but not more than ten at any time). The loss of cases through the re-

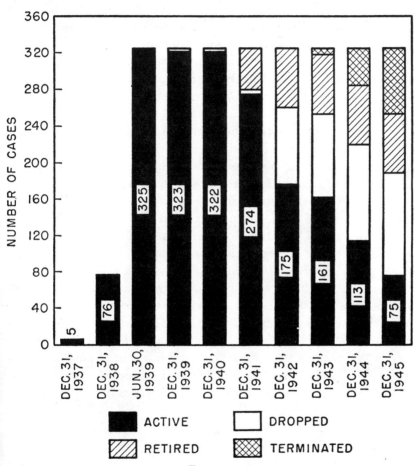

FIGURE 7

ANNUAL INCREASE AND DECREASE IN TREATMENT CASE LOAD

tirement of the average boys, through the death of a few, through the removal of some to other communities and through conditions brought on directly or indirectly by the war caused an annual decrease in the case load until less than one-fourth of the original numbers remained in the treatment program by December, 1945 (see Figure 7).

Each counselor applied his special skills to the particular boys assigned to him, supplemented by the professional counseling of psychiatrists, psychologists, pediatricians, tutors and social workers. Aid in the solution of special problems was sought through the help of the church, the home, and the school, together with the many hospitals, clinics, and social agencies in the community. A great deal of attention was given to problems of school adjustment, health, recreation, and the family, in addition to the counseling and case work applied directly to the boy in fostering his growth and development. The religious development emphasized by Dr. Cabot at the outset of treatment received relatively little attention from the counselors. Only one counselor (who considered herself "spiritually minded") devoted much time and thought to the religious training of the boys assigned to her. The chief reason suggested for the light touch in this area was the reluctance of the counselors to cross denominational lines. It will be recalled that 61 percent of the total group were from Catholic families while only 26 percent of the counselors were of that faith. The counselors, as a rule, with the one exception, hesitated to discuss religion with a boy or family of another faith.

In brief, it might be said that the treatment program comprised a wide variety of services from removing nits from a boy's head to preparing him for higher education. One boy summarized the program as he saw it, "They taught me the name of snakes, what to do in case of fire, how to make a boat, and how not to steal and hop trucks." What was the ultimate effect of this great amount of attention to a selected group of boys? The answer constitutes a major problem in evaluation.

CHAPTER XIII

THE BOY JUDGES
THE TREATMENT

WHAT DID THE BOY HIMSELF THINK OF THIS ELABORATE PROGRAM that was focused on his problems? It will be refreshing to hear his opinion, before we enter into the technical analysis of his conduct or attempt to evaluate more objectively the results of our work. These judgments are not, of course, a final test. The honesty and friendliness of the boys do not, alone, warrant us in accepting their statements at face value. One boy, for example, having a warm, friendly feeling for his counselor, stated that the Study was "tops," overlooking the fact that his fundamental problems remained un-solved. In his case there was no doubt that he enjoyed the attention he received but there was considerable doubt as to how much he benefited therefrom. Another boy at the conclusion of the program, when asked "What did he [the counselor] do for you as you look back at it now?" replied, "He told me what to do—what's right and wrong—*not to fool around with girls.* It gives a boy a good feeling to have an older person outside the family to tell you what's right and wrong—someone to take an interest in you." And yet, twenty-two months later he was sent to a correctional institution on a five-year sentence for a sex offense.

THE BOY'S OWN STORY

The boy's own story has always had its special fascination. His bluntness, his ability to see through pretense, his colorful language, make his viewpoint interesting and furnish helpful hints to case workers. Such testimony bridges the gap between the idealized framework of the project as seen by the staff and its actual impact upon the boy. The more important member of the counselor-boy relationship should not remain a "silent partner."

We studied the opinions of the boys at the termination of the project. Three methods were used to get a sample of opinions: (1) interviews, (2) questionnaires, and (3) letters spontaneously written by boys to their respective counselors.

The Sample Interviewed. It was not possible to go to each of the 325 boys in the treatment group for an appraisal of the Study. A sample consisting of one-third of the group was considered sufficient, the boy's availability for an interview and his length of acquaintance with the Study being the chief determining factors. It was evident that little would be gained by interviewing the 65 boys who had been retired early from the program; it was obvious also that the 71 boys dropped in 1943 or earlier would have less to say about the Study than those who had been retained for a longer period. Five boys had died, reducing the number to 184. It was soon discovered that interviews could not be arranged with all of these: 41 were in the armed services, 9 were living outside Cambridge and Somerville; 7 could not be found; and 4 were confined in hospitals or institutions for mental cases. Thus a nucleus of 123 boys remained for interviewing locally. Of these, 118 (95.5 percent) were found and their opinions recorded. Only one of the boys refused to give his frank opinions about the Study. He consented to the interview but protested that the interviewer had no right to question him and that the questions asked were "too personal." [1]

Thus, approximately one-third of the total treatment group of 325 boys, including practically all of the most active cases then available, three-fifths of the institutionalized delinquents, and about 45 percent of the boys who had been brought into juvenile court during the treatment program, were interviewed. The sample also included eight boys who were known as "uncooperative cases" for part or all of the treatment period.

The Interviewing Staff. Six experienced interviewers were employed who had had no previous association with the Study. Four of the interviewers were college graduates studying for a doctoral degree in psychology or sociology; the fifth was a social worker, and the sixth was a college senior who was writing a thesis on the technique of the interview. All but the social worker were men. Prior

---

[1] A short time after the interview this boy was committed to a State hospital with a diagnosis of schizophrenia.

to their employment none of the interviewers had been informed about the Study. They were given a boy's name and address and were instructed to attempt to find him, to arrange for an interview with him at his home or at any convenient place and to ask him certain questions concerning his association with the Study. The interviewers were informed that the Study was a research project, that it was interested in the prevention of delinquency and that it had been known to a number of boys in Cambridge and Somerville. They knew little else about it. They were thus not likely to ask the boys leading questions or to influence them in their replies. A list of questions was given them with instructions as to how these questions should be used, though they were permitted flexibility in their approach.[2]

They were asked to explain that they were sent by a local organization which had sponsored a youth program and now wanted to find out whether the program had been of value and how the boy reacted to it. The interviewers did not mention the name of the Study unless the boy could not recall it. Usually the interviewer memorized the questions and took verbatim notes of the replies. It was sometimes necessary to explain that many boys were being interviewed and it was necessary to take notes in order to avoid confusion. Only on rare occasions did the boy object to this technique or show any reticence when the interviewer took out his pad and pencil.

On the whole, the interviewers found it easy to gain rapport with the boys, most of whom recalled the Study and the names of their most recent counselors; the majority were willing to express their own viewpoint.[3] The interviewer concluded his written report with a statement of his general impressions of the boy's sincerity. In almost every case the interviewer believed that the boy had expressed his honest opinion.

The first interview was undertaken seven months after the treatment program ended. The interviewing continued for a period of 16 months. Three-fourths of the boys were 18, 19, or 20 years old at the time they were interviewed; the youngest was almost 13, the oldest 21.

[2] See Appendix C for a copy of the questions and directions for interviewers.
[3] For excerpts from these interviews see pp. 159–171.

The Questionnaires. To reach the boys in the service, a questionnaire was prepared incorporating most of the questions with which the interviewer had been supplied [4] and was sent to approximately 43 boys. This was evidently considered a rather formidable document, for only nine were returned.

The Letters. Many letters were received from boys during their camping experiences while treatment was in progress, but during and immediately following the end of the war when so many of the boys were in some branch of the service, there was a great increase in letter writing. (Many boys were still writing letters to their counselors in 1949.) Over 100 letters received by the counselors in 1945, 1946 and 1947 (and a few prior to that time) reveal a wide variety of opinions concerning the Study. As a sampling of opinion the letters, of course, are inferior to the interview, for boys who were critical of the Study would be unlikely to write letters to their counselors. None of the boys were asked to write. There is no reason to doubt the sincerity of statements made by boys who chose to keep in touch with their counselors.[5]

The Boys' Judgments of the Study. Expressions of opinions ranged from high praise to complete rejection. On the whole, the general tenor of the replies was favorable to the Study. Even in the interviews more than half of the boys expressed a belief that the Study was of some value to them personally.[6]

The following excerpts comprise a selection from 40 percent of the interviews, from six of the nine returned questionnaires, and a relatively small proportion of the many letters received. The excerpts from the interviews and questionnaire replies may be considered *representative* of the total for only those were omitted that were particularly unclear or irrelevant, or that substantially duplicated an opinion that has been included.[7]

---

[4] A copy of this questionnaire appears in Appendix C.

[5] Two of the letter writers were also included among the interviewees.

[6] It was difficult to classify the replies in such a way as to indicate the degree of the boys' acceptance or rejection of the Study for the opinions were sometimes mixed or lacking in clarity and definiteness. Yet, Dr. Helen L. Witmer, in her evaluation reports (Chap. XXV) made a rough classification of the judgments of the boys interviewed as follows (1) The Study was very worth while, 40.7 percent; (2) somewhat worth while, 16.9 percent; (3) had dubious value, 14.4 per cent; and (4) was of little or no value, 28.0 percent.

[7] Opinions numbered 1 to 47 were expressed orally in interviews, those numbered 48 to 53 in questionnaire replies. Those numbered 54 to 59 are extracts from letters.

A. EXCERPTS FROM INTERVIEWS

1. She [counselor] was more than a nurse. She was sort of—closer than an aunt—well, she seemed to know what was wrong and she could take out your hidden thoughts. If you had just a little trouble on your mind, she'd dig and find it right off. She has a good knowledge of children right down to the last act. She could always get around some-one—if the child wouldn't say nothing, she'd get around another way and in a few minutes this one would be talking to her. I never had anything seriously affecting myself. I mean trouble. I couldn't get along with teachers and she told me I'd have to go half way with the teachers and sort of made me feel that the teachers were there to help me and not to sort of push me around.

Personally I think it [Study] is a good thing. It could help a fellow in the long run and he'll feel that someone cares for him and the whole world isn't against him. This organization sent quite a few fellows to the camps. Fellows got away from the city and that helps a lot. When you get into life, you probably pick up a trade with your hands or maybe through your mind. This organization helps develop that.

The last fellow [counselor] was really tops with me. He really tried to help me out in everything. I mean as far as talking about the opposite sex. He helped me out and fixed me up as far as not picking anything up out of the street and whatnot. In other words, he straightened me out in the facts of life and told me right down from the ground floor up. It wasn't sort of like I had to tell him anything. I didn't have to tell him nothing. Nothing was forced. It's not like in school where you have to do something or else. It was sort of like an every-day friend you might meet on the street—only more so.

2. I don't know what he [counselor] was trying to do. I don't know whether he was trying to prove something or disprove something. He just came along, that's all. He was all right, too. He was a good friend. He said to bring my troubles to him but I really didn't need any help.

3. Mr. B. came down to the house. I met him in school. He took me to the circus. He was trying to keep me off the street and he took me to camp, baseball games. They were very good men. Mr. B. was swell. Others were also but I didn't have them as much. We talked about problems. They always wanted to help us out. I was going through that wild age then. He used to come down. I used to respect him for keeping me out of trouble. Just about all they did was to keep me out of trouble. It doesn't seem important but it was. I would have no one to tell my problems to except Mr. B. and Mr. S. We used to have a lot of arguments at home. They probably stopped me from stealing and things like that. Poor kids with no money—nothing to do—nobody to care about them—would be helped by this [the Study]. A kid feels lost in the world—he starts stealing—it ruins his life. If they had somebody like Mr. B. and

Mr. S. things would be different. To know that someone wants to take care of things—then you won't think that you're nobody.

4. They were trying to keep kids busy—keep them out of trouble. I guess they didn't have much luck with me. I just couldn't keep out of trouble. He came down—he was a nice guy—we used to see a lot of each other and then he left and another fellow took over his route. They did a lot for me. They used to give me a chance to do things I never would have been able to do before. I could never afford to go to a camp. S. and I used to go horseback riding every Saturday.

5. I looked up to him like a son looks up to his father. You see I never knew my real father and my stepfather died when I was seven or eight years old. I looked forward to seeing him whenever I got in trouble. You know, when the cat's away the mice must play. He had a wonderful personality. He was always ready to talk to you about different things. He knew about everything I had ever done—good or bad. How I don't know. He was just an all-around good buddy. He helped me correct my faults before they got a good grip on me. I don't know what they would have become if he hadn't helped me. [The boy says he is planning to become a police officer.]

6. [A persistent delinquent, Peter was interviewed in the prison where he was serving a sentence for robbery. He commented as follows on his counselor's technique:] He just didn't understand. He was a nice fellow but he didn't understand me. If I did things—after I had done them— he'd tell me not to do them and to be good and they were not right to do. [When asked if the program helped him, he said,] Well, usually it was too late. Before they tell you what not to do, you've already done it.

7. [Ronald characterized the work of the counselor as a benevolent racket.] It looked pretty good to me. It was a position—not a job—something that I'd like to have [and yet he added that his counselor was like a "guardian"]. No foolin', he really took care of us. He helped me mostly with my mother. My mother has asthma. He got her into the hospital for an operation. I used to go to the Study every afternoon for about a year and a half. You have to keep occupied and stay out of trouble. They had everything down pat. Ya, they knew what they were doing—they had a good program.

8. He is a swell fellow. He used to come down to school and then he'd help me with my studies. He took me to ball games. I was up to his house a few times. We did all kinds of different things. He used to advise me. Once or twice I got into deep trouble. He helped me see the right side of things. They used to give me physical exams, also mental ones. You see, these tests sort of helped me to know just what I could do. He was a swell guy. He really took a personal interest in your affairs. You could see them anytime. I always felt free. They always had time for you. They were always waiting with an open hand. If it hadn't been for B. I don't

know what I would have done. B. was a swell Joe. B. is more like my father than my real father. I just can't say enough in favor of it. They have certainly been wonderful to me. B. showed me that people really could get along together.

9. It was a good organization. They helped some of the kids out with their trouble. Something they couldn't speak to their parents about. You know parents don't tell their kids much about the facts of life and kids start worrying about it. Well, at the Study they'd talk it over with you. They could explain it to you so you could understand. You didn't mind talking about it to them. They had a personality so you didn't mind. They made it sound all right. They did some tutoring up there. You know, the schools won't do that after school hours and if a kid has trouble in school, it's just too bad for him, but the Study—why, they'd try to find out what was wrong and help you out on it. It took care of my teeth, too. They sent me to camp one year. I thought it was a good idea but I got homesick and had to come home and they sent me back the next year and I got homesick again.

[When asked if he thought the counselors were prying into his personal affairs, he said,] No, I didn't figure they were prying. We didn't have to be in the Study if we didn't want to. If I didn't want to see Mr. N., why I could go up to his face and tell him not to come any more, but I didn't feel that way about it.

[He was puzzled as to his own selection for the program.] I couldn't figure out anything definite so I just thought, well, if they wanted to help—okay. Let them help if they could. I didn't figure they could do anything at all but they did. They did a lot of good even though there were some who didn't like it and thought they were prying, but I didn't figure it that way. I'd say it did one hundred per cent more good than harm.

10. They did good for me. I got very favorable feelings about them. I seen him [counselor] since I was nine years old. They gave me encouragement. They did a lot of good for me and I hope they start it up again, maybe not for me but for my kids when they grow up. They need something like that, Yeh, so it's like I tell you, they helped me out a lot. [Throughout the interview this boy gave little concrete evidence that the Study had helped; as a matter of fact, he has probably been in court more often than any of the other boys and was returned to a correctional institution 13 months after this interview.]

11. [Nelson, a rather sickly boy, remembered the Study because they] just help people who weren't feeling well and who needed some doctor's care. I called her [his first counselor] once when my teeth hurted and she had them fixed. [He didn't care for the rest of the program. His next counselor] wanted me to go swimming or go some other places but I'd rather go with the gang. I suppose it was a good thing if a fellow was

interested in it. I wasn't interested. My father was very suspicious about it, but they were all right. They took care of me when I was sick. They helped me out.

12. [Philip, one of the average boys who was dropped in 1943, said he remembered only one of the two counselors he had had.] I really wasn't very much interested in it. I don't remember too much about it anyway. I was only six or seven years old at the time. [He was actually ten years old when the first counselor started work with him.] He was always trying to help us in various ways but there wasn't very much he could do for me. You know, I didn't need any help but if it hadn't been for them I would probably never have seen a football game.

13. [Mark said,] We used to hop trucks. If we didn't like the kids on the street corner, we used to belt them in the face—jump buildings. Foolish days—I think so now. [When asked what the counselor had done for him, he replied,] He helped make me a character. I was shy, then I was wild, now I'm medium.

14. I had a lot of fun with him. He taught a lot of us to drive and they taught you not to steal, not to hop trucks. They said it won't get you anywhere to steal, not to argue with people older than you are, especially old ladies—like kids in the street playing cards; sometimes ladies speak to them and they are awfully fresh to them.

15. He used to take us to the "Y," to baseball games, hikes and picnics, trying to keep the fellows off the streets and to meet fellows. He was more or less like a social worker but he is more like a good friend of the family. Very few got arrested while this program was going on but after it stopped, that's when it happened.

16. He took me to the airport but he did a lot of other things, helped me with school and when I got held back for a year, he got me up at Washington Avenue, got a teacher to give me some examinations to find out what I knew and what I didn't know and what I was supposed to know. He told me to keep out of trouble while I was going up to the Study. He was a great fellow. He tended me—took care of me. He was a nice fellow. [When asked what he would say Mr. S.'s job was, Oscar said,] "They were sort of guardians to me—to see that I had a good time. It was sort of like a house of fun. He learned me how to swim, too. They never charged nothing for camp or for anything that we did. It never cost nothin'."

17. [Brian was described as a child] difficult to understand; secretive, extremely sullen, restless and nervous. [He said,] Once I saw a psychiatrist up there but he started asking me all sorts of questions so I just kept quiet. I don't go for that sort of stuff. Anytime somebody starts to write down what I say I just keep quiet. They don't get anything out of me. Whenever anyone starts to study me, I can't go for that but Miss A. kept me out of trouble, I guess. She used to talk to me all the time. I went to court once. I didn't say anything. Then they had some psychia-

trist who started to ask me questions. I wouldn't tell them nothing. I made believe I didn't know but I was burning inside. Most of the things that bothered me I never told her. That's just like me. There are a lot of things I want to find out and want to ask about them but I just can't seem able to. I can never ask questions. All my life it's been like that. I want to know so many things but I just wait and see if I get the answer later on. If she had been a man, it might have been easy to talk to her about some things. You know they are pretty good up there. For instance, telling a fellow where babies come from. She can take out a book and show you rather than kids getting it in the wrong way but I can't ask people questions. That's why this thing wasn't just for me. It wasn't the right thing. I decided that all they wanted to do was study you.

18. [Guy at first said that he got nothing out of the Study but on further questioning he said,] Whatever I wanted to do or whatever I had to say they would listen to me. I wanted more education. That's what I wanted mostly and they tried to help me with that. I guess I was just too dumb, too thick. They did give me some help in reading and writing but I couldn't catch it. They tried their best with me. It isn't their fault that I couldn't learn.

19. It was all right. They were trying to build me up. They gave us physical examinations, blood tests—took pictures. You know, with your clothes off. They wanted me to eat vegetables but I don't like vegetables. They gave me some pills, too. I never would take them—I never could swallow pills. [When asked how they built him up, he said,] It didn't do nothin'. It didn't do a thing for me. You got to eat vegetables to grow but I tried it once and I didn't like it. It didn't work with me. They just wasted their time. It helped some kids a lot—growing—got them to eat better food. They didn't tell me what they were doing so I didn't go up there any more.

20. [Dominic started his delinquencies toward the end of the treatment program and continued after its termination. He said,] I don't remember too much about it. It didn't make much difference to me. It isn't very important. I had too much else to do. The camp was all right, swimming and stuff like that, but I never did see him [counselor] very often anyway.

21. They gave you physical examinations. They took care of my teeth. They'd take care of your eyes too, if you needed it. It was free. It seemed that the money was left by some woman who died. I liked the camping and the recreation the best. I think it did help the fellows.

22. I didn't know what it was all about. They taught me how to drive. N. [last counselor] was a good egg but I didn't like all the questions. They were too personal. I'm not too much interested. I liked E. [first counselor]. She was a lady. She was tall, very nice. She never asked personal questions. They helped me out a couple of times, psychologi-

cally I guess. I wanted to quit school and go to work. They told me education was more important. I wanted to join the Navy and they still told me education was more important. They had a fund from a fellow that died. They were interested in taking you off the hands of your parents so you wouldn't roam the streets. Whatever you wanted to do they did. I went to get some of the physical examinations, go on picnics and things like that. They told us to come see them when we had problems. I used to go, but not with the very personal ones; I answered those myself.

23.   I wasn't very much interested in it. I didn't care very much about it. I wondered why anybody would come down and take an interest in me like that or take me out, but I never figured it out. I didn't think I ought to ask. I didn't think it was any of my business. I wasn't interested. There wasn't anything going on. It was like an insurance business, just a lot of offices there. After I got into trouble, he [counselor] sort of slacked off. I guess he thought I was a lost cause. Well, they didn't do anything. Nothing came out of it. [During the latter part of the Study the counselor neglected this case. It was during that period that the boy got into trouble. The early years of the counselor-boy relationship were quite different. Recalling those years, Edmund said,] 'It was just like going out with any of the other fellows, like going to a show with one of your friends, but, of course, with him you couldn't get into trouble. That was the difference.

24.   [Orrin, one of the older boys who was not a very active case, said,] Looking back I can see it's a good thing but I couldn't see it then. I was just a kid. I wasn't interested in that sort of thing. She [counselor] tried to get me to go to camp. I wasn't interested. You see, I'm not the type. I have never been interested in clubs. She used to ask for your ideas about this and that. We never bothered with personal questions. I don't want to bother anyone with my troubles, except maybe Dad. I really don't know just what the organization was for anyway.

25.   Well, about ten years ago I was in school. These people used to go around and were interested in backward children. I couldn't read or write and I should have been able to. I used to read backwards so they helped me along. They even brought me over to Boston University one summer so I could study and learn how to read and write. She [counselor] was all right. She used to do a lot of things for us. That was the trouble though—she used to do too many things. You know how you don't like anybody who tries to do too much for you. She used to tell my mother, "Have him come in early at night. See that he doesn't stay out so late"—you know, stuff like that. I didn't like that. I didn't appreciate her. I didn't get to know her and like her until the end of this whole thing. Then I realized as I grew up that she was right. She used to take me out to dinner. Sometimes I'd call her and take her out to dinner.

I met Dr. Cabot before he died. That was a pretty good idea. Now they've stopped the Study and they are all doing some research. They are writing up everything that happened. The idea is to see if you give fellows a break, whether they go bad or they don't go bad. There's a fellow that I have to meet [referring to the boy in the control group matched with him] who is just like me. He looks like me and he acts like me. Now they are going to find out who turned out better. I'm supposed to meet him this year. I'm very much interested. They gave me my faith back in things. I was pretty discouraged. I couldn't read. I thought everything was against me. Then they showed me how easy it was to read and I looked at this differently. I used to get into a lot of trouble in school. Miss A. would always come down and help me out so I figured since she was helping me out, I'd get into more trouble, so I did. Then one day I found out. She didn't come down, so I learned. After all, they're going to play you card for card and trump for trump. You can't beat them.

The Study is a pretty good thing. It keeps kids from going bad. It keeps them off the street. It keeps them busy. There were a couple of others at the Study, too. They are more like cops. Sometimes social workers are cops. They used to ask you if you smoked. Then they used to ask you if you drank and if you didn't know the ropes, you'd tell them, but I didn't—I was too smart. There was a psychiatrist. I remember going to see him. I didn't like him. He said, "Tell me all the things you have been afraid to tell everybody else," but I didn't. I don't believe in Confession.

26. I don't remember much about it. Anyway, I never went down to the place. They used to come here once in a while. I don't like that kind of stuff. I'd rather stick here and kick around with the gang. I never do like to go places with people very much. I didn't go to camp. He tried to get me to go to camp but I never went. I didn't have much to do with them. Maybe that sort of thing is okay for some people. I don't know— I wasn't interested. I'd rather stay here.

27. They helped you when you were in trouble and sometimes they helped you stay out. I had bad kidneys [enuresis]. He helped me with those. He wasn't a doctor but he was real scientific-like. I could talk to him any old way.

28. [Miles, a strong, hyperactive, little boy who was a behavior problem with symptoms suggestive of epilepsy, but who didn't have a delinquent record, said:] I had an awful lot of workers. They bought me sundaes and talked to me. Mr. P. was all right. He took me out and bought me ice cream. He talked to me. He fixed things up with the teachers. Mr. O., he had hair that used to stick up. He was funny. He bought me ice cream and took me to baseball games. He talked to me all the time. It helped me. It gave me something to do. I used to steal all the time but I don't do that any more.

29. [Many of the boys expressed a very natural desire to have a club that they could run themselves. Angelo, a persistent delinquent, said:]

Give the fellows the chance of having the feeling of running it them-selves. They don't want to be looked after too much. At the Study we never got a chance to do anything for ourselves. Everything was done for us. If you wanted to make something—these people—they practi-cally saw that it was done for you. While I was with them [his counselors] they kept me active. Since then I got my neck caught. After they left, I lost all interest. Mr. N. didn't know how to handle me. He lacked something. I don't know what it was. The first two counselors were okay. They tried to keep me busy but when they weren't around, I guess I went with the wrong gang. I used to break in at night. Go in a window and get the things. We'd work in a group of three or four.

[Although the boy seemed to like his counselors, particularly the first two, he was delinquent all during the treatment period. He said,] It was okay during the daytime but they should have something during the night, something for us to do to keep us busy. [It was during the night that he used to break into stores.]

30. I can't say enough for the Study. I can't say enough for Mr. B. He was swell. We did a lot of things. It kept you busy. I can't tell you how much the Study has done for me. I wish it could keep on going and take care of all the boys. If I had any money, I would give some to it.

31. [Gordon said he used to see his counselor every day or every other day.] I would say that it did help to see me so often. It didn't give me a chance to get into mischief. Most everyone used to be able to make a fool out of me. Now they can't do it so often. The kids would laugh be-cause I couldn't read but now I still play dumb and they think I still am dumb but I know what they are talking about. I can read and use big words, too. I just let them think I'm dumb. I know I'm not. She [coun-selor] was trying to see me get ahead. To be up with everybody else, not to be lagging behind, to always be in there pitching. When I got in hot water, she always got me out. Some boys when they find that someone is interested in them will go ahead and do things and prosper but when nobody cares what you do, you might just as well go out and do what you please.

32. [Dexter, probably our most loquacious boy, said,] The most im-portant part they did to help my family was when Mr. F. seen that my sister was able to go to a heart specialist. This was the only thing they did as far as I'm concerned. All they seemed to do was ask me how "the problem child" was getting along. They didn't do me any good. Mr. K. knew damn well that I wasn't getting along in school.

Of course, if I was running this Youth Study I'd start a regular gym-nasium and see that they got any kind of hospital care they needed—see that they were tutored in any subjects that they lacked and if they were overworked and had to work hard for a living, to stop that and get on the ball and study instead of wasting your time working.

Mr. F. wanted to teach me how to box. He wanted to sort of win me over to his way of thinking. Of course, at that time he felt as though I was very highly emotional and very much like my father and flew off the handle, but actually I wasn't like that at all. They didn't draw the right opinion of me.

His intentions were to help me in school—to have me box—sort of win me over to his way of being easy going and everything. He was a hell of a nice guy but at that time he left and another fellow who didn't do any good whatever came.

It didn't do me any good because they didn't help me. He didn't tutor me—he was always too busy. He didn't say to me, "Now, work only a few hours a day and study hard."

It made me feel as though it was something similar to a reform school, you might say, trying to see how "the problem child" was getting along, trying to straighten me out, but actually they went a miserable way around doing it. Before you start there's three strikes against you already. They think, "Oh, gee, this guy's a problem child—oh, gee, we've got to treat him like one." They should treat you just like anybody else.

They lacked dancing school—they lacked a machine shop—libraries and things like that. I wasn't advancing. I didn't feel as though I was progressing. A guy coming up seeing how I was getting along! What the heck! Sure, I'm getting along. If you get into any trouble, they visited me just like a regular truant officer—just like being on probation or something. You'd only make a boy want to be crooked because you'd say to a fellow, "How are you getting along? How are you? Are you being a good boy? Are you doing this and that?" That only makes a boy feel like, "Good God, all this guy gives is a nuisance." In plain language you'd say, "Good gravy, this looks like a truant officer," and you'd actually get sore and you'd say, "Oh, gee, here he comes again."

33. I'd have gone to Shirley [the Industrial School for delinquents] if it hadn't been for S. I'm sure of it. He didn't ask me any personal questions. I didn't have to make appointments. I could come in any time. I used to call him about six and go home with him for supper. I met his wife. I joined all the clubs but since S. has stopped coming, I haven't gone to any of these places. I've gone back to the pool room. There's nothing else to do.

34. [This boy had a strong attachment to his counselor.] She did a lot for me. Let me tell you what kind of person she is. She is walking down the street and she sees some kid who looks as though they're not taking good care of him and she'll take him home to his mother and she'll write out a prescription and give his mother money and tell her to buy things for him. That's the kind of a woman she is. She just wants to make this world pretty. She has so many things to do I don't know how she ever does them. You know what I'd like I'd like for you to take me around with you sometime and ask some fellow and if he said Miss A. was no good, I'd punch him in the nose, because he's wrong!

35. [Asked what he thought about the program, Burt said,] Mr. B. came down about seven years ago. He was awfully nice to me and helped me out a lot and taught me lots of things. He was a fine man. I didn't know what to think about it then. I was just a kid full of ambition. I had trouble in school. I didn't like the teachers. They didn't understand but Mr. B. came along and picked me up. If it hadn't been for him, I wouldn't be where I am today. I didn't know what to think of him at first. I had to feel him out. I didn't open up to him. Kept things to myself, but later I trusted him more. I'd tell him everything. I'd go to him with problems.

[Asked if it helped him, Burt said,] It sure did. Mr. B. sent me to an academy. He kept me steady. He helped my mother socially—no—financially. We never had no money. We were always poor. My father's on the bum, you know. I wouldn't be where I am today if it hadn't been for Mr. B. There should be more of it. He proved you could work things through. He told me all about juvenile delinquency. It's really a tough problem. They've got time on their hands and no place to go. You've got to understand a kid and work on his symptoms. At first I didn't know about social workers. You know, I didn't know what they were like but I learned and I'd do what they wanted. They should have more social workers. When kids start stealing, they shouldn't put them in jail. They should take them and tell them about things. It's worth it to spend the money. It's too bad the Foundation is closing. If people would set up more foundations like this and help kids, this would be a better country to live in. If it hadn't been for that, I wouldn't be where I am today. I've got ambition. I'm going places.

36. [Duncan was a feeble-minded child who never learned to read. The staff spent a great deal of time with him attempting to give him the fundamentals of reading and writing but with little success. To Duncan the purpose of the Study was] to help a boy learn to read and write like me. I don't think they took any [boys] unless they couldn't read or write. It's a good thing for people like us to try to do things like that. I know I'll never forget what they did for me. Who would people like me turn to if they didn't have places to teach you and help you get jobs and things?

37. They had a camp and some doctors. I never participated. I hardly ever went there. Mr. N. came down and tried to see if he could help me out. [Asked if he helped him any, he said,] No, I didn't like him. He used to come down about twice a week but I was always out. He did catch me at home a couple of times. He used to ask me all kinds of questions. Looking back at it now I can sort of see what he was trying to do but then I thought he was just trying to butt in. Anyway we were just a bunch of wild kids.

38. I was in the fourth grade [it was actually the sixth] when I first came across this [the Study] and I was sick. I had rheumatic fever. She

[his counselor] got me two specialists to examine me. They were Viennese who escaped from Europe. She got me all kinds of examinations to find out how I was. She got me into the hospital, too. They tried out new things on me to see if they would work. They saw to it that I got a doctor and while I was at home they got me a nurse.

I was very shy, too and sort of backward. Miss A. worked on that. I was scared of people—nervous, you know. Miss A. helped me get over that. Sometimes I was stubborn but she didn't mind that. She encouraged me to stand up for what I felt. She didn't want me to be just a yes-man. She didn't make me do anything I didn't want to do. She influenced my parents, too. I've never had any money but she got them to send me to college and she got a high school teacher interested in me who gave me aptitude tests. She got me into meeting more young people and to go to dances and get acquainted with girls. I didn't know very many people then—I was nervous with them. I resisted at first but finally I got so I liked it all right.

I was kind of wobbly in English so Miss A. sent me to summer camp. The Study helped me a lot. I have come a long way since then.

39. To tell the truth, it never did me any good. I only went to see them once. I didn't like to make the trip over there. [He lived a long distance from the Study office.] They sent me to camp twice. That was very nice and I enjoyed talking to them but I just didn't like it, that's all.

40. [Chester, a persistent delinquent as a youngster, said,] I never went for clubs. I never liked them. I don't see how it can help a fellow to go play checkers and read a book. That is no good. That stuff doesn't help a fellow. Mr. D. used to help me out by talking to me. When I used to get into jams, he'd help me and then sometimes he'd help me so I didn't get into them. He claimed he liked me better than any kid he went with—I suppose he meant it, too. I used to like him a lot. He used to help me out of a hell of a lot of jams.

41. Yeh, I went up there and they kept taking blood out of every one of my fingers and then the guy started to take it out of my arm and I quit. It got monotonous having them take blood all the time. They had a doctor up there. They began to stick needles into my fingers and every day I'd come back and I'd look at my fingers and they began taking so much blood out of them, my fingers began to shrink so the knuckles started to stick out. Now I have big knuckles just because of that. I can't stand hospitals. I hate to get cut. [As for his counselor, Brad said,] Oh, he was all right but I didn't like him after awhile. You couldn't depend on him.

42. Sometimes they used to help fellows out who had trouble in school. I never had any trouble so they never had to help me out. [This was a strange statement coming from a boy who had many hours of special tutoring by staff tutors and other services over a period of seven

years.] I didn't see what I was going up there for. That's about all I can tell you. I went to a club up there, woodworking or something. I thought it was a lot of baloney and a waste of money, if you want my honest opinion.

43. I enjoyed it very much. They sent me to camp for two summers. I have nothing but good things to say about it. We used to go to all sorts of places together. It was good to me. What surprised me—I used to wonder why anyone would talk like that or take such an interest in people.

44. [When asked what changes he'd like to make if the program started over again, Lew said,] I can't think of anything. I think it would be swell just the way it was. They did all that they could for me.

45. She wanted to keep me from running around with some of the boys in the gang and doing things I shouldn't, like breaking into a store, staying out of school and things like that. She said if I ever wanted to make anything out of myself after I got out of school and got a good job, I would have to have some education. For the best jobs you've got to have a college education. She was always trying to get me to use my spare time after school some way but I just didn't seem to like to. She wanted me to schedule my time instead of just doing things when I felt like it. I guess I got set in my ways, just always drifting away from the schedule. It just never seemed to work. It was never very interesting, it was too dull. There was always something else I would just as soon do just when it came up. I didn't like to have things all planned out like that—somebody else telling you what to do—always some kind of competition. Somebody had to be better than somebody else. It's better with a bunch of fellows that think a lot of each other and somebody isn't always trying to show how good they are. If you do something wrong, why, they understand. They don't look down on you for it.

I just can't stand routine. They wanted to get me interested in things and to plan to do things but it didn't work so well with me. I sort of drifted away from it. Right now I can't think of anything it did for me. Well, they did one thing though, they got me interested in my health. They took me to see a child specialist and the dentist took out some ulcerated teeth.

[Ambrose was also impressed by the fact that the tutor was so friendly with him in contrast to his teacher.] She really liked me; she took me right into her home, introduced me to her family. She told me I should act in her house just like I was in my own house. She really was nice to me. She took an interest in me.

46. Mr. N. was one of the best friends I ever had. If I ever needed him, I could always rely on him. I quit school when I was 16. He was mad at that. He was always a good friend. He would always help me. I liked him a lot and the kids always told me, Mr. N. liked me. When the kids would say, "What the hell is N. to you?" I would say, "I don't

know. It's probably because he knows my mother." Everything I asked for—anything within reason—they'd give to us. They gave us a basketball and a football. You could do anything you wanted there and it wouldn't cost you a cent. Mr. N. taught me how to drive. The kids loved to go to the office. They were treated good. They went to picnics and parties.

47. [This little colored boy was aware of some racial discrimination in his neighborhood and found it very difficult to accept the counselors from the Study. One counselor, in particular, he said,] was prejudiced in a racial sort of way. When I found that out, I wouldn't be home when he came around so he didn't see me when he wanted to. [It was difficult for this boy to accept help.] They used to help me out with some school work, but I don't like people to help me. I'm the kind that can't take help. I'd rather do things for myself.

[Because of certain personality handicaps Leon was referred by the Study to a psychiatrist in a local clinic whom he saw for a period of two or three months. When asked what the psychiatrist did, he said,] Oh, I'd sit down and talk to him for about a half hour. He'd ask me a lot of simple questions but I never paid much attention to him. If I didn't want to answer anything or didn't like anybody or didn't want to do anything for 'em, I'd just sit there and every once in awhile if he asked me I'd give some sort of an answer that didn't make much sense. I guess he gave up after a while and told me not to come back.

B. EXCERPTS FROM QUESTIONNAIRES

48. I had a little trouble, mostly kid stuff, like breaking windows, playing hookey from school. The Study always helped me. They were swell to me. I really can't put it into words how much I appreciate it. [In answer to the question how delinquency can be prevented, he said,] By more clubs like the Study. They done all they could for me. They were wonderful. They tried to keep the boys busy so they would keep out of trouble. Speaking for myself I do think they succeeded. It made me have more respect for my mother and father. The best thing about it was the people working in it.

49. Gee, if it hadn't been for Miss A. I'd have been in Sing Sing or a place like that. I'm sure of that. They succeeded all right. They have cured me from my bad habits, my rash—diseases—keep me out of trouble mostly.

50. I believe that the sex education was the most important part of the program. I've got in trouble both in school and in the neighborhood. Yes, the men in the Study helped me as much as they could. They succeeded to a minor extent. It would help a lot of people if they opened another study in other communities but I'm one of the boys who just didn't care what happened to me, [said Leroy, who continued his delinquencies and is now confined in a prison.]

51. I can't be sure of what they wanted to do but whatever it was, it was pleasant for me and I got more value out of it personally than the value of all the money invested in it. Everything I did with them was of my own will. The best thing about the Study was an understanding adult who was also a good friend and not his business to punish you but to advise you, someone who could have confidence in and tell to what you would be afraid to tell your parents. [Asked what the worst thing about the Study was he said,] There wasn't enough of it.

The Study more or less kept me occupied and interested in not getting into trouble. My greatest trouble was being board at my neighborhood at times and looking forward to Study activities kept me from leaving it at times.

Take me to New York—give me a million dollars, or something out of a dream—yes, I'd have liked that but what they gave me was much more valuable and showed me life can be even better than a dream.

52. I was in trouble many times when I was younger, both in school and in the neighborhood and just about everywhere at the time. I believe if it hadn't been for the helpful understanding of the Study, I might be in some reformatory now. It was through them that I was given the chance to move to the country and make something of myself. I think in the majority of their pupils they have succeeded. What I liked best about the Study was their idea to help and show the pupils what a good clean life can do for the people who are more or less inclined toward delinquency.

53. I think they did everything they could have done without me asking for more. I can still remember when I uster call Miss A. my Ferry Godmother back in gramma school and junior high school. I was a year or two back on my age and they put me on my feet againe. I once hated school but they taught me that it was the best thing for me and that I could use it in later years. I'm glad they helped me. They gave me the idea that school was important and helped me to believe it. School builds up your mind.

C. EXCERPTS FROM LETTERS

54. You're all swell friends. You're all tops. I'll call you all when I hit South Station and we'll go out and have a hell of a time. And this time dinner's on me.

55. How old are you anyway? I bet your old enuf to be my grandma. Am I nosey? But no kidding you're the best friend a guy ever had and that's no kidding. Tank you for believing in me. Also thanks for the loan. I took my girl out and had a swell time.

56. You've been better to me than my own father and I'll do everything in my power to make you proud of me. I'll deeply appreciate your picture. With deepest admiration.

57. [Spencer, from a warship stationed at Shanghai, China, wrote to

his counselor:] In your letter you asked what my opinion is about the Study. To me, I think it is a swell organization and that it helps us fellas in many ways. For instance, you take a fella that hasn't many friends, introduce him to some boys, let him enjoy himself in play and working with these other boys, he becomes interested in games and learns what friendship really is. Give him a break and usually he'll come out on the top. I think, if every boy has some kind of responsibility he will have confidence in himself and that some day he will be a great leader in whatever rode he chooses to lead in. It may be he wants to become a banker, director, priest or engineer, no matter which one it is, two to one, he comes out to be a respectable person and a good citizen.

I have mom, you and Mrs. P. to thank for keeping me on the right road. True I've been in trouble many times, if you had not the patience to tell me what right from wrong is, I doubt if I could have gotten along. Putting me into boys camp was a swell thing for me. There I've made many friends and earned my way to become a counselor and a leader in different sports.

You want to know what the Study did to help me? First of all, I think friendship had everything to do with it. When you, Dr. V., Mrs. T. and others acted friendly with me, I put my trust into your hands and knew whatever you thought was best for me.

The thing that I think I enjoyed most was you helping me to try to become a leader. How to go about it and to use a little of psychology. Then the talks I had with Dr. V. about sexes and other things. Most of the sexes of I've learned was with the fellas. Then when I met Dr. V. I learned more and still more in this outfit. That's one thing is always kept a secret. Whenever I spoke about it at home my mother would think it's a sacrilege to talk of such things. I think it should be brought out in the open, I can't see anything bad about it, in fact it's a good education for girls and boys, then they'll be more careful.

58. To one who has been like a mother to me. Love and a kiss from me to you. I can never pay you for all you've done. I've read one book— "Pice of Mine."

59. Situation with my folks couldn't be better. My mother loves me more than ever and that makes me feel good inside. You gave me a new light on all things in general and words can't express my deep gratitude and thanks. Throughout the rest of my life I will remember what you have done, and hope your fine organization will rise again.

CHAPTER XIV

WHO IS A
JUVENILE DELINQUENT?

SOME AUTHORITIES CONSIDER THE DELINQUENT A "PROBLEM CHILD" who is beyond parental control; others characterize him as a "socially maladjusted youth"; while a few bluntly term him a "youthful criminal." On the other hand, Father Flanagan of Boys Town said, "There is no such thing as a bad boy." Some have urged that we abandon the term juvenile delinquent altogether, substituting delinquent parents or delinquent communities.[1] And yet, in spite of all this disagreement, the question, Who is and who is not a delinquent, is fundamental to research in this field.

DIVERSE OUTCOMES FOR FIVE DELINQUENT BOYS

Before discussing further the concept of "delinquency," let us glance at five illustrations of boys who engaged in certain prohibited acts.

Bobby, aged ten, a "good" boy from a respectable home, tries to "thumb" a ride on the way to school but without success. Nothing happens.

Joe, whose father has a criminal record and whose mother is unable to keep an eye on her seven children, enjoys the sport of snowballing with other boys on their way home from school. No one is hurt, but a police officer sees him, recognizes him as a tough kid

---

[1] Sociologists sometimes define a delinquent in terms of the social forces impinging upon him, minimizing the boy's own responsibility for his behavior. Porterfield, for example, states, "It is not altogether facetious to define the juvenile delinquent as a friendless young person who does not live in a good home or in a college dormitory; who is not old enough to enter business or a profession for himself, or to run for the legislature; but who has offended some part of a rather peevish and irresponsible community, and been charged with the necessity of being responsible and other than peevish himself" (Austin L. Porterfield, *Youth in Trouble*, Fort Worth, The Leo Potishman Foundation, 1946, p. 46).

from another neighborhood and rushes him off to the police station to be held as a juvenile delinquent.

Charlie, a bright, attractive Italian boy of ten, on many different occasions sneaks various articles of value out of the local five-and-ten-cent store. Charlie is clever and is not detected. He gets away with it; in fact, he is praised for his smartness by his father and boasts about it to his friends.

Dick, for the first and only time in his life, steals a small sum of money from the cash register of his employer. When caught, he is penitent, readily admits his guilt and is adjudged delinquent.

Howard, who never stole anything or committed any serious offense, engages in sex play with another boy. The boy reports the incident. Howard is brought into court. With shame and humiliation he answers the persistent questions of the police and the court psychiatrist. The offense shocks the public. He is labeled a "sex offender"—a concept of strongly emotional tone. "Sex offenders" are "dangerous," "potential murderers." The newspapers editorially start a crusade against all sex offenders following the report of a sex murder contemporaneously committed by another boy. Though Howard is quite harmless, he is caught in the maelstrom of public opinion and is "put away for the protection of society."

Let us look at these five cases from different points of view:

DELINQUENT BY DEFINITION

All five of these boys are delinquent by definition, for in Massachusetts, where these acts occurred, a juvenile delinquent is defined as "a child between seven and seventeen who violates any city ordinance or town by-law or commits an offense not punishable by death." [2]

The position that we are here taking is that a delinquent child is what the law says he is. In Massachusetts the law is brief and direct, defining a delinquent as one who violates ordinances or commits certain punishable offenses. In practically all other states a broader concept of delinquency has been adopted, not focusing on the com-

[2] Sec. 52, Chap. 119 of the General Laws. During the treatment program and up until January 1, 1949, this section of the law read: "A child between seven and seventeen who violates any city ordinance or town by-law or commits an offense not punishable by death or by imprisonment for life."

mitment of criminal offenses but on the general moral behavior of the child.[3] To accept the view sometimes adopted by researchers that a child is not a delinquent until his wrongdoing is detected leads to strange consequences. In a recent English enquiry into juvenile delinquency, for example, is a statement: "Juvenile delinquents can be exactly defined; they are those belonging to a particular age group who have been shown to the satisfaction of a court of law to have committed certain acts." [4] By such a definition the persistent but undetected thief is not a delinquent, while the boy who is brought into court for a minor offense *is* so labeled. This definition does not necessarily parallel a boy's antisocial behavior. It applies only if certain events occur, usually beyond a child's control; namely, discovery and arrest by the authorities.

Bobby, the hitchhiker, and Joe, the snowballer, each violated a city ordinance.[5] The fact that one was not taken into custody and the other was depended partly on chance. In Bobby's case no police officer was present; in any event, probably no detention would have followed the violation, while Joe's arrest depended not only upon the chance presence of a police officer but upon the officer's discretion based upon extraneous factors. Charlie's behavior, though constituting a series of thefts that were far from trivial, did not result in a court appearance because Charlie had, for a time at least, outwitted the officials. Dick's theft from the cash register was relatively serious and clear-cut, and because it was a bungling job became immediately known to the authorities. Howard's sex conduct aroused deep apprehension in his neighborhood. The attendant newspaper publicity made commitment almost inevitable, much to Howard's surprise and consternation. Thus in Massachusetts, as in all states, a juvenile delinquent may be a trivial offender or he may be a serious offender, a first offender or a repeater. Nevertheless,

[3] Sol Rubin, "The Legal Character of Juvenile Delinquency," *Annals of the American Academy of Political and Social Science,* Vol. 261 (1949), p. 1.

[4] A. M. Carr-Saunders, Hermann Mannheim, and E. C. Rhodes, *Young Offenders: an Enquiry into Juvenile Delinquency* (New York, The Macmillan Company, 1944), p. 146.

[5] Bobby had violated Sec. 1 of Art. 4 of Chap. 28 of the City Ordinances of Cambridge which reads: "It shall be unlawful for any person to stand in a roadway for the purpose of soliciting a ride from the operator of any motor vehicle." Joe violated Sec. 17 of Chap. 19 of the city ordinances: "No person shall play ball or throw a stone or a snowball or other missile in any street or upon or from any bridge." These acts may not have constituted violations of city ordinances in other cities in this State.

our studies have shown that exceedingly few boys who are delinquent-by-definition are adjudged delinquent by a court.[6] Most delinquencies committed by boys would, of course, ordinarily be considered trivial. No doubt *all* of our 650 boys at some time after age seven and before seventeen committed some violation of a city ordinance and could thus be defined as delinquent! These five boys categorized as delinquent-by-definition have little in common. They are placed in the same class not because of any psychological trait, characteristic, or motive that is common to all, but because the behavior of each one comes within a legal definition that covers a wide variety of offenses.

DELINQUENT BY OFFICIAL ADJUDICATION

Most research studies in delinquency, recognizing the fact that no generalizations can be drawn from such divergent behavior, have chosen as their subject matter only children who have been adjudged delinquent by a court.[7] This limitation has certain obvious advantages. Boys who have committed the most trivial offenses seldom reach this point in the legal process. Each case is first screened by the police or other officials before a legal determination is made that the boy or girl is or is not delinquent. It should be kept in mind that in the application of the laws relating to juvenile delinquency the court may consider all of the surrounding circumstances of the case. The judge need not confine his examination to the question of the guilt or innocence of the specific act charged, as he must in dealing with adult offenders. The court's powers are in this respect broad and discretionary, partaking of the character of an equity court. The technical offense with which the boy is charged therefore should not be considered necessarily the most

6 Fred J. Murphy, Mary M. Shirley, and Helen L. Witmer, "The Incidence of Hidden Delinquency," *American Journal of Orthopsychiatry*, XVI (1946), 686–696.

7 Representative of this type of research are studies by the Gluecks, by Healy and Bronner, by Merrill and others. The boys studied by the Gluecks, for example, in their analysis of the effectiveness of the Boston Juvenile Court and the Judge Baker Foundation clinic comprised 1000 cases referred by the court. (Sheldon and Eleanor T. Glueck, *One Thousand Juvenile Delinquents*, Cambridge, Harvard University Press, 1934.) William Healy and Augusta F. Bronner, in their *New Light on Delinquency and Its Treatment* (New Haven, Yale University Press, 1936) compare boys officially charged with delinquency in court and their non-delinquent siblings. Merrill, in comparing non-delinquent school children with delinquent children, takes as representative delinquents boys and girls referred to the juvenile court in a rural county in California. (Maud A. Merrill, *Problems of Child Delinquency*, New York, Houghton Mifflin Company, 1947.)

important factor in the case. Such charge may be a cover for a rather bad total situation. This condition, of course, decreases the meaningfulness of research studies based solely on offenses listed in the official court docket.

Of the five boys in our illustration, all delinquent by definition, only Joe, Dick, and Howard are delinquent by official adjudication, one for a trival offense and two for more serious offenses. Bobby, the hitchhiker, might or might not have been found delinquent if a police officer had been present and had made an arrest. In all likelihood this violation of a city ordinance would have been overlooked. Nevertheless boys are *sometimes* brought into court for trivial violations, usually when accompanied by aggravating circumstances. Charlie, the clever thief, whose antisocial acts were more extensive than the others, is actually not delinquent by official adjudication. Basic factors in an adjudication of delinquency are many. Some of them, in addition to the law itself, are: the nature of the act and the manner in which it is performed; the presence or the knowledge of the police; the use of official discretion; the previous behavior of the child in question; the degree to which the officials, presumably sensitive to public opinion, are angered, annoyed, or shocked; their philosophy of punishment and their theory of discipline; and innumerable other more or less extraneous and often purely fortuitous circumstances. Obviously, boys may be adjudged delinquent for one offense or for many; for armed robbery or for playing ball in the street; or not adjudged delinquent at all, though committing a serious offense. Within this official delinquent group, incomplete as it is, the variety of circumstances is generally baffling. An adjudged delinquent may be seven years old or 17; a girl or a boy; an incidental first offender or one who is appearing in court for the first time after a long series of undetected acts. He may be feebleminded or brilliant; from a good home or a bad one; healthy or ill. He may even be virtually guiltless of the offense charged against him. His act may have reflected a long-standing antisocial attitude or it may have been simply a boyish prank. It may have been the first step toward a criminal career or a chance episode never to be repeated and soon to be forgotten.[8]

[8] We do not mean to imply that those officially adjudged delinquent represent a random sample of a true cross section of the boy and girl populations. Countless

DELINQUENT BY OFFICIAL COMMITMENT

Some research studies in delinquency deal only with those who have been committed by a court to an institution for delinquents.[9] Usually, but not always, these boys are more serious offenders who have been given a second or third chance on probation before commitment. To that extent they are a more highly selected group of lawbreakers. The individual differences, however, are still great within the group. The normal are thrown in with the neurotic, the defective, and the psychopathic. Some of the committed boys are tough lads whose criminality continues after release; others, more amenable to treatment, profit by their experience and make a good adjustment to life after their discharge from the institution. Some, no doubt, would have become better citizens if they had not been committed. Of the five boys in our illustration only the sex offender, Howard, may be considered a "delinquent by official commitment," though it is not evident that his behavior was more serious or harmful to society than that of the others.

DELINQUENT BY A SELECTED STANDARD

In any discussion of the causation, treatment, and prevention of delinquency it would be more meaningful to classify delinquents in terms that go beyond the act itself and that cut across official barriers.

Who is the real delinquent—the boy who is making a career of delinquency? We have seen that such a boy is not necessarily one who is a delinquent-by-definition only, for that category includes *all* delinquents; nor is he the officially adjudged delinquent, nor

---

studies have shown that certain factors are more frequently found in the lives of adjudged delinquents than in those who are never brought into court. In treating the delinquents as a group, for example, it has been found that delinquents come from poorer neighborhoods than non-delinquents; their I.Q.'s are lower; their homes are less adequate, and so on (see Chap. XVI). In other words, some common factors appear in the official delinquent *group* with greater frequency than in the non-delinquent *group* and yet the differences between the individuals within the groups are considerable.

[9] The Gluecks' study of the inmates of Concord Reformatory is an outstanding example of this sort of research (*500 Criminal Careers*, New York, Alfred A. Knopf, 1930). Most of the numerous psychometric studies of delinquents have been made in institutions where group tests are most readily administered. For a number of such studies the reader is referred to P. S. de Q. Cabot, *Juvenile Delinquency: a Critical Annotated Bibliography* (New York, The H. W. Wilson Company, 1946).

even the boy who has been committed to an institution for delinquents, and yet we cannot get away entirely from the legal concept. The neurotic boy who sits at home planning his crimes but does nothing more than brood over his fancied exploits is not a delinquent in the eyes of the law, nor as that term is ordinarily understood, no matter how maladjusted he might be by other standards. Some overt act or some pattern of behavior is basic to the concept of delinquency. As the foundation of the criminal law is the protection of society, a delinquent's acts must involve some injury or threat to another person or to himself, or deprive others of their property rights, or undermine the moral or legal foundations of government.

We found in our studies that in seeking for the real delinquents three important concepts must be taken into consideration: (a) the seriousness of the behavior, (b) its frequency, and (c) the attitude of the offender toward a lawfully constituted society. These three concepts are the basis for our selected standard or criterion for the measurement of the degree of delinquency. We shall now explain these concepts.

A. Seriousness. Delinquent offenses can be roughly arranged in a continuum of seriousness, from the least serious to the most serious, as they affect the peace and security of society. In Chapter XX we show how offenses (not boys) were thus classified. The classifiers in that case were law-enforcement authorities who, after years of practical dealings with juvenile offenses, had developed a "feel" for the seriousness of an offense merely by noting its legal appellation, though admitting the existence of borderline cases and the necessity for individualizing in terms of mitigating circumstances. In dealing with the individual offender, the mitigating circumstances may become all important. We must know not only what offense was committed but we must appraise the actor as well as the act itself and its consequences. In this way, we can make a rough value judgment pertaining to the seriousness of the boy's behavior as it affects society. For example, the average larceny case brought before the court (in, say, an unbroken series of 1,000 cases) is considered by the authorities to be less serious than the average of a similar series of robbery cases. If we are focusing upon the individual, however, we may find that a given robbery is less serious than a certain larceny committed by another boy. John may, for example, by threats of harm, force another boy to give up ten cents, which in this case could be considered robbery. Jack, on the other hand, may steal a thousand dollars from a bank, which under the circumstances constitutes larceny. Obviously in this illustration the authorities consider Jack's offense (larceny) more serious. In the cases now before us we have enough information about the offense, its surrounding circumstances, and its ultimate consequences to warrant such an individualized judgment.

B. Frequency. The factor of frequency is also fundamental to the consideration of the harm or danger to society. A boy, for example, committing an offense (trivial or serious) over and over again in spite of warnings and punishments cannot be put in the same category as a boy who commits the offense only once. A continuing pattern of antisocial behavior may distinguish the real delinquent from the incidental or occasional offender.

C. Attitude. The attitude of the person toward authority is another important concept. In the building of a delinquent career over a period of time the boy's attitude toward the rights and obligations of himself and others is obviously an essential element. It might well differentiate the purely impulsive or careless, though frequent, offender from one who is defiant of authority and who is building up a general attitude that might have sufficient momentum to carry him along the road to habitual criminality. Attitude in relation to frequency and seriousness often turns the scales toward a delinquent career.[10]

10 The nature of an offender's attitude toward constituted authority in any society is crucial to an understanding of his behavior and reformation. One of the authors of this volume in a previous study of the attitudes of inmates of a state prison found it helpful in evaluating a case-work program to divide the prison population into four groups in respect to one variable—attitude toward society. These groups are, I: Men with strong, aggressive, antisocial attitudes that seemed to bar any successful readjustment to society. II: Men with attitudes that are less fixed and not so irreconcilable as those of the first group. The attitudes of these men are less deeply rooted or have already begun to modify through the impact of other influences, or are approaching a period of emotional disorganization when they are susceptible to other forces. III: Men in this group do not have antisocial attitudes. Their criminal behavior did not arise out of deeply motivated criminal drives and their attitudes are not characterized by aggression or defiance of society. IV: Men whose persistent claims of innocence carry some plausibility and whose real attitudes toward society cannot be determined until we discover the true facts relating to their alleged offenses.

Obviously, it would be extravagant to hope for successful rehabilitation of Group I

We must consider all *three* concepts as they are related to each other. Does the child commit serious offenses? Does he frequently or infrequently commit serious acts? Does he commit minor violations frequently? How does he judge his own behavior? Has he a general attitude of defiance?

RECLASSIFYING OUR DELINQUENTS

A study of each boy's career makes it possible to classify him in terms of these three criteria. Five categories or groups are used to represent a continuum from the most delinquent to the least delinquent. Each boy may be a delinquent by definition, for, as we have pointed out, probably every boy in Cambridge and Somerville has violated some city ordinance.

Group I (The Most Delinquent). Here we place boys who have shown a persistent pattern of antisocial behavior, with serious consequences for society. These boys, as a rule, have shown a reckless, defiant or irresponsible attitude toward others. Usually, but not necessarily, these boys have been officially adjudged delinquent at some time in their careers before the age of 17, and many of them have been committed to an institution.

Group II (The Ordinary Delinquent). Boys in this group have been less persistent or have committed less serious offenses or have shown a less well-integrated antisocial attitude than boys in Group I, and yet they have quite definitely offended against society on a number of occasions. They are presumably less likely to continue.

Group III (The Occasional Delinquent). Boys in this group have been noticeably inconsistent in their behavior and their attitudes. At times they have been delinquent, though never very seriously or persistently. For longer periods of time they have been law-abiding. They are obviously less addicted to delinquent behavior than those in Group II. They represent a mid-point between the most and the least delinquent.

---

by case work, as that technique is usually practiced in a prison, but such efforts should be concentrated on those in Group II, which, incidentally, constituted the largest group. Group III needs little attention from the point of view of rehabilitation, and to attempt case work with Group IV without further information might be wasteful as well as tactless. (Edwin Powers, *Individualization of Treatment as Illustrated by Studies of Fifty Cases; a Report on the Development of Penological Treatment at Norfolk Prison Colony in Massachusetts,* New York, Bureau of Social Hygiene, Inc., 1940, 209–264.)

Group IV (The Seldom Delinquent). These boys have not been considered serious delinquents nor have they been frequent offenders. Delinquency was not habitual with them nor typical of their behavior. Their offenses were, on the whole, minor ones and their delinquent behavior has generally been given up as they matured. Relatively few of these boys appeared in court; some may have appeared for relatively minor offenses.

Group V (The Least Delinquent). The boys in this group have committed no delinquency at all other than minor violations. Most of them were not known to the police. They have shown a normal respect for authority. What offenses they may have committed have not been characteristic of them, nor were they serious or repeated. Some of these boys may have appeared in court for minor offenses.

In respect to such a scheme the five boys in our illustration might be grouped as follows:

Charlie would be placed in Group I, the most delinquent group. Though Charlie was not officially adjudged delinquent he was a clever thief who boasted of his ability to outwit the police and who committed a long series of antisocial acts. Each stealing episode may have been relatively minor, but the pattern continued with every reason to presume that the boy was going to persist in his criminality.

Joe, who violated a minor city ordinance relating to snowballing, had committed no other delinquencies known to the authorities until his case was thoroughly examined by the court and the probation officer. It was discovered that he had been staying out late at night and truanting from school, and that he was mildly antisocial in his attitudes, though up to this time he had made no appearance in court. He seemed to be less defiant and persistent than Charlie and his offenses were less serious. These considerations led to placement in Group II, for we are here considering the boy in his total relations to society rather than the isolated act for which he was brought into court.

Dick, who committed only one serious delinquent offense (larceny from the cash register), is difficult to classify. Though generally law-abiding, his attitude toward the authorities had been inconsistent. For the most part he is considered to be a fairly normal youngster who now and then breaks out into some act socially disapproved. Group III seems to be an appropriate placement for him.

Howard, the only one in our illustration who was committed to an institution, was not a persistent delinquent. His only misstep was a single sex episode which upon examination did not reflect an anti-social attitude and would not be considered by many people particularly serious. He is expected to outgrow this experience and may make a good adjustment to society, provided society's handling of this offense does not harm him too much. He seems to be appropriately placed in Group IV.

Bobby falls readily into Group V, for though he is a delinquent by definition, he has done nothing to harm himself or others. He has a respectful attitude toward authority. His attempt to "thumb a ride" was not an act which he thought was particularly wrong or dangerous. He did not even know he had violated a city ordinance. No harm resulted to himself or others.

We can thus see how a classification by legal concepts differs from a classification by selected criteria as judged by those who are well acquainted with the boys and who are able to appraise the total situation—the boy in his relationship to society. Table 26 shows these differences.

TABLE 26

*Classification of Five Boys by Legal Criteria and
by Selected Standards of Delinquency*

	LEGAL CRITERIA			
Boy	*Definition*	*Adjudication*	*Commitment*	*Selected Standard*
Charlie	Yes	No	No	I: Most Delinquent
Joe	Yes	Yes	No	II: Ordinary Delinquent
Dick	Yes	Yes	No	III: Occasional Delinquent
Howard	Yes	Yes	Yes	IV: Seldom Delinquent
Bobby	Yes	No	No	V: Least Delinquent

CLASSIFYING THE STUDY BOYS

Adopting the classification plan just described, we can now separate at least part of our total population into the five groups which range from "the most delinquent" to "the least delinquent."

It was not possible to classify each of the 650 boys in the Study. Some had died; some had been retired at an early age and others were dropped from the program before reaching their 17th birthday, as described in previous chapters.[11]

Furthermore, no boy in the treatment group could be classified unless he was well known to the classifiers. No C-boy likewise could be classified unless he had been interviewed (after his 17th birthday) or unless his record during the ages of seven to 17 was well known. The groups under consideration were thus limited to 120 T-boys and 116 C-boys.

The classification was carried out by two staff members. One had been employed by the Study for ten years, one for four; both had been counselors. The 120 T-boys were personally known to one or both of them for a period of four to eight years. Extensive material had been collected pertaining to the personal history of each boy. Boys in the control group were, of course, less well known. One classifier personally interviewed each of these boys, with the exception of the six or seven who were institutionalized and about whom the Study had extensive information. The classifiers kept in mind the three criteria for "selected standard" and based their decision upon the boy's behavior and attitudes from the time he was first known to the Study (all of these boys were then under 12) until his 17th birthday. A few of the boys may commit offenses after they pass their 17th birthdays and others no doubt will commit further delinquencies, given sufficient time, but the behavior following the 17th birthday was not considered in making the judgments. It was necessary to anchor the judgments at a fixed period in the boy's life in order that boys of widely varying ages might be comparable throughout the entire group.

Although the judgments did not depend solely upon the presence or absence of an official record, no classification was made until the records of the State Board of Probation and the police records in Cambridge and Somerville had been checked. Commitments to correctional schools or the Massachusetts Reformatory or the House of

[11] No classification could fairly be made unless a boy had reached his 17th birthday, for ages 15 and 16 were found to be the peak for overt delinquencies. It was, in fact, necessary to wait until a boy had attained the age of 17½ in order to allow time for the recording in the central office of the Board of Probation of all official records entered in the courts of original jurisdiction throughout the State. At least one-third of the total group had not yet reached that age at the time the first classification was undertaken.

Correction for the county in which the Study was located were also noted. In no case was a boy included if the Study had lost track of him at any time prior to his 17th birthday. In short, the behavior of these boys, both official and unofficial, was well known. Each classifier made his rating independently. In two-thirds of the cases there was an immediate independent agreement; in the remaining one-third a thorough discussion of the case was necessary to reach an agreement.

Of the 236 older boys in the treatment and control groups they classified 31 as "the most delinquent" boys (Group I), 33 as "ordinary delinquents" (Group II), 12 as "occasional delinquents" (Group III), 41 as "seldom delinquent" (Group IV), and 119 as "the least delinquent" (Group V).

Dividing our boys into these five groups made it possible to determine to what extent factors commonly associated with official delinquents were present in the lives of boys who exhibited varying degrees of delinquency (see Chapter XVI). In the process of evaluating the treatment program, however, we cannot compare the 116 C-boys who were distributed in these five groups with our 120 T-boys similarly distributed, for they were not matched groups. Moreover, they were not representative of the total matched groups from which they were drawn.

CHAPTER XV

"MOST DELINQUENT" BOYS

WHILE TREATMENT WAS IN PROGRESS A NUMBER OF THE STUDY BOYS became delinquent in spite of the counselors' best efforts. One could observe not only the continuation of delinquent habits deeply rooted when the Study first became acquainted with the boys, but the building of delinquent habits in boys who were not overt delinquents when first known.

Among the older members of the treatment group were found 15 boys whom we have designated our "most delinquent" (Group I), following the classification scheme described in the previous chapter. The lives of nine of these boys are here reported in brief case studies in order to depict the patterns of circumstances that prevailed, and in order to shed some light upon etiological factors. To these reports has been added another case study of a persistently delinquent boy who was too young to be included in the classification of boys described in the last chapter.[1]

HOW DELINQUENT WERE THEY?

These 15 boys showed a generally persistent pattern of antisocial behavior, leading in each case to one or more court appearances. Some may yet "straighten out" as they mature, others will continue to provide material for our courts and penal institutions. All of them were, of course, delinquent by definition. All were also delinquent by adjudication. Fourteen were committed to correctional institutions; six were committed more than once; 11 continued their delinquent behavior after the age of 17. The total number of separate offenses with which these 15 boys were officially charged in court was 75. Their unofficial offenses amounted to many times

---

[1] This case is the first to be presented in this series. See p. 189.

this number. The records showed a wide variety of delinquencies ranging from stubbornness to robbery (Table 27).

TABLE 27

*List of Offenses Charged against
15 "Most Delinquent" Boys* [a]

Offense	Number of Charges
Larceny (or attempt)	21
Breaking and entering (or attempt)	14
Use of auto without authority	7
Serious traffic violations [b]	7
Sex offenses	4
Drunkenness	4
Assault and battery	3
Assault and battery with dangerous weapon	2
Robbery	2
Stubbornness	2
Malicious injury to property	2
Carrying dangerous weapon	1
Receiving stolen property	1
Conspiracy to commit crime	1
Miscellaneous	4
Total	75

[a] Average age of the boys at the time the court records were cleared was 20.0. The age range was from 18.0 to 21.7.

[b] Minor traffic violations, such as not stopping for traffic signals, have been omitted from this table. Truancy, which is not technically a delinquent act, but considered in Massachusetts under a separate chapter of the law entitled, "School Offenders and County Training Schools" (Chap. 77 of the General Laws) has also been omitted. All but two of the 15 boys were truants. One of these two was a boy whose only offenses were sex affairs with other boys.

In these studies we describe the influences surrounding the boys in their homes and neighborhoods and the boys' reactions to these influences. We are not here particularly concerned with an evaluation of the counselor's work. Obviously in no case was the counselor successful in preventing the boy from developing a delinquent career.

In reworking our extensive material on the life histories of these boys we have been highly selective.[2] Yet in the process of selection

[2] Obviously, to present the data in brief form and to conceal identity, vastly more material was omitted than included. In these 15 cases we have on file approximately

we have endeavored to give an integrated picture of the boys' struggle—in most cases an unhappy and unsuccessful struggle—against adverse influences.

CASE STUDIES

PEEWEE [3]

Peewee, an undersized, attractive little boy, was longing to get out again. He had been forced to stay indoors every evening for a week as punishment for his last fire-setting escapade. Setting fires had been fun for Peewee ever since he was six years old. He loved to see the leaping flames and to hear the fire engines screeching through the streets. Now he was almost ten and his mother was worried about him.

"But don't you know that that's a dangerous thing to do, Peewee?" his counselor once said to him.

"Oh, gee," he replied with a smile, "that last one was only a little fire." He was referring to a fire he had started in a vacant house at a cost of $1,000 to the owner. He had two other fires to his "credit" at that time but they had been brought under control soon after discovery.

"But why do you do it, Peewee?" he was asked.

"Oh, I don't know," he said, "I set fires when I don't like people. It makes my heart pound faster."

He explained how he usually dug a small hole in the ground, put bits of paper in the hole and watched them burn. "If no one comes, that means no one cares. If anybody does come, that means that someone does care." Sometimes he admitted he runs away because he gets scared when the fire starts but if no one comes he goes back to it.

On this particular night Peewee had begged his mother to let him out. He promised to be a good boy. She couldn't resist his pleas. He left by the front door, half walking, half running down the street.

1,700 pages (single-spaced typing on 8" by 11" paper) of "running records," in addition to hundreds of miscellaneous documents, letters, and reports. On the other hand, information concerning the very early life of the child is unfortunately meager.

[3] White boy. Father born in U.S.; mother born in Italy. Siblings: Two older half sisters. Health: Good. Intelligence: Dull normal to borderline. Religion: Catholic. Neighborhood rating: 0. Delinquency prognosis: −1 at age 6 years, 10 months. Age when treatment started: 7 years, 2 months; when treatment ended: 13 years, 9 months. Number of counselors: Three.

He headed directly for the high school. The building was completely dark. Peewee almost lost his nerve. He was afraid of the dark. In fact, he had been afraid of many things. Going over a bridge, for example, always terrified him; that is, if there was water beneath the bridge. He was afraid it might collapse. He often dreamed about drowning. He once dreamed he was a fish and he stayed under water for a whole day. Sometimes sharks chased him. Peewee always got away but once a shark warned him, "Never mind, I'll get you next time. I'll get you sooner or later!"

Peewee was sure there were haunted houses in this neighborhood. He knew about ghosts or "spoogies" as he called them. Maybe there were ghosts in the school building. He hesitated. Should he run home again? He fingered the matches in his pocket. He looked down at the dry grass near the building. The grass was soon blazing merrily. The fire burned brightly for only a few minutes but it gave him courage. Seeing a red brick in the frozen earth he gave it a kick. It came loose. "A brick is like a key," he thought, "it will let you in." With it he broke the glass in the rear door of the school. Reaching his right hand inside he turned the knob. He had never been in this school before. He did not know where the light switch was but it was not hard to find. Setting fire to a building, he knew, wasn't easy. Nothing burns very well until you get it started. He went to the domestic science rooms. He knew he could set fire to the upholstery of one of the chairs because he had started fires that way before. He left by the side door and ran to the street. "Now," he thought, "this will be a real fire and the fire engines will come."

The night watchman, making his rounds, sounded the alarm shortly after the fire started. By the time the first fire truck arrived great billows of smoke were emanating from the basement rooms. The fire was shortly under control but the damage exceeded $500. Then the search for the culprit began. Peewee's reputation as a "firebug" focused suspicion on him. He was found on the street not far from the scene, willing, almost eager, to admit that he started it. "I just wanted to have a little fun," he said.

The judge took a sterner view of the "fun," labeled this boy a "menace to society," and sent him forthwith to the state school for delinquents, where he was the youngest of all the boys committed to that school.

The newspaper publicity focused attention on this little fellow. Who was he? What kind of home did he come from? Couldn't somebody cure him of this habit? Everyone said the boy was cute, this little boy with the tousled hair, blue eyes, and appealing manner. He seemed never to have grown up physically or mentally. In fact, he got a pretty poor start. Prematurely born, he weighed but four pounds at birth. At twelve and a half, a physical examination showed that he was "still in a state of complete infantilism." The psychologists, too, were impressed with his immaturity. "A small, undersized boy who looks nearer six than eight years old," said one. "He is such a harmless looking little fellow," said another psychologist who examined him at the school for delinquents, "Quite likely the smallest boy in the colony, contrasting sharply with the older, larger, and seemingly tougher youths at the school. I infer too few instances of positive joy in Peewee's life. He smiles to be sure, but I should be surprised if he really laughs much. This lack of high animal spirits suggests that he has not had much fun in life and is starved for fun and amusement. Is that what he provides for himself by his extensive 'fireworks'?"

School, at any rate, had not afforded Peewee much fun. It seemed to his teachers as though he did not want to learn, for he would not pay attention. He wasn't rough or aggressive. "He is a surprising child in many ways," his teacher said. "He looks so innocent. He is so affectionate, is engaging in his ways but you could never depend on him to tell the truth. He is a very spoiled boy who has no respect for authority. Always wants his own way. Perhaps he'll wake up next year and do better work," she said with the perennial hope of a teacher.

But next year he was no better. She placed him at a desk close to her, apart from the others. "He has to be watched," she said. "He'll just fool away his time. He'll steal, too, if he gets the chance. He likes to go through the pockets in the coatroom." Nevertheless, she was quite fond of him. Everyone, in fact, seemed to like Peewee because he responded so well to affection. He did not appear to be a stupid boy—"childish" would be a more appropriate characterization.[4]

[4] The psychologist who examined him when he was ten and a half years old said, "It was clear that he was not feebleminded. I base this upon his honest and con-

After two years in the first grade he was given a conditional promotion, but second grade work proved to be too much for him and
he was transferred to a special class where he remained. Individual
tutoring by his counselor (twice a week for four months) was given
up, for the boy did not buckle down to work. "I would like to
know how to write when I grow up," he explained to the counselor,
excusing himself. *"But not now! Now,* I want to color. Do you think
I am a good colorer? You can go home and tell your mother you
know a boy who knows how to color." At age nine he had learned
to write his first name but not his last. He hadn't yet learned the
days of the week. When he was 11 years old he was asked a few questions to test his sophistication of the world outside of his own home.

Q. How old is the earth in which we live?
A. Fifteen years.

Q. How far away is the sun?
A. Ten miles.

Q. How many miles around the earth is it?
A. I can't count after 100.

Q. How many people live in the United States?
A. Five thousand.

Q. Which city in this State has the most people?
A. U.S.A.

Q. Name all the states in New England.
A. (He said that he couldn't name any of them.)

Q. What is the date today?
A. (He made an error of 13 years.)

Being of a gentle disposition he was generally affectionate
toward animals. He cried bitterly when he lost his little dog. But
for some strange reason he had shown no liking for rabbits. One
day he went into a neighbor's yard and killed two pet rabbits by

sistent statements about likes and dislikes, his willingness to stick to a repetitious,
mildly intellectual task, his awareness of social norms along with some indications of
a 'moral sense,' plus occasional bits of insight into his own nature. I should estimate
his 'true' I.Q. range as falling between 80 and 90; only severe cultural deprivation,
poor test rapport and affective barriers would drop him below the 80 I.Q. line." His
Binet I.Q. scores at age 6.8, 8.6, and 9.6 were 86, 73, and 75, respectively.

wringing their necks. On another occasion he had killed a chicken, "because," he said, "it pecked at me."

The neighbors were talking. The mother felt ashamed to go out on the street. She knew people were saying, "There goes Peewee's mother. That boy's nuts. Why don't they send him away?" Someone suggested to the father (before the counselor entered the case) that he take the boy to a doctor. He knew about the big psychopathic hospital in Boston for he was once a patient there himself, so he took his son there. His father had so frequently warned him that some day he would be sent away, that Peewee was scared. "Perhaps," he thought, "this is the place where they will lock me up." He decided he wouldn't talk when he sat down in the office of the psychiatrist. The father, who was present at the interview, embarrassed at the boy's silence, shouted at him: "They're going to strap you or tie you in a chair—you better talk!" The psychiatrist attempted to calm the boy's fears but Peewee was determined to keep his silence. A second interview was scheduled, this time without the father, and more cooperation was obtained. The psychiatrist did not think the boy was psychotic but he was immature and had little conception of right and wrong. He showed no emotional reaction to the discussion of his fire-setting habits. Perhaps, the psychiatrist suggested, a better environment under adequate supervision would help. Perhaps it would, but the mother did not want to give up the boy.

She admitted that Peewee had had a poor start in life, but what could she do? She had found it extremely difficult to manage her own life. Her mother had deserted her when she was an infant. A stepmother had brought her up. "I always thought stepmothers were *supposed* to be bad," she said, "mine was anyway." And so she had run away and had found a man who was, at least temporarily, interested in her. After a little girl was born she had married this man, but her unhappiness continued. Shortly after a second child, a girl, was born to them the husband deserted and she had secured a divorce. Soon the man who was to become Peewee's father came into her life. Never able to make a success of anything he undertook, he had drifted from one job to another, finding some release from his worries in the local taverns. Three years after Peewee was born to this couple the mother had married the father, thus legitimizing Peewee. When Peewee was nine the father died of pneumonia. Public funds and loans from friends helped the mother make a new start. She went to work in a factory.

Peewee was poorly supervised. His two older half-sisters (three and six years older than himself) had little time for him. His mother gave him what time she could spare. She tried her best to reason with him. Neither parent had resorted to corporal punishment except on rare occasions. The father had held over the boy's head the constant threat of "reform school," but Peewee had no idea what a reform school was supposed to be. He became very curious about it and he asked whomever he thought would know, even strangers, "What kind of food do they give you there?" "How do they treat you?" "How far away is it?"

The first counselor who visited the mother shortly after Peewee's seventh birthday found the parents eager for help. "My boy is known all over town for his bad behavior," his mother said. The janitor of the apartment, too, was complaining about this child: "The kid's always up to some kind of deviltry and he's a firebug to boot."

In the course of the next six or seven years three counselors explored the possibility of offering Peewee every variety of treatment available to the Study. Physical, psychological, and psychiatric examinations were frequently given. Recreational opportunities were provided, and he was placed on a farm for one summer. Attempts were made to place the boy permanently, but without success. A Catholic home had heard of his reputation as a firebug and would not consider him. A permanent farm placement was not practical, for during a trial placement he had twice set fire to a chicken coop which almost caused disaster. There was, in fact, no place for this child outside of his own home—or a correctional school.

Nothing unusual in respect to health was revealed after five physical examinations, other than the fact that the boy was immature and undersize for his age. Several psychiatric examinations were given. One psychiatrist who saw the boy when he was nine believed that the fire-setting was "only the case of a simple-minded boy who liked to see smoke and flames. There is apparently no deeper motivation." Another psychiatrist who examined the boy three or four years later thought there were difficulties below the surface. "He sets fires, he says, because he doesn't like people. Even now he imagines setting fires to the houses of people he doesn't like —for instance, boys who pick on him. He makes the point he never sets fires when he is feeling good and getting along well with people." Further psychiatric examinations were suggested and plans for psychotherapy were considered. Though seemingly a classic case of pyromania, the psychiatrists, whose calendars were already overcrowded during these war years, were not eager to attempt therapy with a boy who intellectually was probably not able to respond adequately. No psychiatrist, in fact, could be found at that time who would undertake the long and patient therapy that such a difficult case seemed to require.

After the boy returned from the correctional school where he had been sent following the high school fire, he returned home and found that his mother was interested in another man, an Italian widower with seven children of his own. Two months later the couple were married and the children of the two families were thrown together. The household became unmanageable. The new step-brothers and sisters were well behaved, but Peewee was the black sheep of the family. He felt he did not belong in the family. Everyone blamed him when anything happened. Peewee recalled the pleasant time he had had on the farm one summer. He said, "I would like to leave home and live in the country. Maybe if I set another fire they will send me to the country, because the court does that sometimes." He tried to set a fire in a coalyard. He was again apprehended and was returned to the correctional school, not to the farm. There he remained for another year. His behavior there was good and he attempted no fires at the school.

On his return home (his age was then 12 years and three months) life again proved to be unpleasant. The counselor sent him to a summer camp. There he made a poor adjustment, stealing small articles from other campers. He begged to be sent home. He resumed school in the fall but with no success in his studies.

One Sunday he was sent out by his mother to buy a newspaper. He was then 13 years, four months. Joined by another boy he broke into the home of a war veteran who had been collecting guns. They took the guns, explaining later when they were discovered, that they thought they might sell the guns in order to buy a bugle. Peewee told the police he was sorry he caused so much trouble and he begged them not to send him back to the correctional school. "I only done two crimes," he said. Nevertheless, his probation officer returned him to the school, for there seemed to be no alternative.

When the Study came to an end Peewee was still in the correctional school. The Study turned over the case to another agency but seven months after Peewee was released he was again in trouble. One day he decided to stay out of school all day. He went off by himself. He went into a neighbor's barn and found a comfortable place in the hayloft where he could look at some comic books he had taken with him. There he lit a candle which he "happened" to have with him. After he finished reading he left the candle burning close to a pile of loose hay. Shortly after midnight the fire was discovered and considerable damage was done. Peewee again was quite willing to admit his part in this episode. After an examination by the state psychiatrist he was taken to court and committed to a state defective delinquent colony where he will probably remain for some time, possibly for life.

PETER [5]

Peter holds no grudge against his father. "He didn't beat me very hard," the boy said. "I got only what I deserved. He just beat me like any father beats his kid when he is bad but I guess it didn't do me any good." Peter never got very well acquainted with his father. When Peter was a baby his father concluded that ten years of married life was enough. He had decided to live apart from his family—to be free and independent of his wife and four children, yet he always kept in touch with them and was generally on call if his children were in trouble. He seemed to show a real interest in Peter only when the boy was "acting up"; otherwise he was quite indifferent.

But Peter still holds vivid memories of certain occasions when his father, called home by his mother, would deal out stern punishment

---

[5] Negro boy. Birthplace of parents: U.S. Siblings: Two older sisters, one older brother. Health: Good. Intelligence: Borderline. Religion: Protestant. Neighborhood rating: +2. Delinquency prognosis: —2 at age 11 years, 1 month. Age when treatment started: 11 years, 6 months; when treatment ended: 15 years, 11 months. Number of counselors: One.

to the children who had been "bad" during his absence. After administering the beatings, he would again disappear, though he continued to live in the neighborhood.

Those who knew Peter's father said he wasn't a bad sort. He was a fluent talker and a person of some intelligence. There was a marked resemblance between Peter and his father in features and in general body-build. One got the impression that the father was self-centered and a difficult person to get along with. He wasn't particularly interested in beating the boy, the mother said. "He just wasn't interested one way or the other." He was a good worker and held his job as a truck driver for many years, continuing his sporadic support of the family. "I have kept on friendly terms with him," his wife said, "for the children's sake. The boys stay with him in the summer while I go to work."

The four children were denied parental supervision during the daytime. The mother had to work in order to provide enough food for the growing children. She took in a boarder, too, after her husband left—a man about her own age who sometimes substituted for the father as a disciplinarian in the home. She was a pleasant, friendly, but unhappy woman, burdened and harassed by her many responsibilities. She had provided her children with a clean, comfortable home and had worked hard to supply them with a few comforts and adequate food. She prayed for them and "just hoped for the best." She could not understand why Peter and his older brother always seemed to be getting into trouble. She thought that a little beating now and then by herself or an occasional whipping with a leather strap wielded by the husky father would cure them of their "wildness."

Peter had been free to roam around by himself ever since he was three. During the day some kindly neighbor was usually willing to look after him; if not, his two sisters (who were 14 and 15 years old when Peter was three) were entrusted with this responsibility. Peter's brother, three years older, sometimes took a hand, but Peter couldn't stand his "bossiness." He refused to submit to his dictation and constant quarrels over the years prevented any strong tie between these two boys.

Peter had no deep affection for anyone. He had no close friends. His habit of accusing his friends whenever he was suspected of stealing and his fondness for "bullying" the younger kids may have accounted for his unpopularity. Toward his father he alternated between anger and admiration. The counselor who spent a good deal of time with Peter said, "He does not seem capable of any real depth of feeling. He is unimpressed alike by the court, by the probation officer, by the school teachers and the father's whipping. . . . As long as you are not trying to make him change his ways or do something which he does not want to do, the youngster (then 12 years old) is an extremely friendly chap and quite likeable indeed. He seems to be rather fond of me and wants to please me, but that desire to please is not deep-rooted and I have no real hold on the boy."

Very early in life Peter learned that he could avoid doing things that he didn't like doing. He found as he grew older that he could skip school occasionally and stay out late at night and get away with it. "You know, I never did mind my mother," Peter said later, "if I wanted to go out I just went out. I used to go out a lot at night." His mother observed sorrowfully, "Peter likes his own way in things." She didn't feel that she could do much about disciplining him. She came home very tired from a day's work. She liked to sit down in the evening and talk with her boys but she admitted that such opportunities were rare. "Many a time I didn't see Peter for days at a time except to look in at him when he was asleep," she said. She was worried about the poor reports from school describing Peter as "a very restless, talkative boy (then in the fourth grade); very untidy and careless in everything he does. He is a leader among the boys but teases and quarrels with them. He has never finished anything without constant supervision." During the next school year his behavior had not improved. The teacher remarked, "The other children are a bit afraid of him. He is the captain of the baseball team and he usually has two whacks at bat to their one because they give in to him. He is quite a fighter. They give in to him in almost everything. He has been bothering some of the smaller children outside after school and they come back to me terrified, saying that Peter is going to give them a licking. He has formed a colored clique in my room, something that did not exist before. One day he brought me a gift which I think he must have stolen."

When Peter was 11, his teacher was impressed with his vivid imagination. She said that if they talked about South America in school, Peter would claim that his father had been there and had brought back all sorts of interesting things. If the teacher mentioned New York City, Peter would pop up with the contribution that he had been to that city and he would offer to tell the class about it. The counselor discovered this same tendency when he took Peter on trips with other boys. "You could not mention any incident or point out an object," the counselor said, "without Peter having had some very exciting experience connected with it. We passed a half-smashed boat in the Charles River which had been wrecked during the hurricane. At the sight of this Peter told the most colorful story of how he had been there when the boat was sinking with four or five little boys on board and of how he and another boy had thrown them a rope and had helped to save them. . . . It did not seem to bother him later in our trip, however, to tell several other stories of where he had been during the hurricane."

Peter loved action. He was healthy, well-built, dynamic. "He had a mind of his own," his older sister said, "and he wouldn't do what we told him to. He was always hanging around with the worst crowd and half the time we didn't know where he was. He never liked school. I think this was because he was too active, always on the move, always looking for excitement and adventure. He loved things that were risky. If he went swimming with the boys, he wanted to dive from the highest place. He would come home with tall stories of how he did this and that, and he was always the hero."

His numerous minor exploits of truancy and stealing preceded his first serious offense at the age of 11 and a half. One evening he broke into the school building to pick up a bicycle that he had seen there. Failing to find the object of his search, he went directly to the headmaster's office and there got his "revenge." (The headmaster had frequently given Peter a "bad" report to take home.) Peter upset the desk, mussed up the papers and then his eyes fastened on the small school radio. Tucking the radio under his arm he sneaked out of the building. The next day he was at once suspected and questioned by the police. He admitted the theft with a boastful air but refused to tell what he had done with the radio. The "cops" couldn't make him tell. He enjoyed being driven off in the police car, observed by the other children. "He is basking and glorying in the attention that he is receiving from the police," the teacher said, "and is not worried about the situation at all." The court placed him on probation with the condition that he make restitution. When he failed to do so, the school principal demanded that the court take further action. "The boy should be sent away— that's what reform schools are for—kids like him."

At this point the counselor from the Study entered the picture, a little late, but the school authorities hoped it was not too late to curb the boy's antisocial tendencies. The counselor was readily accepted by the family. The mother always "went to pieces" when Peter got into trouble and she was grateful for outside help. The police, too, welcomed any assistance that could be given. They characterized Peter as a "lying, mean kid with whom you can't do a darn thing." He bragged about his exploits but generally whined and cried when the officers got tough.

The counselor, realizing that Peter was at a crisis in his life, sought to coordinate the work of the schools and the court. The schoolmaster said that Peter was not a dull student. He was doing passing work but he was a "real nuisance." He would beat up little white boys, pushing them into the bushes and spitting on them. Sometimes he used his knife and he cut one little boy "rather badly." To the counselor the most glaring problem was the lack of home supervision. The schoolmaster said something would have to be done about his increasing truancy. If the parents could not discipline Peter then someone else must use a strong hand. The court, on the recommendation of the counselor and the probation officer, sent him to a temporary home in another city, where Peter seemed to do well. He said he was glad to get away from his home town to a city "where they don't know me at all, where they're not always blaming things on me." Now for the first time he openly expressed resentment against his parents. His father, he said, had been beating him again after hearing about the theft of the radio. His mother, Peter said, was always going away and leaving him. Others were "picking on him" because he was a Negro. He began to feel sorry for himself.

The best solution the father could think of was to send the boy far away. "Why not send him to some school in the South?" he said. "I tell you, that boy is driving me crazy. He steals money from me and from the people upstairs. I tell you, Mr. D., I'm scared I'm going to kill him some day. I whip him and whip him and whip him and the harder I whip him, the less effect it has and some day I'm going to whip him so hard I'll kill the boy."

After the boy returned from a summer camp in his 12th year, a child-placement agency was consulted. The mother at that time was seriously ill and the father was determined on a plan for getting Peter out of town where he would not cause him any further embarrassment. "Send him away," he said. "I can't manage him any more. Send him anywhere. I'll try to pay for it." The placement agency arranged for a foster home. During the next few years Peter was shifted from one foster home to another, changing schools at each new placement. At each school he got into new difficulties with the teachers and the principal; teasing, bullying and stealing became more and more habitual with him. As he grew older and stronger he became more surly and assaultive. Strict discipline was applied, and in one school corporal punishment was administered. Again the school took the logical course. The boy was unmanageable because he had been allowed to "get away with it"; therefore he should be more strictly dealt with.

In one school the principal declared he was "fed up with the policy of punishing other students but not punishing Peter." Peter's foster mother had insisted that Peter should not be punished because he was "nervous." The case worker (from the agency that placed Peter under the care of this foster mother) intervened in the argument and assured the principal that Peter should not be treated differently and should never be excused from *just* punishment. The principal, thereupon, summoned Peter to the office and pronounced this judgment upon him; "Now I'm going to punish you for what you have done in the past few months!" At this school Peter had been accused of nothing more serious than a series of minor incidents such as talking without permission, humming in class, and annoying the teacher in many little ways. On the other hand, he was active in the Scouts, was singing in the church choir, and was in other respects generally well behaved. He received this pronouncement with surprise but said nothing. The principal proceeded to give him a good beating on the hand with a ruler, hitting him so vigorously that the teacher who was present intervened. The principal replied to the teacher, "I want to beat this boy until he cries, so the other children will see that I'm playing no favorites. I'm running this school and I don't need any advice from the mothers." When Peter went home that day he talked about "getting even" but his foster mother calmed him down. She believed that this school had a reputation for being anti-Negro and she didn't know what she could do about it. Peter now felt sure he was being "picked on" and he threatened to run away. He truanted a few times but eventually fell into line.

For the balance of the school year Peter's behavior seemed to follow a cycle from bad to good and back to bad again. The case worker from the child-placing agency had many heart-to-heart talks with him and devoted much time to Peter's problems, attempting to keep him from doing anything drastic.

About a year later Peter, rebelling against any authoritative approach, suddenly disappeared. He was then 15 years old but he looked more mature. For about two years he dropped out of sight. He was on his own and no special effort was made to locate him. When he returned during his 17th year from his travels around the country he had learned something about the way a Negro is treated in the South. He had developed a fondness for alcohol and he learned, too, from hanging around the taverns, that a drunkard is an easy victim. From this time on he was involved in one offense after another, rolling drunks or robbing them on the street. He met two other boys who joined him in these exciting adventures. "We did a lot of stealing," he admitted. Then one day an almost fatal assault with a knife on a protesting victim landed Peter in a state prison for a long period of years. He is there now, and in the same prison with his older brother, who is also serving a long sentence for an assault with a dangerous weapon.

WILBUR [6]

"Where is my daddy?" Wilbur asked when he was seven. "Never mind your daddy," his mother replied sharply, "he's in jail now

[6] White boy. Birthplace of parents: U.S. Siblings: One older sister and one younger brother, four step-siblings. Health: Good. Intelligence: Average. Religion: Protestant. Neighborhood rating: —5. Delinquency prognosis: —3 at age 9 years, 3 months. Age when treatment started: 10 years, 6 months; when treatment ended: 17. Number of counselors: Six.

[for non-support]. He's no damned good! And you're going to jail, too, if you keep on snitching from my pocketbook. You're too damned fresh. I'm going to get married next year and you'll have a new daddy and he'll see that you cut out your foolishness." "But why do I have a new daddy?" Wilbur asked. "You're too smart," his mother snapped. "Now mind your own business!"

His mother could not bring herself to tell him the truth. She saw no point in telling him of the hard struggle that she had had in a family of nine children; how *her* father had been abusive; how he had deserted his family and had been brought into court for non-support; how she had never gotten beyond the third grade, for her family "were never much interested in educating her"; how she met a man when she was 14 and had her first baby, a little girl who is Wilbur's older sister; how three years later Wilbur was born and two years after that another boy. The father of these children was then in jail for non-support. He had promised the judge to marry the mother but she didn't care if he didn't keep his promise. She was now going to marry someone else anyway and she thought that was all Wilbur need know.

Wilbur's new father didn't like Wilbur. He thought it wasn't so bad for the boy to steal from his mother but when ten-year-old Wilbur began stealing money from neighbors that was too much. Wilbur's mother did not share this hostility toward her boy, although she announced to the social worker who visited the home (when Wilbur was nine years old), and in the boy's presence, that he was a "bad boy," saying, "I have had more trouble with him than anyone else." At other times she defended the boy, saying he was "really a good kid." Her most bitter arguments with her husband were over Wilbur. She did not think it was right to beat him so often. "After all," she said, "he's a wonderful child—except for stealing."

The stepfather told Wilbur that he was a "bastard" and explained the meaning of the word to him. He made him feel ashamed. The continued beatings of the boy together with the drinking on the part of both parents had been brought to the attention of a social agency when Wilbur was eight. The agency's representative reported that the boy's face was bruised by a blow given by his drunken stepfather. The mother said the stepfather abused the child even when he was sober and she had frequently sent the boy over to her sister's house that he might escape further punishment. The social worker did not know what to do. The case was referred to a placement agency. The agency refused to accept the case and referred it to a home for children. They, too, rejected the case, saying it was not the type they could do much for.

When he was nine and a half, Wilbur was sent to a guidance clinic. There foster-home placement was recommended but no home or institution could be found that would accept him, for by that time he was known as a particularly difficult "problem child." The record read, "Eats and sleeps poorly, slight lisp. Is a behavior problem in school. Likes to be out of the house."

The boy did not like school. He was a frequent truant, the teacher said, "for no adequate reason." At least he couldn't *give* an adequate reason. There seemed to be no alternative, and the child was taken to court by the attendance officer on a complaint of truancy and was immediately sent to a county training school where he remained under close supervision for almost *four* years. The mother did not protest. She had told the teacher the boy should be sent to a reform school as she could not control him.

The counselor from the Study did not enter the case until after Wilbur had been sent to the training school. After gaining the co-operation of the boy's mother the counselor made a visit to the institution. He introduced himself but the boy did not respond with friendliness. The boy's aunt, with whom he had spent many a day as a refugee from his own home, had remarked upon the "peculiar" behavior of the boy. "There's one strange thing about him," she said, "in all the years that he had been at my house he has never showed any affection toward me. He has never kissed me goodnight as my own children would. He just wouldn't respond—I never understood why. . . . I always blamed his mother for his trouble. She didn't want him from the minute he was born and her second husband didn't want a thing to do with him."

The counselor found him to be a sullen child. He did not want to talk. As the years wore on there seemed to be little change in the boy in this respect. He seldom unburdened himself to strangers and it was difficult, even for one who knew him well, to stimulate any conversation concerning himself. He seemed to have no close friends. Various counselors reported the boy as morose, brooding, and suspicious. One counselor admitted that he was never really accepted by the boy as a friend. As he phrased it, Wilbur was becoming "more hardened, more skillful in parrying blows to his ego and more capable of sublimating his desires for affection." Another counselor, trying his best to get the boy's confidence, wrote, "The boy is very much locked up inside and does not seem able to trust anyone." He was tight-lipped, independent. He characteristically rejected specific offers of help. It was difficult for him to accept kindnesses or to thank one for offering assistance. He became independent and did not take part in cooperative ventures with friends. He failed to attend his sister's wedding: "I just forgot," he explained.

If Wilbur thought that by being taken out of his home and placed under the supervision of the officials at the school he would be protected from physical beatings, he was sadly mistaken. During the three years and ten months of his stay there he developed an intense hatred for the cottage master and the superintendent, both of whom used to beat him, he said, quite frequently. When visited by his counselor he was just recovering from a bloody nose, which he claimed had been caused by a blow from the big fist of the cottage master. "How often are you beaten?" he was asked. "About five times a week," he said. "I'm not beaten any more than the other boys. The master uses a large stick and hits us on the hands but sometimes he uses his fists. We're not allowed to fool at the table. We can't talk much to each other and we must always do what we're told."

Wilbur exhibited a streak of stubbornness while at the school. His conduct report was "Unsatisfactory." That's one reason why he stayed so long, he said, for release depended upon good behavior. Only the boy who did just as he was told would get the coveted award—release.

The mother found it difficult to make the long trip to the training school and visited him only twice in four years. She knew that if she brought the boy home there would be continued fights with his stepfather. She wished that he could be placed in a good home but she said, "I know a private family couldn't control him and then there would be more trouble." Wilbur was always hoping that some day he might go back to his true father, but when released from jail the father returned to his alcoholic habits and finally was swallowed up by the Army.

Wilbur gave up caring about keeping up his family ties. His mother said, "He doesn't talk much or particularly care whether we visit him." On his release from the training school he returned home but shifted back and forth between his own home and that of his mother's sister. School failures, truancy, petty stealing, gambling, drinking, and loafing characterized the next few years. A short spell of Army life was marked by time spent in disciplinary barracks for minor infractions. On discharge he managed to hold a few odd jobs but not for long. Everything he had ever undertaken seemed to end in failure. At age 18 years, 6 months, he was again arrested for burglary. Another criminal career is well on its way.

TONY [7]

Tony's father said proudly that his boy was "the darndest chisler and the smartest of the lot." He had started stealing in his seventh year, or possibly earlier, taking little things from stores or "clipping" watches, pens, or trinkets wherever he could find them, even from his friends. Usually he got away with it. He always worked alone and he was pretty shrewd about it. When caught he would deny it for a time but when he saw that he could not divert the blame to someone else he usually said he stole "to help my mother as she needs the money."

Tony was his father's favorite. He was spared the severe discipline administered to the others for he had never been a husky child. He had developed chorea when he was ten and spent six weeks in the hospital and, in later years, many weeks in various convalescent homes. The father said, "I don't beat him on account of his health. I'd probably kill him if I started giving him a beating."

The father was an interesting young fellow, bright and resourceful, with unusual skill for mechanical things. He had held a number

---

[7] White boy. Birthplace of parents: U.S. Siblings: One older sister, one older brother, two younger sisters, three younger brothers. Health: Fair. Intelligence: Average. Religion: Catholic. Neighborhood rating: —5. Delinquency prognosis: —2 at age 8 years, 9 months. Age when treatment started: 9 years, 3 months; when treatment ended: 16. Number of counselors: Three.

of highly technical jobs but was frequently laid off from work. Sometimes he had to quit because of a recurrence of an old T.B. condition; at other times he was laid off because he couldn't get along with his fellow workers. He was self-centered in the extreme, contentious and cynical. He lived his own life and even though the large family was very crowded in four dingy rooms the father had set aside one entire room for himself in which he could tinker with his mechanical "inventions." As a child he, too, had been a delinquent and most of his brothers and sisters in a very large family had had criminal records for stealing or assault. He also had been charged with assault and his wife had called the police on more than one occasion when he gave her a beating. She had no respect for him and there was constant quarreling within the home. He made no attempt to conceal the fact that there were plenty of other women in his life. Tony knew about all this and openly expressed hostility to his father.

At times the family was well able to take care of itself; at other times they depended upon public welfare agencies. No one knew when the father was going to give up his job and take a long "vacation." The family was constantly moving about but always lived in the worst neighborhoods. Most of Tony's cousins who lived near by were delinquent too but they were not as smart as Tony. Tony could steal for weeks at a time without being caught.

Tony's mother was long-suffering and devoted to her children. He gave her the most trouble. She knew of no way to stop his stealing. "Tony just looks at you," she complained, "and he lies and he grins and nothing you say or do seems to have any effect." When Tony was 11 she said in a letter to a foster home: "You see, he has gotten away with so much stealing before I knew about it. I guess it would be hard to break him of it, if it can be done at all. I was always expecting a police officer at my door because of his stealing. He is quite easy to get around in a way, but if you try to make him do things he pouts and sulks and cries. He complains about his head hurting him. He seems to think it is the sun that gives him headaches and his stomach bothers him a lot. I have tried over and over again to figure it out and the closest I get is he must have a very nervous system. He gives me the opinion that he worries a lot, about what, I can't seem to grasp." She didn't have a great deal of time to spend with Tony because she had to take over most of the burden of caring for the children, as the father usually had his own interests. She was worn out by years of continuous poverty and almost yearly child-bearing. (In 12 years of marriage she had ten pregnancies—two of the children died.) She had married very young and looked ten years older than her years.

Everyone who knew Tony said he was a likeable, attractive youngster, bright and "as clever a thief as one would want to meet." In school he was not particularly a problem to the teacher, though she was aware of his stealing propensities. Teachers found him at times to be self-centered and independent and they knew he truanted when he felt like it, but he was bright enough to do his schoolwork. He failed of promotion only one year.

His petty stealing on every possible occasion led one to believe that it was almost compulsive with him. Tony explained how he operated. "I started out pretty small. I would pick up an ashtray and then it got to big things. I was pretty good at it. I used to walk over and look at it—the next thing I knew—you know, it was gone. They'd fish me and couldn't find it because it was up my sleeve. . . . I think it's all the parents' fault. The parents ought to give the kids money to take care of them. The kids shouldn't have to go out and steal for it."

A long-continued series of psychiatric interviews disclosed a very neurotic child, full of guilt and fears. He told the psychiatrist that he hated his father and he was continually afraid he was going to lose his mother's love. He had a great deal of hostility toward his siblings. He retained many of his childish ways and was unabashed about sucking his thumb in public, even at age 11. He had an abnormally strong desire for approval. He was moody in the extreme and showed little affection for anyone.

He developed a relatively strong friendship for his counselor, who spent a great deal of time with him. "I like him best in the world!" he said to another staff member. He also became attached to the psychiatrist though this attachment alternated with periods of anger. To retain the friendship of these people he was constantly promising to give up stealing. He would say, "I won't steal any more. I can stop. I did stop this summer." But he couldn't seem to resist for long the opportunities confronting him. He would even

steal from the psychiatrist's office or from the medical center where
he was receiving treatment for his chorea.

From the point of view of the police, commitment to correctional school was inevitable for this child, and he was sent there at
the age of 12 years, 10 months. He was paroled within a year but
the record shows he was not cured of his habit of taking property
whenever he was so moved. He claimed he did not plan his thefts
any more. "I don't know why I steal," he said, "my fingers run away
with me. A guy's a sucker to leave money hanging around. It takes
a lot of courage to get away with stealing. Ya gotta be smart—it's
exciting!" Truanting and disobedience at home led to a recommit-
ment following several beatings by his father. He didn't like the
restricted life at the correctional school. He showed his dislike by
running away on four different occasions. Each time he was caught
and returned.

At the age of 16 years and 2 months he was released into the community. The war and the commitments to the correctional school
interfered with psychiatric treatment for Tony and shortly thereafter the last counselor assigned to him wrote, "I believe that Tony
is definitely headed for a criminal career." Nothing further is
known of the boy except that within a few months he had signed up
for three years in the Army.

DOMINIC [8]

Neither his second grade teacher nor his counselor, who became
acquainted with Dominic at the age of ten, thought that he was
going to be a delinquent boy. He lacked aggressiveness. He was
quiet and shy. No one knew him very well. "He is not the kind," his
counselor said, "to snuggle up to a social worker and tell his inner-
most thoughts." A dull, fearful child who seemed to want to make
friends but didn't quite know how. It was obvious that he was underweight and that his teeth had been badly neglected, but in other
respects he seemed to be a fairly healthy boy.

No one, least of all the boy himself, understood the pressures that

[8] White boy. Birthplace of parents: Italy. Siblings: One older sister, one younger
sister, three younger brothers, ten step-siblings. Health: Good. Intelligence: Borderline. Religion: Catholic. Neighborhood rating: —4. Delinquency prognosis: —2 at
age 10. Age when treatment started: 10 years, 7 months; when treatment ended: 17.
Number of counselors: Four.

were brought to bear on Dominic. No one had much time for him. He was the second of six children of Italian-born parents. Each parent had been previously married and Dominic had ten step-brothers and sisters. Three of them had been involved in criminal activities. Most of the older stepchildren had left the home by the time Dominic was born. The father's income was meager, but the children had adequate food and clothing, for the older ones were working and helped to support the family. The home, located in a delinquency area, was overcrowded, though clean and fairly com-fortably furnished.

Of the younger children Dominic was the only one to give the family any concern. "I worry all the time," his mother said. She had not been well since her first husband died. She was very tired. "I've had too many children," she said, for in addition to being step-mother to four she had twelve of her own. She complained of nerv-ousness and severe headaches and sometimes suffered from vertigo.

His parents did not understand why Dominic did not like to go to school. The father thought that the school was too easy with him. "All I ask for my boy," he said, "is for a teacher who will hit him if he does wrong. Boys get away with too much these days." After two years in the first grade and two in the third Dominic at age 11 was promoted to the fourth grade but was scarcely able to do the work required of the smaller children in his class. The bright little boys in his room made him mad. "See, you dummy," his mother shouted at him, "you got to go to the special class," and Dominic went to special class. But some days he just wouldn't go to school at all. He wandered around the streets by himself. Sometimes he went with a gang of boys who were well known to the police and who were con-stantly being watched. His family knew about his truanting. The father said that beating the boy didn't seem to help. Sometimes he said he felt sick after beating the boy because the lad was such a frail-looking youngster. He hated to do it but he knew no other way of punishing him. Everyone had been too easy with Dominic, he thought. Once the father tied him to a bedpost. Dominic got a good beating that time but he kept on truanting and continued his petty stealing. He remained the black sheep among the younger children of the family. The Catholic sister in the parochial school said it was necessary to "break the child's will." She punished him almost daily. She made him kneel down and ask forgiveness and she lectured him frequently in the presence of the other children. Dominic didn't like this treatment. "The teachers pick on me all the time," he said.

An unhappy child, he had no sense of achievement or of being appreciated by others. In fact, he had little respect for himself. Everyone said he was dumb and he could not deny it—he didn't even try. The school's harshness and the duplication of the family pattern of rejection and punishment was alleviated somewhat by periods of truanting. Willfulness and stubbornness at home were followed by slyness and petty stealing in a neighborhood where such things brought some rewards.

At 18, Dominic is confined in a tiny cell behind steel bars in a "house of correction." He is sitting at a little iron table and slowly writing out in his immature handwriting a letter to a former counselor. "I can see now that I have made a serious mistake against society and the people of my family," he writes. "I am writing this letter in hopes you can help me get back to my family. I would be most grateful for anything you can do to help me get released from this institution. I was sentenced for a period of six months [for stealing]. I will be waiting to hear from you soon. Thank you very much. Respectfully yours, Dominic."

BERNARD [9]

Bernard's Polish-born parents were kindly, plodding, respectable people whose five other children were well behaved. The only reason they could give for Bernard's waywardness was that he was influenced by the "bad" boys in the neighborhood, one of the poorest sections of the city. The probation officer, the teachers, and the counselor from the Study agreed that Bernard was dominated by "a gang of thieves." Most of those who knew Bernard believed that if he had been brought up in a better neighborhood he might not have gotten into trouble at all. Bernard, too, was aware of these influences. He said, "They come and call for me and when I get with

[9] White boy. Birthplace of parents: Poland. Siblings: Two older sisters, two older brothers, one younger brother. Health: Fair. Intelligence: Average. Religion: Catholic. Neighborhood rating: −5. Delinquency prognosis: −2 at age 9 years, 6 months. Age when treatment started: 10 years, 4 months; when treatment ended: 17. Number of counselors: Two.

them we get doing things. That's the trouble—no matter who I play with people say they're the wrong kids. What am I going to do?"

Bernard was a shy, slender child, obviously underweight and noticeably lacking in energy. He found little satisfaction anywhere. His home consisted of a little "flat" in a three-family dwelling. It was crowded, dark, and poorly furnished. "A feeling of hopelessness seems to hang over this family group," wrote the counselor when the boy was 11. "There's no spontaneity, no laughter there." Bernard's father was an honest, hard-working man but rather ineffectual. He was an unskilled laborer, frequently out of work. During the time of his unemployment Bernard's mother had to take on odd jobs and at the same time do the housework for her family of eight. She showed an interest in Bernard and some affection, but admitted she did not understand him or know how to control him when he wished to stay out on the streets at night. In spite of punishments by the parents Bernard insisted on choosing his own friends. "He always chooses the bad boys," the mother said. She remained a stranger to a good part of the American culture in which the boy was growing up and never learned to speak English well enough to get along without the help of the older children as interpreters. She asked Bernard's older brother to keep him in line. Bernard resented the frequent cuffings the brother gave him.

Bernard found no satisfaction in his schoolwork. Though of average intelligence he had to repeat the second grade. The teacher thought he was lazy and just didn't care. "A definite lack of interest," she said. When school became too uncomfortable for him he would fall asleep in his seat. "I think he lacks ambition," his second grade teacher said. "On some occasions too I would question his honesty (cheating in spelling and that sort of thing) but when he is caught he seems genuinely sorry."

Bernard was a sickly looking child and always felt inferior about his puny physique. When he was asked (at age 14) "If you could not be yourself, what three persons would you rather be?" he replied, "First, the president; second, a movie star; and third, somebody popular." He also said he would "like to be a hero," but he admitted to his counselor that he often wished he had never been born. The only enjoyment he got was in the company of the tougher boys in the neighborhood. Because of his delicate appearance and his timidity he was never accepted as a leader but he was a ready follower and he was well liked by the other boys.

The counselor did much to improve the boy's health, trying to overcome his "marked lassitude and easy fatigability." He was taken to physicians and medical clinics, but no physical basis could be found for his sickly appearance. He was provided with some recreational opportunities. He was sent to camp. He was given special individual tutoring for a long period of time. He improved in his schoolwork and he enjoyed the friendship of an older person. He promised his counselor he would break off his delinquent activities. "Bobby" (a well-known delinquent in that neighborhood) "is always trying to get the kids to do something like break into a bakery," Bernard said to his counselor, "but I ain't going to do it."

The counselor had many long talks with the boy, trying to persuade him to get to bed early, to pay more attention to his work, and to keep away from the delinquent gangs. Bernard tried his best to please his counselor, who was genuinely fond of him. He said to the boy when he heard that he was getting into some difficulty (Bernard was then about 14), "Bernie, in my book you've always been a darn good kid. I know from the past several times when the other kids were all getting into trouble you were always the one who backed out and got away from that trouble. I always counted on you in that way, Bernard, and I was always proud of you and felt happy about it. I guess you know that I felt that way. Now look, Bernard, I've heard some things about you getting mixed up with the Caruso kids and young Conti and stealing from the trucks." At this point Bernard interrupted the talk by crying and trying to say in his faint little voice that he had been stealing but he didn't know why he did it and he promised that he would not do it again. "You know I won't," he said with earnestness. The counselor added that the boy seemed so penitent and sincere that he was utterly convinced that he wouldn't steal again after this talk.

The teacher, too, had a talk with the boy. She said, "You know, Bernard, Mr. D. has really put you on a pedestal. He thinks you're a wonderful boy and I don't know how he will feel if he hears about you truanting." The boy broke into tears, visibly affected by the thought that he was not being fair to his counselor.

The counselor felt reassured and began to see Bernard at less frequent intervals. Bernard returned to his old haunts and his old companions. "They came calling for me again," he said, "and I went with them and before I knew it we were in it again. I could have stopped—they didn't make me do it—but when they asked me, somehow I just went ahead with them."

For about six months following his 14th birthday he was involved in a series of larcenies and store breaks. Finally the law caught up with him. As he sat in the visiting room of the correctional school, to which the judge had promptly committed him, he said, "I kept out of trouble when he [the counselor] was around." He felt genuinely remorseful about his confinement. The correctional officer described him as "an awfully weak stick." "I don't know when I've seen a boy cry so much on coming up here," he commented. "He's been slobbering all over the place."

The counselor visited him at the correctional school. Bernard renewed his crying, realizing that he had let his friend down, and he reassured him that he would not be led into this trouble again. When the counselor left the Study shortly after this interview he was again confident that Bernard would keep out of trouble. His prediction might have come true if he had continued his association with the boy, but the necessity of assigning a new counselor, a stranger to the boy, destroyed the continuity of treatment.

For quite a long time Bernard kept out of trouble, but around his 16th birthday he and another boy committed a series of slightly more sophisticated crimes. They broke into five garages, stealing various items from cars, and even siphoning gasoline which they were able to sell. For these offenses he was sent to another correctional school, where again he was repentant and vowed he would never get into trouble again.

Later, at age 18 years, 4 months, reflecting upon his brief career in crime, he said, "I had nothing to do. That's why I got into trouble. Hanging around the corner—no place to go—wanting to go to a lot of places but I didn't have any money so we used to clip things. But I straighened out. I've decided to work for my money now." Apparently he meant it.

NORMAN [10]

Norman's father was a God-fearing man. On Sundays, putting aside his work clothes, he would occupy the pulpit of the church and as lay preacher give forthright warnings of the punishments awaiting those who fail to keep the Ten Commandments. His strong religious views had a harsh and uncompromising quality. He ruled over his family with a firm hand. By virtue of his own intelligence and industry he had earned the respect of his neighbors and his employers. He had one cross that was hard to bear—two of his boys would not toe the mark. Norman, the youngest, particularly was a thorn in his side, flouting the Fifth Commandment—"Honor thy father and thy mother." Any child who cast a shadow of sin over this deeply religious family felt the stern hand of this minister of God laid upon him. Norman experienced this hard fact early in life, very early according to his mother. In listening to the mother's story of Norman's first lesson in obedience and respect one could understand why his mother, a kind and intelligent person, was heartbroken over this child. "My husband," she said, "has always been a stern man, a hard man. He always whipped the boys all the time they were growing up, particularly Norman. One time I'll never forget as long as I live and I'll never forgive him for it. When Norman was a little baby—just two years old, toddling around—we lived in an old house with the window sill down close to the ground. Baby Norman came along and put a little pile of sand on the window sill outside. My husband was sitting down reading inside the house near the window. He yelled, jumped from his chair, and ran out and pulled that little baby in through the door, dragging him along the floor by one arm. Then he got his cat-o-nine-tails that he always had with the wire braided into little knots in the leather strap and then he started whipping that child with all the strength he had. I jumped over to help the baby. I thought my husband had gone crazy. I thought he'd kill the baby. He flung me hard across the floor. I hit the wall. I was hurt a bit and I lay there while he took

---

[10] Negro boy. Birthplace of parents: British West Indies. Siblings: Two older sisters, one younger sister, two older brothers. Health: Good. Intelligence: Average. Religion: Protestant. Neighborhood rating: —3. Delinquency prognosis: —2 at age 10 years, 11 months. Age when treatment started: 11 years, 5 months; when treatment ended: 16 years, 9 months. Number of counselors: One.

a kick at me and kept on whipping that baby. Baby Norman was so hurt he couldn't cry out. I thought he was dead, the blood came and my husband kept whipping. That was fourteen years ago and I can see it just as plain as though it was yesterday."

The paternal whippings continued with terrible regularity as the boy grew older and into adolescence; yet the father was losing the fight for the boy's love and respect. The child's temper tantrums continued with greater violence as Norman grew in stature and strength. This turn of events baffled a father whose own childhood memories were filled with horrible beatings by his father. After all, didn't he grow up to be a man respected in his community? Perhaps beatings were not enough. The father restricted the boy's activities in the home; the playing of marbles was forbidden, no radio was allowed in the home. Sunday mornings and afternoons, church attendance was compulsory for all. One evening a week had to be given to the church. The boy was denied earthly possessions that most boys crave—sled, bike, roller skates—and to make life's burdens a little harder to bear, Norman was not allowed to sell papers or to shine shoes to earn a little spending money. All his friends were earning money this way. His mother said, "I could not blame him for doing it on the sly."

The boy grew up to be "hateful" and "stubborn." This least attractive-looking of six children developed into an awkward adolescent. One finds this description of him shortly after his 15th birthday. "His low brow, his thick, flabby lips, the dangling arms, the glowering countenance all give him an ape-like appearance." During the next year he affected the clothing worn by the zoot-suiters indicative of his membership in a small, informal group of rather troublesome Negro boys of his age who were "looking for trouble, carrying knives, and as often as not, finding the trouble for which they sought."

It seemed strange to the father that this boy of his of average intelligence was so "strong-willed" as to neglect his opportunities for an education. He refused to study. He often ran away from school or just didn't bother to go. He was forced to repeat the first grade and later the fifth. His teacher observed that Norman was "spiteful, cruel, and hardboiled." "He is a peculiar child," his fifth grade teacher said. No one could quite understand him. At times he would be cheerful, respectful, and pleasant. At other times he would strike a mood of sullenness, sustained for a considerable length of time, punctuated by outbreaks of such violence that he was considered a dangerous boy, and soon earned the title of the most disliked boy in the school. "He seems to think," his fifth grade teacher said, "that you are picking on him all the time. On two or three different occasions he has thrown things at me and at different teachers. He has thrown chairs at me and at Mr. W. (the schoolmaster). He is smart enough if he will do the work. He wants to be the boss and do what he feels like. He once threw a music book in my face and in the same tantrum gave me an awful cut with his nails on the back of my arm. . . . He threw a book at the fourth grade teacher. . . . Sometimes he is actually too lazy to put his name on his paper. When I jibed him for this he signed his next paper 'Mr. Nobody.' "

Life at home and in school was frustrating, but there were satisfactions in this neighborhood where opportunities for pleasant companionship appealed to his gregarious nature. "I steal because it is a pleasure," he wrote in his school composition when the topic for the day was "Myself." At the age of 12 he was finding increasing pleasure in breaking into stores. He found his greatest satisfactions in associating with boys whom the police had suspected of much "deviltry." In such a group Norman's courage, his physical strength, and his toughness were highly valued. He became a fighter to be feared. In speaking of Norman, another tough boy in the neighborhood said, "Boy, I sure would hate to tangle with that guy when he's mad. He's plain murder, that's what he is. Little choppy punches." Norman was proud of his own strength. He said, "I do not know why I fight—I just get mad." Though he did not understand his own motivations he had his reasons. "I'm always being picked on because I'm colored—that's the trouble—always picking on me."

At home, his mother said, he received more than his share of the beatings dealt out by the father. The oldest child "was the father's pet," the mother said, "and he got off easy." The next oldest, Wesley, "He got some awful beatings, too.[11] Norman, he was the youngest, but I don't know why he got it so hard and heavy."

By the time a counselor from the Study was sent to see the boy he was 11½ years old and attending the fifth grade in the public

[11] Wesley, too, became a persistent delinquent.

schools where he was considered a "serious problem." There he had a reputation for defiance of authority, for stealing, for fighting, and for temper outbursts expressed with superior physical strength which frightened the teacher. The record states that "he had a remarkable capacity for making people dislike him." From the teacher's point of view this was an understatement. He became the outstanding boy in that school. The master of the school gave up in despair. His final pronouncement was, "A licking will do him a lot of good." The master regretted that the law would not allow him to take matters in his own hands. The teachers, too, said the boy "needs a firm hand." The counselor from the Study thought the boy needed a friend, saying, hopefully, before he actually met the lad, "My friendly and non-clinical interest might just possibly compensate for the father's stern and extremely critical attitude toward the boy."

The treatment program planned and carried through by the counselor was a varied one. He had many heart-to-heart talks with Norman. He took him on sight-seeing trips, sent him to camp in the summers, arranged for a temporary foster-home placement, acted as liaison between the home and the school, the police and the courts. He saw that the boy had adequate physical examinations and he arranged for a special psychiatric study. Throughout the period of treatment, which lasted more than four and a half years, the counselor spent countless hours and much ingenuity in trying to change the boy's attitudes. He had many interviews with the parents and received the warm and sympathetic support of Norman's mother. The boy at times showed great affection for the counselor and once said to him, "You are the only one who is not picking on me." The counselor felt rewarded by the parental cooperation, though the father's sternness was not relaxed. The father, in shaking hands with the counselor, said, "I want to thank you, Mr. D., for all the help you've been with my boy." The boy's good behavior, however, was not long-sustained for he would, for reasons unknown to anyone, suddenly throw off all restraint and break out in assaultive conduct that brought him immediately to the attention of the police. Periods of bad behavior were followed by periods of good behavior with corresponding fluctuations in the hopes and despairs of the counselor. When he was about 13½ Norman was sent to the correctional school for nine months for larceny.

The boy was taken to a child-guidance clinic. The psychiatrist observed that the boy "seems fundamentally and constitutionally to belong to the hyper-irritable, hyper-excitable group as evidenced by his constant activity, nervous irritability, early convulsive episodes, and his temper outbursts, usually assaultive in their character." Intensive, psychoanalytic therapy was recommended in the form of interviews five days a week for an indefinite period of time, but the recommendation proved to be completely impracticable. No therapist was available and the boy probably would not have consented to such a time-consuming program. The diagnosis of the police officer who knew him well was less technical: "He is just a mean little rat!"

By the time the boy had reached the age of 15 years and 8 months, he had acquired an unsavory reputation with the police, the probation officers, the court, and the school authorities. Norman experienced a renewal of his feeling that he was being "picked on." At this time the boy related the story of his encounter with an officer of the police force. He said he was walking along the street, "minding my own business," when the officer, driving up in a car, yelled at him as he passed in front of the car, "Get out of my way you black bastard!" When Norman did not move quickly enough the officer jumped out of the car and punched him in the face. The record states, "Norman returned home, very ugly of mood and the mother had quite a job on her hands to talk him out of retaliation." The mother felt that what the boy needed was love. "I treat my boys with love, Mr. D. I feel that love is the greatest thing in the world and that's what my boys need. I want to give them things, I want them to love me—and you know Norman—he can be sour, mean and hard to get along with, with most anyone else sometimes, but he looks at me sometimes and he smiles so sweet and I know that boy loves me." But his mother's love and the counselor's efforts could not seem to rid this boy of his periodic temper outbursts. The psychiatrist raised the question of some organic or constitutional difficulty, but the neurological examinations were negative. To attribute Norman's behavior to some vague theory of "predisposition" or "constitutional endowment" would not have been unusual in a case of this sort, though it would have added little to our understanding of his motivations.

At this time, along with many other boys, he became involved in a disturbance in a movie house. Four of the boys, including Norman, were arrested, but Norman alone was sent to the correctional school, feeling greatly discriminated against.

This brief biographical sketch closes on a tragic and anticlimactic note. A year and a half after this boy had been released from the correctional school he met with a fatal accident at the age of 17 years, 4 months. The mother commented, "Norman was always a hard-luck boy."

JACK [12]

"Everybody in my neighborhood steals—they're all crooks—that is, all of them but me. I don't steal." Jack uttered this impressive statement when he was a 12-year-old, many pounds underweight, pale and sickly looking. His high, thin voice was in keeping with his paleness and slight build.

Jack's harassed mother told quite a different story. She said Jack had been stealing ever since he was a very small boy and she had to get the police after him herself. When first visited by a social worker from the Study, Jack, at age ten and a half, was the typical "problem child"—disobedient, willful, given to violent temper tantrums accompanied by vulgar expressions. He was fussy about food. In fact, his mother said, "He never wants to eat anything. The only thing he likes is coffee. He never did like vegetables and he refuses them. He is now ten and a half and he wants to stay up late at night. He has been a very sickly child. I can't do anything with him."

Sickness, in fact, had plagued Jack all his young life. He was not a well baby and as an infant of two and a half he was hospitalized for "general debility." From that time on he suffered from colds and

[12] White boy. Father born in U.S.; mother born in Canada. Siblings: One older sister, one older brother, one younger sister, and one younger brother. Health: Poor. Intelligence: Low average. Religion: Protestant. Neighborhood rating: —4. Delinquency prognosis: —3 at age 10 years, 3 months. Age when treatment started: 10 years, 6 months; when treatment ended: 17. Number of counselors: Three.

tonsilitis. During his fourth year he had pneumonia, boils, swollen glands, and chicken pox. At five he was thought to be afflicted with tuberculosis. He looked like a tuberculous child—thin, pale, flat-chested, sickly. Almost every year after that he was given chest X-rays. He spent some time in a sanatorium but a clear diagnosis of tuberculosis was never made. He had whooping cough at seven and at eight was sent to a convalescent home for a short time because of anemia and was readmitted to the home a year later because of mal-nutrition. Bronchitis, pneumonia, and a ruptured appendix fol-lowed in turn. The hospital placed him on the "danger list" and his mother did not know whether he would live to see his 12th birth-day. During adolescence his illnesses continued, the diagnosis gen-erally being pneumonia or bronchitis.

Schoolwork was difficult for this boy of low average intelligence who had missed so many days because of illness. He didn't like school anyway. He stayed out whenever he could. He began to fol-low the path of his older brother, who was constantly being checked by the police. Bikes and other objects in the neighborhood that didn't belong to him had an exciting appeal for him. His mother, never in good health herself, had little energy for the responsibil-ities of caring for her four children. His father was living in another town, for the parents had separated when Jack was five and were divorced seven years later. The father was of little help. He occa-sionally sent money home, as he was able to earn a good living as a technician. He took little interest in Jack and Jack had no love for him. He was described as "a man of black moods, very much embit-tered and sharp-spoken; brutal in his beatings of the wife and chil-dren. The children are deathly afraid of him and they run upstairs to the neighbor's apartment when he does come home from time to time to beat them up."

The mother did not approve of beating the children. Jack was too sickly a child, she thought, to be punished. What could be done with him? She did not know. He was surly, impudent, demanding, and constantly whining for what he wanted. Although overprotec-tive, the mother showed little real affection toward the boy, but she encouraged him in using his illness as a protection against punish-ment by the courts. When he got into trouble she was his strongest defender. She developed bitter hostility toward the police and the probation officers, an attitude shared by the boy, who became cynical and antisocial in his attitudes.

With no strong hand to guide him at home Jack drifted about the city and took part with other delinquent friends in a number of exciting adventures with other people's cars. The adventures finally culminated in his confinement in a correctional school. There his antisocial attitudes were quite evident. He later characterized the school in these words: "They treated you like murderers. They beat you—they handcuffed you—they're no good." Discipline of any kind was annoying to this boy. He couldn't stand living in a school where he was told what to do and what not to do. He soon ran away from the school and joined the Army. "Perhaps the war will make a man of him," his mother said.

BILLY [13]

For many years Billy had been in the habit of shuffling into a store and slyly slipping some coveted object into his pocket. Once he stole a pair of shoes from the home of a friend. He showed little feeling of guilt about his stealing. Even at age 11 and 12 it seemed to him the natural thing to do. "I'd never have nuthin' if I didn't steal," he said. That sentiment was the tragic summary of the situation in which he found himself.

Born into a family where living conditions were at a bare minimum, he had become accustomed to deprivation very early in life. "The filthiest home in Cambridge," a city official had written in the record. "All we get to eat," Billy said, "is stale cake from the bakery and tea or coffee. I like milk but I never get any milk. If we have any my mother has to give it to my baby brothers and sisters. We never sit down to eat. There are not enough chairs." Billy might have added, "There were too many children." At age 13 he had to compete for food with five younger brothers and one older sister and a few years later with two baby sisters. The father, an alcoholic, was not able to provide adequate support, even if he had been steadily employed. He had been seriously ill with pneumonia followed by

---

[13] White boy. Birthplace of parents: U.S. Siblings: One older sister, two younger sisters, five younger brothers. Health: Fair. Intelligence: Average. Religion: Catholic. Neighborhood rating: —4. Delinquency prognosis: —4 at age 10. Age when treatment started: 11 years, 1 month; when treatment ended: 17. Number of counselors: One.

acute laryngitis, when Billy was six years old. A stocky, red-faced, explosive person, he had a belligerent attitude toward the police, the teachers, and the many social workers that visited this family over the years. He complained frequently of shortness of breath and inability to do hard work. He was never a well man during Billy's youth and he died suddenly of a heart attack in Billy's sixteenth year. Billy returned home for the funeral (for he was a runaway at this time) but the mother said, "We couldn't stand him around. He was swearing at everyone and calling us all vile names. No one can do anything with him. He steals and drinks and uses vile language."

Billy was brought up with no knowledge of cleanliness, good manners, or any sound sense of morality or consideration for others. There were no cultural interests in the home. The mother said, "Give me a piece of gum and 'True Stories' and I'm okay." Billy hated his father bitterly. He recalled the days when his father used to hover over him when he was a small boy striving to earn money shining shoes. The father would take the money as fast as the boy earned it and get himself a drink. "My father and mother always beat me [for stealing] and I go out and do it all over again," he said. He found that he could wander around the streets at night and even stay out all night without the family particularly caring. He was then 12. His first court appearance was at the age of eight. When he was ten he had developed a fear of the cops. He said, "They take you away and put a knife in you and kill you."

His mother was an affectionate person, dull and untidy and yet with a warm feeling for her children. Billy, however, did not receive much of her affection, for from the time when he was two years old a baby was born to this family every year or two. The mother didn't have much time for Billy. Billy says, "She never kissed me goodnight. She says I'm so bad and naughty that she wouldn't do anything for me but beat me." She always adored each new baby that came along, spending most of her time with it, neglecting the other children. No doubt Billy was a problem to her. "He tells lies," she complained. "He is stubborn if you try to force him." The psychiatrist's impression was that "a great deal of the boy's difficulty lies in a constitutional, emotional instability." This opinion cast a sort of hopelessness over the treatment plans for Billy. The mother said, "He is so lazy you couldn't even shame him."

Nearly everyone who knew him had the same characterization— "just lazy." The doctor referred to this trait as "a low energy level." His mother said, "I scare him; I offer him pennies; I hit him—but nothing helps. I'd put him away if I thought it would do any good. I hope he can go to camp because I don't want him hanging around all summer." Besides, she pointed out, she had too many children to feed.

The counselor, who did a great deal to bolster the morale of this family, sent Billy off to a farm for the summer where he would get special care. The mother's parting advice to him was, "Don't you dare steal nuthin' and be sure and send me your money." In spite of this explicit advice Billy stole a watch at the farm and the farmer's wife made him go to confession. Billy said that at home he never confesses to the priests "because they might hit you." He finally had to be returned home because he refused to do the farm chores.

Billy wasn't exactly stupid although he certainly gave that impression. Tests showed that his intellectual abilities were within the normal range, but he was almost completely devoid of motivation. From his shuffling gait and hangdog look one could see that nothing particularly mattered to him. He stayed in the first grade for almost four years. He was completely disgusted with school. Some of his teachers were in turn disgusted with him. His mouth open, sometimes drooling, this ungainly, slovenly child presented an unattractive picture. No one was surprised when he truanted and kept on truanting. He was always afraid that the teacher was going to hit him. Fortunately they did not treat him this way, for the father had said, "For every licking he gets in school I'll give him one ten times worse."

The counselor came into his life when Billy was 11 years old. For the first time Billy found out something about cleanliness. He had a chance "to see how the other half lives." He learned something about good food and manners. These new experiences seemed to reinforce his rejection of his family. He realized that his home wasn't a decent place to live in. His hatred of his father increased as the boy became older and his rejection of his mother was quite complete. She said she had tried to reason with him, "but he don't care for nobody. He's a champion liar. Sometimes he sits in a daze as though he don't pay attention."

Several times Billy ran away from home. He was brought into court for being a stubborn child and soon thereafter became involved in a series of delinquencies. He didn't care for life at the correctional school either so he ran away. No one could find him. No one cared particularly whether they found him or not. He was not seen for some time. Later it was learned that he was spending time in a jail in another state—an unfortunate, lonely youth with no training, no ambition, and no friends.

EMIL [14]

The psychiatrist at the guidance clinic who interviewed this boy when he was nine years old and already involved in "a tremendous amount of delinquency—stealing, breaking into the school, truancy, sex affairs, etc.," found "the whole case perfectly clear as far as this boy's upbringing and experiences are concerned. The question put to us is whether the boy shows abnormal characteristics. I feel certain that there is no evidence of this here upon our single examination. Considering his experience and conflicts about them, the phenomena may have been only normal reactions. The boy is living under terrible and immoral conditions."

A visitor from the Study who first went to the home when Emil was six, found him dirty, ragged, cold and hungry. In appearance he was the typical neglected child, with ambling gait, streetwise manner and no childish spontaneity of expression. He didn't make friends easily. Adults considered him a queer boy; sometimes shy, sometimes sulky, with a fixed, tense smile. He was easily given to tears and sometimes he would sob hysterically when talking about his mother who, he feared, didn't love him. At the correctional school where he was committed after a series of thefts he frequently dreamed that his mother had died.

Generally he was silent and withdrawn. He did not care for any of the recreational activities available to children in the city in which he lived. He didn't know how to play. The only one in the family whom he seemed to like was an older brother, Raymond, a

[14] White boy. Father born in Canada; mother born in U.S. Siblings: One older sister, two older brothers, three younger sisters, one younger brother. Health: Fair. Intelligence: Borderline. Religion: Catholic. Neighborhood rating: —4. Delinquency prognosis: —3 at age 8 years, 6 months. Age when treatment started: 8 years, 8 months; when treatment ended: 15 years, 6 months. Number of counselors: Two.

notorious delinquent. His younger brother was a delinquent, too, but the oldest boy was an accomplished thief and a surprisingly good tutor. He taught Emil how to steal and what kind of stealing was serious and liable to end in a sentence to the penitentiary. Once he said to Emil, "It's okay—go ahead and steal. Take the things; it's the only way to get them. Supposin' ya do get caught, they give you a chance, and then another chance, and then probation—then suspended sentence—oh, you can get away with it a whole lot of times. Then suppose they do send you away, so what? It's a swell place. You'll like it. You won't get anything good unless you take it anyway." As a matter of fact, at the correctional school the food and general living conditions were superior to that which his parents could offer him at home.[15]

The police said (when Emil was eight) "both those kids are going around to the stores stealing all sorts of stuff. They take it home and also to the home of a Mrs. ——. We are very, very sure that these women are sending the children out to steal. You can't imagine all the stuff we found in the home. They had stolen dresses, a ski suit, shoes, games, belts, trousers, and other stuff. They used to have a five-year-old girl go around with them. [Emil's mother] had most of the stuff hidden in a closet."

The mother admitted that the boy was continually stealing, though she denied she had any part in it. She said, "When he get out of school he steal more. He make great trouble for me, I betcha. I want to put him away. I want him to go away. I can't do nothing with him." It was not long after this that Emil was sent to the correctional school. His mother was brought into court for contributing to the boy's stealing.

The father stated his point of view: "You can't talk to Emil. You talk—nuthin' happens. He doesn't know what you're talking about. He just look at you and he do what he please. You beat him —it make no difference. You try to make him be good—no matter what you do it doesn't help. What the hell kind of a life is this? Trouble all the time with my kids. [His daughters, too, were getting into difficulties.] Work like hell for $17 a week. [For a family of ten.] Get 40 cents for beer on Saturday; money gone on Monday." Emil

---

[15] Raymond was considered a psychopathic boy if not a pre-psychotic. He is now in the State Prison on a charge of armed robbery.

said the money was generally gone on Saturday and he and his brothers never got any food on that day. The home was always dirty and smelly and the family was charged with neglect when Emil was seven. The father was proud of one thing. "I never stole a cent in my life," he said but he did not mention the fact that he had been in court on four or five different occasions for drunkenness, disturbing the peace, and assault and battery. He worked hard when he was sober. Emil had no use for him; in fact, he said he hated his father and when he thought his parents were going to discipline him he ran away. He frequently remained away from home for long periods.

Taking Emil out of the home was the only "solution" to his problems. Within a period of a few years the boy found himself in seven different foster homes, each time being forced to leave because he was stealing from the foster parents or because his sex activities with other boys in the home were more than they could stand. Emil, in fact, was highly sophisticated in sexual matters, claiming to have had his first sex experience at age nine. The father countenanced the immorality and sometimes he himself would bring immoral women to the home.

When Emil was 14 his mother and father separated and the mother invited the boy to come back from one of the foster homes to stay with her. After three days she said she didn't want him any more and she sent him to his father. The father had little time for Emil and another series of delinquent episodes occurred. Emil was then returned to the correctional school. There he used to cry for his mother. "My mother must be dead," he said to his counselor. "She must be dead! She must be dead!" he sobbed. He was assured that she was alive but he insisted, "I know she's dead. I worry about it all the time. If she isn't dead, why doesn't she come to see me? She doesn't even answer my letters!" Later he wrote to his counselor, "Have you found out if my mother wants me? I hope she dous. I'll do the worke for her. I'll do everything that she wants me to do. I love my mother." But the mother was "too busy" to write or to visit him more than once during his stay at the school and on that occasion the counselor had made the arrangements and urged her to go.

Emil's progress through school was very slow, partly because he was continually changing homes and never was able to get a good start in his schoolwork. Of borderline intelligence, he found the work difficult, but, strangely enough, he was a fairly well-behaved child when he was attending school.

From the age of 12 to 15 if Emil wasn't in a foster home he was usually in the correctional school where he was first committed at the age of 11. He was paroled and returned to the school four times. His last return followed the stealing of a car from the foster home in which he seemed to be making such a good adjustment. In that home everyone was optimistic about him. He was apparently happy there. No one knew exactly why he decided to steal a car from his foster parents and thus "spoil it all." What sort of an adolescent "brainstorm" struck this 15-year-old boy? Up to this time the counselor considered the case a success. His foster mother was very fond of him and thought the boy was happy in her home. She had taught him cooking, gardening and farming and when he stole her car and with two other boys drove it to New York she was heartbroken. The boy was soon apprehended and returned to the correctional school. After his parole he joined the Army.

The last counselor, disillusioned at this turn of events, said, "I have come to believe more and more that this boy is none other than a constitutional psychopathic inferior."

CHAPTER XVI

WHAT MAKES THEM DELINQUENT?

Not all of the homes just described lacked the basic requirements for good standards of health and material care. Yet all of them were inadequate, in most cases deplorably so, in meeting the fundamental psychological needs of the boys for affection and self-esteem. From this handful of cases alone, one is not justified in concluding that all serious delinquents come from homes like these or that all such homes always produce delinquent children. Before attempting any generalizations as to the formation of delinquent patterns of behavior, let us compare some of the homes of the "most delinquent" boys with the homes of those who were delinquent to a lesser degree.

Home Visitors' Ratings of the Homes. As we learned in Chapter IV, visitors went to the home of each boy prior to the beginning of the treatment program to get basic information concerning the boy and his family. The boys were at that time from five to 11 years old. After one or more interviews with the mother or the father each visitor wrote a report briefly summarizing the general conditions of the home as observed by her. The standard of living was rated on the familiar 11-point scale, ranging from −5 through 0 to +5. Homes that were thought by the visitor to be "best able to maintain the highest standard of living from the point of view of health and decency" were rated +5. Homes judged least able to maintain such standards were rated −5. Intermediate ratings were used to indicate standards between these extremes. The standard of living concept was defined as "the domestic economy which a family is able to keep, depending both on income and the family's good sense in using the income to maintain standards of health and decency," but had nothing to do with the psychological relationship between the parent and the child.

The home visitors at the same time rated each home as "a place likely or unlikely to produce delinquency." A rating of —5 represented an extreme probability of delinquency among the children from this home. A rating of +5 indicated the reverse: that a boy living in this home was very unlikely to become delinquent. The ratings were made on the basis of the more or less obvious influences prevailing in the home without regard to the personality of the boy living there.

The visitor did not look for any particular factor or combination of factors. The ratings were impressionistic, based on the total picture as observed during the interview in the home and on any supplementary information already on file. Frequently the visitor was acquainted with the reputation of the family, especially as to homes where the standards were below normal.

We can now compare the homes of the "most delinquent" boys with the homes of those who were less delinquent, in respect to these two ratings. Table 28 shows the distribution of the "standard of living" ratings.

"Standard of Living" Ratings. Column 1 of Table 28 shows how the various ratings on the 11-point scale have been grouped for convenience. Minus five and plus five ratings were used rarely by the visitors and have therefore been placed in the same category with the minus four, minus three, and the plus four, plus three ratings, respectively. Column 2 shows how the 31 "most delinquent" boys have been distributed into these five categories. To the 15 T-boys we have added the 16 "most delinquent" among the older C-boys. The frequencies and the percentages are indicated. Column 3 gives similar information relating to the boys (both T and C) who were classified (as described in Chapter XIV) as "ordinary delinquents." Group III ("occasional delinquents") has been omitted because in this category there were only 12 boys, a group that when broken into sub-groups is too small for making comparisons. Columns 4 and 5 give the data similarly for Groups IV and V, the T- and C-boys who were classified as "seldom delinquent" and "least delinquent" respectively. Column 6 gives the ratings for 64 T-boys who were retired from the program as described in Chap-

TABLE 28

Comparative Ratings of Homes of Delinquent and Non-delinquent (T and C) Boys in Respect to "Standard of Living"

(1) Ratings	(2) Group I		(3) Group II		(4) Group IV		(5) Group V		(6) Retired		(7) Total	
	Number	Percent	Number	Percent	Number	Percent	Number	Percent	Number	Percent	Number	Percent
−5 −4 −3 (least able)	10	32.3	13	39.4	18	45.0	28	23.5	4	6.2	73	25.4
−2 −1	8	25.8	4	12.1	5	12.5	24	20.2	9	14.1	50	17.4
0	4	12.9	1	3.0	3	7.5	7	5.9	1	1.6	16	5.6
+1 +2	9	29.0	9	27.3	13	32.5	51	42.8	27	42.2	109	38.0
+3 +4 +5 (most able)	0	—	6	18.2	1	2.5	9	7.6	23	35.9	39	13.6
Total	31	100.0	33	100.0	40	100.0	119	100.0	64	100.0	287	100.0
Average	−1.13		−0.73		−1.58		−0.19		+1.48			

TABLE 29

Comparative Ratings of Homes of Delinquent and Non-delinquent (T and C) Boys in Respect to Likelihood of Producing Delinquency

(1) Ratings	(2) Group I		(3) Group II		(4) Group IV		(5) Group V		(6) Retired		(7) Total	
	Number	Percent	Number	Percent	Number	Percent	Number	Percent	Number	Percent	Number	Percent
−5 −4 −3 (most likely)	11	35.5	12	37.5	15	38.5	27	22.7	1	1.6	66	23.2
−2 −1	14	45.1	7	21.9	12	30.8	26	21.8	10	15.6	69	24.2
0	4	12.9	5	15.6	8	20.5	16	13.4	3	4.7	36	12.6
+1 +2	2	6.5	4	12.5	3	7.7	41	34.5	19	29.7	69	24.2
+3 +4 +5 (least likely)	0	—	4	12.5	1	2.5	9	7.6	31	48.4	45	15.8
Total	31	100.0	32	100.0	39	100.0	119	100.0	64	100.0	285	100.0
Average	−1.90		−1.19		−1.90		−0.32		+1.95			

ter XI, and Column 7 gives the totals for all groups. It will be recalled that the retired group was made up of boys who had always been rated on the plus side of the delinquency-prediction scale; who had no problems with which the Study could deal; who at the time of referral were not known to the police or probation officers; who were not originally referred as difficult and who were, and remained, on the whole, relatively well-adjusted boys. Originally there were 65 in this group but one has been omitted because he was in court on a minor delinquency charge. The other 64 have been entirely free of any delinquency known to the police or courts. We can therefore consider that the retired group comprises the high average boys who have conformed most closely to legal precepts and the mores of the culture.

It is evident from this table that no direct relationship was found between the *degree* of delinquency in Groups I to V and the standard of living. Nevertheless, none of the "most delinquent" boys come from the homes with highest standards and very few (6.2 percent) of the retired boys come from the worst homes in this respect. The average ratings of the homes of the "most delinquent" boys is not significantly lower than the average of the ratings of the homes of boys who were less delinquent (Group II and Group IV). In fact, the homes of the boys in Group IV were rated slightly lower (on the average) than the homes of the "most delinquent" boys. This rating, it will be recalled, emphasizes the capacity of the home to maintain decent standards which is a function of the family's economic status. We know from other evidence that the high average boys (the retired boys, Column 6) come from homes in sections of the city where rents are considerably higher and where economic conditions make possible higher standards of living. It is not surprising, then, that the homes of this group of boys received on the whole the highest ratings.

It appears that not all of these boys from homes with the lowest standards are seriously delinquent, nor can we say that all of the "most delinquent" boys come from such homes. In fact, the table shows that 29 percent of Group I (the "most delinquent") boys come from plus homes in respect to this rating, while 20 percent of the retired boys come from minus homes. The other boys come from homes that, on the average, were minus in respect to this rating but did not show a decreasing standard of living in direct correspondence with the increasing degree of delinquent behavior. We must look for additional factors.

Ratings of Homes as to Likelihood of Producing Delinquency. Again in Table 29 [1] we see no great differences between the homes of the "most delinquent boys" (Group I) and the homes of the boys who were less delinquent (Group II and Group IV), though the least delinquent boys (Group V) and those who were retired obviously come from homes which for the most part do not show the usual signs which the home visitors might interpret as delinquency-producing. At the same time there are within each group large individual differences. Seventeen percent of the retired boys in fact come from homes that the visitors thought were likely to produce delinquency, while 30 percent of the "ordinary delinquents" (Group II) and "most delinquent" (Group I) come from homes that did not show evident signs of being delinquency-producing. However, it was not infrequently found that a Study boy from a delinquency-producing home was not in fact delinquent in any serious sense but had one or more siblings who were.

So far as the quality of homes is concerned we find in these two tables confirmation of the view that research studies in delinquency invariably reach; namely, that delinquent behavior in any given case depends on a variety of factors and that no generalization can be drawn as to any single factor that will apply exclusively to delinquent boys.[2] At the same time, by our method of initial ratings, we do find that inadequacy characterizes the homes of the "most delinquent" boys much more frequently than it does the homes of the "least delinquent" boys.

Broken Homes. Though the "most delinquent" boys' homes were in many respects inadequate, they were not necessarily broken homes in the sense in which that term is usually understood, that is, broken by the absence of one or both parents.

[1] Columns 1 to 7 correspond to the columns of the same number in Table 28. Columns 3 and 4 in Table 29 each show one less rating than the comparable columns in Table 28, for the reason that the ratings were not available in these two cases.

[2] The conclusion arrived at by a recent English research in juvenile delinquency is typical: "We never discovered that all delinquents have been subject to one kind of influence or show some distinctive characteristic, while all our controls (non-delinquent) have been free from such influence or do not exhibit that characteristic" (A. M. Carr-Saunders, Hermann Mannheim, and E. C. Rhodes, *Young Offenders: an Enquiry into Juvenile Delinquency,* New York, The Macmillan Co., 1944, p. 151).

Of our 31 "most delinquent" boys we found only nine in homes from which one or both parents were permanently absent during the boys' first twelve years, and in all but four of these families a stepparent was present during all or part of that period. The presence of parents in the home is, of course, no guarantee of a healthy atmosphere for the proper growth and development of the boy. Disharmony, conflict, and unwise discipline may be more damaging to the development of mature personalities than the total absence of one or both parents.

Our limited data do not yield anything new on the statistical problem of the relationship of broken homes to delinquency. Many other studies have shown that the proportion of delinquents from broken homes is high, the range being roughly between 30 to 50 percent. The Gluecks' study, for example, dealing with delinquents in Massachusetts, reports that in 48 percent of 966 cases the homes were broken by the death of one or both parents, or by desertion, separation or divorce, or by the prolonged absence of one or both parents because of illness or imprisonment. "The probability that non-delinquents have so high an incidence of inadequate homes is remote," they report.[3] Merrill, in her contrast of delinquents and non-delinquents, shows that 50.7 percent of the delinquents came from broken homes in which one or both parents were divorced, separated, dead, or had deserted, in contrast with 26.7 percent of the controls.[4] What seems to be a more important consideration is the proportion of homes that are psychologically broken: "The best evidence . . . points to the conclusion that broken homes are not nearly so serious as a causal factor in producing delinquents as disorganized homes. It is not physical absence of the father or even the mother but a fault of the human relationship which causes the child to go astray."[5]

Ratings of Social Aspects of the Homes. What were some of the social characteristics of these homes? Examination of our "most delinquent" cases gives the reader an opportunity to draw his own conclusions as to the wholesomeness of family life in this special

[3] Sheldon and Eleanor T. Glueck, *One Thousand Juvenile Delinquents* (Cambridge, Harvard University Press, 1934), pp. 75–76.
[4] Maud A. Merrill, *Problems of Child Delinquency* (New York, Houghton Mifflin, 1947), p. 66.
[5] Charles W. Coulter, "Family Disorganization as a Causal Factor in Delinquency and Crime," *Federal Probation,* XII (1948), 13–17.

group. Many different combinations of adverse factors were found. In spite of the complexity of the total picture Dr. Witmer makes a rough grouping of families into three types from the point of view of the prevailing mores.[6] This grouping does not take into account the quality of the parents' affection but only the socially approved interest in and concern for their children. For example, a home was considered good if the parents were faithful to each other, did not quarrel excessively, provided adequate food, shelter, and clothing for the children, were not too harsh in their discipline, and were at least reasonably kind. Families that were studied from this point of view were placed in the following three categories: (1) Good homes, that is, homes where the social aspects seemed to be more or less conventional; (2) Fair homes, that is, homes demonstrating various combinations of good and bad characteristics from a social point of view; (3) Poor homes, that is, homes where there were relatively few factors that might be considered favorable from a social point of view.

How do the homes of our 15 "most delinquent" boys compare with those of the less delinquent? Table 30 shows the distribution of our five groups in respect to the rating of social aspects of the home.[7] By giving "good" ratings a value of 3, "fair" ratings 2, and "poor" 1 we can compare the average point values for each group.

TABLE 30

Comparison of Homes of Delinquent and Non-delinquent Boys in Respect to Social Aspects

DELINQUENCY JUDGMENTS

Social Aspects Ratings	(Most Delinquent) I	II	III	IV	(Least Delinquent) V	Total
Good: 3 points	2	5	1	2	46	56
Fair: 2 points	6	8	6	8	17	45
Poor: 1 point	7	4	4	3	1	19
Total	15	17	11	13	64	120
Average Point Values	1.7	2.1	1.7	1.9	2.7	

[6] For a description of the methods used in this analysis of the social aspects of the home see Chap. XXII.

[7] The C-boys and the retired T-boys have been omitted from this table, for the factors upon which this classification was based were not available as to them.

We see that more than two-thirds of the "least delinquent" (Group V) boys come from homes that were more or less conventional in their social aspects. The striking characteristic of this table is that the distribution of Group V in these three classes of "good," "fair," and "poor" is markedly different from the distribution of the other four groups. On the other hand, there seems to be very little difference in this respect in the distribution of the four groups as compared with each other.

Ratings of Emotional Aspects of the Homes. It has frequently been said that a seriously delinquent boy must be one who has not received adequate affection from either or both of his parents. A rough classification of cases in terms of ratings of adequacy of parental affection and interest was made on the basis of a study of the comprehensive case histories.[8] Let us check these ratings with our delinquency judgments.

Families where the parental affection toward the children and interest in them seemed to be relatively "good" were placed in Category A even though their behavior might have been far from ideal from a mental hygiene point of view. In Category B were placed cases in which the parental attitudes of affection and interest seemed neither particularly favorable nor unfavorable, while in Category C were found cases in which the parents' attitudes were obviously unfavorable to the moral development of the child. Implicit in this classification is the assumption not only that parental affection is important but that certain kinds of parental affection are favorable and certain kinds unfavorable to the proper development of a child. Too much affection, for example, might prove harmful. In other words, affection was not thought of as a trait that could be measured on a continuum, one extreme of which would represent great affection, the other extreme the absence of affection. This characteristic was judged qualitatively by one who had had many years of experience with case work and with child guidance clinics and who, therefore, was in a position to characterize the homes from a study of the case records in accordance with the usual clinical standards.

Table 31 shows how the boys in the treatment group who were

8 For a description of the methods used in this analysis of the emotional aspects of the home see Chap. XXII.

"most delinquent" compared in parental affection and interest to boys who were less delinquent.[9]

TABLE 31

Comparison of Homes of Delinquent and Non-delinquent Boys in Respect to Parental Affection and Interest

DELINQUENCY JUDGMENTS

Parental Affection and Interest	(Most Delinquent) I	II	III	IV	(Least Delinquent) V	Total
Good: 3 points	0	1	1	1	35	38
Fair: 2 points	3	5	7	7	19	41
Poor: 1 point	12	11	3	5	10	41
Total	15	17	11	13	64	120
Average Point Values	1.2	1.3	1.8	1.7	2.4	

Again we find that the "least delinquent" group of boys is markedly different from the other groups which, though smaller in numbers, show proportionately more cases at the "poor" end of the scale. It is interesting to note that none of the 15 "most delinquent" boys, nine of whose cases were briefly sketched in the previous chapter, had parents who were rated "good" in respect to affection and interest. It is also noteworthy that only ten of the 64 boys who were "least delinquent" had parents whose affection and interest was "poor." [10] We cannot say that wherever there are inadequate parents we always find delinquents, nor that all delinquents have inadequate parents, though there is a marked trend in both of these directions.[11]

[9] The C-boys and the retired T-boys have been omitted from this table, for the factors upon which this classification was based were not available as to them.

[10] The importance of wholesome family interrelationships in developing sound social attitudes in the growing child has been emphasized by all students of the problem of delinquency. See Maud A. Merrill, *Problems of Child Delinquency* (New York, Houghton Mifflin, 1947), Chap. III; William C. Kvaraceus, *Juvenile Delinquency and the School* (Yonkers, World Book, 1945), Chap. VIII; William Healy and Augusta F. Bronner, *New Light on Delinquency and Its Treatment* (New Haven, Yale University Press, 1936), Chap. III; Sheldon and Eleanor T. Glueck, *One Thousand Juvenile Delinquents*, Chap. V.

[11] A non-delinquent, of course, may, but usually did not, come from a home where there were delinquent brothers. On the other hand, frequently a delinquent boy had delinquent brothers. Of the 31 (T and C) "most delinquent" boys, one had no brothers. Of the remaining boys, 15 had one brother with a court record, three had two, one had

Where Are the Delinquents' Homes Located? Numerous studies have demonstrated that delinquent boys, as a rule, come from homes located in areas that have become highly industrialized, physically deteriorated, and overcrowded.[12] Such areas comprise most of the low-rental sections of the city where housing is inadequate and where most of the foreign-born families live. Our delinquency survey described in Chapter II showed that the homes of boys who were delinquent in a four-year period prior to the commencement of the Study program followed such a distribution in the two cities. In Cambridge, for example, there were relatively few delinquents living in the old residential areas adjoining and to the west of Harvard University; in Somerville, most of the delinquents came from the homes in the eastern half of the city adjoining business and industrialized districts.

Prior to the beginning of the treatment program a study was made of the influences surrounding the home of each boy (see Chapter IV). An observer recorded the nature of the living conditions in the area close to the boy's home, the nearness of the home to railroad yards, taverns and junk yards, the available recreational facilities, and the general "quality" of that section of the city. Notice was also taken of the presence or absence in contiguous territory of homes of boys who had become delinquent as shown on the spot maps previously described (see Chapter II). The observer then rated that particular locality in terms of its likelihood or unlikelihood of exerting an adverse influence upon any child living there, not taking into account personal factors such as the characteristics

---

three, two had four, one had five. Eight had brothers without court records. In brief, of the 31 boys 22, or 71.0 percent, had one or more brothers who were in court.

12 The pioneer work in this field was carried on in Chicago by Clifford R. Shaw and his colleagues. Many studies in different parts of the country have shown that delinquency is generally concentrated in certain well-defined areas in the overcrowded and disorganized sections of cities close to the central business and industrial areas. See C. R. Shaw, H. D. McKay, *et al.*, *Juvenile Delinquency and Urban Areas* (Chicago, University of Chicago Press, 1942); T. Earl Sullenger, *Social Determinants in Juvenile Delinquency* (New York, Wiley, 1936); William C. Kvaraceus, *Juvenile Delinquency and the School*; Sheldon and Eleanor T. Glueck, *One Thousand Juvenile Delinquents*; C. R. Shaw, H. D. McKay, and J. F. McDonald, *Brothers in Crime* (Chicago, University of Chicago Press, 1938). See also Sophia M. Robison, *Can Delinquency be Measured* (New York, Columbia University Press, 1936). In this book (p. 210) Robison states "the theory of the inverse ratio of the delinquency rate for an area with its distance from the center of the city, said to be established by the Chicago and other city studies has been shown to be invalid and inappropriate for New York City."

of the parents or the boy himself. The familiar 11-point scale was used, ranging from +5 through 0 to —5, +5 indicating the very favorable neighborhoods with the most wholesome influences, —5 the very unfavorable and least wholesome, and 0 representing the mid-point on the scale. Figure 8 shows the distribution of scale points for 323 boys in the treatment group.

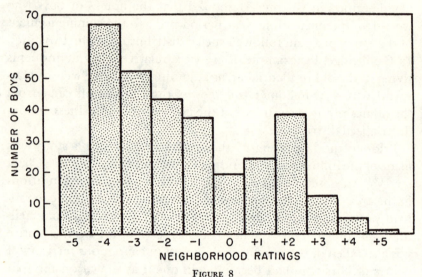

FIGURE 8

NEIGHBORHOOD RATINGS OF THE HOMES OF 323 T-BOYS

This figure makes it clear that our total group was not equally distributed throughout the favorable and unfavorable areas of the two cities. As we have already learned, our 650 boys did not represent a true cross section of the boy population but were deliberately weighted with difficult boys from the most unfavorable sections of the two cities.

The ratings were accompanied by a brief statement of the particular factors upon which they were based. One observer rated all neighborhoods of the Cambridge boys; another, in a similar manner, rated the Somerville neighborhoods, the two raters having first agreed on values after comparing notes on 12 homes rated by each observer independently. In this study we shall call these ratings "neighborhood ratings."

Some nine to ten years later it was possible to compare the ratings with the outcomes of the boys coming from homes in rated areas. Were those who later became delinquent the boys who lived in minus or unfavorable neighborhoods? Did the boys who refrained from delinquent behavior throughout the treatment period usually come from the more favorable areas?

Let us first compare the neighborhood ratings with the delinquency judgments following the general plan described above where the "most delinquent" and the less delinquent were compared in respect to various social standards.

Table 32 shows the distribution of neighborhood ratings among the four delinquency groups (omitting Group III as there were too few cases in that category).

TABLE 32

Comparison of Neighborhood Ratings of Delinquent Boys

DELINQUENCY JUDGMENTS

Neighborhood Ratings	GROUP I Number	Per- cent	GROUP II Number	Per- cent	GROUP IV Number	Per- cent	GROUP V Number	Per- cent	TOTAL Number	Per- cent
−5 −4 −3 "Very unfavorable"	14	45.2	15	45.4	22	53.7	52	44.4	103	46.4
−2 −1 "Unfavorable"	7	22.6	10	30.3	14	34.1	41	35.0	72	32.4
0 "Neutral"	4	12.9	2	6.1	0	..	4	3.4	10	4.5
+1 +2 "Favorable"	6	19.3	4	12.1	5	12.2	14	12.1	29	13.1
+3 +4 +5 "Very favorable"	0	..	2	6.1	0	..	6	5.1	8	3.6
Total	31	100.0	33	100.0	41	100.0	117	100.0	222	100.0

In examining this table one should keep in mind the fact that most of our boys (after the retired, non-difficult boys had been deducted) came from the poorer neighborhoods, as was seen in Figure 8 above. Table 32 does not offer any evidence that there is a direct correspondence between seriousness and frequency of delinquent behavior and the character of the neighborhood. The home areas of the "most delinquent" boys are not as a rule more unfavorable than those of the less delinquent. In fact the less favorable areas showed a higher proportion of "least delinquent" homes than of "most delinquent." [13] Of Group V, 79.4 percent lived in the minus areas, compared to 67.8 percent of Group I. It is also evident that 19.3 percent of Group I boys lived in plus areas, compared to 17.2 percent of Group V boys.

Most of the research in delinquency areas contrasts adjudicated or committed delinquents with non-delinquent boys rather than with boys of varying degrees of delinquent behavior. Let us now check these neighborhood ratings in the conventional way with one group of non-delinquents and two groups of delinquents.

Group A comprised 45 delinquents who were committed to correctional institutions.

Group B consisted of 94 boys from both the treatment and control groups who were found delinquent in court but for some reason were not committed to correctional institutions, presumably because the judges did not consider their offenses serious enough.

Group C consists of 62 retired boys who, as previously pointed out, were not delinquent (except for possible minor violations) and were never in court or known to the police or to their counselors as delinquents.[14]

How many boys from the non-delinquent and the delinquent groups came from very favorable or favorable neighborhoods? As shown in Table 33 about a third of the non-delinquents (33.9 percent) came from very favorable or favorable neighborhoods, while only 17.0 percent of the adjudicated but non-committed delinquents came from such neighborhoods. Not one of the committed boys spent his early life in a very favorable neighborhood, though 13.3 percent of them had lived in favorable neighborhoods.

How many boys from the delinquent and non-delinquent groups came from the unfavorable or very unfavorable neighborhoods? As shown in Table 33 most of the committed boys (73.4 percent) and a very large proportion of the delinquent but non-committed boys (79.8 percent) came from homes located in unfavorable or very unfavorable neighborhoods. It was also found that 58.1 percent of the non-delinquent boys came from such neighborhoods.

[13] We must again warn the reader against a too hasty conclusion from Table 32, for we are here correlating the boy's neighborhood with his behavior, without regard to the fact that the behavior of his siblings may have been quite different.

[14] This group has been more fully described in Chap. XI. They had no court record down to July 1, 1948, at which time their average age was 19.

TABLE 33

"Non-delinquent" Boys Compared with Adjudicated and Committed Delinquent Boys in Respect to Neighborhood Ratings

Neighborhood Ratings	GROUP A		GROUP B		GROUP C		TOTAL	
	Number	Percent	Number	Percent	Number	Percent	Number	Percent
+5 +4 +3 "Very favorable"	0	0.0	3	3.2	6	9.7	9	4.5
+2 +1 "Favorable"	6	13.3	13	13.8	15	24.2	34	16.9
0 "Neutral"	6	13.3	3	3.2	5	8.0	14	7.0
−1 −2 "Unfavorable"	8	17.8	22	23.4	14	22.6	44	21.9
−3 −4 −5 "Very unfavorable"	25	55.6	53	56.4	22	35.5	100	49.7
Total	45	100.0	94	100.0	62	100.0	201	100.0

It is evident that the delinquents did not invariably come from unfavorable neighborhoods, although a large majority of them did. It is equally true that a substantial number of boys who lived in these same unfavorable neighborhoods did not become delinquent. Delinquents and non-delinquents live side by side. (See Figure 9.) Though our data concern only a small proportion of the total population of the two cities, as a general rule even in the very unfavorable areas there are to be found more non-delinquents than delinquents. It is obvious that the character of the neighborhood does not alone determine the boy's adjustment to society.

THE BOY GIVES HIS OPINION

Approximately 75 T-boys, after the termination of the program, were asked for their opinions on the causation and prevention of delinquency and for their appraisal of the law-enforcement agencies. The group interviewed included both delinquent and non-delinquent boys, most of whom were then between the ages of 18 and 21. The questions were asked during informal interviews which have been previously described (see Chapter XIII). We cannot, of course, expect deep insight from these boys as to the psychological and sociological influences basic to delinquent behavior but we find their views illuminating and well worth considering in our study of juvenile crime.

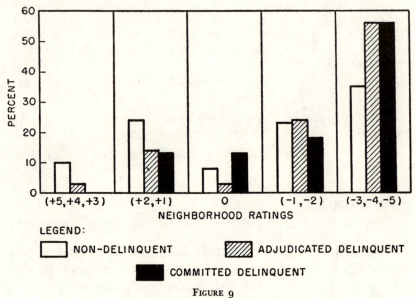

LEGEND:

☐ NON-DELINQUENT   ▨ ADJUDICATED DELINQUENT

■ COMMITTED DELINQUENT

FIGURE 9

COMPARISON OF NON-DELINQUENTS, ADJUDICATED DELIN-QUENTS, AND COMMITTED DELINQUENTS AS TO NEIGHBORHOOD RATINGS

QUESTION 1: WHAT DO YOU THINK MAKES KIDS GET INTO TROUBLE?

The delinquent boys may have been more vivid in their replies but no substantial differences in content were found between the answers of those who had been in court for delinquent behavior and those who had not.

Companions. About one-third of the replies attributed delinquency to the influence of companions. To say that another boy led them into trouble is the obvious way to avoid the rebuke that usually follows the acceptance of full responsibility. However, there is no doubt that most of the delinquents did have delinquent companions.[15] Some typical replies were as follows:

15 In a study made at the Massachusetts Reformatory the Gluecks found that "95 per cent of the youths had bad associates prior to sentence to the Reformatory" (Sheldon and Eleanor T. Glueck, *500 Criminal Careers,* New York, Alfred A. Knopf, 1930, p. 127).

1. Wrong crowd. The younger fellow catches on; he goes with someone who is older, more experienced. Ya, the older fellow says "Come on, see what we can do—steal a car and get away with it"; and they kept on doing it until they do get caught.

2. Ya, that's it [the gang]. Of course, he has to want to himself, too—there's something to that. Now you take this Skippy O'Toole of Water Street and myself—when we're separated we're okay, but every time we get together we have nothing to do we start getting ideas and start doing things. So after this last time Skippy said to me, "You stay down where you are on Fiske Avenue and I'll stay here on Water Street. That way none of us will get into trouble." When we're apart we're okay but when we're together there's always trouble.

3. It's going around with the wrong gang. Probably kids over on the other side of town. You know, they get in with a gang a little older and they want to be big shots, and show off. They go around with older guys who are a little wiser than they are so they do things they wouldn't do by themselves. That's the trouble with the coming generation, you know. I guess it's the war or something but the parents seem to work because of the war and the mother isn't home and they don't have very much time with the kids so the kids go wrong. I never been in trouble myself. I never had occasion to. I never went around with any guys like that.

Use of Leisure Time. Another third emphasized the importance of the general environment outside the home. Many of the boys who lived in the more deteriorated portions of the city said there was just nothing to do, the principal occupation of "hanging around" often leading to trouble. From our observation of these boys it was evident that the most delinquent did not care to utilize the facilities even when organized recreation was available. They preferred the street, or the vacant stores or shanties where they sometimes established their own clubs. If known to the neighborhood houses at all these boys were known as "nuisances." None was a "member in good standing" of any of the organized youth groups such as the "Y" or the Scouts. It is significant that such boys could not tolerate a recreational organization where rules were enforced. They had evidently not been well conditioned to obedience, to forgoing immediate pleasures for the greater good of all. Their characterization of the "Y" or the Scouts as "sissy" organizations may have been defense reactions to assure themselves of their own "masculinity."

1. Oh, they have nuthin' to do, you know. Time on their hands. They'd just as easily do something bad as something good. There were three fellows I remember. They walked down the street and they saw a truck so they got in and started fooling around. Next thing you knew they were way down on Springfield Street in the truck. Then they got picked up. But they didn't know—they just didn't have anything to do.

2. Well, when fellows are younger they didn't get any enjoyment out of them [playgrounds]. We used to go play at the Thompson Field. Well, there'd be older kids playing there—about 16 or 17 years old. We'd go to play and they'd kick us off because we were younger kids so we'd go play in the middle of the street and the ladies would kick and beef and call the cops. The cops would chase us off the street. So we'd jump roofs, hop trucks, steal, hop rides on trolleys. . . . Ya, we wouldn't take any more [than food] because it would look like our parents couldn't afford things. They couldn't. Everyone's poor around here. Well, we used to take an empty bag. We'd go in the store. We'd pick up some food— canned goods and fruit and walk out with it.

3. When a fellow thinks his family doesn't like him and he doesn't care it is pretty easy for him to cross the line and become a crook. He needs someone to sway him. If they are brought up in poverty—brought up in the street and the families have no time to teach them—they would take a lot of swaying.

Other Factors. The remaining third of the replies dealt with a variety of topics, difficult to classify, in this order: parental neglect, having no money, seeing attractive objects in the store, wanting to be a "big shot" and so on. No boy mentioned the influence of the movies, radio, or "comic" books. The striking fact about the boys' opinions of causation was that few of them placed the blame upon the parents. The delinquent boy himself rarely expressed the view that family influences were the chief factors in his own delinquent behavior. Parents, too, were frequently unable or unwilling to admit that their own child could be "such a bad boy." They pointed to the evil influences of the neighbor's children—"those kids led my boy into trouble." Sometimes they faced the problem as one having its roots in their own home. The remedy in such cases was usually corporal punishment. Some of the typical replies in these categories follow:

1. Some get into trouble because they have bad families, but I had a good family. I know I got into trouble because I wanted to be a big shot. I used to hang around with an older crowd. I've been getting into trouble since I was a kid. At first it wasn't to get any money or anything

like that. It was just for the thrill—you know, the thrill of stealing or the thrill of somebody chasing you—that was fun. When I was ten we used to break into box cars and go through them. When we were kids we'd just pick up fruit. When we were six we used to go into the Five and Ten and steal bottles of perfume from the counter. We didn't need any perfume—we didn't want it—we'd take it to school and put it into the inkwells. We used to hop rides—just for the thrill and then also because it was something you shouldn't do. I think I still like the thrill but I wouldn't do it. I wouldn't do anything else now because I'm afraid of getting caught—that's what keeps me from doing it.

2. When children get into trouble my belief is that to a certain extent it is right in the family itself. A kid grows up and he's spoiled—the mother's got two or three or four babies in the house—maybe she's got a whole family of kids. She doesn't know what the kids are doing or she doesn't give a damn what they're doing. She wants the kids all right but on the other hand she . . . don't know what the hell to do with them all so the kids are running around in rags. . . . They see candy—they see fruit—something they want to steal. They haven't got it themself so they wish they could have it. Maybe they see some kid walk off with some candy; sure, why shouldn't he, if he hasn't got it. Maybe his mother doesn't give him hell.

4. My people never took me out or to a show or any place with them. If I wanted to go to the show . . . I'd have to go out and clip it. You see, that was some of the things—my brothers used to get money and I didn't. Like there were Christmases and I was wrong and my mother would buy my brother something and my older brother something and I wouldn't get nuthin'. I don't like to mention these things because I know I was wrong and I feel wrong anyway. Three in a bed. I used to sleep at the end—you know—two this way and one that way. You'd just have part of the blankets on ya like that and even if I wanted to swop with my younger brother I couldn't.

QUESTION 2: WHAT DO YOU THINK KEEPS A KID STRAIGHT?

Here again we found no substantial differences between the answers given by the "most delinquent" and the less delinquent boys. Almost half of the replies related to the topic of keeping busy. Most of the boys seemed to feel that if one had something "to occupy his mind" such as an interesting hobby or some occupation he would not be delinquent. A few mentioned the effectiveness of good parental control and discipline. A few others urged the importance of a club or an organization, such as the Study. Some of the typical replies to this question:

1. Delinquency can be prevented not by restrictions and punishment but by companionship, teaching and occupations. If left alone boys will choose what they want to do. But who knows what and where—a city dump, stealing pears or apples? Good, but breaking into a small shop or railroad car, stealing a bicycle, perhaps even an auto—not good. With a guiding hand the choice will be just as pleasant to them plus educational.

2. If cops wouldn't nab kids and be ready right away to send them to reform school, if they would study them, work with them like the Study did, they'd all come out smooth. Organizations with things for kids to do—all kinds of sports, recreation mostly—would help.

3. Parents should take more of an interest in what their children are doing: Like giving an allowance for small things fellows want—then they don't steal—the petty things; to keep them off the street.

QUESTION 3: DO YOU THINK "COPS" ARE FAIR?

Some of the boys did not reply to this question or said they did not know, but of the 46 who answered, 22 thought the "cops" were fair, 13 thought they were sometimes fair and sometimes not, 11 believed they were not fair. Here we find that those who had been in difficulties with the law generally expressed hostility toward the "cops." Some typical replies follow (the first four replies were given by boys who had been adjudged delinquent, the next four replies by boys who had not):

1. No good. Like when I was caught taking the clothes out of the Bishop Store. The police, they issued several warrants on me for stealing things. You know, they had cases on their books that weren't closed, so they wanted to make a closed case so they picked on me. They said they had my fingerprints and everything.

2. No. Well, see, like they had me one time—they jump on you—they say, "This is the one that did it"; they get you all mixed up—you say things you didn't mean and then they take you upstairs and point to books, radios, wires, everything, and say, "You took it—you took it." Sure, I robbed, but I didn't take *all* the things!

3. No, sir! They were a bunch of bastards and they still are today! Cops are no good! At least, I find them that way. A cop ain't supposed to put a hand on anyone, but these cops—they all got rackets and I know they have. I'm old now and I know the rackets they run. Maybe some cops are on the level but they're all getting graft. They know where the bookie offices are. I know where they are myself. I know where the gambling is. The young kids like—younger than me are startin' to go in now—regular set-up—pool room right in

back where there's more Goddamn games goin' on from Friday till Monday morning. Well, anyways, this cop walks in the station and he's always insultin' me. He's always calling me, "You little fresh, you little bastard." He'd belt me or anything that they felt like doing. They know they have authority. I seen a cop once—he was off duty—he had his uniform off—stinkin' drunk! Things like that ain't goin' ta make a world you know! People aren't going to trust each other in anything.

4. Oh, once a guy gets into trouble or they get his name they're on his neck all the time—they're always trying to pin something on him.

5. I think they're human. If a policeman makes a mistake it is more dramatized. They arrest someone; if it's the wrong person, they can be sued. But if things go wrong and they don't arrest someone then they are fired. To me, the cops I know are swell fellows.

6. No. If something goes wrong in some other part of the town, wherever it might be, if a colored fellow did it—well, this is the first place [the area more heavily populated with Negroes] they come to. Well, I guess maybe one time probably kids did do something that got us in bad and ever since then they've always come down here first when things go wrong. Doesn't seem fair to me.

7. Sure—fair as we are. A cop is doing his duty and is paid for it.

8. Well, to tell you the truth, I don't. I don't think they're fair at all. A cop can be in the wrong and you can't do anything to him. But *you* can be in the wrong and he can certainly give it to you.

QUESTION 4: DO YOU THINK THE COURTS ARE FAIR?

Some of the boys who had not been in court said they had no opinion on this matter. Of the 31 who expressed an opinion, 16 thought the courts were fair, four thought they were fair at times and unfair at other times, while 11 thought the courts were not fair. We find that those with court experience had less respect for the courts. Of the 11 who thought the courts were not fair, nine had actually been in court. Of the 16 boys who gave replies favorable to the courts, ten had never been in court. To state it another way, of the 15 boys who had been in court, nine did not think the courts were fair. Of the 12 boys who had not been in court only two considered the courts unfair. The following replies were given by boys with court experiences:

1. You go up there and they just open a big book and they close it again and then it's all over.

2. They're no good. You don't have a chance. When you go up there you're not supposed to know nuttin'—the judge does all the talking

and you can't say anything. I was on probation four and a half years for that. Well, they gave me six months and then I used to break probation—instead of going up every week I'd skip a week or so and they'd keep adding on. Everything they do is supposed to be right. You're not supposed to know anything. It's the same thing now. I drive a truck—if you get out of line and right away they give you a ticket. Well, I'll get even with them.

3. Oh, I can't understand them. You read in the paper one guy steals a car and he gets sent away and then you read about another guy that steals a car and he gets let off. Why up the street here there was a gang that stole about 20 cars—two or three of them got away with nothing. The rest of them were sent away. And me, all I did was this one thing but they had to bring up my past—juvenile they called it—so they sent me away.

4. Well, I don't know how it is now but two or three years ago they were pretty rugged. They would rather send a fellow away than to do anything for him. As soon as a guy got into trouble they wanted to send him someplace.

QUESTION 5: WHAT DO YOU THINK ABOUT "REFORM" SCHOOLS?

With one or two exceptions the boys who had not been to "reform" schools replied that they had heard the schools were "pretty bad." The schools had a poor reputation among boys in general. Only three of the 18 who had some knowledge of these schools spoke favorably of them. The others considered them "unfair," "bad," "too strict," and so on. Correctional schools are no longer officially called "reform" schools.[16] Responding to the newer philosophy of treatment and rehabilitation they are designed to help a boy make a better adjustment to life and to educate him scholastically, vocationally, and morally. Yet to practically all boys—delinquent and non-delinquent alike—these institutions are known as "reformatories," "places where they punish you," or "schools of crime." So long as parents, teachers, and the police use these institutions as threats or as places of last resort where "bad boys" are sent, this interpretation will persist. When a judge, denouncing a boy for being "bad," sends him away for the protection of society, can one expect the boy to look upon the institution to which he is committed against his will, as a "school" rather than a "juvenile prison"? To

16 In Massachusetts the Lyman School for Boys at Westborough, the Industrial School for older boys at Shirley, and the Industrial School for girls at Lancaster are known as "training schools."

such boys these institutions constitute an integral part of society's system of punishment for, they believe, a boy is "sentenced" to these institutions for his juvenile "crimes" just as an adult who robs and steals is sentenced to a prison. It would be unrealistic at the present time for a boy to think otherwise.[17]

Some opinions of boys who had been to correctional schools follow:

1. I didn't like the place. I used to run away. I had run away once and then they picked me up and brought me back and then put me in another cottage for ten months. I ran away again. [He was caught and again returned.] They were good guys. They're all okay. Those masters were some of the best guys you ever met. The master, Mr. Y.—he's okay. I got plenty of black eyes from him—but that's something else. He was a good guy.

2. I was at X twice and they used to treat the kids pretty rough over there. I used to get a punch in the nose every morning. Then they used to have a stick. They used to bring it down on my hand a hundred times. They carry a little leather strap around in their pockets and give it to the kids over the fanny. I ran away five times. There was an old guy up there, he got this kid [a runaway] and he started to hit him and a young guy was there with a club in case the kid should fight back. The older guy hit the kid three times until he knocked the kid out. Boy, I'd like to go up there sometime and clean them out!

3. I felt pretty bitter. I got in some trouble up there. There was some fellow there who used to carry a knife. One of the other fellows said he was going to tell on him and I told him if he did I'd punch his face in. One of the guys that guards us came over to me one day when I was standing in the yard near a wall and they hit me and I hit the brick wall and they kept on hitting me. My head hit the wall a few times and I fell down. I wasn't conscious and yet I wasn't unconscious. I made up my mind to get even with them. They kicked me a few times in the back. When I got a chance I ran away. Boy, I wish I could see some of those guys now out here. Boy, if I had one of them out here I'd show them!

4. Those schools aren't any good—the X school and the Y school. They're terrible. Everyone says so. I was up there. They beat you. They handcuff you and kick you. Sure, they feed you slop. When the inspectors come out from Boston they have good food and treat you good, but the schools don't do anyone any good.

[17] On January 1, 1949, three years after the close of the treatment program a new method of committing delinquent boys and girls became effective in Massachusetts. The court now cannot commit delinquents directly to the juvenile training schools but may commit them to the custody of a newly created Youth Service Board which has been given broad powers over the care, treatment and disposition of such cases. (Chap. 310 of the Acts of 1948).

CONCLUSIONS

The Study did not have as large a number of serious delinquents as some previous studies, yet our intimate acquaintance with a small group of delinquents enables us to contribute some insights pertaining to the questions raised in this chapter.

Extent of Delinquency. Technically, probably every child now over 17 years old in Cambridge and Somerville had been a delinquent boy by definition and yet very few delinquent acts led to court appearances.[18] The term "juvenile delinquent" indiscriminately used has, therefore, little intrinsic meaning. In a study of 114 boys intimately known to our staff it was estimated that less than 1.5 percent of the many offenses committed by these boys resulted in official action.[19] Furthermore, many boys who did appear in court had been charged with relatively minor offenses. Of the 188 boys who were brought into court charged with 482 offenses at one time or another, only 68, or 36.3 percent, were committed to a correctional institution.[20] The boys who appeared in juvenile court represented a small proportion of all boys of juvenile court age. Not more than 1 or 2 percent of all boys between the ages of seven and 17 were brought into court in any given year. This fact holds true in most sections of the country where delinquency rates have been computed.[21]

From this evidence and the observations of our staff it is obvious that delinquency in its more *serious* forms is not the most common youth problem, though no doubt the most dramatic. Often it arouses our emotions of aggression and compels us to action because it is a threat to our sense of security. In considering the welfare of youth in general, however, delinquency-prevention cannot be compared in importance to the problem of academic education, of physical and mental health, of vocational training, or of the broader problem of personal relationships.[22]

---

[18] See Chap. XIV, pp. 176–176.

[19] Fred J. Murphy, Mary M. Shirley, and Helen M. Witmer, "The Incidence of Hidden Delinquency," *American Journal of Orthopsychiatry*, XVI (1946), 686–696.

[20] These figures include both T- and C-boys. See Tables 59 and 60, p. 336.

[21] See Chap. II.

[22] It will be recalled that one of the objectives of the Study—the prevention of delinquency—was reformulated to embrace the larger goal of character development. The counselors endeavored not simply to prevent Joe from stealing apples but to

Most of our 188 boys who were brought into the juvenile court have not so far continued their delinquencies into their late teens or early twenties. Presumably relatively few of the C-boys, and we believe (for reasons to be given later) even fewer of the T-boys, will become future criminals; and yet juvenile delinquents are popularly thought of as destined to become criminals later in life. Jacob Panken, a noted justice of the New York City Children's Court wrote, "It must be underscored time and again that the delinquent child of today, unless he is saved, is the adult criminal of tomorrow." [23] The validity of the judge's remark rests heavily upon the phrase "unless he is saved." Our evidence, at any rate, does not suggest that most of the boys who as youngsters committed delinquent offenses even of a fairly serious nature continued their antisocial behavior beyond the age of 17.[24] Most of these boys were evidently "saved" either through the efforts of some person or institution or by the deterrent forces in the community or by the natural processes of maturation which bring about a lessening of the desire for adventure and excitement.[25]

Our Study also showed that relatively few of the boys who were committed to correctional institutions prior to the age of 17 were later committed to adult institutions within the few years in which we have followed their careers. Although a large proportion of adult criminals, at least of those who are confined in our prisons

---

help him develop his potentialities for good citizenship. Delinquency prevention, in brief, was not narrowly construed in terms of preventing specific kinds of behavior. One could not, in any practical way, isolate the problem of the boy's delinquent conduct from the concern about the boy's health, or his dissatisfaction with school, or the discipline in his home.

[23] Jacob Panken, *The Child Speaks* (New York, Henry Holt, 1941), p. 3.

[24] This statement is based on an examination of court records when the boys were of an average age of 19 years, 10 months.

[25] The Gluecks, in their research studies of ex-inmates of the Concord Reformatory and in their follow-up studies of juvenile delinquents referred by the juvenile court to the Judge Baker Foundation clinic, were the first to point out the statistical confirmation of the factor of maturation in accounting for reformation. They found that delinquency runs a fairly steady and predictable course; that some underlying process in the lives of some of these youthful offenders accounts for a falling-off in criminality following youthful offenses—a process they have called "maturation." They did not find this decrease in criminality at any certain age but at a certain distance from the time the boys first began to be delinquent. See Sheldon and Eleanor T. Glueck, *Juvenile Delinquents Grown Up* (New York, The Commonwealth Fund, 1940), Chap. III, and *Later Criminal Careers* (New York, The Commonwealth Fund, 1937), Chap. X.

today, were at one time delinquent boys, we believe it is far from true that a substantial proportion of erstwhile delinquent boys spend any part of their adult years in prison. Boys, for example, who committed delinquent acts for the fun of it, or as Judge Panken phrases it, "from pure deviltry rather than in response to a criminal drive," [26] or because they have been swept along with a social group who are committing such acts—and these boys make up a large proportion of the offender group—do not become serious offenders or professional criminals in later life.[27]

The Homes. Our "most delinquent" boys came from homes where the standard of living was lower and the evidences of delinquency-producing factors more obvious than in the homes of the least delinquent boys; and yet, there are so many exceptions to the general rule that again we find no point-for-point correspondence between the *degree* of delinquent behavior and the character of the home in these respects. More closely related to delinquent behavior are the social and emotional aspects of the home.

We conclude that the child's greatest need within the family circle is the affection of his parents. The deprivation of parental affection early in life we found to be a common phenomenon in the lives of many of our most serious delinquents.[28] The quality of the parents' love of the child, we believe, will have much to do in later years with the child's love of the world. A child, too, must have an adequate feeling of his own importance. Many delinquents overcompensate for this lack by wanting to be "big shots," by bullying younger children, or by defying those in authority. A sub-group of T-boys with poor prognoses (in terms of our delinquency rating scale) who did not become seriously delinquent was compared with

[26] *The Child Speaks,* p. 3.

[27] A longer period of time is needed, of course, to verify this apparent trend.

[28] We cannot conclude, however, that when these important psychological needs are not met delinquency invariably results. Why some boys express their disappointments and frustrations in other than antisocial ways depends on a complex pattern of factors. William Healy and Augusta F. Bronner, in *New Light on Delinquency and Its Treatment* (New Haven, Yale University Press, 1936), made a direct attack on this problem through a comparative study of delinquents and their non-delinquent siblings. Studying 75 non-delinquents coming from homes where the circumstances were inimical, they found that the boy escaped from delinquency through more satisfactory affectional relationships within the home or through fortuitous circumstances such as having physical handicaps, having special interests, being particularly non-aggressive, retiring or shy.

another sub-group having equally poor prognoses who sought expression in frequent and serious antisocial behavior. A considerably larger proportion of the former came from homes where the mothers were able to give the child warm and genuine affection.

The Neighborhood. More delinquents live in the poorer, more deteriorated, and less attractive areas of the city where living standards are below average, than in the residential sections of the city. The adverse influences of such areas may account for much of the delinquent behavior but there is no direct correspondence between the *seriousness* or *frequency* of the delinquent behavior and the character of the neighborhood in which the offender lives. Many of the least delinquent boys, for example, as well as the most delinquent, live in the unfavorable areas. We also find that the most delinquent boys do not always live in the worst areas. One vital fact about boys who live in the so-called "delinquency areas" is that there are far more boys there who are *not* officially known to the police or courts than there are adjudicated delinquents. The statement made by Dr. Sheldon Glueck that "even in the most marked interstitial area nine-tenths of the children do *not* become delinquent" would apply to Cambridge and Somerville if by delinquent one means a child adjudicated delinquent by a court.[29]

The Run-of-the-Mine Delinquents. The bulk of the transitory delinquents came from homes with at least the minimum of good standards, and yet for a time the boys became involved in a number of delinquent episodes, responding to the unwholesome forces within the community. (Homes where moral standards were lax or where the boy found nothing to absorb his interests probably produced a larger proportion of transitory delinquents.) They were delinquent largely because of social habits; they lived in neighborhoods where their closest friends were delinquent or on the verge of delinquency. To gamble on Sunday, steal rides on trolleys, and then to engage in petty stealing, which at times developed into more

[29] Sheldon Glueck, *Crime Causation* (National Probation Association Yearbook, 1941), p. 91. The term "interstitial area," as used by Frederic M. Thrasher, in *The Gang* (Chicago, University of Chicago Press, 1937), refers roughly to that section of the city between the industrial and residential areas. Generally, this area is one that has deteriorated; that was formerly a residential district, from which the more well-to-do residents have moved out as business and industry have encroached upon it. What remains then becomes distinctly an interstitial phase of the growth of the city.

daring and exciting exploits, constituted behavior quite acceptable in one's own group. They gave little deliberate thought to the rightness or wrongness of their acts until they came up against the reality of arrest and court appearance. Most of them were not fundamentally inferior to non-delinquents in the better section of the city. We do not believe it is accurate, then, to say that delinquency is always symptomatic of personal maladjustment. These boys are not psychologically sick. They are not particularly maladjusted within their own culture. Their habits of committing antisocial acts are acquired just as the other habits common to their particular group are acquired. They are not outstandingly unhappy or neurotic compared to the non-delinquent child living under the same conditions. Most of these boys, when they mature, look back upon their reckless quest for excitement as "kid stuff." They soon develop a realization that they have outgrown that sort of thing.

The relatively few who advance from minor delinquencies into more serious crimes are generally those who are relatively less happy, more self-centered, and less able to respond with affection. They are the ones, by and large, who spent their early years in homes where they were denied the affection and attention essential to the development of wholesome personalities and they are the ones who are most likely to constitute a large proportion of our future prison population.

To understand what makes a boy delinquent these rough generalizations may serve as a guide. But we cannot overlook the uniqueness of personality. Each boy responds to a different combination of forces—usually unknown to himself. To determine why any given boy is delinquent we must study *that* particular boy.

CHAPTER XVII

THE SCHOOL MEETS
THE DELINQUENT
BOY

WE HAVE REVIEWED SOME OF THE FAMILY AND NEIGHBORHOOD INFLU-
ences surrounding our "most delinquent" boys. Here we follow
them into the classrooms. Were any of these delinquents, when
subjected to the stricter and more evenly administered discipline
of their teachers in the first few grades of the public school, considered average, well-behaved children?

IS THE DELINQUENT A PROBLEM CHILD IN SCHOOL?

Let us examine this question from the point of view of the teachers. We have already described the method of obtaining teachers'
opinions through personal interviews and through the personality
sketches they wrote on the Trait Record Cards (see Chapter IV).
These opinions were expressed when the average age of the boys was
about nine and a half, and usually before their delinquencies had
been committed or had become extensive. Most of the boys were
then in the second or third grade. Even at that early stage, many of
these boys had a reputation for petty stealing and were well on the
way toward a delinquent career. We cannot say, therefore, that they
were non-delinquent, though all but about 2 percent had had no
court experience. The opinions were not necessarily directed to the
single question of delinquency but the teachers were, of course, acquainted with the objectives of the Study. They described the boys'
personalities and their general behavior, but there was a tendency
to dwell upon the kind of behavior that would ordinarily be disturbing to classroom routine and decorum. If the boy had annoying traits the teacher seemed to be well aware of his activities and

she had much to say about his personality. If, on the other hand, he was well behaved she had relatively little to say about him. We placed the children in three groups, as they were differentiated by teachers' opinions.

1. Good. The child in this category is generally spoken of as well behaved. He has good intentions, is usually attentive, conforms at least fairly well to rules, and makes a reasonable effort to cooperate.

2. Fair. In this group are boys who are lacking in interest in schoolwork, are occasionally disobedient and uncooperative, but not outstanding as school problems. Generally these children are willing to conform but their behavior is marked by occasional reversals. On the whole, they are neither very good nor very bad from the teachers' point of view.

3. Bad. These children are the rebels of the class, frquently violating the rules, upsetting the good order of the classroom, puzzling, annoying or exasperating the teacher.

The teachers' opinions of our 31 "most delinquent" boys (15 T-boys and 16 C-boys) might thus be distributed, as follows: Good, 2; Fair, 9; Bad, 20.

What kind of behavior seemed to indicate that in future years (before or after they had left school) these boys would be problems for the police, the courts, the correctional schools, and, in some cases, the prisons? We present here a representative sample of descriptions made by teachers *before* the delinquent careers of the boys had fully developed.[1] Nonconformity, rebelliousness, truancy mark the cases. Boys who misbehaved outside of school seldom were inclined to good behavior in the classroom, as shown by the teachers' descriptions. In quite a few cases the boy's reputation for being a "terror" had preceded him and the teacher was on the alert for any expression of unacceptable conduct.

1. *Bernard* (Age 9 years, 6 months; in the third grade). A kind of wild Indian, hard to manage and just not especially interested in his work. His work is very disorderly and smoochy. Has played truant several times this year. Seems to be in with a rather wild gang outside. He is quite disorderly about his personal appearance. His hands and face are cleaned up at home but he seems to get himself very dirty in school. They (his gang) are hard to manage in school. Absolutely nothing seems to faze

1 This one-third sample was randomly chosen.

Bernard. Will take a good strapping by the headmaster and not be bothered by it at all. He spits on his paper, always has a lot of paraphernalia in his desk, such as bits of string, tin, mirror, and tracing paper. He will play happily with these for hours if you would let him. Is not malicious, even though he will punch people and knock them down. It is not for fighting's sake that he fights but just because he is a rough boy. Will admit anything, is brazen as brass. There seems to be no way to deal with him. Scolding and coaxing are of no avail. He will simply stand there expressionless.

2. *Norman* (Age 10 years, 10 months; in the fifth grade). A peculiar boy. Seems to think you are picking on him all the time. On two or three different occasions he has thrown things at me and at different teachers. He has thrown chairs at me, at a substitute and at Mr. W. Is smart enough, if he will do the work. Never wants to sit still long. Can be terribly angry at you, and two minutes later be very friendly. Sometimes he lies. Has played truant for a couple of days. Was with George with whom he chums. George is a little villain like Norman. They like to hop trucks and streetcars. Norman takes liberties like walking out to get a drink of water without asking permission. He wants to be the boss and do what he feels like. Sometimes he comes to school very neat and tidy. Other times decidedly not. Once threw a music book in my face, and in the same tantrum gave me an awful cut with his nails on the back of my arm. He is now being marked for conduct every hour and has to report to the office before and after school. Home conditions seem very poor. I was at the home. It seems quite bare of furniture. All the children sleep in one bed. When he gets angry at the other children he will throw anything that is handy at them. They usually punch him first now when they see him getting angry at them. He threw a book at the fourth grade teacher. He is a very healthy boy. He is doing well enough in his studies to get by. Is just about passing, but could do much better. Sometimes is actually too lazy to put his name on his paper.

3. *Frank* (Age 9 years, 7 months; in special class). This is his first year in special class. Is lazy, careless and untidy. Have definite proof that he steals. A penknife was missed from the teacher's desk. When Frank was accused of taking it, it was returned the next day by his brother Leonard who said that Frank had taken it and had forgotten to give it back. Is always hitting someone in the classroom. Is helpful in cleaning the room and other such tasks. He makes friends easily and loses them quickly. Will make a friend in order to obtain something. Is a shy youngster. Teacher does not seem to think that he is as stupid as he seems to be. Gets smaller children into trouble by getting them to do something he is afraid to do. Cries very easily, seems to be able to turn on the tears at will. Is very sneaky but not so much so in his relationships

with other children as with teacher. Parents are quite good to him. Father is very, very strict. Beats children to correct them. Frank is regular in attendance and punctual. His desk is just a mass of jumbled papers, pencils, toys, and other things. Is quite selfish. Is not impulsive; schemes and plans before doing a thing. Smokes, but most of these boys do.

4. *Wilbur* (Age 8 years; in the first grade). Wilbur is a very restless type. He leaves his seat on the slightest excuse. When spoken to or corrected he seems to be resentful and will not answer—just shrugs his shoulders, hands on his hips and bites his lips. He is rough with the other children. I have also had complaints about swearing when he is outside of school.

5. *Robert* (Age 10 years, 5 months; in the special class). Has to be driven to do school work. Two years in Grade I. Two years in Grade II. One year in third. Now in second year in special. A follower. School attendance perfect. Punctual. Not truthful. Robert and others had brought some toy guns to school—later found to have been "lifted" from store. Then school discovered Robert had been on probation when nine years old. Quick and alert in social relationships. Hard boiled. Can hold his own. Accepted by group of children. Not impulsive. Harbors a grudge and is revengeful. Is boisterous. Makes a fuss about his work. A grand flourisher. Has air of braggadocio. Responds to praise. Little brother in same room is very good worker and is very amenable.

6. *Michael* (Age 8 years, 11 months; in the third grade). Very poorly cared for child. Very good writer. Very poor in arithmetic and cannot read what he writes. Is generous, kind, and very impulsive. Has been a truant several times. Seems always to be looking for someone to be giving him something. Hangs out at the commissary. Runs errands for the men there and they give him some of their lunch. Has no mother. She died when he was a baby. He complains a lot for a child. Seems neurotic. Complains of being dizzy and having a pain in his head. Seems sleepy. That may be because he gets up at 5 A.M. when his father goes to work. Is a regular "he man" all right, is "up and at them," ready to put up his hands to fight at a minute's notice. May be inclined to take things if not carefully watched. Is the sort who may get into trouble. Is likable but easily led. Does not seem to have any particular friends. Is very much of a daydreamer. Shows a lack of muscular coordination, tripping and falling all the time. Squirms around in his chair so much that every now and then he falls out of his seat onto the floor.

7. *Andrew* (Age 10 years, 5 months; in the third grade). A character! Cute and likable but a terror. His mother died in a sanitarium for T.B.

about four years ago. The children have been with a grandmother since then. She goes on "bats" for a week or so at a time. Andrew has been two years in each of the first and second grades. He will run around the room in wild fashion, but has become a little better in regard to this. Is a little fox. Will beam at the supervisor when she comes in. Means to do all right but cannot seem to keep it up long. He ran out of the school when told to go to the headmaster. Was not found until 7 o'clock at the square. He had stolen some oranges to keep going. Is very excitable outside the school. Liked very much by the boys and by the girls, too. Will promise you anything. His handwork is poor. His reading is improving. He cannot seem to write words; he can spell very well aloud. Has a lot of personality; will play up to a teacher and make her like him. His father has had a hard time. All the family have head lice. Father would never consent to any sort of medical attention for teeth, eyes, or anything like that. Father used to have to wash all their clothes. The oldest girls are "toughs." The oldest girl beat up a teacher. Andrew steals from all the stores. He once took five cents of the teacher's money. The oldest sister also steals from stores and clotheslines.

8. *George* (Age 10 years, 7 months; in the fourth grade). George has been my problem for two years. Last year he was impossible. This year he is a little better. He is an intelligent child, and can use his head and ask very intelligent questions, but is saucy and impudent, and wants his own way. Sprawled in late seventeen times with a "What are you going to do about it?" attitude. His mother is one who takes the attitude that what her children do is right, and that they must not be punished. George is very argumentative with the other boys. He plays baseball very well. Could be a leader, and might be one in a very short time. His mother took him to the Guidance Center last year. She has an older boy whom she thinks is God's gift to the world but George does not see it that way. The final report from the Guidance Center was that George was a child who would cause her a great deal of trouble later on. He is a healthy boy. Is fidgety. Gets very resentful and sulky when corrected. Is a daydreamer of the imaginative sort. Will ask many intelligent questions after a spell of daydreams.

9. *Neil* (Age 9 years, 6 months; in the third grade). I cannot seem to pin anything on him in the room although I hear that he gets into a lot of trouble outside. He has stolen a lot of money from his home. He spends a lot of his time on the street. Played truant a few times. He was caught and punished. He plays with bad companions who are older boys. Neil once threw stones at another school class and swore terribly at a teacher. He is fair in his studies; will be promoted. I did not get much cooperation from the home. The father and mother would say

that they were doing their best, but did not seem to do anything. Both Neil and his sister are inclined to be untidy and slack. He is a healthy boy.

10. *Jack* (Age 10 years, 1 month; in the third grade). Is a very difficult boy. Plays truant continually. Is always unkempt. His home conditions are not at all what they should be. His mother knows about the truanting, but will do nothing about it. You can always hear his voice above the others in the classroom. Scholastically his is average third grade. He likes to fight in the yard and outside school. Something of a tease. I think he steals outside the school. He has been acting suspiciously in the Five and Ten and he has taken some small things in school. The mother of another pupil said she had seen Jack and his brother stealing in stores. He swears quite a bit. Lies. Is nervous and fidgety.

We see that, as a general rule, our "most delinquent" boys are, in their earlier years, nonconformists in the classroom. (Only two or three of the 31 did not give such indications.) And yet, not all boys who were problems to their teachers were necessarily delinquent or pre-delinquent. A considerable number of the restless, inattentive, and annoying schoolchildren were not in later years involved in larceny, burglary, assaults, or other serious acts against society.

IS THE DELINQUENT A MISFIT IN SCHOOL?

It is to be expected that continued inattention, lack of motivation for schoolwork, and disobedience would be accompanied by unsatisfactory school achievement resulting in the failure of the child to be promoted regularly from one grade to another. In a few cases a child was denied promotion because of his conduct, not because of his grades. Failure to be promoted generally accentuated the child's dissatisfaction with school and led to further disobedience. A comparison of the delinquent child with the less delinquent or the non-delinquent, in respect to grade retardation, establishes the point that the delinquent child fails to be promoted annually to the next higher grade more often than the non-delinquent child. Table 34 shows the number of grades, on the average, that the children in each category were retarded.

The "most delinquent" boys, it is evident, are relatively frequently retarded—seven out of 15 were retarded three or more times or placed in special class or vocational school, while none of

TABLE 34

Relative Retardation of Delinquent and Less Delinquent Boys
(Up to Beginning of Grade VI)

	DELINQUENCY JUDGMENTS					
Retardation	I	II	IV	V	Retired	Total
None	1	2	2	15	50	70
One year	2	6	6	17	10	41
Two years	5	3	3	13	4	28
Three years or more [a]	7	6	2	19	0	34
Total	15	17	13	64	64	173

[a] Includes placement in the "special class" or the vocational school.

the retired boys was retarded more than two grades. We note, however, a good deal of retardation in the groups that were "least delinquent" and in the intermediate groups. In short, while retardation alone is not an indication of delinquency, few of the "most delinquent" boys are able to achieve regular annual promotions.[2]

IS THE DELINQUENT INTELLECTUALLY HANDICAPPED?

We cannot assume that retardation was due necessarily either to the boys' poor conduct or to lack of motivation for schoolwork, though the latter factor must have played a large part.[3] The lack of native intellectual capacity may have had some part in the maladjustment picture. We now compare the boys (in these same categories of delinquency) who were given individual intelligence tests administered by the staff psychologists, using the Stanford-Binet Revised Test.

This table clearly differentiates in I.Q. the average "most delinquent" boy from the average retired boy. (The retired boys, it will be remembered, were the boys with the fewest problems and with a minimum of misbehavior.) The "most delinquent" boys also

2 The Gluecks found that of 935 delinquents who were in court, only 145 boys (15.5 percent) were *not* retarded in school. They also found that school retardation and poor conduct in school were two of the six factors most closely related to posttreatment failure (Sheldon and Eleanor T. Glueck, *One Thousand Juvenile Delinquents*). Kvaraceus found in his study of 661 delinquents that 43.5 percent had repeated one term (one half year) or more, compared to 17 percent for the total school population (William C. Kvaraceus, *Juvenile Delinquency and the School*).

3 In Chap. XI the differences in motivation for school work between the delinquent and the non-delinquent were indicated.

TABLE 35

Distribution of Average I.Q.'s of Delinquent and Less Delinquent Boys
(Stanford-Binet Revised Test)

DELINQUENCY JUDGMENTS

	I	II	IV	V	*Retired* [a]
Number	14	16	13	62	31
Average I.Q.	87.3	95.6	94.9	92.5	103.0

[a] Of the 64 retired boys, 31 had been given the Binet tests and are therefore included here.

achieved as a group a lower average I.Q. than any of the other groups.

We conclude that there is no evidence from these limited data to show any substantial correspondence between intellectual capacity and severity or frequency of delinquent behavior, although those whose antisocial behavior seems to be most persistent are found on the average to have I.Q.s below 90, which is considerably below the average for those with the fewest problems.[4]

IS THE DELINQUENT A TRUANT?

All research studies dealing with the delinquent boy and the school have demonstrated a close relationship between delinquent behavior and truancy from school.[5] Boys who are less able to do the required work and who are more frequently retarded are forced to sit in a classroom where the younger and brighter children outdistance them. It is easy to see how under such circumstances school attendance becomes a progressively unhappy experience. The simplest way for such a child to avoid humiliation or boredom is to stay out as long as he can "get away with it." He evidently finds his deepest satisfactions outside of school, generally in a socially disapproved manner. The result is a high correlation between delinquent behavior and truancy.

[4] The studies of the relationship between intelligence and delinquency are too numerous to list here. The delinquent child has generally been found to be in the *dull normal* group. For specific references to these studies, see P. S. de Q. Cabot, *Juvenile Delinquency; a Critical Annotated Bibliography* (New York, H. W. Wilson, 1946).

[5] All studies in this field confirm the fact that delinquents truant far more frequently than non-delinquents. Kvaraceus (*Juvenile Delinquency and the School*, pp. 144–145) examined the findings of six research projects dealing with the incidence of truancy among delinquents, showing percentages of delinquents who were found to be truants ranging from 25 to 66.

TABLE 36

Distribution of Truants

DELINQUENCY JUDGMENTS

	I	II	IV	V	Retired
Number of boys	15	17	13	64	64
Number of truants	13	14	8	12	0
Percent of truants	86.7	82.4	61.5	18.8	0

Table 36 shows the distribution of truancy in our delinquent and non-delinquent groups. By "truant" we mean a boy of school age who intentionally stays away from school for no other reason than that he does not wish to go. Before placing him in the class of truant we noted that he absented himself without parental excuse not once or twice but at least on three or four different occasions over a period of weeks or months.[6]

The data given in Table 36 are taken from our case records, for the counselors were generally well aware of the truancy whether or not it was officially recorded in the office of the attendance supervisor. We had, of course, no comparable data for C-boys.

Thirteen of our 15 "most delinquent" T-boys were truants. Our next most delinquent group (Group II) was also actively truant to about the same degree, and yet our "seldom delinquents" (Group IV) and particularly our "least delinquent" boys (Group V) truanted far less frequently. We note that not one of our retired boys was a truant.

We conclude from these data that truancy is closely related to delinquent behavior, more closely in fact than the intelligence quotient or the degree of retardation.

COMPARISON OF PERSONALITY TRAITS

One cannot describe the personality of *the* delinquent boy: we can describe only the personality of *a* delinquent boy. John, for example, who was declared to be a delinquent because he had broken into a store one night and rifled a cash register, is as different in personality from Joe, who was adjudicated a delinquent be-

---

6 Unauthorized absences occurring only once or twice or occurring more frequently but within a single week or two and not recurring were not recorded as truancy in Table 36.

cause his mother said he was a "stubborn child," as John's behavior is different from Joe's. These two boys bore little resemblance to each other in physique, intelligence, or motivation. The "causes" of their delinquencies were not in any respect similar. The only common factors between them seemed to be that they were both boys between the ages of seven and 17 and both were officially declared delinquent by an individual called a judge.[7]

Nevertheless, in dealing with school children it is wise to be on guard against certain kinds of overt behavior that may indicate possible future difficulty. Such behavior may be symptomatic of pre-delinquency in a given case, because on the average it is more characteristic of delinquents than non-delinquents. The question, then, can be stated: Have any specific personality traits been observed by teachers more frequently among boys who are or who become delinquents than among those who are never delinquent in any serious sense?

DIFFERENTIATING DELINQUENTS FROM NON-DELINQUENTS BY TEACHERS' RATINGS

Two instruments were used by the teachers before the beginning of the treatment program that were believed to point to the danger

[7] And yet, in contrasting large groups of adjudicated delinquents with non-delinquents significant differences can be demonstrated when group averages are compared as to certain factors such as intelligence or emotional stability. For a review of the literature dealing with a variety of factors differentiating delinquents and criminals from others, see Milton Metfessel and Constance Lovell, "Recent Literature on Individual Correlates of Crime," *Psychological Bulletin*, XXXIX (1942), 133–164.

Merrill summarizes the factors which have been found by personality tests to differentiate the delinquents from the non-delinquents. The two groups, *as such*, differ significantly, she reports, in (1) emotional stability, (2) emotional maturity, (3) traits characterizing the psychopathic personality, (4) social adjustment, (5) personal attitudes, (6) problem behavior, and (7) honesty. See Maud A. Merrill, *Problems of Child Delinquency* (New York, Houghton Mifflin, 1947), pp. 40–41.

The proportion of delinquents who come from inadequate homes and inferior neighborhoods is, to give another example, higher than the proportion of non-delinquents from such homes and such neighborhoods. We also have shown that the delinquent boy, on the average, is more frequently a problem child in school and more frequently truants when he finds life unbearable in the classroom. But we cannot overlook the fact that in the distribution of any of these factors there is much overlapping. In other words, though delinquents and non-delinquents differ as *groups* the differences between the individuals in the groups are greater than the differences between the groups themselves. This fact, of course, does not make diagnosis or prediction easier and is a warning to those dealing with the practical problem of treatment that they must always consider the delinquent as an individual with his own private reasons for behaving as he does.

signs of behavior. One was the Trait Record Card, already described.[8] This card listed a number of undesirable traits or characteristics grouped in eight categories. The second instrument was the Descriptive Rating Scale which contained 26 items relating to behavior and personality which the teachers rated on a five-point scale.[9]

Let us first compare our "most delinquent" boys with our "least delinquent" boys in respect to the number of unfavorable items checked on the Trait Record Card for the boys in each group, who were then about nine years old. Group I consisted of 29 of our "most delinquent" boys. (In two of the 31 cases of "most delinquent" boys adequate information was lacking.) Group V consisted of 73 of our "least delinquent" boys.[10]

Table 37 shows the percentage of boys in each group who, according to the teachers' observations, were completely free of any unfavorable behavior in any of the eight categories.

TABLE 37

Comparison of "Most" and "Least" Delinquent Boys in Respect to Absence of Undesirable Behavior as Noted by Teachers of First Five Grades

		ABSENCE OF UNDESIRABLE BEHAVIOR (IN PERCENT)		
Behavior Categories *(Trait Record Card)*	*Number of Items*	*Group I*	*Group V*	*Group V minus Group I*
A. Troublemaking	14	20.7	43.8	23.1
B. Neurotic behavior	11	31.0	53.4	22.4
C. Show-off	7	41.4	64.4	23.0
D. Retiring	14	41.4	31.5	−9.9
E. Aggressive	16	31.0	52.1	21.1
F. Submissive	13	31.0	50.7	19.7
G. Antisocial	7	72.4	90.4	18.0
H. Undesirable habits	11	17.2	47.9	30.7

Table 38 shows the average occurrence of a trait checked by the teachers for each of the two groups. It is evident from these tables

8 See Chap. IV. A copy of this card appears in Appendix C.
9 See Chap. IV. A copy of this scale appears in Appendix C.
10 In order to differentiate more sharply the "most delinquent" from the "least delinquent," we have omitted 46 of the 119 boys in Group V who had appeared before the Crime Prevention Bureau or before the court for even a minor offense; this leaves 73 boys who were not known to the staff for any delinquent behavior other than technical and minor infractions of the law.

that, of the 102, the boys who became the most delinquent were more frequently characterized as: troublemaking, aggressive, having show-off behavior, having undesirable habits, submissive, neurotic, and antisocial. The "least delinquent" group slightly exceeded the "most delinquent" group in the average number of undesirable items classified as "retiring behavior." This category included such items as "is seclusive," "is shy," "is self-effacing," "lacks self-confidence," and so on.

TABLE 38

Comparison of "Most" and "Least" Delinquent Boys in Respect to Undesirable Behavior as Noted by Teachers in First Five Grades

Behavior Categories (Trait Record Card)	Number of Items	AVERAGE NUMBER OF ITEMS CHECKED		
		Group I	Group V	Group I minus Group V
A. Troublemaking	14	4.2	2.4	1.8
B. Neurotic behavior	11	1.6	1.0	.6
C. Show-off	7	2.4	.9	1.5
D. Retiring	14	1.4	1.7	—.3
E. Aggressive	16	3.9	1.6	2.3
F. Submissive	13	1.8	1.5	.3
G. Antisocial	7	.7	.1	.6
H. Undesirable habits	11	2.2	1.2	1.0

Not all of the "most delinquent" boys, of course, were "bad"; nor were all of the "least delinquent" boys "good," in the eyes of their teachers. In fact, we found one "least delinquent" boy who received more checks in the category of troublemaking behavior than any of the "most delinquent" boys; there were ten "least delinquent" boys with three or more checks in the category of aggressive reactions; there were 14 "least delinquent" boys with three or more checks in the category of undesirable habits. Conversely, in each of the categories we find a number of "most delinquent" boys with no checks whatsoever. Nevertheless, the boys who later demonstrated serious antisocial behavior clearly had more than their share of undesirable traits in their early school years.

We now compare the same groups of boys in respect to 12 of the 26 items on the Descriptive Rating Scale that proved to be discriminating (Table 39).

TABLE 39

"Most Delinquent" Compared with "Least Delinquent" Boys in Respect to Traits Observed by Teachers in the First Few Grades ("Descriptive Rating Scale") [a]

		PERCENTAGES		
Characteristic	Manifestation	Group I [b] ("Most delinquent")	Group V [c] ("Least delinquent")	Difference between Groups I and V
1. Restlessness	(a) "Constantly on the move; irritable; fussing with hands, impatient."	55.6	17.4	38.2
2. Courage	(e) "Dare-devil."	52.0	14.5	37.5
3. Interest in schoolwork	(a) "Negativistic toward learning"; or (b) "Amenable but negligent."	74.1	38.0	36.1
4. Moods	At one extreme or the other: (a, b) "Stolid; impassive"; "Generally inexpressive"; or (d, e) "Has strong and frequent changes of mood"; "Has periods of extreme elation or depression."	82.6	47.5	35.1
5. Easygoing	(e) "Irresponsible and entirely carefree."	53.8	18.8	35.0
6. Sensitive to others	(a) "Cruel; spiteful; sarcastic; hard-boiled."	58.3	23.3	35.0
7. Flexibility	(a) "Stubborn, hidebound; nonconformist."	40.0	7.6	32.4
8. Attention	(a) "Distractible; jumps rapidly from one thing to another"; (b) "Difficult to keep at task until completed."	83.3	51.5	31.8
9. Talkative	(d) "Talks more than his share"; (e) "Jabbers; very loquacious."	59.3	27.9	31.4
10. Self-confidence	(e) "Cocksure"; (d) "Quite self-confident."	57.1	26.2	30.9
11. Impulsive	(a) "Impulsive; bolts; acts on the spur of the moment"; (b) "Frequently unreflective and imprudent."	82.6	53.7	28.9
12. Personal appearance	(a) "Very slovenly; unkempt"; (b) "Rather negligent."	55.5	27.1	28.4

[a] Only 12 of the 26 items—those that proved to be the most discriminating—are here tabulated.
[b] Number = 21 to 27.
[c] Number = 60 to 71.

270 THE SCHOOL MEETS THE DELINQUENT BOY

These boys of eight, nine, and ten who later became seriously delinquent were observed by their teachers to be less amenable to classroom routine more frequently than were the "least delinquent" boys. It is interesting to note in Table 39 that "restlessness" was the characteristic that most frequently distinguished the delinquent boy. Healy and Bronner in their study of delinquents contrasted with their non-delinquent siblings also found that this trait was most characteristic of the delinquent child. "Great restlessness or overactivity," they wrote, "was found reported by parents, teachers and others to be a habitual characteristic of the delinquent. . . . In this category—and we repeat that we are enumerating only those who showed this type of behavior to a most unusual or abnormal degree—we found one-third of our total number of delinquents— 53 cases. We are forced to agree with some other students of behavior problems that hyperactivity on the part of children is strongly related to the appearance of delinquency. In our series no other single personality characteristic is found in any exaggerated degree so frequently." [11]

No one of the items of these two instruments was the exclusive possession of the delinquents nor were there more than three or four of the delinquents with an extreme rating on *all* of the items. There were also a few non-delinquents who had a similarly high rating. Evidently, the individual delinquent is not a sub-species of human being in possession of factors common to his sub-species that are not found in the non-delinquent.

THE DELINQUENTS AND THE MALADJUSTED COMPARED

Many boys scoring high on these items are "pseudo-delinquents" —that is, maladjusted children who might like to (but dare not) break out into antisocial behavior. Pursuing this idea further we took three other groups of children (mostly nine- and ten-year-olds at the time the teachers' ratings were made):

A. A group of 29 boys later placed in our "most delinquent" category;

B. A group of 31 boys later placed in our "least delinquent" cate-

[11] William Healy and Augusta F. Bronner, *New Light on Delinquency and Its Treatment* (New Haven, Yale University Press, 1936), pp. 44–45.

gory who were not adjudicated delinquent but were poorly adjusted to life;

C. A group of 21 boys later placed in our "least delinquent" category who were well adjusted to life.[12]

Comparing the ratings of the three groups on these items we found that the maladjusted non-delinquent resembled the delinquent boy, though his ratings were not as extreme on the items mentioned. In fact, in every one of the eight items taken from the Descriptive Rating Scale we found that the boy who was not delinquent, but nevertheless unhappy and poorly adjusted to school routine, possessed the traits common to the delinquent more frequently than the well-adjusted boy did. The same finding was true as to the items on the Trait Record Card (with the exception of aggressive behavior). In other words, in trying to select a future delinquent we unavoidably include in our group a number of boys who will not be delinquent in the years to come and yet will need guidance and help in making a happy adjustment to life. It is doubtful if any test or rating scale can make the sharp distinction at the first or second grade level between the boy who is not now delinquent, but is going to express his reaction to frustration in a manner that is punishable, from the boy who will express his reactions in a socially undesirable but unpunishable manner. (We should keep in mind that a delinquent act is punishable, an act that is not punishable is not delinquent.) Thus, for every maladjusted child who expressed himself by serious social misconduct outside of school there are innumerable maladjusted children who do not. The latter do not call attention to themselves because their behavior lacks the dramatic quality that characterizes the delinquent's conduct. The school might better concern itself then, not with the restricted and somewhat negative problem of delinquency-prevention as such, but with the problems of all children, who, in the pursuit of happiness, express hostility toward others or toward themselves alone.[13]

[12] The criteria for "poor and good adjustment to life" are discussed in Chap. XXII.

[13] For a discussion of the school's responsibility in respect to this problem, see Edwin Powers, "The School's Responsibility for the Early Detection of Delinquency-Prone Children," *Harvard Educational Review*, XIX (1949), 80–86

SUMMARY

The "most delinquent" boys were, with very few exceptions, outstanding problems to their schoolteachers. They were, on the whole, misfits in the school program, had below normal intellectual capacity (on the average) and failed of promotion far more frequently than boys who were less delinquent. The most striking characteristic of the boy who later became a serious problem for the police and courts was his tendency to escape, by frequent truanting, from the uncomfortable situation in which he found himself.

The future delinquent also showed early in his school career characteristic ways of behaving that distinguished the most serious of them as a group from the least serious. Generally, potential serious delinquents were readily spotted by their teachers. On the other hand, many boys who later were maladjusted but not seriously delinquent were also behavior problems in school. It is useful also to identify boys who are problems to their teachers, though not necessarily future delinquents, for most of these boys are in need of understanding and guidance. The distinction between these two types of boys may be difficult to make in many cases, but becomes more or less academic, for both kinds of boys need attention.

CHAPTER XVIII

CAN DELINQUENCY
BE PREDICTED?

ONE OF THE LITTLE BOYS REFERRED TO THE STUDY TEN YEARS AGO BY his fourth grade teacher with the comment that he was a "restless, talkative boy" who "just wants to get into mischief" is now in a state prison. Another boy from the third grade whose home life was "most unsatisfactory" and whom the teacher found necessary "to watch and correct most carefully" is serving a long term in a federal penitentiary. A third boy reported as a truant when nine years old is now in a house of correction for stealing goods from a freight car. A number of other boys known to the Study when they were under 12 years old are similarly confined or are on parole from a correctional institution or a juvenile training school.

Were these outcomes foreshadowed by the boys' early pre-delinquent behavior? Could one have predicted correctly that some boys would, in a few years, be "enemies of society" while others would be good citizens?

A growing number of studies suggest that human behavior can be predicted in a general way. Scholastic achievement in college, for example, and vocational success and failure can be foretold within limits.[1] To some extent the probable adjustment to society of prisoners following their release from confinement can be predicted.[2] There have also been attempts to identify those youngsters who later in life would become delinquent, but to the writer's knowl-

---

[1] The references on prediction are too numerous to mention here. In a 1941 Social Science Research Council Publication (Bulletin No. 48), Paul Horst presents a bibliography of studies relating to prediction in the fields of marriage, criminal recidivism, school and vocational success (pp. 152–156).

[2] For studies prior to 1942 see R. M. Allen, "A Review of Parole Prediction Literature," *Journal of Criminal Law and Criminology*, XXXII (1942), 548. See also Elio D. Monachesi, "American Studies in the Prediction of Recidivism," *Journal of Criminal Law and Criminology*, XLI (1950), 268–289.

edge none has reported a checking of its predictions in later years.

From the records of the Study a partial investigation of this problem can be made, for there are available (a) delinquency predictions pertaining to boys under the age of 12, (b) recorded observations of these same boys whose growth and development have been followed over a period of nine or ten years, and (c) judgments made at the end of that period of time as to whether each boy had or had not developed a delinquent career, and, if so, to what extent.

SUBJECTS OF THE PREDICTION STUDY

The subjects comprise 100 T-boys and 100 C-boys. Of the treatment group only the older boys were chosen—those over 17 at the time the delinquency judgments were made, and only those whose life histories were sufficiently well known to warrant a judgment. From a list arranged chronologically by ages the first 100 boys were selected. A similar procedure was used to select 100 C-boys. This second group had, of course, not been so closely followed throughout the intervening period as the T-boys, but in each case school and official records had been kept and their careers were well known. Each C-boy was personally interviewed just prior to the final judgment, with the exception of six or seven boys who had been confined to institutions, but in such cases ample records of the boy's delinquencies and attitudes were available to the Study.[3]

PREDICTIONS BY A COMMITTEE OF THREE

The Original Predictions. As previously described (Chapter V), a committee of three who had had training and practical experience in dealing with youthful and adult criminals had made a predictive rating for 782 boys (including of course the 200 boys who were subjects of this study), indicating their judgments as to the probability of delinquent careers. At the time such ratings were made none of the 200 boys had reached the age of 12. The age distribution is shown in Table 40.

---

[3] One hundred and thirty-six of the oldest C-boys were omitted for lack of sufficient information to warrant a valid rating. Younger C-boys (though over 17) had to be included in order to make up the required number. The average age of boys in the control group was approximately six months less than the average for the T-boys. It is thus evident that the two selected groups were not matched as individuals or as groups. The usefulness of the matching plan described in Chap. VI will be more apparent in subsequent chapters on evaluation.

TABLE 40

Ages of the 200 Subjects at the Time of the Original Predictions

Age in Years	T-Boys	C-Boys	Total	Percent
8 to 9	0	14	14	7.0
9 to 10	28	33	61	30.5
10 to 11	47	31	78	39.0
11 to 12	25	22	47	23.5
Total	100	100	200	100.0

The predictive scale, it will be recalled, ranged from a minus five, indicating an extreme probability that the boy would develop a delinquent career in the ensuing years, through zero, to a plus five, indicating an extreme probability that he would not develop such a career. A zero rating indicated that there were no apparent probabilities in either direction, or that the chances seemed to be equal that the boy would go toward or away from delinquency. In making their predictions on the total group of 782 boys the predictors seldom used the extreme ratings.[4] In the sample of 200 boys here studied there happened to be no minus five, plus four, or plus five predictions. The distribution of predictions appears in Table 41. The table shows that 69 percent of the 200 boys here studied were predicted as probable future delinquents (−1 to −4), 25 percent as probable non-delinquents (+1 to +3), with 6 percent reflecting an uncertain prediction (0).

TABLE 41

Original Predictive Ratings of the 200 Boys

Rating	T-Boys	C-Boys	Total	Percent
−5	0	0	0	. .
−4	3	1	4	2.0
−3	12	10	22	11.0
−2	35	26	61	30.5
−1	20	31	51	25.5
0	7	5	12	6.0
+1	13	8	21	10.5
+2	9	18	27	13.5
+3	1	1	2	1.0
+4	0	0	0	. .
+5	0	0	0	. .
Total	100	100	200	100.0

[4] In this chapter those who made the original predictions are referred to as "predictors"; those who later checked the predictions are called "judges."

The Basis of the Original Predictions. Comprehensive data on the personal and social lives of these boys were available to the predictors (see Chapter V). This material represented a wide variety of information dealing with the mental and physical condition of the boy, his progress in school, his adjustment to his family and to the world, and a brief review of his parentage and the family picture. Little was known of the boy's heredity or of the first few years of his life. For practical reasons, it was impossible to arrange for personal interviews between the predictors and the boys which might have revealed more significant psychological data. Nevertheless, the material available to the predictors was reasonably adequate in regard to the objective factors in the boy's behavior and environment.

The Concept of Delinquent Career. The predictors, in placing a boy on the minus side, did not thereby predict that he would commit only one delinquent act (regardless of its general nature), nor in placing him on the plus side did they predict that he would never commit any delinquent act. In other words, they were not concerned merely with technical violations or the presence or absence of an official record. They had in mind the prediction of "a delinquent career" which may or may not have been officially recorded in the dockets of the court. It was evident to the predictors, as it was to the counselors later, that there is no necessary relationship between behavior and appearance in court.[5] The concept of a delinquent career was broader than this. A subjective criterion was adopted, the three essential ingredients of which were the frequency of offenses, their seriousness, and the boy's attitude toward society.[6]

How the Original Predictions Were Made. After making a predictive rating the predictors were asked to state the chief factors upon which they thought it had been based. Subsequently these factors were enumerated and it was possible to compile 52 headings under which all of the variables they listed as important in their decisions could be placed.[7] Twenty-one of the 52 factors most frequently mentioned by the judges were as follows, in this order:

[5] As pointed out in Chap. II, there are no infallible comprehensive quantitative indices of delinquent behavior. See S. M. Robison, *Can Delinquency Be Measured?* (New York, Columbia University Press, 1936).

[6] We have explained the meanings of these terms in Chap. XIV.

[7] See Donald W. Taylor, "An Analysis of Predictions of Delinquency Based on Case Studies," *Journal of Abnormal and Social Psychology*, XLII (1947), 45–56. The findings of Taylor's report are summarized in the present volume, Chap. V, pp. 58–59.

1. Home (generally adequate or inadequate)
2. Neighborhood
3. Intelligence
4. Status of Father
5. Parent-Boy Attitude
6. Standard of Living
7. Family Delinquency
8. Discipline in the Home
9. Attitude toward Authority
10. Status of Mother
11. Personality Disorders
12. Social Adjustment
13. Number of Children in Family
14. Chronological Age
15. Health
16. Ordinal Rank among Siblings
17. Status of Siblings
18. School Retardation
19. School Accomplishment
20. Unbroken or Broken Home
21. Behavior

We may assume that to the judges this list comprises the most important factors in the available information. It is conceivable that other factors might have had more weight had they been present in the record, such as the very early history of the child. What weight the predictors consciously or unconsciously assigned to any factors or what interrelationships impressed them as important is not known. Presumably they selected factors most commonly associated with delinquent and criminal behavior as reported in other research studies, or drawn from their own extensive experience with delinquents and criminals.

The predictors had in mind the probable behavior of the boy in question during the interval (five to nine years) between the prediction and the boy's 17th birthday. The predictors, not knowing which boys would be placed in the treatment group, made their predictions on the assumption that boys would or would not become delinquent if no special treatment, such as that offered by the Study, were given them. The control group, therefore, becomes the only "pure" group in checking the predictions. Each group will be separately considered.

Checking the Original Predictions. After the original predictions were made (1937 to 1938) nine to ten years elapsed before the 200 cases were reexamined on the hypothesis that the delinquent probabilities can be checked after a period of years by a delinquency rating based on a scale showing the extent to which delinquency actually developed. It was not always possible, however, when the second ratings were made, to assign a boy confidently and precisely to one of the 11 steps on the scale, even when his career was well known. The 11 points were therefore telescoped into five corre-

278   CAN DELINQUENCY BE PREDICTED?

sponding categories (Groups I to V inclusive). Table 42 shows how the 11 points were regrouped.

TABLE 42

Comparison of Original Predictions and Judgments of Outcomes

Original Predictions (1937–38)		Judgments of Outcomes (1947–48)	
(−5) −4 −3	Highest probability of delinquent career	Group I	Boys who developed the most delinquent careers
−2 −1	Moderate probability of delinquent career	Group II	Boys who developed moderate delinquent careers—the ordinary delinquent
0	Mid-point; no probability in either direction	Group III	The mid-point; boys who were not consistently delinquent or non-delinquent — the occasional delinquent
+1 +2	Moderate probability of non-delinquency	Group IV	Boys who were moderately free of delinquency—the seldom delinquent
+3 (+4) (+5)	Highest probability of non-delinquency	Group V	Boys who were least delinquent

NOTE: It will be recalled (Table 41) that steps −5, +4 and +5 were not used in the original predictive ratings on this sample of 200 boys, though they were used sparingly on some of the 782 predicted cases.

The method used by two judges in analyzing and judging each of these 200 boys nine to ten years later, placing them in five groups ranging from "most" to "least" delinquent, has already been described (see Chapter XIV, pp. 182–183). Table 43 shows the distribution of the boys' ages at the time the judgments were made.

Each judge made his rating independently, placing each of the

TABLE 43

Approximate Ages of the Subjects at Time of Final Judgments

Age in Years	T-Boys	C-Boys	Total	Percent
17 to 18	0	3	3	1.5
18 to 19	3	23	26	13.0
19 to 20	36	31	67	33.5
20 to 21	45	27	72	36.0
21 to 22	16	16	32	16.0
Total	100	100	200	100.0

boys in one of the five groups. In two-thirds of the cases there was an independent agreement; the remaining one-third of the cases were discussed by the two judges until an agreement was reached.

Findings. Table 44 shows the distribution of the final judgments compared to the original predictions for T-boys.

TABLE 44

Comparison of Original Predictions and Final Judgments
for 100 T-Boys

Original Predictions	FINAL JUDGMENTS					
	I	*II*	*III*	*IV*	*V*	*Total*
−5 −4 −3	6	1	0	3	5	15
−2 −1	4	12	5	8	26	55
0	0	0	2	0	5	7
+1 +2	0	1	2	1	18	22
+3 +4 +5	0	0	0	0	1	1
Total	10	14	9	12	55	100

From the above table we find that:

1. In 22 of the 100 cases there was perfect agreement between the predictors and the judges.

2. Of the 70 boys with a minus (delinquent) prediction only 23 were later judged delinquent (Groups I and II).

3. Of the 23 boys with a plus (non-delinquent) prediction, 20 were later judged seldom or least delinquent (Groups IV and V).

4. Of the 24 boys who were judged delinquent (Groups I and II) 23 had been so predicted (rated minus), but of the 67 boys who were judged seldom or least delinquent (Groups IV and V) only 20 had been so predicted (rated plus).

The outstanding feature of this table is the overprediction of delinquency. Of those who ultimately became delinquent, delinquency had been successfully predicted (with one exception). However, many more boys were predicted delinquent than actually became so. The table thus shows an interesting asymmetry: the judges predicted delinquency very well indeed in the cases where it did occur, but predicted it much too often in cases where it did not. The correlation between these two sets of ratings for the T-boys is .44 which is significantly different from zero.[8]

[8] To gauge the strength of the relationship between predictions and subsequent judgments the tetrachoric correlation coefficient was used, drawing the lines of

Checking the Predictions on C-Boys. As boys in the treatment group were subject to the case-work efforts of the counselors who were particularly concerned with preventing the minus boys from becoming delinquent, thus defeating the predictions on that group, one might assume that the fact that so many boys who were predicted delinquent did not become so was due to the work of the counselors. Let us then check the predictions on the C-boys.

Table 45 shows the distribution of the final judgments in terms of the original predictions for the 100 C-boys.

TABLE 45

Comparison of Original Predictions and Final Judgments for 100 C-Boys

	FINAL JUDGMENTS					
Original Predictions	I	II	III	IV	V	Total
−5 −4 −3	4	3	0	3	1	11
−1 −2	11	9	0	16	21	57
0	1	0	0	1	3	5
+1 +2	0	3	0	2	21	26
+3 +4 +5	0	0	0	0	1	1
Total	16	15	0	22	47	100

Findings. From the above table it is seen that:

1. In 16 of the 100 cases there was perfect agreement between the predictors and the judges.

2. Of the 68 boys with a minus (delinquent) prediction only 27 were later judged delinquent (Groups I and II).

3. Of the 27 boys with a plus (non-delinquent) prediction 24 were later judged seldom or least delinquent (Groups IV and V).

4. Of the 31 judged delinquent (Groups I and II) 27 had been so predicted (rated minus), but of the 69 boys judged seldom or least delinquent (Groups IV and V) only 24 had been so predicted (rated plus).

dichotomy at zero and Group III respectively. It is not certain that the assumptions made for the use of this statistic (continuity of variables and rectilinearity of regression) were fully met. The distributions of the two sets of ratings, moreover, seemed to deviate from normality. Bearing these limitations in mind, we can, nevertheless, use the tetrachoric coefficient as an approximate measure of the degree of correspondence between predictions and later judgments. The standard error of a tetrachoric correlation of zero obtained from data such as those in Table 44 is .17 so that $t = 2.59$. The probability of obtaining a coefficient as large, or larger, by chance alone is .01.

Again we find the judges predicted delinquency very well in cases in which it did occur but predicted it much too often. The correlation between the predictions and the later judgments for the C-boys is .54. Again the coefficient is significantly different from zero.[9] If a significantly lower coefficient were obtained for the treatment group than for the control group this fact might, as we have said, constitute some evidence for successful treatment. A rough but adequate test of significance of the difference between the two correlation coefficients was carried out. No conclusive evidence could be found that the prediction for the control group was significantly better than for the treatment group though in both cases the predictions were better than chance.[10]

Checking the Predictions on the Combined Treatment and Control Groups. The treatment and control groups were combined and the predictions and final judgments were compared in the same manner. The correlation between these two ratings of the 200 cases was found to be .49, also significantly above chance.[11] As the predictions of T-boys did not significantly differ from the predictions of C-boys we have here omitted the table and the specific findings for the combined groups.

PREDICTIONS BY TEACHERS

It has frequently been claimed that teachers of children in the lower grades of the public schools can distinguish future delinquents from other boys in the classroom, the assumption being that there are dependable signs of probable delinquent behavior.

Basis of the Prediction. The teachers of each of the 200 boys were asked to give a concise but comprehensive report of the boy's personality and behavior in an interview with a staff member. These interviews were held at about the same time as the predictors were

[9] Here $t = 3.18$. The probability of obtaining such a large coefficient by chance is also less than .01.

[10] The standard error of the difference was estimated with the aid of the formula given by Charles C. Peters and Walter R. Van Voorhis, *Statistical Procedures and Their Mathematical Bases* (State College, Pa., 1935), p. 372 ff. A t-value of .50 was obtained, showing clearly that the difference between the two coefficients is not significant. As an additional check, a chi-square test was performed to test the hypothesis that predictions for C-boys were not more successful than predictions for T-boys. This hypothesis could not be rejected (probability of chance relationship .50).

[11] Here $t = 4.08$, probability of chance less than .01.

making their independent predictions. The interviews were informal and in most cases the teacher's remarks were taken down verbatim. Questions were directed particularly to the boy's general behavior and attitudes. All of the 200 boys were at that time pupils in one of the first five grades of the public schools. Approximately 90 percent of the interviews were held in the second half of the school year, thus giving the teacher ample opportunity for knowing the boy.[12]

The teachers were not asked to use the scale adopted by the predictors, for it is doubtful if so many individuals would have employed this scale with a common interpretation. Furthermore, teachers would probably have been reluctant to identify the future delinquent if they had been asked to rate him on a delinquency scale. Another method had to be devised. One of the directors of the Study, after interviewing the teacher in each case, or studying the reports of another member of the staff who interviewed the teacher, checked that point on the prognostic scale that he believed represented the rating the teacher herself might have assigned. These predictions then are not, strictly speaking, teachers' predictions but careful approximations of them.[13]

Checking the Teachers' Predictions. The teachers' predictions were compared with the subsequent judgments in the same manner as the ratings of the original predictors were compared. (See Tables 46 and 47.)

TABLE 46

*Comparison of Teachers' Predictions and Final Judgments
for 100 T-Boys*

Teachers' Predictions	FINAL JUDGMENTS					
	I	II	III	IV	V	Total
−3 −4 −5	8	4	1	8	8	29
−1 −2	1	7	2	1	15	26
0	1	2	2	2	7	14
+1 +2	0	1	3	1	14	19
+3 +4 +5	0	0	1	0	11	12
Total	10	14	9	12	55	100

[12] The methods used in obtaining these opinions were described in Chap. IV. Samples of the interviews were given in Chap. XIV.

[13] For convenience, we shall refer to them as teachers' predictions in this chapter.

From Table 46, which compares the teachers' predictions on the T-boys with the final delinquency judgments, it is seen that:

1. In 29 of the 100 cases there was perfect agreement between the teachers and the judges.

2. Of the 55 boys with a minus (delinquent) prediction only 20 were later judged delinquent (Groups I and II).

3. Of the 31 boys with a plus (non-delinquent) prediction 26 were later judged seldom or least delinquent (Groups IV and V).

4. Of the 24 boys who were judged delinquent (Groups I and II) 20 had been so predicted (rated minus), but of the 67 boys who were judged seldom or least delinquent (Groups IV and V) only 26 had been so predicted (rated plus).

Again we see the same general pattern: accurate predictions for boys who became definitely delinquent or definitely non-delinquent, accompanied by a sizable overprediction of delinquency. Treating the data in the same way as was done in the case of the original predictions we obtain a tetrachoric correlation coefficient of .35 between teachers' predictions and later judgments.[14]

Examining the teachers' predictions of 100 C-boys (Table 47) and comparing them with later judgments of delinquency we find:

TABLE 47

Comparison of Teachers' Predictions and Final Judgments for 100 C-Boys

	FINAL JUDGMENTS					
Teachers' Predictions	*I*	*II*	*III*	*IV*	*V*	*Total*
−3 −4 −5	9	4	0	4	4	21
−1 −2	4	7	0	8	10	29
0	1	4	0	2	9	16
+1 +2	2	0	0	7	16	25
+3 +4 +5	0	0	0	1	8	9
Total	16	15	0	22	47	100

1. In 31 of the 100 cases there was perfect agreement between the teachers and the judges.

2. Of the 50 boys with a minus (delinquent) prediction only 24 were later judged to be delinquent (Groups I and II).

14 This coefficient is just significantly different from zero ($t = 2.19$, chance probability being between .02 and .05).

3. Of the 34 boys with a plus (non-delinquent) prediction 32 were later judged seldom or least delinquent (Groups IV and V).

4. Of the 31 boys judged delinquent (Groups I and II) 24 had been so predicted (rated minus) but of the 69 judged seldom or least delinquent (Groups IV and V) only 32 had been so predicted (rated plus).

Here we find a slightly higher tetrachoric correlation coefficient (.59) [15] than in the prediction of T-boys by the teachers or in the prediction of either T- or C-boys by the original predictors.

Again we may ask whether the teachers' predictions were more efficient for the control group than for the treatment group. There is a suggestive trend in that direction, though the difference between the correlation of .35 (for the treatment group) and the correlation of .59 (for the control group) falls short of statistical significance.[16] It must be kept in mind, however, that both the rating scales and the statistics employed are fairly rough. Considering the consistency of the results obtained both from teachers and judges one can conclude that there is a trend, at least, of greater efficiency for the control group predictions than for those of the treatment group. This difference may possibly be taken as slight presumptive evidence for the effectiveness of the treatment program.

Checking the Teachers' Predictions on the Combined Treatment and Control Groups. If we combine the treatment and control groups we obtain a coefficient, using the same method, of .48 between the teachers' predictions and the final judgments of delinquency. As in all of the above instances the coefficient is significantly different from zero.[17]

In general it was found that teachers in formal reports interpreted in terms of points on a scale predicting delinquency or non-delinquency do predict such behavior at a better-than-chance level. Boys who later became "most delinquent" were generally identified. As in the case of the predictions described in the preceding section (original predictions) they overpredict delinquency; that is,

[15] Here $t = 3.70$, P $= .01$.

[16] This difference between the correlations for the treatment and control groups yields a t of 1.26 and a P value of .20. Similarly, a chi-square formula testing the hypothesis that predictions for C-boys are no more efficient than predictions for T-boys yielded a P value of .50.

[17] Here $t = 4.00$, chance probability being less than .01.

they include in their delinquency predictions many cases where such behavior does not subsequently occur.

PREDICTIVE VALUE OF A BEHAVIOR RATING SCALE

None of the many rating scales, schedules, or questionnaires used in the Study had any known validity in predicting delinquent behavior, with the possible exception of the Haggerty-Olson-Wickman Behavior Rating Schedule.[18] This schedule was designed to measure the problem tendencies of children from the kindergarten to the 12th grade by comparing them with children of the same age in respect to score values measuring specific aspects of behavior and personality. The scale was not constructed specifically for predicting delinquent behavior, its emphasis being on the measurement of "problem tendencies." Dr. Olson, however, one of the authors of the scale, has claimed for it some validity in its ability to select from a large number of school children those who later actually appeared in juvenile court. He obtained "problem tendency" scores for approximately 3,000 school children. Six years later the status of approximately 1,500 children who were first tested in the first grade of 15 representative schools was compared with the scores. Olson found that the mean "problem tendency" score for children who were brought into court because of dependency and neglect was no greater than the mean for children in general, but the averages for children who were brought into court for delinquent behavior were much higher than those for children in general. He also found that the scores differentiated the group in terms of types of offenses. Boys brought into court for stealing had received on the average higher scores than boys who were brought into court for minor offenses. The scores increased successively as the disposition of the court became more severe. Boys committed to the training school had received higher scores than boys placed on probation. Olson thus found a clear relationship between a child's behavior in school as reflected in scores based upon teachers' ratings and the delinquent behavior of these same children six years later.[19]

[18] M. E. Haggerty, W. C. Olson, and E. K. Wickman, *Haggerty-Olson-Wickman Behavior Rating Schedules* (Yonkers, World Book, 1930); *The Nineteen-forty Mental Measurements Yearbook* (Highland Park, N.J., The Mental Measurements Yearbook, 1941), pp. 1222–23.

[19] Willard C. Olson, *Child Development* (Boston, Heath and Company, 1949), pp. 238–245.

The scale consists of Schedule A and Schedule B. The former comprises a list of 15 kinds of behavior, such as lying, defiance of discipline, speech difficulty, which are checked by the boys' teachers for frequency of occurrence. Frequencies are given weighted values. Schedule B consists of 35 questions grouped into four divisions relating to the child's intellectual, physical, social, and emotional traits. Each question is accompanied by a five-point rating scale of descriptive phrases. The teacher checks the phrase which she thinks most aptly fits the boy under consideration. Each position on the scale has a weighted value, in general the extremes receiving higher weightings than the intermediate positions.[20] For example, one of the 35 questions related to the boy's ethical conduct:

Is his behavior (honesty, morals, etc.) generally acceptable to ordinary social standards?

Unacceptable, Extreme Violations	Occasional Violations	Ordinarily Acceptable	Always Acceptable	Bends Backward, Very Rigid Standards
(5)	(4)	(3)	(1)	(2)

The range of scores on Schedule B was 35 to 175. The usefulness of the scale (and, of course, its validity) is subject to the accuracy and insight of the teachers using it. Frequently, we believe, a teacher could not resist the tendency to rate an annoying child "bad" on nearly all counts, and an "average" or a less conspicuous child at the mid-point on each question.

These scales were checked by the teachers of the T- and C-boys during the years 1938–41 inclusive.[21] To allow for a lapse of nine to ten years between the return of the scales and the final judgments of delinquency we have selected only those scales checked in 1938. It was during this year, too, that the greatest number of teacher interviews were held. Most of the predictors' ratings were also completed in 1938 or the early part of 1939. (See Table 40 for boys' ages at this time.)

To verify or check the scores on this rating scale as indicators of future delinquency or non-delinquency, several methods are possible.

[20] The Descriptive Rating Scale, devised by the Study's research staff and described in Chap. IV, was constructed on this pattern.

[21] The scales were usually checked at the end of each of the school years after the teachers had acquired some familiarity with the boys.

METHOD A

The scale scores can be compared to the same post-treatment judgments used in checking the original predictions and the teachers' predictions as described in the preceding sections. In doing so, however, we are beset with several new problems. In the first place we could not say that our "most delinquent" boys (Group I) could be expected to score within any definite range, as compared to the less delinquent. Secondly, our distribution of scores as well as our distribution of boys within the five categories did not show a constant increment of change. Taking a small sample of 88 T- and C-boys for whom we have H.O.W. scores (Schedule B) we plotted the distribution of scores on a chart showing the relationship between the delinquency judgments and the scale scores. We found that two-thirds of the delinquency judgments fell into Group V and that three-fourths of the scale scores fell below the mid-point of the range (50 to 150). Such a distribution does not lend itself well to the determination of a product-moment correlation coefficient. A biserial correlation was then computed which seemed to be more appropriate for this peculiar distribution and the relatively small number of cases, dichotomizing the delinquency judgments between Group V and lower than Group V and treating the rating scale scores as a continuous variable. A value of —.23 was obtained, a coefficient barely above chance.[22]

From these results we cannot say that Schedule B has any predictive value in terms of our concept of delinquency. Our finding, of course, for the reasons given, is inconclusive. It did not seem worth while to make the same computation on Schedule A, where by inspection the distribution appeared to be similar.

METHOD B

We now compare the means of the scale scores obtained for each of the delinquency judgments (Groups I, II, IV and V). We shall omit Group III, for the number of cases in that group for which the scale scores are available was so small as to be negligible.

Let us first compare the means of the scores of Schedule A for each of the four groups.

[22] $t = 1.92$, P between 5 and 10 percent.

TABLE 48

Scores on Schedule A of the "H.O.W." Schedule Compared with Delinquency Judgments for 193 T- and C-Boys [a]

Delinquency Judgment Groups	SCORES FOR T-BOYS		SCORES FOR C-BOYS		T AND C SCORES COMBINED		
	Number	Mean	Number	Mean	Number	Mean	Range
I ("Most delinquent")	12	63.1	14	49.9	26	56.0	0–139
II	16	40.8	15	47.4	31	44.0	4–116
IV	12	38.7	22	38.0	34	38.3	0–119
V ("Least delinquent")	57	36.5	45	29.9	102	33.6	0–118

[a] For 523 unselected cases (Ts and Cs) for which the "H.O.W." scores (Schedule A) were available, a range of 0–154 and a mean of 33.7 was found; for 54 retired (plus) T-boys, a range of 0–62 and a mean of 11.9.

From this table it appears that our "most delinquent" boys (Group I) had, on the average, a significantly higher scale score (the higher the score the greater number of problems) than our "least delinquent" boys (Group V); and yet the intermediate groups were not very different from each other in this respect. There is much overlapping. Some boys in Group I received a lower score than many of the boys in Group V and some of the boys in Group V received a higher score than many of the boys in Group I.

Again we cannot say that Schedule A showed special predictive value in terms of our concept of delinquency, though there was an evident trend toward correct prediction, the delinquent groups having a proportionately smaller number of low (non-problem) scores than those who were less delinquent.

Schedule B scores, similarly treated, led to the same general conclusions.

METHOD C

Rather than rely upon our delinquency judgments to check or verify the H.O.W. scales let us take three groups of boys who by their own behavior over a period of nine to ten years distributed themselves in three different groups.

1. The first group consists of 51 (T-boys only) whom we considered our high average, relatively non-delinquent group. They

are drawn from our pool of 65 retired cases.[23] We shall call these boys our "non-delinquents."

2. Our second group of boys we shall define for present purposes as our "mildly delinquent" boys. Each of these 47 boys (both Ts and Cs) had been delinquent as evidenced by two or more appearances before the Crime Prevention Bureau of the Cambridge Police Department, but his behavior (up to an average age of about 19 or 20) had not been delinquent enough from the point of view of the police official to result in a court appearance.

3. Our third group is composed of those among the treatment and control delinquents who have not only appeared in court but have been committed to a correctional institution. We shall call these the "committed delinquents."

Table 49 shows the mean scale scores for Schedule B together with the range and the deviation for each of these three groups.

TABLE 49

Scores on Schedule B of the "H.O.W." Schedule for Non-delinquent and Delinquent Groups

	Number	Mean	Range	Standard Deviation	Standard Error
Non-Delinquents	51	63.33	49–94	10.60	1.49
Mild Delinquents	47	88.85	58–143	17.34	2.53
Committed Delinquents	36	91.39	55–140	19.68	3.28

Schedule B scores differentiate the "non-delinquents" from the "mildly delinquent" and the "committed delinquents." The difference between the means of the first and second and the first and third groups in Table 49 appears greater than a chance expectancy.[24] There is no significant difference, however, between the "mildly delinquent" and the "committed" delinquent."[25]

[23] See Chap. XI for a description of the retired category. Originally 65 boys were retired. One has been omitted from our group because he had made two appearances before the Crime Prevention Bureau. Thirteen other cases were omitted also because there were no available H.O.W. scores for them.

[24] The difference in mean scores between the "non-delinquent" and the "mildly delinquent" is over eight and one-half times the standard error of the difference, the difference between the "non-delinquent" and the "committed delinquent" seven and one-half times the standard error of the differences. These differences then, are clearly significant. P is less than .01.

[25] Observed difference only .61 times the standard error of the difference. P between .50 and .60.

Conclusions as to the Predictive Value of the "H.O.W." Behavior Rating Schedule. This rating scale, designed to show the extent of behavior problems in school children representing the discrepancy between the child's capacity to adjust and the demands of his environment, was checked by different methods to determine its value as a device for specifically predicting delinquency. We found some degree of correspondence between high problem scores and delinquent behavior. Trends observed in the distribution of scores indicated that the future delinquent is more often the problem child in school than the non-delinquent, but the overlapping in the distribution for groups ranging from "non-delinquent" to "delinquent" was so marked that we cannot say that either Schedule A or Schedule B will correctly spot pre-delinquency. As a group result, however, the scores did differentiate the "most delinquent" from the "least delinquent," and the "committed delinquents" from the "non-delinquents."

SUMMARY AND DISCUSSION

1. One of the aims of social science is the prediction of behavior. Our data give us opportunities to study the forecasting of delinquency in three ways: by experts dealing with children's records around age nine; by teachers of the same children at the same age; by a scale designed to assess problem behavior, also used at about the same age.

2. The experts succeeded above chance in predicting delinquency.

3. The teachers succeeded about as well as the experts.

4. Both experts and teachers overpredicted delinquency. They almost always spotted a pre-delinquent who became in fact a serious delinquent, but they predicted delinquency in many cases when it did not materialize in serious form.

5. These data did not tell us *why* overprediction occurred. It may have been due in part to a mental set in a delinquency-prevention framework. Probably more important, however, was the lack of an intimate knowledge of the young boy as a person. The boys who were overpredicted generally showed the usual signs of delinquency, but presumably personality was the crucial factor. (The

reader will recall that the predictors did not have an opportunity of interviewing the boy himself although they had before them information gathered by others relating to the personality of the boy.) Much of the available information dealt with the obvious rather than with the more subtle or dynamic aspects of the boy's character. Healy and Bronner have shown how boys living in the same home with delinquent brothers did not become delinquent. The delinquent brother they "almost universally found to be the one who at some stage of his development had been blocked in his needs for satisfying relationships in his family circle." [26] Some of these intimate factors were probably not known to the predictors at this early stage in the boy's life. Moreover, unforeseeable events—moving to a better neighborhood after the prediction was made, or the father's securing a better job—occasionally made a difference in the outcome.

Strictly speaking, we cannot say with certainty that the predictors overpredicted delinquency. All we can say is that their predictions did not agree completely with the second set of judges. The latter may have been too lenient in their judgments of delinquency. In other words, the criterion by which the predictive measures were validated may have been inadequate. On the other hand, the predictors may have underestimated the strength of the character-building forces in the community. It is reasonable to assume (even allowing for some overprediction in the direction of delinquency) that the church, the school, and the public and private social agencies were effective delinquency-prevention forces. Seldom do we hear the question, Why is there not more delinquency? Seldom does one know or appreciate the extent of preventive work constantly going on. Indeed, there is less need for concern over the fact that there is so much delinquency than there is reason for optimism over the fact that there is so little, in the face of so many adverse circumstances.

6. The Behavior Rating Schedule as a group test differentiates by its scores those boys who later in life become "most delinquent" and/or are committed, from those who are "least delinquent" and are not committed. However, as a device solely for correctly spot-

[26] See in Chap. XVI, note 28.

ting the pre-delinquent its predictive value is not high. Many boys with high problem scores are not necessarily antisocial in any serious overt manner.

7. If the predictions as to the minus C-boys had been more successful than the predictions for the minus T-boys we might draw an inference as to the success of the counselors' efforts, for it was their aim, of course, to turn minus boys from their delinquent goals. No significant differences, however, were found in the accuracy of predictions of Ts as compared to Cs.

This indirect method of evaluating the work of the counselors is fortunately not the only one available. We turn our attention now to other methods and to the major research problem; namely, the evaluation of the treatment program.

CHAPTER XIX

EVALUATION
DURING THE COURSE
OF TREATMENT

THE ULTIMATE VALUE OF THE COUNSELORS' WORK COULD NOT, OF course, be determined until the end of the treatment program or later. Nevertheless, it seemed advisable to make two checks during the course of treatment in order to reveal whatever trends might be under way. In 1941 and again in 1943, small groups of treatment boys were compared with their control twins. An answer was sought to the question: "Has the treatment program been able to effect a sufficient degree of character development so that by selected objective tests such effects will be apparent when the treatment and control groups are compared?" It was assumed by the research staff that if the treatment were effective during the first few years, some gains should then be obvious and measurable. At any rate, a plan for a systematic self-evaluation in midstream as a guide and incentive for more effective work was decided upon.

THE SAMPLES USED

It was neither necessary nor practicable to measure all boys in both groups. Satisfactory samples could be selected that would be sufficiently representative to indicate existing trends. In the first evaluation survey (1941–42) a sample of approximately 60 T-boys, who were receiving varying degrees of attention from their counselors over a two-and-a-half to three-year period, was compared with a like number of C-boys with whom they had been matched. This sample was a cross section of the 264 boys who were at that time still in the treatment program.[1] It was so constructed that it reflected

[1] Sixty-one of the 325 boys were no longer receiving help from the counselors when this survey began in 1941. Of the 61, two had died, approximately six had moved out

point for point the characteristics of the larger group in terms of the 20 variables used in the matching process (see Chapter VI). Submitted to a statistical analysis it was shown that the sample of T-boys was as well matched with its corresponding C-boys as the total groups were matched with each other. Furthermore, the sample contained the same proportions of boys who were being most intensively and least intensively treated.

In the second survey (1943) no attempt was made to use a "stratified" sample, representing a statistical cross section. On the contrary, the boys who became the subjects of the second survey were chosen from the group who happened to be at that time still in the treatment program and who had received major treatment emphasis. Some boys were excluded from the survey simply because they were not available for testing. Although a selection on this basis had the disadvantage of not being sufficiently representative of the total group to warrant generalizations in respect to the total program, it served the purpose of contrasting the boys upon whom the counselors had concentrated their best efforts with their non-treated control twins. Such a procedure, it was held, ought certainly to show differential and measurable gains in the treatment group, if any existed.

LIMITATIONS

Certain inevitable limitations beset these two evaluation studies. In the first place, no group tests, as such, could be administered; for neither the T- nor the C-boys were ever assembled in groups; each boy had to be sought out in the community or in the school and there personally tested or interviewed. The amount of time consumed in visiting the boys' homes was large. (In the second survey, visits to the home which consumed so large a proportion of the time of the first surveyors were omitted.) In the second place, completely comparable information about both groups was not available. As for the C-boys, the information in the files was restricted to school reports, official records of delinquency, and some scattered information. The parents of the C-boys were unfamiliar with the Study and thus the investigators could not expect, on a single visit, to bring

---

of the field of operations and the balance had been permanently retired from the treatment program, as explained in Chap. XI.

back the most pertinent and revealing information. On the other hand, a parent of a T-boy whose attitudes and habits of living were well known to the counselor would probably not attempt to give a false or inconsistent picture; yet on the whole the investigators did not believe that there was any particular bias arising out of the fact that one group was better known to the Study than the other.

THE FIRST SURVEY

Method. The first survey, under the supervision of Dr. Turner, the research psychologist, was begun in the spring of 1941 and completed in the fall of 1942. During the middle of this period (that is, about January 1942), the mean age of the boys was 13 years and 3 months. These boys had been in the program, on the average, for a period of two years and seven months. The survey data were based upon interviews with boys, their families, and their teachers, and consisted of various ratings and test scores. The measures used were administered by six persons who had had no part in the treatment program. Three of the six carried the major burden (92 percent of the home and school visits). To avoid bias, each investigator examined about as many T-boys as C-boys. He did not know the matched pairs, although, of course, when visiting the home he knew in advance whether he was interviewing the mother of a T-boy or the mother of a C-boy. In the latter case he had to explain the Study or reacquaint the parent with its purposes. The work was arduous and time-consuming, for frequently many visits (as many as twelve in one case) had to be made to a home before a convenient interview could be arranged; yet the cooperation of parents and boys was good. In only four out of 120 instances (one T- and three C-cases) were the investigators unable to get the parents' consent to an interview. In only five out of 120 instances (two T- and three C-cases) boys could not be located or would not consent to be interviewed.

THE SELECTION OF MEASURING INSTRUMENTS

In seeking for adequate measures it was necessary to choose tests that would apply to boys of approximately thirteen years of age; that would not arouse hostility or cause embarrassment; that could be conveniently handled by the investigator; that would admit of quantitative measurements; and above all, that would seek to bring out important, relevant aspects of the boy's development. Also tests were desired that had some known or demonstrable reliability and validity. Since few existing instruments seemed to meet all of these conditions, some measures were especially devised.

Fourteen different tests were chosen and administered to the boys in the sample. Before the scores were tabulated, it was evident that some of these measures fell below the desired standard of adequacy and relevancy. It was also clear that, though a chosen test was both adequate in itself and relevant to the purposes of the survey, it might for practical reasons be impossible for an investigator to get all the data called for.

The series of fourteen measures may be divided into two parts. The first comprises the tests that proved to be reasonably satisfactory from the point of view of adequacy, relevancy, and practicality after the testing program was concluded. In the second division are placed those that were less adequate and that should be considered separately in the computation of scores.

Division I	*Division II*
1. Vineland Social Maturity Scale	1. The Fels Parent-Behavior Ratings
2. Furfey's Test for Developmental Age	2. The Boys' Activities Schedule
3. The California Test of Personality (one section)	3. Boys' Interest Schedule
4. The Haggerty-Olson-Wickman Schedules	4. Boys' Vocational Future Ratings
5. The Altruism Scale	5. The California Test of Personality (all but one section)
6. School Records (marks, conduct, and retardation)	6. School Schedule A
7. Contacts with Cambridge Police	
8. Official Court Records	

DIVISION I

1. The Vineland Social Maturity Scale.[2] This was administered by an investigator to one of the parents of the boy, generally the mother, on a visit to the home. It seeks to determine from her answers to specific questions the boy's degree of self-reliance and social

[2] E. A. Doll, "Annotated Bibliography on the Vineland Society Maturity Scale," *Journal of Consulting Psychology,* IV (1940), 123–132.

maturity. For example, the investigator asked the parent if the boy characteristically (not under pressure) "writes occasional short letters" or "makes telephone calls by himself" or "exercises complete care of dress" or "goes to bed unassisted," and so on. After noting her answer the interpreter had to decide whether in his opinion the boy would be scored plus or minus on the item in question. This scale was used because it seemed to be particularly relevant to one of the aims of the counselors; namely, to increase a boy's self-reliance and general development. The test results showed that there were no significant differences in the scores of T- and C-boys, the arithmetical means for the Ts and Cs being 105.4 and 104.6 respectively.

2. *Furfey Developmental Quotient.*[3] This was also designed to measure a boy's growth and development toward more mature interests and choices. The schedule is filled out by the boy himself, who must indicate his choice between certain paired items. For example, a boy is asked to choose between "going on scout hikes" and "knocking flies," or "collecting stamps" and "playing cowboys and Indians." He is also asked to make choices between possible future businesses or occupations, the books he would like to read, things he would like to have and see and think about. This test was included as a standardized scale for measuring maturity of interests up to 15 years of age. When scored, the arithmetical means for the treatment boys was practically identical with that of the control boys (97.5 for Ts, 97.4 for Cs, 100.0 being the normal quotient).

3. *California Test of Personality.*[4] Purporting to measure a boy's adjustment to his family, school, and community, this test presents a series of questions such as, "Would you rather plan your own work than to have someone else plan it for you?" or "Do you like to speak or sing before other people?" As a diagnostic measure it proved to be disappointing in its application to the Study boys. After it was administered, each part of the test was correlated with careful ratings of certain Study boys well known to the counselors in regard to the pertinent aspects of his adjustment. It was found that only one section (Section 2D on Family Relations) seemed to have any material

[3] Paul H. Furfey, "A Revised Scale for Measuring Developmental Age in Boys," *Child Development,* II (1931), 102–114.

[4] Devised by Louis T. Thorpe, Willis W. Clark, and Ernest W. Tiegs, for Grades Four to Nine (published by California Test Bureau, Los Angeles, California).

validity; or, in other words, only one aspect of the test correlated reasonably well $(r = +.54)$ with the counselor's opinions of the T-boys' personalities. Only this part of the test, dealing with the boy's relation to his parents, has been placed in Division I. He was asked to say "yes" or "no" to such questions as, "Do you have a hard time because it seems that your folks hardly ever have enough money?" or "Do you sometimes feel like running away from home?" or "Have you often felt that your folks thought you would not amount to anything?" The scores of the T-boys on this section of the test showed a mean of 10.1 compared to a mean of 9.6 for the C-boys. This difference was not significant.

4. The "H.O.W." Schedule.[5] This schedule, to be checked by the boy's teacher, consisted of two parts. Part A listed 15 behavior problems commonly met with in the school, such as cheating, lying, unnecessary tardiness, sex offenses, and so on. It called for a checking of the frequency of occurrences from "never occurred" to "frequent occurrence." A high score indicated the seriousness of the problems. Part B consisted of 35 rating scales pertaining to the boy's intellectual interests, his general appearance, his social behavior, and his personality. A high score here also indicated unfavorable trends. On both parts of the schedule the T-boys achieved the lowest ("most favorable") score; though again the differences were not great. (The arithmetical mean for T-boys was 30.5 on Schedule A, 79.2 on Schedule B; for C-boys 34.6 on Schedule A, 82.6 on Schedule B.)

5. The Altruism Scale. In his search for some apparent and measurable aspects of character or conscience, the director of the investigation devised a test somewhat similar to Willoughby's Scale of Emotional Maturity, pertaining to the trait of altruism, in contrast to selfishness or egocentricity—a boy's ability to consider the needs and attitudes of others and his ability to react accordingly.[6] It was

---

[5] M. E. Haggerty, W. C. Olson, and E. K. Wickman, *Haggerty-Olson-Wickman Behavior Rating Schedules* (Yonkers, World Book, 1930); see Chap. XVIII, for a discussion of the predictive value of this test. W. C. Olson, "The Clinical Use of Behavior Rating Schedules," *Journal of Juvenile Research,* XV (1931), 237–245. E. K. Wickman, *Teachers and Behavior Problems* (New York, Commonwealth Fund, 1938). W. C. Olson, "Utilization of the H.O.W. Behavior Rating Schedules," *Childhood Education,* IX (1933), 350–359.

[6] This test has been described by its author, W. D. Turner, in "Altruism and Its Measurement in Children," *Journal of Abnormal and Social Psychology,* XLIII (1948), 502–516.

believed that this trait or characteristic is basic to good citizenship. The scale was composed of thirty items representing rather common situations in which children, pre-adolescents and adolescents might find themselves. The investigator obtained his information about the boy's behavior solely from the parent, generally the mother, in a home interview. The mother, for example, was asked how her boy behaved when losing in a competitive activity or game. The mother might state that the boy lost his temper or she might describe his behavior as what would ordinarily be called "being a good sport." The investigator continued the series of questions to determine whether or not the boy usually behaved with due regard for the feelings and the rights of other people. Difficulty was experienced at first in scoring the replies, for the interpretation was impressionistic. Although mothers might tend to picture their boys in brighter colors than they deserved, the investigator believed that any constant error in this regard would be found with equal frequency in both groups. When the test was scored it was found that both groups obtained approximately the same scores. The arithmetic mean score favored the T-boys, being slightly, but not significantly, greater than for the C-boys (32.1 compared with 31.0).

6. *School Records.*[7] It was found in the school year 1941–42 that the grade distribution for the T-boys was approximately the same as that for the C-boys. A study was then made of the average marks of each of the pupils for that year to see whether the T-boys had achieved better grades. In spite of the fact that many of the T-boys were receiving special tutoring, the C-boys' grades were slightly higher. The arithmetical mean for the T-boys was 2.83 and for the C-boys 2.93 (grades were transmuted to a scale ranging from one to five before the arithmetic mean was determined). This difference also was not great.

The teacher's rating on the boy's school conduct during that same year was also obtained. In respect to this factor we find almost identical scores; 3.38 for the T-boys and 3.47 for the C-boys (a low score being preferable). When the paired twins alone (95 pairs) were taken, the mean difference between the two was found to be .01 in favor of the T-boys—obviously an insignificant difference.

---

[7] In comparing the treatment and control groups in terms of school records, police reports and court records all available cases were used rather than the smaller sample.

The number of grades retarded was also computed for 171 T-boys and 173 C-boys. The T-boys, on the average, had repeated at this time .082 grades; the C-boys .139 grades—a difference favoring the T-boys, possibly significant statistically.

7. *Police Reports.* The Crime Prevention Bureau of the Cambridge Police Department had been operating a few years before the survey was made and was cooperative in furnishing data on the number of appearances made in respect to actual and suspected delinquent behavior. Information was obtained as to the number of Study boys appearing before it during a 13 months' period beginning September, 1941. This group comprised 274 matched pairs rather than the smaller survey samples. Only two-thirds of this group lived in Cambridge yet occasionally a few of the Somerville boys appeared before the Cambridge Bureau. The records show that there were 34 T-boys (42 appearances) appearing before the Bureau as compared to 35 C-boys (49 appearances).[8]

8. *Official Court Records.* Official records obtained from the Massachusetts Board of Probation showed that 16 T-boys compared to 11 C-boys out of the group of 274 Ts and Cs had been brought officially into court for same alleged delinquency.[9]

DIVISION II

The following measures proved to have been less adequate and relevant and are here listed with the reasons for so characterizing them.

1. The Fels Parent-Behavior Rating Scales.[10] This scale attempts to rate the adjustment of the home. It proved to be unsatisfactory for the following reasons: (a) It dealt chiefly with the parent-boy relationship which the counselors could not have been expected to alter appreciably in the first few years of treatment, for during that period the visits to the family were, on the average, no more frequent than nine to 12 times per family per year, and on most of

[8] A subsequent analysis for the calendar year 1942 showed that there were 57 T-boys and 60 C-boys before the Bureau. (See Chap. XX for a further comparison of T- and C-boys in this respect.)

[9] In addition to these 27 boys there were seven T-boys who had been in court *prior* to the commencement of treatment and five C-boys who had been in court during this same pre-treatment interval.

[10] Horace Champney, *Fels Parent-Behavior Rating Scales* (Yellow Springs, Ohio, Antioch Press, 1939).

these occasions no intensive effort was made to change the parents' attitudes. (b) Only five or ten minutes of the home visit by the investigator were devoted directly to the Fels Scales (although further pertinent information may have been acquired during the course of the administration of the Vineland and Altruism Scales). (c) The investigators (who, of course, were not acquainted with the families) found that the scoring depended very largely on interpretative judgments. They expressed a lack of confidence in their ability to evaluate the family on "its general internal adjustment" in its "day-by-day relationships" on the basis of a single interview with only one parent. Of the 30 scored items of this scale it was found that the T-boys slightly excelled the C-boys on 19 items, whereas the C-boys showed a better score on six. On five items it was impossible to determine which group was favored. There were, however, no differences that could be considered statistically significant between the groups on these 25 items.

2. *The Activities Schedule.* Administered to the boy in school, this questionnaire attempted to assay the variety and concentration of his preferred activities by asking him to check various activities, indicating the approximate frequency ("never," "once or twice," "five or six times," "almost daily") with which he had taken part during the three weeks immediately preceding. The list of 125 items covered a wide range from "reading the New Republic" to "playing games with girls." It appeared after the tests were administered that valid differences between the two groups, if any existed, could probably not be shown for the following reasons: (a) The tests were not all administered at the same time. It was therefore impossible, for example, to compare answers to the question "How frequently have you played croquet during the past three weeks?" when the test was administered to some boys in January and to others in June. (b) There was no differential weighting of scores. All answers, for example, that indicated "almost daily" participation in certain activities were equally evaluated. Thus, a boy stating that he "almost daily" "visited art galleries" received on that item the same score as a boy who answered that he "almost daily" had "met a new girl." The measurement of the frequency of activities regardless of the quality of the activity raised some question as to just what this schedule purported to measure. Some counselors maintained that

they were not trying to develop overactivity indiscriminately in their boys. (c) The directions given to the boys were not always clear to them. The investigators found, for example, that boys who frequently engaged in a certain activity but who had not done so in the past three weeks, possibly because of seasonal conditions, did not always check the item "never." Probably few of the boys carried out the instructions literally. The extent of this error was unknown. (d) The investigators discovered that 14 of the 125 items were unintelligible to some of the boys and had to be explained to them. It was suspected that some boys who did not understand an item were reluctant to ask about it but checked it nevertheless. The arithmetical mean for T-boys was higher (more favorable) than for the C-boys (22.8 compared to 18.9) but the difference is not statistically significant.

3. *The Interests Schedule.* This schedule, consisting of 125 items, was similar to the Activities Schedule. The boy was instructed to indicate how often "during the next three weeks" he *would like* to do the things mentioned. There was a wide variety of items such as "do housework," "collect stamps," "go to the movies," "hear symphony concerts," "read the Atlantic Monthly." This schedule was inadequate for substantially the same reasons given in respect to the Activities Schedule. The arithmetical means of the scores showed a slight but insignificant advantage for the C-boys (30.2 compared to 28.1).

4. *The Boy's Vocational Future.* This was an attempt, by means of a conversation on the subject, to rate "the boy's sense of his own vocational future" and to disclose "any promise of the boy's status as a potential good citizen." Because of its extreme subjectivity and because it seemed to have little relevancy in relation to the work of the counselor the test was unsatisfactory. Most of the boys at this age were ambitious to be "airplane pilots." Of the six items on this questionnaire, four favored the T-boys, but on only one of the four was the difference probably statistically significant.

5. *The California Test of Personality.*[11] As stated, all but one section of this test was inadequate because of its lack of correlation with ratings by counselors. Of the 14 sub-divisions (one division

[11] See note 4, above.

relating to family relations has already been considered under Division I, above) the arithmetical means of the scores favored the T-boys in ten cases and the C-boys in four cases. An analysis of the scores showed that none of the differences was statistically significant.

6. *School Ratings by Counselors.* Teachers were interviewed concerning 16 aspects of the boy's behavior in school, such as industriousness, promptness, self-reliance, and so on. The interviewers then rated the boy on a five-point scale on the basis of such comments. It is doubtful if such ratings could be considered impartial, inasmuch as all T-boys were rated by their own counselors who interviewed their teachers, while the C-boys were rated by the director of the survey. It was found that of the four (out of 16) parts of the schedule where a significant difference was obtained between the scores of the two groups the T-boys received the higher score in three.

RESULTS OF FIRST SURVEY

1. Table 50 shows that six of the eight measures in Division I favored the T-boys although in no case was the difference in scores between the matched pairs considered statistically significant.

2. Four of the six measures in Division II favored the T-boys, while one favored the C-boys and one showed no differential score between the two groups, although again the difference in the scores was not statistically significant with the exception of five separate items, four of which favored the treatment group.

3. Combining all 14 measures, we find the treatment group achieved a higher score in ten measures, the control group in three; there was no differentiating in one measure. Splitting some of the larger measures into items that could be separately scored, we find that in the total of 79 measures or items, the treatment group excelled in 55.

4. In examining the official records we do not find any consistent trends. Ratings on school marks and school conduct are very similar in both groups (the T-boys were slightly superior in conduct, the C-boys in marks). We find fewer T-boys appearing before the Crime Prevention Bureau of the Police Department (although again the

TABLE 50

Differences between T- and C-Boys in Measurements Used in the First Evaluative Survey

DIVISION I

A	B		C		D	E	F	
	Number of Cases		Arithmetical Means		Matched Pairs [a]	Statistical Significance	Difference Favoring	
Name of Measure	T	C	T	C			T	C
1. Vineland Social Maturity	56	56	105.4	104.6	52	None	..	C
2. Furfey's Developmental Age	58	57	97.5	97.4	55	None	T	..
3. California Personality Test (Sec. 2)	58	56	10.1	9.6	54	None	T	..
4. "H.O.W."								
Part A	60	59	30.5	34.6	59	None	T	..
Part B	60	59	79.2	82.6	59	None	T	..
5. Altruism	59	57	32.1	31.0	56	None	T	..
6. School Records								
A. Marks	167	169	2.83	2.93	96	P[b]	..	C
B. Conduct	151	160	3.38	3.47	95	None	T	..
C. Retardation	171	173	.082	.139	73	P[b]	T	..
7. Police Contacts	274	274	.15	.18	274	None	T	..
8. Official Court Records	274	274	.10	.06	274	None	..	C

DIVISION II

A	B		C		D	E	F	
Name of Measure	Number of Cases		Arithmetical Means		Matched Pairs [a]	Statistical Significance	Difference Favoring	
	T	C	T	C			T	C
1. Fels Parent-Behavior	58–59	55–56	59.3	57.2	54–55	1 item, Yes 27 items, None 2 items, D [c]	19 T 5	6 C Neither
2. Activities	58	57	22.8	18.9	55	None	T	..
3. Interests	57	57	28.1	30.2	54	None	..	C
4. Vocational Future	52–55	49–55	2.64	2.50	42–51	5 items, None 1 item, D [c]	4 T	2 C
5. Personality (Sec. 2D)	58	56	22.04	21.95	54	None	10 T	4 C
6. School Ratings	60	60	3.19	3.12	60	4 items, Yes 1 item, D [c] 11 items, None	8 T	8 C

Total of measures (Divisions I and II) favoring T or C   10   3

Total items in Divisions I and II combined   55   24

[a] The statistical significance was determined upon the basis of these matched pairs.

[b] P = Possibly.

[c] D = Doubtful.

difference between the Ts and Cs in this respect is small and doubt-ful), but more of the T-boys than the C-boys were officially brought to court.

Discussion. In general, the majority of minor differences favoring the treatment sample would probably not be attained by chance. Such differences are apparent whether we consider the measures of Division I alone (measures that were considered more adequate and relevant to the survey) or whether we consider Divisions I and II combined. The small differences in the individual ratings do not, however, prove that any significant gains, as measured by this survey, were made by the counselors during the first few years of treatment.

A variety of statistical procedures was applied to the data. By weighting certain of the survey variables that seemed to be more dependable and relevant, it was found that in terms of a composite of 18 of such variables the slight differences between the T-boys and the C-boys were not significantly increased. Pursuing the analysis further, it was found that the survey scores which seemed to have the highest correlation (more than plus .50) with a criterion based on counselors' judgments of their own effectiveness indicated again a slight superiority for the T-boys but with a difference too small to be significant. In other words, by concentrating on those tests that seemed to be most valid either subjectively or in terms of this criterion, the slight group differences failed to become further accentuated.

A small group of cases that the counselors themselves believed had most profited by treatment was also selected to determine whether or not the survey tests would show greater differences here than on the total sample. Again it was found that the results were inconclusive: boys who the counselors thought had shown improvement received a slightly lower score than the C-boys on some tests and a higher score on others. The most intensively treated did not show any superiority in the tests over those least intensively treated. Yet it is true that even if we progressively eliminate from consideration those measures that were less appropriately designed or less effectively administered, the majority of small differences in favor of the treatment sample group persists.

From an examination of the police and court records it is clear that in the first few years of the treatment program the counselors were *not*, by and large, preventing T-boys from committing acts that led to apprehension and/or court appearances less frequently than would ordinarily have occurred without the counselors' services.

Although no marked trends emerge from this first attempt at evaluation the survey was valuable in pointing out the difficulties of appraising psychological growth and maturity by the use of tests and rating scales that rely heavily on subjective interpretations. Although the counselors were not convinced that their efforts were fairly reflected in the test scores, or that the effect of their treatment techniques could be assessed at this time by any method, still the survey did help to stimulate them to a better effort.

We do not presume to interpret the finding that although virtually none of the individual measures is statistically significant yet a majority of them favor the T-boys. In very few, if any cases, was a systematic bias on the part of the investigators in favor of T-boys possible. The ratio of measures favoring T-boys could not be fully accounted for, assuming such a bias. It seems rather that one of the two following explanations of this slight but recurrent trend must be adopted. The reader may take his choice. (1) Chance may conceivably account for the distribution of slight differences in favor of T-boys. (No satisfactory method seems to have been devised statistically to assess the significance of an array of differences in one direction when none of the differences individually can be considered significant.) (2) The counselors may have been making *slight* but scarcely measurable progress within the first two or three years of the treatment program. This interpretation, more favorable to the Study, may reasonably be accepted, provided our final evaluations (after more years of treatment) turn out to be in the same direction.

THE SECOND SURVEY

The new Director of Research, Dr. George W. Hartmann, organized and supervised the second survey in 1942 and 1943. Though changes had occurred in the administration of the Study and even in the methods of treatment since the first survey, the objectives were still focused on the general "social, physical, intellectual, and spiritual growth" of the Study boys and on the prevention of delinquency in particular.

This survey, like the first, sought to discover if there were any measurable differences between the T-boys and the C-boys, who had not been in touch with the treatment staff. Such a comparison was made in respect to scores achieved on selected ratings and schedules, differing considerably from those employed in the first survey. It was believed that if treatment was at all effective, some evidences of "trends" should be discernible after approximately four years of intensive effort and that such "trends" could be reduced to quantitative terms.[12]

Use of a Sample. The second survey differed from the first in the nature of its sample. Whereas the first survey employed a "stratified" sample, the second covered only T-boys readily available at the time. Some 100 boys were, in 1943, receiving relatively intensive treatment. Of these, there were 56 whom the counselors were seeing most frequently and who could be most easily reached and made available for testing. Inferences as to the effectiveness of the total treatment program could not, of course, be drawn from measurements of a non-representative sample comprising only 17 percent of the original group, yet score differences on selected measures between the 56 T-boys and their 56 matched twins might shed considerable light on the effectiveness of the program in respect to the smaller group, provided the measures were adequate and the two segments of the total populations were well matched. Moreover, if any differences existed between the treatment and control groups as a result of treatment, it should be most clearly revealed in an analysis of the intensively treated group.

How well this 17 percent segment was matched with the corresponding controls was difficult to determine. Though it had been established that the total groups, as such, were well matched (see Chapter VI) one could not expect the members of each pair to be well matched, in view of the natural diversity of personalities. The individual boy-with-boy matching was attempted subject to these

---

[12] By January, 1943, the boys had reached an average age of 15 years, 1 month, and had been in treatment for a period of time varying from three years, seven months, to five years, one month.

limitations, but, it will be recalled, the real substance of the matching resided in the set matching, that is, in the matching of small interdependent groups. If, therefore, we selected certain T-boys for testing without any regard to the sets, we could not be sure that such sub-groups would be as well matched as the original parent groups. Therefore, the 56 pairs were examined to determine the degree of divergence from the matching standard maintained for the original groups. The analysis was confined to only one, but a very important one, of the matching variables—the Selection Committee prognostic ratings.[13] It was found that though the total treatment group of 325 boys contained about as many minus boys as the control group (see Table 17, Chapter VI), the sub-group of 56 T-boys contained a heavier load of minus cases. This finding was not surprising, for it had been the rule to retain for continued treatment those boys who were in most need, and such boys, of course, were more likely to be minus boys. It was found that among the 56 pairs there were 26 minus twos or minus threes in the treatment group but only 15 such ratings in the corresponding control group. It was also found that, in 24 out of 26 instances in which there was some discrepancy between the treatment and control prognostic ratings in the two sub-groups, the lower rating (indicative of greater likelihood of being delinquent) fell to the T-boys. To correct this obvious bias in this non-representative sample, all pairs in which a discrepancy of even one point in the pre-treatment rating was found were dropped from the final computations. This step reduced the sample to 30 matched pairs, perfectly equated as to the original pre-treatment ratings. How well they were matched in other respects was impractical to determine at this point, although it seemed a reasonable assumption that the quality of the matching would be sufficiently adequate for a fair comparison.

Selecting Adequate Measures. Again we were faced with the difficulty of finding adequate instruments to measure slight increments of growth. As less than one-third of the 30 pairs had been included in the first survey, the idea of adopting the same measures used in that survey was abandoned. The evaluation was based more directly on the specific goals that the counselors had in mind. It will be recalled that the Director of Research had already broken down

13 For an explanation of the Selection Committee ratings, see Chap. V.

the broad statement of objectives into 15 specific areas of improvement that the counselors agreed were vital. These factors were listed in Chapter XII.

It was evident that tests, questionnaires, or rating scales could not be devised to tap *each one* of these areas, nor was it possible to give each area equal weight. Some areas could not be so clearly defined as to be easily measured. Nevertheless, a variety of special rating scales and tests was designed that could be quickly and easily administered to boys and their schoolteachers. Home visits and interviews with parents which had consumed such an excessive amount of time in the first survey were omitted. Altogether 17 separate instruments were used as a trial procedure and administered by the Director of Research assisted by the staff psychologist and the research assistant. Most of the measures were administered in the schools, where the boys were most conveniently found.

Adequate and Inadequate Measures. Although a wide variety of measures was used, it was again impossible to determine, until after they had been tried out, which of them seemed to be adequate. On the basis of a subsequent review of the 17 different measures it was apparent at once that three of them were obviously inadequate and should not be considered at all in the final tabulation of scores.[14]

[14] The three measures discarded because of inadequacy or irrelevancy were:

1. *The Revised Minnesota Paper Form Board Test* which measures the capacity to identify a geometrical pattern when broken into its constituent parts and presented in different spatial arrangements. This test did not seem to tap any of the special areas of particular concern to the counselors. It presumably had more to do with a general intelligence factor, or, more specifically, a higher order of visualization, not particularly subject to improvement by the counselors' efforts.

2. *A Tool Information Test* which purported to measure a boy's familiarity with 40 tools used by carpenters, plumbers, mechanics, and cooks. (This is a sub-test of the Detroit Mechanical Aptitude Test.) The acquisition of information of this sort seemed, upon analysis, to be only tangential to the purposes of the counselors.

3. *A Test of Orientation.* This test, original with Dr. Hartmann, contained a series of 22 questions designed to yield a picture of the boy's familiarity with his immediate surroundings, his elementary geographical and astronomical concepts as well as his orientation in time. He was asked, for instance, "How old is the earth on which we live?" "How far away is the moon?" "How far away is the sun?" "How many people live in the U.S.?" "Which city in Massachusetts has the most people?" "Name the New England states." Both groups did so poorly on this test that we concluded it was pitched at too high a level. As the test had not been previously given there was also considerable doubt about the best method of scoring the answers.

The scores achieved by the treatment and control groups on these three tests showed in no case any significant differences.

The remaining 14 tests were then analyzed in various ways. The total survey group of 112 boys (56 pairs) was split into smaller sub-groups chosen in such a way that they could be defined as "high" or "low" with regard to a number of variables, for example, "high" versus "low" in terms of (a) the Selection Committee ratings; (b) the average ratings on the Rogers-Hartmann Factor Analysis charts checked by the counselors (see Chapter XII, p. 147); (c) "successful" versus "unsuccessful" cases as judged by the counselors; and (d) boys who had become officially delinquent versus those who had not. It was then possible to find the measures that seemed to correlate most highly with these four criteria. The subjects used to determine the degree of correlation were the 56 T-boys originally selected rather than the 30 finally chosen for this second evaluation. The 14 tests were placed into two equal divisions; Division I representing the seven measures that had the highest degree of correlation with the criteria mentioned, Division II the seven measures that had the lowest degree of correlation.

DIVISION I

The following seven measures are listed in order of their discriminating power, starting with the most discriminating, that is, those that correlated most highly with the four criteria mentioned.

1. The Trait Record Card Differential. Each of the boys' teachers was supplied with a Trait Record Card on which he or she was asked to check the boy's undesirable habits or traits. The cards were identical with those given to the teachers before the treatment program was launched (see Chapter IV). A comparison was made between the number of items checked on the Trait Record Card in 1943 and the number checked in the pre-treatment period (1936–1939). (The 1943 cards were not, of course, checked by the same teachers who had made the pre-treatment judgments some three to five years earlier.) If a boy seemed to possess fewer undesirable traits in 1943 than during the pre-treatment period he might arbitrarily be called an "improved" case. Strangely enough, for both the C- and the T-boys *more* undesirable traits or items were checked in 1943 than previously (possibly because they were older and more overt in their behavior), though there was a differential rate between the two groups: the C-boys had acquired a greater increment of undesirable traits than the T-boys. The score differences between the two groups was, however, of doubtful significance.

2. *Teachers' Ratings*. Many of the boys were then in junior high school or high school where they had several teachers. The teacher believed to know the boy most intimately was given a printed booklet listing a number of qualities or characteristics—posture, skin condition, cleanliness, general health, conversational ability, quality of voice, courtesy, ability to get along with others, recognition and praise by others, sense of humor, timidity, irritability, dependability, helpfulness, industriousness, initiative, happiness, efficiency, and sympathy.[15] The teacher was asked to evaluate each of these in reference to each of the boys by placing a check at some point along a scale ranging from the "least desirable" to the "most desirable" manifestations of the quality in question. She was also asked to check opinions concerning the boy's intellectual curiosity and drive, scientific approach, practical competence, and group leadership. The mean scores for the two groups showed no significant differences.

3. *An Ethical Discrimination Test*. This measure was an attempt to tap the boy's less tangible attitudes and qualities of character. His sophistication about ethical issues and his ability to verbalize his moral discriminations were assessed by means of his comments concerning a series of short stories descriptive of moral or immoral behavior. A boy's answers to such questions as "Who did 'more wrong' "? "Who deserves more punishment?" and so on, were presumed to test his ability to discriminate wrong intentions from wrong outcomes, and to compare the relative "goodness" or "badness" of the actor's intentions. Other stories read to the boy were designed to test his sense of justice and responsibility and to show the extent to which he had overcome local group-centeredness. The T-boys achieved a significantly higher score on this test.

4. *Honesty*. The investigator read three questions in the nature of practically insoluble problems and gave the boys the opportunity of replying merely, "Yes, I got it" without the necessity of indicating their solutions or answers. They were thus presented with the opportunity for dishonesty and their behavior in this respect was

[15] See Appendix C for a copy of this booklet.

noted and scored. It was interesting to observe, incidentally, that the boys who showed a high level of ethical judgment when asked to verbalize about ethical problems (on the Ethical Discrimination Test) and at the same time most readily gave dishonest answers on the Honesty Test were those whom the counselors had considered their "least successful" cases. A certain moral glibness seemed to accompany the "immoral" behavior of the very difficult boys. On the whole, the T-boys showed a higher "honesty score."

5. *Superstitions.*[16] This questionnaire was concerned with the general area of maturity of attitudes and the boy's degree of emancipation from unfounded or magical beliefs. He was given a list of 34 so-called superstitions which had been collected partly from the boys themselves and partly from the literature. The boy was asked to indicate which he considered to be true or justified. The differences in scores, favoring the T-boys, were of doubtful significance.

6. *Composite Research Staff Ratings.* The three members of the research staff who administered the tests and schedules and who therefore had a good opportunity of observing the boy at first hand were asked to rate him in terms of the first eight qualities or traits appearing on the Teachers' Rating Schedule described above. All of these eight manifestations were of such nature that they could be readily observed on a first meeting. The T-boys and C-boys were compared in terms of the composite ratings of the three investigators. No significant differences in scores appeared.

7. *The Columbia Vocabulary Test.*[17] The treatment and control groups were well equated in terms of intelligence test scores.[18] It was believed that it would be relevant to administer at least one vocabulary test to see what differences, if any, might be disclosed in respect to the acquisition of new words as a result of school and life experiences and, in the case of the T-boys, the friendship with their counselors. The T-boys showed a slightly higher vocabulary score.

[16] See Appendix C for a copy of this questionnaire.

[17] Irene Gansel, and H. E. Garrett, *Columbia Vocabulary Test* (New York, Psychological Corporation, 1939).

[18] On the Kuhlmann-Anderson Group Test of Intelligence the 30 T-boys had scored a mean of 95.10, the 30 C-boys a mean of 95.07.

DIVISION II

The following seven measures, similarly validated in terms of the four selected "high" and "low" factors, were found to be less discriminating (that is, having relatively lower correlation coefficients).

1. The Game of Threes.[19] The boy was asked to record his answers to 26 different choices, such as "Name the three things you do that you like most." "If you had only three wishes and they could come true—what would they be?" "Of what three things are you most afraid?" "If I were my father the three things I would try to do for the family are?" "What are the three finest books you have ever read?" "The three things I would like to do first if I ever had a million dollars." Although this was an interesting test, eliciting answers that were revealing of the boy's maturity and attitudes, its chief difficulty lay in its scoring method. A simple over-all impression, rather than a separate score on each item, furnished the investigator with a rating on a five-point scale, ranging from "extremely childish" to "a systematic and well-developed pattern of ideals." The scores did not significantly differentiate boys who were presumably making most progress toward the ultimate goals of the Study from those who were not. The control group as a whole achieved a slightly higher score.

2. A "Euphorimeter" devised by the Director of Research (as a minor modification of Hornell Hart's "Chart of Happiness") was considered a sort of "happiness questionnaire." The answers were taken as indications of the relative prevalence and intensity of feelings of gloom or glee. Essentially this was a measure of mood level, or of the individual's sense of well-being. Some of the questions were: "Do you worry about the future?" "Do you think you ought to be happier than you are?" "How often do you feel guilty about anything?" "How peppy do you feel?" Whether or not this called for too much insight and frankness on the part of the boy, we do not know, but at any rate, the test proved to be non-discriminating between groups of a very divergent nature. The control group did slightly better but the differences between the two groups were of doubtful significance.

[19] See Appendix C for a copy of this schedule.

3. *An Accuracy Test* was devised by Dr. Hartmann. Within a four-minute time limit, a boy was asked to underline ordinary words hidden or buried in lines of pied type. Careless individuals tend to show a high rate of omissions. The test might have been more effective if more time had been allowed so that there would have been a greater spread in scores. As it was, it proved to be not only non-discriminating but probably did not tap any special area with which the counselors were particularly concerned. Group scores were very similar.

4. *Morale Questionnaire.* This related to the boy's personal satisfactions in a number of spheres—school, neighborhood, family, and friendships. "Yes," "No," or "Uncertain" specified answers to 30 statements such as, "If a fellow only tried hard enough, he can get ahead on the jobs he wants to get." "I would rather live any other place than where I'm living now." "If I should die today, it would not make any difference to most of the people who know me." The answers were expected to give a rough estimate of the boy's *morale.* This test likewise yielded mean scores that did not show significant differences between the treatment and control groups.

5. *Income Expectations.* A boy was asked, "How much a week do you think you should be earning about ten years from now?" No significant differences could be found between the two groups on the scores obtained from this test. As the question was phrased in terms of the acquisition of money one could not say whether a high or low score was closest to the ideal of good citizenship or the kind of character development the counselors were striving for.

6. *Number of Friends.* In this test an attempt was made to get an approximate picture of the boy's social relationships. However, the only method used was an inquiry of the boy himself as to the number of friends and associates he had. He was asked to write their names on a card and to rank them in order of preference. Here again, one had no check on the boy's honesty and insight. There were no significant differences in the scores for the two groups.

7. *The Strength-of-Grip Test.* The degree of strength of a boy's hand grip was determined by a dynamometer. The T- and C-boys were fairly evenly balanced. It was regretted that a thorough physical examination could not have been given to each of the T- and

C-boys in the sample in view of the great amount of time spent by the counselors on health problems, but time and staff limitations precluded such an ambitious plan.

RESULTS

1. On all of the seven tests reported here as more valid, the T-boys achieved a higher (more desirable or more favorable) score than their control twins. A close examination discloses the fact that the margin of the difference between the two groups is not great. In three of the tests, however (The Ethical Discrimination Test, The Honesty Test, and The Vocabulary Test) the differences were statistically significant. The fact that on all seven of these tests the T-boys excelled, though to a slight degree, indicated a pattern of differences statistically in favor of the T-boys. This showing reflects at least an appreciable *trend* in the desired direction (see Table 51).

TABLE 51

Mean Scores on Tests, Schedules, and Ratings in Division I for 30 Matched Pairs

| | MEAN SCORE | | | | |
Name of Test	Ts	Cs	Differ- ence	Signifi- cant	Favor- ing
1. T.R.C. (differential)	4.42	5.11	0.69	D a	T
2. Teachers' Ratings	33.07	32.07	1.00	No	T
3. Ethical Discrimination	16.33	15.83	0.50	Yes	T
4. Honesty	3.40	3.10	0.30	Yes	T
5. Superstitions	9.73	10.77	1.04	D	T
6. Composite Research Staff Ratings	34.10	33.83	0.27	No	T
7. Vocabulary Test	32.62	29.52	3.10	Yes	T

a D = Doubtful.

2. On the seven tests reported here as least discriminating, the C-boys achieved a slightly higher (a more desirable or more favorable) score than their treatment twins on four of the tests. On two of the tests it was impossible to tell definitely which group was favored. On the remaining test the score favored the treatment group. In only one case, however (The Game of Threes Test) was there a definitely significant difference between the scores of the two groups and in this case the scores favored the C-boys (see Table 52).

TABLE 52

Mean Scores on Tests, Schedules, and Ratings in Division II for 30 Matched Pairs

		MEAN SCORE		Differ-	Signifi-	Favor-
Name of Test		Ts	Cs	ence	cant	ing
1. Game of Threes		1.35	1.89	.54	Yes	C
2. Euphorimeter		234.48	262.07	27.59	P a	C
3. Accuracy:						
Part A		35.66	32.87	2.79	No	T
Part B		27.83	27.70	.13	No	
4. Morale		98.90	105.17	6.27	No	C
5. Income Expectations		47.47	51.37	3.90	No	?
6. Number of Friends		13.00	12.33	.67	No	?
7. Grip		69.24	69.90	.66	No	C

a P = Possibly.

3. Considering only the measures in both the discriminating and non-discriminating groups where a significant difference was obtained between the scores of the T- and C-boys, we find that the differences favored the T-boys on three occasions and the C-boys on one.

4. In brief, a second survey of a sample of the treatment group and its corresponding controls again revealed no great differences in scores achieved on a variety of tests, schedules, and ratings. Nevertheless, a definite *trend* was apparent in favor of the treatment group, a trend that was somewhat more significant than that found in the first evaluation.

DISCUSSION

A quantitative measurement of treatment gains while the program was in operation presented a number of practical problems. Administering tests without disturbing case-work relationships, for example, or explaining the purpose of the research to the parents who feared the counselor might be more interested in studying their child than in helping him, called for ingenuity and skill on the part of the research staff. Their greatest concern, however, was with questions of methodology, for little was known about how character develops or what constitutes good character or good citizenship.

Can such intangibles as social and spiritual growth, for example, be measured with scientific precision? In brief, how to evaluate a character-building program is a puzzle at the frontiers of science.

Three approaches to evaluation seemed to be within the realm of practical achievement: (1) the use of tests, questionnaires, and rating scales of diverse sorts; (2) the use of delinquency statistics; and (3) clinical judgments based on studies of individual cases.

For these two interim surveys the principal method adopted was the test method. A few delinquency statistics were used but a thorough comparison of the treatment and control groups in terms of police, court and commitment records was reserved for a terminal evaluation which is reported in the next chapter. The method of clinical evaluation was also adopted as a terminal evaluation and is reported in Chapters XXI to XXIX.

The difficulty of finding measures relevant to the objectives of the Study and adaptable to the peculiar conditions confronting the research staff has been related in the preceding pages. Many of the standardized personality tests were not suitable and a few tests and scales had to be invented. The future evaluators in this difficult area might find some lessons of value in our successes and failures in attempting to devise suitable measures and thus take us further along the road to better techniques of evaluation. The most promising tests, we believe, are those based on ratings by those who know the boys well, such as the teachers. The least promising tests and questionnaires seemed to be those filled out by the boy himself that depended so much on his insight and honesty.

The test measures used in these two interim surveys were not designed to show the degree of progress made by any individual T-boy during the treatment program, for they were not administered to the boy before the program started. It was hoped merely that they would reveal any existing and measurable differences between the T- and C-boys in respect to relevant factors.

It was found that the slight trend toward treatment success apparent in the first survey was a bit more evident in the second. Unfortunately, at the termination of treatment none of these tests could be repeated. In the first place, too few of the measures brought out significant differences. Secondly, it would have been difficult to locate the same individuals and to have tested them, for so many of them at the termination of treatment were still in the armed services or in the Merchant Marine. Therefore, in our final evaluation we relied on our two remaining methods—delinquency statistics and clinical judgments.

CHAPTER XX

WAS DELINQUENT BEHAVIOR PREVENTED?

THIS CHAPTER DEALS WITH AN EVALUATION OF THE STUDY SOLELY AS A delinquency-prevention program. Subsequent chapters appraise the character-building efforts of the counselors in achieving the objectives of the Study as more broadly conceived. Our experimental hypothesis was simple. If the counselors' work had been reasonably successful, then the C-boys, who had been denied the services of experienced and talented personal counselors, should show a proportionately higher frequency of delinquent behavior. The question we are seeking to answer is, Did this enduring, personal relationship of counselor and boy actually prevent the pre-delinquent child from becoming a delinquent youth?

USEFULNESS OF THE CONTROL GROUP

The usefulness of the control group is apparent, for if there had been none we could not interpret the following outcomes: (1) Not more than one-third of the older boys in the treatment group whose careers were closely followed and who appeared to be pre-delinquent boys when under 12, actually became delinquents in any serious sense. (2) Surprisingly few (less than one-sixth) of the boys who were rated on the minus side by the predictors were actually committed to correctional institutions. (3) The counselors believed that the Study's program had "substantially benefited" about two-thirds of the boys whom it served. (4) Considerably more than half of the boys acknowledged that they had been helped by their association with the Study.[1] Obviously, these facts alone do not prove

---

[1] These points are reviewed by Edwin Powers in "An Experiment in Prevention of Delinquency," *Annals of the American Academy of Political and Social Science*, CCLXI (1949), 77–88.

that the outcome would have been any different without the intervention of the counselors. The control group was therefore indispensable in measuring the effectiveness of the counselors' work.

The C-boys, of course, did not live in a social vacuum. Though receiving no help from the counselors we cannot assume that they received no help at all. On the contrary, we know that many, if not all, of the C-boys in the usual course of events received guidance from their families, the school, and the church, and a few were aided by the social agencies in the two cities. It is impossible for us to measure the extent of this help. All the Study could hope to show, therefore, was what its treatment amounted to *over and above* the influences ordinarily brought to bear upon a child in these communities; or, to state it another way, whether coordinated and sustained counseling or personal case work was better than a more sporadic variety. We know little about the forces that were actually brought to bear upon the C-boys; however, the case work to which some of them were exposed was undoubtedly good, and perhaps less sporadic than we assume. Nor were the Study services always over and above what was ordinarily given to the boys in the community, for sometimes the Study was, in a sense, a substitute for other agencies. There was some evidence to show, for example, that members of the treatment group participated less frequently than non-Study boys in the activities of other youth agencies. In other words, it seemed that the counselors' services were not always supplementary but were sometimes in lieu of other services, and one could not be sure that a substitution was better in each case than the help the boy would have received had the Study not been in existence. By and large, however, we believe that a comparison between the T-boys and C-boys can be based upon the fact that the T-boys received a *special* kind of service, not available to the controls, having the unique features of a continuous, friendly relationship of an older counselor. Did this special service keep them out of trouble?

Before examining the statistical findings let us first consider the time factor.

1. How Long Did the Period of Treatment Continue? Under the original plan each boy was to have received ten years of continuous counseling. As the onset of treatment was staggered over a period of many months from November, 1937, to May, 1939, the termination of the relationships was to have been reached sometime between November, 1947, and May, 1949. For reasons stated in previous chapters the program fell short of realization by a number of years, as shown graphically in Figure 7, Chapter XII, p. 153.

For more than three-fourths of the group the counselors' visits ceased before the official close on December 31, 1945. The boys who were retired from the treatment program early in its operation received on the average only about two and one half years of attention from the counselors; those who were dropped were seen for only four years and two months on the average; while those boys who were terminated (after reaching their 17th birthdays) were, on the average, in touch with their counselors for a period of five years and 11 months. There were, in fact, only 75 boys who were carried from the very beginning of the treatment program to its official termination. For them treatment extended for an average period of six years and nine months (with a range from eight years and one month to six years and seven months). For the entire group of 325 boys who were originally nominated for treatment, the average length of the treatment period was no more than four years and ten months.

On the other hand, in many cases the counselor-boy relationship was continued beyond the official closing of the case, for the boys, reluctant to accept the fact that the program had suddenly come to an end, persisted in seeing their counselors. Some of the counselors, too, after they had left the Study, were eager to continue the relationships which for some developed into more or less permanent friendships. Indeed, several of the counselors expressed the opinion that they would probably continue an interest in some of their boys for the rest of their lives. A genuine, friendly relationship does not end on a given date, yet for purposes of research one must take the view that intensive, supervised treatment came to an end December 31, 1945.

2. *At What Point in Time Should an Evaluation Be Undertaken?* A final evaluation taken too soon after termination might not take account of an important period of assimilation and maturation. The counselors believed that noticeable, or at least measurable, effects of treatment would not necessarily appear until the boy became older and was better able to assimilate and profit by the experience he had been through. The real criteria, they maintained, would not be how high a score the boy achieved on a special test

given during or immediately following the conclusion of the program but how well he had matured, how well he had carried on in life and how he had borne his responsibilities as a citizen. Delinquent habits that had acquired some momentum *before* treatment got under way may naturally have continued for some time into the period of treatment. The factor of maturation therefore becomes important. How well did the boys adjust to adult life? Carrying this point of view to its logical extreme, one might defer evaluation until the subjects had lived out their entire span of life, which would extend beyond the life of the research, its sponsors, and its personnel. By waiting too long before assessing the results of the program one might also run the risk of losing sight of many of the boys who had left home after reaching the age of 17 or 18. To wait until the boy had married and settled down or had taken up a vocation would no doubt be an extravagant interpretation of what Dr. Richard C. Cabot meant when he said, in speaking generally of evaluations of social work, "a reasonable period of time" should elapse before the results could be judged.[2] July 1, 1948, may not have been the optimum point in time for a terminal evaluation, for approximately one-ninth of the entire group had not yet reached the age of 17. Nevertheless, a comparison of the delinquent behavior of the treatment and control groups during the continuance of and shortly after the end of the treatment program could then be made to reveal trends as well as the current incidence of delinquent behavior. At some later date we hope to explore the extent to which boys in both groups continued their delinquent behavior into adulthood.

Our comparison of the treatment and control groups in respect to delinquent behavior is confined to official records, because of insufficient data relating to the offenses of C-boys unknown to the police and courts. We shall consider offenses known to the police in Cambridge, court appearances (frequency and seriousness), and commitments to juvenile or correctional institutions.

COMPARISON OF THE T- AND C-BOYS IN RESPECT TO POLICE STATISTICS IN CAMBRIDGE

This comparison is based upon the records of the Crime Preven-

[2] *Proceedings of the National Conference of Social Work* (Chicago, University of Chicago Press, 1931), pp. 16–17.

tion Bureau of the Police Department in the City of Cambridge.[3] Through the courtesy of its officials an examination was made of the records on file from its inception in 1938 through 1946, the year following the termination of the treatment program. Most of the cases appearing before this Bureau were handled in an informal manner after an investigation and interview with the boy and his parents. Relatively few cases were referred to the district court for disposition, for most of the offenses were of a minor nature. Nevertheless, they represented behavior that was sufficiently harmful or annoying to come to the attention of the police.

Table 53 shows the total number of T- and C-boys who appeared before the Bureau in a given period.

TABLE 53

Number of Boys Appearing before the Crime Prevention Bureau from 1938 to 1946, Inclusive

Number of Appearances	Number of Boys	
	T	C
One	49	49
Two or more	65	52
Total	114	101

Table 54 shows the total number of T- and C-boys who appeared before the Bureau two or more times during this period of time.

TABLE 54

Distribution of Frequency of Appearance before the Crime Prevention Bureau from 1938 to 1946, Inclusive

	T	C	Preponderance
The Less Frequent Repeaters:			
2 times	65	52	T
3 times	45	36	T
4 times	30	25	T
The More Frequent Repeaters:			
5 times	13	19	C
6 times	7	14	C
7 times	5	5	..
8 times	3	4	C

[3] The organization and function of this Bureau is described in Chap. XII.

FINDINGS

1. The number of T-boys who made only one appearance before the Bureau equals the number of C-boys making only one appearance.

2. The number of T-boys who appeared two or more times exceeds the number of C-boys who were repeaters.

3. The number of T-boys who appeared before the Bureau exceeded the number of C-boys (53 percent of the total were T-boys).

4. From 1938 to 1946 inclusive, 282 T-boys and 256 C-boys appeared before the Bureau. The average number of appearances per boy was similar in the two groups—2.45 for T-boys compared to 2.53 for C-boys.

5. The number of T-boys appearing two or more times, three or more times, and four or more times exceeded the number of C-boys who appeared a like number of times, but the C-boys exceeded the T-boys in making five or more, six or more, or eight or more appearances. The number of T- and C-boys making at least seven appearances was equal.

CONCLUSIONS

Throughout the treatment period the counselors were evidently not successful in preventing boys from committing offenses that brought them to the attention of the police in Cambridge (where two-thirds of them resided). Indeed, the counselors seem to have had no positive effect whatever in this respect, as measured by the number of T-boys appearing before the Bureau in comparison with a matched group equal in number who did not receive this special counseling service. The number of boys who appeared, as well as the total number of appearances, was greater for the treatment group than for the control group.[4] It can be said, nevertheless, that there was a *slight* preponderance of C-boys among the most active recidivists.

[4] Just why the T-boys showed a slightly excessive number of appearances over the C-boys we cannot say. The counselors did not believe, naturally, that their influence was adverse; they offered the alternative explanation that more T-boys were known to the police by the very fact that the counselors had discussed some of their cases with them. Also, in a few cases, counselors reported T-boys directly to the police in the first instance "for the boy's own good." Furthermore, as we pointed out in Chap. VI (pp. 78–79) the treatment group had a slight preponderance of minus ratings, though this difference may have been negligible.

COMPARISON OF THE T- AND C-BOYS IN RESPECT TO FREQUENCY OF
COURT APPEARANCES

Through the courtesy of the Massachusetts Commissioner of
Probation all cases were cleared through the state probation files as
of July 1, 1948. In the central files the names of all boys who had
been brought into any state or county court on a delinquent or
criminal charge were noted. Offenses committed outside the State
were disregarded in these comparisons. From these data the following tabulations are derived.

1. We first compare the frequency of offenses and of court appearances of the 325 T-boys and the 325 C-boys as of July 1, 1948,
regardless of age at that time or the length of time the T-boys had
remained in the treatment group.[5]

Court Appearances	T	C
Number of boys	96	92
Number of offenses	264	218

2. We now compare the T-boys who had reached the age of 17
before July 1, 1948, with the C-boys matched with them in respect
to the frequency of court appearances.[6] This comparison concerns
only 89.8 percent of the total group of 650 boys, for 10.2 percent
were at that time still under 17. As the treatment and control groups
were matched closely for age the number in each group who were
under 17 on that date is approximately the same.

Court Appearances	T	C
Number of boys	68	63
Number of offenses	141	132

3. Compared to C-boys, how many T-boys committed offenses
for which they were brought into court *after* their 17th birthdays?
Table 55 shows the distribution of the number of offenses charged
against T- and C-boys between their 17th and 22d birthdays.
The distribution of ages at that time (July 1, 1948) for the 650 boys
is as follows: Under 17, 10.2 percent; 17-year-olds, 10.8 percent; 18-
year-olds, 14.2 percent; 19-year-olds, 18.5 percent; 20-year-olds, 24.7

5 The oldest boy was then 21.9, the youngest 14.4, the median about 19.10.
6 It will be recalled that 17 is the upper age limit in this State for juvenile delinquency as defined by statute.

percent; and 21-year-olds, 21.6 percent. We find here that the number of T-boys who committed offenses in their 18th, or 19th, or 20th, or 21st years exceeded the number of C-boys, and also that the number of offenses committed by them was larger.

TABLE 55

Number of Boys in Court and Number of Offenses Charged against Them between Their 17th and 22d Birthdays

	Number in Court	Number of Offenses
T-boys: 17th year	21	30
C-boys: 17th year	27	40
T-boys: 18th year	20	36
C-boys: 18th year	14	19
T-boys: 19th year	23	37
C-boys: 19th year	13	19
T-boys: 20th year	12	13
C-boys: 20th year	6	8
T-boys: 21st year	3	7
C-boys: 21st year	..	..
Total Number of Offenders	T 123	
	C 86	

4. Were the boys who remained with the Study for a longer consecutive period and who presumably were the recipients of more intensive and extensive efforts of the counselors less delinquent or more delinquent than their matched controls? To answer this question we now compare the official delinquent records of the 74 boys who were in the treatment program from the beginning to the end, together with the 68 boys whose cases were not terminated until they had reached their 17th birthdays, with 142 C-boys who were originally matched with these T-boys.[7]

Some of the T-boys had already been in court before the counselor's first visit. Others were well on their way toward delinquency before the assigned counselor had become acquainted with the boy and his family or could consider himself a friend. Ob-

[7] There were 75 boys in the treatment program from the beginning to the end and 72 terminated cases, but five of this group were matched with C-boys who died or had left the State and were lost sight of relatively early in the program. These five pairs were therefore omitted in order to make both groups comparable in age and number.

viously, we would not expect the friendship of the counselor to have an immediate effect on the boy's delinquent habits. To allow for a "warming-up" period, therefore, we are not tabulating here any possible court appearances prior to 1940.[8]

Comparing the 142 boys in the T-group who received the most extensive treatment with the 142 boys matched with them in the C-group during a six-year period commencing eight months (on the average) after treatment began and terminating July 1, 1948, we find:

Court Appearances	T	C
Number of boys	60	48
Number of offenses	171	121

Again we find an excess of T-offenders. In this analysis a higher proportion of T-boys than was evident in the previous analyses might be due to selective factors appearing subsequent to the matching. Boys retained for treatment were, as a rule, those whose problems persisted. Presumably these two original groups (325 T-boys and 325 C-boys) were well matched at the outset, but it does not follow that a sub-group of 142 T-boys selected on the basis of factors arising after the original matching would still be as well matched with their 142 C-twins. This point has already been discussed in Chapter XIV.

COMPARISON OF T- AND C-BOYS IN RESPECT TO SERIOUSNESS OF OFFENSES

We have so far considered the boys' delinquent behavior quantitatively without regard to the nature of the offenses committed. Did either group commit more serious offenses than the other? To answer this question we must first determine the relative degrees of seriousness of the various offenses. As we have previously maintained (Chapter XIV, pp. 179–182) the seriousness of any given offense cannot be judged without knowing the details of the act and its consequences. It is impossible for us to make this individual appraisal for we do not have the necessary information concerning our C-boys. In dealing with large groups of cases, however, one can

[8] It will be recalled that 76.6 percent of the first visits to boys were made during the first five months of 1939. Only 21.8 percent of the cases were commenced in 1938, and 1.5 percent in 1937.

assign a numerical value to each offense as a sort of average or composite of all acts that are given that offense name. Individual variations due to the particular circumstances of the case are lost but would probably be equally balanced in the two groups.

Can "Seriousness" Be Measured? Can we then assume that the seriousness of various types of delinquent offenses can be quantified on a linear scale from least to most serious? Clark devised a scale made up of delinquent acts classified into 14 different groups.[9] Durea, taking these same 14 delinquencies, found a score value for each offense by using the method of paired comparisons.[10] Arranging the 14 offenses in 91 different pairs, he recorded the decisions of 45 psychologists, 15 sociologists, 28 juvenile judges, and 31 graduate students who were asked to choose which offense in each pair they judged the more serious. By using the Thurstone formula he arrived at a numerical value for each offense. He found, for example, that murder, highway robbery, and arson were, in that order, the three most serious, while malicious mischief, vagrancy, and truancy were the least serious. The other eight offenses were distributed between the two extremes. He did not find that the linear scale showed increments of equal steps. He did not provide the judges with a definition of "seriousness," but presumed that each judge would use that term as he ordinarily understood it. The circumstances surrounding each offense were not described; an offense was judged in the abstract.

This scale is of little use in our analysis of the problem of seriousness, for our list comprised 69 rather than 14 different offenses. Four of the 14 offenses in Durea's list are not found in ours.

We are here using the term "seriousness" as it is ordinarily understood by two groups of law-enforcement authorities—the police and probation officers. These officials play a significant role in determining what shall be done with the offender. Their decision is probably largely determined by the gravity of the offense as they understand that concept in their routine work. Our board of judges was comprised of four police officers (two from Cambridge and two

9 W. W. Clark, "Whittier Scale for Grading Juvenile Offenses," *California Bureau of Juvenile Research,* 1922, Bulletin 11.

10 Mervin A. Durea, "An Experimental Study of Attitudes toward Juvenile Delinquency," *Journal of Applied Psychology,* XVII (1933), 522–534.

from Somerville) who, for many years, had been specializing in the problems of juvenile delinquents, and four probation officers from three courts who had also been assigned to work exclusively with the delinquent child. Each officer was asked to rate each offense on a scale comprising four steps: (1) least serious, (2) fairly serious, (3) serious, and (4) most serious. These officials, of course, were not given any information about the special circumstances of the offenses listed. They were merely asked, "How serious do you ordinarily consider an offense of this sort? You have had many larceny cases for example; some are serious; some, of course, are less serious. How serious do you consider larceny *on the average* as compared to these other offenses?" No attempt was made to define the word "serious" nor did any officer ask for the meaning of the word. Each offense was thus given a numerical rating by each of the eight officers.

The judges, independently ranking each offense, substantially agreed as to the degree of seriousness on 41 (59.4 percent) of the 69 offenses. All eight judges placed 17 offenses in the same category; seven of the eight agreed as to 16 other offenses, while six of the eight agreed as to eight. Only 13 offenses (18.8 percent) were placed in three different categories. No offense rated "most serious" by one judge was rated "least serious" by another; or vice versa.

Table 56 lists the offenses in order of seriousness and indicates the frequency of commission. Each offense has been given a numerical value in accordance with the category into which it was placed by the judges. Offenses judged "least serious" were given a value of one; "fairly serious" a value of two; "serious" a value of three; and "most serious," four. The total value was divided by the number of judges. (Drunkenness, for example, was ranked by the eight judges 2-2-3-2-3-2-2-3, giving a total of 19 which, divided by 8, gives a numerical value of 2.38). The eight traffic violations that were unanimously rated "least serious" have been grouped into one class, which in our table we have called "minor traffic violations." [11]

[11] These offenses are: (1) Failing to stop at stop-sign, (2) Driving to left of streetcar, (3) Not provided with mechanical device, (4) Not slowing down, (5) Not slowing down at intersection, (6) Not keeping to right at intersection, (7) One-way street violation, and (8) Unlicensed hack driver.

TABLE 56

Index of Offenses Committed by T- and C-Boys in Order of Seriousness as Judged by Law-Enforcement Authorities

		Number of Offenses	
Seriousness Index	*Offense Name*	T	C
	A. LEAST SERIOUS (1.00–1.74)		
1.00	Minor traffic violations	17	12
1.00	Occupying the street (loitering)	1	0
1.00	Stealing ride on streetcar	0	2
1.00	Violating fish and game laws	1	0
1.13	Breaking glass	1	0
1.13	Crossing through-way	2	1
1.13	No auto inspection sticker	4	3
1.13	Present at game on Lord's Day	0	2
1.13	Using profane language	1	0
1.13	Trespassing	1	1
1.13	Turning water on in hydrant	0	1
1.25	Committing a nuisance	1	0
1.25	Disturbing the peace	4	5
1.25	Not obeying traffic control	2	1
1.25	Trespassing on the railroad	2	3
1.38	Refusing to stop	1	0
1.38	Runaway	5	7
1.50	Speeding	13	7
1.50	Stubbornness	5	5
1.63	Habitual absentee	8	3
1.63	No license	7	4
		76	57
	B. FAIRLY SERIOUS (1.75–2.49)		
1.75	Operating without insurance	2	1
1.75	Refusing to obey police officer	1	1
1.75	Rude and disorderly	2	0
1.75	Driving unregistered auto	5	2
2.00	Destroying city property	7	3
2.00	False fire alarm	2	0
2.00	Peeping Tom	1	0
2.00	Violating regulations of training school	1	0
2.13	Going away after traffic accident	1	1
2.25	Assault and battery	7	6
2.25	Threats of assault	0	1
2.38	Drunkenness	20	16
2.38	Operating car to endanger	3	0
		52	31

TABLE 56 (*continued*)

Seriousness Index	Offense Name	Number of Offenses T	C
	C. SERIOUS (2.50–3.24)		
2.50	Accessory to the fact of larceny	0	1
2.63	Altering number plates on car	1	0
2.63	Operating after revocation of license	3	0
2.63	Using auto without authority	20	12
2.71	Conspiracy (in connection with larceny)	2	0
2.75	Attempting larceny	4	7
2.75	Receiving stolen property	4	5
2.88	Exposing person	0	1
2.88	Operating under the influence of liquor	3	0
2.88	Setting fire	0	1
3.00	Larceny	44	36
3.13	Breaking and entering (or attempt) not in the nighttime	7	9
		88	72
	D. MOST SERIOUS (3.25–4.00)		
3.25	Lewdness	2	2
3.33	Indecent assault and battery	0	4
3.38	Carrying dangerous weapon	4	0
3.50	Breaking and entering (or attempt) in the nighttime	32	40
3.50	Unnatural and lascivious acts	1	2
3.63	Assault and battery with dangerous weapon	2	0
3.63	Possession of burglary tools	1	0
3.88	Abusing female child	1	1
3.88	Arson	2	1
3.88	Carnal abuse	0	1
3.88	Robbery, unarmed	2	2
3.88	Sodomy	0	1
4.00	Assault with intent to rape	1	0
4.00	Manslaughter	0	1
4.00	Robbery, armed	0	2
4.00	Robbery by force and violence	0	1
		48	58

We can now compare the tabulated offenses to see whether, on the whole, the more serious offenses were committed by the T- or the C-boys. From Table 56, where the offenses have been grouped into the four categories, it is evident that (a) slightly more offenses were judged "serious" or "most serious" (55.2 percent) than "fairly" or "least serious." (b) Although the total number of offenses committed by the T-boys (264) considerably exceeded the number of offenses by C-boys (218) as noted on p. 326, nevertheless the distribution into categories of seriousness differed considerably. Of the offenses committed by the C-boys, 59.6 percent were placed in the two more serious categories as compared to 51.5 percent committed by the T-boys. (c) In the category of "most serious" offenses the C-boys exceeded the T-boys in number of offenses committed (58 compared to 48). Also, more C-boys (35) than T-boys (30) committed such offenses. In comparing the proportion of such offenses to the total in the series (Table 57 and Figure 10), we also find that a larger proportion of "most serious" offenses were committed by C-boys (26.6 percent) than by T-boys (18.2 percent). (d) Taken as a whole, the average index of offenses was slightly less serious for T-boys (2.41) than for C-boys (2.56).

TABLE 57

T- and C-Boys Compared as to Seriousness Category of Offenses

	NUMBER OF BOYS		NUMBER OF OFFENSES					
Seriousness Category	T	C	T	*Percent*	C	*Percent*	*Total*	*Percent*
A. Least Serious	50	42	76	28.8	57	26.2	133	27.6
B. Fairly Serious	37	22	52	19.7	31	14.2	83	17.2
C. Serious	46	45	88	33.3	72	33.0	160	33.2
D. Most Serious	30	35	48	18.2	58	26.6	106	22.0
Total			264	100.0	218	100.0	482	100.0

The two groups can again be compared as to seriousness and frequency of offenses by computing the delinquency index for the 96 T-boys and the 92 C-boys. Each boy who had committed one or more offenses in either group was given a delinquency index number made up of the sum of the weighted seriousness values for each of the offenses he committed. For example, a boy committing larceny with a seriousness value of 3.00, manslaughter with a seriousness value of 4.00, and four minor traffic violations (with a total seriousness value of 4.00) would have a delinquency index of 11. In Table 58 we see how the boys are distributed in respect to this factor.

TABLE 58

T- and C-Boys Compared in Respect to Seriousness of Offenses

Seriousness Index	T-Boys	Percent	C-Boys	Percent
1.0–2.9	31	32.3	33	35.9
3.0–4.9	18	18.7	19	20.6
5.0–6.9	15	15.6	15	16.3
7.0–8.9	8	8.3	4	4.3
9.0–10.9	7	7.3	8	8.7
11.0–12.9	7	7.3	3	3.3
13.0–14.9	2	2.1	1	1.0
15.0–16.9	2	2.1	3	3.3
17.0–18.9	2	2.1	0	0.0
19.0–and over	4	4.2	6	6.5
Total	96	100.0	92	100.0

This table reflects the close resemblance between the two groups. Here we find that six C-boys, compared to four T-boys, are found to have a seriousness index of 19.0 (due in part to frequency of offenses committed) or over and yet we find more T-boys than C-boys more frequently committing offenses having a seriousness index of over 7.0. We also see that of all T-offenders 33.4 percent have a seriousness index of 7.0 or greater compared to 27.1 percent of the C-offenders. Though the T-boys have committed, on the whole, more offenses in the aggregate and more T-boys than C-boys have committed the "serious" offenses, there is some evidence, though slight, that the *most* serious offenders are in the control group.

COMPARISON OF THE T- AND C-BOYS IN RESPECT TO COMMITMENTS TO CORRECTIONAL INSTITUTIONS

Another way to measure "seriousness" may be by noting the incidence of commitments in the two groups, for the more serious delinquent presumably is the boy who was committed to a correctional institution on the theory that he could not be expected to make a satisfactory adjustment to society while living in his own home. We have maintained (Chapter XIV) that this presumption is not necessarily true in the individual case but, by and large, in considering delinquents in groups rather than individually, commitment to an institution is a reasonable indication that the delinquent behavior of the group has been serious and/or persistent as judged by the court. We now compare the 325 T-boys and the 325 C-boys in respect to commitments, from the beginning of the Study down to November 1, 1948, a span of almost ten years for most of the group.

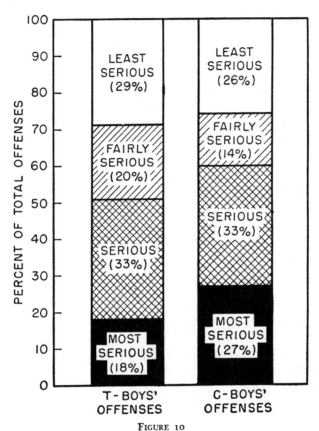

FIGURE 10

THE RELATIVE SERIOUSNESS OF OFFENSES IN THE T AND C GROUPS

1. Table 59 compares the number of T-boys with the number of C-boys who were committed to correctional institutions for juveniles in this State. Eighteen of the 23 T-boys were committed while they were still in the treatment program. None was committed prior to the beginning of the program.

TABLE 59

Commitments of T-Boys and C-Boys to Correctional Institutions for Juveniles from the Beginning of Treatment to November 1, 1948

	COMMITMENTS			PERCENT OF TOTAL	
Institution	T	C	Total	T	C
Lyman School for Boys	9	13	22	40.9	59.0
Industrial School	14	9	23	60.9	38.1
Total	23	22	45	51.1	48.9

2. Table 60 compares the number of T-boys with the number of C-boys who were committed to institutions for older offenders. Seven of the eight T-boys were committed after they were no longer in the treatment program.

TABLE 60

Commitments of T-Boys and C-Boys to Correctional Institutions for Older Offenders from the Beginning of Treatment to November 1, 1948

	COMMITMENTS			PERCENT OF TOTAL	
Institution	T	C	Total	T	C
Massachusetts Reformatory	2	8	10	20.0	80.0
House of Correction [a]	5	5	10	50.0	50.0
State Prison	1	2	3	33.3	66.6
Total	8	15	23	34.8	65.2

[a] The Houses of Correction referred to here are the county institutions in Middlesex County in which Cambridge and Somerville are located and in Suffolk County in which the adjacent city of Boston is located.

3. Some of the boys were committed to two of the institutions and a few were committed to three, as follows: committed to 2 institutions, 3 T-boys, 7 C-boys; committed to 3 institutions, 1 T-boy, 2 C-boys.

FINDINGS

1. An almost identical number of T- and C-boys were committed to institutions for juvenile offenders: 23 T-boys and 22 C-boys.

2. More C-boys than T-boys were committed to institutions for older offenders: 8 T-boys compared to 15 C-boys. Although the total numbers were small, the control group is almost double the treatment group in this respect.

3. C-boys were more frequently committed to more than one institution: 4 T-boys compared to 9 C-boys.

GENERAL CONCLUSIONS

From our comparison of the delinquent behavior of the T- and C-boys two main conclusions can be drawn:

1. The special work of the counselors was no more effective than the usual forces in the community in preventing boys from committing delinquent acts. Evidence for this conclusion was found in our analysis of official records. We found in the records of the Cambridge Crime Prevention Bureau that more T-boys appeared before this Bureau than C-boys. From a study of court records it appeared that slightly more T-boys were in court than C-boys, regardless of age or the number of years in the Study, and again a preponderance of T-boys appeared when analyzed by age into two groups—under and over 17. In considering only the boys who presumably were the recipients of more intensive and extensive efforts of the counselors we found again that the T-boys had more official records than the C-boys matched with them. In appraising the seriousness of the offenses of the two groups we found a striking similarity in degree, although the control group showed a slight trend toward more serious offenses; and, finally, from the records of commitments to institutions we found close correspondence between the T- and C-boys, with a slight preponderance of C-boys.

2. Our second conclusion is that, though the counselors were unable to stop the advance of young boys into delinquency with any greater success than the usual deterrent forces in the community, some of the boys were evidently deflected from delinquent careers which, without the counselors' help, might have resulted in continued or more serious violations. Thus, the evidence seems to point to the fact that, though the first stages of delinquency are not wholly averted when starting treatment at the eight-to-ten-year level, the later and more serious stages may to some degree be curtailed. Evidence for this conclusion was found in the analysis of official records which showed that the more frequent repeaters (Police Bureau statistics) and the more serious offenders (court statistics) were more often in the control group, though the differences

were not large. We found, however, considerable preponderance of C-boys committed to institutions for older offenders.

DISCUSSION

Our belief (admittedly based on slight evidence) that in the next decade there will be a preponderance of adult criminals in our control group as compared to our treatment group must, of course, be checked at some later date. We cannot now be sure that the present trends will be continued.

As we have insisted throughout, officially recorded delinquent behavior is not the whole story. We have already shown that many boys known to us have committed delinquent acts but have not been apprehended and that many boys who were apprehended and adjudged delinquent were minor offenders who did not repeat their delinquent acts. We have also seen how many of the boys expressed the opinion that they were helped by the Study in spite of the fact that they were officially adjudged delinquent.

We should give up the idea, so frequently expressed, that when a boy is brought into juvenile court his future is blighted. An official record in the juvenile court should not and does not stigmatize the boy throughout the rest of his life. Moreover, appearance in court may be a therapeutic experience for a child. Indeed, there were more than a few cases where the counselor himself directed the child to the court for the child's own good.[12] Thus, one or two court appearances constitute a poor criterion for measuring a boy's constructive growth of personality. We have already pointed out that the making of good citizens was the broader objective on which the Study was based. In many cases, even in the lives of some of the adjudged delinquents, emotional conflicts were alleviated, practical problems were dealt with successfully, and the boys were given greater confidence to face life. Evaluation of the program, therefore, must not rest alone on a study of official records. The next chapters will deal with an analysis of the character-building effects of the counselors' work.

---

[12] Counselors, of course, in carrying out their treatment plans could not follow the strict demands of research. In calling to the attention of the police or the courts their own T-boys they may have thrown a slight bias into the final tabulation of appearances before these authorities. (See note 4, p. 325.)

PART II. EVALUATION

By Helen L. Witmer

CHAPTER XXI

PLAN OF EVALUATION

THE STUDY, AS HAS BEEN SHOWN IN THE PRECEDING CHAPTERS, WAS designed to test the hypothesis that many difficult boys would be deflected from antisocial behavior and become youths of good character if they were provided with the continued friendship and wise counsel of adults who were deeply interested in them and who could secure for them access to such community services as they required. By the time the service program neared its end it became apparent that as a means of delinquency prevention the plan had not been markedly successful. Nevertheless, sponsors of the Study and those who had been members of the staff were inclined to believe that the counselors' services had been useful to many boys and that much had been learned in the course of the work that would be of interest and value to social workers. Accordingly, toward the end of the treatment program a research staff composed of individuals not connected with the Study was engaged to "evaluate" the work of the counselors. This and the following chapters constitute this research staff's report on how they conducted the study and what they found.

The question initially posed for investigation has been stated above: Did the specified services to youths of the specified types result in a lessening of delinquency and an increase in good character among them? The answer to the question was to be arrived at by matching two series of boys for certain significant traits, "treating" one series (T-boys) and leaving the other (C-boys) untreated, and by comparing the two groups at the end of about ten years with respect to delinquency records and moral character.

Our first move was to consider whether this scheme for testing results was likely to be adequate. We had two reasons for being in doubt about the suitability of the T-C group comparison as a method of evaluation for our particular purposes. First, that method, at best, does not provide answers that satisfy clinicians, and it was to clinical workers (persons who might use our findings in their work with individual children) that we were asked to direct our report. Second, the conditions of this particular study did not appear to be such as to satisfy the requirements of the control-group method. The reasoning lying back of these statements is as follows.

First, with regard to the clinical objection, we must consider the nature of findings based on control-group comparisons. The logic of the control-group method is well known; less frequently considered is its applicability to a clinical situation. The control-group method is a statistical method, relying on the principle of the stability of large numbers and referring to average effects rather than to individual performance. According to that principle, the behavior of the individual units under consideration (the boys in our case) may vary widely in reaction to numerous and diverse influences; the range and distribution of the variations will, however, remain constant from group to group and from time to time unless some new and important factor intervenes. That factor (the Study's services in our case) may not affect the behavior of all the units, but if it affects any significant number of them the distribution will be altered and the effectiveness of the new factor will be demonstrated. In any individual case, however, we will not know whether it was the new factor or one or more of the old factors that produced the beneficent results. Moreover, even if no significant differences between study and control groups appear, it is not demonstrated that the new factor was without importance; the most that can be concluded is that the new factor was not more important, on the average, than those previously operating. Even this conclusion may not be justified, for there may be other explanations for the apparent similarity in the behavior of the study and control groups.

Such conclusions do not satisfy the clinical worker, who, by the nature of his task, has little interest in averages. What such a person wants to know is whether there were any cases—even if only a few —in which the introduction of the new factor tipped the balance in a boy's favor. If so, he wants to know which cases these were, so that he may compare them with the others and possibly discover their distinctive traits. He also wants to know whether the organization's services were ever harmful; if so, which services and to which clients? In short, he is not much interested in over-all figures, in the averaging of good and bad. He wants information that he can use in work with individuals, information that will increase the efficiency of his performance.

These considerations were kept in mind in planning the evaluation. Since we hoped to arrive at conclusions that would be clinically useful as well as evaluative of the program as a whole, it seemed clear that the mere comparison of study and control groups would not produce adequate findings. We would have to find some way of determining the value of the services to the individual boys, for only such judgments would provide a basis for determining why the counselors were helpful in some cases and of little or no benefit in others.

The adequacy of the control-group method seemed further questionable by reason of the nature of the problem under consideration. In planning the Study Dr. Cabot was apparently using a medical analogy. He seemed to be assuming that the disorder in question was like a medical disorder, in that it transcended the differences in the subjects in which it appeared, and that the treatment method to be employed was also (like a drug or other medical remedy) sufficiently uniform that variation in its application from case to case could be disregarded. These assumptions may be valid for certain medical experiments but they seemed to us to be dubious for social work. Delinquency and poor character, the disorders the Study sought to remedy, are not analogous to specific diseases, and social services (especially those as heterogeneous as the Study provided) cannot be regarded as having the unitary character of a specific medical remedy. To give a great variety of services to a great variety of boys, each practitioner doing what he thinks best without reference to any commonly held body of theory, seems—control group or no control group—no more a scientific experiment than a medical one would be in which different kinds of medicine were given to patients suffering from different kinds of disorders by doctors who held different theories as to the causes of the illnesses. From such a medical experiment one would not expect significant findings to emerge nor could one be sure about the meaning of any that did appear. This being so, it seemed necessary to reformulate the aim of the Study investigation to take into account the variation in the boys' difficulties and in the kinds of assistance they were given.

Since the medical analogy seemed false with respect to the disorder under consideration and the method of providing aid, we had to consider whether there was a possibility of mistake with respect to goals as well. Dr. Cabot, like most philanthropists and some social workers, stated the goal of social service in long-run terms and talked of prevention of crime, poor character, social irresponsibility, and the like. Social and psychological clinicians are likely to have less ambitious aims. They count their work successful if they have helped their clients to deal with their current social or emotional difficulties. Whether the likelihood of future difficulties is thereby lessened will depend, they say, on the nature of the problems with which they have given help. Physicians follow the same line of reasoning. They treat their patients for specific disorders and hope for amelioration or cure of those disorders rather than for good health in the long run.

The control-group method thus seemed inadequate or inappropriate to the questions at hand, and we were led to the conclusion that a way must be found for making judgments about the value of the Study service case by case. We did not propose to give up the control-group method entirely; we would supplement it, however, and try thereby to overcome some of its most outstanding deficiencies.

Reasoning along these lines, we came to the conclusion that our investigation ought to be directed toward sorting out the kinds of boys the counselors dealt with and the kinds of treatment they were given, and toward trying to discover combinations of boy and treatment method that could be regarded as fairly uniform. This being done, we could, on the one hand, ask to what extent the boys in the various groups appeared to benefit from the counselors' services and, on the other, inquire whether those who did benefit were adjusting better than their controls.

In the search for ways of judging the organization's effectiveness in individual cases three methods used by evaluators of social agency accomplishments were considered: (1) classification of cases on the basis of the degree of social adjustment attained by the time treatment ended; (2) the boys' opinions as to whether or not they had been aided; (3) a subjective estimate by the investigator, on the basis of the case record material, as to the effectiveness of the services. By itself, none of these methods seemed satisfactory. It did seem, however, that a combination of these devices, checked against one another and based on case evaluations of the degree of certainty that help had been given rather than on how much help had been given, might prove fairly trustworthy.

What we did, then, was, first, to make case-by-case judgments as to how sure we were that the boy had benefited from the Study services; and, second, compare these rating with others showing (a) the boys' terminal behavior, (b) the amount of change that had taken place, and (c) the boys' own opinions of the work of the Study. After this was done we had at hand groups of cases classified according to value-of-service. At this point the control-group comparison seemed applicable, for the question now was: Did the boys who were apparently benefited by the Study turn out better than their controls? If the answer was affirmative, not only would the Study program be justified but the distinguishing characteristics of boys who can benefit from such a program could probably be found.

This method of analysis, it seemed to us, overcame some of the faults of the original experimental design. In fact, under this method, it is of advantage that diverse treatment methods were employed with diverse subjects, for this made it possible to test the effectiveness of various combinations of circumstances. Only the fact that the number of cases in the sub-groups would probably become very small would stand in the way of valid conclusions of clinical usefulness. The method, of course, does call for the making of many subjective judgments, including the primary one concerning the effectiveness of the work in individual cases. In this, however, it does not differ very greatly from the original control-group method, for even in the evaluation of probation office records many subjective judgments are required if one is to go beyond the rather meaningless count of court appearances. Moreover, it seemed that it should be possible to show the objective facts on which the investigator's judgments of value were based. All in all, then, this method, it seemed to us, was one to be used carefully and critically; but, if well handled, it should produce findings that would be much more detailed and much more useful clinically than the simple yes or no that results from a control-group comparison.

In the following chapters, then, we shall follow both this method of analysis and the one originally proposed. In spite of the limitations, data about the control boys' adjustment will be utilized as originally planned, and the comparative findings will be examined by various statistical breakdowns, among which will be that of value of service. Chief emphasis, however, will be put upon intragroup comparisons in the series of treated cases, for it is hoped that by such an analysis we can show not only whether the services were useful but which services were of value in particular kinds of cases. Thus, even though the hypothesis of the Study should turn out to be invalid, we would have secured from the data conclusions that were in line with Dr. Cabot's main objective, which was to determine the results of a social work program and draw usable conclusions from it.

One further point must be mentioned before we proceed with the analysis of the data. This evaluation of the organization's effectiveness is based not on the 325 cases that constituted the total series of boys but on 254 of them. The discarded cases were the following: the 65 boys retired from the Study in 1941 because their social adjustment had been uniformly good throughout the period the counselors were in contact with them,[1] and six other boys who either died or moved far away from the Study area within a short time after the service program started. Our reasons for discarding these cases are obvious. We wanted a series of cases that the Study might be expected to have benefited, and it seemed useless to include in it either boys who were served only a short time or boys who, in the counselors' opinion, did not need assistance from the agency.

[1] See Chap. XI for a description of the retirement of cases.

CHAPTER XXII

THE BOYS AND
THEIR FAMILIES

ONE OF THE FIRST QUESTIONS CONFRONTING THE EVALUATORS WAS what kinds of boys the Study had served. As stated in Chapter VIII, 58 percent of the boys were between the ages of 10 and 12 at the time work with them got under way. The range of ages of the total group was from six to 12. Their mean I.Q., as measured by the Stanford-Binet test, was between 92 and 96, with a range from 53 to 149. About 8 percent of the boys were Negroes. A large proportion of the others either had foreign-born parents or parents who were culturally foreign. A third of the boys lived in extremely poor neighborhoods (ratings —3 to —5), and only about a fifth lived in neighborhoods classified as being at the positive or "favorable" end of the scale.

BEHAVIOR DISORDERS

It was also known that the boys varied greatly in the seriousness of their social and emotional maladjustments. Many were regarded by their teachers as "average" boys and were referred as such to the Study. A few were described by the police as persistent delinquents, and a few were said to be so peculiar that they needed psychiatric study. Between these extremes were said to be the majority, the nature of whose difficulties took various forms. For evaluation purposes, categories and figures more definite than these were needed, for we wanted to be able, for example, to relate the type of original difficulty with the results obtained. Accordingly, two sets of categories were devised, the first descriptive of the boys' general adjustment at the time work with them got under way, the second descriptive of the extent of their delinquency, if any.

It is doubtless unnecessary to point out that grouping human beings in accordance with either degree or type of social maladjustment is a very inaccurate procedure. One can quickly be discouraged in the task if he has high standards of precision and dislikes subjective judgments. If, however, one is frankly impressionistic it seems possible to make judgments along common-sense lines that are sufficiently accurate for a study of the kind we were undertaking. This, at any rate, is what we attempted to do. The definitions of categories will be bolstered by case examples which may help to make clearer what we had in mind.

DEGREE OF MALADJUSTMENT

This classification was based on data contained in the counselors' reports of their early contacts with the boys and their families and with others who knew them well. In these information-gathering and rapport-establishing interviews the counselors attempted to size up the situations and to make plans for helping the boys. In compiling data on which to base our judgment about the extent of a boy's maladjustment we did not limit ourselves to a definite period of time or a definite number of preliminary interviews, our aim being to make as accurate a statement as possible about what the boy was like when work with him started—before his behavior might have been changed by reason of the counselor's contact with him.

As a start toward showing the kinds of maladjustment found, a classification system based on the apparent severity of the boys' problems was devised by the writer. Its categories were: Well-adjusted; Mild maladjustment; Considerable social maladjustment; Behavior suggestive of neurosis; Extreme emotional or social maladjustment.

1. Well-adjusted. Nineteen percent of the 254 boys with whom our analysis is concerned originally appeared to be well adjusted. This does not mean that they were paragons of good mental health. They were, however, boys who had friends and interests appropriate to their age and intelligence and who caused little or no trouble or concern in the classroom or at home. Paul, for instance, was referred by his teacher as an average boy. He was a quiet boy, she said, but he had many friends and was interested both in schoolwork and in athletics, even though he could not participate in games because he had a bad heart. Italo was even more clearly well adjusted. He presented no problems at school, was much interested in reading and did acceptable academic work; he was a happy, stable boy, active in church affairs and a leader in his neighborhood gang.

Some of the boys included in this category were not so outgoing as this second example. Arthur, for example, was described as an average, quiet, happy boy, but not a good mixer. Rodney was somewhat shy and tended to daydream. Frederick was quiet, thoughtful, and somewhat uncommunicative and, at the outset of the Study program, played with a group of boys who frequented the railroad yards and hopped trucks. Others asserted themselves more actively and were a bit difficult for the teachers to handle. Allen, for instance, was described as a happy, likable, "regular" boy, but he was inclined to tease other children and to act a bit duller than was compatible with his I.Q. Domaz was a noisy, somewhat aggressive youngster who, however, was well behaved at home and school and in the settlement house which he frequented. In spite of such slight variations from the ideal norm, all the boys in this category appeared at the outset of the Study to be well integrated and to be accepting society's standards in a positive way.

2. *Mild Maladjustment.* In this group, composing 36 percent of the total, the boys' behavior deviated farther from the norm of good social adjustment. Since most of them, like the majority in the Study, were referred by school authorities, much of their maladjustment was described in terms of classroom behavior. A considerable proportion were more or less like Alfred. He was described as forgetful, inattentive, irresponsible, lazy, in trouble with the other children whenever the teacher turned her attention from him. He was said to be spoiled and a show-off but he was not difficult to discipline. Basil also was uninterested in schoolwork, very fidgety and resentful of discipline, but he had a happy disposition and was well liked by the other children. And there was Eric, who also was uninterested in his studies and was rather defiant of discipline. He was not popular with his classmates but he got along fairly well with them. Then there were boys like Ronald and Adam. Ronald's teacher said he was a nice boy but highstrung and very dirty. He was disregarded by the other children in their activities but not ac-

tively disliked by them. The complaints about Adam were that he was listless and slovenly, put forth no effort, and was frequently a truant from school. Irvin was an example of another type of boy included in this group. He was a very bookish boy, precise and sedate, who had few of the usual boy's interests. And Louis was another type—a slow, docile child who did not take his own part in quarrels, was submissive in many ways, and passively accepted an inferior role among his companions and in his family.

In this group also were placed a number of boys whose maladjustment was indicated chiefly by one or two symptoms that were not regarded by the teachers as especially serious. Eugene, for example, was chosen by his teacher as an average boy but she added that he stuttered at times. Donald behaved well as long as the teacher was very patient but he was sullen and had a bad temper when crossed. Charlie was frequently in mischief, breaking windows, tipping over barrels, pestering girls, but he stopped this behavior as soon as his rather delinquent companion moved to another school.

All in all, the boys who were put in this category appeared to have been in need of help of one kind or another but they seemed far from seriously maladjusted. In many cases the aim of such assistance would be one of prevention; that is, it would be provided chiefly in order to keep the boy's maladjustment from becoming worse. In some cases it would seem that some slight environmental change might tip the balance in favor of really good adjustment.[1]

In both Groups 1 and 2 were included a few boys with an I.Q. in the 60's. Those in Group 1 appeared to be clearly well adjusted when their low level of intelligence was taken into consideration; those in Group 2 had problems of about the same character as those of some of the boys described above. Among the best adjusted of these boys was Felix, whose I.Q. ratings ranged from 53 to 60. A tall, well-built boy with a pleasant smile, he created no difficulty at home or in school. Another was Manuel, somewhat brighter, a non-aggressive, hyperactive boy, interested in sports and popular with the others because of his ability as a mimic. In contrast, Teddy

[1] These statements about treatment needs are made by the writer solely on the basis of the symptom picture; they do not refer to the Study planning, which was based on more information about the total situation. The statements are made in order to indicate, from another angle, the degree of difficulty apparently represented by the boys in this category at the time of first acquaintance.

(I.Q. 63; placed in Group 2) was a boy whose school conduct was good but who was persistently enuretic and was regarded as peculiar by the other children.

3. Considerable Social Maladjustment. It will have been noted that Group 2 contained both aggressive, energetic, extroverted boys (to use those words in a non-technical sense) and boys whose symptoms might be suspected of stemming from an emotional conflict of a neurotic nature. This difference in type became much more clear when we attempted to classify the more maladjusted boys, and it was taken into account in the following two categories. Into Group 3 were put the boys who caused considerable trouble in the classroom or who were already involved in delinquent gang activities but who were distinguished from the rest of the maladjusted boys by their ability to make and keep friends; Group 4 was reserved for the friendless boys whose behavior seemed somewhat neurotic.

In Group 3 were placed boys like Morris, who was very disturbing in the classroom because of his mischievous behavior. He was inattentive, irresponsible, always trying to get the other children's attention, and not to be trusted out of the teacher's sight. He had several good friends and many acquaintances, though he was said to pick fights on little provocation. Then there were boys like Carmelo and Gus. Carmelo, at the age of nine, was called a gangster because he got pennies from other children under the threat of beating them up. He was street-wise and self-confident, full of energy and rarely at home. He had many friends, some of whom he led and some of whom he followed. With adults too he was friendly, so long as they made no attempt to correct him. Apparently more maladjusted when first known was Gus, who had such violent temper tantrums at school that the authorities were considering court action. A little investigation showed, however, that this behavior was in line with his mother's tempestuous character and that Gus was very capable of maintaining good relations with people.

Several of the boys in the group were already delinquents. Arnold, for example, was called by the police "one of the worst boys in Cambridge," about to be sentenced to an institution. Bernard was one of a gang caught stealing lights from railroad switches. Spencer was said by his teachers to steal, lie, and stay out late at night. All of these boys, however, had friends of their own age, and their diffi-culties—so far as could be judged by cursory investigations—seemed a reaction to environmental conditions rather than to emo-tional conflict. It seems significant, both for the Study and for the general problem of delinquency, that boys of Group 3 were rela-tively few in number, forming only 8 percent of the total.

4. Behavior Suggestive of Neurosis. The behavior of the boys who were put in Group 4 was so varied as to make description diffi-cult. A considerable number of them had such symptoms as enure-sis, speech defects, tics, nervous mannerisms, odd, erratic behavior. Some had physical complaints for which no physical basis could be found. Some were very effeminate and others spent much time in fantasy. The following examples chosen at random may help to make clearer the kinds of boys who were placed in this category.

Leonard was a slow, fat boy who had few friends and was much given to telling fantastic tales that his mother called lies. His tics and nervous mannerisms made her "wild." At school the teacher was chiefly concerned about his slipshod work and inattentiveness.

Jeremiah was a quiet child who often cried in school. He was very serious and hard-working and put up with much hardship in order to earn money for his family, refusing invitations to games and camp for fear he would lose customers.

Wilfred was a tense, nervous boy, much given to tantrums and unable to sit still. He was called a bully, yet was cowardly and whined if another boy attacked him. Soon after the Study started he became troublesome in school, started to play truant, and was involved in some delinquencies.

Ralph, a sensitive, quiet boy, played only with girls or with boys three or four years younger than himself. He was described as old-maidish and effeminate. Enuresis persisted until he was at least 10 or 11 years old. He was regarded as lazy and ambitionless, doing poorly in school, although he was of average intelligence.

Gerald was a boastful, destructive, show-off sort of boy, moody, sullen, restless, and easily moved to tears. At home he had violent temper tantrums on slight provocation.

Earle seemed dull, slow, and shy, his speech defect making him seem childish beyond his nine years. His contacts with children were meager and he seemed to live in a world of fantasy.

Pat, called the worst boy in the special class (I.Q. 85), was very distractible, silly, attention-seeking, craving of affection. He had enuresis, lisped and stuttered, and was unable to make friends. Thoroughly undisciplined and out of his parents' control, he wandered all over the town and engaged in petty stealing. His chief interests were movies and other solitary forms of recreation.

Boys of this type made up 22 percent of the total here evaluated.

5. *Extreme Emotional or Social Maladjustment.* The boys put in the final category (15 percent) were even more maladjusted than those in Groups 3 and 4, many of them combining the characteristics of these two groups in that they were both "neurotic" and aggressive. The probably neurotic character of their difficulties seemed clear even on brief description, and their aggressive acts appeared to be more serious than those of the boys in Group 3. The following are examples from Group 5.

When Herman was eight years old, his teacher said he had a "mental condition that might develop into something serious." He kicked, bit, and teased the other children, had a complete disregard for authority, indulged in imaginative lying and petty stealing, had enuresis and nightmares.

Norman was regarded as the worst boy in the school. He had an extreme temper and attacked the teacher and the principal, as well as other boys, when crossed, apparently feeling grossly discriminated against. School authorities and the police thought him almost crazy.

Everett was a boy who (at seven or eight years of age) spit at and teased other children and stole petty objects from department stores. He was full of fears and taboos and disapproval of other children's bad behavior. He tried to buy children's affection and always looked worried and nervous.

Terrence was a pale, apathetic daydreamer who by eleven years of age was complaining of headaches and arm and foot pains and had an intense concern about all his bodily functions. He apparently liked being sick and being waited on.

Lawrence had a court record for breaking and entering when only nine. He was a highly nervous, sensitive boy who was very much concerned about a skin ailment that, it was later learned, probably had a psychogenic basis. His delinquencies had a compulsive character and he seemed to arrange matters so that he would be de-tected.

As judged by the descriptions of the boys at the time the Study first became acquainted with them, then, the proportion of boys in these various categories was as follows: Well-adjusted, 19 percent; Mild maladjustment, 36 percent; Considerable social maladjust-ment, 8 percent; Maladjustment suggestive of neurosis, 22 percent; Extreme emotional or social maladjustment, 15 percent. In other words, over half of the boys appeared to be only mildly malad-justed, if at all, while about a seventh had extreme problems. The incidence of difficulties that seemed possibly indicative of neurosis was high, embracing about a third of the cases.

DELINQUENT TENDENCIES

Such an analysis of the kinds of boys chosen for the Study suggests that a considerable proportion of them were not likely to become delinquent. It has already been stated why some well-adjusted boys were deliberately chosen for inclusion: so that the agency should not appear to be serving only boys who were "wild" or "wacky." This policy, however, does not account for the inclusion of a large number of emotionally disturbed children whose personality traits would not appear to be prognostic of delinquency. Not that any-body is certain what the traits prognostic of delinquency are (one of the by-products of this investigation may be some findings on that point), but it is usually thought that delinquent acts are more likely to be committed by "extroverted" than by "introverted" children.

Personality traits, of course, are far from the only criterion by which the likelihood of delinquency is to be judged. It is well known that delinquency is more frequent among the poor than among the well-to-do and among certain cultural groups than among others. Adverse social conditions, both in the home and in the neighborhood, are believed to foster it. Drunkenness, immoral-ity, criminal records on the part of the parents, physical neglect, lack of supervision, low ethical standards, "bad" companions, so on and so on—the alleged social concomitants of delinquency have been listed so often as to be almost self-evident. It was on the basis of traits such as these that many of the boys were thought to be headed for delinquency and were therefore chosen for the Study (see Chapter V).

At the outset of the treatment program, many boys, so far as was known, were neither delinquents nor pre-delinquents, if by the latter term one means associating with delinquents or engaging in conduct that is close to delinquent. Review of the cases from this point of view resulted in the following four categories.

A. With over half the boys (134, or 53 percent) there was no question of delinquency, official or unofficial, when work began. Two-thirds of this group were among those classified above as either well adjusted or only mildly maladjusted. Eleven were severely maladjusted but not at all delinquent.

B. A second group was composed of boys who were very mischievous and annoying in the classroom, not interested in school work, inattentive and distractible. Some of them were pugnacious, frequently getting into quarrels with the other children, while others had many friends and were active, energetic street boys. None of them was known to be delinquent but they had some of the traits that might lead them in that direction. Twelve percent of the boys were of this type.

C. The boys who were put in the third class (18 percent of the total) seemed nearer to being delinquents. Some were associating with delinquents or were members of gangs that frequently got into fights and were suspected of delinquency. A few were so hard to manage in the classroom that court action was threatened. About half were suspected of stealing, largely in school. About half of these boys were classified in Group 2 above, indicating that their general maladjustment seemed to be slight.

D. The final category was composed of boys who were known to have engaged in delinquent types of conduct—mostly stealing or persistent truancy. Some of them already had court records. Nearly half of them were in Group 5 described above. Boys of this type constituted 17 percent of the whole series.

These, then, were the boys with whom the Study started its work. It will have been noted that by either system of classification at least half of the boys appeared to have little wrong with them and that a considerable proportion of those who were considered difficult did not seem to be headed for delinquency so far as could be judged by present conduct. On these points, the Selection Committee, described in a preceding chapter, also passed judgment. By their rather complicated scheme, 37 percent of the 254 boys were rated 0 or +1 to +3, 25 percent were in the −1 category, 27 percent in the −2, while only 11 percent were rated −3 or −4, these ratings referring to likelihood of becoming delinquent, the minus categories indicating the greater likelihood.

HOME CONDITIONS

A child's environment may be considered from several angles. Many persons regard the emotional aspect of the environment as the most important—that which is reflected in the parents' feelings and attitudes toward the child. Others maintain that the social standards of the home are of prime importance, that one cannot expect well-adjusted children to come from homes where child training is disregarded, dirt and disorder prevail, and in which there is laxness in moral standards. Whether the home is broken or not will be regarded by many as of great importance, and housing and general neighborhood conditions will also be deemed factors that must be given serious consideration. Contemplation of this array of complicated factors that must enter into a correct formulation of a child's problems and situation usually leads the research worker either to the conclusion that every child is unique and classification impossible or to the decision to concentrate on one or another aspect which he considers most important. We do not claim to be different from these other research workers, but we shall at least attempt to take into account both the emotional and the social aspects of the boys' situations, if only because there is so much difference of opinion as to which of them should be stressed. Moreover, in our search for the kinds of boys a program like the Study can best serve we cannot afford to disregard any of these hypotheses about cause or concomitants of maladjustment.

In our attempt to define types of boys in terms of emotional and social situations we shall of necessity follow the procedure used in the preceding classifications; that is, only loose, broad categories will be used and boys will be assigned to one or another rather impressionistically. The Study was essentially a service organization even though it had a research purpose. For the most part, its workers were not highly trained in either sociological or psychological observation nor was the objective of their interviews mainly that of diagnosis. This, however, does not in all respects impose a serious limitation on the Study. Our aim, as a matter of fact, is not so much that of scientific analysis as of practical findings—findings, that is, that can be used by social workers to determine which boys can be aided by services of the nature given. These potential users of the findings will not have at hand elaborate studies of the boys they want to serve. To be useful, therefore, our conclusions must be couched in common-sense terms, in terms of observations that can be readily made in a non-clinical situation. Only if correlations can be arrived at from the use of such crude data and broad classifications will a practical purpose be served. In the light of that reasoning it is without apologies that we present the following analysis of the boys' home and neighborhood situations.

HOME CONDITIONS: SOCIAL

To take the most easily classifiable variable first, broken homes were not very frequent among this series of boys, only about a seventh living in homes from which one or both parents were missing. The proportion so handicapped was about as great in the well-adjusted group as among the boys classified as definitely maladjusted. In view of this finding it did not seem worth while to include the marital status of the parents among the important factors to be classified independently. It was used, however, as one of the variables taken into consideration in rating the social aspects of family life.

When other social aspects of family life were looked into, many very adverse situations were found. Choosing at random from among the homes that would seem to be seriously detrimental to a child, we turned up the following.

Edwin's mother was in a sanatarium with tuberculosis, and Edwin was living with his father, who was often drunk and usually neglectful. A neighbor woman tried to supervise the boy a bit but found this hard to do along with her other work. Even before the mother left home there had been much quarreling between husband and wife. The children were unsupervised even then, and there was little money because the father spent most of his small earnings for liquor.

Russell lived with his stepmother, who had been diagnosed psychopathic, and his father, who was incredibly easygoing. The stepmother was often drunk and promiscuous, and she had violent quarrels with both Russell and his sister. She seemed utterly incapable of training the children or of keeping house. The father was apparently undisturbed by the uproar and dirt in which the family lived, his chief interest being in his chickens. He was on W.P.A. when the case opened, but during the war got a job that paid fairly well.

Tommy's mother was a tense, worrying kind of person who was unable to take a firm stand with her children on even serious issues. She was much concerned about the family's poor financial situation. Much of her time was spent in complaining and in quarreling with the neighbors. There was much bickering in the home, and the discipline that was given the children was often harsh and unreasonable. The father was known as a neighborhood character, a mild, eccentric man who was much under his wife's domination.

As even these few illustrations indicate, the possible combinations of adverse factors were very numerous, and the weight to be attached to any one or another of the individual traits defied judgment. It did seem possible, however, to divide the cases roughly into a threefold classification of the good-fair-poor type.[2]

In this classification, an attempt was made to disregard certain of the emotional aspects of the question and to concentrate on the social. Each family situation was looked at from the viewpoint of the prevailing mores, and we considered to what extent the parents behaved toward each other and their children as custom prescribes. Such a way of viewing the matter permitted some latitude when foreign-born families or those of some definite American sub-culture were under consideration. In general, however, the families were rated on the assumption that parents shall be "faithful" to each other, shall not quarrel excessively, shall provide adequate food, shelter, and clothing for the children, shall care for the children's physical needs and instruct them, without harsh discipline, in social rules and customs, that they shall supervise their conduct, guide their development, and handle them with at least a reasonable degree of kindliness. These institutionalized norms of behavior do not take into account the more subtle aspects of parent-

[2] These ratings, like all others, were made by the writer without reference to the boys' terminal adjustment.

child relationships that modern psychology stresses as being of major importance, but they do require that parents shall not abuse or neglect their children and that they shall be interested in them and love them. So highly sanctioned, in fact, is that requirement that few parents can openly avow dislike for their children unless they can adduce some serious fault on the children's part. Accordingly, in classifying the families from a social viewpoint, no account was taken of the quality of the parents' affection for their children; we looked only for whether the parents displayed the socially approved interest in and concern for their children, leaving the more subtle aspects of the emotional relationship for later classification. Grouped on this basis the families were rated A, B, and C with respect to the situation that obtained before the Study measures possibly altered it. Illustrations of these three types follow.

Among the families rated A socially was Eric's. This was a Portuguese family consisting of father, mother, grandmother, and four children. The father was a janitor who had a good work record and a fairly adequate income. The mother worked part-time as a maid. Both parents appeared to be mature, competent people; they were active members of the Baptist church. Their home was an apartment over a store in an area with a high delinquency rate. It was adequately furnished and well kept. The parents and the grandmother were interested in Eric and supervised him closely, probably more closely than was usual in the neighborhood.

Jeremiah's home was also rated A socially. Jeremiah's parents came from Newfoundland and were strict adherents of the Pentecostal faith. The father was a hard-working man, much interested in his children though very strict with them. The mother was much like him in these respects. She was a very good housekeeper and gave the family excellent physical care. They lived for a time in a new housing project; later, with an increase of income under war conditions, they bought a house of their own.

Felix's parents, also rated A from a social viewpoint, were of Polish extraction. The mother was a sandwich maker in a hotel, the father an industrial worker. Together they earned a fair amount of money. Their home was a neat, well-kept apartment in a tenement house on a street in the industrial district. Both parents and older sister were fond of Felix and concerned about his lack of school progress. (His I.Q. was very low.) They supervised him carefully and were eager to do their best for him.

Some of the broken homes were put in this A group, though they were given a distinguishing designation in order that the possible influence of these factors might be looked into later. For instance, Wesley's parents were separated but saw each other from time to time. The mother worked as a cleaning woman and in defense factories. She considered her husband rather worthless but was unemotional about him and did not object to the boy's seeing him. The father, in turn, seemed to be a rather easygoing man who gave Wesley clothes and presents and took him for rides on his truck. Other families in this sub-group were Gilbert's, in which the mother was mentally ill and the children and father (described as kind and sensible) lived with a capable foster mother; Salvatore's, in which the father died and the capable mother brought up her children well on a Department of Welfare allotment; and Stephen's, a family consisting of grandmother and aunts, who were unusually intelligent and socially responsible people.

The B homes had various combinations of good and poor characteristics from a social point of view. Quarreling and other signs of conflict characterized many of them. In a considerable number of cases the father drank to excess and was abusive to wife and children when drunk. Supervision of the children was halfhearted in some of the homes. Housekeeping standards were low in many of them. In a few families there was some immorality. On the other hand, the parents in most of these families were interested in their children's welfare and put a fair amount of effort into training them. The following are some examples from this group.

Carmelo's parents were Italian. The mother was hysterically defensive of her children but supervised them only slightly and often did not know where they were or what they were doing. The father was a downtrodden man, frequently drunk. He had a court record for abusive treatment of his wife and children. One daughter was under the care of the Board of Children's Guardians as a "sex menace." In spite of all this, the family had many loud, merry times together and much pride in each other's small successes. They lived in a run-down tenement house in the midst of considerable dirt except for the parlor, which was neat and well furnished.

Arnold's father was Dutch. He had entered the United States illegally. He had been a gardener, but was out of work when the case opened. He was very poor at that time and was said to condone stealing by the children because the family was in such great need. The mother was a very dull woman, smiling and quiet, entirely dominated by her husband. She did little about either training or supervising the children, leaving most of the household work to her husband. Family conditions were chaotic for some years, but after the father got a good job the arrangements were much better and the strengths in family relationships emerged.

Donald's parents were described as loud, coarse people who indulged in much swearing and bickering. They cheated on relief and looked to political "drag" for aid in getting along. Not much was known about the father (a stepfather, in fact) except that the mother would not let him do much about disciplining the children. She herself disciplined by screaming; she was also very defensive of the children, always blaming others for what the children did. The family lived in very ill-kept rooms in a three-family apartment house in a congested, run-down neighborhood. They suffered from unemployment. In spite of all this, there was much family loyalty.

The proportion of broken homes and illegitimate children was somewhat higher in this group than in the preceding one, an indication, perhaps, of the greater difficulty a single parent encounters in rearing children. Many of the fathers who had deserted the home had previously been drunk and quarrelsome, and the mothers, in spite of their desire to do well, were inadequate in training and disciplining the children. Other mothers were hard-pressed financially and had difficulty in combining earning a living and bringing up the children, so of necessity they often left the children unsupervised. Then there were a few families in which the children were illegitimate and the parental arrangements were very unconventional. For example, in several families the child's grandmother pretended to be his mother, the real mother being either in and out of the family or a constant member who was regarded as the child's older sister. This arrangement, not surprisingly, led to many quarrels and to much confusion about responsibility for child rearing. In other families with illegitimate children the arrangements were less complicated, but even so the children's upbringing was disturbed by conflicting sources of authority and by lack of clarity as to their position.

In the C homes there was little that was favorable from a strictly social point of view. It must be reemphasized, however, that we are making a distinction here between the social and the personal aspects of human relations, for we shall show shortly that some of these socially poorest homes manifested the kind of affectionate relations that are regarded by psychiatrists as psychologically beneficial. The distinction made here, it is agreed, is to a considerable extent an artificial one. We are making it, however, in order to have material for testing the relative importance of these two aspects of family life, as well as for having a basis for classifying cases on the basis of combinations of these two attributes.

The majority of families in the C group were what is conventionally regarded as the "lowest of the low." Drunkenness, promiscuity, dilapidated and filthy homes, and utterly inadequate care of the children were common. For instance, Douglas's father was described by one agency as "the worst drunk and worst bum" known to it. He had frequently been arrested for larceny and breaking and entering. He deserted the family shortly after the boy was born, but maintained some contact with the family up to the time of his death, which occurred when Douglas was about eleven years old. The mother was high-tempered and quarrelsome, alternately indulging and bickering with the children. Five of her ten children had died, some of them apparently from neglect. Home life was almost nonexistent. The mother was away most of the time, the house being used chiefly as a sleeping place. The children, always filthy, wandered around from the home of one relative to another for their meals. In spite of this, Douglas was described by the examining physician as one of the healthiest boys among the Study's clientele.

Oliver's home was fairly similar. The mother was described as an inadequate, weak person, who had no control over the children and was amazingly unconcerned about dangers confronting them. Before the Study entered the case she had been brought into court on the charge of contributing to the children's delinquency. The father was said to be a husky, stable, good-natured person but much given to drunkenness and severe quarrels with his wife. The family living quarters were always in very poor neighborhoods and were filthy and foul-smelling. The children were seriously neglected as to cleanliness and other physical care. Several of them had delinquency records.

Some of the other families in this group were less poverty-stricken

than these but the homes seemed equally unfitted for satisfactory
child rearing. Wilbur, for instance, one of three illegitimate children, lived with his grandparents, his mother, and his stepfather.
The grandmother was called a "high-stepper" and herself had several illegitimate children. An aunt with whom Wilbur lived at times
was also said to be immoral. The stepfather resented his wife's illegitimate children and was especially antagonistic to Wilbur, at times
being actually abusive to him. Throughout his childhood the boy
was essentially without a home, being not much more than barely
tolerated by these various relatives. Several other children in this
C series of cases were equally disliked and tossed about from home
to home, receiving no consistent care or training.

HOME CONDITIONS: EMOTIONAL

As has been said before, many authorities on delinquency and
other forms of social and psychological maladjustment in children
regard as of major importance the emotional relations between
parents and child. Closely associated with this, usually, is the parents' state of mental health. The Study's records contained many
observations which, though not of clinical accuracy, provided material for making judgments on these points. We were, of course,
not able to classify the parents in the diagnostic categories used by
psychiatrists, both because of our own limitations and because of
the unsatisfactory character of many of the observations—necessarily unsatisfactory in that they were not made by trained clinicians. We were tempted at first, however, to use the familiar child
guidance categories of rejection, overprotection, and the like. Even
these, however, were found to be inapplicable in many cases, for in
spite of long contacts with the families some of the counselors did
not record, perhaps did not even observe, the kinds of actions on the
parents' part that such a classification system calls for. In this connection it must be remembered that the Study was deliberately set
up as something other than the usual modern social agency, that its
actual purpose was in part to test whether the kind of work modern
social workers do (and, implicitly, the kind of training they receive)
is necessary. Therefore, in saying that the records did not contain
the kind of data one would expect to find in the records of a child
guidance clinic or a child-placing agency we are not casting asper-

sions on the work; we are merely noting a fact about the data available for the present study.

The records did contain, however, many observations about the parents and about parent-child relations that are of the character of those which sensitive, interested laymen ("lay" in the sense of not being psychiatrically trained) make about human behavior and its accompanying emotions. The net effect was fairly adequate pictures of the emotional conditions under which the boys lived, but pictures that were not sufficiently clear-cut to permit a diagnostic type of classification. The following notes from abstracts of the records, prepared by the writer and her assistants, give some idea of the kind of material we worked from in setting up a classification system; they also indicate the wide range in home conditions.

Kenneth, who was thought to be illegitimate, lived with an aunt who had married a man with nine children and who had five more of her own. She was a haggard-looking woman who claimed much concern about Kenneth, apparently because of her husband's threats to send him away. She was obviously worried lest he get into trouble and was very strict with him. Her husband was very much "down" on Kenneth, the aunt describing his attitude as "not charitable."

Timothy's father was a grouchy, cynical man who suffered from stomach ulcers. Years earlier he had been diagnosed as psychoneurotic. He was openly rejecting of Timothy, frequently calling him a "dope" and predicting a bad outcome for him. He frequently beat his son, openly preferring his daughter. The mother was also antagonistic to Timothy, though she was sometimes a bit affectionate toward him and was interested in his school progress. The mother and the boy quarreled frequently and bitterly and used much "vile" language.

Stanley lived with his grandparents and his mother. His grandfather was an elderly German tailor, rather fond of the boy but accustomed to Old-World standards of discipline and performance. He criticized the boy for being less adept at mechanical pursuits than he himself had been as a child. The grandmother was resentful of having to bring up another family of children. She disapproved of her daughter's lax discipline of Stanley but was afraid to do much about it herself, so she nagged and was critical and very restrictive of the boy but did not punish him. As to the mother, she worked long hours at low wages in a dry-cleaning establishment. She was overprotective and indulgent of Stanley, but said that at times she could kill him. She resented her parents' criticism of her son and pressed him hard for school success, chiefly so she would not be disgraced. She was probably closely tied to her parents, for she was not able to go through with her expressed desire to get an aid-to-dependent-children allowance and set up a home of her own.

Guido's mother was a pleasant, amiable Portuguese woman who was rather lenient with the children, "spoiling" each one as he came along and then brushing him aside in favor of the next younger. She was fond of all her children, however, and interested in their school progress. The father was a friendly, rather forceless person who had a bad temper when drunk. He administered severe corporal punishments to the children, thoughtlessly and indiscriminately. He was fond of all of them but did little for them to show his interest.

Leonard's father was described by his wife at the beginning of the Study as a nearly perfect man—mild-tempered, staying at home evenings, interested in the children, and supporting the family adequately. Later, however, he took to drinking and staying out late with his friends, but at the close of the Study he had reverted to his original behavior. Leonard's mother was a tense, ambitious housewife who put great stress on cleanliness and cooking. She alternately indulged and overcontrolled the boy and pressed him for school success. At the beginning of the Study she had no friends and no interests outside the home, but later she got a war job and made some social contacts.

Rodney's home was very harmonious. His father was a jovial, pleasant man who occasionally was drunk. For several years his work took him away from home but he sent back his pay and maintained close relations with his wife and children. The mother, too, was a pleasant, happy person, a good manager and neat housekeeper. She was very fond of her two children, giving parties for them and maintaining an open house for their friends.

It is clear from these notes that while in some cases one might make a fairly good guess as to the state of the parents' mental health, in others there was not material for even a rough estimate. On the subject of parent-child relations there was more material, but categories sharply discriminating one type of relationship from another were not feasible. Considering this problem we came to the conclusion that the extremes could be easily identified, if at one end were set the cases in which the parents clearly loved the children and were interested in their welfare and at the other end were put those in which the parent-child relationship was very unfavorable. Such a classification system avoids the difficulty of specifying the exact nature of the parent-child relationship; it assumes that it is equally disadvantageous to a child to be openly rejected and abused, to be subjected to alternate indulgence and rebuff, or to be so controlled that independent development is almost impossible. Such an assumption might not be justified if a detailed psychological study were to be undertaken, but it seemed adequate for the purpose of the present investigation, which was not an inquiry into the dynamics of child behavior but a search for the types of boys a Study type of service can benefit.

Even accepting that assumption, we still had to deal with the fact that in most families two parents' attitudes had to be taken into consideration and that some boys did not live with their parents. To cover the first point the classification plan had to allow for various combinations of parental attitudes, while to cover the second some further elaboration had to be made. Before defining the categories that were finally arrived at, however, some examples of the three basic types are in order.

Adequate Affection and Interest. Rodney's parents, described above, are examples of the kind of behavior and attitudes that characterized the parents who were classified as having a good, satisfying relationship with their children. Different culturally, but fairly similar emotionally, was the situation in Bruno's family. Bruno's father, Portuguese, was the boss in the family; he was somewhat severe in his punishments but he was clearly fond of his children and interested in their welfare. Bruno's mother was easygoing and somewhat protective, and family standards of conduct were high. Another cultural variant was seen in Herbert's family, Negroes from the British West Indies. The father was an assistant minister, very serious and proud; he was a strict disciplinarian, insistent that his children conduct themselves in conformity with his social position. He was, however, very fond of Herbert and much interested in his school progress. The mother was a quiet, modest, affectionate woman, eager for her children to be good, neat, clean, and unobtrusive.

Parents who were affectionate toward their children and interested in them were put in this first category even though their behavior in other respects was far from a mental hygiene ideal. An extreme example of this was Gus' mother, cited previously. She was a Sicilian woman who went into rages whenever she thought her children were unfairly treated and who seemed almost paranoid on that subject. She was a hypochondriac who achieved cures for her illnesses through "visions." Although extremely emotional in all her reactions, she managed the children and her household well and was clearly devoted to all her family.

Included also were parents whose love for their children was indubitable but whose relations with each other were far from good. For example, Basil's father was a kind, good-natured man, much interested in his sons and their welfare. The mother was somewhat less devoted but she, too, was proud of Basil and appreciative of his good traits. The parents, however, drank frequently and quarreled excessively with each other. There was much talk of separation and frequent accusations of disloyalty. The home atmosphere, in consequence, was hectic, but the children were apparently not greatly involved in the quarrels. In the classification process the unsatisfactory character of these homes was taken into account under the rating of social conditions. So far as the emotional aspect was concerned, we looked only at parent-child relations, our aim being to separate out the boys who received adequate affection, it being our hunch that this might counterbalance unfavorable factors.

Very Unfavorable Attitudes. The notes on Timothy, above, show one family situation in which the parental attitudes were regarded as very unfavorable. Other examples are the following.

Terrence's mother was a nagging, complaining woman who was very overprotective and indulgent toward her children. She was a vacillating, spineless person, who was always greatly worried but who was not able to be firm about anything. She was both sentimental and irritable and was very fearful that her boys would get into serious trouble.

Reginald's father was excessively alcoholic and abusive. He was very rough and cruel with Reginald, such conduct dating back to the time the boy was an infant. Even when sober he was very demanding and bossed the boy excessively.

Clinton's father, a registered pharmacist, was much better educated than most, but he was very high-strung, nervous, and irritable. He gave such severe punishments when angry that the Society for the Prevention of

Cruelty to Children had been called in. Clinton's mother had been a mental hospital patient and was very changeable in her moods. When feeling well she treated Clinton kindly but at times she, too, was irritable and depressed.

Everett's family situation was an unusual one, in that he lived with his grandmother, mother, and uncle, and that his grandmother was considering adopting him. (He was illegitimate, though his mother had been married for a time.) The grandmother was a very anxious woman, the mother nervous and self-effacing, letting her life be arranged by her mother. Both of these women restricted Everett greatly, put much emphasis on gentility, and continually referred to him as a "poor little kiddo." They treated the boy with pitying indulgence, were unable to be firm with him and yet instilled into him many fears and a sense of guilt. The uncle, too, was a very inadequate man, dominated by the grandmother and not able to do anything for the boy to counteract the influence of the two women.

Moderately Unfavorable Attitudes. The attitudes of many parents were, of course, between the two extremes. In the following cases the parents acted and felt toward their children in ways that seemed detrimental but nevertheless had some positive aspects. (Not that even the parents in the preceding group were wholly negative in their feelings and behavior.)

Luke had been deserted by his mother in infancy and was brought up by his grandparents, his uncle, and an aunt and her husband. The grandmother was fondly indulgent of Luke and his brother. When she died (in 1940) the aunt and her husband set up a home of their own but did not take the boys to live with them, rationalizing that it would not be fair to themselves. The aunt did, however, maintain fairly close contact with the boys throughout the year, and they seemed fairly fond of her.

Roger's mother was a dull woman who had a violent temper. She had considerable affection for her children and gave them fairly good physical care in spite of the chaotic condition of the household. She was, however, rather ambivalent in her attitude toward Roger, who was much disliked by his gypsy stepfather. At one time she would side with Roger against the stepfather and at another she would join with her husband against Roger and say she wanted him out of the home.

Tommy's mother was a worrier; indulged Tommy greatly (he was her favorite) and was inconsistent in her discipline. She was much concerned about her older son's delinquent conduct but she could do nothing about it except complain weakly.

Morris's parents were Barbadoes Negroes, rather isolated and uninterested in social contacts. His mother was a jolly sort of person, but she was very overprotective and dominated Morris, not allowing him to join clubs or go on day trips with the Study workers because she feared he would be hurt. At home she kept him busy doing chores and allowed him very little playtime. That this behavior was not wholly cultural was indicated by the fact that she permitted Morris's somewhat older brother much more freedom, maintaining that he was much more trustworthy.

With these three categories of attitudes and behavior distinguished, we proceeded to set up a system that would take into account the fact that in many cases the attitudes of the two parents differed considerably. In that classification the word "parents" referred to the persons with whom the boy was living when Study work started, foster parents and institutional authorities being excepted. (In the latter cases the attitudes of the boy's own parents were rated if possible.) When the boy was living and had lived for a long time with only one parent, only that parent's attitude was classified. The following were the categories that were used.

1. Both parents affectionate, giving definite evidence of this in pride and interest in the boy and in concern for his welfare.

2. One parent affectionate, the other overprotective or indulgent but clearly devoted to him.

3. Both parents overprotective but clearly devoted to the child.

4. One parent affectionate, the other having some kind of moderately unfavorable attitude.

5. One parent overprotective but devoted, the other having some kind of moderately unfavorable attitude.

6. One parent affectionate; the attitude of the other very unfavorable.

7. One parent overprotective but devoted; the attitude of the other very unfavorable.

8. Attitudes of both parents moderately unfavorable.

9. One parent moderately unfavorable, the other very unfavorable.

10. Both very unfavorable.

In much of the later analysis of data these categories are combined as follows: Group A, categories 1, 2, and 3; Group B, categories 4, 5, 6, and 8; Group C, categories 7, 9, and 10. It is sufficient for our present purpose to note that the boys were about evenly distributed among these three large groups, there being a few more in the middle than in the lowest category.

HOME CONDITIONS: SOCIAL AND EMOTIONAL

Having separated out and classified the two aspects of family life that seemed to be especially important for a boy's character development, we next proceeded to combine them. This process of analysis and synthesis reduced the complexity of the individual cases to manageable proportions and made possible their description in somewhat comparable terms. There were, of course, nine possible combinations of the social and emotional aspects of the homes when they were classified in the threefold manner described above.

These examples are less satisfactory than the preceding ones, for not only was there the usual difficulty of choosing typical cases, but there was the added complication that in the categories of emotional aspects three or four sub-categories were combined. The possible combinations of the ten sub-categories in the emotional-aspect series with the three in the social-aspect series were much too numerous, however, to burden the reader with, so we shall hope the illustrations are sufficient, even though it must be remembered that they represent only a few of the possible combinations. In the following examples of these combinations, the first letter refers to the emotional aspect of the home, the second to the social.

AA. Allen's parents were Italian-born but both spoke English well. They lived in a congested Italian neighborhood but the home was neat and well-kept. When first known to the Study the father was working only intermittently but during the war both he and the mother got good jobs and family finances improved greatly. They were a close-knit family, the mother being a pleasant, energetic woman and the father a soft-spoken, friendly, intelligent man. Both parents were very fond of their children and did all they could to bring them up well.

AB. The father was very easygoing, a steady, hard worker who operated an oil and ice delivery service which brought him a rather undependable income. He seemed a very stable person and was much interested in his children. His wife was a slovenly housekeeper, overwhelmed by her many children and always suffering from asthma and other ailments. She had little control over the children but had warm affection for them, remarking to the worker once in tender amused tones, "Ain't they awful?" She seemed quite content with her lot, getting considerable satisfaction out of dramatizing her ills and engaging in her favorite recreation, Beano. The worker reported that the house was one of the most untidy and dirty she had ever seen. Soiled clothes were piled high on the table; chairs were full of half-eaten food and dirty dishes; dogs, cats, hens, and children played happily in the debris. For all this, the family was close-knit, loyal, industrious, and happy. There was affection to spare, so much so that none of the children seemed hurt when the mother lavishly praised one of them or spoke with great appreciation of another's efforts to make the house a bit tidy.

AC. This was described as a very low-grade family, perhaps feeble-minded. The parents were good-natured, ignorant people, very fond of their children and devoted to each other, but they had no idea how to rear children. The mother seemed very immature and was jealous of anybody of whom Teddy might become fond; she seemed to favor him over his older, somewhat brighter brother. The father was a little more adequate and took a bit more responsibility for child training and care. The house was filthy, as were the children, their language was very rough, and there was much drinking and probably promiscuity. Discipline—what there was of it—was accomplished by much yelling. The various social agencies concerned in the case agreed that it was hopeless to accomplish anything with the family and yet the parents were not sufficiently neglectful for court action.

BA. Compared with other cases in the series, Irvin's father was much better educated and the family had a better income. They lived in a neat, clean, attractively furnished house in a good neighborhood. The father was very resentful of his own mother and her controlling attitude toward him. For some reason he identified Irvin with her and openly preferred his other son. The mother tried to stand as buffer between her husband and his mother and grew very tired of that role. She was more affectionate with Irvin than her husband was and gave him and his brother good care, but she, too, manifested some preference for the younger son.

BB. Roger lived with his stepfather, a gypsy, and his mother, a dull woman who had a violent temper. The stepfather thoroughly disliked his wife's three sons and was especially hostile to Roger. He was very fond of his own three children, born during the years the Study was in contact with the family. The mother had considerable affection for the three older boys but she was torn between husband and son when it came to helping Roger. She would alternately side with and against him in his quarrels with his stepfather. Domestic life in this family was frequently disrupted by the gypsy mode of existence through selling baskets of artificial flowers which the children helped to peddle. The stepfather was very irresponsible in his support of the family but the mother managed to keep up fairly adequate quarters for them and to give the children moderately good physical care. The stepfather was quarrelsome and frequently drunk, and the mother was thought to be promiscuous.

BC. In this family, Portuguese, the father was described by a Study worker as a ghost of a man, so passive and disconnected with reality that he seemed to be sleepwalking. He paid little attention to the children but his long record of drunkenness and abuse (more than 50 arrests on those charges) indicated something of his relationship with them. The mother, described by relief authorities as a slovenly, low-grade person, was attached to the children and kept them close at home. She apparently had the kind of relationship with them that called for little discipline, she being indulgent and somewhat protective and vigorously defensive of them when attacked. Economically the family were in very poor circumstances, and their house, when the Study first knew them, was one of the worst in Cambridge, so bad that the police moved the family from it as uninhabitable. In such a situation the poor physical care the children received was probably to be expected. This, added to the drunkenness, quarreling, and demands on social agencies, created a very unfavorable social situation for Adam, the Study client.

CA. Graham's parents were Armenian. They both punished the boy severely and indulged him excessively, giving him much money and freedom and demanding little in the way of good conduct. They were overeager for school success and were concerned about the boy's poor behavior there. The father was described as a scowling, reserved, suspicious man, the mother as more outgoing and pleasant. The economic situation was favorable, the family owning a small grocery store in a fairly good neighborhood. This store was a hangout for a gang of delinquent boys, some of whom became Graham's friends. The parents were industrious and frugal, providing good physical care for their children and attempting to develop high moral standards in them.

CB. Herman was an illegitimate child who lived with a grandmother who pretended to be his mother but was often called grandmother by the boy. Her attitude was one of indulgent rejection; she could not manage the boy at all, yet resented the implication that she could not. She attributed his poor conduct to the modern generation and often punished him severely. During her final illness Herman lived with his aunt and uncle, described as sensible, stable people. They considered keeping him after the grandmother's death but decided he was too difficult. Herman's own mother came to see him occasionally. She had married a man who had some interest in the boy, but she and her husband apparently never considered offering him a home.

CC. In this Irish family all 10 children were much neglected. The mother was a passive person of low mentality whose chief interest was spiritualism. She was slightly concerned about Pat's health and about his school progress but on the whole she was uninterested in his welfare. Pat felt she disliked him very much. The father was a small-time politician and erstwhile vaudeville player. All the children were dirty and ill-clad (the family was on relief most of the time), wholly unsupervised, and disciplined only by "lickings," which the parents said did no good. The parents engaged in petty illegal activities, had no sense of responsibility, and counted on "drag" for making their way. The children begged and did tap-dancing outside theaters at the parents' instigation and were taught to use their personalities and pathetic appearance to win favors.

The proportion of cases in these various combined categories was as follows: AA, 28.7 percent; AB, 3.2; AC, 1.6; BA, 18.5; BB, 17.2; BC, 3.9; CA, 7.9; CB, 11.4; CC, 6.7. Nine-tenths of one percent were not rated for lack of adequate information.

As was said before, these examples do not adequately typify the various categories, for each category encompassed a great variety of modes of behavior and social situations. The examples do, however, illustrate some of the ways in which the three defined grades of social and emotional aspects of family life combined to produce favorable or unfavorable situations for the children. When joined with the classifications of the boys' individual problems, they serve to define in a fairly adequate manner the kinds of cases the Study chose to deal with.

BEHAVIOR DISORDERS AND HOME CONDITIONS

The combination of ratings with respect to the boys and their homes is shown in Table 61. The table can be read to indicate either the types of cases with which the Study dealt (for example, 34 well-adjusted boys from homes that were emotionally and socially favorable) or the association between home conditions and personal adjustment. Read the latter way, the table shows a considerable relation between these two variables.

None of the well-adjusted boys and only about one in fifteen of those rated as slightly maladjusted came from homes that were classified as C emotionally, while all but three of the extremely maladjusted came from such a home. The proportion from homes rated A emotionally declined sharply as the problem became more severe: Well-adjusted, 80 percent; Slight maladjustment, 39 percent; Considerable social maladjustment, 16 percent; Behavior suggestive of neurosis but not severe, 13 percent; severe maladjustment, none.

TABLE 61

Distribution of Boys According to Original Adjustment and Home Situation

EMOTIONAL-SOCIAL CONDITIONS [a]

Original Groupings	AA	AB	AC	BA	BB	BC	CA	CB	CC	NK [b]	Total
1. Well-adjusted	34	4	2	3	4	2	—	—	—	—	49
2. Slight maladjustment	32	2	1	23	22	5	1	3	2	1	92
3. Considerable social maladjustment	1	2	—	5	6	1	—	4	—	—	19
4. Behavior suggestive of neurosis not extreme	6	—	1	14	12	1	14	5	3	—	56
5. Extreme maladjustment	—	—	—	2	—	1	5	17	12	1	38
Total	73	8	4	47	44	10	20	29	17	2	254

[a] First letter indicates emotional rating; second, social rating.
[b] Not known.

Social aspects of the home were much less important than emotional. Except for Group 5, there was not much variation in the proportion of boys from socially good homes. It will be recalled that this rating took little account of the economic factor but the findings would have been much the same had it done so.

All in all, then, this survey of the boys and their home situations confirms our earlier statement that the counselors worked with a wide variety and wide range of cases. We have stressed here the emotional and social aspects of the homes and the behavior and personality difficulties of the boys on the assumption that these are the variables most relevant to treatability. Weight might also have been given to physical, intellectual, financial, and neighborhood considerations, but the composite picture would have been unduly complicated thereby. Suffice it to say that only a very few boys were physically handicapped or in poor health; that only 14 percent had an I.Q. under 80; and that the great majority lived under poor or fairly poor financial conditions (though the war improved the economic situation for a time), and that the housing and neighborhood situations varied accordingly. The well-adjusted boys aside, these youngsters were doubtless representative of the difficult children in the lower grades of the public schools of the two cities in which the investigation was made, in range of difficulties if not in exact proportions. Such being the case they provided excellent material for testing the Study hypothesis, while their breakdown into the aforementioned categories provides data for our proposed search for the kinds of boys the Study program benefited.

CHAPTER XXIII

THE COUNSELORS AND
THEIR SERVICES

VARIATION IN THE BOYS AND THEIR HOME CIRCUMSTANCES HAVING
been demonstrated, we have next to show the variation in the counselors' working methods and in the services they rendered, for it is
useless to inquire whether the organization's work was successful
unless one can specify fairly definitely what that work consisted of.
To some extent this variation was conditioned by the variation in
the boys' needs; insofar as that was true, type of service is not to be
regarded as an independent factor when results are under consideration. Aside from this reason for variation, however, there was
considerable difference in the individual counselors' characteristic
working methods and in the amount of service the various boys received, and it is this that must be made clear before we undertake
to describe results and to explain why some boys were helped and
others were not.

This analysis of services by quality and quantity must be set
against the background of the main principles of the Study program. It will be recalled that the Study was set up to test the value
of providing needy boys with adult "friends" who would try to discover the reasons for the boys' maladjustment and provide or make
available the needed services. These friends (the counselors) would
seek out the boys rather than wait, in characteristic social-work fashion, for them or their parents to come to the organization and request help. Once the boys were found, the counselors would try to
persuade them to accept the organization's services, largely through
demonstrating in recreational, educational, or health areas how useful they could be. Then, once the counselors were accepted, they
would attempt to maintain contact with the boys throughout adolescence rather than close a case (to use social-work terminology)
when the needed service was rendered.

Another plank in the original platform was that of not restricting the choice of counselors to persons who had formal social-work training. The aim was to employ men and women as counselors who were very much interested in and well disposed toward difficult boys, who presumably could establish friendly relations with them, and who had energy and imagination to give to the job. For the most part these counselors were to proceed with the boys assigned to them as they thought best, using their own native skills and personality and the organization's and the community's resources for the boys' benefit. Early in the Study, advice from the organization's executive was available to them from time to time, especially when plans were analyzed and progress of cases reviewed, and the help of certain specialists was available, but (again contrary to most social-work practice) there was little attempt, in the first few years at least, to provide the kind of supervision that would produce relative uniformity in treatment efforts. In 1941 a supervisor was appointed to guide the counselors' activities somewhat along lines suggested by dynamic psychology, but even then the counselors retained marked individuality in treatment devices and methods.

These variations from current social-work practice were basic to the Study's scheme and account for some of the differences in the character of the individual counselors' work that are described below. The individual differences constitute, however, one of the points to be taken into account when the search for the reasons for success and failure is made.

THE COUNSELORS AND THEIR WORKING METHODS

The most general impression the writer—an outsider called in near the end of the Study to make this evaluation—had of the counselors was that of pleasing personality, great interest in the work, real liking for the boys and their families, good capacity for useful interpersonal relationships, and at least average objectivity about what they were accomplishing. In other words, the reader who is a professional social worker should picture the men and women who were on the Study's staff as individuals much like himself, both in capacity to "relate" to adolescent boys and in unsentimental interest in their welfare.

In spite of this thread of similarity that ran through all the

counselors, there were, of course, wide differences among them. It
has already been mentioned that eight of the nineteen counselors
had professional training for social case work before undertaking
the work, that two were psychologists and one a trained nurse. A
considerable proportion of the others, most of whom had had experience in related fields, studied in schools of social work during
their employment at the Study. Fifteen of them were men, four were
women. In age they varied from 24 to 46 when they began work
with the organization. They were employed for varying lengths of
time, as Figure 6 in Chapter XII indicates.

In an effort to obtain a rough idea of how these various people
carried on their work, samples of their cases were selected at random
and impressionistic descriptions of their characteristic mode of
operation written. It does not seem worth while to cite all of these
brief accounts; the following thirteen are sufficiently representative
to indicate the variation among the counselors.

Counselor D provided most of the typical forms of Study services: with
the boys "trips," camp placement, club memberships, tutoring, physical
examinations, and the like; with the families, counseling in regard to
the boys' problems and assistance with their own difficulties, such as
unemployment, poor health, and legal offenses. On occasion the counselor would give or lend money to parents and sometimes to a boy. He
frequently conferred with social workers, teachers, police and court
officials about his cases, and he visited the boys if they were sent to foster
homes or correctional institutions. His talks with the boys and, to a
considerable extent, with their parents was of the "straight-from-the-
shoulder" variety, and·he often attempted to win their confidence by
telling them of his own experiences as an adolescent. As with most of
the counselors, but to a greater extent than with some of them, his efforts
varied greatly in quantity from case to case. He was usually successful
in establishing good relations with both parents and boys, and in some
cases the boys apparently altered their behavior because of their relationship with him.

Counselor H provided much the same services as Counselor A. In some
instances he did considerable work in regard to general family problems,
while in others he devoted his efforts with the parents largely to explaining the reasons for the boy's behavior and advising them about
how to handle the difficulties. Qualitively his talks with the boys and
their parents differed from those of the preceding counselor, for, like
most of the counselors, he acted in accordance with his own natural bent,

but he, too, did much in the way of advice-giving and general encouragement.

Counselor B utilized the whole range of Study services, but his most typical mode of procedure was to concentrate first on trying to improve a boy's poor schoolwork (a very frequent problem, since most of the boys were referred by teachers), through tutoring and "interpretation" of the boy to the school; if this failed to produce improvement, he was likely to secure first, physical examinations and, that failing, psychiatric. In the meantime he would be talking with the parents, often in an attempt to change their ways of handling the boy. He supplemented this with camp placement, YMCA scholarships or other club memberships, recreational trips for the boys and help with house and job finding, or legal problems, health services, and so on for the family. Parents were usually very friendly toward him and very appreciative of his efforts; the boys, too, were friendly but many of them did not develop a close relationship with him, few of them indulging in those heart-to-heart talks that characterized their relations with some of the other counselors.

Counselor A was a trained nurse, which accounts for the fact that so much of her work with the boys and their families centered around help with problems of a physical nature. She frequently and successfully used her knowledge of health matters both to establish initial rapport and to demonstrate her continuing interest in the boy and his family. Her other characteristic mode of work was that of friendly, somewhat authoritative counseling. This she carried on with both boys and parents, advising, guiding, stimulating, reproving and encouraging, much in the manner of the "friendly visitor" of the early days of social case work. Her other services also had this other-day social-work quality: she sized up the families' needs and attempted to supply what was lacking—jobs, recreational opportunities, tutoring, health care, knowledge of household management and child care, as well as, and far from least, attendance to religious duties. She was much liked by nearly all adults and had a close relationship with many boys, though some boys, especially at adolescence, resented what seemed to them her sentimental approach and control.

Counselor K's services were rather brief and superficial in most of the cases in the sample studied. He would discuss the boys briefly with their teachers, arrange that they attend camp and take them on a few "trips," but otherwise he was not likely to do much for or with them. This way of handling the boys was attributable in part to the fact that he became their counselor after others had straightened out their most pressing problems. With some boys who were still in trouble he did more, especially in regard to court and reform school, encouraging them and their parents and being helpful to them in various concrete ways. He played a "Dutch uncle" role in some of these cases, firmly telling boys and their parents how they ought to behave. In most of the cases studied, his relationships were not very close, though with a few boys a man-to-man feeling developed because of the nature of the material discussed.

Counselor R. In the sample of cases studied, at least, this counselor gave relatively little service. What he did give was likely to involve only the boy, few visits being paid to parents. He secured physical examinations when needed, arranged for tutoring, helped a few boys find jobs, and made the usual camp placements. He taught several boys how to drive an automobile, this being one of their chief desires. In an occasional case he assisted the father or mother to obtain needed medical attention.

Counselor N's most characteristic way of working was to combine frequent "talks" with a boy with participation with him in recreational activities. In the talks, stress was put on problems of adolescence, the counselor having started work with most of his boys at that age period. Girls, sex, smoking, leaving school, holding a job were among the topics most often discussed. Sexual problems were discussed frankly and in considerable detail, the counselor trying to instill in the boys ideals of continence and honor. For recreation he frequently organized swimming parties, as well as making use of "trips" to museums, exhibits, sports events and the like that the other counselors provided. When necessary, this counselor discussed the boy's problems with teachers and court workers and gave assistance to parents with family difficulties, but he did less of this than some of the counselors, concentrating on the boys themselves instead. Many of the boys regarded him as a kind, helpful friend and kept in contact with him after the Study work officially terminated. There was not much evidence, however, that he served as the ego ideal of many of them.

Counselor N also emphasized recreation; he used recreational opportunities and facilities both to develop rapport and to help the boys deal with their problems. He would take the boys on outings of one sort or another, go camping with them, arrange that they join clubs, and so on. He also secured physical examinations as needed, talked with teachers and school authorities when the occasion required, and sometimes helped a boy to secure a job. This counselor was on the Study's staff a rather short time. His relationships were friendly but slight, and in the cases in the sample he accomplished little.

Counselor L confined himself almost wholly to office interviews with the boys, in which he attempted to draw them out with regard to their emotional problems. These efforts were likely to be unsuccessful, being very direct and rather inept. For instance, he would say to a boy that he probably did a lot of thinking about himself and would like to talk about his worries with somebody he could trust. In the course of these conversations he would give some "good advice," which was occasionally accepted, for the boys in the main seemed fond of him. He would also, as the case required, perform some services for the family, but the office interviews were his main reliance in working with the boys.

Counselor F's work was distinguished by attempts (in some cases, successful) to get at the boys' feelings about their difficulties. In the cases in which he worked in this way he was likely to carry on a form of child-guidance case work with the parents, explaining to them the boy's emotional needs and trying to change their ways of handling him. If the situation required, he would concentrate on health, school, or delinquency problems and do considerable work with teachers and police. He used "trips" and other recreation to establish rapport but seldom put chief reliance on such services. He seemed to be somewhat more than usually successful in securing the boys' affection, and the parents too were, for the most part, fond of him.

Counselor E, a woman, provided the typical Study services but in a somewhat different manner from most of the others. Her cases in the sample studied were about evenly divided between those in which she concentrated on the boy and those in which she sought to help him through aiding the parents with the various family problems. She had greater skill and was somewhat more successful than most of the other counselors in learning the parents' and boys' intimate feelings about their problems, and she related her services somewhat more directly to those feelings. Most of the parents were very cordial in their relations with her, and most of the boys seemed fond of her, though some later said that they did not like to have a woman coming to see them.

Counselor C, also a woman, followed two different patterns of procedure. In most cases her chief emphasis was on the boy with particular reference to his recreational needs. She would take these boys on "trips," arrange "Y" and other club memberships for them, send them to camp, and otherwise try to compensate for the poor neighborhoods in which they lived. With this work she combined physical, psychological, and psychiatric examinations if indicated, talks with teachers about the individual boys, occasional "good advice" to the boys and friendly contacts with their parents, making some attempt to modify their adverse attitudes toward the boys. In other cases her services were largely of the family case-work variety. In these she would work largely with the mother, counseling with her about marital problems, difficulties in household management, housing problems, and the like, and she would see little of the boy, though she would arrange that he have some of the same opportunities she secured for her other clients. Parents apparently felt kindly disposed toward this counselor, but close relationships seldom developed. A few boys (in the sample studied) became very fond of her but in even such cases her influence seemed negligible. By chance, probably, this counselor was assigned unusually difficult cases to work with, both boys and parents usually being very much maladjusted.

Counselor S. In most of this counselor's cases service was confined to the boy and not much was done about family problems. Perhaps this was because most of the boys were adolescents by the time he joined the staff. He spent a great deal of time on most of his cases, concentrating chiefly on interviews with the boys, during which many of their problems in social relations were discussed. With one Negro boy, for example, he had many discussions about racial discrimination; with another he talked about his companions and their delinquent acts, the boy's smoking and drinking and his relations with girls. In these talks he played a kind of big-brother role, setting forth the practical reasons for conduct norms. The boys apparently did not regard this as "lecturing" but entered into the discussions avidly; nevertheless few with whom this method was used altered their behavior greatly. In addition to such talks, this counselor arranged for physical examinations when needed, helped the boys secure jobs, discussed their situations with their teachers, took them swimming and riding, and, generally, provided the variety of concrete services the circumstances of the individual case seemed to require. As time went on this counselor apparently began to work more along modern case-work lines, putting more emphasis on ascertaining what the boy himself thought and felt about matters and less on telling him what he ought to do. He was successful in this kind of work in a considerable number of cases.

Something of the variety of the counselors' working methods, as well as some of the common elements (their use of recreation, both in direct participation with the boys and through the use of organized resources, health facilities, psychological examinations, tutoring, and the like) are suggested by the above descriptions, which admittedly do not do justice to the counselors' efforts. Additional indications as to the variety of methods used will be found in Chapters XXVI–XXVIII, in which the work in individual cases is described.

From the above descriptions it can be seen that the work of some counselors might be classified as akin to that usually carried on by "big brother" organizations, except that it was conducted on a full-time, paid basis. The work of others had much in common with the kind of social case work associated with the name of Mary Richmond,[1] while a few counselors at times used modern case-work methods. Such categories are not adequate to provide a basis for accurate classification of cases, however, for most boys had more than one counselor and the intensity and character of the work with them varied from time to time. They may serve, nevertheless,

[1] For a statement of principles see Mary Richmond, *Social Diagnosis* (New York, Russell Sage Foundation, 1917).

to distinguish broadly the main ways in which the boys were served.

How great was the variation in these respects is indicated in the following classification system.

1. Counselors had frequent contact with the boy or did much work in regard to him throughout the whole treatment period. "Frequent" cannot be precisely defined; the general indication is that the counselor usually saw the boy or his parents once each week or fortnight for a considerable period of time and seldom let more than a month elapse between contacts.

2. There were periods (say, three to six months in length) in which little was done, but for the most part the work was like that described above.

3. There were one or more periods of frequent contact but work with the boy was slight at least half of the time.

4. Boy was seen fairly often (say, about once in two weeks tapering off to once a month) for a period of from about nine months to two years, after which little was done with or for him.

5. Rather infrequent contact throughout the case.

6. Very little done with or for the boy.

This variation in amount of service was accounted for in part by the fact that during the war a large number of boys were "dropped," as has been described in Chapter XII. A few such cases, however, were classified as belonging in Categories 1 and 2 due to the fact that much work was done up to that time. The actual distribution of dropped and terminated or closed cases according to the above categories is shown in Table 62.

TABLE 62

Distribution of Dropped and Completed Cases by Frequency of Contact [a]

Category	Dropped	Completed [b]	Total
1	6	43	49
2	4	40	44
3	14	20	34
4	23	11	34
5	21	24	45
6	37	11	48
Total	105	149	254

[a] See text for definitions of categories.
[b] Includes both terminated and closed cases.

Considering only completed cases (the boys who were worked with until they were 17 or until the Study ended), we see that with about two-thirds of the boys close contact was maintained most of the time throughout the period of treatment (Categories 1 and 2) but that with about a fourth, little or rather little was done (Categories 5 and 6). Two-thirds of these latter boys were found on examination to be those who either had very little need for assistance (most of the boys in Category 6 were this kind) or who refused the services of the organization from the outset. Others were about evenly divided between boys who were exceedingly maladjusted and difficult to approach and those who were quickly and rather easily aided. It appears, therefore, that much of the variation in amount of service was attributable to circumstances within the boys' situations rather than to the counselors themselves, and that in most relevant cases the counselors carried out the Study plan of continued contact with the boys.

In this connection it may also be of interest to note, first, that the counselors tended to give most of their attention to the most maladjusted boys and, second, that, by and large, it was the least maladjusted who were dropped. The first point is demonstrated, rather paradoxically, by the fact that among the completed cases the boys with whom the counselors worked least were the ones who turned out best—in the sense that it was in that group that the largest proportion of well-adjusted boys appeared when "terminal adjustment" ratings (see Chapter XXIV) were made. This statement needs correction, however, to take account of the fact that some boys refused service and others did not need help. When these were omitted it was found that the apparent variation in amount of service was fairly closely related to variation in the boys' needs. To a considerable extent the individual counselor's variation from case to case is similarly explainable. There remains, however, the fact that the counselors did differ from one another in over-all way of working, and it is this fact that complicates matters when we attempt to explain the Study's accomplishments.

CHAPTER XXIV

ADJUSTMENT OF
THE TREATED AND
CONTROL BOYS

A STATISTICAL ANALYSIS OF COURT RECORDS, MADE BY THE STUDY staff, showed that only a rather small proportion of the boys who were described by their teachers and others as difficult became delinquents in the legal sense of the word.[1] This good record did not seem attributable to any large extent to the Study's efforts, for an almost equally good showing was made by the boys in the C-group. Prevention of delinquency was, however, only the negative aspect of the Study's aim; it was hoped that through the organization's services socially and emotionally deprived boys would be benefited in ways that would be reflected in character development superior to that of their C-twins. Now, "character" is admittedly a vague word, and only slightly less vague is its sociological counterpart "social adjustment," which, moreover, has connotations regarding the relation of the individual to society that are rather inaccurate. Nevertheless, both of these words have a common-sense meaning that may be sufficiently definite to permit classification of the boys into groups designated "good" and "poor" (and perhaps one or two intermediate categories) and comparison of them on that basis.

With no pretense of great accuracy, then, and with no great liking for the terms employed, we shall classify the boys with respect to how they appeared to be getting along socially, and to some extent, emotionally, when last reported to us by the counselors and shall call that condition their "terminal adjustment."

Unfortunately, this terminal point varied considerably from boy to boy. First, as has been noted in Chapter XII, some boys were

[1] See Chap. XVII.

dropped from the Study, these being largely boys who were making a good social adjustment and who therefore seemed not to be in much need of the counselors' assistance. There were 105 such boys among the 254 we were studying. Some of them were located in 1946, when a follow-up study to be described below was undertaken, and their adjustment at that time was learned. For the others, however (those who could not be reached) we had to use the earlier information and rate their "terminal adjustment" on the basis of what was known about them at the time they were dropped. Second, at the time the service program ended, some boys had not reached seventeen and a half years. Third, some boys kept in touch with their counselors for a long time after they were seventeen and a half. Since it seemed important to know as much as possible about how the boys turned out, the "terminal adjustment" of these boys was that which they were displaying when last known, regardless of how long this was after service to them officially ended.

"Terminal" accordingly refers to no one particular date or period of time either in the life of the boys or in our investigation; instead, it refers to the latest point at which information about a boy could be secured. The boys' ages at that point were as follows: under thirteen, 14; thirteen or fourteen, 39; fifteen or sixteen, 65; seventeen or eighteen, 82; nineteen to twenty-one, 54.

TERMINAL ADJUSTMENT OF TREATED BOYS

In rating the boys, attention was paid chiefly to the social aspects of their behavior. Sociologically speaking, every individual has to relate himself to various institutionally organized groups, the most important of which to an adolescent boy are his family, school, occupational group, voluntary association (for friendship and recreation), and community, especially in its legal aspects. An individual's reputation for good or poor social functioning is based to a considerable degree on the way in which he reacts to the rules of such associations and the manner and extent to which he joins in their activities. Emotional inadequacies and disorders are often indicated by unusual behavior in these areas. Hence, it seemed that by inquiring how a boy was getting along at home, in school, on his job, with regard to friends and associates, recreational interests, and with respect to the law, we should be able to rate him as making a good or poor adjustment or a specified gradation in between these two extremes. Actually, four categories were set up (good, fairly good, rather poor, and poor), and to them several sub-categories were added. In the following paragraphs the extremes (Groups 1 and 4) will be described first and then the intermediate categories (Groups 2 and 3) filled in.

1. Good Social (and Presumably Emotional) Adjustment. Boys were classified as belonging in this group if they got along at least reasonably well [2] at home; if they had friends of their own age and sex, and of the opposite sex if they were old enough; if their work at school was in keeping with their intellectual capacities; if their behavior and performance on a job (if they were of the age to have one) were adequate; if they engaged in satisfying recreational activities; if they were regarded as honest, reliable, cooperative members of the community. If a boy was definitely feebleminded some of these criteria were modified to take that condition into account. For instance, he might not be able to hold paid jobs or to have the kind of friendships better-endowed boys had. He was, however, classified as well adjusted only if he related well to people, if he engaged pleasurably in work and activities that were within his capacity, and if he had a good reputation in the neighborhood.

Example 1. Mark: age 17 years, 5 months; I.Q. 86. This boy's family consisted of his father, a dogmatic, opinionated man who had a severe temper and was often drunk and abusive; his mother, said to be the dominant parent, who was not happy with her husband but was much interested in and very fond of her children; an older brother described as conscientious and outgoing; two younger sisters and two younger brothers, also socially very adequate, although one sister probably had epilepsy.

At 17, when the Study work ended, Mark was a quiet, friendly boy seemingly adequate in all respects. He got along well with his family and had an objective attitude toward his father's drunkenness. He was much liked by other boys and had many friends of both sexes. His interests and activities were normal for his age and social situation. He had left school at 16, not having done well there for the last year or so, probably because of his rather limited intelligence. On leaving school he had secured a job in a restaurant and still had it when last known.

---

[2] This qualification was made to take account of the fact that a certain amount of rebellion against family restrictions is probably normal for boys in adolescence. Actually, almost all the boys who were rated 1 in social adjustment got along well with their parents and siblings.

On the job he did good, steady work and was well regarded by his employer. As to organized recreation he had been an enthusiastic member of a settlement house, Boy Scouts, and other organizations for many years.

Other briefer examples of the kind of adjustment rated 1 are the following. Cornelius at twenty was a very friendly, outgoing boy who was learning on the job to be a chemical technician and was studying mathematics at night. He got along well with his parents and siblings, had many friends, and greatly enjoyed participation in sports. Carmen, a boy with an I.Q. in the low 70's, was found at nineteen to have held a factory job very satisfactorily for two years. He belonged to a neighborhood gang of non-delinquent boys and had much pleasure in their company. He was eager to get into military service and disappointed that he had not been accepted. Family relations were good, though the boy was somewhat teased and criticized by his brighter siblings. Harold, a boy who had had a difficult home situation, was at seventeen on the honor roll of a school in which he had previously been a failing student. He had a job in the home of a faculty member who reported that he was an excellent worker and very trustworthy. The boy himself spoke with affection of the aunt with whom he lived and whose control he formerly resented, while with his mother, who had been much dissatisfied with him, he had a cordial, mature relationship.

4. Poor Adjustment. Boys in this category were at the opposite extreme from those in Group 1. Some were quarrelsome and uncooperative at home; others were so tied to their families that they had no outside interests or contacts. Some had no friends; others associated with delinquent gangs; some had as their only companions a few boys who were antisocial or otherwise clearly maladjusted. Characteristically, these boys did poorly in school even if they had adequate intelligence, while on jobs they were undependable and erratic in performance. Three sub-types were distinguished: (a) those who were maladjusted in all the areas here described; (b) those who were clearly neurotic or psychotic or neurologically disabled; (c) those who were chronic delinquents with long court records. Many of the boys classified as 4c also belonged in 4b, as will be shown in another chapter, but since prevention of delinquency was one of the chief aims of the Study it seemed best to let 4c take precedence over 4b in the classification process.

Example 2. Benny: age 17; I.Q. 101; classified 4a. Benny lived in a ramshackle house on a dead-end street near railroad and coal yards. The neighborhood had a high delinquency rating. His father was a truck driver, a quiet, steady man with considerable interest in his children. His mother had been a factory worker before marriage and took another job of this kind when Benny was about 15. Even before working she was out of the house much of the time and gave the children rather inadequate supervision. Benny's two older brothers were described as shiftless drifters, his sister, next to him in age, was chiefly interested in "the boys," while of the younger children little was known.

Throughout the Study's contact Benny seemed a true gang boy. His intense loyalty to his friends in the gang and his acceptance of their standards apparently kept him from developing any close relationships with adults. He never liked school nor did well there in spite of his adequate intelligence. He was frequently a truant and was suspended several times. At about 15 he told his counselor in considerable detail about the numerous delinquencies of his gang, claiming that he was the only one on whom the police had nothing. When the counselor asked him whether he and his friends were not ashamed of disgracing their families by being brought into court, Benny replied, "No, in the gas-house district the stealing just seems to grow out of boys. Most families feel that going to court is just part of the natural course of events."

Throughout the period of the Study's contact the boy had no steady job. He always claimed he wanted one but when a job was offered or tried for a time it always turned out to be too difficult, too poorly paid, or too time-absorbing. Girls, too, were of little interest to the boy, his one friendship petering out very soon.

In the final review of the case the Study case supervisor said that he regarded the outlook for Benny as poor. His parents were ineffectual people, his father interested but the mother unconcerned. The boy himself was a passive but loyal gang member, who lived by his friends' dictates. A year later, at 18, Benny told his counselor that his gang had been stealing cars, carrying loaded revolvers, and the like; he thought they were "crazy," he would be afraid to do such things. But he gave no indication that he had really changed his habits or his friends.

Example 3. Rex: age 17 years, 5 months; I.Q. 108; classified as 4b. Rex was a boy who had a history of instability and difficult conduct that dated back to at least three years of age. His mother had died when he was a year old, and he had suffered from neglect and abuse in the foster homes in which he was placed. When he was three his father remarried. The father was overstrict with the boy, and the stepmother, though apparently fond of and interested in him, left him in the care of an elderly housekeeper, who found him very difficult to manage. Throughout childhood the boy was overactive, very demanding, and very distractible. At school his attention could seldom be secured and he was regarded as a menace on the playground. He was twice the victim of a homosexual attack, at four and at seven years of age.

The first counselor worked hard on the case for two years. He first attempted to ease the father's pressure on the boy by "interpreting" to the stepmother the reasons for the boy's behavior and advising her how to handle him; later he persuaded the parents to accept psychiatric treatment for him. He had many talks with the teachers about Rex, securing a promotion and special favors for him, and arranged for needed tutoring. He took Rex on frequent trips; sent him to camp, and after child-guidance treatment failed to help, secured the services of a child-placement agency. None of this did much good. Rex was shifted from one to another school or foster home and was finally placed in a well-known residential institution for neurotic children. He did as poorly there as in the previous homes, being always described as flighty, distractible, and shallow in affect. He was seldom delinquent (though after the end of the Study's contact he was put on probation for larceny) but always emotionally very unstable.

Example 4. Wilbur: age 19; I.Q. 91; classified 4c. This boy was one of three illegitimate children in a large family of questionable morals. He lived much of his life in various relatives' homes, his mother's husband disliking him greatly and being abusive to him. From the outset of the Study's contact he seemed a strange, sullen boy with an impenetrable shell of reserve. He had stolen since early childhood and was in the state training school from 10 to 13. There he was constantly in trouble because of his fighting and breaking of rules. He returned home more bitter than when he entered the school and even less accepting of social regulations. For several years he was so frequently a truant that return to the training school was often considered, and he left school as soon as possible. Various jobs were secured for him by the Study counselor but he never kept one for more than a few weeks. His mother, a weak, ineffectual woman, gave in to her husband's refusal to have him in their home and the aunt with whom he found shelter soon became disgusted with him and complained of what she called his lazy, selfish behavior. At 17 he was sentenced to jail for carrying a dangerous weapon and a year later was put on probation for breaking and entering. When last heard of he had joined the Army but was in disciplinary barracks because of having gone AWOL. He was never able to maintain friendships with boys or adults.

Between these two extremes of adjustment two other categories were roughly distinguished, the first consisting of boys whose adjustment seemed fairly good and the second of those whose adjustment was on the poor side. These distinctions were made on the quality rather than on the quantity of socially adequate functioning, although in some cases the distinction between fairly good and fairly poor was made on the basis of the number of areas (family, school, job, friendships, community relations) in which the boy operated adequately. Examples may make clearer than definitions what we mean.

2. *Fairly Good Adjustment.* Two types were distinguished: (a) boys whose adjustment was somewhat less adequate than might be desired but who seemed emotionally healthy and (b) those who were socially conforming but whose rather good social adjustment seemed neurotically determined. The following is an example of an adjustment rated 2a.

Example 5. Zaven: age 18; I.Q. 106. Zaven's mother, a rather unstable Portuguese woman, protected and dominated her children until at adolescence they vigorously protested against such treatment. She preferred her daughters to her sons, thinking them easier to handle. The father was a mild, agreeable man who approved of Zaven and considered him "smart." Zaven was a restless, energetic boy who was rather disobedient in school. In spite of his intelligence he never did well at his studies and never liked school, being two years retarded. Otherwise he was a responsible, sociable boy who had many friends. He started to work at an early age and was always very steady and dependable. He early became interested in girls and saw much of them. In the neighborhood he was a rather sophisticated "street kid"—extroverted, aggressive, engaging in rough-and-tumble fights, and occasionally being involved in unofficial delinquency. He was fond of his mother, very close to his brothers and sisters, and respectful, for the most part, of his father's wishes.

Some of the other boys rated 2a were not quite so well adjusted as this boy. Hank (age 17; I.Q. 89), for example, was a boy who had always been rather reticent with his counselors and a bit suspicious of their intentions. When last interviewed he had had a job at a gasoline station for two years and was apparently well liked by his employer. In school his adjustment had fluctuated with the skill of his teachers and the interest the classes had for him. Toward his family he maintained a rather aloof attitude, claiming to be chiefly interested in how much money he could get from them. His chief spare-time interest was dog racing, a hobby he shared with his employer. In personality he seemed rather tough and belligerent, but these traits were compensated for by warmth and generosity, so that he was well liked by most adults and had a good many friends. As a younger boy he had been involved in some minor delinquencies and was described by the police when only ten years old as a "bully and a braggart but not a bad kid."

The boys rated 2b were characteristically conscientious and reliable workers but were rather limited in friends and interests and had less than satisfactory relations with their families. This, of course, was not the only pattern this rather neurotic type of acceptable social adjustment assumed but it was the most usual one. An example is seen in the case of Orrin (age 20; I.Q. 94) who when last interviewed said he had been on the same job for five years but that he didn't like it and stayed only because it was a job. This boy had always been fearful, had had enuresis for many years, and was overattached to his doting mother, who overprotected him, partly because he had severe nystagmus. He had done well in grade school under the guidance of a very considerate teacher but he had found high school unpleasant and left as soon as he could. He always did well on jobs but had no known interests or ambitions; his recreation consisted of "hanging around."

Another example of this 2b type is seen in Howard (age 19; I.Q. 108), who from the outset of the Study's contact was described as a responsible, serious boy who was striving to take the place of his father who had died when the son was eleven. He apparently never had close friends of his own age and sex (though at sixteen he did have an affair with a fourteen-year-old girl that resulted in pregnancy) and had no interest in the usual boys' sports and other activities. He exhibited much initiative in getting jobs and was always a steady, responsible worker. He did well in the Air Force in spite of being handicapped by air sickness, a disorder that seemed in line with the numerous apparently neurotic ailments he had suffered all his life.

3. Rather Poor Adjustment. This category, also, was subdivided to take into account the difference between the boys who were socially non-conforming and those whose mental health was more obviously poor. Actually, most of the boys in the first subdivision were as emotionally maladjusted as those in the second. The following are examples of these two types, called in subsequent tables 3a and 3b, respectively.

Example 6. Burt: age 18 years, 10 months; I.Q. 99. Burt from the outset was an engaging, likeable boy, very responsive to adults and apparently very open in expressing his feelings about himself and his family. On further acquaintance it seemed that this responsiveness was of a surface nature only, that the boy was really very egocentric, had unrealistic goals for himself, and was the sort that always promises but never fulfills his pledges. He seemed to be constantly in a "manic" state, always voluble in talk and seeking excitement. Throughout the Study's contact he was frequently a truant and involved in petty delinquencies. Although he did fairly adequately in his studies, he annoyed the other children by "silly" behavior, poor sportsmanship, and an abnormally large appetite; they made so much fun of him, he said, that he wanted to leave. His parents were very poor (the father frequently a deserter and the mother in poor health), and Burt claimed great devotion to his mother (who indulged him greatly), but he never kept jobs and frequently asked her for money. He had many illnesses that doctors regarded as neurotic in origin, or at least as attention-seeking devices. When last known he had just left the Merchant Marine, a job at which it had seemed for a time he might do well, especially as he was greatly interested in the activities of the seamen's union. In spite of his careless, irresponsible conduct, Burt avoided serious delinquency. He never seemed greatly disturbed about anything and maintained his plausible, friendly manner throughout all his difficulties.

Example 7. David: age 19; I.Q. 93. At 12, when the Study contact began, David was described as the worst child in his class at school. Acquaintance with him revealed an emotionally insecure boy who had strong feelings of inferiority. He engaged in aggressive, attention-seeking acts that antagonized his parents, teachers, and other boys. He spent most of his time alone; while in a group he always had a chip on his shoulder. He was particularly concerned about what he regarded his smallness (he was really not very short or slight), his stammering, and his having to wear glasses. He was always very much interested in money and saved unusually large amounts of any he was given or earned. His anxiety was usually hidden beneath a "tough" exterior and he could express his feelings only through aggressive acts.

This kind of behavior characterized the boy throughout the Study contact with him. In addition he constantly quarreled with his parents and siblings. He felt, with considerable justification, that his nervous, domineering mother did not like him, and that his father, an ineffectual alcoholic who was often abusive, did not want him in the home. Although he had brief periods of doing well in school, most of the time he was uninterested in his schoolwork, was often a truant, and was disturbing in the classroom. In spite of this he was still in school when last interviewed. At that time he was said to have a few close friends and to be enjoying Y dances and gym activities, but his cynical, "wise-guy" attitude persisted.

Classified according to these categories, the boys who had been Study clients lined up as shown in Table 63. Since final information about the various boys was obtained at different times, the age to which the words "terminal adjustment" refer is included in the table.

TABLE 63

Distribution of Treated Boys by Age and Terminal Adjustment

Terminal Adjustment	Under 13	13–14	15–16	17–18	19–21	Total
1. Good	6	16	16	26	12	76
2. Fairly good:						
a	—	12	22	19	12	65
b	1	3	8	10	9	31
3. Rather poor:						
a	—	1	4	3	6	14
b	—	2	6	8	6	22
4. Poor:						
a	—	—	—	4	—	4
b	1	1	4	5	4	15
c	—	—	3	7	5	15
Not Known	6	4	2	—	—	12
Total	14	39	65	82	54	254

A partial check on the reliability of these ratings is provided by an independent classification of the 109 boys who were over $17\frac{1}{2}$ years of age. This classification was made by two of the Study's staff members for the purpose of analyzing the boys' delinquency records (see Chapter XIV). The following categories were used: [3]

Delinquents, Group I. Boys showing a persistent pattern of anti-social behavior expressed by a disregard and defiance of authority. Their delinquent acts, official and unofficial, have been, as a rule, frequent and serious although in some cases their delinquency may have been expressed by a long series of minor infractions or by only one or two serious offenses.

Delinquents, Group II. Boys who have inhibited their impulses to a greater extent than those in Group I but who have nevertheless shown an unwholesome disregard for authority on occasion. In

[3] Group III is omitted.

general, they lack the aggressiveness and persistence of those in Group I with the result that their offenses are less frequent and less serious.

Non-Delinquents, Group IV. Boys who have shown a fairly consistent attitude of respect toward authority but whose impulsiveness, carelessness, or recklessness may have led them to some involvement in minor delinquencies. If they have committed delinquencies, their acts have been less serious and less frequent than those of the run-of-the-mill delinquent boy. If they do commit such acts, they are usually repentant for them, for they have a more wholesome attitude toward the law.

Non-Delinquents, Group V. There is no doubt about the sincerity of these boys, who are well socialized and definitely respect duly constituted authority. It is possible that they may have committed some delinquent act or acts but, if so, these acts are not typical of them and are rare and not serious. Those who never committed a delinquent act are included in this group.

The cross-classification of the boys according to this system of classification (which, it will be noted, stresses delinquency and pays no attention to other forms of maladjustment) and that used by the writer is shown in Table 64.

TABLE 64

Comparison of T-Boys' Adjustment Ratings According to Two Systems of Classification

	WRITER'S RATINGS				
Study's Ratings	*1*	*2*	*3*	*4*	*Total*
Delinquents					
I	—	—	2	11	13
II	—	4	6	9	19
Non-delinquents					
IV	1	6	4	2	13
V	26	27	10	1	64
Total	27	37	22	23	109

It will be seen that at the extremes there was a great deal of similarity between the ratings. Much of the rest of the apparent diversity was due to the difference in what was being rated: delinquency history versus adjustment when last known. For instance, the two boys in Group I of the Study's delinquency ratings who were not rated as chronic delinquents by the writer were so seriously maladjusted emotionally that it seemed that the rating should stress that fact rather than that they engaged in delinquent acts. One of them was a boy who had a long history of seemingly neurotic delinquency and who in adolescence was diagnosed psychotic. The other was a boy, apparently neurotic, who when last heard about was said to be living with his mother and a new stepfather and working steadily. In Group II the four boys who had a fairly good terminal adjustment rating had earlier shown the kind of behavior described in the definition of Group II. The same was true of the boy in Group IV who was rated 1 in terminal adjustment; he was described as being well adjusted in all respects after several years in a good institution. In Group V most of the extreme discrepancies are accounted for by the fact that the boys, though definitely not delinquent, were seriously maladjusted emotionally. All in all, then, Table 64 indicates a fairly high degree of reliability in the adjustment ratings.

Returning, then, to Table 63, we see that nearly a third of the boys appeared to be making a good adjustment when last known and that somewhat more than a third were rated as doing fairly well. Only 34 out of the 242 whose adjustment could be classified were adjusting very poorly. The younger boys were less likely to be making a poor adjustment than the older ones, but between the ages of 15 and 21 the distributions of adjustment ratings were fairly similar, a fact that would seem to justify disregarding the age factor in subsequent comparisons.

Before the significance of these figures can be considered, one correction must be made: the well-adjusted boys must be omitted. So far as the writer could judge from the descriptions of behavior as reported by the teachers and the Study's home visitors, there were 34 such boys. When they were eliminated from Table 63, Category 1 was decreased by 23, 2a by 6, 3a by 2, and 4c by 1, the final two boys being in the not-known category. The distribution of the remaining 220 boys according to terminal adjustment ratings was then as follows:

1.	Good	53
2a.	Fairly good	59
2b.	Fairly good; neurotic	31
3a.	Rather poor	14
3b.	Rather poor; neurotic	20
4a.	Poor	4
4b.	Poor; neurotic	15
4c.	Poor; delinquent	14
	Not known	10
	Total	220

It thus appears that a fourth of the boys regarded by the original reporters (teachers and home visitors) as more or less maladjusted were doing very well when last known, over a third were doing fairly well, and about a third were adjusting more or less poorly. Only about one in five boys regarded by teachers and others as difficult became seriously maladjusted. At first sight this might seem a tribute to the Study's work, but before such a conclusion can be accepted the cases must be analyzed from other angles.

RELATION OF VARIOUS FACTORS TO TERMINAL ADJUSTMENT

The figures given above indicate that nearly all the boys considered well adjusted by the original reporters remained well adjusted. In fact, only a tenth of them were rated as making a "poor" or "rather poor" adjustment when last known. This suggests that the relation between original and terminal adjustment for the group as a whole must be examined before we credit the organization with having effected great changes in the boys. The relation between original adjustment, as rated in Chapter XXII, and terminal adjustment is shown in Table 65.

First, it will be seen that the number of boys who were rated by the writer as originally well adjusted was 49, about a fifth of the total.[4] In addition, there were 92 whose problems seemed slight. Only 38 of the total 254 boys appeared to be extremely maladjusted at the time the Study counselors first came to know them well. Second, the table indicates that there was considerable relation be-

---

[4] The term "originally" refers to the situation at the time work with the boy got well under way. Some boys who had been described by teachers and other referral persons as somewhat difficult had become well adjusted by the time the counselors started to work with them.

TABLE 65

Relation between Initial and Terminal Adjustment

TERMINAL ADJUSTMENT

Initial Adjustment	1	2a	2b	3a	3b	4a	4b	4c	NK	Total
1. Well-adjusted	34	11	—	2	—	—	—	—	2	49
2. Slight maladjustment	31	36	3	7	1	2	1	4	6	92
3. Considerable social maladjustment	3	9	—	2	2	1	—	2	1	19
4. Maladjustment suggestive of neurosis	8	8	25	3	7	1	2	1	1	56
5. Extreme maladjustment	—	1	3	—	12	—	12	8	2	38
Total	76	65	31	14	22	4	15	15	12	254

tween adjustment at the outset and adjustment when last known. About three-fourths of the boys who originally appeared to be well adjusted remained well adjusted, only two out of the 47 whose terminal adjustment was known being rated as even "rather poor" at the end. In contrast, none of the boys regarded as extremely maladjusted at the outset became really well adjusted, and over half of them remained in the lowest adjustment category. If "considerable social maladjustment" and "maladjustment suggestive of neurosis" are grouped together, it will be seen that there was a progressive decrease in the proportion of boys rated 1 in terminal adjustment and an increase in those rated 3 or 4 as the original maladjustment became more severe. Clearly, the severity of the original maladjustment was a factor in the terminal situation.

In spite of this general relation between original and terminal adjustment, however, there was a difference between the extreme categories and those in the middle. At the extremes the boys tended to maintain their original adjustment ratings; the well-adjusted boys, for the most part, stayed well adjusted, and most of those who were extremely maladjusted remained at least "rather poor." In the mid-categories, on the other hand, an upward tendency was demonstrated. Of the boys originally rated as slightly maladjusted, one-third became well adjusted and about a fifth became worse than they were originally. In the next two categories combined, nearly three-fourths made a good or fairly good adjustment and only a tenth became severely maladjusted. All in all, 101 of the 254 boys improved in adjustment and 24 became less well adjusted as time went by. Great changes for the better or for the worse were rather infrequent, however, being confined to 39 boys in all. These findings suggest that, while the Study was unable to help the severely maladjusted boys make a very good adjustment, its services may have been beneficial to some of the others. This is a point that will be further examined later.[5]

Another factor to be considered as probably influential in the boys' later adjustment, and, if so, a partial explanation of the good showing when the Study ended, is the home situation, for it has already been shown that this factor, especially in its emotional aspects, was closely related to the severity of the boys' original malfunctioning. It has already been noted (Chapter XXII) that more than half of the boys came from homes we rated A in social aspects and that about a third of them lived under favorable emotional conditions. Table 66 shows that the boys' terminal adjustment was fairly closely related to the kind of homes they came from.

Taking the emotional aspect by itself (the first letters in the ratings in Table 66) we see that about 63 percent of the boys from A homes made a very good adjustment, 24 percent of those from B homes, and only one boy out of the 63 from C homes whose adjustments were known. At the other extreme the opposite situation was found; none of the boys from A homes, about 10 percent of those from B homes, and 35 percent of those from C homes were in the lowest adjustment category.

The social aspect of the home was apparently less important. At the extremes there was a definite relationship. Good homes produced a larger proportion of well-adjusted boys than did poor homes but the relationship was not as close as in the preceding comparison. The proportion of boys whose adjustment was rated as fairly good or rather poor was fairly much the same in each type of home.

[5] Chaps. XXVI, XXVIII.

TABLE 66

Relation between Home Situation and Terminal Adjustment

EMOTIONAL-SOCIAL HOME RATING [a]

Terminal Adjustment	AA	AB	AC	BA	BB	BC	CA	CB	CC	NK	Total
1. Good	44	5	3	11	11	1	1	—	—	—	76
2. Fairly good	23	2	1	27	19	6	9	7	2	—	96
3. Rather poor	3	1	—	7	5	—	6	9	5	—	36
4. Poor	—	—	—	1	7	2	4	11	9	—	34
Not Known	3	—	—	1	2	1	—	2	1	2	12
Total	73	8	4	47	44	10	20	29	17	2	254

[a] For definitions, see Chap. XXII.

Another way of considering the figures in Table 66 is to calculate how many boys made an adjustment better or poorer than expectations, on the assumption that boys from A homes, emotionally or socially, should make a 1 or 2 adjustment, those from B homes a 2 or 3, and those from C homes a 3 or 4, these being the categories that contained the majority of such boys. On that assumption, 15 boys made a poorer adjustment than the emotional rating of their homes would lead one to expect, and 44 made a better adjustment. For the social rating the corresponding figures were 39 and 30. This would suggest, on the one hand, that emotional and social were about balanced as predictive factors (the total out of line with expectations being about the same in each case) but, on the other, that social was less important than emotional on the positive side, the table showing that the proportion of boys who were favorably influenced by a good emotional environment was greater than that influenced by a good social environment. All in all, it seems clear that, while the home situation was important, other factors were also influential in the boys' terminal adjustment, one of which, again, might be thought to be the Study's services. The validity of this idea can be tested later by comparison of the Study's effectiveness with boys whose adjustment exceeded expectations and those whose adjustment was worse than anticipated on the basis of their home situations.

We may ask also whether the large proportion of good and fairly good adjustments was in line with the Selection Committee ratings. It will be recalled that this committee originally rated each boy with regard to his likelihood of becoming a delinquent, numerous factors being taken into account in making those judgments (see Chapter V). The rating scale ranged from −5 to +5 but only one boy of the 254 boys was rated as high as +3 and only four as low as −4. A few more than half of these boys were rated −1 or −2, while about a fourth were rated +1 or +2. While it is impossible to equate these ratings with our terminal adjustment categories, it would seem unlikely that the committee expected as many as two-thirds of the boys to be doing well or fairly well.

The relation between the Selection Committee's predictions and the boys' terminal adjustment ratings, shown in Table 67, was far from close. Nearly all the boys who eventually made a very poor adjustment had been rated by the committee on the minus side of the scale but so had more than half of the boys whose terminal adjustment was of the best. Half of the boys rated −4 or −3 were making a good or fairly good adjustment when last known, as compared with three-fourths of those rated +1 and almost all of those rated +2 or +3. Read another way, Table 67 indicates that 57 boys rated −2 or less, eventually made a good or fairly good adjustment, as did 40 others rated −1. These figures contrast with 14 boys rated 0 to +3 who turned out badly (ratings "poor" or "rather poor"). Again the balance seems to be in favor of the Study. Since it was the aim of the Study to overcome the latent delinquent tendencies of the boys, these figures might be taken to indicate that the organization had done so to a considerable extent. This can be determined better, however, when comparison with the control group is made, below.

TABLE 67

Relation between Selection Committee Ratings and Terminal Adjustment of T-Boys

Terminal Adjustment	SELECTION COMMITTEE RATINGS								Total
	−4	−3	−2	−1	0	+1	+2	+3	
1. Good	—	4	19	16	6	15	16	1	77
2. Fairly good	2	7	25	24	9	17	12	—	96
3. Rather poor	—	4	9	10	4	6	2	—	35
4. Poor	2	8	13	9	2	—	—	—	34
Not Known	—	—	3	5	1	2	1	—	12
Total	4	23	69	64	22	40	31	1	254

To sum up, then, about two-thirds of the boys appeared to be adjusting at least fairly well when they were last heard of. This situation was partially attributable to the fact that many of the boys had never been seriously maladjusted, this group constituting nearly three-fourths of those who were rated 1 or 2 terminally. Similarly about 40 percent of the boys were rated 0 or on the plus side by the Selection Committee; three-fourths of that group, also, were among the boys rated as doing at least fairly well when last known. Moreover, about a third of the boys came from homes rated good emotionally and over half of them from homes rated good socially, factors that had been found to be important in the boys' initial adjustment. Ninety percent of the first group and 80 percent of the second were in the satisfactory adjustment categories (1 and 2) when last known. Since boys with these various traits appeared much less frequently among the maladjusted boys, it was concluded that much of the good showing of the series as a whole might be due to these traits rather than to the Study's services. Even if this is granted, however, there remain quite a number of boys who did at least fairly well in spite of considerable initial maladjustment, apparent likelihood of delinquency, and unfavorable home conditions. Later we shall attempt to discover whether in these cases the Study was the decisive factor making for good adjustment. In the meantime we must answer the question whether the control group made a less good showing than these "treated" boys, for it was through such a comparison that the planners of the investigation hoped to determine the organization's efficacy.

FOLLOW-UP OF THE CONTROL BOYS

Determining the present social adjustment of the boys in the control series of cases was a much more difficult task than determining their court records. Data in regard to the latter, insofar as the local courts were concerned, were readily available in the official records of the Massachusetts Board of Probation, while the files of the various state correctional institutions yielded information about the boys who had been committed to their care. Determination of the control boys' social adjustment, however, required visits to them and their families, interviews that were of the sort to yield reasonably valid information about how they were getting along, and the making of judgments on the basis of the material secured. The first problem was to find the control group. It was soon learned that some of them had long since moved away from the Cambridge-Somerville area, that others were in military service and were seldom, if ever, at home, and that a few had died. In some cases it was impossible to locate the boy at all. In addition a few boys refused to be interviewed. All in all, 101 C-boys were lost to the Study for one or another of these reasons, the distribution being as follows:

Address not found	24
Home too distant for interview	16
Military service; never found at home	37
Refused interview	12
Dead	4
Other reasons	8

There were, then, 153 boys about whom reasonably satisfactory information was obtained in one or another of the ways to be described below. For reasons of sampling, however, five of these boys had to be omitted from the comparison with their treated "twins." The situation that necessitated their omission was as follows. At the time the follow-up study was made one T-boy and seven C-boys had been committed to the Massachusetts Reformatory and a total of 18 C-boys and 19 T-boys had been in one or another of the state's penal or correctional institutions. Now, due to the ease of locating them, all the C-boys who were in the reformatory and nine of the others could be interviewed. To have retained all of them in the control sample, however, would have biased it with respect to proportion of committed delinquents. We therefore omitted from the sample two of the seven boys who were in the reformatory and three of the nine others, thus reducing the proportion of committed delinquents in the control sample to eleven, the proportion (7 percent) they constituted in the total control group.[6] We had, then, in the C-group 148 boys about whom information as to present adjustment could be obtained.

[6] The two reformatory boys omitted were those whose ages differed most widely from those of their treatment "twins." The three other C-boys who were dropped from the sample had been in the correctional institutions only once and the only follow-up information secured about them was that contained in the institution's records.

An important question that had to be answered then was whether the 148 treated boys whose controls were to be followed constituted a representative sample of the total number of treated boys in this evaluation study, for only if such were the case would generalization from the sample to the total be justified. The "twins" of the C-boys whose present adjustment was to be determined were, accordingly, listed and compared with the total in the Study group with respect to certain seemingly significant traits: age at time the Study work began, I.Q., number of counselors, value of the Study's services (see Chapter XXV), and adjustment when last known. The averages and proportions were so nearly similar that it was clear that the T-boys whose controls were available for follow-up constituted an unbiased sample of the total. Typical figures were the following:

	Sample (*148*)	Total (*255*)
Mean age at start of Study work	10 years	10 years, 5 months
Mean intelligence quotient	93.0	93.7
Mean number of counselors	2.4	2.5
Value of Study's services [a] (percent)		
Much benefit	20	20
Little or no benefit	41	42
Adjustment when last known (percent)		
Good	32	32
Poor	14	14

[a] See Chap. XXV.

The C-boys who could be reached (the "twins" of the 148 T-boys who were thus found to be representative of the total) were then assumed to be a representative C-sample. We had next to decide what kind of information to try to secure about them. It seemed clear that the follow-up investigation would have to be largely limited to the present situation. It could not be expected that much detail could be elicited about a C-boy's prior history or about his adjustment at just exactly the age at which we had final information concerning his Study twin. All that could be done to remedy the defect due to discrepancies in age was to attempt to locate the T-boys who had been dropped when very young, to bring the records of all the T-boys as much up to date as possible, and to take account of the remaining differences through statistical break-down.

It seemed necessary also to limit the follow-up interviews largely to the boys and their families. While employers, neighbors, and friends might well have been able to give information of value, it did not seem fair to the boys to make such inquiries. We could only hope that the skill of our interviewers, their ability to create the kind of situation in which the boys and their parents would talk freely, would compensate for the obvious lacks in a follow-up study limited to such sources of information. In addition to material secured through these interviews, some data could be obtained from the schools and the Probation Office if boys were in their charge recently. Nevertheless, our main source of information had to be the boys and their parents. This, of course, was the main source in the treated cases also but it was undoubtedly (and unavoidably) true that the picture of the treated boys' adjustment was more detailed, to say the least, than that of the controls.

With these limitations of the follow-up study in mind, a topical outline for guiding and recording the interviews with the C-boys and their parents was drawn up. (The term "topical outline" rather than "schedule" is used deliberately, for we were seeking not easily classifiable answers to a list of detailed questions but such information as would show various aspects of a boy's adjustment and would provide the basis for making a single judgment as to whether it was good, fair, or poor.) In the actual interviews the outline was followed only in the sense that an attempt was made to cover all its points; it was disregarded so far as time sequence was concerned. The points to be covered were these: Informants; House; Neighborhood; Family members; Income; Family relations. In regard to the boy, they were: Job; School; Church; Friends and recreation; Family relations; Military service; Influential adults; General impressions; Social agency, etc., contacts.

In addition to this outline, a questionnaire to be sent to school principals in cases in which the boy was still in school or had left within the last year or two was drawn up. It inquired after scholastic record, school attendance, and behavior in school.

Two counselors on the staff of the Study were chosen as the

follow-up investigators, one a woman and one a man. The man had chief responsibility for locating the boys and for interviewing them, while to the woman was assigned the task of securing pertinent data from the schools and of interviewing the parents, usually the mothers. Both of these counselors had been with the Study for a long time and had demonstrated unusual skill in establishing quick and meaningful rapport with boys and their families. Some of the C-boys were already known to them as friends of boys in the Study group. In addition, these counselors, of course, were well acquainted with the pertinent aspects of the neighborhoods in which most of the boys lived, knew many of the persons (teachers, court workers, social workers) to whom their informants might refer, and, in general, understood the culture, sociologically speaking, of the persons they were to interview. The possible disadvantage of using these persons as follow-up investigators (that they might be biased against the control group) seemed offset by two facts: they did not know the names of the "twins" of the boys they were securing information about, and their personal inclination was to "see the best" in everybody. Moreover, it was not they but the writer who made the adjustment ratings; the investigators confined themselves to reporting what they learned, without making any attempt to evaluate what they found.

EXAMPLE OF INTERVIEWS CONCERNING A CONTROL BOY'S ADJUSTMENT

Interview with Boy

John: A tall, thin lad with a sensitive face and rather effeminate mannerisms; age 19, I.Q. in the low eighties. He seemed frank, cooperative, and interested after I explained my purpose as one of helping us find out about the way boys in his neighborhood live—whether they belong to gangs, at what age they start stealing if at all, how they like school, and the like. He gave the information categorized below.

School. He left school at age 16; was very defensive about school. He found it difficult, but he blamed one teacher as the reason for his quitting, claiming that she used to accuse him of doing things that he did not do. "I couldn't stand that so I quit." He said he reads all right and can do arithmetic but spelling is "tough."

He said that he repeated the third grade twice. The facts, as we have them, are he repeated the third grade three times and the fourth grade twice. He claims that he liked school except for this one teacher.

Jobs. He did not work part-time before leaving school because his father would not let him. Ever since leaving school four years ago he has worked in a candy factory. He likes his job very much and he plans to stay there. "I don't believe in changing around." He mentioned that his father has worked at the same place for 20 or 30 years.

Asked if there was anything in the future that he would like to do he mentioned dress designing. "I notice what girls wear. Maybe some time I can do this; I don't know."

Church. A regular attendant; Roman Catholic.

Leisure time and activities. He is not particularly interested in sports but does like horseback riding, which he started this year for the first time. He also likes swimming and dancing. He was a frequent movie attendant, going about twice a week but he hasn't been to the movies for the last two months since his club now holds his interest. He says he is the life of the party. Somebody will say, "John, pep things up a bit," so he sings or dances and "plays the fool." He has to have a few drinks before he can do these things, however.

Interests. He is interested in music but does not play an instrument. He purchased a victrola-radio about two years ago and he claims to have about $500 worth of records. He is primarily interested in modern dance music. He likes dancing because he likes to have a lot of people around. A number of times and in various connections he stressed that he likes to have a lot of people around him.

Organized activities. Belonged to the City Boys' Club about five years. Thinks he began when he was about seven, going with an older brother until he was shown the way, then was able to find his way over there by himself. Has not belonged to any other organized groups.

Play places. He always played around his own neighborhood until he got older and went to various places to dance, etc. However, he does not go to public dances very much.

Friends. He has a great many friends, at least acquaintances. Two boys are his particular friends. They, too, belong to the Right Wing Club, of which John is the oldest member. Age ranges from 16 to 20; John will be 20 very soon.

The Right Wing Club. Organized about two months ago for the purpose of having a hang-out apparently. John stated, "We used to hang out on a corner. Then a cop would come along and say, 'Break it up, boys.' " The boys had nowhere to go and so decided to form this club. The president of the club is one of his best friends, and John himself was elected vice-president and treasurer. I observed downstairs that he seemed to be the boss and that all the boys were younger than he was, 16 or 17.

Family and relationships. Thinks he gets along well with his family and that he always has. Discipline at home was not too strict, although he told at some length of having to go to bed early even in the summer time. The children were never allowed out after supper, did their studying and then went to bed. He states that sometimes relatives would come to visit and they would be all sitting down on the porch when someone would say, "Where are the kids?" and his mother would say that they were in bed. The other person would say, "Why not let them come down since it's such a hot night?" but the mother would reply, "They are just as cool in bed." John said, "We used to go to sleep very soon."

He gets along well with his father, too, he said. His father is the kind of man who hates to miss a day of work. He gets up early in the morning, around six, straightens up what needs straightening, makes coffee and then goes off to work so that he will have plenty of time to get there. The rest of the family get up after the coffee has been made.

My over-all impression was that this is a family with strong ties.

Health. No complaints as to physical health although he had referred to nervousness. I asked him about this. He said that his stomach rolls and that he sweats inside. When he is in church his stomach will begin to roll and he'll begin to perspire. "But I've never had to leave," he said with pride.

He said he was a bed-wetter until about 14 or 15, attributing this to weak kidneys. He said he was never very much embarrassed about it because his mother never told anyone. He was rejected for military service because of these symptoms, apparently. Judging from his story he told the doctor about them, although he claims they have not occurred for the past two years. He may also have been rejected because of his low intellectual ability.

Girls. Claims he has never had a date as such, although he knows a lot of girls and says the girls like him. His best friend now has a girl but, for himself, he prefers to hang out with the gang.

Sex. I asked him if he ever had any unfortunate sex experiences and he described a brief homosexual encounter.

Smoking. Began at age 16.

Drinking. He does drink but "knows when to stop." He has felt "high" on numerous occasions. He drinks chiefly for social reasons when he goes to a party. Has been drunk only once—on V-J Day. Said about drinking, "It makes you feel good. I like to be happy, and it makes me feel happy."

Delinquencies. He denied all gambling, truancy, or other delinquency. I recalled to his mind a railroad trespass charge in 1935. He said he and some other fellows were in the railroad yard. They had set fire to some strips of paper. One of the bits of paper blew into a car and he leaped in, put the fire out, and when he jumped out he jumped right into the arms of a cop. However, nothing untoward came of this. Evidently the boys had to report about a month later and John said, "The woman told them I was a good boy and I got off."

Interview with Mother

At first the mother did not seem to remember the original home visit I had made but was perfectly willing to talk with me. I read her a little bit of the report I had made of John when he was in the second grade and she said that it fitted him perfectly. She said he still is a very nervous boy and didn't get into the Army because of this nervousness. He was very unhappy about it for a time but soon became reconciled and is now glad that he didn't have to go.

He wasn't enthusiastic about school but he never played truant. He never missed school except when he was ill. He graduated from the seventh grade. He has difficulty in reading, but the mother said it is amazing how well he writes letters. He wrote every night to his friends in the service.

He sings very well. The mother put a record on the victrola that he made himself. He sounded a bit like Frank Sinatra.

One of his evidences of nervousness was the fact that he wet the bed until he was 16. He never was much of an athlete and was more interested in staying around the house with his mother; he liked to knit. However, he did join the Boys' Club with his older brother and he still belongs to this organization. He goes to dances now and then but he much prefers to stay at home and play the radio. He likes the house to be in spic and span order; if he finds it upset, he will turn to and straighten up.

He is working in a candy factory and averages about $30 a week. He is saving his money.

Mother said that none of her boys ever gave her any trouble. I asked if she thought John had been overprotected. She said that the grandmother had overprotected him but now she doesn't interfere too much in their lives. The mother feels that John is a very fine young man but he is perhaps too much like a girl in some ways, especially in his interest in fine things and in fixing things around the house.

He hasn't a girl friend and isn't a bit like his brothers, who are much interested in sports and girls.

He goes to church regularly but he isn't as active a member as his brother, who never misses a day.

The parents would like to move to the country where John could have a garden, because he is very much interested in flowers. He plants windowboxes around the house and would like to have a bigger garden in the yard but the old people who live downstairs want a vegetable garden. They are all saving their money in anticipation of moving to the country as soon as real estate becomes available.

There is no jealousy among her children, the mother said; she has had no trouble with them.

On the basis of such data, the C-boys were classified with regard
to terminal adjustment in accordance with the categories defined
at the beginning of this chapter. No claim is made for a high degree
of accuracy in these ratings, especially in the distinction between
the neurotic sub-types and the others, but in most cases the boy
seemed to fit quite clearly into the category to which he was assigned.

The following examples of C-boys placed in the various adjustment groups serve to illustrate both the kind of data on which the
classification was based and the categories themselves.[7]

1. Good Adjustment

Example 1. Richard: age 19; S.A. 114; K.A. 107. This boy was a high
school graduate who said he had always liked school. From the time he
was 13 until he entered the Army he had had after-school and Saturday
jobs and had worked steadily at them. He had many friends of both
sexes. Some of his boyhood gang had become delinquents and were now
in the reformatory, he said. He was interested in all sports; other interests were stamp collecting and reading novels. He had been a Scout
and a member of the Catholic Youth Organization. Family relations
were good; he and his father and siblings had gone through much
trouble together, he said, after his mother's death when he was 14.

Example 2. Hugh: age 15 years, 9 months; K.A. 97. This boy was in his
first year in the vocational school and expected to continue to gradua-
tion. He said he liked school fairly well. He had had odd jobs for the past
two years. He took much interest in sports and participated actively in
them. His hobbies were repairing old motors and typewriters, and he
liked to read books about scientists. He had many friends in his neighborhood and had a normal amount of interest in girls. He had been a
member of the YMCA and the Scouts since about 12. As to delinquencies, when younger he did a bit of "hopping cars," sneaking admission to
movies, and breaking windows, but he had no delinquency record. His
relations with his family were good.

2a. Fairly Good

Example 3. Cliff: age 17 years, 6 months; K.A. 89; S.A. 72. Having disliked school and been a truant fairly often, this boy left at the earliest

[7] In the following examples K.A. refers to Kuhlmann-Anderson I.Q.; S.B. refers to
Stanford-Binet I.Q.; and S.A. refers to Stanford Achievement test score in relation to
chronological age, i.e., educational quotient.

possible age and found a job. He had worked regularly for several years but was unemployed at the time of the follow-up visit. His hobby was bicycle repairing. He belonged to a gang that "hung around" grilles, went to the movies, and played pool together. He had little interest in girls. Enuresis had persisted till 15; he had a slight stutter. Family relations were said to be satisfactory.

Example 4. Victor: age 19; K.A. 98; S.B. 115. This boy left school at 16 and had frequent job changes before joining the Army, from which he had been recently honorably discharged. As a boy, his mother said, he was watched by the police, and he himself told the follow-up investigator that he was once involved in some stealing but he was scared off by his mother and the police. He was still a member of the Black Crow gang. Family relations appeared to be satisfactory. He had a girl friend, and he was hoping to become an auto mechanic.

2b. *Fairly Good: Neurotic Type*

Example 5. Eddie: age 17; S.A. 76; K.A. 99. A third-year high school student, this boy said he liked school very much and hoped to go on to college. He told of having worked in his father's bakery since 10 years of age and having saved $600. He disapproved of movies, he said, and had never attended one. He had no really close friends, boys or girls, no "dates," and had never engaged in any kind of delinquency. Family relations were close.

3a. *Rather Poor*

Example 6. Walter: age 19; S.A. 73, K.A. 89. A boy with several convictions for delinquency, he was on parole when interviewed. He had no job but was hoping to find one soon. He claimed to be avoiding his former bad companions and to have made new friends. He had the usual adolescent's interests in sports and girls. Family relations were fairly satisfactory.

Example 7. Leo: age 16; K.A. 94; S.A. 106. This boy, who had left school very recently said he had disliked it very much and had played truant most of the time. He apparently had never had a job and still had none but had applied for one. He put forward as his only reason for wanting a job his great interest in baseball and his need for money to participate in the game. His friendships were apparently limited to two boys, though he said he knew many others. Not much was learned about family relations but it seemed likely that they were not very good.

3b. *Rather Poor: Neurotic Type*

Example 8. Dan: age 19 years, 6 months; S.A. 91, S. B. 85. This boy quit school in the eighth grade. He was now working in a bowling alley at low pay. He had been in the Navy, where he had done rather poorly. A Navy psychiatrist had diagnosed his somatic complaints as being neurotic symptoms. The boy had no special friend, according to his own account, but went with a group of boys and had "dates" with one girl. He had never belonged to a club; up to the age of 17 he had engaged in considerable stealing.

4a. Definitely Poor

Example 9. Frank: age 17 years, 6 months; S.A. 62; K.A. 87. This boy was always in much difficulty in school and left at an early age. He changed jobs frequently and was unemployed when interviewed. His delinquency record was rather lengthy and he had twice been in reform school. At the time of the interview he was on parole. He had the usual interests of a dull boy in a delinquent neighborhood and was regarded by his family as very difficult to manage.

4b. Definitely Poor: Neurotic or Otherwise Emotionally Disabled

Example 10. Raymond: age 18 years, 6 months; K.A. 91; S.A. 91. This boy's mother reported that he had always been very nervous, that he never liked school because he resented being bossed, and that he had never held a job for long because he liked to fool around too much. Two months before the interview he had been discharged from the Navy because of stomach ulcers and nervousness. He had few, if any, friends, and had always been, in his mother's opinion, a problem child.

4c. Definitely Poor: Chronic Delinquent

Example 11. Leo: age 15; K.A. 100. This was an aggressive, "hard-boiled" youngster who played truant frequently, disliked school intensely, and was a serious behavior problem there. He spent most of his time "hanging around" and shooting crap, and had little interest even in athletics. He had some friends, one of whom was on parole from a correctional institution. He had engaged extensively in delinquency —had done much stealing and damaging of property—and was a frequent runaway. He apparently greatly enjoyed his boldness in those activities and was said to be getting worse from year to year. He was probably a neurotic boy, being very hostile to authority of any type.

Classified according to these categories the distribution of the 148 C-boys who were followed was as follows: good, 52; fairly good, 58; rather poor, 19; definitely poor, 19. Before comparing these ratings with those of the treated boys their reliability will be tested by comparison with the delinquency ratings made by the Study staff members and described above (see p. 394 this chapter). For that comparison 109 boys were available, those being the boys who were 17½ or older when the ratings were made. The figures are given in Table 68.

TABLE 68

Comparison of C-Boys' Adjustment Ratings According to
Two Systems of Classification

Study's Delinquency Judgments [a]	WRITER'S RATING OF TERMINAL ADJUSTMENT								
	1	2a	2b	3a	3b	4a	4b	4c	Total
I	—	—	—	3	—	1	—	9	13
II	1	2	—	4	4	2	2	—	15
IV	8	12	4	1	1	1	1	—	28
V	30	9	12	—	2	—	—	—	53
Total	39	23	16	8	7	4	3	9	109

[a] See p. 394.

It will be noted that there was little disagreement at the extremes. In addition, when the individual cases were examined, most of the apparent disagreement was found to be largely attributable to differences in the rating systems themselves, the Study's classification of delinquents being concerned with the total history of a boy's career so far as delinquency was concerned and the writer's being concerned with "terminal adjustment" both socially and emotionally considered.

For example, the boy rated 1 by the writer and put in Group II by the Study's raters had been regarded as quite difficult as a youngster, being, according to his own story, a frequent truant and doing much hopping of trucks, fighting as a gang member, and petty stealing until about 15. He had greatly disliked school but had always been much interested in machinery. However, while still in school he had held many jobs and always had many friends. At the time of the follow-up interview he had been steadily employed on one job for three years, had several good friends of both sexes, made a hobby of mechanics, and got along well with his family.

Apparent differences in the ratings in other cases were similarly explainable. When the difference in what was being rated is taken into account, the table demonstrates a high degree of reliability in the classification. With this established, we can make the comparison with the "treated" boys with some assurance that it is justified.

The distribution of the terminal adjustment ratings of the 148 boys in the control series and their "treated twins" is shown in

Table 69. As will be noted the distribution of the two series is strikingly similar. Even granted a certain amount of inaccuracy in the ratings (an inaccuracy that obtained to some extent in the treated series as well as in the control), it would appear difficult to maintain that the presence of Study services made any great difference in the terminal adjustment of the T-boys.

TABLE 69

Distribution of T-Boys and Their C-Twins by Terminal Adjustment Ratings

Terminal Adjustment	T	C
1. Good adjustment	46	52
2a. Fairly good	38	42
2b. Fairly good; neurotic type	21	16
3a. Rather poor	11	9
3b. Rather poor; neurotic type	12	10
4a. Definitely poor	4	4
4b. Definitely poor; neurotic, psychotic, neurological disorder	7	4
4c. Definitely poor; chronic delinquent	9	11
Total	148	148

Before that conclusion can be accepted as established, however, we must see whether age was a factor in the situation. The follow-up study was spread over a considerable period of time (about one and a half years) and a simultaneous follow-up of all the treated boys was not made. Information about the latter boys beyond the time their cases were closed, terminated, or dropped was secured in various ways, if at all. In some cases the boys kept in close touch with their counselors of their own accord. In others, information about them came to the counselors' attention even though they did not see the boys themselves. Some of the boys who were "dropped" at a relatively early age were followed by the male investigator who interviewed the C-boys. In a considerable number of cases, however, nothing was known of the T-boy after work with him ended. Consequently, in 38 cases the C-boy was from two to five years older than his T-twin when his adjustment was rated, while in 20 cases the T-boy was the older by two years or more. This latter situation occurred in cases in which the C-boy was one of the first who were followed and information about the "twin" was secured just as the investigation ended.

The age distribution of the two groups at the time terminal adjustment was rated was as follows:

Age	Treated	Control
11–12	4	0
13–14	13	11
15–16	36	42
17–18	64	51
19–21	31	44
Total	148	148

It will be noted that the number under 17 was the same in the two groups but that there were more boys under 15 in the treatment series and more over 18 in the control.

Age, however, has been shown in Table 63 to have borne rather little relation to adjustment in the treatment series. This was also true in the control group. In both series, for instance, the proportion of boys having a rating of 3 or 4 was, with a few exceptions, about the same in the various age groups, as the following listing of percentages indicates:

Age	Treated	Control
11–12	25	0
13–14	0	36
15–16	31	12
17–18	27	30
19–21	34	38

In spite of the lack of relation between age and adjustment it seemed of interest to make the comparison of the adjustment ratings of pairs of boys whose age difference was not more than one year. The distribution then was that shown in Table 70.

The comparison may also be made on the basis of individual pairs of boys who differed in age by not more than one year (see Table 71). In no two pairs, of course, were the boys really identical; they had, however, been matched fairly closely with respect to a configuration of traits regarded as relevant to social adjustment (see Chapter VI), and it was believed by the planners of the investigation that some degree of similarity between the paired individ-

TABLE 70

Distribution of T-Boys and Their C-Twins by
Terminal Adjustment Ratings
(Age Held Constant)

Terminal Adjustment	T	C
1. Good adjustment	23	27
2a. Fairly good	21	28
2b. Fairly good; neurotic type	13	8
3a. Rather poor	7	8
3b. Rather poor; neurotic type	12	6
4a. Definitely poor	2	1
4b. Definitely poor; neurotic, psychotic, neurological disorder	5	2
4c. Definitely poor; chronic delinquent	8	11
Total	91	91

uals had been established. It seemed fairly justifiable, therefore, to use as one test of the effectiveness of the Study this comparison of individual pairs so long as the emphasis on distribution of ratings within groups was retained.

TABLE 71

Comparison of Paired Boys of Similar Age, with Respect to Terminal Adjustment

T-Boys' Ratings [a]	C-BOYS' RATINGS				
	1	2	3	4	Total
1	8	11	1	3	23
2	9	13	9	3	34
3	5	9	2	3	19
4	5	3	2	5	15
Total	27	36	14	14	91

[a] In this and subsequent comparisons the sub-categories in the terminal adjustment scale are omitted.

The table indicates even more clearly than the comparison of the total distributions that the C-boys were just as likely as the T-boys to achieve a good social adjustment. In 28 pairs of cases the two boys were given an identical rating; in 30 pairs the T-boy was superior and in 33 pairs the C-boy. If Categories 1 and 2 are combined and regarded as good adjustment and Categories 3 and 4 regarded as poor, it will be seen that 55 pairs were similarly rated, while in 16 pairs the T-boy made a superior adjustment and in 22 pairs the C-boy. In other words, in about 40 percent of the pairs a marked difference between the boys appeared, but this difference was just about as likely to be in favor of the C-boy as in favor of the one who was the Study client. The distribution, in short, was that to be expected by chance.

The conclusion that the C-boys turned out just about as well as the boys who had the benefit of the Study's services appears to be further attested by a comparison of the two groups with respect to the Selection Committee ratings. It will be recalled that all the boys chosen for study were rated by a committee with respect to likelihood of delinquency and were paired, to a considerable extent, on that basis. It has been shown above that these predictions were not very accurate so far as the treated boys were concerned, and it was thought that the treated boys' better-than-expected adjustment might be due in part to the influence of the Study. Tabulation of the C-group figures showed, however, that many of the control boys, too, adjusted better than anticipated. The question, then, is: did the T-boys do better than the C-boys of similar Selection Committee rating? The figures are given in Table 72.

With Selection Committee ratings held constant (that is, when T- and C-boys of identical ratings are compared) it is shown in Table 72 that the C-boys did just about as well as the T-boys with respect to terminal adjustment.[8] As has been said before, the Selection Committee ratings and those for terminal adjustment cannot be equated, particularly because the Selection Committee was thinking in terms of delinquency rather than general social adjustment. If, however, for the sake of comparison it is assumed that a boy with a Selection Committee delinquency prognosis of +3 or +2 would be expected to make a "good" adjustment, one with a rating of +1 or 0 to make a "fairly good" adjustment, one with a rating of

[8] Apparently the Selection Committee ratings were no more reliable for the C-group than for the T-boys, perhaps even less so. For example, of the 12 C-boys with Selection Committee ratings from −3 to −5, seven were found to be adjusting at least fairly well when the follow-up study was made. At the other end of the scale the predictions were more accurate: only one of the 24 boys rated +2 or +3 by the Selection Committee was adjusting poorly when last known. As with the T-boys, the terminal adjustments of the C-boys were apparently better on the whole than the committee expected.

TABLE 72

Comparison of T- and C-Boys Regarding Correspondence between Terminal Adjustment and Selection Committee Rating

| Selection Committee Rating | | TERMINAL ADJUSTMENT RATING | | | | |
		1	*2*	*3*	*4*	*Total*
+3	T	—	—	—	—	—
	C	2	1	—	—	3
+2	T	9	6	—	—	15
	C	13	7	1	—	21
+1	T	9	9	4	—	22
	C	4	6	2	1	13
0	T	4	6	1	2	13
	C	1	6	2	2	11
−1	T	11	16	9	6	42
	C	17	21	6	4	48
−2	T	10	16	5	8	39
	C	13	12	8	7	40
−3	T	2	6	3	4	15
	C	1	2	—	4	7
−4	T	—	1	—	1	2
	C	1	2	—	—	3
−5	T	—	—	—	—	—
	C	—	1	—	1	2
Total	T	45	60	22	21	148
	C	52	58	19	19	148

—1 or —2 a "rather poor" adjustment, and one with a lower rating a "poor" adjustment, it will be found in Table 72 that 79 treated boys and 75 controls made a better adjustment than expected and that 27 in each group made a poorer one. In other words, as judged by this test, the C-boys did just about as well as those who had the benefit of the Study's services.[9]

[9] Even if the above assumption about the meaning of the Selection Committee ratings is not justified, the table is of interest in indicating the relative standing of the T- and C-boys, Selection Committee ratings being held constant.

One might be inclined to leave the matter there and conclude that the Study's services were no more effectual in producing good social adjustment than the usual events of boys' lives. This, of course, is what the figures indicate so far as the group as a whole is concerned. The conclusion seems justified, then, that delinquency and social maladjustment are not prevented by programs under which hard-working, well-disposed individuals do all they can to offset the disadvantages under which "difficult" boys live. Since there are many programs, and many proposals for programs, of this general kind, the Study would seem to have been worth while if it did no more than make that point clear.

To one who has studied the records, however, there seems more to it than that. The Study counselors were certain that some of the boys had been significantly aided and some of the case records seemed to substantiate that belief. We must examine the material from that angle, then, and, if the counselors' impressions seem to be correct, consider carefully why this fact was not revealed by the statistics. This search for a further explanation of the figures in Table 71 is also justified by our previously expressed doubt about the validity of the control-group method for the present investigation. As has been said before, the diversity of boys served and the diversity of methods used make one dubious as to just what has been tested by the preceding comparisons. We propose, therefore, before arriving at final conclusions about the effectiveness of this kind of work, to reverse the control-group method, as it were, by attempting to determine case by case whether or not the boys benefited and then seeing whether the T-boys who did benefit made a better terminal adjustment than their C-"twins." By so doing, we assume that the benefit of an organization's services can be more or less accurately assessed by case-record analysis and that the question to be answered through the control group is: Does such benefit make any perceptible difference in the relatively long run?

Judgments as to the organization's effectiveness that are made case by case will also serve an additional purpose: they will provide data through which we may possibly determine the circumstances (in the boys' lives and in the treatment methods) under which the Study was or was not helpful. Social work has much need for such differential statements, for it is obvious that no one type of service will meet the needs of all boys who are in difficulty. The Study's program, of course, did not provide the whole gamut of possible services but it did provide a considerable variety of them to a considerable variety of boys. If we can discover not only that its services, when effective, resulted in better social functioning (as judged by comparison with the C-group) but also with what boys and by what means those services became effective, we should have at hand conclusions of real value to social work.

CHAPTER XXV

VALUE OF
THE STUDY TO
INDIVIDUAL BOYS

TO DETERMINE WHICH BOYS WERE HELPED BY THE STUDY SERVICES
requires the making of difficult decisions. "Helped" to what?
"Value" for what? Those are the basic questions. Reference to the
narrow objectives of the Study suggests that the answer should be
"helped to avoid delinquency"; reference to the broad objective
suggests "value for character development." The impossibility of
determining in any particular case so negative a factor as help in
avoiding something led to the control-group plan, for surely one
can seldom say that such-and-such a boy would have been delinquent if the Study worker had not been on the scene. As to value
for character development, neither the control-group method nor
one of individual analysis would seem of much use, for strength and
depth of character cannot be measured, in spite of the implication
of the terms, nor is it possible to demonstrate that any particular
event or series of events contributed to the development of a boy's
character.

The value or the help that is in question when judgments about
the usefulness of a social agency's services are being made can, however, be defined by reference to the function of social work. This
can be seen when the "value for character development" argument
is pursued a bit further. Stated most generally, the function of social
work is to help individuals deal with the difficulties that stand in
the way of their playing their required part in organized social
groups or in making use of those groups' services. Youth has a culturally prescribed role to play in relation to family, school, job,
neighborhood, government, and informal associations of friends,

but not all individuals are able to play their part adequately or to take advantage of the opportunities afforded by the various social institutions, such as schools and recreational associations. The value of a social agency's services to a particular individual should be judged, then, by whether it helped him play his socially assigned role better—whether, for instance, in consequence of the agency's services he could function better in school, be more law-abiding, relate himself better to his companions, and so on.

Obviously, services can be of value without having such consequences. For example, a boy may go to camp, take art lessons, acquire a good friend without any noticeable change in his general behavior or in his relations with people; the value may lie in his enjoyment of the activities and in the broadening and enrichment of his life. Educational and recreational institutions operate on this basis: their services are given, not to help the individual deal with difficulties that stand in the way of the socialization process, but to further that process by direct methods, and the value of their services is to be judged thereby. The Study, however, was not such an institution, although it used some of those institutions' methods. For example, the Study provided tutoring if boys needed it. Its aim in doing so, however, was not only the direct one of improving the boy's ability to read or understand arithmetical processes, as would be a school's aim. The Study provided this service if the counselor thought that lack of ability to read was handicapping the boy in his social adjustment; the service, therefore, would be judged of value not on the basis of the boy's improvement in reading but by reference to his behavior in school and elsewhere.

The value of the Study services had to be judged, then, not by whether the boys enjoyed the opportunities afforded or by whether their range of interests was broadened or by whether they became closely attached to the counselors, but by whether, through the services, the difficulties that stood in the way of their socialization were lessened and they operated better in family, school, job, and so on. In a sense, then, the value of the Study in individual cases was judged by improvement in what is commonly called "social adjustment." A boy, however, was rated as helped only if it could be shown that obstacles to his social adjustment, either in the boy himself or in his environmental circumstances, were dealt with by the counselors, and the boy, apparently in consequence, functioned better in social relations. Moreover, in the classification system described below, we took into account how sure we were that it was the Study services that had produced the change, a distinction being made between cases in which we were sure the counselors had been helpful and those in which the value of their services seemed dubious.

It will be noted that we are not proposing that a given boy be regarded as helped merely because his adjustment became better, which is the test used in many psychiatric follow-up investigations. We are saying that it is expected that a boy handicapped in a certain way will improve if that handicap is removed. If, therefore, the provision of Study services did remove the handicap and the boy's adjustment did improve, we say that the improvement was due (in part, at least) to those services. In other words, our judgments refer not only to the boy's behavior but to the conditions believed to influence that behavior. These judgments are validated, to some extent, if it can be shown that the boys who were rated as benefited differed from those who were not benefited, both in the nature of their handicaps and in the measures that were used to aid them.

In this evaluation, emphasis was placed on how sure we were that the boy had been helped, not on how good his adjustment became. A boy who was originally very much maladjusted might have received much help and still not be functioning as adequately as another boy who apparently was helped only slightly or perhaps not at all by the counselors' efforts. The extent of relation between amount of help received and terminal social adjustment will be shown later through comparison of the two series of ratings.

A classification of "value of service" requires that each category be sufficiently defined and its limits set sufficiently clearly that competent judges can agree fairly well in the rating of cases. In this study, however, the judgments were made only by the writer; they were not tested by formal submission to other judges, although there was a certain amount of informal checking by reason of the fact that case records were abstracted and rated by several readers (of whom the writer was one) before final judgment was passed. Such a procedure was followed because it was thought that adequate judgments could not be made unless all the records were studied and compared with as much care as was given by the writer to the task; for a larger number of judges that would be too time-consuming a job.

In the following descriptions of categories the considerations that led to the placing of cases in particular groups will be stated, and the cases themselves will later be described and compared. The reader will have at hand, therefore, some of the facts on which the writer's judgments were based and can check the ratings for himself.

VALUE-OF-SERVICE CATEGORIES

In order to compare the boys in these various ways it was necessary, of course, to divide them into groups on the basis of the extent to which they appeared to be benefited by the Study services. We accordingly set up the following descriptive categories, which were arrived at through careful comparison of the individual case records.

A. Boy clearly aided by the services.
B. Services possibly of some assistance but not much change in behavior effected.
C. Little accomplished in spite of friendly relations.
D. Services ineffectual:
    1. Boy or parents refused help.
    2. Work of counselors slight or of poor quality.
    3. Other reasons.
E. Boy did not need help.

Definitions and examples of each of these types will be given below, while in later chapters analyses of all the cases within each category will be made.

It is to be emphasized that it is not the type of service but the changes effected by it that are under consideration here; if we mention type of service, it is only to elaborate upon the nature of its effect. Similarly, we are not primarily classifying the boys' adjustment, although that necessarily entered into the evaluation of how influential the work was. The work might be influential, however, even though a boy did not become well adjusted; conversely, a boy might become well adjusted for reasons other than the receiving of the service. With these reservations, then, the following are the value-of-service categories.

A. Boy Clearly Aided by the Services. In these cases the connection between the boy's improvement in social adjustment and the help given him by the counselors seemed indisputable. This is not to say that the Study was the only beneficial factor in the situation or that the boy became thoroughly well adjusted; in some cases, in fact, the boy had many favorable factors in his environmental situation and never was very maladjusted, while in others he was severely handicapped and made only moderate gains. What we mean, then, by an A rating is that the services appeared to be genuinely helpful and that without them it seems unlikely that the boy would have done as well as he did.

The basis on which such judgments were made varied considerably from case to case. In some the improvement in adjustment followed rapidly when, through the counselor's efforts, certain specific handicaps were removed; in others the good results seemed attributable largely to the work of social or psychiatric agencies whose services the counselor secured for the boy. Examples 1 and 2 illustrate the effects produced in cases of these kinds.

Example 1. Vincent (age 12; I.Q. 90) was an Italian boy whom the school authorities described as a child who was a bully and a daydreamer. They said he had poor work habits, and they suspected him of cheating and stealing. Little of this behavior was evidenced after the Study work started; instead Vincent's chief difficulties were inactivity and sluggishness, called laziness by the teachers. In addition he had severe nightmares and some head jerking and he did very poor work in school.

Vincent's mother was described as a rather neurotic, sickly woman who, when the case was opened, was living with her parents, her husband maintaining a separate dwelling place. She was fond of Vincent but disciplined him severely. The father appeared to be a stable person, interested in and concerned about his five children, but he, too, was very stern with Vincent. After some years the parents resumed their joint household, and life went more smoothly between them. The family was under considerable financial strain (the father was a night watchman), but the house and neighborhood in which they lived were fairly adequate.

During the first year of work with Vincent, chief emphasis was put on tutoring. He was found to be very much lacking in basic knowledge and to have little ability at abstract reasoning. He was interested in being helped. He soon began to do good work at school and his night-mares ceased.

The next year attempts were made to find a physical basis for the boy's difficulties. One doctor suspected epilepsy, another thyroid deficiency, while a psychiatrist said the disorder was functional and that it rep-resented a reaction to the very severe discipline at home. Acting on the latter suggestion, the counselor discussed the matter with the father and found him very willing to try to be less strict. The mother was less quickly responsive to the counselor's suggestions, but, after he allayed her fear that the boy was physically disabled and overcame her defen-siveness, she, too, agreed to change her tactics, remarking that her son always had responded best to an "indirect approach." Vincent himself was relieved to know that the psychiatrist thought there was nothing physically wrong with him. Soon after the parents gave up their severe disciplining, Vincent's nightmares and head jerking ceased and did not return during the following four years in which the counselors were in touch with him. During those latter years very little was done with or for Vincent, partly because he and his family wanted to forget about his "wacky" period.

Example 2. Edwin was considered an average boy by the teacher who referred him to the Study. He was somewhat irritable, however, and somewhat annoying to the other children, and before Study work was started, he was investigated by the Delinquency Squad because of steal-ing schoolbooks. His mother said he lied rather frequently and was very jealous of his sister. He had no close friends but played well with a group of boys. The mother was in a tuberculosis sanatorium when the case opened, and a social agency had arranged for the care of the three younger children in boarding homes. Edwin was living at home with his father, who was frequently drunk, and was partially cared for by a neighbor. Even before the mother left home, there had been consider-able quarreling between the parents, and the children were frequently unsupervised. The mother was very fond of Edwin but the father was said to be harsh with him, though interested in his welfare.

During the first year the counselor had little contact with Edwin beyond taking him to visit his mother and arranging for a camp in which he could remain until another agency active on the case could find a boarding home for him. The counselor visited the mother fairly often, giving her reports on Edwin's progress, which pleased her greatly. The boy was placed with his aunt, who had other foster children, and stayed with her for two years. The aunt then decided that she could keep him no longer, saying he always had been a very difficult child and was becoming harder to handle. She wanted him placed through the Division of Child Guardianship, for which organization she worked, but Edwin disliked this idea very much, not wanting to be a "state child."

During this period of decision the counselor had frequent interviews with the mother and arranged for Edwin to be examined at a child guidance clinic. Not much was discovered about the boy, for the psychiatrist found him unusually reticent, but it was advised that placement through a private agency be arranged, so the Study referred the boy to a children's aid society. That agency found a good foster home for him, and he did well there after a brief period of being very stubborn and defiant of authority. The counselor had considerable correspondence with the mother, who by this time had been sent to a sanatorium in another state, and he took Edwin to visit her once. When this counselor left the Study, the case was dropped, as no service seemed needed beyond, perhaps, keeping the mother cheered.

In other cases the helpfulness of the counselors seemed to derive largely from the emotional relationship established with the boy. In most such cases the counselor acted as a kindly representative of the adult world, and his advice and guidance were accepted by the boy, as were the opportunities he provided for recreation, improvement in health and school progress, and the like.

Example 3. Spencer was a French Canadian boy referred to the Study by his parochial-school teachers because he had done some petty stealing and stayed out late at night. They said he was too old for his age (about 11) but intelligent, sociable, and interested in the usual boy activities. His two brothers nearest to him in age were also semi-delinquent. The parents were quiet, modest people, fond of their seven children though rather nagging and ignorant of their needs.

The work in this case was carried on by one person throughout the period of Study contact. This worker found Spencer a pleasant, friendly boy, very outgoing and much interested in earning money to further his athletic interests. Service in this case was given both to the mother and the boy, though chiefly to the latter. The counselor's relationship with both was very close.

With the mother the counselor had occasional friendly interviews. For example, the mother asked for her help when one of the boys was taken to court for stealing a bicycle; the counselor went with her to court and was able to be of assistance there. In another crisis, of a domestic nature, the counselor helped the mother to see that her taking a job was undermining her husband's self-confidence. Later, when Spencer was an adolescent, she explained to the mother the boy's need for privacy and arranged that he be given his own bed and bureau.

With Spencer the counselor had many interviews in which they discussed his school work, his ambitions, his work plans, sex information, and so on. At the boy's request he was sent to camp for several summers, after the first year in the capacity of a junior counselor. At about 15,

Spencer and one of his brothers were caught attempting to snatch a woman's purse and were put on probation to the counselor. The counselor took Spencer to task for such conduct and later upbraided him when he did not keep his appointments regularly with her. Episodes like these led Spencer to say, "I like her best when she gives me hell."

After the case was terminated and Spencer had entered the Navy, he kept up a lively correspondence with the counselor, discussing his athletic interests, race prejudice, and his worries about his brothers. The counselor's letters usually ended with an admonition to attend faithfully to his religious duties and to set a good example. Once Spencer testified to the value of the counselor's services as follows: "I wonder what would have happened to me if I hadn't met you. I'd be in an institution for sure. I never was able to talk to grown-ups till you came along. When they spoke to me, I'd tell them to go to hell. I couldn't even talk to my mother."

In still other cases the connection between particular acts and attitudes on the part of the counselor and the boy's improvement was less clear, partly because so great a variety of services was given over the years. The net effect, however, seemed to be good. In a sense, these cases show the Study work at its best, in that the long-continued service contemplated by Dr. Cabot was both rendered and found valuable. Because of the diverse nature of the work in these cases it is particularly hard to choose a suitable example. The one described below is a case in which the good results were achieved largely by one counselor, the others giving little or ineffectual service. Other more lengthy cases of the general type will be described in Chapter XXVI, which deals with all the "successful" cases.

Example 4. At the outset Adam was a chronic truant and a listless, slovenly, dull pupil when in school. He was ten and a half years old at that time; his I.Q. was 80. His very unfavorable home situation has been described above (Chapter XXII). To recapitulate briefly. Adam's father was frequently drunk and abusive and often under arrest. His mother was described by the relief authorities as dirty, slovenly, low-grade, and very demanding, and her relatives were regarded as immoral and queer. Close acquaintance, however, showed her to have sincere affection for her children and a desire to further their best interests. The family lived in a house that was condemned as uninhabitable. Of the nine children, several were delinquents.

The first counselor started his contact with Adam by visiting his school. There he found the boy and his siblings so persistently truant that the school authorities had about given the situation up as hopeless. The counselor decided his first aim would be to get Adam to school. During the first few months he had numerous interviews with the mother, the relief authorities, the school principal, the delinquency squad, and so on, listening to their complaints and hoping the police would persist in their plan to break up the family. The children were placed with relatives briefly but the home was soon reestablished and Adam was transferred to a different school. There his attendance became better and the complaints about truancy stopped. This worker had few contacts with the boy or the family after his initial efforts, accepting the other agencies' judgment about the hopelessness of the situation.

The effective work in the case was done in two rather long periods by a worker who was away from the organization for some time in war service. At the time work was started, Adam's older brother was in reform school and Adam was on probation for stealing a bicycle. The counselor very quickly arranged that Adam should go to camp. He then began frequent visits to the mother, discussing with her the boys' predicament and taking her often to see the older son. He helped her to get a legal separation and encouraged her daughter to support her in this decision. From Adam in camp he received several letters, all telling of his gratitude for being sent there. In the fall he helped the boy join a neighborhood house group, which his pals joined also, and he took him frequently to play football on the commons.

On his return from the Army (during which time two other workers had been assigned to the case but had done little), this counselor resumed his frequent visits to the home and continued to talk with the mother about her marital difficulties which, apparently in consequence, became less severe. He assisted Adam in applying for work with the Merchant Marine, which involved some difficulty because of his probation record. In consequence Adam became very friendly and they had talks that were "man to man." The mother did not allow the boy to join the Merchant Marine, but a year or so later Adam sought the counselor's help in getting into the U.S. Coast Guard instead.

Throughout his work with this family the counselor played what he called a "Dutch uncle" role. This combination of authoritative pronouncements and concrete aid seemed very pleasing to them. During the years the family's economic situation improved greatly, the mother became relaxed and happy, and there was great change for the better in Adam's behavior.

B. Services Possibly of Some Assistance But Not Much Change in Behavior Effected. Three types of cases were grouped together in this category—the first two listed in subsequent tables as B1, the other as B2. In B1 were put the cases in which (a) a relatively well-adjusted boy appeared to derive some slight benefit from the concrete services the counselors were able to afford him, and (b) a more maladjusted boy was probably helped but the total effect seemed rather slight.

1. Slight benefit. The following example is that of a rather maladjusted boy who may have benefited slightly from the counselors' efforts.

Example 5. Kevin, nine and a half, was a boy of average intelligence (I.Q. 102) who was described by the police as a wild, troublesome youngster. He had been a patient of a mental hygiene clinic his first year in school. At the time work with him began he had apparently settled down so far as school conduct was concerned and was doing well in his studies. He seemed to most observers, however, a heedless, overactive, unstable boy who was sensitive and eager to please.

Kevin's father had left the family about the time Kevin entered school. He was a man much given to drinking and had been abusive to his wife and children. He was especially unkind to Kevin, his wife said; less so to the younger sister, a tense, nervous child two years younger. The mother was an Italian woman, excitable, restless, seemingly nervous. She reprimanded the children frequently and impulsively but was otherwise overprotective of them, especially of Kevin on account of his health. The family was entirely dependent upon social agencies for support. They lived in a rather poor neighborhood, their dwelling place being the lower floor of a shabby house; later they moved to better quarters and neighborhood.

Kevin had three changes of counselor during the seven years the Study worked with him. All devoted much time and effort to him and his mother. The first one had weekly or more frequent contacts for two and half years, much of his work centering around the treatment of the boy's asthma. The doctors at the hospital to which Kevin was taken tried various remedies, all of which seemed to be of benefit for a time. Kevin was very cooperative about attending the hospital and taking the prescribed medicines. This counselor also frequently discussed with the mother her ways of handling Kevin; he thought she improved somewhat and became a bit less impetuous. Placement away from home was arranged for the sister on the basis of her poor health (both she and Kevin were T.B. suspects) but the mother would not permit this for the son, whom she greatly preferred. The counselor also gave the mother some financial assistance and helped her to find a better house in a better neighborhood.

The second counselor, who worked with Kevin for about two years, put his chief effort into trying to get the boy to discuss his emotional problems, which were believed to underlie the asthma. In this attempt he was almost wholly unsuccessful. Kevin broke many appointments and came chiefly either to get help with arithmetic or to ask for money for medicine for his mother. The mother became rather dependent on this counselor, especially in regard to medical care, and would frequently telephone to ask him to do something for her.

What the final counselor did was not very clear from the record, which consisted chiefly of descriptions of the situation. Apparently in his frequent home visits he talked chiefly about Kevin's school difficulties, with both the mother and the boy. The mother's attitude of dependency continued, so much so that the counselor wondered how the family would get along once the Study contact ended, but Kevin, though he remained friendly, did not develop a close relationship with the counselor.

Over the years Kevin changed from a restless, overactive boy to one who was fat, sluggish, and uninterested in physical activities. At the beginning he had few friends and was afraid of even the smaller boys. At that time he pretended to be a leader and a fighter but actually he engaged in petty stealing in order to buy children's friendship. Later he acquired a few friends. From about the sixth grade on, his schoolwork became steadily worse; he failed at one school and did poor work in a vocational school to which he was transferred. He often played truant. He had a few jobs, which required little skill, but did not keep any of them long. When last interviewed (at 18) he was working, had attacks of asthma less frequently than earlier, and seemed to be getting along better with his mother and his sister, who had returned home a well-adjusted child.

2. *Temporary benefit.* Sub-category B2 was distinguished from the B1 cases by the fact that the benefit afforded was only temporary. The boys in this sub-group were seemingly benefited for a time but, with change of counselors and of working methods, they slipped back into their original state of maladjustment. As will be shown in Chapter XXVI, some of them were basically too disturbed to be expected to benefit from the kind of help the Study could give, while others might have benefited if the counselors had been more persistent or skillful in their efforts. Example 6 is of the latter type.

Example 6. Stanley at twelve was a polite, reserved boy who was considered sly and deceptive by his teachers. His only playmates were children younger than himself and he was often cruel to them. His schoolwork was much behind his ability (I.Q. 98); he was suspected of petty stealing, and he was regarded by the boys as a sissy. He lived with his mother and his grandparents under unfavorable emotional conditions that have been described above (Chapter XXII).

The counselor devoted the first year largely to getting acquainted with the family and taking the boy on trips. She seldom found the mother at home but the grandparents were cordial and pleased to have a visitor. The counselor's attempts to change the grandparents' strict methods of handling the boy were ineffectual. The boy's behavior became much worse, and the mother and grandparents became even more antagonistic to him.

About this time the counselor changed her method. She had a frank talk with Stanley about the purpose of the Study, told him she realized he must feel resentful over the way he was treated at home, and offered to talk matters over with him at weekly intervals. To this the boy responded well. He kept his appointments regularly and began to improve in behavior and schoolwork. Concurrently the counselor had biweekly interviews with the mother, in which, among other matters, the possibility of getting Aid to Dependent Children help and setting up a home of her own was considered with her. Interviews with the boy did not reveal much about his intimate feelings, but he did talk about camp, the possibility of joining in some sort of club activities, and his school situation, and he seemed to be using the relationship effectively.

This favorable state continued for only a few months; then there was a break in the relationship. Perhaps the mother resented the boy's attachment to the counselor, perhaps she was disturbed by some of the facts she herself had revealed, perhaps the boy was disturbed because the counselor aligned herself with the school authorities and lectured him, lightly, about his behavior at school. At any rate, the boy began to do less well, his visits became irregular, and the counselor decided she could be of no more help to the mother, since she seemed incapable of changing her attitude toward Stanley. Shortly it was decided that a male counselor should take the case. From that time on not much was done, except that Stanley was invited to work in the Study's shop, an activity that he greatly enjoyed.

By the time the case was closed Stanley's adjustment had improved somewhat but his schoolwork and his relations with other boys remained poor. (The boys called him a sissy and a "fat slob.") He retained interest in shopwork and in the printer's trade that he was learning at school, but he resented the academic work that was its necessary accompaniment.

C. *Little Accomplished in Spite of Friendly Relations.* The cases in this category were rather misleading in that the parents or the boys regarded the counselors as good and helpful friends, sought their services frequently, and expressed much gratitude for what was done for them. There was little indication, however, that the boys' behavior or personality problems, which were never very severe, improved much or that the boys in any demonstrable way were greatly aided by the counselors' efforts, though the work could not be judged wholly ineffectual.

Example 7. Clinton was referred to the Study by a family welfare society. At school he was described as a queer, erratic boy, likable but irresponsible, and not mixing well with the other children. The parents were better educated and better situated financially than most of the Study clients. The father was a highstrung, nervous, irritable man who used such severe methods in disciplining his two children that he was reported to the Society for the Prevention of Cruelty to Children. The mother was very moody, had once been a patient of a mental hospital. Except when depressed, she treated the children well. House and neighborhood were much above the Study average.

Work in this case was sporadic. At the mother's early request, help was given in securing a tonsillectomy for the boy, for which the mother was very grateful. The story of the reasons for the family's difficulties was obtained (the father had lost his job because of facial paralysis) and assistance was secured when eviction was threatened. The father was helped to find a job, and the older son was encouraged to better his financial situation. Through these and similar efforts the family's economic situation was improved and some of the tension relieved. Not much work was done with the boy. A job at a caddy camp was secured for him several summers, periodic check-ups on his schoolwork were made, and his dislike of vocational school was discussed with him. Intelligence tests were given (I.Q. 90) and the boy was urged not to aim at preparing for a professional career.

When work with the boy ended on his 17th birthday, he was doing adequate work in the vocational school which he had at first disliked, had an after-school job at Woolworth's, and said he was enjoying bowling. Although he reported "everything swell," he did not seem spontaneous or happy, and it seemed doubtful that his adjustment had greatly improved.

D. Study Ineffectual for One or Another Reason. In setting up the sub-categories under this heading we did not attempt to take into account all the kinds of reasons for the lack of effectiveness of the Study's work. In fact the more important of them, from the viewpoint of this evaluation, can be ascertained only by inter-group comparisons. For instance, one cannot say, on the basis of a series of unsuccessful cases alone, that it was the severity of the boys' emotional maladjustment that was the barrier to effective work. Such a conclusion can logically be reached only if comparisons with a series of successful cases show many fewer such boys among the ones who were benefited. Nevertheless, there are certain obvious reasons for lack of success that serve to characterize sub-groups in this category and thus break up the total into comprehensible parts.

1. Offer of service refused. There were some cases in which the boy or more especially his parents were definitely not interested in having a counselor's help. One might argue that the interest of almost any boy and his parents could be aroused if the counselor used the right "approach" or "techniques." We took this debatable proposition into consideration by placing in this category only those cases in which the counselors put forth the usual amount of effort and apparently used the same methods that had been effective in many cases. The cases in this sub-group, then, were those in which the boy or his relatives made it clear that they did not want the Study's services, though they may have been fairly friendly and polite in their refusal and may have permitted visits for a considerable length of time.

Example 8. Herman was a boy of average intelligence who at nine appeared to be seriously maladjusted. He kicked, bit, teased other children, was very restless, made constant bids for attention, and had a complete disregard for authority. In addition, he was enuretic, had severe nightmares, and engaged in imaginative lying. He had been a patient of a child guidance clinic, which had stopped treatment because of lack of cooperation on the relatives' part. Herman's home situation was confused. He was an illegitimate child being reared by his grandmother. She at times claimed he was her child but the boy often called her grandmother. Her attitude toward Herman was one of indulgent rejection; she could not handle him at all, yet she resented the implication of inability and attributed his bad conduct to "the modern generation." During work on the case the grandmother died of cancer, and Herman lived for a time with his aunt and uncle, sensible, stable people. His mother, too, was in the picture occasionally, she having married and having had two other children. She never offered to take Herman home to live with her. Throughout the case, the financial situation of this family was good, and the house and neighborhood of the fairly prosperous variety.

At the outset of the case the grandmother was interested in having help in finding a camp for the boy but she soon obtained one through her own efforts. She strenuously resisted all efforts to get Herman back to the child guidance clinic, her refusal being based on her unwillingness to have him told about his illegitimacy. During this period the boy was taken on a few trips by the counselor, and the counselor had some talks with Herman's teacher about the boy's emotional needs. After the grand-mother's death the counselor had a few talks with the aunt about return to the clinic (which she too refused) and about foster home placement. She herself looked into boarding schools and later arranged for foster home placement through a minister's help. After that, the counselor had occasional contacts with the placement agency and with Herman in his foster homes but did little more than obtain reports about his progress. It was learned that the boy continually fluctuated from good to rather poor behavior and that he was not regarded as extremely maladjusted.

2. *Counselors' work insufficient or poor.* A second group of cases in Category D consisted of those in which the possible effectiveness of the work was not properly tested, for the counselors either did not put forth the usual amount of effort or what they did was of poorer quality than in most cases, a statement that will be docu-mented in Chapter XXVIII. In most of these cases the counselors found the boys or their parents rather uninterested but this atti-tude was not sufficient to account for the slightness of the work done with the boys.

Example 9. James, referred at seven years of age, was described as a slow-moving, stubborn child, unexpressive and babyish. He ate very poorly, was persistently enuretic, and bit his nails. His I.Q. of 84 did not seem to be sufficiently low to account for this behavior. His father was an emotionally maladjusted man who was disagreeable and harsh toward his two children, particularly toward James, whom he disliked especially. He was frequently drunk and had many quarrels with his wife. The mother was apparently fond of James but she was somewhat overprotective and restrictive of him. The family lived in a fairly good neighborhood in a good house their relatives owned but they were fre-quently in financial difficulty.

The mother responded favorably to the first counselor's offer of service, asking immediately for help in getting James to camp, talking readily of his difficulties, and attributing them to the way his father treated him. Camp was secured for the boy for two summers, and he was given some medical examinations. For the most part, however, the counselor confined her efforts to the mother, who was seldom found at home. The counselor tried to get the mother to change the father's behavior toward James, without success, of course; the counselor in-tended to do more for the boy but never got around to it.

The second counselor's efforts were of much the same nature. He was helpful in getting the mother to a mental hospital during a period of mental depression, and he arranged with the hospital for the care of the children while the mother was away. He, too, did little work with James other than arranging for camp and some medical examinations and checking on his school progress. He did finally arrange some tutoring for the boy, which met with some success. In general, however, he considered James an uninteresting boy, uncommunicative and dull, and he felt he could not secure a good relationship with him.

James was fourteen when the Study closed. His enuresis persisted, and he was doing considerable petty stealing. His friendships were shallow, and his general social relations poor. Camp counselors found him negativistic, disobedient, very shy and untrustworthy. In school, however, he was doing fair work; his adjustment there had never been very poor.

Included in this sub-category were a few cases in which not much help was needed but in which the counselors did little toward meeting the slight or temporary problems that did exist. The boys turned out well but the good results could not be attributed to the Study.

Example 10. Gregory was described by his teacher as a quick-tempered boy who held grudges. He was, she said, attention-seeking but likable and "rather a good kid." He did good schoolwork, played with many boys, and was much interested in athletics. The father died when Gregory was a small child. The mother was very fond of the boy; she told of his faults with affection and was proud of his personality and achievements.

Gregory was sent to camp the first summer the counselor worked with him and he was taken on a few trips, but little else was done with him for over two years. When Gregory was thirteen, he was demoted in school because of poor work (he apparently found the impersonal atmosphere of junior high school difficult) and, when returned to his grade, continued to do poor work. The counselor expressed concern about not having kept in touch with the boy, but when he did see him he did little but give him a "pep talk" about doing better. The teacher reported that Gregory was "just crazy about" the counselor and asked that he pay more attention to him; however, little was done. Later Gregory was involved in a minor stealing episode, for which he made restitution. After that the family moved to a good neighborhood and Gregory was changed to another school, after which there was no more difficulty. The counselor felt that his "pep talks" helped Gregory, and it may have been that they did have some effect, since the boy was so fond of him, but the good results in the case seemed attributable chiefly to other factors.

3. Other reasons for failure. In the remaining cases Study efforts proved ineffectual for reasons that must be sought through comparison with the cases in which effective help was given. All that can be said about them here is that little was accomplished even though the counselors put forth at least a moderate amount of effort and the parents were not actively opposed to the work. We state the latter point in this negative way because, actually, there was considerable resistance or at least lack of interest on the part of both parents and boys in many of the cases in this sub-group. We did not think it justifiable, however, to attribute all the lack of success to this one factor alone, so for the time being we disregarded it unless it was so marked as to make the case classifiable in D1, above.

Example 11. Luke was referred to the Study at ten years of age as a non-reader but not as a school disciplinary problem. His I.Q. was 94. He and his brother were living with their paternal grandparents and other relatives, the mother having deserted them in infancy. The grandmother was fondly indulgent of the children. At her death, about a year after Study work started, the aunt, uncle, and grandfather left the house, and the boy's father, stepmother, and three children moved in. These latter people gave Luke and his brother food and shelter but provided little supervision or affection, and the boys drifted around the homes of the various other relatives. All these homes were in rather deteriorated neighborhoods, and there was always considerable financial stress in the families.

Study work started with an attempt to overcome Luke's reading difficulty. Tests showed that Luke could read at his grade level, so tutoring in school rather than more intensive measures was secured for him. Frequent home visits were made, the grandmother and aunt being much pleased to have them, and Luke was taken on several recreational trips. Within a short time, coincident with the grandmother's illness and death, he began to play truant. The counselor had several talks with him about this, after which the truancy subsided. The counselor then began to tutor Luke in arithmetic, with fairly good results. During the tutoring sessions the boy told of his resentment against his mother for deserting him. In consequence an interview with a psychiatrist was arranged. The psychiatrist thought the boy needed treatment but Luke did not keep the appointments that were arranged for him. Throughout this period of two years or so the counselor had frequent contact with the various families concerned.

The next counselor (Luke was now about thirteen) tried to do something about the truancy, which was continuing, by securing a physical examination to see whether there was a physical basis for the frequent absences. He also spent much time listening to the aunt complain about how unsuitable a home the boy's father and stepmother were maintaining for the children. About this time Luke disappeared from home. His parents claimed to have no knowledge of his whereabouts, but on his return six months later it was learned he had been living with his uncle. Shortly after, he used his aunt's car without a driving license and for this offense was put on probation. Shortly he was caught attempting to steal a car and was sentenced to reform school. The counselor made one visit to him at that school and subsequently discussed his situation with his aunt.

When the third counselor entered the case, Luke was fifteen; just out of reform school, he was working for a milk company. This counselor had frequent interviews with Luke over a two-year period. In them Luke's various difficulties were discussed, and the boy claimed that he had given up his delinquent companions. During this time he lost several jobs, was involved in various semi-delinquent activities, and began drinking. The counselor increased his efforts, seeing Luke for weekly interviews about matters that were bothering him. They talked of such things as how to know when one is in love, why it is wrong to wear a veteran's pin when one has not been in military service, why punctuality, honesty, and responsibility are needed on jobs. In addition, the counselor took Luke on numerous recreational trips. Luke seemed to enjoy the talks but did not alter his conduct, which went from bad to worse.

When last known Luke at seventeen had obtained his parents' permission to marry a girl from a deprived family of rather poor reputation. He had a job driving a truck. There was little evidence that he would be any more honest or reliable on this job than he had been on earlier ones.

E. No Need for the Study's Help. Finally there was a considerable number of cases in which there was little or no need for the services of the Study; hence it was impossible to judge the value of the services that were given. For the most part the boys in this category had been referred to the organization to meet its request for "average" or well-adjusted youngsters. To many of the boys in this category only slight service was given but some were seen at fairly frequent intervals over a considerable period of time. More than half of these cases were dropped when war conditions forced the organization to retrench.

Example 12 is an illustration of the cases in which little work was done.

Example 12. Wesley was a quiet, slightly shy boy of ten (I.Q. 105) when he was referred to the Study as an average youngster. He tended to play with children somewhat younger than himself but he always had friends. In school he was polite, docile, and well behaved. He was greatly interested in airplanes and was determined to work in connection with them when he grew up.

The parents were separated. The mother was a pleasant person, very fond of Wesley and objective about him. She worked as a cleaning woman and in factories during the war. She considered her husband worthless but was unemotional about him and did not object to Wesley's seeing him. Little was learned about the man but he probably was fond of Wesley, for he gave the boy clothes and gifts and took him for rides in his truck. The family lived in a tenement building in a commercial section of town, the apartment being neat and adequately furnished.

From the outset Wesley was pleased to take trips with the counselor, and his mother had no objections. The counselor visited the boy about once in two months. After a few years of such contacts the mother inquired about medical service and asked for help with a sinus condition. When Wesley was about thirteen, his schoolwork became poor, but no reason for the change was discovered. Tutoring was arranged and he accepted it for a time, but not much was accomplished. The counselor's attempts to discover emotional problems were without avail. When last heard from, at sixteen, Wesley was still not doing very well in school but was hoping to do better. His mother said he had become much less silent. He had friends and interests normal to his age. His great interest in aeronautics had persisted and he was studying that subject in high school.

A more complicated case, illustrative of the boys with whom more work was done, is described in Example 13. These are rather puzzling cases to evaluate, for in them much work was done in regard to family problems, presumably because it was feared the existing unsatisfactory conditions would affect the boys adversely. In spite of much work the family problems persisted but the boys continued to be well adjusted.

Example 13. Ronald at eight years old (I.Q. 99) was described by his teacher as a nice boy, though highstrung and very dirty, so much so that the children avoided him. His father was a friendly, easygoing man, much interested in his children. He worked hard but was often in financial difficulties because he would not press his customers to pay their bills. The mother was an extremely slovenly housekeeper, overwhelmed by many children and chronic asthma; she seemed quite content and got great pleasure out of dramatizing her condition. She was warmly affectionate; in fact, the first counselor described the family as one of the happiest, most united he had ever met, even though the dirt and disorder of the house were extreme.

Since there were no outstanding problems in the boy, the first counselor concentrated on the mother, attempting to better her health. He got her to an allergy clinic but she would not accept the doctor's recommendation to get rid of the family dog. He also tried to help her understand her sister's point of view, when the sister, in an attempt at neatness, threw some discarded furniture out of the window and let the children burn it. None of these attempts proved especially successful, but the mother became very devoted to the counselor.

With Ronald the counselor spent much time, chiefly on recreational trips. He got the boy a scholarship at the YMCA, which Ronald used a few months until his best friend was expelled. He helped the school nurse get glasses for the boy, and he sent the boy to camp for the summer. After a year of so Ronald began to come to the Study headquarters for chats with the counselor and to work in the shop. Membership in the Boys' Club was secured at about this time but was of only passing interest to Ronald.

The second counselor saw Ronald about once a month for several years. He, too, visited the home and listened to the mother's complaints about her poor health, once taking her to a hospital for an examination. Since Ronald had no problems, this counselor regarded his job as one of standing by in case of need. He did considerable work with Ronald's younger and rather difficult brother, to which the boy responded fairly well.

When the Study contact ended, Ronald was a neat, clean-cut boy of seventeen, with normal friendships and interests. The family's financial situation and standard of living had improved greatly.

The distribution of boys according to these categories of value of service, sub-divided to indicate whether the case was dropped or was carried through to completion (that is, to the end of the Study or to the boy's 17th birthday) is set forth in Table 73. Before considering the significance of these figures, however, we want to show the extent of correspondence between these ratings and two other types of data by which the accomplishments of social agencies are frequently judged.

CORRESPONDENCE WITH OTHER TESTS OF ACCOMPLISHMENT

Social agencies frequently test the effectiveness of their services by describing either how well adjusted their clients became by the time work with them ended or how much they improved during the period of contact. Figures with respect to these two points have been presented in the preceding chapter, where it was shown that about a third of the boys were very well adjusted and another third fairly well adjusted when last known, and that this represented improvement over the original situation in about 40 percent of the cases. Since much the same situation was found in the control group,

TABLE 73

Distribution of Boys by Value and Duration of Study Service

	DURATION OF SERVICE			
	DROPPED	COMPLETED	TOTAL	
Value of Service			*Number*	*Percent*
A. Definitely beneficial	16	33	49	19
B. Possibly beneficial				
1. Slight benefit	2	22	24	10
2. Temporary benefit	3	10	13	5
C. Little accomplished in spite of friendly relations	5	15	20	8
D. Clearly ineffectual				
1. Offer of service refused	18	2	20	8
2. Work insufficient or poor	27	17	44	17
3. Other reasons	10	34	44	17
E. No need for help	24	16	40	16
Total	105	149	254	100

however, it was not at all certain that this fairly good showing could be attributed to the counselor's efforts.

In Table 74 the extent of correspondence between the terminal adjustment ratings and those referring to value of service is indicated. It will be noted that only a third of the well-adjusted boys and less than a fourth of those rated fairly good in adjustment were boys whom the Study clearly appeared to have benefited. At the same time, a fifth of the boys whose terminal adjustment was rated

TABLE 74

Relation between Value of Service and Terminal Adjustment

	VALUE OF SERVICE							
Terminal Adjustment	*A*	*B*	*C*	*D3*	*D1*	*D2*	*E*	*Total*
1. Good	26	2	2	—	5	11	30	76
2a. Fairly good	13	12	6	5	7	16	6	65
2b. Fairly good; neurotic	9	9	5	2	1	5	—	31
3a. Rather poor	—	3	4	1	1	4	1	14
3b. Rather poor; neurotic	—	5	2	9	2	4	—	22
4a. Poor	—	—	1	3	—	—	—	4
4b. Poor; neurotic or psychotic	—	6	—	8	—	1	—	15
4c. Chronic delinquent	—	—	—	14	—	1	—	15
Not known	1	—	—	2	4	2	3	12
Total	49	37	20	44	20	44	40	254

poor seemed possibly to have been helped somewhat by the counselors. The table thus shows that the value-of-service judgments were not based on terminal adjustment alone. It also suggests that, in spite of the control findings, the good showing of some boys may have been attributable, in part at least, to the counselors' services.

In Table 75 this possibility is further explored by comparison of the value-of-service ratings of the boys who improved greatly during the period of Study contact with those who made little improvement or became less well adjusted. We have earlier pointed out the impossibility of making accurate judgments about improvement in social adjustment or character, since most children have their ups and downs and since standards vary from one age to another. Nevertheless, an attempt at judgment on this point was made by noting the extent of difference between initial and terminal adjustment ratings [1] (see Table 65, Chapter XXIV), the following scale being used:

I. *Boy became better adjusted*
   a. Initial rating 5; terminal rating 1, 2, or 3
   b. Initial rating 3 or 4; terminal rating 1 or 2
   c. Initial rating 2; terminal rating 1
II. *Boy became less well adjusted*
   a. Initial rating 1; terminal rating 3 or 4
   b. Initial rating 2; terminal rating 3 or 4
   c. Initial rating 3 or 4; terminal rating 4
III. *Boy remained the same*
IV. *Terminal adjustment not known*

Table 75 again demonstrates that the value-of-service ratings were not based primarily upon adjustment or change in adjustment, for of the 101 who became better adjusted only 35 were rated as clearly benefited by the organization's services, while four of the 24 who became worse seemed possibly to have been helped somewhat. Among those who became better adjusted, those whom the counselors appeared to have aided were more likely to be boys who made a slight change (and that from a fairly good to a good adjustment)

---

[1] It will be recalled that the initial ratings were made on a five-point scale, in which values 3 and 4 differed in quality but perhaps not in degree of maladjustment (Chap. XXII), while the terminal adjustment ratings (Chap. XXIV) were made on a four-point scale.

than boys who changed greatly. This rather important finding is in line with data to be presented later. If correct, it would help to explain the lack of difference between the Study and control series, for such slight improvement might well have taken place in the absence of the counselors' help.

TABLE 75

Relation between Value of Service and Degree of Change in Adjustment

Change in Adjustment	VALUE OF SERVICE									Total
	A	B	C	D_3	Total	D_1	D_2	E	Total	
I. Became better										
a	3	4	1	7	15	1	1	—	2	17
b	17	14	7	5	43	2	7	—	9	52
c	15	1	1	—	17	3	10	2	15	32
Total	35	19	9	12	75	6	18	2	26	101
II. Became worse										
a	—	—	1	—	1	—	—	1	—	2
b	—	3	2	5	10	1	4	—	5	15
c	—	1	1	4	6	—	1	—	1	7
Total	—	4	4	9	17	1	5	1	6	24
III. Remained same	13	14	7	21	55	9	19	34	62	117
IV. Not known	1	—	—	2	3	4	2	3	9	12
Total	49	37	20	44	150	20	44	40	103	254

A third test of results sometimes employed by social agencies is that secured by asking the clients, sometime after service is ended, whether they had benefited. Material on this point for the present study was provided by an independent investigation conducted by graduate students, this study being made one to two years after the Study period of service had ended (see Chapter XIII).

For this follow-up investigation boys were selected by the Study executive on the basis of availability. One hundred and eighteen boys were interviewed. Tabulation of their distribution among the value-of-service categories indicated that, while they did not constitute a proportional sample of all the categories (very few, for example, of those who refused to participate being included), marked "successes" and marked "failures" were equally represented among them.[2]

The investigators presented themselves to the boys as persons who were unconnected with and largely ignorant of the Study program. In soliciting opinions of it they said either that somebody was considering setting up such a program in another city or that the people who had provided the money for the Study's activities wanted to find out what the boys thought of the program. They asked the boys, among other questions, what the organization's purpose was, how they happened to be invited to join in its activities, who their counselors were, how they liked the program, what they thought its value to themselves and others had been.

All but one or two of the 118 boys selected for interviewing were willing to talk to the investigators. The great majority appeared to express their opinions very frankly, though there was, of course, much variation in their articulateness. Widely different opinions about the value of the Study were expressed. Categorized they were as follows:

1a. Some boys were highly enthusiastic about the program, thought the services had been of great benefit to them, and stressed especially the value of their personal relationships with the counselors and the intangible benefits secured.

Lester. When asked whether he thought this program was something that could keep a fellow straight, Lester replied, "Yes, it's hard not to, when you know they'll ask you why and how—ask you for the story. You're in good with them, so you just don't do things. You know them so well you tell them the inner things—they get them out of you. Yah, they make you feel at ease; they're easy to talk to. And sometimes when you're trying to say something, they help you say it."

2 ——————

Value of Service	In Sample	Total	Percent in Sample
A	27	51	53
B	23	35	66
C	13	20	65
D1	2	20	10
D2	13	44	30
D3	24	44	55
E	16	40	40
Total	118	254	46

1b. Others talked chiefly in terms of the "concrete" assistance. These boys stressed such services as tutoring, medical care, recreation, aid when in difficulty with the police, and said that they had been definitely helped thereby.

Spike. "I have nothing but good to say for the Study." He went on to describe the program largely in terms of recreation, the good times he had with the counselors and the boys he met at the Study. He also mentioned the help given him in finding jobs.

Eliot. This boy stressed recreation, help with schoolwork, help when he was in court. "The aim of the Study was to make a regular guy out of you." It was chiefly useful, he said, for "kids that haven't got much—money, intelligence, things other kids have, such as bikes. It keeps them busy and off the streets."

1c. Still others were not quite so explicit about being helped. They said they appreciated greatly the counselor's friendship but did not say specifically that they had followed the advice they received.

Julius. "N was one of the best friends I ever had. If I ever needed him, I could always rely on him. A lot of times I went to him with problems and asked him what to do. When I quit school, my brother got mad, so I asked N and he told me the best thing was to go back. But I quit because my mother needed the money. . . . A lot of times I could get along better with N than with my brothers and sisters. They'd tell him to tell me what to do and I'd do it faster than for them."

2. Other boys were somewhat less enthusiastic. Some of them spoke in affectionate terms of their counselors but were a bit uncertain as to whether they had been helped. Others were rather vague about the value of the program as a whole but mentioned some services that had been helpful.

Pasquale. "The aim of the Study was to make good citizens, to develop talents." It was of use to him because of the tutoring provided and because "they had my ears fixed, so people don't laugh at me so much anymore." "The program can lead a guy but the rest is up to him." He apparently was not sure that he had been helped greatly.

Cornelius. His counselor was very nice, this boy said, and helped him with schoolwork and by securing medical care and sending him to camp. The Study "helped some kids to get self-confident"; for himself he "didn't have much to do with it."

3. Some boys were more dubious about Study benefits. "It was okay," some of them said, unenthusiastically. "It was a good thing, I suppose, but I didn't go there much," said others. "It was all right for kids who were in trouble but I didn't need it." Such remarks, as well as the rather frequent comment that they remembered little about the organization, were characteristic of these boys.

4. Finally, some boys (4a) were either very ambivalent about the organization or (4b) said its services were of little value to them, though in some single aspect its work may have been useful, or (4c) were certain that the whole program was valueless.

Buddy. "They kept me out of trouble—they thought!" The boy went on to tell about various escapades then and now, making it clear that he paid little attention to what the counselors or his parents thought. "Most of the fellows went along for the ride. That's what I did. We used to go different places. It gave you something to do. I'd make things in the woodworking shop. I liked to do those things. I miss them now."

Nearly half of the 118 boys interviewed expressed opinions of the first type, nearly a third made replies of the second or third type, while about a fourth were clearly skeptical of the organization's value. These proportions cannot be immediately generalized to refer to the total group of boys served by the Study, since the sample of boys interviewed contained somewhat disproportionate shares of the various value-of-service groups described above. If attention is confined, however, to the 87 boys in the most significant groups (A, B, C and D3), and the boys who either did not need, did not want, or were not adequately given service are omitted, this discrepancy between the sample and the total population almost disappears. We find, then, in this representative sample of boys who needed and more or less accepted help and were given service in line with the organization's intentions that about a half thought the service of value, a third were more or less dubious, and about a fourth said they had received little, if any, benefit from it (see Table 76).

Just what were the characteristics of the boys who expressed these various types of opinions is a question of interest, but our desire here is to show to what extent the boys' opinions coincided with the judgments arrived at by the writer on the basis of the case record material. The relationship is shown in Table 76.

TABLE 76

Boys' Opinions and Writer's Judgments of Value of Study Service

Boys' Opinions	WRITER'S JUDGMENTS OF VALUE OF SERVICE							
	A	B	C	D1	D2	D3	E	Total
1. Study very worth while								
a. Conduct influenced by relationship with counselor	14	1	1	—	—	1	1	18
b. Benefited by material services	10	2	1	—	3	3	5	24
c. Services appreciated; effect on conduct not mentioned	—	3	3	—	—	—	—	6
2. Somewhat worth while	3	8	4	—	—	4	1	20
3. Dubious value	—	3	2	—	2	4	6	17
4. Little or no value	—	6	2	2	8	12	3	33
Total	27	23	13	2	13	24	16	118

Apparently almost all the boys whom the writer rated as having been definitely benefited by the organization's services would have agreed with that judgment. Twenty-three others also described the Study as very worth while, but most of them did not make it so clear that they thought their conduct had been influenced by the counselors' efforts. Apparently a boy might have the highest regard for his counselor and appreciation of what he had done for him and yet not credit the counselor with having changed his behavior greatly. This was the sort of appreciation of the Study expressed by most of the boys not rated as being clearly benefited.

Two-thirds of the boys who had not benefited (D3) were dubious about the value of the Study or said that it had been of little or no use to them. The boys who refused the offer of service and those with whom little or poor work was done (D1, D2) were also largely in agreement with the writer that the organization had not helped them. Characteristically, most of the boys in Category C, those who had had very friendly relations with their counselors but did not appear to have benefited significantly, reported that they liked the Study very much, as did about a fourth of those in Categories B1 and B2, whose case records seemed to indicate that what benefit they had received had been slight or only temporary.

A review of the most striking exceptions to the agreement between the boys and the writer (the four cases in Category D3 in which the boys said they greatly appreciated what their counselors had done for them) provides some clues as to reasons for the divergence in opinion.

Two of these four boys described the value of the Study in terms of their personal relations with the counselors. One said briefly, "They were like your own folks." The other, a very verbose individual said, "I wouldn't be where I am today if it weren't for Mr. B. He taught me to understand loyalty and trust and respect. He was like a father—no, like an official. He didn't tell me I had to do anything—just gave me advice and suggested. . . ." The case records showed both of these boys to be very unstable emotionally, perhaps of psychopathic personality, as judged by their "smooth" ways, their constant promises to do better, their ability to use people for their own interests. The one boy had a long record of delinquency and was in the state reformatory at the time of the follow-up interview. The other had joined the Merchant Marine and was passionately devoted to the seamen's union; shortly thereafter he quit the service and stayed around home, as irresponsible and immature as always.

The two other boys stated explicitly that they considered the Study chiefly worth while because it helped them to stay out of delinquency by keeping them busy. The testimony of one of them seemed rather unreliable, for he was somewhat drunk at the time of the interview; taken at its face value, the benefit he derived was that of "encouragement" when "in trouble" (meaning when delinquent) in return for which he was willing to tell the counselor "anything he wanted to know." The other, a boy with a long history of emotional maladjustment and inability to relate well to people, said that the Study was important to him for its help when he was in difficulty with the police and for providing a place where he could play. "There's nothing to do around these streets," he said. "The nearest playground is a mile and a half off in the 'nigger' section and they beat you up if you go there."

From this it seems clear that the boys' opinions of the value of the Study cannot be accepted at face value but must be judged in relation to the whole story of the organization's contact with them and their personality make-up. An enthusiastic endorsement of the organization may mean only that the speaker is one who is accustomed to telling adults what he thinks they want to hear, or it may indicate a dependent individual's liking for being kept in line or out of difficulty, or it may mean that the client greatly enjoyed certain of the organization's activities or appreciated the counselors' friendship without necessarily being greatly influenced thereby. Or there may be other explanations that the cases so far examined do not reveal. The point of importance is that testimony as to an organization's value to an individual must itself be evaluated—which leaves the research worker in the awkward position of maintaining that his own judgments are more valid than those of the persons who received the organization's services.

In spite of this rather disappointing conclusion, Table 76 is of value in confirming to a considerable extent the judgments arrived at in the previous section of this chapter. One of our objectives in that analysis, it will be recalled, was to find the boys who were clearly benefited by Study services so that we might compare their terminal adjustment with that of their control twins. It was reassuring, therefore, to discover that all but three of the boys in the sample who had been classified as clearly benefited stated that the Study had helped them very much, and that those three (boys with whom the Study had worked briefly) said that they had been aided by some particular service. At the other end of the scale, two-thirds of the boys classified as not having benefited (D2 and D3) stated frankly that they were dubious about the value of the services or that the services had been more or less useless; most of the others were the maladjusted boys described above. The opinions of most of those in the other categories (those who claimed more value from the organization than the writer thought justified by the case records) could be accounted for by facts much like those described in the divergent cases above. It is with considerable confidence, therefore, that we proceed with the further analysis of the findings with respect to these value-of-service groups.

IMPLICATIONS OF THE FINDINGS

Returning now to an analysis of the figures in Table 73 (the distribution of boys according to these categories of value-of-service, sub-divided to show whether the case was "dropped" or completed), we note that the data can be considered from two angles: (1) that of the group as a whole, which would indicate what the Study accomplished with the total series of boys under consideration here,[3] and (2) that of the boys who needed and accepted the organization's help and were given service of the type the organization deemed adequate.

Viewed from the first angle, about a fifth of the boys appeared to have been definitely aided by the Study and another tenth got some slight benefit from its services. The rest, for one reason or another, did not appear to have been appreciably helped by the organization's work. This latter fact—that two-thirds or more of the boys were not significantly affected by the help given—would seem to go far toward explaining why the later social adjustment of the T-boys did not differ from that of the controls.

The second angle from which the figures may be considered is of chief importance to those who are interested in the social work implications of the data. Such persons want to know, (1) what proportion of boys responded to this offer of service, which was so contrary to present-day social work practice (that is, soliciting the interest of the boys and their parents rather than waiting for them to seek the organization's help); (2) what was accomplished with those who especially needed the organization's help; (3) were better results obtained with those the Study worked with to the end than with those who were "dropped?"

1. The figures indicate that only 20 boys of the 254 (8 percent) who were approached by Study counselors either refused to have anything to do with the organization or soon lost interest. In some cases this was their own decision; in others, that of their parents. (See Chapter XXVII for a detailed analysis.) These were, of course, not all the boys who were "resistive"; they were, however, the only ones who were so resistive that the counselors did not have an opportunity to demonstrate what their services might consist of. It would seem, therefore, that "difficult" boys and their parents are not likely to object to being approached by a social worker who offers help.

In drawing this conclusion, one must consider, however, the kind

---

[3] Here, as elsewhere in this second part of the volume, "total" refers to the 254 boys, not to the 325 on the Study's original list (see Chap. XXI).

of help the Study offered, as described in Part I. Briefly, it was an offer to provide some recreational opportunities, help with school work, access to health services, and the like. Parents and boys, in the main, accepted such offers with pleasure. This response was in marked contrast to one reported by a skilled social case worker.[4] This case worker visited parents of delinquents and offered them help with their troubles. She did not secure nearly so favorable a response as did the Study counselors. Apparently, then, it was the specificity of the Study's offer, as well as the nature of it, that secured the favorable response.

2. In determining what proportion of boys were significantly aided by the Study, the 20 boys who refused the offer of service should be omitted from the total. So, too, should the 40 who were found to be so well adjusted that what the organization could do for them could be of little or no benefit from the viewpoint of social-work objectives. Then, if we are interested in learning what could have been accomplished rather than what was accomplished by work of this kind, the 44 boys with whom the work was below the agency's standards should also be dropped from consideration. Such omissions constitute 41 percent of the total series of cases and leave us with 150 boys who needed and accepted Study service and were given assistance of the type that seemed to be in keeping with what the organization aimed to provide. One-third of these boys (see Table 73) were clearly benefited by the help they received, about a fourth got slight or temporary benefit, and the rest (42 percent) got little or no help, as far as the writer could see. Whether this is a good or poor showing is difficult to determine, for comparable figures from other types of social agencies are lacking, though it is known that child guidance clinics usually fail to help about a fourth of their patients.[5]

3. There were some differences in accomplishments with the boys who were dropped [6] and those with whom work was carried on until completion, as defined in the plan of the Study. There were,

[4] Bertha Capen Reynolds, "Between Client and Community," *Smith College Studies in Social Work*, V (1934), 43–97.

[5] Helen L. Witmer, "A Comparison of Treatment Results in Various Types of Child Guidance Clinics," *American Journal of Orthopsychiatry*, V (1939), 351–361.

[6] Our figures for "dropped" boys, as stated earlier, omit the six who died or moved away soon after work with them started. Evaluation of results with these boys was clearly impossible.

of course, among the dropped cases more boys who refused the offer of service and more who had little or no need for it. These constituted 40 percent of the dropped boys and only 12 percent of the others. With such cases omitted, as well as those with whom inadequate work was done, the proportion of boys who benefited definitely or slightly was 41 percent in the dropped series and 29 percent in the series in which service was carried on until the planned-for termination. The proportion of cases in which the Study clearly failed, even though the work was carried on in accordance with the agency's standards, was higher in the latter group than in the former. Stated another way, a third of the boys whom the Study clearly helped were boys who were dropped rather early in the course of service.

These findings suggest that the long-time contact the Study planned on is not always necessary, that some boys can be aided in a relatively short time. To this may be added the fact (revealed through the analysis of cases to be reported in the following chapters) that to many boys the really effective service was given, and improvement in their social adjustment was secured, long before contact with them ended. With some exceptions, then, the lengthy period of contact called for by the Study plan did not appear to be needed by all the boys.

All in all, these findings suggest that if the intake of the Study had been limited in accordance with usual social-agency practice (to those who need and want the service) and if all the work had been up to the Study's standards, the boys who clearly benefited would have been fairly numerous. Their proportion in the total might have been even higher than the one-third noted above, for "wanting help" would probably have been defined in such a way that some of the boys with whom the Study failed would not have been accepted as clients. Such a limiting of intake, however, was contrary to one of the basic principles of the Study; in fact, it was this practice of most social agencies that was one of the points at issue when the organization was set up. From that point of view, then, one of the chief findings is that only 8 percent of the 254 boys and their families definitely refused or lacked interest in the Study's offer of help. This would imply that the Study's plan of going out to the families of boys who are thought to be in need of help is usually successful in arousing interest. Such an offer results, however, in only about a third of the boys being helped to improve in social functioning. We are left, then, with the conclusion that the Study's plan cannot be universally recommended; and we want to know, more than ever, who were the boys whom it did help.

COMPARISON WITH THE CONTROL GROUP

As will be recalled, in determining the value of the Study service to individual boys, we had two objectives aside from that of judging the program's effectiveness. The one objective was to provide a basis for discovering the distinguishing characteristics of the circumstances under which the Study's type of program can be helpful to difficult boys. This question will be answered in the subsequent chapters. The other objective was to provide data for analyzing further why the T-boys were apparently doing no better than their C-twins at the time their social adjustment was rated. At the end of the preceding chapter it was pointed out that this statement was true only when the two series of boys were considered as wholes, that there were pairs of cases in which the T-boy was functioning better than his twin. The question was raised whether these were the boys who had benefited significantly from the organization's work. The classification according to value of service makes it possible to answer that question.

Unfortunately for definite findings, the number of boys available for comparison is small. Of the 51 boys rated A (definitely benefited by the Study) there were only 15 whose C-twins' social adjustment was ascertained at the same age. (In 15 other cases the C-twin was located but there was a difference of more than a year in the ages of the pair when social adjustment was rated.) These 15 form about the same proportion of the total sample of 91, however, as the 51 do of total population, so they are probably representative of the whole.

When these 15 pairs of boys were compared with respect to terminal adjustment, it was found that in 11 pairs the T-boy had a better rating than his control, in only one pair did he have a poorer rating, and there were three pairs in which the rating was similar. These 11 boys accounted for more than a third of the cases in the total series in which the T-boy was doing better than the control.

454   VALUE OF STUDY TO INDIVIDUAL BOYS

(See Table 77 below.) Much the same was true when the comparison was made without respect to age. There were then 30 boys to be compared. In that case, 16 of the T-boys had a higher rating and four a lower rating than their C-twins. These 16 again constituted a third of the pairs of that type. In spite of the small number of cases involved, these differences were found to be statistically significant.

At the other end of the scale the opposite condition obtained. Among the 19 pairs of boys of the same age in which the T-boys were not benefited by the Study (rating D3) the C-boy made the better adjustment in 10 cases and the T-boy in three; in six pairs the ratings were similar. When the comparison was made irrespective of age, the C-boy was found to be doing better in 16 out of 27 pairs, the T-boy in four, while similar ratings appeared in seven pairs.

In Table 77 comparable figures are presented for all the value-of-service categories, these being grouped in descending likelihood of the T-boys' adjustment being favorably influenced by the Study. It will be seen that in the first two categories (that in which the

TABLE 77

Distribution of Relative Adjustment Ratings of T- and C-Boys by Value-of-Service Categories

TERMINAL ADJUSTMENT

| | T AND C OF SIMILAR AGE | | | | IRRESPECTIVE OF AGE | | | |
| | T | C | | | | T | C | |
Value of Service	Same	Better	Better	Total	Same	Better	Better	Total
A. Clearly benefited	3	11	1	15	10	16	4	30
E. Help not needed	6	6	1	13	9	10	3	22
B1. Slight benefit	4	3	6	13	6	5	6	17
B2. Temporary benefit	1	—	3	4	1	1	4	6
C. Benefit dubious	4	2	3	9	4	2	5	11
D1. Refused help	1	1	2	4	2	3	5	10
D2. No benefit: poor work	4	3	7	14	6	7	12	25
D3. No benefit	6	3	10	19	7	4	16	27
Total	29	29	33	91	45	48	55	148

boys did not seem to need the organization's services—and that in which they clearly benefited) the number of pairs in which the T-boy excelled in adjustment far outnumbered those in which the C-boy excelled. In the second group of categories (that in which the boys either benefited only slightly or refused the offer of service) there was the distribution of ratings that was to be expected by chance. In the third group, in which little if anything was accomplished with the boys, the C-boys made a much better showing than did the T-boys.

In spite of the rather small number of cases the consistency of these findings lends weight to the conclusion that when the Study services were effectual most of the boys did function better socially than their C-twins. This conclusion can be accepted, however, only if its opposite is also accepted: that some of the boys who were not benefited may have been handicapped in social adjustment by the organization's efforts. If this is true, we can conclude that the apparent chance distribution of terminal adjustment ratings noted in the preceding chapter was due to the fact that the good effects of the Study were counterbalanced by the poor.

Whether the Study actually had harmful effects as well as good effects is very difficult to demonstrate. Nevertheless, in the following chapters an attempt to answer that question will be made by means of individual case analysis. The chief aim in these chapters is, however, to arrive at some conclusions regarding the conditions under which the Study's type of service is profitable.

CHAPTER XXVI

HOW AND WITH WHOM
GOOD RESULTS
WERE SECURED

THE FINDING THAT SOME BOYS WERE SIGNIFICANTLY AIDED BY THE Study's services but that many were not benefited is of importance, of course, but much more valuable to planners of services to problem boys would be a reasonably precise formulation of the circumstances under which benefit to boys can be secured. Such a formulation should have reference both to the boys themselves and their environmental circumstances and to the methods used in helping them. It is the aim of this and the following three chapters to arrive at such a statement.

The problem will be attacked from two angles. First, we shall analyze the cases in which the services seemed of most value to the boys, sub-dividing them into groups in which fairly similar working methods were used. In these sub-groups an attempt will be made to discern uniformities in the case situations, which may give a lead to the circumstances under which the given method is effective. Second, we shall test these findings by reference to the cases in which the Study services proved to be of dubious or little value. By this double checking it may be possible to arrive at diagnostic and treatment formulations that are applicable in specified types of situations. The present chapter deals with the first of these attempts.

SUB-GROUP 1: REMOVAL OF SPECIFIC HANDICAPS [1]

The first sub-group of the 49 successful cases to be examined is that in which the boys benefited through the discovery and removal of specific handicaps to good social relationships. Many of these

[1] Sub-groups are numbered for later reference.

handicaps lay in the boys themselves but some were found in parents' or teachers' ways of handling them. Usually one particular handicap was found and attention concentrated on it, with other incidental services being given in addition; in some cases, however, a considerable amount of time was spent on discovering what the handicap was, in the course of which numerous services were provided.

This is a kind of service that has a common-sense appeal. This boy, says the enthusiastic layman, has a bad nose and throat condition; that one is cross-eyed; that one doesn't participate in athletics for fear of hurting his heart; some boys have a reading disability that keeps them from progressing in school and makes them feel inferior; others are running wild on the streets for lack of better recreational facilities; others don't get along with their teachers. Clear up the physical difficulties, provide tutoring, give them membership cards for the "Y," explain to the teachers what is wrong, and all will be well. Many programs of delinquency prevention are based on such reasoning. It seems especially important, therefore, to discover under what circumstances boys are helped to become better adjusted socially by such measures.

It seems a significant finding that in only 22 cases did the boy's improvement appear to be chiefly attributable to his having received this sort of help. Help along these lines was, of course, given to many other boys in the total series of 254, so it is apparent that not much reliance can be put upon such simple measures as a means of helping socially maladjusted boys. This conclusion is greatly strengthened by the discovery of the kinds of boys that were benefited by measures of this sort.

Review of the case material showed that nearly all of the twenty-two were boys whose problems, at the outset, appeared to be slight or non-existent—problems that were rated 1 or 2 according to the categories described in Chapter XXII. In addition, most of them came from families in which the parent-child relationships were very favorable and which were rated A from the social point of view. In only six cases were the parents' attitudes rated as somewhat adverse and in all but one of them that attitude (either overprotection or overstrict discipline) stemmed from the parents' interest in and concern about the boy. In the one exceptional case (described below) the mother was very erratic and self-centered but the father was very fond of the boy. In short, only one of these boys lived under adverse social or emotional conditions and none appeared to be severely maladjusted.

As an example of the majority of the boys Allen may be cited. He was a happy, likable boy who had no noticeable problems until he was about twelve (he became a T-boy at ten), when he began being something of a clown and mischief-maker in school and was finally demoted. His parents, Italian-born, were affectionate, energetic people, much interested in their children's welfare and less "old-world" in their habits than many of their neighbors. They maintained a pleasant, well-kept home in a congested neighborhood; their income was marginal but increased considerably as the children grew older. Study services to Allen included a tonsillectomy and a "Y" scholarship, but the service that was most clearly beneficial was one of mediation between him and the school at the time his behavior was creating difficulties. He was helped with his school difficulties at his own request. The counselor talked with the principal, who then secured the mother's participation in school activities and greater interest in the boy's school progress.

Another case of this sort was that of Carl, a docile, well-behaved boy who had several friends but seemed rather withdrawn. Again there was a high degree of affection and solidarity in the family. Carl was teased by the other children about his squint and was called "four-eyes" when he secured glasses. After the counselor arranged for an eye operation that corrected the "crossed" condition, Carl became more confident and easier in his relations with his schoolmates and was no longer so retiring.

One boy in this sub-group whose original adjustment was less good and whose home situation was rather unfavorable was Owen. His mother was an aggressive, defensive woman who used extremely poor measures in controlling her children, but the father, even-tempered and mild, said of Owen, "He won't do much with books but he's a good bright boy for getting along with people." They lived in a comfortable house in an Italian residential area. Owen was described by his teacher as lovable but extremely restless and distractible and constantly stealing and lying at school. He proved to be a feeble-minded boy who, though he did not benefit much from the tutoring which the Study gave, gained a great deal in self-confidence and self-discipline from the tutor's kindly attention and concentration on simple tasks he could learn to perform. As he grew better adjusted, his mother became more accepting of his limitations, with consequent improvement in behavior on his part, and she was willing to permit special class placement. In that class he had a very understanding teacher, who carried on the work the tutor had started.

The only other boy whose adjustment at first seemed rather poor was Barry. A long series of illnesses and unstable home conditions had changed him from an alert, responsive child to one who was listless, apathetic, and fearful. It was found that the chief disturbing factor was his psychotic father. After the father was committed to a mental hospital through the Study's efforts, and the school and recreation situation was improved Barry became much more alert and spontaneous, and his I.Q. advanced from 65 to 80. These latter two cases represent the use of somewhat less tangible means of assistance than the others described above but they have in common with them the speedy improvement in a boy's adjustment with the removal of conditions that were handicapping to him.

Another characteristic of these cases was that, with minor exceptions, the parents from the outset were very cordial to the counselors; most of them not only were willing that the boys participate in the Study but also had specific ideas about the areas in which help was needed. To be precise, only two rather overprotective mothers were somewhat dubious about the project, and their objections were easily overcome. The parents and the boys remained cordial to the counselors throughout the period of contact.

What these findings suggest is that if a boy has a rather obvious handicap to his social adjustment (a reading disability, a physical disorder, a teacher who does not understand him, a father who is too strict or is mentally disturbed) he is likely to be greatly benefited by the removal of the handicap (literally or figuratively speaking) only if his maladjustment is not very severe (that is, if he has many positive personality traits), if his home situation is socially favorable, if his parents are kindly disposed toward him, and if they want help. Under less favorable circumstances, apparently, the removal of such handicaps—useful as that action may be—will not be sufficient to effect important changes in behavior or personality.

SUB-GROUP 2: COUNSELOR ACCEPTED AS PARENT-SUPPLEMENT OR SUBSTITUTE

In the next type of case the good results seemed attributable to the fact that the boy became greatly attached to the counselor, accepted his standards, took his advice, and put to good use the opportunities that were made available to him. The counselor, in short, acted as a representative of the conventional adult world and its requirements. More closely analyzed, the activities of the counselors appeared to be such as supplemented those of the mothers and fathers in their parental role. Just as wise and loving parents do, the counselors let the boys know what society expected of them in the way of conduct, counseled with them regarding the difficulties they had in living up to those standards, showed displeasure occasionally in a kindly way, urged and encouraged them in the use of their abilities, arranged for needed recreational, educational, and health services, and so on. Such an attempt to make up for parental deficiencies characterized many of the cases in the total Study series but in only eleven cases did the boys' improvement seem chiefly attributable to the fact that he reacted to the counselor as to a loving parent or adult friend and used his help accordingly.

The search for similarities among the cases in which this happened led to the conclusion that this reaction occurred chiefly among boys who came from emotionally satisfying homes that diverged considerably from the predominating cultural pattern. This was true of nine of these eleven boys. The parents had real affection for the boys but, for one reason or another (usually cultural), did not provide the stimulus and backing the boys needed to take advantage of the opportunity schools, clinics, and the like afford. These parents' deficiencies were social rather than emotional; they loved their children but, because of cultural differences or personal inadequacy, they could not pass on to them the "American heritage." They were, however, not only willing but eager to have the agency's services, and the boys themselves were reaching out for help. All of these boys were doing well when last known.

Such a conclusion seems to "make sense" psychologically. It suggests that these were boys who formed attachments not because of emotional deprivation but because they were emotionally healthy and could trust people. Their parents, too, were sufficiently secure to share their children with others, could release them even to those whose standards were somewhat different from their own, and could let their children be different from themselves. Fiction pictures the deprived child who attaches himself to the kind benefactor, follows his bidding and models himself after him. This study gives little backing for any such conception. Apparently most children who can form this kind of attachment and can accept and profit from this parent-substitute kind of service are already emotionally quite healthy, even though perhaps socially and economically deprived. The following three cases are illustrative of this group of boys and the work done with them.

Lester. This bright Portuguese boy (I.Q. 112) was overactive and rather stubborn in school and not working up to his ability. The parents, foreign-born, were very indulgent of Lester, rather amused at his misbehavior, and very fond of him, as he was of them. Both parents were very friendly to the counselors and appreciative of their interest. The first two counselors had a rather casual relationship with the boy, concentrating chiefly on such services as a "Y" scholarship, camp, and attention to dental care, none of which were much needed so far as the boy's social adjustment was concerned. In fact, during the three years or so of their contact there was little wrong with that adjustment.

By the time Lester was thirteen school was beginning to be something of a problem to him. His parents supplied no backing for his remaining in school, and Lester himself often felt, as he said, disgusted with it. The new counselor visited him frequently, took him on camping trips, and engaged in sports with him, but he put chief emphasis on the school difficulty. He continually assured Lester of his ability to progress in school, urged him to finish high school, and urged him to take a mature attitude toward his dislike of the teachers and the studies. The boy discussed these matters seriously whenever he was discouraged or in difficulty, often saying he was staying in school only to please the counselor. He accepted other of the counselor's standards, even dropping a friend after the counselor objected to him.

Throughout this period it was clear that the counselor was urging decisions and trying to supply motivations that the parents were indifferent about; nevertheless the parents remained very friendly and put up no objections to the boy's following the counselor's advice. In a follow-up interview when Lester was eighteen, he said that the Study could keep boys straight because they would hate to disappoint their counselors by doing wrong. He said that the last counselor had helped him express his "inner thoughts" and that he felt at ease with him. Families, he added, are a bad influence when they let boys make up their own minds.

Luigi. A boy with a serious heart condition resulting from rheumatic fever, Luigi was inattentive and disinterested in schoolwork, nervous, a fussy eater, fearful of medical treatment. Although sickness and a retiring personality handicapped him in group activity, he made friends quite easily, especially with adults. His parents were old-world Italians; the mother was overindulgent, the father quiet and respected by the children. When Study services were offered, the mother expressed great eagerness to have a friend, urged the counselor to take a house near hers so she could see her more often. She was unwilling, however, to impose the restrictions on Luigi that his physical condition required, saying that resting was childish and that the boy liked nothing but Italian foods.

The second counselor, a nurse, concentrated her attention on Luigi, making many arrangements with other organizations—convalescent home, school, and so on—that facilitated his adjustment to the limitations his heart condition imposed. She discussed with the boy many times the need to take responsibility for his own care, helped him overcome his shyness, and provided both a job opportunity and the emotional backing to make use of it. In short, she did the things an intelligent, resourceful parent would have done, and the boy responded as to a loved parent. By the time service ended, the boy's heart had compensated well, and he was being very mature about his remaining limitations. In a follow-up interview at twenty, Luigi placed great emphasis on the care he had received from his counselor. He seemed to feel that the whole pattern of his development was influenced by her, and he gave her credit for helping him overcome his shyness and acquire a vocational aim.

Oliver. The police described Oliver at ten as a boy with whom they could do nothing. He apparently was urged on in delinquency by his mother and by an older brother, both of whom had a long police record. In addition, he was a very restless, high-strung boy, subject to severe nightmares and temper outbursts. He was not a gang member but always had a few friends; his schoolwork and behavior were reasonably good.

Oliver's parents were French Canadians. The family lived in a filthy house, and the children were very much neglected. The mother was an inadequate, weak person with no control over the children, amazingly unconcerned about dangers confronting them. The father was a good-natured man, unable to understand why his children were so difficult. The family income, until the war, was very low, and the neighborhood in which they lived delinquent. In spite of their limitations and their violent quarrels, the parents were fond of their children and interested, though ineffectually, in their progress.

The mother was cordial to the counselor from the outset. "I know you come for to help my boys," she said. Oliver also developed a close attachment, even in the first interview. From the very start the counselor used his usual method of friendly "lecturing," pointing out the unwiseness of stealing and suggesting that Oliver keep himself cleaner. He had many contacts with the boy for the first six months, keeping in touch with the Delinquency Squad concerning him, getting reading tests made and tutoring started, providing a membership card for the "Y" (which Oliver very much enjoyed), and sending him to camp, where he was voted the best boy. There were later some stormy years in which Oliver was in and out of foster homes on court order but, throughout, the counselor maintained his contact and his friendly guidance and the boy remained greatly attached to him and responsive to his advice. In a long, follow-up interview at eighteen Oliver said, "D helped me out a lot. It wasn't like one fellow taking care of another—we were more like pals. . . . The Study gave me somebody to lean on when I needed it."

The two boys who did not fit the above description were neurotic boys whose home situations were very unfavorable emotionally and socially. Neither boy became at all well adjusted until he left home in late adolescence to join the Navy. The boys have since left military service and appear to be adjusting fairly well. Just how much of the improvement was due to the Study cannot be determined, of course, but it seems indubitable that the counselors' support was important and that the later improvement is to be attributed in part to it.

The significant factors in the counselors' work in these cases were, probably, the steadfastness of the counselors' attention, the strength of the boys' attachment, and the desire on the parents' part to have their sons helped. Since the ultimate adjustment of these two boys was so different from that of most of their kind (see Chapter XXVII) a more detailed description of the cases seems warranted.

Lawrence. Age 11–17; I.Q. 82. Lawrence was a highly nervous, sensitive boy who had a chronic skin ailment that flared up whenever he engaged in stealing, which he did frequently and seemingly compulsively. As he grew older he became very erratic, was unable to stick to jobs, and continued to be involved in delinquency that was sure to be detected.

The father was a quiet, patient man, so passive that he made no objection to his wife's drinking or to her promiscuous sexual relations in their own home. The mother, who appeared to be a sweet, ineffectual person without the least control over her children, was diagnosed at a mental hospital as probably having an organic brain disease. Lawrence was fond of his father and was in considerable emotional conflict about his mother and her behavior and her rather rejecting attitude toward him, being resentful and yet desirous of her approval. At home there was less bickering and quarreling than might have been expected, due chiefly to the father's meekness. The mother's housekeeping standards were very low and the family moved frequently, always to dilapidated tenements in areas of much delinquency.

The counselors put a great deal of effort into getting the skin condition diagnosed and treated, for it was a source of great discomfort and shame to the boy. The condition would clear up while he was in a hospital or otherwise out of his home, as he was rather frequently, on court order because of his delinquencies, but it would soon flare up when he returned. Whether he was in or out of foster homes or correctional institutions the counselors kept in close contact with him, one counselor in particular, who had him in her charge for four years, playing the part of guide and friend to an unusual degree.

This counselor would urge and encourage Lawrence, exhort and befriend him. At one time she bought him clothes when he was ashamed of his poor appearance. Time and again she tried to explain the emotional basis of the skin ailment to his mother and urged her to follow the doctor's recommendations. She worked indefatigably with teachers and probation officers on the boy's behalf. Often the parents expressed gratitude toward her, as did the teachers and the boy himself. All the effort seemed rather fruitless, however, until Lawrence was old enough to join the Navy. There he did quite well and has continued a satisfactory adjustment ever since, being now married and in a home of his own. The counselor continued her contact with him long after the Study closed. To the follow-up investigator Lawrence said, "I'd be dead now or in Sing Sing maybe if it hadn't been for them."

Terrence. Age 11–17; I.Q. 106. Terrence was a frail, nervous boy who complained frequently of headaches and arm and leg pains for which doctors could find no physical basis. He was very meticulous and orderly, with a marked striving for perfection. He did very poorly in school, especially in arithmetic, in spite of much tutoring. In general, he was apathetic, abstracted, and very forgetful. Toward the end of the Study contact with him he became involved in a series of delinquent activities that seemed neurotically motivated. A psychiatrist at that time described him as a serious mental case.

The mother was a nagging, complaining person, continually worrying. She overprotected and indulged her children greatly and was not able to be firm about anything. The father was very irritable and very stingy, refusing to provide adequately for his family even though he had a good income. There was much quarreling between the parents; when Terrence was fourteen the father deserted. The basic difficulty seemed to be that the mother, a "spineless" person, could never, for all her nagging and fear that the boy might get into trouble, be firm with him, and that the father was a person whose example the boy could not follow, for he was very irritable and selfish, interested only in his own pleasure, and did many things (such as "stepping out" with other women) of which the boy disapproved. The favorable factor in this case was that both the boy and the parents wanted the counselor's help.

The counselor was most persistent in his efforts. The first year he concentrated on tutoring the boy, for he was failing in school and exasperating the teacher by his lack of interest and defiant behavior. Tutoring was only moderately successful but the teachers became interested and cooperative, with the result that the boy's behavior became much better. Terrence continued, however, to be lethargic, absent-minded, and distracted, so psychiatric treatment was secured. This, too, was temporarily successful but the psychiatrist finally decided that the situation was rather hopeless, since the boy was not strong enough to take responsibility for anything, always following the path of least resistance, and there was nobody at home who would be firm with him. The counselor persisted nevertheless, discussing camp, recreation, jobs with the boy and giving the mother emotional support when home affairs became too difficult for her. In spite of this the boy became involved in a series of rather serious delinquencies, not being able to resist temptation even when his getting into the Navy (his own desire) depended upon a minimum of conformity. Through all the vicissitudes the counselor stood by him. It was wartime, the military authorities were lenient, and the boy got into the Navy, where, in spite of occasional periods of feeling miserable, he did well.

When interviewed later, the boy told an independent investigator that his counselor was a swell fellow who helped him with his studies, took him places, and advised him when in trouble. "It was wonderful," he said. "I always felt free. He always had time for you. . . . If it hadn't been for him I don't know what I'd have done. He was more like a father than my real father. I'd die if I turned out like my real father, but he says I won't; there's nothing hereditary about it."

These cases suggest, then, that some very maladjusted boys from very inadequate homes can be helped if they relate positively to a counselor, if close contact is maintained for a period of years, and if they can get away from home and into a stable environment.

SUB-GROUP 3: PARENTS PREVAILED ON TO ALTER THEIR BEHAVIOR

In another small group of cases, three in number, the boys benefited greatly from the counselors' efforts largely because of changes
effected in their parents' behavior through a combination of friendship and moral suasion. Since this was a treatment method that was
frequently used, the small number of cases in which it appeared to
be the decisive factor in the good results seems significant. In these
cases the usual services of making various facilities available to the
boys and of standing by them in periods of stress were also given.
The work with these parents was somewhat like that with the boys
in the preceding group of cases. In these cases the family picture
seemed unfavorable at the outset and most of the boys were considerably maladjusted. The following brief descriptions attest to
that.

Gus. At time of referral, Gus was in serious difficulty in school, the result
of numerous violent fights not only with children but with teachers, and
court action was being considered. His father was a calm, placid, peasant-
like Italian, but his mother, a Sicilian, was given to extreme rages,
usually over what she considered unfair treatment of her children. She
was very belligerent with the school authorities but at home she seemed
to manage the children well and was much interested in their school
success. Family life in general was tempestuous, with much laughing and
much quarreling. The mother, from an American point of view, seemed
both paranoid and hypochondriacal but perhaps she was only a "typical
Sicilian."

Roland. Referred as a boy who lied, stole, played truant, and was generally stubborn, Roland (I.Q. 105) was high-strung, impulsive, constantly
in difficulty in school though doing well academically. His mother had
died when he was seven. He and his brother were living in a boarding
house with four other orphans, of whom Roland was jealous. The father,
a heavy drinker, paid for their support but saw little of them. The foster
mother seemed rather ambivalent about Roland, whose only source of
emotional satisfaction appeared to be his teacher.

Adam. A boy with an I.Q. of 80, Adam was not a behavior problem but
was listless, slovenly, and a chronic truant. He lived with his parents,
Portuguese, and eight siblings in a house so inadequate that when the
police discovered it (in the course of arresting the father for about the
fiftieth time) the family were moved to another dwelling. The mother
was considered feeble-minded and utterly incompetent by the school

authorities, the police, and the relief workers, while the father was a chronic drunkard, abusive, and frequently a deserter. To the counselor, however, the mother showed herself as one who was sincerely devoted to her children and who tried to do her inadequate best for them, confining her screaming and other "queer" behavior to the authorities who refused her constant requests for aid.

The work with these parents varied greatly from case to case. Perhaps a brief description of what was done with the mother of Gus and the father of Roland will indicate its character.

Gus (continued). The work in this case started with a visit to the school because of the emergency nature of the referral. There the teachers described how violently the boy had behaved recently when ordered to do something. They said they thought the mother was crazy, so extreme were her words and acts when the least complaint about her children's behavior was made. The counselor offered to act as a buffer between mother and teacher, an offer that was accepted with pleasure but doubt as to its success.

The counselor next called on Gus's mother and opened the conversation by saying that he was interested in Gus and was wanting to help him in any way he could. He identified himself as a friend of the nurse who had made the first contact on behalf of the Study a month earlier. The mother, having liked the nurse very much, received the counselor cordially. Once in the house and introduced to Gus and his brothers the counselor inquired about their after-school activities, learned that they sold newspapers, and thereupon told of his own experiences in that line, stressing the economic difficulties. The mother and the boys were delighted. After the boys left the room, the mother launched in a dramatic description of her troubles with the school authorities, saying she felt so strongly about this that it made her sick. The counselor told her that her oldest son's teacher liked him very much and that she was a fine teacher. He reminded her that even with that teacher she had had disputes and asked her whether it was not true that she and teachers were both trying to work for the boy's good. The mother agreed that this was so. After some general conversation and a hint that if the boys did not behave better, their license to sell newspapers might be taken away, the counselor left.

In the next interview, about a month later, the mother said the teachers had complained about her eldest son's conduct and that she had gone to his defense. The counselor listened carefully, then gently reminded her of their joint interest in the boys and stated calmly that the boys might be sent to a reform school if they became too troublesome and the family got too bad a reputation. He suggested that instead of going to the teachers when the boys were in difficulty, the mother call him and they would talk about the matter. At that the mother became quieter and agreed to follow the plan. A few weeks later, when the next school incident occurred, she started to go to the school but came to the Study office instead and was less violent in her tirade than previously. After that—various kinds of help having been given to Gus in the meantime—the mother consistently discussed her difficulties with the counselor. Visits were made to the home two or three times a week for the first six months; after that about once in two weeks, and later even less frequently, for the counselor wanted to avoid being drawn in on settling many family problems.

In regard to Gus, a check-up at school revealed that within a month his behavior had improved greatly. The teacher asked that he be tested for reading disability, since he was doing so poorly in reading. Gus very much wanted help, as did his mother, so arrangements were made for his being studied at a university reading clinic. There it was found that his disability was very marked. After hearing the story of the family and school situation, the clinic authorities agreed, in spite of a long waiting list, to admit him to their classes and waive the fees. Gus made rapid progress and was much liked by all the clinic staff. For about a year Gus had his schoolwork at the university clinic. On his return to public school the counselor paid special attention to helping him adjust there; described the problem to the new teacher, urged the boy on when he began to be somewhat lazy, and, the next year, helped him to enter a school in which he would have an unusually good teacher.

In the five years that this counselor worked with Gus and his family, various other problems, of course, came up, and various other services were given. There was, for instance, a brief period in which Gus played truant. The counselor firmly rebuked the boy for staying out of school and the mother for permitting him to do so. Then there was a time when the police took away the boy's shoeshine box because he was working beyond the legal hours. The counselor talked to the police and they agreed to let Gus sell newspapers even though he was under the legal age. To the mother the counselor frequently gave advice and encouragement, especially when she was ill and depressed, and helped by various acts to keep the family out of hot water.

All in all, work in this case went very smoothly after the first month or so, though the mother continued to seek help on various matters and to be very excitable. The results of the services were rather spectacular. Without the Study's help Gus might well have become a delinquent, for he was getting a bad reputation in school and was making very little progress there. He did, however, have very great assets, chief of which (not mentioned above) were his very attractive personality and his ability to arouse the interest and sympathy of adults. The clinic workers liked him greatly, an elderly professor at the university took a special interest in him, and his first employer gave him much encouragement. The school authorities said the improvement in the boy and his family was incredible.

In this case there were the positive traits of family solidarity, parental affection for the boy, interest on the part of the school and the reading clinic, and basic stability and charm in the boy's personality. The difficulties—very real ones—were primarily cultural, and it may have been that with the mother the counselor played a role that was culturally acceptable to her—that of a kind but firm and authoritative advisor.

Such an array of favorable traits was not present in the other cases in this sub-group, however. In that of Roland, for instance, there seemed at the outset little to work with. The initial situation is described above. Work was carried on as follows.

Roland (continued). As with Gus, the work involved both the boy and his parent, in this case the father. From the beginning Roland was under the custody of a child placement agency so the social work throughout was on a "cooperative" basis. The counselor, a warm, motherly person, interested herself in Roland's needs, spiritual and physical. She tried to arouse his interest in being an altar boy, obtained music lessons for him, arranged a series of examinations for possible congenital syphilis, and conferred with the placement workers about the disadvantages of his foster home.

When a new foster home was secured, Roland adjusted well at first but soon began stealing from the foster father and from women's purses at church. The counselor visited him, talked with the foster mother, who seemed to be very tolerant of this behavior, and took Roland on several trips. After some time, however, the boy again began stealing at church. Court action was not taken but the foster parents asked that he be removed, as they had not been able to win his affection.

In the next home there was the same sequence of events but this time the foster mother agreed to keep him in spite of this behavior, Roland having in the meantime had some interviews with the Study psychiatrist. The boy stayed in that home several years, the counselor visiting him at intervals and trying to encourage him in various ways. Later he was transferred to an industrial school, where again he proved to be unreliable.

In the meantime, the counselor was having a lengthy correspondence with the father. He was working as a lumberjack in a rural state. Contact started when the counselor requested that the father come to Boston for a blood test at the time Roland was being examined for syphilis. After some delay, he did so, and had some interviews with the counselor at the Study office. After he returned to his job, he began a voluminous correspondence with her about his children's care. In these letters he began to question the wisdom of his actions and to seek other ways of fulfilling his parental duties. For example, after several years he wrote, "I voluntarily let the children drift to state control believing they would get above average care, and that the children and I would be free of obligation to any relative or individual. I'd rather be in debt to the public as a whole. I'm beginning to see that the children prefer a father and a home of their own to whatever society can provide. No matter how much I try to justify my actions I feel that I have terribly let my kids down." Letters in this vein, running to as much as fifteen pages, continued for several years. By 1941 (the case had opened in 1937) the father was writing in rather wishful but unreal terms about taking his children to live with him. He claimed to be making an effort to give up drinking, and it was clear that he enjoyed the solitude of the woods.

In 1943 he wrote that he had married a widow with four children about the ages of his own and that she was helping him to reconstitute a home. The counselor replied, saying she was proud of him and hoped that he could reunite his family. Soon after he brought his wife to Boston to introduce her to the children and to visit the counselor. He tried to get the children released from public care but without success. Two years later, however, at the father's request, the counselor secured Roland's release from the industrial school and his return home. Once there the boy apparently did well, becoming very much attached to his stepmother. When last heard of he was in the Navy, doing well but longing to be home.

Such an account of the events cannot convey the flavor of the correspondence between Roland's father and the counselor. The counselor, throughout, gave much advice, continually encouraged the man, emphasized his duty as a father, and urged him to take religion seriously. In his last letter the father wrote of her help as follows:

"I can only say that you personally gave me courage and confidence in the work you are doing. I never felt entirely helpless when I knew you were backing me up to get back to a normal Christian life. My hopes for myself and the children have been exceeded. There have been times when the going was rough and my self-respect almost zero—and I never thought it would be possible for me to enjoy the simple pleasure and satisfaction of having a home and family together. I sincerely believe it was you personally that gave me back a home and my children. It is fortunate that youth in particular has your help."

There is much about the psycho-dynamics of this case that is not clear, but it will be noted that, again, there was both affection for the boy on a parent's part and some elements of strength in the boy (otherwise he probably would not so easily have become fond of his stepmother). These favorable traits, however, were far from evident at the outset, and much credit for the change must be given to the counselor for bringing them to light. In spite of the unexpectedly good results in these two cases, however, one must admit that there was much of chance about the outcome. Actually, these counselors used similar methods in other cases without anything like so much benefit accruing. What we have in such cases, it seems to the writer, is a chance meeting of two personalities that dovetail in services and needs. The counselors were not so much utilizing professional skills as "being themselves." And it happened that the kind of self they possessed met the clients' needs.

Some confirmation of this is found in the case of Adam, which culturally was somewhat like that of Gus. The initial situation has been described above.

Adam (continued). There were four counselors in this case, in which an ignorant, protective Portuguese mother, very much handicapped financially and socially, was trying to bring up eight children with little assistance from her husband. The first counselor, largely on the basis of police and social agency reports, regarded the family as hopeless. While he had a kind and tolerant attitude toward the mother and her suspicion of him as a "sex fiend" because of his sudden seeking out her son for attention, he made little attempt to get to know her and he hoped that the police would break up the family permanently. The next two counselors were also unsuccessful in influencing the family in their rather brief periods of contact. In spite of sympathy for the family, they too failed to get close to either mother or boy.

The fourth counselor entered the case at a time when the boy was on probation and one of his brothers was in reform school. Perhaps because he recognized the mother's deep concern for the boys and repeatedly assured her of their basic good qualities, this counselor was accepted by the mother as a good friend. He helped her to get a legal separation from her drunken husband, sustained her again and again in her decision not to let him return, and advised her to let him drink in moderation when she did finally take him back. For the boy he secured an admission to a summer camp that he much desired, took him on recreational trips, and helped him get into the Merchant Marine. Much of this counselor's assistance to both boy and mother was of a concrete nature, but it was accompanied by many discussions in which the counselor upheld the side of law and order. He described himself as a sort of "Dutch uncle" to the family, supporting the mother through many difficult decisions and making many firm pronouncements when she was wavering. Through these efforts the mother's morale improved greatly and she provided a much more satisfying home for the children.

Such work may be regarded as a perspicacious use of authoritative methods rather than a chance meeting of congenial personalities. However that may be, success apparently requires the presence of parental concern about and interest in the children and the discernment of such feelings by the counselor, for it is to that concern and interest that the emotional appeal of the counselor is made, and authority enters in only after a relationship based on mutual interest in the children has been established. The method seems to work best with individuals who are culturally accustomed to advice and remonstrances from persons in authority or who are emotionally dependent on such support. This combination of traits in the client and use of the method by the counselor was apparently rare in our series of cases, for only three boys were classified as being greatly helped in this way.

SUB-GROUP 4: HELPED CHIEFLY THROUGH OTHER AGENCIES

In another small group of cases, five in number, the benefit to the boy seemed to come chiefly through the work of other organizations—psychiatric or child welfare—but the Study played the important part of securing these services for the boys, for it is unlikely that the parents would or could have done so unaided. Preceding this referral to other agencies (and, in most cases, subsequent to it), the counselors had established friendly relations with the boys and their parents, had been of service to them in various concrete ways, but had been unable to effect marked changes in the boys' behavior. In connection with the placement, they were of definite service. For example, in three cases the counselors found foster homes or schools that were particularly adapted to these boys' needs, previous ones secured by other agencies having proved of little use. In another case the counselor discovered how much the boy dreaded being a state charge and therefore arranged that he be placed through a private agency. In addition, in several cases the counselors stimulated the parents to demonstrate more clearly their interest in their sons' behavior, and this bolstered the boys considerably.

In these cases the aid usually secured was foster-home or institutional placement, preceded in several cases by a diagnostic study by a child guidance clinic. In one instance, however, the service secured was psychiatric treatment, this being a case in which family relations were strong and the boy's difficulty a definite psychiatric disorder. Disregarding this single case of psychiatric treatment, we may inquire under what circumstances parents can accept and boys benefit from placement outside the home. So far as can be judged by the similarities in this small series of cases, it seems that this form of assistance is beneficial (1) if the parents are too immature to deal with the boy's problem or are physically unable to provide a home for him, but have affection for him that can be mobilized in his interest, (2) if they want the boy to be placed, and (3) if the boy himself is willing to leave home. None of these boys was seriously maladjusted emotionally but several of them were on the verge of delinquency. The following two cases are illustrative of this series.

Claude. Age 11; I.Q. 94. When first known Claude was a frail nervous boy with an exaggerated lack of self-confidence. He was afraid of the rough boys in the neighborhood (a very poor one with a high delinquency rate) and confined his friendship to a few other physically weak boys. He had some artistic talent, which his father was eager to see developed, he himself having some such ability.

The father was an invalid, and the mother too had many ailments. The father's relationship with Claude was a very close one. The mother, rather limited in intelligence, was a somewhat martyr-like person, more than usually attached to her own mother and dependent on her. She shifted some of this dependence to the first counselor, saying at one time that she was like a mother to her.

The first counselor gave the mother much emotional support and helped her to secure needed medical care, leaving as much as possible of the initiative to her, however. She also helped her find better living quarters and qualify for state aid to dependent children, thus securing a somewhat higher income for the family. Her work with Claude was concentrated on building his self-confidence, partly through medical services and camp. At adolescence the boy developed anxiety attacks, for which psychiatric treatment was secured. Good results were obtained, not only with respect to the neurotic symptoms but in general adjustment.

The second counselor did little with the parents. Instead, he worked chiefly with the boy, giving him much guidance in regard to jobs, school, friends, sex problems, and the like. The relationship between the counselor and the boy was friendly but not unusually close.

Francis. Age 12; I.Q. 81. This boy was originally described as being un-dependable, lying his way out of school situations and stealing there occasionally. He did poor work in school and had some nervous habits, such as nail-biting and enuresis. He always had a few friends, but picked quarrels easily and was not generally liked. A child psychiatrist described him as "a dull boy with no strong affectional tie to anybody." The mother was a pleasant rather ineffectual woman, indecisive in discipline, eager to do what was "right," and seeking advice. She nagged Francis frequently, compared him unfavorably with his siblings, and, though she had some affection for him, could not show it in a way the boy could understand. The father had died when Francis was four, and the mother felt very inadequate in handling her five children.

The first counselor found the mother eager for help, especially with the school problem. She thought Francis needed male supervision and was considering sending him to industrial school. The work consisted at first of about monthly visits to the mother and recreational trips for Francis. Work with the mother was largely of the good-advice type; it was not certain that she acted on the recommendations. Camp and a "Y" membership were secured for Francis.

At about fourteen the boy became increasingly hard to manage. Some-time later, because of increased stealing and sex interest, the advice of a child guidance clinic was sought and at its recommendation foster-home care was secured. This did not work out well, but placement in a farm school apparently met his needs and he did very well there, his good adjustment continuing when he returned home. In connection with this placement it is to be noted that before Francis went there, his mother, at the counselor's suggestion, did several things for him that convinced him of her love. Contacts with another counselor, after Francis left the school, were not especially fruitful, the boy not being much interested in the discussions the counselor tried to initiate. When last heard of he was doing well in the Navy.

One other case might be added to this group, though it differed considerably from these in that the boy and the parents were much more maladjusted and the counselor's help lay, not in securing the placement which was ultimately so beneficial (though the counselor had attempted to do so), but in providing emotional support preceding and during placement. As in the preceding cases, chief credit for aiding the boy must go to the other agencies but, to some extent, the Study's services perhaps made the good results possible.

Franklin. Age 10–16; I.Q. 116. This bright boy, shy and immature, displayed no difficult behavior in school but from the very beginning was most reluctant to attend. His truancy, which probably represented a school phobia (for he could not make himself attend school even when under police scrutiny) continued over the years, becoming so excessive that the boy was finally sent to a farm school by the court. At home he was considered very disobedient and hard to manage. He had some nervous mannerisms and would vomit when under special strain.

The father was an untidy, uncouth man who at first seemed to have little interest in the boy but later expressed concern that a good school be found for him. The mother was a vague, disoriented neurotic whose chief concern was her physical ailments. She was entirely inadequate in dealing with Franklin and said frankly that she wished he were a girl, as girls are less bother. She often expressed a desire to have him put away. She gave him attention only when he was ill and seemed to like to take him to hospitals. The family lived in a dark, damp basement in a residential area, although their income was not excessively low.

The first counselor had only four interviews with Franklin in the first two years. The boy responded very well to him and obviously liked him, but when an attempt was made to renew the friendship after Franklin was in difficulty because of lengthy truancy the boy rather rejected the counselor's advances. The counselor did, however, visit him frequently for a time and tried to arrange placement away from home.

The second counselor found Franklin making a fair adjustment in school but being markedly unhappy and anxious. Soon his truancy began again; it became so excessive that court action was started by the truant officer. At this time Franklin talked to the counselor about fearing insanity and spoke often of death and accidents. The counselor spent much time with the boy during this period, sometimes staying with him nearly all day. In spite of promises, Franklin could not get himself to go to school. The court insisted upon placement, and the boy was put in a school that did not permit the counselor to visit him. Franklin adjusted fairly well in the school, and later, when transferred to a "junior republic," became one of the most prominent and successful boys in the institution. The counselor maintained contact with him through his parents and occasional letters, but it was probably the Republic workers who were of chief help to the boy.

In spite of the less favorable home circumstances and the correspondingly more serious emotional disorder in this boy, the case has some elements in common with those described above. Specifically, these parents, too, were willing that the boy be placed away from home, and the boy, while panicky when he first heard he must leave, was not wholly opposed to the move. The parents' affection for the boy was much less than in the preceding cases but the father, erratic as he was, evidenced after a time some real interest in his son, wanted him to go to a "nice" school, and was appreciative of the Study's efforts in the boy's behalf. Accordingly, our previous findings as to the conditions under which placement proves beneficial can probably stand.

SUB-GROUP 5: MODERN CASE-WORK METHODS USED

In the preceding three groups of cases—especially in the last two —the good results seemed attributable to service on the part of the counselors that was the kind a strong, wise, loving friend might give. It was directed to the needs in the situations; it was based in many of the cases on strong emotional attachment (often of a two-way nature); but it lacked that non-judgmental character, that use of the client-worker relationship to effect release of inhibited feelings on which modern case work relies. Modern case work is chiefly distinguished from the kind of social work generally carried on by the Study counselors by the fact that its practitioners seldom give advice, cite ethical precepts, warn of the consequences of antisocial behavior, or urge particular courses of action. Instead, modern case workers help their clients to express their feelings about unpleasant or difficult situations and to formulate plans for dealing with them that are consonant with their own desires.

There were seven cases in which the benefit the boy received from his contact with the Study appeared to be attributable to the counselor's use of this case-work method. Not all the counselors of these boys were professionally trained case workers, but in these cases they conducted their work along modern case-work lines.

As in the previous sub-groups of cases, we want to know both how this work was done and to what sort of boy it was helpful. To answer the last question first, all but one of these seven boys appeared to be somewhat neurotic (Category 4 in Chapter XXII) and at least half of them had parents whose attitudes were highly unfavorable. The following are brief descriptions of these aspects of the boys and their situations as they appeared at or near the outset of the work, arranged roughly in ascending order of difficulty.

Mario. Age 16; I.Q. 73. Described by his older brother, who was in charge of the household, as sensitive and imaginative and still mourning the death of his mother (two years earlier), Mario was found to be a stable boy of unusually high ethical standards, loyal to his family and friends. At the time Study contact began, however, he was restless and inattentive in school and was attempting to copy an older delinquent brother by acting tough. The father was away from home most of the time, with the result that Mario was given little supervision or physical care.

Matthew. Age 12; I.Q. 99. A high-strung, tense boy who bit his nails, Matthew had an eye tic and enuresis. He was seclusive and had few friends, the only ones being six- and seven-year-old children. The father, a garment worker, was very strict with the boy and constantly criticized him, greatly preferring Matthew's younger sister. The mother had a good relationship with the boy and seemed fairly wise in her handling of him. She blamed her husband for Matthew's behavior. Both parents wanted him in the Study, the father because he was worried about what would happen to the boy if he continued as he was.

Keith. Age 7; I.Q. 84. Keith was a repressed, withdrawn little boy, apathetic and completely lacking in confidence. Very timid about new experiences, he was known in school as a sissy, and was much given to lying and distorting circumstances in order to control situations. His father seemed a stable, mild-mannered man, insistent, in Italian fashion, on being the head of the household. He took a major part in doing things for the children and was protective of them, and his relationship with Keith seemed good. The mother was a dull, very neurotic woman, diagnosed as schizophrenic at one time during the Study's contact. She was excitable and ineffectual in handling her children and was especially rejecting of Keith, whom she often punished severely. Her selfishness and attempts to absolve herself from blame seemed to be copied by the boy. Both parents received the first counselor cordially, being much interested in the offered services of medical care.

Maurice. Age 12; I.Q. 101. The teacher, a very exacting person, described Maurice as markedly inattentive, unable to get along with the other children, constantly enuretic. His mother was disturbed about his frequent crying, his unwillingness to put forth effort, and his feeling that everybody was against him. He had very few friends and those much younger children. To the counselor he said, "I feel sick and rotten. I'd like to kill the kids."

Maurice and his parents lived in a residential area in a neat and attractive house. The father, a very insecure, immature person, was dependent on his wife and resentful of the children. He was making a barely adequate income as an insurance salesman. He had always disliked Maurice and definitely favored the other two children. The mother, an exacting, rigid person, had little patience with the boy, punished him severely for his enuresis, often humiliated him by ridiculing his fears and passivity, and labeled all his attempts at independence "sneakiness." From the first she was desirous of the counselor's help, saying she wanted to discuss with him her difficulties with Maurice and asking him to return.

Lew. Age 8; I.Q. 78. The school authorities referred Lew to the Study as a difficult, retarded boy who was in a daze, "peculiar," dirty and untidy, and a conduct problem. Lew was soon found to have many fears associated with school and a skin condition that flared up when the home situation was especially difficult. Otherwise he was a well-developed boy with social poise that gave him an appearance of greater intelligence than he possessed. The parents at first seemed to be interested in him and understanding of his trouble, but longer acquaintance showed them immature and inadequate and resentful of the boy. The father drank frequently and was abusive; when responsible for Lew's care (during separation from his wife) he neglected the boy grossly. The mother too was neglectful of the children's welfare. She was frequently sick, drank heavily, and seemed to be deteriorating. She was endearing to Lew when with him but obviously wanted somebody else to take responsibility for him. Both parents, after some discussion, accepted the counselor's offer of help with schoolwork and recreation.

Sydney. Age 7; I.Q. 105. A very nervous, restless, hyperactive child, Sydney was always in trouble with other children and did poor work at school. He was exceedingly aggressive, critical of other children, always trying to dominate situations and rebelling against all restrictions, attempting to escape unpleasant situations by evasion and dishonesty. He felt his rejection by other children keenly and was sensitive to his lack of school progress. He had an overpolite approach to adults which could not conceal his basic antagonism. A neurological examination revealed a possibly unstable cortical functioning.

The parents were Portuguese of good family, the father having had some college training. They separated early in the Study period of contact and not much was learned about the father's relationship with Sydney except that it was definitely better than the mother's. The mother was a very unstable person, diagnosed psychoneurotic and clearly rejecting of her son. She could never handle him calmly and never succeeded in either liking him or disciplining him. She greeted the counselor eagerly at the time of the initial visit and immediately started talking about her difficulties with her husband.

Harold. Age 9; I.Q. 104. This boy was described by both teacher and mother at the beginning of the Study's contact as increasingly lying and stealing in a shrewd, deliberate manner. He said he wanted to be a clever crook. He had various nervous mannerisms and was doing rather poor work in school. Later acquaintance showed him to be a boy of strong mood changes. His periods of disturbance, characterized by disinterest in school and withdrawal from group activities, corresponded to periods of excessive strain at home.

Harold had an unsettled home life, living with one or another of his relatives while his mother worked. His parents had separated when he was five. Little was learned about the father but Harold said he was not as bad as described by the relatives, that he had been companionable with him and that he would like to live with his father were it not for his new wife. The mother was a very ambitious, cold woman, dogmatic and inflexible in her dealings with Harold. She apparently had never wanted him, had no guilt about her rejection of him, and regarded him chiefly as an obstacle to her desire for economic success. The relatives disapproved of her and were stern and critical with Harold. The counselor, on her first visit, was greeted enthusiastically by the mother, who said she needed "expert guidance" and help in finding a home for the boy.

The kind of case-work service given by the counselors to these boys and their families is illustrated below. For three of the boys foster homes or institutions were found, but this was done only after numerous interviews with them and their parents, in which they expressed their feelings and desires and became more accepting of the situation.

Maurice (continued). When the counselor, a woman, first called at the home, the mother was rather curt, but she was quickly won over when the counselor sympathized with her illness. She then described her present problem with Maurice and asked the counselor to return. After that, for almost three years, very frequent visits were made, the counselor talking with the mother and the boy separately, on the mother's suggestion.

The mother frequently talked about the general family relationships and her feelings about her husband and relatives, but the counselor did not make much response to this, other than accepting it factually. Instead most of the interviews were spent in telling the mother why Maurice behaved as he did, why the mother was impatient with him, and what the boy needed from her. The mother already had considerable insight into Maurice's needs and, apparently, the counselor's support enabled her to handle him better. Having got rid of some of her irritation about the family situation, the mother was able to give Maurice more approval and fewer scoldings. Her relationship with the counselor was close; she said the counselor was the only woman she had ever been able to talk to.

In the meantime the counselor developed a close relationship with Maurice, emphasized his achievements and praised his efforts. Medical advice about his enuresis, camp placement, and talks with the teacher were among the counselor's helpful services to the boy, but the chief value seemed to come from her interest in him, which gave him a sense of importance. He was often affectionate with her, in a way that he could not be with his mother. During this period there was constant improvement in the boy's behavior. His enuresis decreased considerably, and he developed greater self-reliance. He joined a military brigade, organized a club, and took much interest in chemical experiments. Adolescence brought some rather healthy aggressiveness, the extremes of which were mitigated by a summer farm placement. He began to be somewhat ambivalent about being singled out for attention by the counselor, however.

A period of about six months elapsed between counselors. When the second counselor called, the mother was cordial and reported Maurice pretty well settled. Within a few months, however, he began playing truant and being very defiant, and had become involved in rather serious stealing with a gang of boys. (He was then between 15 and 16.) The parents were very emotional about all this, called the boy "half rotten," and wondered whether he should be sent to court or to a psychiatrist. The counselor then began much the same kind of work the previous one carried on. He had long talks with Maurice about his feelings about parental restrictions and nagging, his relationship with his father, sex, and his reactions to authority. He did not moralize but merely gave the boy an opportunity to express himself and come to some conclusions about his behavior. Maurice became very free with the counselor and much less defensive of his actions. The counselor saw him once or twice a month, taking him to dinner or talking with him in the agency's office. Meanwhile the counselor reviewed with the mother why her son was behaving in this way and why he needed the reassurance of his parents' affection. He found it possible to discuss with the mother the effects of her early rejection of Maurice, for she talked freely of her feelings in that period.

Within a year or so relationships within the family improved greatly. Maurice began to feel free to talk about his problems with his mother, and she was quite wise in her handling of his remarks. The parents became pleased with Maurice in various ways, and what criticisms they had to make were much less emotionally tinged. After trying unsuccessfully to get into the Navy, the boy obtained a good job and did well at it. The mother expressed regret when told the Study was closing, saying, "It was a good place."

Harold (continued). The first of the two counselors in this case decided after a few interviews with the mother and about ten with Harold that the mother was so rejecting that the only thing to do was to help her find a boarding school for the boy, as she desired. The counselor did, however, persuade the mother to buy glasses for Harold and gave the teacher some suggestions about handling the boy, both of which measures seemed to be of some benefit. With Harold he talked about the advantages and disadvantages of leaving home. The boy was very eager to see the counselor and to spend time with him alone; he accepted the idea of placement well, regarding it as inevitable.

Once in the school, Harold did rather poorly for about a year but later (he remained there for seven years) improved greatly and became very popular. The mother never visited him, and the school permitted Harold short vacations only, for he regressed greatly every time he went home. The counselor made about four visits to him during the first two years, each time at the boy's request. Later, becoming better adjusted, Harold became less interested in maintaining contact with the counselor.

After seven years, against the Study's advice, Harold returned to live with his mother, although she did not want him there. He then moved to his great-aunt's home, where he also had trouble. A visit to that home by a second counselor revealed Harold again maladjusted, doing poorly in school and spending much time in solitude. The great-aunt, who nagged at him continually, asked the counselor for help, and Harold also said he'd like to see him. During the following year and a half, the counselor had many interviews with the boy and a considerable number with the aunt. To the aunt he gave sympathy and praise, appreciating her difficulties, at her age, in dealing with this problem boy. He urged her to praise the boy and make fewer demands on him, and he discussed with her some plans for improving the school situation. He also enlisted the principal's interest in giving the boy another chance in public school, having secured intelligence tests that indicated adequate ability.

With Harold the counselor had weekly interviews for a year and a half. At first the boy was suspicious that what he told the counselor would be repeated, but this attitude was soon replaced by complete confidence. The counselor consistently encouraged Harold in regard to his ability to achieve (the boy said his family regarded him as a bum, so he was going to be that) but also emphasized his responsibility in the matter. Harold brought to the counselor his problems about adjusting to his aunt's requirements, his resentment of her and his mother, and the usual problems of adolescence. For example, he said he much disliked having his mother use his allowance as punishment or reward, to which the counselor replied by telling him that some people cannot express themselves in affectionate ways. When, however, the counselor felt that the boy's allowance was really inadequate he supplemented it for a time, discussing with Harold ways of using the money well.

In a later follow-up interview Harold described his relationship with this counselor as one of father and son. He said he used his talks with the counselor to get rid of his "beefs." During the period of contact he raised his school grades from failing to A and B, took an active interest in school affairs, and began to speak of his great-aunt with affection, saying their arguments were short-lived and that he no longer felt rebellious. The great-aunt, too, said she was well satisfied with the boy. He visited his mother and reported that she seemed more pleased with him. The counselor's relationship with the boy tapered off gradually, Harold using the later interviews to report successes rather than to discuss problems. When last heard of (at 17, two years after the Study closed) he was still in school and doing very well.

Now, for further indications as to when this type of case-work service is called for and when it will succeed. We have already noted that the boys who benefited from this form of help displayed behavior symptoms that are often regarded as neurotic in character, although whether they actually represented the solution of an unconscious emotional conflict is difficult to say. In all these cases the home situation was very poor emotionally; in one or two, one parent was reasonably well disposed toward the boy, but in the others the attitude of both parents was such as to make the prospect of securing good results with the boys very dubious. Nevertheless, there was a hopeful element in the parents' desire for assistance with regard to the boys, and it was that which distinguished these cases from many other somewhat similar ones that will be described in subsequent chapters.

Reviewing this whole series of cases in which the boys clearly benefited from the counselors' services, we see, then, that the good results are largely to be attributed to services of the type that the organization originally set out to perform—those of friendly study, counseling, and the procurement of assistance of health, recreational, educational, and other agencies whose services were needed. The boys who were aided by such methods were, for the most part, those whose problems were never very severe and whose home situations, both emotionally and socially, were at least fairly adequate. Almost half, in fact, were boys with only mild problems and from good homes. With the few whose problems and home situations were of the worst order, modern social case-work methods were used. In all situations the parents were willing and, in many cases, eager to have the boys helped with their difficulties, and the boys were pleased to have the counselors' attention. These, then, appear to have been the necessary conditions for the receipt of marked benefit from the organization's efforts. Whether they are the sufficient conditions can be determined only after the other cases are examined.

CHAPTER XXVII

THE BOYS WHO WERE
NOT HELPED

THE CONTRAST WITH THESE CASES IN WHICH THE STUDY WORK WAS definitely beneficial is most clearly seen in the cases in which little or nothing was accomplished. There were 108 such cases, nearly half of the total in which aid was needed. Some reasons why this proportion was so large have been suggested in Chapter XXVI; more definite findings on that subject should emerge from an analysis of the individual cases.

Two reasons for the failure to accomplish much in these cases is shown in the classification scheme itself. First, in 20 of the 108 cases the boys were definitely disinterested in or opposed to the Study and early made their feelings clear. The counselors did what they could to overcome these attitudes but without success. Not that all the other boys received the Study's offer of assistance with enthusiasm and were highly cooperative throughout, but in these particular cases the boys or their parents made it clear immediately or very soon that they did not want help. Second, in 44 cases it seemed to the writer that the counselors failed to give service commensurate with need. There remain, then, 44 cases in which, in spite of (in many cases) much effort on the part of the counselors and in spite of at least a moderate display of interest on the part of the clients, the boys' social adjustment did not improve in consequence of the aid received. This latter group presents the most interesting problem for analysis. The cases in the first two groups will be reviewed first, however, in order to show under what circumstances the Study's offer was refused and in what ways the help given was inadequate.

SUB-GROUP 6: COUNSELORS' OFFER OF HELP REFUSED

In spite of the apparent simplicity of this first category of reasons for failure, there were several variations in the way the parents or boys in these 20 cases made it clear that they did not want the counselors' services. In some cases they said so at the outset; in others, the lack of interest was made clear as work progressed. In a few cases they were willing to accept certain material services but showed obvious lack of interest in doing anything about the real problems. Sometimes a definite reason was given for the refusal—a dislike of charity, a fear that the worker was a truant officer or some such official, a suspicion that there must be something malevolent about the organization's purposes. Sometimes the parents or boys were polite and friendly but simply "not interested." Along with this refusal of service there was, of course, variation in the counselors' methods, persistence, and ingenuity, so that in some cases it was difficult to say whether the lack of interest should be attributed to the boy's attitude or the counselor's ability. Time may also have been a factor, for some counselors regarded their case loads as too large.

It must be emphasized that these were not the only cases in which lack of interest and resistance to service was found. In many instances, as will be shown later, the work was blocked by the parents' or boy's lack of genuine concern about the problems or by their emotional inability to form the kind of relationship on the basis of which good results could be secured. The kind of case that is under consideration here is the one in which the refusal of help was so overt and made so soon after the initial contact that work was definitely barred.

The most clear-cut cases of this type were the ones in which a parent explicitly said he did not want the counselor to see the boy. It seems a commentary either on the politeness and forbearance of the poor or on the counselors' friendliness that there was only one case in which this happened and the mother persisted in her refusal of service. This was one of the rather few families with middle-class standards. The parents were said by the teachers to be intelligent, pleasant people, interested in their children. The mother told the counselor that she was busy but perhaps could see him some other time. To a later investigator she pretended at first not to be the person he was seeking and then said, "Why do you come around sneaking and spying? My boy is all right and we don't want to have anything to do with that organization. Go back to the place you came from and tear up every word you've written."

In five other cases the parents early made it clear that they did not want the agency's attention. One Italian mother kept insisting the counselor must be a truant officer and, when that doubt was finally dispelled, inquired, "Why you like Theodore better than the others?" and remained suspicious of the counselor's intentions. Another, French Canadian, thought the visitor a welfare worker who would take her son away; although she later said that the counselor might talk with the boy, she obviously avoided letting this happen. In two cases in which the families lived in a good residential neighborhood it was the grandmother who blocked aid. In the final case the mother was obviously paranoid, a subject of special concern being her feeble-minded daughter. After her first suspicions were allayed and some recreational and medical services secured, her anxiety flared up again and she said, "You're not really interested in Bill, you're coming here to get Marjorie." Even then the counselor did not cease her efforts on the boy's behalf, but finally the case had to be dropped because the mother was so vituperative.

In six cases the counselors were received more cordially but the parents were very dubious about wanting help and made no effort to back them up in their efforts. In one Italian family, for instance, the mother said on the first call, "He's a good boy; he's doing all right. He just doesn't like school," while on later visits the boy's sisters professed interest but said their father would not permit anything to be done. The father eventually did agree to letting the boy join the Scouts and expressed interest in having him transfer to trade school but about this time the counselor left the agency and his successor did little to continue the contact. In another case the mother, after having on several occasions refused to let the counselor talk with the boy, said, "If you come only once in a while I won't throw you out." After health and intelligence examinations were secured and the teacher was talked with several times, the boy said his mother wanted to know what was wrong with him. No further progress in giving help was made and the case was finally dropped, although the boy's adjustment seemed somewhat less good than at the outset.

In two other cases, somewhat comparable with these, the parents seemed superficially to want the agency's assistance but indicated by their actions that this was not really so. One of these was a very "low-grade" family, the parents probably feeble-minded and the house one of the very poorest in the whole series of cases; these parents were glad to have clothing and medical care provided, but they saw nothing to be concerned about in their son's persistent enuresis and inability to make friends. (The boy had an I.Q. of 68 and the gross muscular incoordination and indistinct speech of the severely handicapped.) The other situation was a very complicated one, involving illegitimacy, a grandmother who pretended to be the boy's mother, and middle-class social status. Placement of the child was desired but the assistance of the church rather than the Study was sought.

In the other six cases it was the boy rather than the parents whose interest could not be aroused, although in some of these cases the parents, too, were either unconcerned or so involved in the boy's problem that they could not support work that he was opposed to.

As to the characteristics of these boys who did not develop a friendly relationship with the counselors, it is difficult to generalize. Two of them were unsupervised little street gamins whose chief pleasure was gang life. Their parents were willing to have the counselors try to improve recreational and school activities but the boys themselves were very indifferent. Another boy, of somewhat higher economic status, was also chiefly influenced by his gang and especially resented the fact that the counselor was a woman. By the time a man was assigned to the case the boy was getting along so well that little attempt was made to work with him. In contrast to these, there was one boy whose extreme shyness and uncommunicativeness was impenetrable either by the two counselors who tried to help him or by a psychiatrist in a child guidance clinic. The boy finally said directly that he wanted to live in his own way and not be bothered. Two other boys were friendly, responsive individuals as seen in school and clubs but they were rather immature and resentful of any demands put on them. They were willing to accompany the counselors on recreational trips and otherwise have a good time with them but when efforts were made to interest them in discussion of their problems they became antagonistic and could not be reached.

As indicated by the descriptions of their difficulties at the time the Study tried to help them and by their adjustment when last heard of, about half of the boys in this group really needed some sort of assistance. Five others were rated as only moderately well adjusted at the time of last contact. Originally, in regard to behavior symptoms and home conditions, the boys did not differ significantly from the series as a whole. A third of them apparently had only minor problems and belonged to families rated AA emotionally and socially. (It will be recalled that AA gives no indication of economic status.) At the other extreme were four boys from homes rated C emotionally. There was, accordingly, no identifiable type of boy or family that refused the offer of service. All that can be said on the point, then, is that such cases were encountered, that they comprised a surprisingly small proportion of the total, and that (of course) nothing could be accomplished under such circumstances.

Counselors' Efforts Insufficient or Poor. The second obvious reason for lack of accomplishment with the boys was found in the inadequacy of the work in certain cases. Since one of our objectives in this part of the study is to discover what kinds of services are adequate under specified conditions, it may seem illogical to say at the outset that some work was not as good as it should have been. Again, however, as in the previous category of reasons for failure, it does not seem necessary to overlook common-sense considerations in pursuit of an ideal of strict logic. Hence to say, for instance, that some cases failed because the counselors put forth very little effort seems a justifiable statement if the evidence is produced.

It must be reemphasized in connection with these cases that what is under consideration here is not whether the boys became better adjusted over the years but whether their better adjustment seemed attributable to the counselors' efforts. In other words, "failure" in this study does not mean that the boy adjusted poorly but that the Study failed to help him. Many of the boys in the group under consideration here might not be regarded by social case workers as in need of help, it being thought that they and their parents could deal with the slight problems unassisted. The Study, however, operated on the theory of giving help with all discoverable difficulties—of being a friend in need—if any need could be found. Under such a theory it seems appropriate to label a case a failure when a counselor saw problems but did little if anything about them.

Three sub-groups were found in this category of explanation of failure. The first was composed of cases in which, apparently, little help was needed but the counselors failed to give even that little help. The second and third comprised more serious cases. In these, either the work was too slight in view of the difficulties of the situation or it was obviously poor or inappropriate to the existing conditions.

SUB-GROUP 7: LITTLE HELP NEEDED BUT THAT LITTLE NOT GIVEN

There were 20 boys in the first of these three sub-groups. Ten of them came from homes rated AA and AB and their problems at the outset seemed slight. The homes of the other 10 were less satisfying emotionally, being rated B, but these boys, too, were clearly not very maladjusted. Five boys remained active cases until they were 17 or until the agency's work ended; the others were dropped at the time the case load was reduced.

A random selection of these cases will illustrate what we mean by insufficiency of effort on the part of the counselors.

Nicholas. Age 10 years, 6 months; I.Q. 114. This boy, the oldest of seven siblings, was referred to the Study as an average boy. He was very adequate and able to meet difficult situations maturely. His prime desire was to help his mother. The father was periodically a heavy drinker and at such times required constant care from his wife and Nicholas. The mother was frequently ill and at one time was diagnosed psychoneurotic. She was very fond of Nicholas, considerate of his health and welfare, and protected him and the other children against her husband's irritability when drunk. Nicholas seemed to consider his father pathetic rather than to be blamed (a reflection of his mother's attitude), though he became somewhat contemptuous of him as he got older.

There were two counselors in this case. The first had very few contacts with Nicholas, but she visited the mother about once a month for a year or so and made arrangements for Nicholas to have a "Y" scholarship, ear examinations, and camp one summer. She saw the boy so infrequently that she did not know for some months that he was playing truant or that he had been put on probation for larceny.

For about six months the second counselor had rather frequent interviews with Nicholas, in which plans for his future were discussed. The boy, however, decided to leave school and join the Merchant Marine, where he apparently did well. Throughout the case the relationship between counselors and clients was friendly but superficial.

Zaven. Age 10; I.Q. 106. This was the younger of two brothers who were Study clients. Much work was done with the other brother, while Zaven was somewhat neglected. Referred by a school as restless, rather disobedient, frequently acting silly, Zaven was found to be a responsible, social extrovert who had never liked school and was two years retarded. The mother was an unstable Portuguese woman, very protective and dominating toward her children. She and the father both approved of Zaven, considering him "smart."

Again there were two counselors on the case. The first concentrated on the family problems and saw little of Zaven except when she occasionally included him on trips with his brother. The second was much involved in work with the older brother and paid little attention to the younger boy until he was about 14, when he was involved in delinquency and did particularly poorly in school. At that time the counselor had some talks with the boy about his behavior but did not accomplish much. He also arranged for tutoring, which was moderately successful. Two years later he tried to put more effort into his work with the boy but it was largely of a recreational nature. Attempts to interest Zaven in discussion of problems of adolescence were unsuccessful.

When last heard of, eleven of these boys were making a very good social adjustment and eight were doing somewhat less well, being rated 2 instead of 1 in social adjustment. The adjustment of one boy was classified as unknown. Nineteen of these boys originally had only slight problems while the twentieth had practically no difficulties. These facts would appear to confirm our earlier statement that these boys were not much in need of help.

One wonders, however, whether some of the eight boys whose final rating was 2 might not have been helped to do even better if the counselors had put forth greater effort. Four of these boys came from homes rated A in parent-child relationships. Three had mothers who were dominating and overprotective and fathers who were stable individuals. The eighth lived under unfavorable home conditions, socially and emotionally, being much disliked by his gypsy father. This boy, however, was bright and self-reliant, and it seemed that he might have made an even better adjustment if the work had been directed toward him instead of his mother.

These are conditions that have been shown above to be favorable to the Study type of effort. These eight cases, then, may constitute one small part of the explanation why the final social adjustment of the T-boys was not better than that of the controls.

SUB-GROUP 8: CONSIDERABLE HELP NEEDED

The second sub-group—that in which there was greater need for the agency's help but the counselors' efforts were rather slight—contained eleven cases, eight of which were dropped when the agency's case load was reduced. None of these boys had consistent affection from either parent; two lived under definitely unfavorable emotional conditions. The problems of over half of the boys did not seem especially serious at the outset, but greater difficulties appeared as time went by. When last known, however, seven of the eleven appeared to be making a fairly satisfactory adjustment (rating 2), one was classified as socially satisfactory but rather neurotic (2a), two were doing pretty poorly (3), while the last was in a correctional institution.

About the work with seven of these boys there is little to be said except that it was much slighter than was typical of the counselors' usual efforts. Why this was so could not be determined from the case records. It may well be that not much could have been accomplished with four of the boys by the usual Study methods, for their difficulties seemed to represent deep-seated reactions to indecisive, rather neurotic parents. These four were the brightest of the seven boys, their I.Q.'s ranging from 95 to 109. The other three were very dull boys, with I.Q.'s in the seventies. It seems possible that these three could have been aided if the counselors had put forth greater effort, for in these cases there was indication both of interest in being helped and of fairly constructive attitudes on the part of the parents. As it was, two of the boys did not turn out badly, being rated 2 in final adjustment, but the third had a fairly long record of delinquencies. This third boy, the last in the group of seven, a seemingly mature lad of normal intelligence and from a good home, had been worked with for several years but, as the boy later put it, the counselor "slacked off" just about the time he was needed most and the boy committed several offenses.

The following is an example from this sub-group.

Stuart. Age 7 years, 6 months; I.Q. 75. Stuart was described by his teacher as very restless and stubborn in school and given to severe temper tantrums. He was unable to make friends and kept to himself, but he was fairly responsive when alone with the teacher. His mother found him difficult to manage, especially after his baby sister's birth. Acquaintance with the family revealed that the mother both overprotected Stuart and compared him unfavorably with his sister. The father was alternately indulgent and severe, being very much disappointed in the boy's limited mentality, which he regarded as a reflection of his own inadequacy.

The first contact in this case was made with the father. He described at length his attempt to help Stuart learn his school lessons and admitted that he become too excited and scared the boy. "We will work together to help Stuart," he said to the counselor and urged her to come as often as she liked to see the boy and himself. This responsive attitude on the part of the father continued in the subsequent visits. Unfortunately, the counselor gave little time to this case, and it was finally dropped on the ground that the boy was doing as well as could be expected.

In the other three cases in the total group of eleven, reasons for not carrying on the needed kind of work with the boys was clearer. The situations were ones that are familiar to child guidance workers and have been found to call for especially skillful work if anything at all is to be accomplished. In one instance neither mother nor boy (the father was not seen) had much sense of need for help with the problem regarded by the counselor as important—the boy's poor schoolwork (his I.Q. was 114). Moreover, the counselor was not able to give much time to the case. In the other two cases, in which work was carried on chiefly with the mother, the counselors found the mother's subtly controlling attitudes impossible to deal with, and they did not get beyond them to work with the boys themselves. Child guidance experience suggests that the work probably would not have been effective even if they had done so, for usually in such cases both parents' and children's attitudes and feelings must change if good results are to eventuate. That this principle operated in the Study also is suggested by the findings in regard to the successful cases.

SUB-GROUP 9: COUNSELORS' MISTAKES

In the third sub-group, the one in which the lack of accomplishment seemed due in part to poor work on the part of the counselors, there were thirteen cases. In four of them the counselors became so involved in work with the mother or other members of the family that they neglected to do much with or for the boy, even though in some instances the boy gave definite evidence of liking the counselor and seeking his favor. In the other cases, although work was centered on the boy, the error lay chiefly in a somewhat punitive attitude toward the boy or a failure to recognize his bids for attention and interest, or in concentration on one problem or form of service while the boy obviously needed some other.

The first of these types is illustrated by the following case. In it the counselor spent much time and effort on various members of the family and was helpful to them but did less than was needed with the boy.

Chris. Age 10 years, 11 months, to 17 years; I.Q. 89. This lad was always very erratic in his behavior but responded well to people who displayed an interest in him. He was closely attached to his gang, followed the lead of the very delinquent boys who were its members, and thought anything the gang did was right. He was suspicious of anybody who tried to guide him and so was usually regarded as sly and cunning. His family life was difficult, for his mother was psychotic much of the time (manic-depressive), his father overanxious for the children to earn money and give it to him, and his brother feeble-minded and very unstable. Positive factors in the suitation for Chris were that he was his mother's favorite and that his father had considerable affection for all the children even though he had little ability to control them.

Work centered on the mother and on the feeble-minded, unstable brother, the counselor for nine years giving every sort of assistance that lay in her power. She secured camps and medical services for the children, arranged for their church attendance and confirmation, checked on their school behavior, and provided tutoring for several of them. She arranged for the mother's hospitalization when her psychosis flared up (she was in a hospital for three years), and before and after that had frequent interviews with her which provided an outlet for her pent-up feelings. She also talked with the father frequently and advised him how to handle the children. Her work with the feeble-minded brother was intensive and seemed to provide him such support that he improved remarkably. Only Chris was somewhat neglected. The counselor did discuss his difficulties with his teachers and provide tutoring for him, take him on some trips, and attempt to give him some good advice about giving up his gang but she never secured his real interest nor had much influence over him. That the boy might have formed a closer attachment was suggested by his liking for the shop instructor at the Study and his expressed desire that a male member of the staff come to see him.

It seemed unquestionable that the counselor was a real help to the family and therefore may have benefited Chris indirectly. The boy, however, became increasingly involved with his delinquent gang and, although escaping a court record, participated in many delinquent activities. At one time he claimed to have found $200. He gave the money to his father, who bought bonds with it. The counselor, convinced that a theft had occurred, took Chris and his father to court but the theft could not be proved. The father, perhaps feeling guilty about the matter, did not continue the hostility to the counselor that this act of hers at first provoked, but Chris became more sullen and reticent than ever. Nevertheless, the boy did not remain wholly antagonistc, for when last known he was writing letters to the counselor from his military post in Alaska.

In some cases of the second type the basic error was made of alienating the boy's latent interest by actions that showed the counselor aligned against him, emotionally as well as factually.

Martin. This boy had a personality that apparently was obnoxious to everybody. His tutor said he was the most "aggravating" boy she had ever worked with; the principal and teachers called him "pesty" and would put forth little effort to help him; even the counselors were so annoyed by his "polite but officious" manner that they could not view him objectively or recognize the insecurity that occasioned his behavior.

The first counselor had very few interviews with the boy and thought that his behavior was not such as to warrant "treatment." The second saw him much more frequently, but took a cold, moralistic attitude toward him, thinking that the boy's demanding behavior should be controlled by counterdemands on his part. Although he suspected that the boy wanted a close personal relationship he permitted group contacts only, specifically swimming parties which the boy disliked because he could not swim well. Undoubtedly the boy was spoiled and demanding, for his extremely dominant mother indulged him excessively and rewarded him alike for success or failure. Nevertheless, it was clear that the counselors, in trying to force the boy to give up his annoying behavior without first securing his affection, were highly unsuccessful.

Wallace. With this boy, when delinquent at eight and nine years of age, the counselor used a very stern, authoritative approach, centering each interview upon the boy's stealing and saying he did not believe his denials of the acts. He told the child he could go to camp only if he were good. It was not surprising, therefore, that the boy said he preferred selling magazines to engaging in the activities that the counselor suggested or that, some years later with another counselor, he avoided interviews and said he did not come to the Study office because there were things to do that were more fun.

In other cases the counselors ignored or missed the significance of the boys' bids for their attention and interest. Such examples were noted as a boy pressing for specific dates for next visits to be set; another spontaneously discussing his difficulties at school and home even though the counselor visited him only about once in three months and did little but take him on recreational trips; and one saying frankly that he'd rather pal around with the counselor than do anything else. Isolated instances of such actions on the counselors' part were found in many cases but in those under consideration here such mistakes characterized so much of the work that its failure seemed attributable to them.

In the final two cases in which failure seemed attributable to the counselors' mistakes the error lay in over-all planning or in not following through on leads to boys' needs that were plainly given.

In the first of these two cases the parents had problems that child guidance clinics find rather often in Jewish families. They were very sensitive about their cultural status and eager for financial success; they indulged the boy and greatly dominated and controlled him; they were concerned about his poor eating habits and resentful that he did not appreciate all that was being done for him. In addition, the mother was clearly neurotic, of a rather paranoid type. The first counselor tried to meet this difficult situation by advising the mother how to handle the boy with regard to his excessive energy and did nothing in response to her own freely expressed feelings of resentment toward the boy. The second, intent on avoiding involvement with the mother, did not find time to follow through on her request that he try to build up in the boy a pride in being Jewish. The third, desirous of stimulating the boy's intellectual activities, apparently did not know how to proceed when the boy spontaneously started talking about his feelings about himself and his parents, and he became involved in home visits in which mother and boy vied for his attention.

The other of these two cases had some similar elements, although the most striking aspect of the picture was this very bright but probably neurotic boy's interest in intellectual pursuits and unusual hobbies. The mistake was made in following along the lines of the boy's interests to the exclusion of his emotional problems, which the boy gave rather clear evidence of being concerned about. In this case the counselors rather deliberately "held the boy off" in much the same manner as his father did and thus refused him the warm relationship he seemed to be seeking.

Whether the boys could have been helped if these various kinds of mistakes had not been made is difficult to determine. It is to be noted, however, that while none of the boys came from homes that were rated A in emotional relationships (a condition that characterized such a large proportion of the cases in which the boys benefited greatly), there were five cases in which parents' attitudes toward the boy were not very destructive and in which the boy seemed eager for the counselor's attention. Perhaps these five could have been aided. Two of them appeared to be making a neurotic type of adjustment when last heard from, and two were socially maladjusted. Little was known of the fifth boy after he was ten years old, for he moved out of town at that time. The other eight boys had homes that were definitely unfavorable emotionally, being rated C. As will be shown shortly, few boys from such homes were helped by the counselors' efforts. Nearly all these boys were classified as neurotic on the basis of final information about their adjustment. It is probable that these boys would not have responded very well even if the counselors' work had been more adroit; nevertheless, that lack of adroitness must be counted as one element in the failure.

Study Ineffectual for Other Reasons. The above explanations of reasons for failure—the parents' or boys' clear lack of interest in having the agency's services and the counselors' mistakes or lack of effort—seemed to account for somewhat more than half of the cases classified as unsuccessful. The remaining "failures" numbered 44. Analysis of these cases disclosed many situations that seemed too difficult emotionally for Study types of service to reach, if one is to credit the findings of child guidance and other psychiatric studies. In many of them there was a combination of a serious neurotic or other psychiatric disorder on the part of the boy and a very adverse relationship between him and his parents. In others, as well as in many of these cases, genuine cooperation could not be secured, both parents and boys being very ambivalent in their interest in altering the existing unsatisfactory situation.

SUB-GROUP 10: EXTREME EMOTIONAL MALADJUSTMENT

The most striking cases of the first of these two types were 22 in which the parent-child relationships had been classified as C and the boy's initial problems as 5; that is, the emotional situation in the home was very destructive to the boy and his problems from the outset appeared to be very severe. Only two of these boys had an I.Q. under normal, and even they were not seriously retarded. In some of these cases the boy was subjected to cruel treatment at home or was seriously disliked and neglected; in others he was over-indulged by his very weak, ineffectual mother and severely punished by his father, who had little affection for him. As would be expected, few of these boys could form constructive relationships with anybody. Many of them were described as sullen, defiant, aggressive, very demanding, given to temper outbursts on slight provocation. Some seemed psychopathic, having a surface "smoothness" and charm but seemingly lacking in all sense of guilt about their misdeeds. Others were thought to be neurologically disabled, though this diagnosis was never certain.

The following are some examples from this group.

Conrad. This Negro boy was an illegitimate child whose intellectually retarded mother severely rejected him from birth. He lived most of his life with his grandmother, his mother sharing the home. The grandmother had much higher standards than the mother and did her duty by Conrad, but she was stern and perfectionistic, striving after middle-class standards. For two years, when about ten, the boy had a stepfather, but this man was not allowed to have any part in handling the boy.

Conrad was quarrelsome and jealous and unable to make friends. He engaged in persistent stealing and lying all during the Study contact with him. He was under psychiatric treatment for about six months and was regarded by the therapist as having a severe character neurosis and to be lacking in a sense of guilt.

Chester. This boy's home was in the most delinquent neighborhood in Cambridge. His father, a constant drinker and gambler, severely abusive to his wife and children, was killed when Chester was four. The mother was an excitable, quarrelsome person who was frequently sick; she was fatalistic about her children's difficulties. "Put them all in institutions;" she said; "they're all going to Hell anyway."

Chester at nine was described as sullen, defiant, and aggressive. A psychologist who examined him said the boy did not know how to give a spontaneous expression to his feelings. "Everyone expects the worst of me," the boy said, and he lived up to his reputation by apparently compulsive cruelty, destruction of property, and other acts that seemed designed deliberately to antagonize.

Wilbur. He was one of three illegitimate children. His mother was a weak, ineffectual person, not much interested in him. They lived for a time with her mother and sister, both of dubious morals. The mother later married a man who much disliked her children, particularly Wilbur, and would not live in the same house with them. Throughout his childhood the boy was essentially without a home, wandering around from one relative to another, without affection from anybody. He was described as a strange, sullen, moody boy, resentful of everything and everyone. He had stolen since early childhood. By the time the Study work with him started he had been committed to a training school, where he was often in trouble because of his rebellious behavior. His various counselors described him as a boy who had built a shell around himself that they were unable to penetrate.

Henry. The father seemed to be a friendly, worried person. He saw little of his son and, though he said he liked the boy, his only way of disciplining him was to beat him. He used his minor political influence to cover up the boy's delinquencies and save the family's good name. Henry's mother was an excitable, tense woman, much concerned about her health and often near "nervous prostration." She was considered peculiar by the neighbors. She had much guilt about Henry's behavior and many explanations to account for it, ranging from an old head injury to her own nervousness and his being spoiled by his grandmother. Although she said that at times she'd like to kill him, she always defended the boy, sided with him in all his escapades, and always let him do as he pleased. She readily accepted the counselor's offer of help and yet told Henry the worker was trying to get him into a hospital to see whether he was crazy.

Peewee. From early childhood this boy's home situation was very unstable. His mother, a nervous, sickly woman, had divorced his father and left the boy with his aunt for four years. The aunt would lock the child up for hours at a time. When he was about five his mother remarried, the new father being a drunkard with a long police record. This man, who apparently never had much to do with Peewee, died of epilepsy when the boy was nine. The mother was alternately severe with and indulgent of her son; she was utterly incapable of managing him and always glad to have him out of the home.

Peewee, I.Q. 74, was always excessively immature in his behavior, as well as being very retarded physically. To the counselors he was rather appealing in his baby fashion, very talkative and imaginative. Great apprehensiveness was indicated by his dreams and phantasies. He was usually cheerful unless questioned closely about his activities, when he would become very hostile. He was much given to stealing and setting fires; while he seemed to know his acts were wrong, he had no sense of guilt about them. He told the counselor that when he set a fire his heart pounded and he found the situation very exciting.

Angelo. The father was a strutting, self-righteous, excitable man, who gave the impression at first of being a conscientious father. It was soon found, however, that he blamed his wife severely for indulging Angelo, and he himself beat and stormed at the boy and threatened to send him away. The mother was a pleasant but very ineffectual person, totally unable to manage Angelo, even when he was very young. It was not so much that she overprotected him as that, out of inability to do anything else, she left him to do exactly as he pleased.

Angelo, who was first seen when he was only seven years old, bit his nails excessively, slept very poorly, and had enuresis. Soon he took to truancy and stealing, which became worse as the years went by. He was both overactive and tense but had a "smooth," very polite way of talking. He always professed great interest in "going straight" and much appreciation of the counselors' efforts to help him. He was, however, completely unable or unwilling to control his impulse to do whatever he desired at the moment. Both school and court workers were taken in by his "line" and were reluctant to be firm with him, year after year giving him a "last chance."

With only a few exceptions the counselors put a great deal of effort into working with these boys. They stood by them through thick and thin, urging and encouraging them, trying to find activities that interested them, arranging for examinations to discover the reason for their maladjustment, talking with their parents and teachers and others about how to handle them and what to do about them. Foster homes were found for about half of the boys, and psychiatric examination and treatment were secured for many. All in all, in most of these cases the Study's theory of treatment was well carried out but to little or no avail.

This failure could not be attributed to lack of a close relationship with parents and boys, for this usual precondition for successful work was present in some cases, although in others it was lacking. There was variation from case to case, of course, in the counselors' methods and skill and in the amount of time spent with the boys and their families, but in no case were there the serious mistakes that have been described above. It is true, from a psychiatric point of view, that much of the work seemed futile (the attempts, for instance, to give good advice to obviously weak and ineffectual parents or to urge very unstable boys to do better), but these efforts were in line with the original Study theory, and the results only testify to that theory's insufficiency when seriously maladjusted boys are the subjects. It is to be noted, however, that in the few cases in which rather long-continued psychiatric treatment was secured the results were ultimately no better, though some progress was temporarily made with one or two boys. Final judgment as to whether boys of this type are wholly unamenable to the Study sort of treatment must be reserved until the cases in other categories are examined. So far it can be said, however, that practically none of them benefited greatly, for there was only one boy like this in the group of successful cases.

The adjustment of these boys when last known was definitely unsatisfactory. Seven of them were rated 3a (fairly poor adjustment of a neurotic type), one was in category 4a (very poor but not a chronic delinquent), while the rest were both chronically delinquent and seriously neurotic or otherwise emotionally disabled. We shall have more to say about this latter group in connection with chronic delinquency.[1] As to the others, we can say only that the behavior these intellectually adequate boys displayed at the outset continued throughout the period of contact and that from the first they were clearly either neurotic, psychopathic, or neurologically damaged children.

To this group of seriously maladjusted boys from unsatisfying homes may be added four others whose problems did not seem quite so extreme at the outset but who were later found to be seriously neurotic. Most of what has been said above applies to these cases as well. The boys' adjustment when last known was as unsatisfactory as that of the boys described above, three being chronic delinquents and the other apparently even more neurotic than when treatment started.

Three of these four boys were interviewed by the independent

1 See Chap. XXIX.

follow-up investigators. One of them (who between ten and twelve years of age had had many interviews with a counselor whom he described at the time as his only real friend) denied that he had gone to the Study often and said that he had not permitted the counselor to help him. Another said, "Nobody can help you; you have to help yourself. Social workers try to understand you but they can't." The third very belligerently denied all knowledge of the organization, while his perhaps psychotic mother added, "You people are always bothering us. Our whole family is queer; that's why people are always coming around."

All in all, then, over half of the cases classified as failures despite the Study's adequate efforts involved seriously maladjusted boys from very destructive homes. That they were not helped by the kind of services the Study afforded can occasion no surprise.

SUB-GROUP 11: OTHER EXTREME HANDICAPS

Another four boys in this series of unsuccessful cases had in common psychological or social handicaps that the Study could neither remove nor offset. In one case this was extreme feeble-mindedness in an erratic, impulsive boy whose father was a very inadequate, unemployed drunkard and whose mother, a conscientious, hard-working woman, was worn down by the cares of her household. Institutional placement seemed the only answer to the problem but it could not be secured. The mother finally sent the boy to live with some relatives in the country, where he was said to do well.

Another boy suffered from idiopathic epilepsy. The counselor tried to interest the parents in institutional placement but they were unconcerned. When placement was secured through court action, in connection with some flagrant delinquency, the boy adjusted fairly well but he rapidly deteriorated when he returned to his very poor home.

In the other two cases, extreme social maladjustment was coupled with fairly affectionate parent-child relationships. One of these boys lived in utter disorder and filth with his incredibly easygoing and affectionate father and a stepmother, diagnosed psychopathic, who was quite incapable of keeping house and rearing him and his sister. The other's home situation was almost as bad. His father, a spoiled son of an overprotective mother, was selfish and promiscuous; he left his family of wife and nine children soon after the Study work started. The mother of this boy was affectionate and interested in him but she was very unstable, of low intelligence, and unable to keep her house in even a semblance of order or to give the children the minimum of training. Probably because of the affection they received these boys adjusted remarkably well as youngsters, but with adolescence and a decline in their already bad home situations they became resentful and unconforming. The one became involved in serious delinquency; the other, in spite of many delinquent friends, had no court record. In these two cases chief attention was given to the parents and nothing particularly purposeful was done with the boys. The failure may therefore have been due to the inappropriateness of the counselors' efforts.

SUB-GROUPS 12 AND 13: NO DESIRE FOR HELP

Of the remaining sixteen boys in this group that did not benefit from the agency's services, ten came from about as poor homes as those described above, while the others lived under more favorable circumstances emotionally. The problems originally appeared to be less serious than those in the preceding sub-group. Some of the boys were described as unusually reticent and inarticulate, others as typical delinquents who got so much satisfaction from their gang companions that they felt little need of the counselors. Several were boys who were doing fairly well considering the serious handicaps under which they lived. The lack of success with most of these boys seemed chiefly attributable to the absence of a sense of need for the kind of help that would improve their social adjustment. In some cases it was the parents, especially the mothers, who rendered the counselors' efforts ineffectual for this reason; in others it was the boys themselves who could not be reached. Two sub-groups were distinguishable.

Sub-group 12 was represented by seven cases in which the mother was very indulgent or overprotective or overcontrolling and either wanted to use the counselor to increase her control over the boy or seemed to have no sense of problem with him. Most of these were economically and culturally middle-class people, in contrast to the working class status of most of the Study's cases. Overprotective mothers are well known to child guidance workers, who probably encounter them more frequently than the Study counselors did. The overprotective attitude usually engenders a corresponding lack of sense of need on the part of the child. Two examples follow.

Otto. Age 11–15; I.Q. 107. There was never any question of delinquency on the part of this boy. Teachers and counselors were concerned, however, about his almost compulsive drive for perfection, which showed itself in tension and anxiety when there was any possibility that he might fail to reach the highest academic standards. His mother's prohibitions kept him from leading a normal boy's life but he did not rebel. He was accepted by the other children in his class but was not regarded by them as a "regular fellow."

The father, rather unsuccessful in business, was described by his wife as irritable with Otto, leaving all decisions about the boy to her. (She regarded her husband as a very inadequate man.) The mother was extremely controlling in her relation to the boy. She would not allow him to play with the children in the neighborhood, regarding it as beneath her social status, took complete charge of his reading and his extracurricular activities, rushed to the school to complain whenever his marks fell below A, and, generally, did not permit him to have a life of his own. She was full of theories and explanations about his behavior and her own actions regarding it, for the most part feeling that he was doing very well.

This mother from the outset was eager for the counselor's interest in the boy. She was willing to have him see Otto alone but was determined that he should set forth a definite program of what he expected to accomplish with the boy. Her own interviews with the counselor she kept on a definitely social basis, firmly using him as backing for her ideas. Only once did she ask for specific help—concerning a teacher whom Otto did not like. At that time the counselor tried to suggest that her standards for the boy were too high, but the mother denied that she was asking for more than average, saying that Otto's standards were his own.

A second counselor aroused much antagonism in the mother by advocating activities for Otto to which she was opposed. That episode practically ended the work on the case, a third counselor having only one interview. Throughout this time the boy was seen only infrequently. To all the counselor's attempts to elicit the boy's feelings about the way he was treated by his parents, he received almost direct quotations of the mother's point of view. The boy's only concern seemed to be that he might antagonize his teacher and so receive lower marks than he and his mother would want.

Cosmo. Age 7 years, 7 months to 14 years, 7 months; I.Q. 121. This bright Italian boy was an aggressive, self-confident, spoiled child, rivalrous with his older, duller brother. In spite of his intelligence he did very poor work in school and was constantly in mischief in the classroom. In and out of school he was pugnacious with the other children, sulky, bossy, always wanting to be the center of attention. Enuresis persisted until ten, when he apparently gave it up in order to go to camp.

Cosmo's mother was very lenient and indulgent with him. She was not at all concerned about his behavior difficulties, not even minding the bed-wetting. She was not defensive of him, in the manner of some Italian mothers, but just pleasantly unconcerned except when things went especially badly and then she had no idea what she could do. His father was more bothered by Cosmo's behavior but did nothing about it except storm around occasionally and accuse his wife of spoiling the boy.

Cosmo was taken on many recreational trips by his counselors; physical examinations and psychological examinations were secured, and reports of his superior intelligence were given to the teachers. He was sent to camp and art school, which he liked for a time. Slight attempts were made to urge the mother to change her ways of handling Cosmo but to no avail. She remained friendly with the counselors but unconcerned about Cosmo's behavior. Cosmo, too, was consistently friendly but did not develop a close relationship. His conduct continued about the same throughout the years.

Sub-group 13 was quite the reverse of this. Instead of enveloping their sons with a neurotic kind of affection that bound the boys to them and prevented emotional growth, the mothers of the nine boys in this sub-group were indifferent and unconcerned. The boys in turn, instead of being overattached to their mothers, went outside the family for satisfaction of their emotional needs and found in gang life what they missed at home. Some of these boys were reticent or inarticulate, traits that the counselors found baffling, sometimes irritating, and at least uninteresting. Other boys were friendly and likable and were described as having pleasing personalities. (Significantly, it was these latter boys who had the least unsatisfactory home conditions.) Few of the boys seemed to feel any real need of the counselors' help, though some maintained friendly relations with them. All of these boys had adequate intelligence, two having an I.Q. above 110.

Chief emphasis in most of these cases was put on finding or providing better recreational facilities for the boy, in describing the home situation to the teachers, in securing tutoring and physical examinations when needed. Little work was done with the families. In only one or two cases did a counselor get close enough to the boy to be consulted about his personal problem and even then the relationship was not sustained. In many case records the counselors were very definite in their statements that the boy's interest could not be secured.

Ross. Age 10–15; I.Q. 83. Ross's father, an engineer on a fishing boat, was a steady drinker who had had several mental hospital commitments with the diagnosis of Korsakoff's syndrome. He was said to be cruel to his children. The mother was a dull, ineffectual woman who seemed completely without concern about her children and without ability to handle them, though she made a pretense of discussing ways of doing so. She had once been diagnosed as a psychopathic personality. She did not favor any of her nine children nor was she deliberately neglectful or cruel to them. The children got along with each other fairly well but all seemed uninterested in bettering their situation.

Ross was a pleasant, somewhat lethargic boy who got along well with his gang. His behavior grew worse with time, for he became less interested in school, more given to delinquent activities, and, though often complaining about lack of play opportunities, less willing to put forth any effort to change his recreational habits. The first counselor put considerable effort into separating the boy from his gang by providing better leisure-time activities and talking with him about the risks he was running in engaging in petty delinquency. Later counselors found him unresponsive, as the first did also, and made little attempt to help him. Neither the boy nor his mother ever asked for assistance, and there was no evidence that they cared much whether the counselors came to see them or not.

Alexander. Age 12–17; I.Q. 116. The mother was a nervous, rather unhappy person who felt she could not discipline or supervise her son adequately because her husband was so irritable with him. Actually, she herself was too weak to exercise any control over him and not really much concerned about his behavior. The father, too, was indifferent to the boy's conduct so long as he stayed out from under foot and did not cause inconvenience. The family lived in a rough neighborhood and had little income.

Alexander was first described as a gregarious, energetic boy, rather self-centered. He disliked school and was frequently a truant. His friends were a gang of delinquent boys, who, like himself, spent most of their time on the streets, playing and getting into mischief. Alexander seemed wholly irresponsible, unwilling to do anything that was even slightly unpleasant to him, such as attending school or practicing for the band. He left school at fifteen and had a very chequered job history after that.

Chief emphasis in the early work with Alexander was on getting him to accept and use a "Y" membership, without much success. Slight attempts were made to influence the boy and his mother by good advice. Alexander was untouched by these efforts, and the mother, while giving lip service to the suggestion that she be firmer with him, felt that her son's companions were to blame. Alexander was very friendly with the first counselor, making rather frequent calls at her home, but her influence over him was negligible. The second, a man, made many visits to the home and thought he had a good relationship with the boy. Actually, he seldom saw Alexander, and his services were little used unless the boy wanted something from him, such as having a court charge "fixed."

Since these boys were the delinquent type for which the Study was originally designed, the failure with them is particularly striking, even though understandable. Whether most cases of this sort were unsuccessfully handled cannot be answered, however, until all are examined. When last heard about, two of these boys were adjusting fairly well, the adjustment of four was rated as rather poor or very poor, and the remaining three were chronic delinquents.

SUMMARY

Reviewing this analysis of reasons why the counselors were unsuccessful in so many cases, we see fairly obvious explanations accounting for most of them. First, in about a fifth of these failures the offer of service was either openly refused by parents or by boys from the start or soon rendered ineffective by disinterest. Second, in nearly half, the failure seemed due in part at least to inadequate or poor work on the part of the counselors, in the sense that either less was done than the situation called for or obviously poor methods were used. The former was the more frequent fault; it occurred most often in cases in which the boy's need apparently was not great—in other words, in cases that were dropped because of pressure of staff time. It is only in retrospect and in the light of the findings in regard to the most successful cases that this discontinuance of work with fairly well-adjusted boys is seen to be important. It was the Study's understandable aim to give chief attention to the most needy boys, but it appears—so far in our analysis at least—that, if good results were desired, more would have been gained by concentrating on those who were less maladjusted.[2]

[2] For confirmation of this point see Chap. XXIX.

Third, and in line with what has just been said, a little more than a fifth of the failures seemed attributable largely to social, emotional, or (in one case) mental handicaps that were beyond the counselors' power to deal with. For the most part, the boys so classified were very neurotic and the parent-child relationships so lacking in healthy elements that there was little with which the counselors could work. In these cases, as in those in the following group, the Study program encountered the stumbling-block that child guidance workers are so familiar with—the inability or unwillingness of the boys to mobilize sufficient strength to overcome the forces that pull them in the direction of non-conformity to social requirements.

Fourth, and finally, in a sixth of the cases the boys' genuine interest in being helped could not be secured, even though these boys and their parents did not reject the Study at the outset. In some cases the mother-boy relationship was too close to permit the use of the counselor's assistance; in others the parents were rather indifferent to the boy and his welfare, and the boy had, in a sense, substituted gang loyalty for family attachment and was thus unlikely to turn to any adult for help.

There were, then, three main elements in these failure cases, though not all of them were present in each: the boys' disinterst in the service offered, the counselors' lacks in time and skill, and the severity of the boys' handicaps, chiefly emotional in nature. In all these respects the contrast with the successful cases described in the preceding chapter is great. There, for the most part, the boys and their families were eager for the agency's assistance, the help that was given was (in both quality and time devoted to it) adequate to the boys' needs, and the boys' handicaps, in many cases, did not lie in the sphere of the emotions or, if they did, were counterbalanced by healthy elements in their personality and in the parent-child relationships. In most of the successful cases all three of these favorable elements were present; in many of the failures all were missing.

The extent of the difference between the successes and the failures is shown best by eliminating the cases in which failure was due either to the clients' explicit refusal of the agency's services or to poor work on the part of the counselors. Considering, then, the boys' "original" adjustment ratings we find among the successfully treated cases 29 of the 49 boys originally classified as in good mental health or as having only a slight problem, and only one of those classified as seriously maladjusted. In contrast, among the failures there were no boys rated as originally well adjusted and only seven of the 44 whose problems were rated as slight. Half of these boys who were not helped were originally classified as seriously maladjusted.

The ratings on the emotional-social aspects of the boys' homes are equally striking. Nearly half of the boys who benefited greatly came from homes rated A emotionally; there were no such homes among the boys with whom little or nothing was accomplished. At the other extreme about an eighth of the successes and nearly three-fourths of the failures came from homes where the emotional situation was rated C. Two-thirds of the first group, as contrasted with one-fourth of the second, had homes rated A socially, while the proportion from C homes was a tenth in the successful group and about a fourth among the failures.

It was in the cases rated B emotionally that factors other than the home situation were especially important in differentiating the successes from the failures. In record after record of boys definitely aided it is stated that the boy and his parents seemed very fond of the counselor and eager to have his help. For example, Alvin, a rather unstable boy with a complex and difficult family situation, told his counselor, "You are the only person I can really talk to," and his employer reported, "The family say you are the only one who can do anything with Alvin." In contrast, among the failures the inability of the counselors to establish good working relationships was strikingly apparent. Among the cases of this sort were boys described by their counselors in such terms as stolid, inarticulate, or indifferent; the parents, though moderately fond of the boys, were said to be rather unconcerned about their welfare.

Then, too, in the B cases in which the boys benefited, the counselors' working methods seemed more skilled or more appropriate to the situations than in those in which they were not helped, though it is difficult to document this point without giving much detail. The difference lay partly in the fact that the counselors concentrated on the boys instead of becoming greatly involved in trying to alleviate hopeless family difficulties; and partly in the fact that, perhaps by chance, they struck the right note in their dealings with the parents, so that the positive rather than the negative elements in the situations were accentuated.

All in all, then, after a detailed analysis of the case records is made there seems to be little mystery as to why the counselors were able to help some of the boys so greatly while with others their efforts were of little avail. This clarity, however, has been achieved by comparing extremes. Whether it will remain after the less clear-cut cases are examined is yet to be determined.

Possibly Harmful Effects of the Study. In reviewing the cases in which the boys were not benefited we aimed not only to show what kinds of boys these were but also to discover whether some of them might have been harmed. This latter question had to be considered because the statistical findings in Chapter XXIV showed that at the time of follow-up a significant proportion of boys with whom the counselors failed were more socially maladjusted than their control "twins."

To suggest that social work activities may be actually harmful may seem rather shocking, so accustomed are we to thinking that well-intentioned actions in the field of human relations can at worst be only ineffectual. Such a point of view, of course, is not maintained in the field of medical or psychological therapy, where it is well recognized that under certain circumstances a specified form of treatment may make matters worse. In social work, however, where friendly counseling and the provision of various forms of concrete assistance are the services afforded, it is seldom thought that damage can be done. Nevertheless, if it can happen, it is very important that practitioners know what kinds of actions may be harmful and by what signs "social treatment" is contra-indicated.

At first thought it seems very difficult, perhaps impossible, to demonstrate that a given boy's adjustment was made worse by a counselor's efforts to help him. We have, however, attempted to demonstrate the opposite in a previous series of cases—that under certain circumstances certain types of service benefited boys—so the apparent difficulty may lie more in the unfamiliarity of the argument than in its logic.

When good results were under consideration we first identified the cases in which boys' social adjustment apparently improved after some period of contact with the organization. These cases were then examined to see what the counselors had done, if anything, that might be regarded as causally related to the change in the boys' condition. In so doing, we necessarily had in mind some scientific or common-sense principles regarding the causes of social maladjustment and possible remedies. In other words, back of the case analysis lay certain assumptions as to why boys might benefit from services such as those the Study provided. These assumptions had regard both to the traits of the boys and their home situations and to the kind of work that was done with them.

The analysis of reasons for failure followed similar lines. After determining which boys did not improve or became worse, we looked to see whether there were factors in the boys themselves or in the services they received that would theoretically be associated with poor results. For example, we attributed failure in a considerable number of cases to lack of interest on the boys' part, while in others the work of the counselors did not appear to be up to standard. In the other cases, in which Study services failed to help the boys, lack of success was attributed chiefly to various traits of the boys themselves and their home situations, and little attention was paid to the counselors' working methods. It was in this group of cases (C3) that the comparison with the control group revealed that some boys had possibly been harmed by their contact with the organization. Our present objective is to discover whether there were any such boys and, if so, to what the possible damage might be attributed. The fact that the nature of the organization's activities has not been closely analyzed in this series provides a clue with which to begin.

The search for reasons for good results was facilitated by the fact that we had certain ideas as to how they might have been achieved. It seemed reasonable to suppose, for instance, that when a boy's behavior improved after the removal of some handicap or the resolution of some conflict situation in his family there was a causal connection between the two events. Our search for the ways, if any, in which harm was done to the boys obviously also requires preliminary ideas as to how this result might come about, and it is here that we run into difficulties, for ideas in this area are less plentiful than in the other. It is possible, however, to start with one assumption on the negative side; it seems rather unlikely that boys could be harmed by "concrete" services provided in the kindly, interested, sympathetic Study manner, especially if these were given in such a way as not to produce guilt. Providing tutoring and recreational opportunities, taking a boy for physical examinations and arranging for his medical care, "interpreting" his behavior to his teachers—it seems rather unlikely that such services in and of themselves could be detrimental. If any possible harm could follow upon such work it would come, it seems, from the emotions aroused in the boys by such actions, from their emotional response to the persons who provided the services. If this is so, we can pretty well eliminate from the list of possibly harmed boys those who did not form close relationships with the counselors; such boys may not have benefited but it seems rather unlikely that they could have been hurt. The acceptance of this assumption thus narrows the search to boys who were attached to their counselors and calls for consideration of ways in which such an attachment could be detrimental. We shall leave these speculations, however, until the cases themselves are examined, for otherwise the range of possibilities opened up is too large.

In the descriptive analysis above, the boys who were not benefited were classified according to the apparent reasons for the failure. The search may well start with the categories within the D3 group described on p. 496, for this grouping was made partly along the lines of the boys' response to Study efforts. In two of the categories (Subgroups 12 and 13) failure of the Study to be of benefit seemed attributable to the boys' or their parents' lack of interest in being helped; in the other two it was the severity of the boys' disabilities that seemed to stand in the way.

Now it would seem unlikely that the boys in these first two categories could have been harmed by the counselors' attention, for, by definition, they did not participate sufficiently to have exposed themselves psychologically to that danger. Review of the cases substantiated that conclusion. Several of them have been described above. (Otto, p. 503, Cosmo, p. 503, Ross, p. 505, Alexander, p. 505.) The work in the other cases was similarly superficial, in the sense that either the counselors had little contact with the boys or, if they did give them much attention, they confined their efforts to activities (such as providing recreational opportunities, tutoring, medical examinations, and the like) that did not touch upon the boys' emotional problems. As has been said before, it seems rather unlikely that such services could have adversely influenced the boys' adjustment.

If this reasoning is correct, if any boys were harmed by the Study's attention they are to be found among the severely maladjusted youngsters in Sub-groups 10 or 11. These were boys who from the outset were recognized as greatly handicapped; all those whose difficulties lay in the emotional sphere remained maladjusted. Review of the cases indicated that the boys for whom we were searching were probably in this latter group, but even in that group there were many for whom the Study's services could be scarcely considered detrimental. With some of these boys the Study played a subordinate role to that of other organizations, the counselors maintained friendly contact with the boys and, in some cases, secured the other organizations' services for them but did not gain much influence over the boys otherwise.

An example is the work done with Rex. This very unstable, aggressive boy apparently suffered from early emotional deprivation and overstrict handling by his father, for which his stepmother was unable to compensate. The first Study counselor had bi-monthly interviews with the stepmother for the first two years in the hope of relieving the tense situation. Treatment by a child guidance clinic was secured for the boy, and considerable time was spent in telling the teacher about his difficulties. When the boy's conduct became worse, the help of a child-placing agency was secured, through whose efforts the boy was sent to a succession of foster homes and schools for maladjusted youngsters, all without success. This counselor, as well as the second one, left most of the work with the boy to these other agencies, though he did take him on some trips, sent him to camp, and wrote to him when he was at school. Rex seemed to use the counselors, especially the second one, chiefly as a source of material assistance and at times tried to play them off against the other agency social workers. While it was clear that the Study accomplished little if anything with this boy, there seemed little reason to believe that the counselors' efforts made matters worse than they would have been otherwise.

With other boys in this series, Study work, though not beneficial, could not be considered detrimental because it was only after long and persistent effort that the boy evinced even slight interest in the proffered services. It seemed unlikely that the little they did accept and the modicum of a relationship they permitted to develop could have been harmful. In still other cases much of the counselors' efforts went into work rather remote from the boy and his parents, so far as engaging their emotions is concerned. For instance, with Miles, an excessively hyperactive boy, much time was spent on securing a diagnosis, epilepsy at one time being suspected. The many interviews with the mother were largely centered about securing her permission for physical examinations, while with Miles himself little was done except providing much, and ineffectual, tutoring. The boy was taken on a few trips and sent to camp for two summers but it was only near the time of termination that interviews were held that seemed to have any real appeal for him.

Our search for the boys who may possibly have been harmed narrows down, then, to a group of severely maladjusted youngsters who at one time or another became very much attached to their counselors and, probably, emotionally dependent upon them. We have already seen that such a relationship formed the basis for successful work in some cases. In the series of boys who were clearly benefited there were some striking examples of such accomplishments. Some of the boys so helped were basically well-adjusted individuals whom the counselors served in the capacity of supplements to well-disposed but ignorant or immature parents (Sub-group 2). The others, among whom were some very neurotic boys, were aided either by unusually skilled use of the relationship (Sub-group 5) or by unusually persistent work of the typical Study variety. Since the boys under consideration here were more or less like this latter group in emotional incapacity, our attention is directed to the ways in which their relationship with the counselors was handled.

Examination of the cases from this point of view revealed two major types of possibly harmful mistakes that were made by the counselors: breaking off of contact after a close relationship had been established, and using the relationship in a way that was psychologically unsound in view of the character of the boy's emotional problem. The avoidance of this latter type of mistake presupposes, of course, a knowledge of psychiatry and skill in the use of psycho-therapeutic measures to which the counselors did not pretend and which was largely outside the Study's plan. Nevertheless, since it seems that the boys with whom such mistakes in treatment were made were the only ones likely to have been made worse by some of their experiences with the counselors, it seems important to indicate the nature of the possible errors.

An example of the first type of error, unavoidable perhaps, but possibly damaging nevertheless, is shown in the case of Leroy, who may also have suffered from unwise handling on the part of the last counselor.

Leroy (I.Q. 86) was an alert, rather furtive gang member when work with him started at the age of ten; in behavior and personality he became progressively more unstable as time went by. His father had died about six months before, and Leroy, his favorite, was much upset by the death. The mother, casual to the point of neglect in her care of her five children, was very indifferent toward Leroy; she later became definitely hostile to him and their quarrels became extreme. She and the boy's older sister were promiscuous in their sexual affairs, and life in the home was very quarrelsome and confused.

The first counselor, a woman, tried to build up Leroy's self-confidence. She arranged that he go to camp several summers, secured a "Y" membership for him, and throughout one winter tutored him regularly. Leroy seemed reticent with her but it was clear that he liked her very much and enjoyed the attentions the tutoring sessions provided. He felt very unhappy when she left the Study. On her departure, a male counselor instituted weekly interviews with the boy, attempting to use various play-therapy techniques. In these interviews Leroy indicated hostile feelings toward his mother, intense curiosity about sex, and concern about death. To the counselor's attempt to interpret the meaning of his play he responded by avoiding interviews for several months. His attachment to the counselor was quite clear, however. He had a painful farewell interview with this counselor, at which time he also asked why the first counselor had to leave. A few days later he was put on probation for breaking windows, this delinquency following several stealing episodes.

The third counselor's working method seemed chiefly that of responding to nearly all the boy's requests, such as taking Leroy and his friends on overnight trips to the family's tumble-down cabin, where the boys became very boisterous and pretty much out of hand, and of letting him come with his friends to his own home, where Leroy ransacked desk drawers and closets in search of objects of interest. The counselor did this, apparently, in the hope of off-setting the mother's bad treatment of the boy and of giving him an opportunity to escape from the turmoil of his home. Throughout the period, however, Leroy became an even more serious truant from school and often stayed away from home all night, once leaving entirely for three weeks. He was eventually sentenced to a school for truants. After release he did better for a time, then began his usual erratic going on and off jobs, and finally falsified his age (with the counselor's consent) and tried to enlist. The last report (from his mother) told of his desertion from the Army, stealing of a car, and attempted murder of a policeman.

It is impossible to prove, of course, that the severance of the happy relationship with the first two counselors, which duplicated in a sense the boy's loss of his affectionate father, was a factor in the decline in social adjustment. It seems psychologically plausible, however, that the boy would have been better off if the emotional involvement, inherent especially in the kind of work the second counselor attempted, had never occurred if it were not to be followed through to a satisfactory close. In addition, the overindulgent attitude of the third counselor may also have been harmful.

An example of the second type of error is shown in the following case.

Willard (I.Q. 75) was at eleven a small, slight boy, much given to aggressive talk and tales of numerous misdeeds. He continually stressed his "badness" and said that his stealing, smoking, fighting were bad habits that could not be broken. As he grew older he became increasingly moody. Willard's parents were Italians who did not speak English, so not much was learned regarding their feelings about the boy, but they seemed indifferent to his welfare. His older siblings, who took some responsibility for him, themselves engaged in illegal activities but tried to keep Willard out of trouble. His home was a well-kept apartment in one of the worst of the community's delinquency areas.

The first counselor, who worked with the boy for about two years, had at least monthly interviews with him alone, and, in addition, tutoring was provided. The counselor tried to tell the boy that his attitudes of being tough and bullying were only creating difficulties and that his boasts were without real basis. He treated all the boy's talk of being bad as pure phantasy and, although he knew of some minor delinquencies being committed by the boy, said nothing about them but tried to influence Willard toward better conduct. Willard was very fond of this counselor, often said he appreciated his interest, described him as his only real friend, and yet kept saying that the counselor should not waste time on him. He revealed much ambivalence or guilt toward other persons also. Regarding the teacher, for example, he said, "I'm a tough guy. I'm not a teacher's pet. I don't want people to be nice to me." Regarding his family he would say at one time that they were too nice to him and at another that none in his family except his mother liked him and that even she wanted to get rid of him. By the end of this counselor's contact Willard was becoming more difficult in the classroom and was terrorizing other children.

The next counselor had only one interview with the boy during the month that he was assigned to the case. In that interview, in response to the counselor's saying that he must be a boy who was afraid of himself Willard said, "That's the trouble. I've got two minds. One tells me to do good things and the other bad things. Everyone has tried to help me but they can't." Following this talk Willard's behavior in school became very much worse. He said to the teacher, "I don't want no one coming around here to help me. They can't do anything for me."

The next counselor put most of his effort into winning Willard's confidence by providing various forms of recreation for the gang to which the boy was by this time greatly attached and by taking a very lenient attitude toward the gang's behavior. Willard at first avoided this counselor, then tolerated him for a time, and then, in spite of many attempts on the counselor's part to seek him out, avoided him entirely. A follow-up interviewer found him very nervous; he protested that he had seldom gone to the Study and recalled only his last counselor's name. He was working as an auto mechanic; his chief interest was in making cars go very fast.

Again, proof of the damage done cannot be established, but it seems likely that this boy found very discouraging the lack of understanding of his feelings (indicated by the denial of his being bad) on the part of the counselor who seemed to love him and to whom he was so much devoted. The counselor's kindliness, coupled with his exhortations to do better, may have only added to the boy's guilt; the boy seemed to be seeking recognition of his badness and help in dealing with it, and he may have had to act worse and worse when his feelings were denied.

In other boys other complicated emotional reactions seemed evident, lack of understanding of which may have adversely influenced development. For example, one boy, regarded even at eleven as a potential homosexual, became very fond of his counselor and described him as a "grand man" and, except for one person, his only

THE BOYS WHO WERE NOT HELPED

friend. It seemed noteworthy that with the other person the boy played a passive homosexual role and that against both him and the counselor he committed aggressive acts of stealing and running away. Before the counselor began his work, the boy had been having some success in making the best of a bad home situation. It may be that the counselor's friendship and his encouragement in regard to leaving home may have aroused emotions in the boy with which he could deal only destructively.

In the two other cases, sensitive, solitary boys, physically and emotionally neglected at home, did fairly well for a time under the kindly, affectionate ministrations of a counselor whom they came to like very much. When, however, the counselor, in one case, turned her attention for a time to the problems of the boy's rejecting mother and, in the other case, reported the boy to the court after he failed his probation appointments, insecurities were apparently aroused and the boys reacted accordingly. As in the cases described above in more detail, no proof can be given that these various kinds of failure to recognize the nature of their feelings adversely affected the boys' adjustment, but if any boys were hurt by the Study efforts it seems that it must have been those whose attachment to the counselors could have made them vulnerable.

In all, there were eight boys who seemed to the writer possibly somewhat harmed by the counselors' efforts. All of them were boys definitely maladjusted from the outset, and there is little reason to believe that they would have become well adjusted if they had not come in contact with the organization. It is only in a relative sense, then, that the Study's services were possibly detrimental; were it not for the comparison with the control group one would probably have said only that these boys were not benefited, not that they were harmed. If, however, the statistics comparing T- and C-boys are to be believed, and if these eight were boys whose terminal adjustment was somewhat less good than it might otherwise have been, the conclusion to be drawn is that organizations that provide services of the "friendship" type (that is, that do not have psychiatrically trained staffs) must proceed very cautiously in encouraging the development of close relationships with seriously maladjusted individuals. Such a relationship can occasionally be very constructive, but an untrained worker always runs the risk of breaking trust with a neurotic boy whose sensitivities he does not understand or of increasing his anxiety and guilt. It would seem better, for the most part, that untrained counselors should be helped to recognize individuals such as these and thereby avoid the close involvement that may follow upon discussion of personal problems.

CHAPTER XXVIII

THE DUBIOUS CASES

IN THE CLASSIFICATION SYSTEM DESCRIBED IN CHAPTER XXV CATE-
gories of results of service were described that might be combined
under the heading "dubious." These consisted of (1) cases in which
not much was accomplished, but the boys and/or their parents
were so friendly with the counselors and so appreciative of their
assistance that it seemed incorrect to describe the work as wholly
unavailing; (2) cases in which the counselors seemed to be helpful
to the boys for a time but afterwards the boys again lapsed into
difficulties; (3) cases in which the counselors' efforts were possibly
beneficial but there was no certainty that this was so. Most of the
boys in the first category were never very maladjusted, while many
in the second group had serious problems throughout the period of
contact. The three categories of cases will be analyzed separately
below, in an effort to see to what extent they confirm or refute the
conclusions already drawn.

NOT MUCH ACCOMPLISHED IN SPITE OF FRIENDLY RELATIONS

The twenty boys in the first series varied widely in type of home
situation and in the seriousness of behavior disorders. A few had
homes rated AA or AB emotionally and socially; [1] most came from
BA or BB homes, and a few lived under emotional conditions rated
C. As to behavior disorders, about half seemed to have few if any
difficulties at the outset (ratings 1 or 2), and only one boy was so
maladjusted as to be placed in the lowest category. Most of these
boys, accordingly, were not as handicapped as those with whom the
Study failed; on the other hand, few of them were as favorably situated as the boys with whom the counselors were most successful.
This position midway, as it were, between the successes and the failures is not, however, sufficient explanation of why the counselors

---

[1] See Chap. XXII for definitions of categories.

did not accomplish much with these boys in spite of the friendly relations that were established with them. For such an explanation we must examine the cases as wholes.

Close study revealed situations that had much in common with the cases previously described. A few more or less paralleled those in which the boys were clearly benefited by the counselors' services, so the question had to be asked, why was it that these favorably situated boys were not helped? Many, on the other hand, had so much in common with the failures that the lack of success did not seem surprising. They will be described below under these headings.

SUB-GROUP 14: CASES PARALLELING THOSE OF BOYS WHO BENEFITED

Among the boys who clearly benefited from the Study's services was a relatively large number whose problems were rather slight and who came from homes that were emotionally and socially adequate. With many of these boys, it may be recalled, the good results were secured through the discovery and removal of specific handicaps to their social adjustment—a reading disability, for example, or a physical defect, or an adverse form of behavior on a parent's part.

There were five boys with somewhat similar characteristics in the series under consideration but they remained much the same from the beginning to the end of the counselors' work with them. Comparison of these cases suggests that the reason for the unsatisfactory outcome lay in the counselors' inability to discover the cause of the difficulty and to deal with it directly.

Two of these boys the counselors regarded as uninteresting or baffling. The boys were inarticulate, uncommunicative, or shy and retiring, and it was these traits that made work with them difficult.

One of these boys had these traits to such an extreme degree that this in itself constituted his chief problem. He was otherwise socially adequate, with the usual boy's interests and activities, but in all situations, at home as well as elsewhere, he was monosyllabic. A psychiatrist who examined him thought that he might be in an early stage of Parkinson's disease, but this diagnosis was not established, as the boy refused a second examination. Neither of two counselors was able to draw him out or to discover what lay back of this attitude, so the case was dropped as unsuitable for further effort, especially since the boy was getting along fairly well.

The other inarticulate boy's problem was chiefly that of doing much poorer schoolwork than would be expected from his I.Q. of 102 and of taking jobs that were beyond his physical capacity. Several counselors tried to reach him without apparent success, though the boy on follow-up told the independent investigator that the last of the counselors had been "a real friend, not a person hired to do this work." Part of the problem may have lain in the boy's fear of tuberculosis, his father and sister having died of that disease and he himself being rather frail; if so, the counselors did not elicit that concern, though the boy persistently showed reluctance to have chest examinations. When last seen, this boy had successfully finished his period of Army service; he gave no evidence of his former reticence.

In the three other cases the counselors' inability to get at the root of the problem seemed attributable in part to the use of rather poor methods.

One of these boys was hyperactive, pugnacious, demanding, and rather "spoiled." Several of his counselors did little with him, and the one who saw him most frequently felt that his problems were very elusive. Little was done to help the boy be less jealous of his brother, who was also a client, though some of his actions suggested that this was an important factor in the maladjustment.

Another of the boys was dull (I.Q. 70), had a severe reading disability, and stuttered, but it was chiefly his petty stealing that got him into trouble. The first two counselors' work with this boy was rather trivial and undirected, for they considered him too dull to be worth their efforts, but even the third counselor, who made an attempt to discuss the stealing, did not try to discover why the boy behaved as he did. This counselor felt that he made no impression, but the boy said near the end of his period of contact, "If you come here long enough you never forget this place." When last heard of, at sixteen, he had quit school and was "loafing." His stealing had never led to court action.

In the final of the three cases the counselors' mistakes were those of commission rather than omission. This bright boy was energetic and outgoing and had many friends; for a time, however, he did poor schoolwork and engaged in some minor stealing, and he had enuresis at least up to thirteen, when the counselor's work ended because the family moved away. Work with this boy centered chiefly on the enuresis, which was diagnosed by a doctor as not due to organic causes. What it was due to was not discovered. The counselor put so much pressure on the boy and his mother to take measures to deal with the problem that they were put on the defensive. Nevertheless, they remained interested in having the counselor visit them, chiefly because he provided recreation.

The chief difference between these cases and those in which the boys benefited greatly from the Study's services seems to lie in the counselors' working methods. In the latter cases there was a close correspondence between boys' needs and counselors' efforts, and the skills employed were appropriate to the objectives. Just the opposite was true of the cases described above, although the work in them was not outstandingly poor. Perhaps the cases were more difficult than the others, in that these boys were shy or dull and the reasons for their problems not very serious. Perhaps they were less interesting to the counselors. Whatever the reason, review of the cases and comparison of them with those rated A suggests that more is needed for successful work of the Study type than friendly relations and favorable home conditions; such service calls for direction and skill, just as do other forms of social work.

In four other cases the parallel with those in which the boys were greatly helped lay chiefly in the methods the counselors used. In two of these cases the situation contained elements less favorable to success, while in the other two cases the rather poor results seemed due, in part at least, to the counselors' lack of skill.

SUB-GROUP 15

The first of the four cases was one in which the counselor played the role of parent-supplement to a boy whose mother was foreign-born and whose father was dead. This Portuguese boy with an I.Q. of 86 was described by his teacher as an aggressive, bossy child who cheated and stole and made himself generally disliked in the classroom. The counselor, however, found him energetic, likable, capable of good relationships, and having many friends. He lived in a delinquent neighborhood and had inadequate supervision, though his mother was somewhat overprotective of him in a typical South-European way. The boy became very much attached to the counselor and manifested considerable desire to live up to what she expected of him but, in spite of this, he continued to be unstable in school and on jobs, doing well under specially favorable conditions and becoming irritable and resentful when things did not go quite right. For example, he tried to get out of the Navy by pretending that he could not write and yet did well in military service after that particular episode was straightened out, partly by an appeal for loyalty to the counselor.

Comparison of this case with those in the successful group which were somewhat like it suggests that the difference in outcome is to be attributed to the difference in the emotional tone of the home. It may be recalled that in most of the successful cases the parents were very fond of the boys and family relationships were very good. The boys' attachment to the counselors seemed a result of strength rather than weakness. In the present case, on the contrary, the father was dead and the mother, fond but overprotective, had a somewhat paranoid attitude that was copied by her children. In addition, the boy's oldest brother, a dull inadequate youth who constantly complained and criticized and treated the boy roughly, was a decidedly bad factor in the home. The counselor apparently could not offset these unfavorable influences, though his friendship was probably of some value to the boy.

Much the same comment might be made on the second case. This boy was a delicate, sensitive child in a sturdy, rough Italian family. He was bad-tempered and sullen when crossed and greatly resented authority, traits that frequently got him into trouble in school. His mother, described as a loud, coarse woman, engaged in much bickering and swearing, cheated on relief and depended on political "drag" for getting along. She was violently defensive of her children when they were criticized and yet was inconsistent and irregular in her discipline at home. She did not permit the stepfather, whom the boy liked, to have anything to do with child training. The chief emphasis in this case was on bettering this mother's relations with the school authorities, for it was clear that her violent demands there hurt her children's reputation. The counselor thought she was somewhat effective in this, but reports of improvement in the boy's behavior were always followed by new difficulties, with the same silly, disturbing, sullen behavior being displayed. By sixteen the boy described himself as so nervous he could not eat or sleep. He had always been a "human dynamo" (the counselor's words) with respect to jobs, but his mother was now putting great pressure on him to make "big money." When interviewed by an independent investigator after the Study closed the boy said the counselor had been a friend to whom he could tell all his troubles and that he felt he could still go to her, though he had not done so in the last two years. He had had a job as a shoe repair worker for the last five years and liked it.

These two cases, then, seem to confirm our earlier conclusion that this sort of work, in which reliance is put on influencing boys through personal attachment, is not likely to be very successful unless the boys live under favorable emotional conditions at home.

SUB-GROUP 16

With the next two boys attempts were made at a case-work kind of treatment, which was probably appropriate to the problems presented, in that the boys were somewhat neurotic and the parents' attitudes unfavorable, but the case work was not very skillfully carried out. In addition, the parents were not especially interested in having the boys helped, and they were not included in the case-work efforts, services to them being of the usual Study type, friendly interest and concrete services.

Both of these boys were fearful, shy youngsters, and enuretic. The one came from a Greek-Italian family that was very "old-world" in its standards, the parents stressing academic success (the boy's I.Q. was 92), hard work, no play, and no contacts with outsiders. The father was domineering; he was fond of the boy but did not show his feelings very clearly. The other boy lived under even less favorable circumstances. His father was a boastful, garrulous extrovert, fond of the children but very strict with them and given to outbursts of temper. He died when the boy was fourteen. After his death the home became very disorganized, for the mother was a tense, worrying kind of person, immature and self-centered, and unable to maintain order or discipline, so the home was dirty, meals irregular, and there were many fights.

With the first boy the first two counselors felt that they accomplished little. They had worked in the usual way of providing recreational opportunities, health examinations, and advice to the parents. By the time the third counselor got the case the boy was fifteen and considered very nervous. This counselor was able to engage the boy in interviews that revealed his resentment of his father's domination and insistence on his following Greek customs. The counselor was unable, however, to follow through on this and to use his relationship with the boy therapeutically. The boy, after a show of independence in which he formed a friendship with a delinquent boy (which the counselor persuaded him to renounce), retired into his old patterns and made no further attempt to break away from his home.

The other boy had five different counselors, several of whom attempted to help him through interviews of a psychotherapeutic type: play activities through which it was hoped he would find an outlet for repressed aggression, free association interviews, and the like. The boy was very fond of the first and the last counselors but neither of them thought he benefited noticeably from their efforts, for the personality traits with which he started persisted throughout. The boy himself, in a follow-up interview, said he liked the last counselor best but he gave the impression that he had not been much helped.

It is obvious that neither in the extent of the parents' interest nor in quality of work done were these two cases the equal of those in the successful series in which good results were obtained by the use of modern case-work methods. In these cases friendly relations and the boy's appreciation of the agency's services were not a sufficient basis for great help, one or another of the other necessary favorable factors being missing.

This conclusion, in fact, applies to all the cases so far described in this series of "dubious" results. In one way or another an element that made for successful work was lacking. In most of the cases it was the counselors' methods that seemed at fault, while in a few it was the home circumstances that were not sufficiently favorable.

The friendly relationships between counselors and boys could not compensate for these lacks, though the boys may have benefited slightly in some rather obscure way.

CASES RESEMBLING THOSE OF BOYS WHO WERE NOT HELPED

Very different from these cases were those that resembled the failures rather than the successes. Here the question is not why the results were poorer but what were the unfavorable circumstances that set a limit to the usefulness of services even when good relationships were secured.

SUB-GROUP 17

The first group of this sort comprises four boys whose home situations were about as bad as those of the majority of the failures and whose problems were only slightly less extreme. The chief difference beween them and the failures was that these boys were more or less aware of how they felt about the way they were treated at home. Perhaps in consequence they were better able to relate to the counselors, but this ability was not enough to offset their handicaps.

The record of the work with the most maladjusted of these boys is illustrative of the futility of attempting to change deep-set, probably neurotic patterns in parent-child relations by the common-sense method of appeal to reason and the provision of needed services.

Reginald. Age 11–17; I.Q. 73. This was a very effeminate boy, both in appearance and interests. He disliked all boyish games and hobbies and, when first known, was chiefly interested in "baby sitting," knitting, and making clothes. His teacher considered him timid, sneaky, stubborn, and very nervous. There was some possibility that he had had chorea. Before Study work with him started he had been a patient of a child guidance clinic; there institutional placement had been recommended.

Reginald's home situation was most unsatisfying to him, though economically fairly good. His father was excessively alcoholic and cruel to his wife and children, having abused Reginald since infancy. The mother was a meek, timid person, always trusting that her husband would change. She was very fond of all her children but especially of Reginald, whom she felt she had to protect especially, both because of his delicate health and because of his father's treatment of him. She had trained all the children to be unusually polite; all of them were tense and nervous.

The counselor had a long, close contact with this boy and his parents and was much liked by all of them, even though they seldom took his advice. His attempts at changing the home situation included urging the father to treat the boy more kindly, discussing with the mother the possibility of court action against her husband or separation from him, talking with the boy about leaving school and home, to both of which desires the father was opposed. Help was also given in regard to the boy's health, the father's legal difficulties, and jobs for both father and son. Little was done about the boy's effeminacy; medical study contra-indicated endocrine therapy. The boy was always frank in his expression of dislike for his father but otherwise revealed little of his feelings, although he was somewhat confidential with the shop instructor at the Study office.

As time went by, this boy's effeminacy became more marked, and he regarded himself as weak and ailing. On jobs he worked hard and conscientiously. He never had friends of his own age, for other boys regarded him as queer, but he did have a "best friend" in a middle-aged man who took him on trips. He finally enlisted in the Navy and apparently got along satisfactorily there until he had a serious accident. After a medical discharge he returned home more maladjusted than ever—very unsettled, no sense of family responsibility, unrealistic about jobs, and eager for excitement. The counselor and others tried to help him, and a job that seemed in line with his early interests was secured. On this job, however, the boy made a very unsatisfying marriage, had a "nervous breakdown," secured a divorce, and eventually found work he liked in a mental hospital. Meanwhile his mother continued to have trouble with her husband, obtained a court order against him (instead of having him committed as the counselor advised), and eventually let him come back home.

All in all, then, the case ended much as it began. From many points of view it would be rated a complete failure. It may be, however, that the emotional support which the counselor gave, while not adequate to change the situation or better the boy's adjustment, was of some intangible value, for the boy, after he came home from the Navy, told an independent investigator, "Mr. B. was like a father to me. He always gave good advice. But there were some problems that were too personal; I couldn't discuss them with him."

The other three boys were equally or more handicapped in their home situations, and they too developed into neurotic, socially maladjusted boys in spite of great efforts on the part of the counselors and in spite of the friendship that grew up between them. For example, one of the boys, when first known, was a sensitive, passive child with few friends and little interest in recreational activities.

His father, a chronic drunkard, had left the family shortly after the boy's birth. His mother, too, drank excessively, was constantly on the move, and never provided an even moderately satisfactory home for the boy. This boy, like the preceding one, was in the Navy for a time, was discharged because of "nervousness," and seemed to be drifting in the direction of a shiftless adulthood when last known. Yet he, too, reported to an independent investigator that the Study was of much help. Its value, he said, lay in "knowing somebody who wants to take care of things for you. Then you don't think you are nobody."

Even interviews of the type we designated "case work" in Chapter XXVI were apparently insufficient to help such boys. Work of this sort was done with one boy whose compulsive, excitable mother frankly hated him and whose father stood passively by while the two engaged in physical combat. The boy, who from the outset was open in his dislike of his mother, seemed to benefit for a time from the interviews and from psychiatric treatment that was secured for him at about the same time, and he made a real effort to view his mother's treatment of him objectively. The mother, however, in spite of interviews of the same type, became antagonistic toward the counselor, saying he created a barrier between her and her son. When last heard about, this boy was in the Navy, where he was very unhappy and depressed, even threatening suicide.

SUB-GROUP 18

A fifth boy might be added to Sub-group 17 because his situation was comparable to that of the two among the failures whose homes were socially very unsatisfactory but who, for a time at least, received adequate affection from very inadequate parents. Like those boys, this lad maintained a good social adjustment for many years, but at adolescence—so it seemed—the affection he received did not compensate for the emotional turmoil of the home and he became a delinquent. In this case, in which excessive drinking and quarreling between the parents ended in temporary separation, attempts were made to help the mother with her marital problem and to elicit from the boy his feelings about it. Neither of these attempts was very skillfully executed and nothing was accomplished by them, though both mother and son were very appreciative of the counselor's friendship. After the case was closed the parents sought out the counselor because their difficulties had become much worse, and they then seemed able to benefit somewhat from his help. The boy, however, had become a member of a delinquent gang and was put on suspended sentence to reform school. When interviewed by an independent investigator he was reticent and suspicious.

All in all, then, the agency's experience with these boys appears to confirm the conclusion of the preceding chapter that seriously maladjusted boys from homes that provide little or no satisfaction for emotional needs seldom show much improvement under the services such an organization can render. This apparently is true even when the boys become very fond of the counselors and credit them with having been of assistance, although in such cases one is tempted to say that the boys may have received temporary emotional support.

SUB-GROUP 19

The third group of cases that paralleled the failures bore some resemblance to those in which the failure seemed attributable to the counselors' inability to penetrate the overclose mother-boy relationship. These mothers, it will be recalled, were overprotective and dominating, and they tried to use the counselors to increase their control over their sons. The four mothers in the present series were not so neurotic nor so deeply involved with the boys as those with whom the work wholly failed, and they were appreciative of such of the counselors' services as were in line with their desires, such as tutoring or helping the boy when he was in difficulty with the court. In spite of this friendliness, the attempts to overcome the mothers' overprotective or controlling attitudes were as unavailing as in the failure cases. In this connection it is to be noted that in two cases these attempts consisted of rather direct attacks on the problem (specific advice as to what to do) while in the third there was the slower drawing-out of feeling about the matter that characterizes social case work in this kind of situation. In the fourth case no work was done with the parents.

Two of the four families were Negroes from the Barbados, people of high standards, rigid disciplinarians. One of the mothers was described as moody, discontented, often complaining of ailments; the other as jolly but rather isolated, interested only in her own family. The son of the first was a very quiet, retiring, dull boy (I.Q. 67), of the second a mischievous, distractible youngster (I.Q. 92) who was uninterested in school. In both cases considerable work was done toward effecting better school adjustment or securing more recreation, but in both attempts the counselors encountered considerable resistance from the mothers. Advising the mothers in regard to handling the boys was even more unsuccessful. Both women, however, were appreciative of services that were in line with their desires, such as accompanying the one boy to court and on his probation office visits and giving the mother of the other small loans of money. Both boys reported to the independent investigators that they liked their counselors very much, but they thought of the agency chiefly in terms of recreation or educational service. Neither had ever been especially maladjusted, and both continued about as they were when the counselors made their first contacts with them.

The third case was even more like those described among the failures. This mother was a rigid, compulsive person who put great stress on cleanliness and good home management and who worried greatly about her health. Toward her son, a slow, fat, passive boy with tics and nervous mannerisms, she was alternately indulgent and demanding, and she leaned on him for support and affection when her husband's drinking became extreme. The counselor used a combination of parent education and case-work methods with this woman, trying to get her to see that much of the boy's nervousness was due to the pressure she put upon him, advising her to give the boy sex instruction, and listening for hours to her descriptions of her early childhood and her difficulties with her husband. None of these efforts accomplished much, but the mother frequently told the counselor that she was the only person to whom she could turn for help. To the boy the counselor offered tutoring (which did little to improve his arithmetic), trips with other boys when he complained that he had no friends, and camp, which he consistently refused because he thought he would be homesick. The boy did, for one winter, find pleasure in the shopwork at the Study headquarters, and it was this that he mentioned chiefly in a follow-up interview. At the time of that interview the boy, then sixteen, was described by his father as still nervous but he had several friends and was interested in athletics.

These findings in regard to work with overprotective, controlling mothers, especially those who are neurotically involved with their sons, are in line with those of child guidance workers. It is generally recognized in child guidance clinics that women of this sort can be helped only if they are very much concerned about their children's behavior (which, apparently, was not true of these mothers) and if they are handled so skillfully that their emotional defenses are not aroused. Unless they can be helped, it is unlikely that their children will improve greatly in social adjustment.

SUB-GROUP 20

The final two boys whose cases somewhat paralleled the failures were the energetic, outgoing, young-delinquent type described in the preceding chapter. They differed from these failures, however, in that they came from close-knit, loyal families of foreign background. It is somewhat questionable whether they should be included in the group under consideration here, for their relations with the counselors were at times far from friendly. Their parents, however, were very appreciative of the counselors' efforts, so the classification seemed fairly valid.

The reactions of these two boys to the counselors may be of significance for work with young delinquents. These boys were very "touchy," quick to sense slights or imagined lack of interest on the part of the counselors, and they resented any implication that their families were less capable than other boys'. They responded well to favorable changes in their environmental circumstances. In both cases lack of skill in the management of the counselors' relationship with the boy was evidenced; in both it was difficult to determine whether the agency had been of help. One boy's eventual good adjustment was definitely related to favorable changes that took place in the family quite outside the counselors' activities, while the other boy did not change greatly. The latter boy gave an independent investigator the impression that he had not been much interested in what the Study had to offer.

This review of the cases in which not much was accomplished in spite of friendly relations and expressions of appreciation on the part of the boys or their parents leads, then, to the conclusion that the relationship must be "used" correctly if it is to be effective. It must be used, in some cases, to discover what lies back of a boy's behavior difficulties, in others how he and his parents feel about the problem; it must be used at all times to convey to the boy the counselor's continuing interest in him and appreciation of his difficulties. Working methods must be adapted to a boy's needs (the big-brother type of work, for instance, seems to be applicable only when the boy's parents are well disposed toward him), and there are some types of extreme maladjustment that even close friendship does not remedy. These conclusions must be checked, of course, against the findings in the final two series of cases, but so far they appear to be warranted.

TEMPORARY IMPROVEMENT SECURED

In thirteen cases the boys improved for a time (in consequence, apparently, of the close attention given them or secured for them by the counselors), but this improvement was not sustained. All of these boys were definitely maladjusted in one way or another and none had a really favorable home. Two sub-types are distinguishable; one consisted of feeble-minded or neurologically handicapped boys who probably would have required lifelong attention, their home conditions being what they were, and the other consisted of potentially capable boys whose lack of sustained gain seemed attributable, in part at least, to variation in the kind and amount of assistance they received from the counselors. In other words, in the first sub-type the boys' regression was probably inevitable, while in the second the boys could perhaps have achieved a better adjustment if the counselors had continued their helpful efforts.

SUB-GROUP 21

There were five boys of the first sub-type. Two were feeble-minded, one was an epileptic, and the fourth—a questionable case for this category—was a boy of little intelligence who became psychotic at fifteen. The fifth boy, perhaps post-encephalitic, was very limited in intelligence and displayed behavior bordering on the psychotic. In all cases the parents' attitudes were definitely unfavorable to the utilization of what limited capacities the boys had.

One of these boys had an I.Q. of 64, a bad speech defect, and such poor muscular coordination that he was teased by other children and could not participate in play with them. His father, hospitalized as a psychopath, was fond of him, but his mother, a tense, highstrung woman of borderline intelligence, nagged him continually and compared him unfavorably with his bright brother. Two counselors made unsuccessful attempts to tutor the boy; when that failed and his behavior became too extreme for the teacher to handle, they tried to get him into an institution. He was accepted for placement but the judge would not commit him. Another counselor was then assigned to the case. He visited the boy and his mother frequently and was accepted by them as a friend. He was able to persuade the mother to ignore some of the boy's problems and to let him attend a work camp. He spent much time with the boy and was very patient with him, taking him to his own home when the mother was sick, finding him a job as a dishwasher, accompanying him to his place of employment until he knew the route well, teaching him to tell time, and generally supporting and encouraging him. A fourth counselor was assigned to the case when this man left the Study, and he, too, was helpful to the boy in much the same manner. For nearly two years the boy held a job of a "sheltered" type but after the Study closed and he left this job he again slumped; the last report of his adjustment (at twenty years of age) told of his being unemployed and hard to manage, given to temper tantrums, fights, and drinking.

Even less was accomplished in the other four cases. These boys, too, improved when given much attention and affection by the counselors or when in an institution, but they, too, could not sustain these gains.

One of these was a boy with an I.Q. of 56 and some cerebral damage; he became calmer and less nervous under a tutor's kindly attention but did not get along at all well in an institution. Another, thought to be post-encephalitic, did fairly well when sent to a school for the feeble-minded, but relapsed when released.

A third, a boy of adequate intelligence, had had a skull fracture at five and was thought to be epileptic; he had visual agnosia, a true word blindness, and could not learn to read. His mother was an utterly ineffectual person, incapable of exerting any control over her children, while his father was quick-tempered and rough but rather fond of the boy. This boy became very much attached to the counselor, sought her approval, and improved greatly for a time. As soon as the counselor left for the summer, however, the boy became much involved in delinquent activities and from that time on went downhill. His parents later sent him to live with relatives in the country, where he again did well for a time in an atmosphere of affection. This home proved, however, to be overstimulating to the boy (it was a rough boarding house) and his wild rages and delinquencies returned. He was later killed in an accident.

The fourth, whose I.Q. when measured for admission to special class was 56 but on other tests was found to be as high as 85, was an exceedingly nervous, unhappy child who at twelve talked of wanting to be killed and of committing suicide. He was a large, awkward boy, very garrulous (asking questions much like those of a three-year-old), and yet withdrawn and given to phantasy. The father was an extremely immature, unstable man who treated the boy badly, making fun of him, comparing him with his bright, capable brother, and beating him severely. The mother was somewhat more understanding of his needs but ineffectual in supervising or training him. The boy became fond of the counselor and other workers in the agency and improved greatly during a period in which he was given weekly lessons in speech and deportment, and his mother, at the counselor's advice, became less severe with him. He was admitted to the sixth grade in school, behaved acceptably there, and did well in camp and in an institution. Within a year, however, he got into difficulty with the police and a long history of perverted sexual practices was uncovered. There was some evidence of psychotic trends at that time. Within the next year he was committed to a mental hospital and has been in such an institution ever since.

As has been said before, it seems unlikely that anything except constant supervision in a favorable environment would have kept these boys functioning adequately.

SUB-GROUP 22

Most of the eight boys in the second sub-type were also severely handicapped youngsters, emotionally if not intellectually. Their good response during the periods in which the counselors worked closely with them suggests, however, that they might have maintained some gain if more attention had been paid to them. This seemed especially true of the one boy whose home conditions were only moderately unfavorable and whose parents were interested in having help with him. This very friendly, gregarious boy had strong feelings of insecurity and inferiority, especially with respect to his intelligence (I.Q. 73). His father was a good-natured man, interested in his children and their problems, though rather discouraged about the boy's lack of intellectual ability. The mother was less fond of him and desirous at times of having him "sent away"; she was, nevertheless, conscientious in caring for the boy and willing to try out some of the counselors' suggestions. Only one of four counselors gave much attention to the case. That counselor, for a time, had frequent interviews of a case-work type, to which the boy responded well. The gain was not sustained however, and when last known the boy was drifting in a listless, dissatisfied manner. In a follow-up interview he and his mother spoke appreciatively of the counselor who had worked closely with them, regretting that they never saw enough of him. As the boy said, "He was someone you could trust."

With this one exception, these boys lived under very unfavorable home conditions (all being rated C in parent-child relations), one parent being what Dr. David Levy calls overprotective out of guilt, and the other very neglectful or cruel. The boys' responses varied. Several were timid and seclusive, much given to phantasy; two acted "crazy" or clownish to secure attention; several were irritable and pugnacious; one was a socially conforming neurotic. None of these boys was able to have really friendly relations with other children.

Work with these boys followed one of two patterns: either frequent activities resembling case work on the part of one counselor (or, in one case, treatment in a psychiatric clinic) under which the boy improved, followed by less frequent contacts by subsequent counselors and retrogression on the boy's part; or intermittent work of the typical Study type supplemented by foster home placement. The following case is illustrative of the first pattern, which was used in six of the seven cases.

Pat. Age 9–16; I.Q. 85. When first referred to the Study, Pat was described as the worst boy in his class, distractible, silly, attention-seeking, boastful, and impudent. He stuttered, had enuresis, and engaged in petty stealing. He had no friends, his chief interests being movies and other solitary pursuits. Thoroughly undisciplined and out of control, he wandered at will over the town, his parents unconcerned about his being away.

Pat was one of ten children, all much neglected and unsupervised. His mother, passive and perhaps feeble-minded, was chiefly interested in spiritualism. Pat felt much disliked by her. His father, a minor politician, engaged in petty illegal activities, looked to "drag" to achieve his desires, and used the children to get money by tap-dancing and begging outside theaters. The family had been relief recipients for years.

The first counselor developed a close relationship with Pat, evidenced by his delight in seeing her and his giving her little gifts. She first tried to secure better recreation for him and to get his speech defect remedied through extensive dental repair. These efforts were not very successful, partly because the parents would take no responsibility and the counselor was unable to alter their general attitudes toward the boy. Later, when the boy had been promoted but was doing poorly in reading, tutoring was secured, which pleased him. He continued, however, to have periods of defiance and discouragement because of his feelings about the way he was treated at home. Mingled with these services were frequent interviews between the boy and the counselor, in which Pat felt sufficiently comfortable to tell the counselor a bit about what was bothering him—chiefly his mother's dislike of him and his own dislike of school. The counselor did not utilize these confessions very skillfully, but she did retain the boy's friendship. Throughout this period his behavior in the classroom improved somewhat, though he still was unable to make friends.

The second counselor tried to use psychotherapeutic methods, asking the boy about his dreams and soliciting free associations. Pat was willing to tell his dreams, but nothing was accomplished by this device and many appointments were broken. The next counselor apparently did little with him, and the fourth's work consisted of occasional outings. It was only with the first counselor that the boy improved; except for the school progress he made with her, he remained pretty much as at the beginning. In an interview with an independent investigator he said that the counselors were trying to build him up physically but they were just wasting their time, as he wouldn't take pills and didn't like the other medical advice. He did, however, like his first counselor very much; he said she was a "friend" he could always trust.

The other five cases were fairly similar to this one; nothing could be accomplished with the parents, but the boys improved during the period the counselors paid close attention to them and let them express their feelings, or when (as in one case) psychiatric treatment was secured. In the seventh case the service was more typical of that usually given by Study workers and included foster home placement. The boy did well under the tutoring provided and while in the foster home. After he returned from the foster home and the counselor's visits became infrequent he, too, relapsed. Whether these boys could have been permanently helped if close contact had been maintained, is, of course, an open question, but if one may judge by some cases to be described later in this chapter (Sub-group 26) it would seem that they might have benefited, especially after they got away from home.

When last heard about, only one of the eight boys in the second sub-type was getting along even fairly well, and that boy's behavior had been poor until he got out of his home by joining the Army. Three boys were making a socially acceptable but neurotic type of adjustment and the others were definitely maladjusted.

BOYS SOMEWHAT BENEFITED

The last group of cases to be considered contains some of the most interesting in the whole series, those of boys who were helped to make a moderately good adjustment despite great odds. Like the other groups, this consisted of a wide range of cases with respect to factors so far found to be significant—severity of the original disorder and extent of maladjustment in the home. Five of the 27 boys in the group appeared from the outset to be very maladjusted, while eleven had problems that were rated as negligible or slight. As to their homes, seven were rated AA or AB (the first letter referring to the emotional and the second to the social aspects), fifteen BA or BB, while five boys came from homes classified C emotionally, two of these being C socially as well. The first and the last of these, at least, pose different questions for the investigator, for of the first we want to know why the Study services were not more effective, while of the second the question is how so much was achieved.

SUB-GROUP 23

To consider the seven boys from the best homes first, the reasons for the relative lack of accomplishment were found to be rather clear. Two of these were boys with I.Q.'s in the low sixties. The only problem was the fact that the parents were unwilling to admit the extent of the handicap and so were somewhat too ambitious for the boys. The counselors were able to offer some help in this respect and to be of some use in providing better recreation for the boys but, for the most part, the continued and fairly satisfactory adjustment of the boys was attributable to the parents' own efforts and to their kindly attitudes.

Another boy was dull and inarticulate and uninterested in contacts with adults—traits, as has already been shown, the counselors found difficult or uninteresting. In another case, the father did not want the counselors to work with the boy, though he professed interest in the Study and used the counselors' services in making school and job arrangements for his son. In two other cases the boys were friendly with the counselors but the main reasons for their maladjustment were not discovered. The one was a frail, sensitive, effeminate boy who had an artificial eye, the other an introverted, phantasying child who adjusted to others by acting the clown. Various services proved useful in the immediate situation, but the boys continued much as they had started, not seriously maladjusted but not greatly benefited either.

In the seventh case the boy had improved greatly by the end of the contact with him, but only part of the change could be credited to the Study. This was a case somewhat like several mentioned before in which the boy lived under very poor social conditions but received fairly adequate affection. This boy committed many petty delinquencies, both while his family life was rather disrupted and after it was proceeding more smoothly. The counselors maintained close contact with him, arranging with the court that he be kept out of correctional school, acting as probation officers, talking with him, advising and guiding him, and generally being "big brothers." In the meantime family life greatly improved. It had once been so disorganized (with the mother feeble-minded, a sister a sex delinquent, and the father bitter and resentful about his unemployment) that all the children had been placed in foster homes by court order. The Study had some part in that improvement, for the counselor found the father a job and gave him other sorts of assistance, but part of the change seemed attributable to the parents' good mental health and to the children's being older and thus able to manage the household. In this case, then, it was difficult to determine just how much the Study accomplished, but the boy spoke in glowing terms of the counselors to an independent investigator, saying he was trying to use their methods with his younger brother. Perhaps the explanation of the long time it took for the counselors' efforts to be effective is to be found in the nature of the boy's interests and activities, for he was the gregarious, gang type that Study efforts often did not reach.

The explanation of why these boys from emotionally good homes did not benefit more from the agency's services is thus to be found in factors that have already been shown to be adverse: insufficient interest in being helped, personality traits that handicapped progress, and inability on the counselors' part to discover the reason for the maladjustment.

Statistics cited in the preceding chapter have indicated that about half the boys who were most helped and a third of those with whom the counselors failed came from homes rated B in parent-child relationships. There was also a high proportion of boys from such homes in the present series of boys who were somewhat helped—15 out of the total 27. Such figures suggest that it may not be the relative inadequacy of the home but the character of the inadequacy that is important. This is a point that can be determined, however, only through comparison of the various groups.

SUB-GROUP 24

Taking these fifteen cases by themselves, without reference to others that were rated B, we find in eleven of them parents who were overprotective or overstrict, these attitudes deriving to a considerable extent from cultural conditions. For example, there were a number of excitable, protective Portuguese or Italian mothers who tried hard to keep firm control over their sons even in adolescence, several French Canadians or Newfoundlanders who were overstrict according to American standards, several Negroes who were overcontrolling in an attempt to keep the boys from bad companions and who were very "touchy" about their treatment by white people. In reaction, perhaps, the boys were either aggressive and demanding, to cover up feelings of inadequacy, or retiring and given to daydreams and phantasies. These boys tended to become rather attached to a particular counselor and to modify their conduct somewhat in response to his efforts, but their behavior did not become wholly or consistently satisfactory.

These situations were qualitatively different from the overprotective ones listed among the failures, for these mothers and sons did not have that tight, negative sort of attachment to each other that the counselors found impossible to penetrate, and the counselors were consequently better able to secure their friendship. The mothers (and fathers too in some cases) in the present group were, however, equally impossible to influence so far as their feelings and behavior toward the boys were concerned, for they were quite convinced that they were acting in their sons' interests. They were, however, pleased to have or to let the boys have other services the counselors had to offer—recreation, camp, help with school and jobs, and so on—and the boys benefited to some extent from such efforts. Though these boys were freer to accept the counselors' friendship than were the neurotically overprotected boys, neither they nor their parents had the same amount of interest in being helped that those in the successful series had. In addition, the counselors were seldom consistent in their efforts. They tended to have frequent contacts with the boys for a time and then to see them rather infrequently; consequently they did not follow up on the good relationships they did establish or utilize them very well in the boys' behalf. There were, accordingly, several reasons why those boys benefited only moderately from the Study services; the chief, however, seemed to be that the counselors could neither change the situation that was causing the boys' difficulties nor offset it, as we shall see they did for a few boys who were overtly disliked by their parents.

Among the services performed for some of these boys was the kind that had been effective in the series of successful cases: the removal or modification of specific handicaps to their social adjustment. For one boy, for example, who had very bad eyesight, placement in a sight-saving class was secured, and the teacher's interest was aroused by a description of his unfavorable home situation. For another an operation on ears that protruded badly and contributed to his "goofy" appearance was procured. These services and the others that accompanied them, however, could not counterbalance the overprotection that these nervous, inadequate boys received at home, though the boys were temporarily made happier by reason of them. This finding is in line with the earlier conclusion about this kind of work: that it is successful only when the particular handicap under consideration is the basic reason for the boy's maladjustment and home conditions are favorable.

It would seem, then, that the typical methods used by the counselors are not very suitable for boys who are overprotected or overcontrolled and who either submit rather neurotically to this treatment or who rebel against it. The boys were helped slightly by what the counselors had to offer but the majority remained considerably maladjusted. None of them was rated as well adjusted when last known.

SUB-GROUP 25

The other four boys in this group from moderately poor homes had parents who were rather indifferent to them or actually disliked them, and who were chiefly concerned about their own difficulties. In this respect the cases bore considerable resemblance to those in the successful series in which parents and boys benefited from services of a case-work nature. Such work was attempted with only one of these families, however, and it was confined to the boy. Three of these boys were nervous, aggressive, quick-tempered youngsters who were hard to manage, while one was a passive, babyish child with seemingly neurotic fears. Two of these boys resolved their difficulties largely through their own efforts, though the counselors were somewhat useful to them in such ways as helping with school arrangements and discussing sex problems and other personal matters. For one boy whose father had deserted and whose mother was very resentful, the counselors acted as a kind of substitute father. They were not able to be as useful in this respect as in the successful cases of this type, the underlying strength in family relations that characterized those cases being lacking and the boy being too involved in the parents' quarrel wholly to accept a substitute. In the fourth case attempts at case work were made by the counselors but, since the irritating situation at home continued unabated (the grandmother being overindulgent and the promiscuous mother arousing jealousy), not much change in the boy was secured.

The reasons for the relative lack of success in these cases seem much the same as in the preceding ones; in both groups they can be determined with any certainty only when comparison with the others that involved moderately poor homes is made. It seems significant, however, that nearly all these boys were reacting with insecurity and nervousness to unfavorable attitudes on the part of the parents. Child guidance workers have found that with such children they are unlikely to succeed unless the parents' attitudes improve. Since this change in attitude was not accomplished in the present cases, it may be that the rather slight results with the boys are to be attributed largely to that fact.

SUB-GROUP 26

The most interesting sub-group of boys in this series of cases in which Study services were possibly beneficial is that in which the home conditions (emotional and, in a considerable proportion of cases, social as well) were very poor and the boys were seriously maladjusted. This is a type of case that our analysis so far has shown to be usually unsuccessful, even though friendly and close relations with the boys and their parents develop. Why this should be so seems obvious. Here, however, we have two boys who, in spite of markedly unfavorable personality and home conditions, seemed to derive some benefit from the counselors services. Detailed description seems called for.

In severity of maladjustment and unfavorableness of home conditions these boys were somewhat like two of those described in Sub-group 2 (Chapter XXVI) as aided by their close attachment to the counselors. Like these boys, the present two had the counselors' continuous support and services, but with them the end results were less good. In this connection it seems significant that in all four cases Study efforts seemed to accomplish little more than holding the line as long as the boys remained at home or in foster homes from which they were likely to be removed at any time. If, however, they escaped from that stress and strain, the benefit of the counselors' supportive measures showed up more clearly. This is what happened in the two cases listed as definitely benefited, while the two boys under present consideration never secured a really stable environment.

Dwight. Age 10–17; I.Q. 73. This boy was first described as overactive, rebellious, defiant of his teachers, acting silly or tough in an effort to get attention. Although his aggressive behavior became somewhat less marked later, he never adjusted well in a group, clinging to single children and joining in delinquencies to win favor. He was always very insecure and seemed to be trying to find some permanent attachment; he was always very responsive to adults. A psychiatrist who examined him described him as a constitutional inferior, handicapped physically and intellectually, for he had had several attacks of rheumatic fever and a neurological examination indicated possible epilepsy.

The boy's home situation was unpleasant throughout. He was an illegitimate child whose mother had boarded him in a foster home from birth to fifteen. The mother never showed any interest in him, never came to see him, and once when he was ill said it would be just as well if he died. The foster mother somewhat overprotected and indulged him but at the same time continually reminded him that she had taken him when he was an "ugly baby" because his mother did not want him. When he was fifteen his mother took him home but she would not admit that he was her child. His stepfather, a man well known and respected in the community, made no objection to having the boy in his home and seemed to have a good but casual relationship with him.

Study work started when Dwight was in the foster home. The first counselor secured better recreation for him, persuaded the foster mother to give him better supervision, and himself played the role of a substitute father, putting great stress on the boy's making an effort to be good. Dwight responded well to this as long as the counselor made frequent visits but when, for a period, he visited him only infrequently the boy again lapsed into his old patterns.

The second counselor concluded that, whatever the cause of the difficulties, what the boy most needed was support and counsel, and he acted in that capacity for three years. At about this time the foster mother died, and Dwight was returned to his own home. Dwight clung to the counselor during this period, and the counselor visited him frequently. The boy became especially upset when he learned that what he thought was a new foster mother was his real mother; later when she specifically denied this, he ran away from home, engaged in fire-setting, and was most irritable and demanding when he eventually returned.

Throughout this period the counselor had frequent interviews, in which the boy expressed his resentment of the way he was treated at home and his inability to keep from joining other boys in delinquent activities. The parents were pleased to have the counselor work with the boy, and they accepted his advice about recreational activities for him.

With the boy's delinquent activities, however, they became increasingly impatient; they were much ashamed of being called to the police's attention, and they were pleased when he was finally sentenced to the state training school. Dwight adjusted well in this school, as also in a convalescent home to which he was sent when he had another attack of rheumatic fever.

From that time on he was in and out of his own home, his foster siblings' homes, hospitals, ranches, and so on. He gave up delinquent activities but became irresponsible about jobs and health and when last known was in a hospital with a serious heart condition. He always did better away from home than with his parents but had no real stability anywhere. It seemed, however, that the counselor, through giving constant emotional support and many times making practical arrangements that nobody else would secure, at least kept this boy from a serious delinquent career.

Emil. Age 9–16; I.Q. 81. When first known, Emil was a miserably neglected child, filthy dirty, clothed in rags, and having no spontaneity of gesture or expression. He had abrupt, seemingly unexplainable mood changes and varied from silent, unresponsive daydreaming to exhibitionistic attention-seeking behavior. He did much fanciful lying. He was never antagonistic or hostile but seemed unable to respond to friendly advances. He often engaged in disconnected, rambling monologues and once in school suddenly began slapping himself in the face in a very excited fashion.

Home conditions were extremely bad, the parents being utterly unconcerned about their children's welfare and quite incapable of supervising them. The Society for the Prevention of Cruelty to Children had once reported conditions of extreme neglect but had not prosecuted. Two siblings were chronic delinquents; one brother, considered psychotic, had an unusually long record. The mother, once sentenced for contributing to her children's delinquency, was a dull, inadequate woman who quite openly favored one son and actively disliked Emil. The father, often drunk and abusive, was somewhat more competent but he too had little interest in Emil.

The first counselor worked with both Emil and his more outgoing brother, who was also a Study boy. He did not appear to make much headway with Emil, who was passively jealous of his brother, but the boy did indicate that he was interested in the counselor's attention. The counselor then discussed with the parents the question of foster placement for Emil, who had been in court on a charge of stealing. They and the boy had no objection, so placement through the state agency was arranged. Within the next three years Emil was in five different foster homes, doing well when he was the only child, but enuretic, engaging in sex activities, and stealing when he had to share the homes with others.

During this period he began to be more openly interested in the coun- selor, especially when things went badly for him in the foster homes. He was then sent to a reform school, where he adjusted fairly well but became very homesick and fearful that his mother had died. Returning home he got along well for a time but, home conditions being worse than before, soon lapsed and became what his siblings called crazily aggres- sive. The counselor took to seeing him very frequently, and the boy showed his interest by frequent requests for his company.

The second counselor continued this kind of attention until the boy was again put in a foster home. From that time on the story was much as before, though the periods of good conduct in foster homes and the reform school, to which he was returned for a time, were longer. Delin- quencies became less numerous, the enuresis disappeared, and, in gen- eral, the boy improved, though he still remained unstable. When last heard about, he was in another state living with his mother, who had remarried, and he had a steady job. While it is unlikely that this boy had become well adjusted, it seems probable that the counselors had been helpful in keeping him from becoming a criminal. Throughout, he turned to the counselors when he was in difficulty, maintaining his contact with the first one even after he had left the Study's employ.

All in all, then, these boys, like the others in this series labeled "dubious," had some of the characteristics of the boys with whom the Study succeeded and some of those of the boys with whom the work failed. This, in itself, would seem confirming evidence that the division into groups was justified. What we want to know now is what our findings add up to for the series of cases as a whole; in other words, whether some fairly precise formulation can be arrived at that will identify the boys to whom and the services through which effective help can be given.

CHAPTER XXIX

WHY THE COUNSELORS
WERE NOT MORE
SUCCESSFUL

THE REASONS FOR THE STUDY'S FAILURE TO PRODUCE A MARKED LES-
sening in the incidence of delinquency and poor social adjustment
become clear when the conditions under which good results were
secured are compared with those that obtained in the other cases.
The individual case analyses presented in the preceding chapters
suggest that the significant factors can be isolated and that good results are likely to occur only when the factors are present in favorable combination. These factors appear to be: (1) the emotional
maladjustment in the home and in the boy is not too extreme;
(2) the boy and, usually, his parents desire help with the problem;
(3) the counselors' services are consistently and skillfully related to
the source of the difficulty. In the following sections of the chapter
these and other points will be considered individually, and an attempt will be made to state more precisely the conditions under
which good results were secured. After this has been done it should
be rather easy to see why the T-boys did not turn out much better
than the boys in the C-group.

AGE AND INTELLIGENCE OF LITTLE IMPORTANCE

Before proceeding with the more refined analysis of the figures,
two points of frequent interest may be cleared up: whether the
results were better when the work with the boys was started at an
early age, and whether bright boys were more amenable to help
than dull ones. The figures are given in Table 78. There, as in subsequent tables, the boys who refused the organization's offer of service (D1), those who were not adequately served according to the

organization's standards (D2), and those who were found not to need help (E) are separated from the others so that attention may be concentrated on the others.

Table 78 indicates that the boy's age at the time work was begun had little if any bearing on whether he was significantly benefited. The counselors were just about as likely to be able to help boys who were eleven or twelve when work started as boys who were under nine. Similarly, they were about as able to be helpful to dull boys as to those whose intelligence was average or better. These two traits can be disregarded, then, in the search for why the Study succeeded in helping some boys and not others.

TABLE 78

Relation of Age and Intelligence to Benefit Derived

Age at Start of Work	VALUE OF SERVICE [a]									
	A	B	C	D_3	Total	D_1	D_2	E	Total	Total
Under 9	10	10	4	6	30	2	10	9	21	51
9–10	21	13	12	23	69	7	21	17	45	114
11–12	18	14	4	15	51	11	13	14	38	89
Total	49	37	20	44	150	20	44	40	104	254
I.Q.										
Under 80	6	8	5	5	24	3	6	3	12	36
80–89	11	10	4	6	31	7	12	12	31	62
90–109	26	16	9	29	80	10	22	19	51	131
110 and over	6	3	2	4	15	—	4	6	10	25
Total	49	37	20	44	150	20	44	40	104	254

[a] *Code.* A: Clearly beneficial. B: Possibly beneficial; not much change effected. C: Little accomplished in spite of friendly relations. D_3: Clearly ineffectual. D_1: Offer of service refused. D_2: Counselors' work slight or poor. E: No help needed.

DEGREE AND NATURE OF THE EMOTIONAL MALADJUSTMENT ARE OF SIGNIFICANCE

It has already been shown that the character and severity of the boys' problems when work began were related to the degree of social adjustment later achieved (see Chapter XXIV), and the preceding analyses of individual cases have indicated that these characteristics were also often important factors in the counselors' ability to be of help. In Tables 79 to 82 the statistics on this point are set forth. In Table 79 the comparison is made in terms of the initial adjustment ratings previously employed,[1] while in Table 80 the categories referring to the delinquent tendencies apparent in the boys at the outset of Study work are used.[2]

TABLE 79

Relation of Initial Adjustment to Benefit Derived

| Initial Adjustment | VALUE OF SERVICE | | | | | | | | | |
	A	B	C	D3	Total	D1	D2	E	Total	Total
1. Well-adjusted	6	2	3	—	11	3	1	34	38	49
2. Slight mal-adjustment	23	10	6	7	46	11	29	6	46	92
3. Definite social maladjustment	2	4	3	6	15	2	2	—	4	19
4. Maladjustment suggestive of neurosis but not extreme	15	13	7	8	43	2	11	—	13	56
5. Extreme mal-adjustment	3	8	1	23	35	2	1	—	3	38
Total	49	37	20	44	150	20	44	40	104	254

As has been indicated previously, most of the well-adjusted boys were found not to be in need of Study service. Though contact with them was maintained for some time, ratings as to the value of the organization's service to most of them were not attempted. Most of the few who were rated (because apparently needed service was given) benefited to at least some extent. The more important comparison, however, is to be found in the other categories in the table. There it is seen that there was a definite relation between the apparent severity of the original maladjustment and the amount of benefit a boy received from the work of the organization. Half of the boys whose maladjustment appeared to be slight, about a third of the boys who seemed to be mildly neurotic, and only three out of the 35 who were extremely maladjusted benefited significantly. It will be noted also that only a small proportion of the boys originally classified as socially, rather than emotionally, maladjusted were definitely helped. Apparently, the kinds of service the Study had

[1] For definitions, see Chap. XXII; for use in table see Chap. XXIV, Table 65.
[2] For definitions, see Chap. XXII.

to offer were more likely to be useful to fairly well-adjusted boys and to those who were somewhat neurotic than to the severely maladjusted and those mischievous, energetic, aggressive boys who were in rebellion against society's restrictions. This finding suggests that an organization like the Study is unlikely to be able to help serious delinquents. The figures in Tables 80 to 83 give more information on this point.

The value of the services to boys of presumably delinquent make-up is first tested in Table 80, in which the categories (described in Chapter XXII under the heading of "delinquent tendencies") refer to the boys' behavior when first known to the Study. The categories are as follows:

1. No question of delinquency, though the boy may have been emotionally maladjusted

2. Very mischievous and annoying in school

3. Associating with delinquents; much fighting; suspected of minor delinquency

4. Considerable truancy, stealing, or court record for delinquency

TABLE 80

Relation of Original Delinquent Tendencies to Benefit Derived

Delinquent Tendencies	VALUE OF SERVICE									
	A	B	C	D_3	Total	D_1	D_2	E	Total	Total
1. None	22	11	10	12	55	13	26	38	77	132
2. Very mischievous	4	12	5	5	26	2	6	—	8	34
3. Delinquent companions	13	7	3	8	31	2	9	1	12	43
4. Actual delinquency	10	7	2	19	38	3	3	1	7	45
Total	49	37	20	44	150	20	44	40	104	254

Apparently only the boys in the last of these categories were especially unamenable to the counselors' efforts. Even so, half of them (if they needed and accepted help and were given adequate service) were at least somewhat benefited. It appears, then, that a history of delinquency at an early age or of behavior suggestive of future delinquency did not serve as a criterion differentiating the boys whom the Study helped from the others whom it was unlikely to benefit.

With later delinquency the story is somewhat different, as Table 81 indicates. The categories used in that table were the following, the boys being classified by the writer on the basis of data in the case records, both official and unofficial delinquencies being included.

1. No delinquency

2. One or two delinquent episodes of a minor nature or a reputation at time of referral for petty stealing

3. Petty stealing or other delinquency of a minor nature that persisted for some time

4. Several fairly serious offenses or a period of being rather habitually delinquent

5. Persistent and at least fairly serious delinquency

TABLE 81

Relation of Extent and Character of Delinquent Behavior to Benefit Derived

Extent of Delinquency	VALUE OF SERVICE									
	A	B	C	D_3	Total	D_1	D_2	E	Total	Total
1. None	23	11	9	10	53	14	20	32	66	119
2. Few minor episodes	9	6	4	—	19	4	10	5	19	38
3. Fairly frequent; minor	8	9	5	3	25	2	7	3	12	37
4. Fairly frequent; more serious	7	9	1	8	25	—	5	—	5	30
5. Persistent and fairly serious	2	2	1	23	28	—	2	—	2	30
Total	49	37	20	44	150	20	44	40	104	254

As the table shows, among the boys adequately served, less than a fifth of the persistent delinquents were even slightly benefited as contrasted with about three-fifths of those in the other categories. Since, however, these other categories contained many boys who engaged in delinquency at one time or another, we can conclude only that it is the rather serious, persistent delinquent who is very unlikely to benefit, not that all delinquents are unamenable to help.

This finding is confirmed and elaborated upon when the delinquency categories made by two staff members are used.[3] These persons studied the records of approximately 100 T-boys who had reached the age of 17½ years and about whose life careers much was known. They divided the boys into five groups: most delinquent, ordinary delinquent, occasional delinquent, seldom delinquent, and least delinquent. Comparing these classifications with those made with respect to value of service, we find that a little less than a fifth of the adequately served delinquents benefited (and those dubiously) as contrasted with three-fourths of the non-delinquents. Since some of the boys classified by the staff members as essentially non-delinquent did occasionally engage in delinquent acts, the conclusion seems justified that it is not the occasional delinquent act but the behavior that is characteristically antisocial

TABLE 82

Relation between Staff Judgments of Delinquency and Benefit Derived

Delinquency Judgments	VALUE OF SERVICE									
	A	B	C	D3	Total	D1	D2	E	Total	Total
1. Most delinquent	—	2	—	11	13	—	6	—	6	19
2. Ordinary delinquent	—	2	—	10	12	—	—	—	—	12
3. Seldom delinquent	4	5	1	3	13	—	—	—	—	13
5. Least delinquent	17	13	7	4	41	3	8	12	23	64
Total	21	22	8	28	79	3	14	12	29	108

that marks the kind of boy who did not respond favorably to the Study services. As has been previously stated, many boys of this kind were seriously neurotic as well, so our first conclusion seems justified: the Study was most likely to benefit fairly well-adjusted boys or those whose unconscious emotional conflicts, not very severe, were internalized rather than "acted out."

[3] See Chap. XIV.

HOME SITUATION IS ALSO IMPORTANT

It has already been shown that a boy's adjustment is fairly closely related to the kind of home he comes from, especially to its emotional aspects (Chapter XXII, Table 61 and Chapter XXV, Table 66). That this factor also bore considerable relation to whether or not a boy responded well to Study services has been indicated in the preceding chapters devoted to case analysis. We have next to show the extent of that relationship statistically, for it seems that this factor, like the character of the boy's problem, may serve to distinguish boys who probably can be helped by Study-like services from those who probably cannot. The figures on this point are given in Table 83.

TABLE 83

Relation of Emotional Aspects of Home Conditions to Benefit Derived

Home Ratings	VALUE OF SERVICE									
	A	B	C	D_3	Total	D_1	D_2	E	Total	Total
A	21	7	5	..	33	7	11	34	52	85
B	21	19	11	14	65	7	23	6	36	101
C	7	11	4	30	52	4	10	..	14	66
NK a	..	..	..	..	..	2	..	..	2	2
Total	49	37	20	44	150	20	44	40	104	254

a Not known.

Two-thirds of the boys who came from homes rated A in their emotional aspects (see Chapter XXII) and who needed and wanted the organization's services and were given adequate help clearly benefited. This contrasts with one-third of the boys from homes rated B and less than a seventh of the boys from homes rated C. At the other end of the scale none of the boys from A homes were in the group classified as definitely not helped, while that category contained about a fifth of the boys from B homes and three-fifths of those from C homes.

With the social aspects of the homes the relation to value of service was less close. Half of the boys from A homes who needed, wanted, and received adequate service and a fifth of those from B or C homes definitely benefited; one seventh from A homes and about half from the other types were not helped. While these are differences of some importance, they are clearly not as great as those found when the emotional aspect of the home was examined.

"Emotional aspects," it will be recalled, referred chiefly to the favorable or unfavorable character of the parents' attitudes, the extent of their affection for the boys and interest in their welfare. The term did not refer to the emotional maturity or emotional health of the parents, their relations with each other and with the other children, or the wisdom of their ways of handling the boys, though these were often interrelated characteristics. "Social aspects" referred to the institutionalized norms of parental conduct, such as those of financial support, home management, child care and training. What the above figures suggest, then, is that in selecting boys for service an organization like the Study would be well advised to pay more attention to the parents' attitudes toward the boys than to whether the home conditions are good or bad in the conventional sense of the word, and to choose for service those needy and interested boys whose parents are fairly well disposed toward them.

FRIENDLY RELATIONS ARE NOT ENOUGH

In spite of the preceding findings not all fairly well-adjusted boys and not all who came from fairly good homes benefited, even though they were in need of help, accepted the offer of service, and were treated in a way that seemed reasonably consistent with the Study's standards. Nor did all the severely maladjusted and those from very unfavorable homes fail to benefit. The easy answer would be that whether the boys benefited or not depended upon whether the counselors were able to win their confidence, were able to become the kind of friend that was envisaged in the original plan. To a certain extent this was found to be true but it, too, was not the whole story.

The Study started with the hypothesis that what maladjusted boys most need is the friendship of an adult who can discover the reasons for their difficulties and bring about the needed changes. It was assumed that the prime need would usually be for a guide and counselor, a strong, kind person who would stand by the boy through all adversities and provide the ego ideal that was probably lacking in his life, although it was recognized that material services would also play an important part.

The preceding review of the cases suggests that this hypothesis was only partially correct. For the most part the boys who clearly benefited from the organization's help were those who already had good relations with their parents and who were more in need of material services than of inspirational guidance. There were, of course, exceptions to this, instances in which the "guide, counselor and friend" aspect of the work was of major importance, but even in most of these cases strong, healthy parent-child relationships provided the basis for the boy's ability to benefit from such help. It may be that some of the boys with whom little observable was accomplished were heartened by the counselors' friendship and kept from more serious maladjustment by it, but this is largely speculation, based on the fact that boys and parents liked the counselors and expressed appreciation of what they had done.

Among the 44 boys with whom nothing seemed to be accomplished were some with whom the counselors were able to establish friendly relations and a few who became closely attached to the counselors. The kinds of relationships that developed were classifiable as follows:

1. Close relationship impossible (boy feeble-minded or case handled largely by another agency), 6
2. Boy clearly resistant throughout period of contact, 3
3. Boy usually resistant but at times showed interest in being helped, 7
4. Boy fairly friendly but relationship superficial throughout, 17
5. Relationship close at first; boy later resistant, 2
6. Relationship close most of the time, 9

Insofar as these boys were resistant to the counselors' efforts they differed from the boys who benefited. The chief difference between these boys' behavior and that of the boys in the A group lay, however, in the quality of their relationship with the counselors, this, naturally, being affected by their neurotic disorders. The counselors, being for the most part untrained in the use of psychiatric skills, were apparently not able to utilize in the neurotic boys' behalf the kind of relationship that developed between them. To have been able to do so would have required knowledge about psychological disorders far beyond that contemplated in the Study arrangements; hence this statement is not made in criticism. Nevertheless, it is a fact that some of the maladjusted boys gave evidence of wanting more help, or a different kind of help, than they received.

We conclude, therefore, that friendliness between a boy and a counselor is a necessary but not sufficient condition for the giving of assistance with behavior disorders. Most boys regarded the counselors as their friends but nevertheless many were not significantly aided. What is needed in addition is, first, on the boy's part, a sense of need for help, and, second, on the counselor's part, an ability to adapt "treatment" efforts to the individual boy's personality make-up, especially when the boy is emotionally maladjusted. This leads us, then, to examine the relation of the kind of service given to the results achieved, and to study more closely the kinds of boys who responded to the particular types of assistance rendered.

SERVICE MUST BE APPROPRIATE TO THE NATURE OF THE DIFFICULTIES

From all that has been said so far it is clear that it is useless to consider type of service apart from the type of boy served. Some indications of the difference in personality between the boys who benefited and those who did not have been revealed in the statistics above and in the case comparisons set forth in the preceding chapters. Fairly well-adjusted boys were likely to benefit, while those neurotically delinquent or otherwise seriously neurotic were usually not greatly aided. There were exceptions to this rule, however, and to some extent the exceptions are explainable in terms of the type of help given. It is clear, therefore, that the important question of correlation between type of boy and type of service requires more analysis than has so far been given to it.

If the term "problem" is used to denote the total configuration of boy and parents and home situation interacting to create the difficulties with which the Study was concerned, the review of the cases suggests that there are identifiable types of boys with which the counselors were able to be effective, as well as types with which failure was likely, and that within these types certain methods were useful and certain were not. The formula for which we are seeking in order to account for the Study's results therefore requires checking on all three aspects of the cases concurrently.

A. Good Parent-Child Relations; Boy Somewhat Maladjusted. It has already been noted that in cases in which relationships were very good (even though there was much about the home that was otherwise unfavorable, sometimes even to an extreme degree) the boys' difficulties were likely to respond easily to the counselors' services. The "problem" in these cases consisted largely of the parents' not having the ability or knowledge or cultural standards to give the boy all that he needed for the best utilization of his capacities. In such cases, good results were secured when the counselors discovered what it was that was lacking or at fault and instituted measures to correct the difficulty. (They were usually able to do this, for the difficulty did not lie in the area of parent-child relations.) Health, education, or recreational services were what many of these boys needed; in a few cases, advice and encouragement to the boy and his parents supplemented the parents' own efforts and were beneficial (see Sub-groups 1, 2, 3, pp. 456–472).

Twenty-one out of the 50 boys who were not seriously maladjusted and whose homes were rated A in parent-child relationships benefited from such services. In 11 of the cases in which the work was not effective the fault lay with the counselors, in that they put very little effort into helping the boys with their slight problems (see Sub-group 7, pp. 489–491). Most of these cases were dropped at the time of reorganization. In 10 other cases the parents either refused from the outset to have anything to do with the Study or showed little interest in having the boy helped, though they may have made some slight use of the counselors' services (Sub-groups 6, 23). In all the rest the counselors were not able to discover what was the reason for the boy's disabilities, most of these boys being inarticulate and unresponsive (Sub-groups 14, 23). In short, with reasonably well-adjusted boys from emotionally good homes the counselors were effective when help was desired and the counselors could discover what was wrong.

B. Very Unfavorable Parent-Child Relations; Boy Severely Maladjusted. To go to the other extreme next, we have noted several times that the likelihood of success was very slight in cases rated C in parent-child relations, especially in those in which the boy from the outset appeared to be very maladjusted. There were 24 such cases among the failures, four in the group in which it seemed that perhaps something may have been accomplished (Sub-group 17), five in which some benefit was secured temporarily (Sub-groups 21, 22), and five in the group classified as possibly benefited (Sub-group 26). In addition, there was one such boy among the cases in which the parents refused all service. Such a distribution speaks for itself, but it is important to try to determine whether the few boys who were helped are distinguishable from the others, either on the basis of their own traits or on the basis of the kind of service they were given, for it was from the ranks of these very maladjusted boys that most of the more serious delinquents came.

Close comparison of the cases revealed that within the general category of extreme maladjustment in the boy and extremely unfavorable parent-child relationships several types were to be distinguished.

First, there were thirteen boys who were greatly overprotected or overindulged or completely undisciplined, some by mothers who felt very guilty about their actual dislike of their sons, others by mothers whose real feelings were not known but who were extremely weak, ineffectual, neurotic individuals (Sub-group 27). Some of these boys were closely involved in their mothers' neuroses and were guilty and anxious; others seemed unable to control their actions and to have little emotional conflict about always insisting on having their own way. Three of them have been described in a preceding chapter (Sub-groups 10, 26). Other examples are the following:

Everett. Age 6 years, 10 months, to 12; I.Q. 99. This boy was being brought up by his dominating, anxious, overprotective grandmother, his inadequate, submissive mother, and his weak, often-unemployed uncle. The boy was illegitimate, and his relatives, with pitying indulgence, always referred to him as "the poor little kiddo." None of the adults was able to be firm with him, yet they instilled into him many fears and much sense of guilt. He was permitted no child companions because the neighborhood in which they lived was a rough one, so at school he tried to buy children's favor. In this he was never successful, for he spit at them, teased them, and generally displayed no ability for cooperative relationships. At home he was very hard to manage, indulging in abusive language, trying to play one adult off against the other, and being emotionally distraught.

Jack. Age 10 years, 6 months, to 17; I.Q. 85. The father's attitude varied from disinterest to abuse; when Jack was twelve he left home permanently. The mother was a weak, dull woman who expressed much concern about her children but gave them very inadequate care. She was quite unable to control them; they taunted her for her ineffectiveness. She constantly nagged Jack about his bad companions, yet when he was in trouble she always blamed others, regarded all actions against her children as unfair, and encouraged them to use illness as protection against being punished. She exploited all her contacts with employers and relief workers for her children's benefit. Jack, in reaction, was very aggressive, negative, demanding, insolent, much given to profanity and to temper tantrums to get his own way. He tried to avoid all unpleasant situations and was, generally, caustic, surly, and cocky.

A second sub-group (28) of extremely maladjusted boys consisted of twelve who were rejected and in some cases grossly neglected by their parents and whose reactions were of the paranoid or the self-punishing or the psychopathic variety. In consequence of these emotional defenses the boys were unable to form close relationships with anybody, the counselors characteristically describing them as boys to whom they could not get close or who "used" them for what they could get out of them.

Wilbur. Age 10 years, 6 months, to 17; I.Q. 91. This was a boy essentially without a home, his mother, his aunt, and his grandparents providing little more than shelter. He was one of three illegitimate children, both his mother and his grandmother being promiscuous. His mother was a weak, indecisive person who had little interest in the boy; his stepfather so much resented him that he left the family when Wilbur returned to live with them; his grandmother compared him unfavorably with her son of about the same age, and only an aunt, with whom he lived occasionally when things got too bad elsewhere, showed the least affection for him. It was accordingly not strange that Wilbur became a sullen, moody boy, resentful of everybody. He was repeatedly described in the Study's record as having a shell around him that the counselors could not penetrate.

Willard. Age 10 years, 8 months, to 17; I.Q. 75. Not much was known about how Willard's parents felt about him, for they did not speak English, but they seemed indifferent to his welfare. His oldest brother, a confirmed law-offender, had chief charge of him. Willard complained that he was treated like a baby, that nobody in his family liked him, that even his mother wanted to get rid of him by sending him to reform school. He was a quiet but moody boy, much given to aggressive talk. He continually stressed his "badness," over which he said he had no control. He claimed he was a "tough guy," that he didn't want people to be nice to him, that the counselor should not pay so much attention to him, he didn't deserve it. "I don't want anybody coming around to help me," he said, "They can't do anything for me. I've got two minds. One tells me to do good things and the other one bad things. Everyone has tried to help me but they can't."

Tony. Age 9 years, 3 months, to 16; I.Q. 92. Tony belonged to a family with a history of two generations of immorality, delinquency, and dependency. The father was an egocentric man interested in his family only as they contributed to his feelings of superiority or when their behavior gave him an opportunity to flaunt some authority. He had a great admiration for any person who could beat the law. Tony was the favorite because his father considered him the smartest of the children, but he was also resented because the boy's ill health hampered the father in using his usual method of discipline, severe beatings. Whenever the boy was in difficulty, through illness or delinquency, the father's first thought was to send him away. The mother seemed genuinely fond of and concerned about the children but she was completely apathetic and incompetent. Tony himself was an extremely moody boy with a faculty of winning adults by seeming to seek their approval and attention. Temporarily he could adapt to any person or situation very well but, though jealous, he could not form a close relationship with anybody. He stole continuously, derived great pleasure from doing so, lied about it with no sense of guilt, and boasted of deeds that had escaped police attention. He was always demanding material evidence of people's affection for him.

With neither of these two types of boys could the counselors make any headway, whatever measures they used. The psychological reasons for the failure are quite clear. Boys of the first type had no incentive to seek a counselor's friendship, some of them being already overwhelmed with restrictive affection and others having no desire to subject themselves to the kind of discipline that a close relationship with a counselor involved. With boys of the other type, the whole personality was organized against interpersonal relationship; to have been beneficial the counselors would have had to effect a complete personality change in these boys.

In these cases, method of work was apparently not important. Chief emphasis was sometimes put on the parents in an attempt to persuade them to treat the boys differently; in others much time was spent in searching for an organic cause of the disability; in others much work was done with the boys themselves and many opportunities for recreation, tutoring, and so on, were made available; for some, foster home or institutional placement was secured. Regardless of what was done, the results were negligible.

A third type of extreme maladjustment (Sub-group 29) was found in twelve boys who differed from the preceding chiefly in their desire for attention and affection. Some of them were somewhat less disturbed emotionally than the previous boys, and their home situations, while definitely unfavorable, were not quite so destructive, in that one parent or the other had a modicum of interest in the boy and, in some cases, some interest in having help with him. Most of these boys were seriously neglected, physically and emotionally; others felt disliked by their disinterested or antagonistic parents; two were nagged and overrestricted by parents and relatives who had little affection for them or so little strength of character that their attempts at discipline were utterly ineffectual. Some of these boys have been described in Sub-groups 2 (a), 17, 22, 26 in previous chapters.

With some of these boys moderately good results were secured, temporarily or by the end of the treatment program. It has been shown that the decisive factor was the persistency of the counselors' efforts. These emotionally needy boys responded fairly well when the counselors spent considerable time with them and demonstrated in this way their affection and interest. They speedily relapsed, however, when that attention was withdrawn. Only when the attention was sustained and when the boys got out of their unsatisfying homes into the emotionally neutral atmosphere of military service or a good institution did they sustain their gains. This conclusion was stated in the preceding chapter. It is confirmed by the examination of the four cases of this type in which the Study did not succeed. In two of these cases the counselors did not continue the close attention that was given at the start; in the third most of their efforts went into getting a diagnosis of the boy's condition and little time was spent with him alone; in the fourth, most of the work was done by placement agencies.

We conclude, therefore, that within the category of very much maladjusted boys from very unfavorable homes are a few who can be somewhat helped (in the sense of being emotionally supported until such time as environmental conditions become more favorable) if a counselor will give them much and consistent attention. These boys are distinguishable from the many with whom such efforts are futile by the fact that the parents have a little interest in the boy, expressed in some manner other than excessive protection and indulgence, and the boy himself is seeking rather than repelling friendship with an adult. In such cases, then, the nature of the problem and the nature of the service rendered are equally important in determining the outcome.

C. Parents Overprotective or Overindulgent. So much for the extremes. Another type of problem with which good results were seldom secured was that in which the trouble lay in the parents' overcontrol, overprotection, or overindulgence. This failure occurred even though the boys had not become seriously neurotic and even though there was an element of genuine affection in the parents' attitudes. Some of the extreme cases of this type have been listed with the preceding category of problems (Sub-group 27); others have been described under the heading of overprotection or overcontrol in various parts of the preceding chapters (Sub-groups 8, 12, 19, 24).

Two sub-types are to be distinguished: that in which the reason for the parents' attitude was primarily emotional and that in which cultural standards and beliefs played a major role. With cases of the first sub-type the counselors were uniformly unsuccessful, not being able to penetrate the close mother-son relationship or to deal with mothers who hoped to secure through them increased control over their sons (Sub-groups 8, 12, 19). With the second sub-type the counselors were sometimes able to provide recreation, tutoring, medical services, and the like, but attempts at altering the parents' ways of handling the boys were almost always unsuccessful (Sub-group 24). These attempts usually took the form of direct advice. Perhaps some of the parents might have changed their behavior if case-work methods had been employed, but this possibility was not put to the test.

D. *Home Extremely Poor Socially*. Another type of problem (occurring rarely as the main reason for a boy's difficulty) was that in which the social inadequacies of the home were so extreme as to counterbalance the parents' affection and concern for the boy's welfare (Sub-group 32). It has been shown that counselors were usually not able to help boys whose homes were of this type (Sub-groups 11, 18). In only two out of eight cases of this sort were the boys definitely benefited (Sub-groups 2, 3), though two others might have been helped had the counselors been more persistent or more skillful in their work (Sub-groups 21, 9).

Sub-group 33, the socially inadequate category, might be expanded to include all the 31 homes rated C in their social aspects, for it is popularly believed that children who live under such extremely disadvantageous social conditions are beyond assistance. In 17 of these homes unfavorable emotional conditions paralleled the unfavorable social ones, the rating given the home being CC. Only two of these 17 boys were clearly benefited by the organization's work; with one case-work methods were used (Sub-group 5), while the other was one of the emotionally needy boys mentioned above (Sub-group 2a) to whom the counselor gave unusually close and persistent attention. In 12 cases nothing was accomplished, although in two of them the parents and boys were very friendly and appreciative. Two boys were somewhat benefited as long as the counselors gave them much attention (Sub-group 22) and one improved slightly with the help of an unusually persistent counselor (Sub-group 29).[4]

With the 14 boys who came from homes less destructive emotionally, although socially very inadequate, better results were secured. Three of them were found to require little, if any, help; in two cases the parents refused the offer of assistance, and one boy was among those inadequately served by his counselors. The methods used in the three cases in which the boys were most helped had one trait in common—that the counselors tried to compensate for the parents' inadequacies. This was done in various ways: by a close relationship with and direct services to the boy (2), by improving

4 Figures in parentheses in the following pages refer to Sub-groups.

the mother's morale (3), or by removing the boy from the home, parents and boy being willing (4). This method of compensation was also used with success with another boy (21) as long as the counselor continued with it. On the counselor's departure, however, the boy rapidly declined and did not do well again until his parents sent him to live with relatives in the country.

With the four boys from this kind of home who were not helped the counselors' work was very different. With one, crude attempts at psychotherapy were made (16); with another, little was done by several counselors, while the one who did most seemed to ignore the boy's chief difficulty, jealousy of his sibling (14). The third boy, too, received little help (11), the counselors concentrating most of their attention on his inadequate and neglectful mother, and this was largely true in the fourth case also (11).

In this kind of case, then (the kind in which home conditions are very poor socially but not emotionally), it is particularly clear that service must be appropriate to the nature of the difficulty. Since the difficulty consists chiefly of the parents' inadequacies in child care and training, it is not surprising to find that those boys were helped for whom, in one way or another, this difficulty was surmounted. Usually it was impossible to improve the home situation (though this was done in one case); hence, the successful efforts usually consisted of making up to the boys for the parents' inadequacies—by finding a good school for the boy in one case, and by supplementing the parents' efforts in others.

E. Boy Persistently Delinquent. As has been shown before, Study services were usually ineffectual with seriously delinquent boys (Sub-group 34). (See Tables 81 and 82 above.) Since the original purpose of the organization was largely that of delinquency prevention, this point calls for further examination, especially with reference to the boys' personality make-up and the kind of work that was done with them. The boys to be considered are those listed in Table 81 (Sub-groups 4 and 5) as being habitually and rather seriously delinquent for fairly long periods of time. The table indicates that nine of these 53 boys were significantly benefited by Study services and that 31 of them were not at all helped. A comparison of these two groups may indicate some of the reasons for the difference.

Most of the boys with whom the counselors worked unsuccessfully had the kind of personality traits or lived under the kind of home conditions that have already been shown to be unresponsive to Study efforts. Eight of them were boys, not obviously neurotic, who usually shunned close relations with adults and apparently found in street life the satisfactions they missed at home. Many of these boys had parents who were indifferent to them, or rather disliked them, or at least paid little attention to them. Some of them were described by the counselors as inarticulate or reticent (13, 20, 2); others were outgoing and friendly, but they never became closely attached to their counselors. Eighteen others were the extremely neurotic boys from very unfavorable homes who had the kind of personality that proved impervious to all attempts at help (27, 28). Two others from equally poor homes were greatly handicapped intellectually or neurologically; direct work with them was impossible, and their parents were uninterested in having help from the counselors.

There remain, then, only three delinquent boys for whom the organization's failure to help may be possibly attributed to treatment methods. One of these boys has been included above in the groups of boys from homes that were disadvantageous socially but not emotionally. There it was pointed out that the treatment error, as judged by comparison with the successfully treated boys, lay in the counselor's concentrating attention chiefly on the parents instead of utilizing the boy's attachment to him to make up, in part, for the parents' inadequacies. The other two were the kind of neurotic children who, being emotionally deprived (29) at home, seek love and attention from outsiders. With one of these boys the counselor at first had a close relationship and the boy profited from it; later, the counselor transferred much of her attention to his rejecting mother, at which point the boy withdrew his interest and went on his delinquent way. With the other boy very little was done, other social agencies assuming chief responsibility.

The nine delinquent boys who benefited were like these latter three boys in personality, being either fairly stable youngsters from emotionally favorable homes or the neurotic type that seeks the affectionate relations denied them by the parents. The counselors, in their work with these boys, in one way or another, offset or overcame the deficiencies of the parents that had been responsible, more or less, for the boys' delinquent behavior.

With two emotionally stable boys this help was supplementary to the parents' well-intentioned but inadequate efforts; the counselors, having secured the boys' affection, gave them the kind of backing and practical assistance their parents, loving as they were, could not supply (2). With three neurotic boys the character of the work was much the same, but much more time and patience were required of the counselors and the good effects of their work did not show up until the boys left home (Sub-group 2, cases of Lawrence and Terrence). With two boys the parental inadequacies were circumvented by foster-home or institutional placement (4), this being agreeable to both parents and boys,[5] while in the final two cases good relations between the boys and their parents were restored through unusually sensitive work on the part of the counselors (3, 5).

The contrast between the delinquents who were aided by the Study and those with whom the work failed is, then, quite clear. It lay both in the personality of the boys and in the kind of work that was done with them. The best of work proved fruitless when interest could not be secured. This happened when the boys were either the type that finds in gang affection and loyalties a substitute for parents' interest or the neurotic type whose defenses operate against close relations with people. If the boy's interest was secured (which proved to be the case when he was either fairly stable or was emotionally disposed to form close attachments) it proved to be necessary, with a few exceptions, to concentrate on the boy rather than on the parents. Only if the parents were open to change of attitude toward the boy was close work with them justified. Otherwise, the chief objective of the counselors' work in the successful cases was to compensate the boys for the parents' inadequacies, either by direct services to them or by securing them new homes.

F. Boy Rather Neurotic. One final type remains to be discussed— the somewhat neurotic boy whom statistics previously presented

---

[5] It is noteworthy that in these two cases the counselors gave most of their time to the mothers rather than to the boys, in spite of the fact that the boys evidenced interest in adults' attention. The boys improved only after placement had provided them with the affectionate relations they were seeking.

show to have a fairly good chance of being helped by the Study. There were 43 boys classified as appearing to have, early in the Study's contact, a maladjustment that was "suggestive of neurosis but not extreme." Table 79 indicated that a third of those boys, provided they wanted help and received service consistent with the program, were definitely benefited and that about a fifth were clearly not helped.

Review of these cases showed that most of the eight failures in this group of 43 were in one or another of the five preceding categories. Two were boys from very unfavorable homes whom closer acquaintance showed to be much more neurotic than at first suspected. They have been included (see 27 and 28) with boys whose personality make-up precluded the establishment of close boy-counselor relationships. Four were greatly overprotected or over-controlled sons of very neurotic mothers, another type with which good results were never secured (see 12, 30). There remained, then, only two boys of the type under consideration here. With one of these boys the counselor was unable to develop a friendly relationship, probably because he let the boy identify him with the probation officer. With the other, the original good relationship petered out after the counselor began to give much attention to the boy's rejecting mother.

This elimination of most of the eight failures in this category (on the basis of their not being correctly assigned to the category or on the basis of mistakes on the counselors' part) would appear to strengthen the conclusion that the Study was usually able to be helpful to slightly neurotic boys.

Review of the cases of the 15 boys of this type who were helped indicated, however, that five of them were aided by methods we have designated modern social case work rather than those typical of the Study program (5). These, for the most part, were boys from emotionally unfavorable homes. Through careful, sensitive handling of parents' and boy's feelings about their situation the counselors were able either to improve the home situation or to free the boy to leave home.

With the other boys, methods more usual to the Study were used. Four of the boys were among the nine delinquents described above as helped by measures designed to offset their parents' inadequacies.

Four others were boys from homes that emotionally were at least somewhat favorable; they were aided by rather simple measures that alleviated some stress to which they were exposed (1). For the final two boys the help of other agencies was secured, one for psychiatric treatment of an acute disorder and the other for foster home placement. In spite of the variation in method, however, the cases do have this in common: the measures used were directly related to the causes of the boys' difficulties and did not spread out to all manner of problems in the rest of the family.

CONCLUSIONS REGARDING APPROPRIATE CASES AND SERVICES

We conclude, then, that there are identifiable types of problems with which efforts of the Study type are likely to be successful and types with which they are likely to fail. The character of the parent-child relationship is an important indicator of what the probable outcome of service will be, but this is not the sole criterion. Another important factor appears in the nature of the boy's personality and of his emotional "defenses." The counselors were chiefly successful in working with boys who were socially, physically, or mentally handicapped, but who were relatively healthy in personality and whose parents were either emotionally healthy or somewhat dependent and immature. They were also able to be of considerable service to a few boys who were emotionally very much maladjusted and who came from very unhealthy homes, psychologically considered. The trait that distinguished these few boys from the many of this type who were not helped was their obvious seeking for attention and affection—to which must be added the counselors' corresponding and consistent response.

Given the proper type of problem (that is, the kind of boy and home situation that usually proves amenable to Study efforts) it was necessary that proper treatment methods be employed. With some fairly well-adjusted boys from socially and emotionally adequate homes the method that proved helpful consisted of removing some specific handicap that stood in the way of wholly adequate functioning. This was true to some extent in all cases in which the counselor's ability to help the boy depended upon a close relationship between them. With most boys, the effective treatment method was one that, in one way or another, offset the parental inadequacies. A few somewhat neurotic boys were aided by services through which good parent-child relations were established. This usually required the use of modern case-work methods, although occasionally direct advice and encouragement were effectively employed with immature or culturally handicapped parents (35). In most cases, however, little was accomplished in the way of changing parents' attitudes (the "direct advice" method being the one usually employed), and attempts to work with parents to the exclusion, or the relative ignoring, of the boy proved ineffectual or actually detrimental. The chief method, then, by which good results were achieved was that of giving most attention to the boy and subordinating work with the family to that requirement, the aim of this boy-centered work being to offset parental inadequacies.

Various devices were used to offset the parents' inadequacies. For some boys the counselor acted as a parent-supplement, providing the knowledge and encouragement and access to educational, medical, or recreational resources that more sophisticated parents would themselves supply. For other boys the counselors' affectionate guidance proved a substitute for parental lacks. For some boys, sometimes through the assistance of other agencies, new homes were found. Given a boy of the requisite personality make-up and a counselor who did not make serious blunders, one or another of these measures usually proved effective in meeting the boy's chief lack—parents who could give him both adequate affection and the kind of material help and guidance that life in our complicated society requires.

If the boy was seriously emotionally maladjusted and yet was the type that sought the friendship of adults and so was likely to be amenable to treatment, it was especially necessary that contact with him be both long sustained and sensitively attuned to his needs, and that nothing (such as interest in other members of the family or a counselor's departure) be permitted to arouse in him the sense of being let down or rejected. Since cases of that kind were fairly numerous [6] and since failure to handle the relationship well accounted for some of the unsuccessful results, it would seem that this aspect

[6] Most of the successful cases were of that type, with the exception of those rather simple ones in which good results were accomplished by the removal of specific handicaps.

of treatment is one that should be given more attention than is usual in programs of the Study type.

All in all, then, success in the Study work was dependent on the boy's being of the requisite personality make-up and having some desire to be aided in dealing with his difficulties, and on the counselor's being able to ascertain where the trouble lay and to direct his efforts accordingly. Such a statement applies equally well, of course, to all social case work and, perhaps, to psychotherapy as well. The distinguishing characteristics of the Study's program were its assumption of responsibility in seeking out its clients, its long-continued service to them, and the rather naive and common-sense method its counselors usually employed. What we think we have established above is that the kinds of boys who can respond well to such a program can be designated and that for those boys there are certain identifiable kinds of services that prove effective.

THE CONCLUSION TESTED

The conclusion (that when the counselors gave the appropriate services the program was helpful to certain types of boys) can perhaps be best tested by examining the results secured by one particular member of the staff. This person (we shall call her Counselor A) best exemplified the Study principles—in the kind of work she did, in her own personality, and in the fact that, for the most part, she made the original contact with her clients and continued her contact with them throughout the period of the Study and after. Counselor A was the first to be chosen by Dr. Cabot for the staff. She was a long-time colleague of Dr. Cabot's and was regarded by him as the type of guide, counselor, and friend that he had in mind when he set forth his hypothesis.[7] Counselor A and her work have been described as follows by a member of the staff:

The worker, a nurse, who is unprejudiced by formal social work training, threw herself wholeheartedly into the family, doing whatever the situation at the moment seemed to warrant. It is impossible to put her into any category in relation to her approach to the family, for her role changed with each new situation. She was kindly, she was indulgent, she was critical, she was demanding, she was authoritative, and she was at

[7] Margaret G. Reilly and Robert A. Young, "Agency-Initiated Treatment of a Potentially Delinquent Boy," *American Journal of Orthopsychiatry*, XVI (1946), 697–706, for a detailed description of this counselor's work with one boy.

times threatening. But over all was her sincerity, which held the whole structure of her relationship together. Naturally, she brought into her work her own philosophies and disciplines. Being a nurse, her work was influenced by the nursing point of view. Being "spiritually minded," a term she often used in speaking of herself, she gave a great deal of attention to religious values. But throughout she never lost sight of the practical and reality aspect of the various family situations with which she was confronted.

At the very end of our investigation and with little expectation of significant findings, we tabulated the value-of-service ratings of the boys assigned to this counselor and compared them with the ratings of the other boys. The results, shown in Table 84, make it clear that this counselor was much more frequently successful and much less frequently unsuccessful in being helpful to boys than were the other counselors.

TABLE 84

Value-of-Service Ratings of Counselor A's Cases as Compared with Total Series

Value of Service	Counselor A Throughout	Counselor A Part-time	Total	Other Counselors	Total
A	8	2	10	39	49
B	7	4	11	26	37
C	2	—	2	18	20
D3	2	1	3	41	44
D1	1	—	1	19	20
D2	1	1	2	42	44
E	4	1	5	35	40
Total	25	9	34	220	254

NOTE: The proportion of A and B cases in Counselor A's whole series was 62 per-cent; in that served by other counselors it was 30. The difference and its standard error being 32 ± 8.9, this outcome is very unlikely to have occurred by chance.

This difference may not be wholly attributable to the counselor's working methods (described in Chapter XXIII, p. 379). In addition to having the kind of personality Dr. Cabot desired and in addition to carrying on her work in the manner that he prescribed, this counselor worked continuously with most of her clients, while most of the other boys had from two to four counselors during the Study period. The table, then, must be read not as necessarily indicating poorer work on the part of the rest of the counselors. It does suggest, however, that the results were less good when the Study plan was not carried out with the consistency that Dr. Cabot envisaged.

Analyzed in more detail, Table 84 indicates that, when carried out strictly in accordance with Dr. Cabot's plan (that is, by Counselor A), the services resulted in about one-third of the boys being clearly helped (A), another third perhaps being aided somewhat (B), and the rest, for one reason or another, being unaffected significantly. About half of this latter third, however, was made up of boys who either did not need help or refused the offer of service, and only three out of 34 boys served by Counselor A proved definitely unamenable to services. Of the boys who needed and accepted assistance, 36 percent of Counselor A's clients clearly benefited, as compared with 23 percent of those served by other counselors. When the cases rated A and B are combined, it is found that the proportion is increased to 75 percent of Counselor A's boys as compared with 39 percent of those of other counselors.

These rather startling findings reinforce rather than cast doubt upon the conclusions arrived at above, for the difference between the results secured by this counselor and the combined others appear to be attributable largely to the methods employed rather than to the nature of the boy's personality and problems. This is variously indicated.

First, comparison of the "original behavior" ratings and the home-condition ratings of the boys assigned to this counselor with those of the boys assigned to the other counselors showed an almost similar distribution. Apparently, then, this counselor's good results were not due to her having been given "easier" cases.

Second, it is clear from Table 84 that Counselor A had a much smaller proportion of boys classified as not benefited because too little work or inadequate work was done with them (D2). Only 6 percent of her series as contrasted with nearly 20 percent in the other series were cases of this sort.

Third, the kinds of boys this counselor was most successful with were apparently much the same as those the other counselors could help. It has been shown in Chapter XXV that most of the boys rated A in value of service were fairly healthy boys emotionally. Most of the few who were not so classified were aided by modern case-work methods, a way of working that Counselor A did not employ. Similarly, at the other extreme, this counselor was like the others in seldom being able to be of much help to severely neurotic boys who came from emotionally disadvantageous homes. All of her marked failures were of this type. One of these boys perhaps could have been helped had Counselor A not shifted attention from him to his mother, for he was the affection-seeking type counselors were otherwise successful with (see 2). Another of her failures was the paranoid type that shuns close relationships, while the third was an overindulged but severely rejected boy whose personality verged on the psychopathic. Two other severely maladjusted boys (listed in the B group in Table 84) were aided temporarily; their relapse occurred when the counselor made the mistake (exemplified in so many cases of the other counselors) of withdrawing her attention from them.

This counselor's superiority in results, then, seems attributable to her being more consistent and more persistent in her efforts than were the other counselors, taken as a group. It was not that she could work with boys they failed with; rather it was that, given a boy of one or another of the proper types, she worked so steadily and with such devotion to the boy's welfare that she was nearly always able to be of value to him.

The results Counselor A secured, then, may probably be regarded as the limit of what is to be expected from a program of the Study type. If the plan could have been carried out wholly as Dr. Cabot envisaged, the proportion of boys helped would have been considerably increased. Even so, the program would have left unaided the kinds of grossly handicapped boys described above. It is that fact that, in our opinion, goes far toward explaining the lack of difference between the treatment and control groups in terminal adjustment ratings.

WHY THE STUDY WAS NOT MORE SUCCESSFUL

In the light of the preceding analysis it may seem unnecessary to try to sum up why the counselors' services did not significantly lessen the incidence of delinquency and generally poor social functioning in the T-group as compared with the C-group. The answer, it seems clear, is to be found largely in the fact that the kinds of boys who usually become persistent delinquents or otherwise seriously maladjusted individuals are not the sort whose difficulties, largely emotional in nature, can be reached by the kinds of service the Study provided. In other words, Dr. Cabot's hypothesis (that what is needed to prevent delinquency and to foster good character development is the presence of an adult "friend" who will stand by the boy through thick and thin and make available to him the opportunities and the moral guidance that parents normally supply) appears to be disproved. The hypothesis was not rendered wholly invalid by the Study, however, for although this kind of work seldom prevented delinquency it has been shown that in certain kinds of cases "friendship" of the type Dr. Cabot envisaged did prove to be valuable. What we seem to have discovered, then, is the kind of "feller" that needs this kind of friend! What kind of "feller" that is and what the friendship must be like have been described in considerable detail above.

As to why the Study was not successful in significantly altering the distribution of adjustment ratings, we have, first, then, this fact that the Study group contained many boys who were too sick emotionally to respond favorably to the type of help the Study characteristically afforded. Second, there were at the other extreme a considerable number of boys (deliberately included in the group) who were emotionally healthy and very unlikely to become delinquents; in other words, a group of boys who did not need the counselors' services. Third, there were some boys who refused the offer of service, either directly and from the outset or indirectly by their passive resistance. Fourth, there were some who were poorly served by the counselors, either by being given much less attention than the plan called for (this was due, in part, to the exigencies of the wartime situation) or by being served in ways that our research has shown to be ineffectual.

When these four types of boys are eliminated from the series, there remain only about 50 boys whose delinquency records and general adjustment might be expected to be better than their controls. This is not a large proportion of the total; nevertheless it would seem to be large enough to affect the relative distribution of terminal adjustment ratings, so we have still to account for the lack of difference in the two groups.

One possible explanation is found in figures, previously cited, that indicate the amount of change that took place in adjustment ratings between the beginning and end of the program (Table 65 Chapter XXIV). Of the 49 boys who were clearly benefited, 35 had a higher rating at the end than at the beginning. This contrasted favorably with the boys who were not helped (that is, the 205 others in the whole series), for only a third of them improved over the years as judged by this test. This was taken as one indication that the work had really been useful to certain boys. These latter figures can be used in another way, however, to serve our present purpose. On the one hand, they may set a minimum for the proportion of the C-boys whose behavior improved, for the improvement in these boys whom the Study failed to benefit cannot be attributed to the counselors' work. Interpreted in this way, the figures suggest that at least a third of the C-boys improved despite the absence of this kind of help. On the other hand, the figures also suggest that at least a third of the T-boys who were helped might have improved even if the services had not been given. These could be boys for whom services were immediately helpful rather than preventive of breakdown in the long run, or they could be boys in whom the Study produced a qualitative rather than a quantitative change (see Chapter XXI). Deducting this one third from the 35 clearly benefited boys whose adjustment was found to have improved at the end of the program, we are left with only 20 boys whose adjustment would be expected to be better than that of their C-twins.

To this possible explanation of the lack of difference between the terminal adjustment ratings of T- and C-boys must be added one earlier presented (Chapter XXV): that the improvement in some boys was counterbalanced to some extent by the harm done to others. We were not able to be at all definite as to how many boys were adversely affected by the counselors' efforts, but it would not need to be a great many to counterbalance the 20 mentioned above, especially since some leeway must be allowed for error in the ratings in general. In this connection another point, not so far mentioned, is of interest: few of the boys whose adjustment improved greatly were in the group classified as benefited. To put it differently, the benefit the boys derived was seldom such as to make a great change in their adjustment ratings (see Table 65, Chapter XXIV). Putting these facts together (that some T-boys may have been made worse and that others improved only slightly so far as adjustment ratings are concerned), we see how it could have happened that the T- and C-boys' terminal adjustment ratings were so similarly distributed, even though it is clear that the services were beneficial to some boys.

To these various explanations of the lack of difference between the T- and C-group ratings must be added another suggested by the analysis of services appropriate to specific types of maladjustment that has been made earlier in this chapter. It was there concluded that not only did the Study attempt to serve many boys whose needs were beyond the capacity of this program to meet but also the counselors rather frequently did not use the proper methods with the boys they might have aided. The higher proportion of good results obtained by one counselor would seem to testify to this conclusion. Careful review of the case records suggests that there may have been as many as 20 other boys who might have achieved a better adjustment if the counselors had carried on their work in the ways our research has shown to be most effective.

A final possibility is that the C-boys received from other organizations approximately the same amount of help with their difficulties that the T-boys received from the Study. This possibility was explored in an investigation carried on independently of this main study, one that inquired into the extent to which the casework agencies of Greater Boston gave assistance to the C-boys.[8] It was found that less than 10 percent of an unbiased sample of C-boys became clients of psychiatric clinics or of social agencies that offer assistance in dealing with social adjustment difficulties. Moreover, in none of these cases were the treatment efforts at all successful: one boy had to be committed to a mental hospital, another was sent to prison, and in the other cases the social workers were unable to effect needed changes in the parents' attitudes toward the boys.

We are left, then, with rather contradictory evidence with regard to whether the C-boys got from others the help the T-boys got. It

[8] Sylvia J. Fuhrer, "Are Social Agencies Reaching Seriously Maladjusted Children?" Unpublished thesis, Smith College School for Social Work. Abstracted in *Smith College Studies in Social Work*, XVII (1946), 152.

would appear that the C-boys the clinics and case-work agencies failed to aid were probably the same kind the Study failed to help; nevertheless, it seems clear that none of the less maladjusted C-boys received from such organizations the kind of individual attention the Study successfully afforded to some boys. The greater participation of the C-boys in the activities of the group-work and recreational agencies might be regarded as making up for this lack, since the Study, too, did much work of a recreational nature. It will have been noted, however, that the benefit boys derived from the Study seemed attributable more to individualized services than to the general recreational activities, useful as the latter may have been in establishing rapport and providing the boys with needed opportunities. All in all, then, it seems rather doubtful that the lack of difference in outcome in T- and C-cases is to be explained on this basis.

CHAPTER XXX

RECOMMENDATIONS FOR
FUTURE PROGRAMS

IN THE LIGHT OF ALL THIS THE READER MAY WONDER WHETHER PRO-
grams of the Study type should be set up elsewhere or, at least, what
recommendations for work with difficult boys emerge from this
study. The finding that few true delinquents were significantly
helped by the work of the organization and that the C-boys turned
out about as well on the average as did those who received the organization's services might be taken to indicate that the expenditure of time and money was useless, except to demonstrate that
something other than this sort of service is needed if assistance is
to be given to difficult boys. Our more detailed analysis of the cases
has indicated, however, that the chief conclusion need not be quite
so gloomy as this. Some boys did benefit and others might have benefited if the counselors had worked with equal skill in all cases.
Those who did benefit usually made a better terminal adjustment
than their C-twins. The distinguishing characteristics of these boys
have been fairly well isolated, as have the characteristics of the service by which they were helped; these are facts that can be used in
differential planning for problem children. What the investigation
does show, then, is not that work of the Study type is useless but
that its usefulness is limited, and that no such generous, ambitious,
but professionally rather naive program can diminish to any considerable extent that persistent problem, juvenile delinquency.

How juvenile delinquents can be helped to assume more socially
acceptable modes of behavior the investigation did not indicate,
other than to suggest that, with certain types of boys, efforts that
compensate for the parents' lacks may sometimes be fruitful. For
the most part, however, it was not with serious delinquents that the
counselors were successful. The program, set up originally for de-

linquency-prevention, proved most beneficial to socially disadvantaged boys (some of whom were rather neurotic) whose delinquent behavior, if it existed at all, was transient in character, and whose chief problems were of another nature. It is toward children other than confirmed delinquents, or children who are unlikely to become confirmed delinquents, then, that programs of the Study type should be directed if the counselor's time and the organization's money are to be used most fruitfully. As to the Study itself, it seems a very worth while expenditure of funds to have demonstrated this, for throughout the United States programs more or less like it are being proposed and set up, and much effort is being put on preventing delinquency by befriending delinquent boys and making accessible to them the various resources of the community.

Even though the services did not prove helpful to the majority of true delinquents, the Study did serve a further purpose by providing some indications as to how boys who are likely to become persistent delinquents can be distinguished from other problem children. No universally valid means of doing this was discovered; probably it cannot be discovered, for human behavior is far from wholly determinate and predictable. We did find, however, that most of the boys who persisted in delinquency in spite of all efforts made to help them were seriously neurotic youngsters from homes that were very unsatisfying emotionally. These traits were discovered very early in the organization's contact with the boys. Very few boys with such traits were aided; those who were aided differed from the others in the character of their emotional defenses. To know which boys are likely to become chronically delinquent is the first step toward the elimination of the condition. That the Study provided some data on this point is therefore perhaps sufficient; it is not incumbent upon a research program to supply all the answers. Having some idea which boys are likely to continue with careers of delinquency and, probably, crime, other clinical research workers can go on from there and test out other means of prevention.

As to the kinds of boys a service such as the Study can help, they are fairly well identifiable on the basis of the degree of seriousness of their disorders, their personality make-up, the character of the parent-child relationships, and their interest in receiving assistance. In this respect too, then, the research was worth while, for this information can be used by persons who have the responsibility of deciding in individual cases what kind of treatment shall be provided for problem children and to what kind of organization a given child shall be referred. Such persons, of course, will have to have the kind of training and ability that enables them to make such differential diagnoses. To such individuals the findings of the research should prove very useful.

So much for the value of the findings for diagnosticians and for those organizations that provide services of the usual Study type. We must consider also to what extent the two principles by which the work of the Study was distinguished from that of most other organizations proved to be valid: the principle that the clients should be sought out and offered service rather than be waited for at the application desk, and the principle that contact with the clients should be continued for years rather than ended when the problem at issue seems to be cleared up. Some data pertinent to this question have been presented in the preceding chapters but a closer analysis must be made here, for these were important points in the plan.

As to the first principle, the great majority of boys and their parents appeared at the outset to be pleased with the counselors' offer of service, and very few explicitly refused it. In the total series of 254 cases there were only 20 in which the parents or the boy made it clear from the start or fairly early in the program that they did not want to have anything to do with the organization. These cases, 8 percent of the total, have been described in Chapter XXVII, where it was shown that attitudes ranging from middle-class dislike of outside help to paranoid reactions characterized the parents, while the boys who refused service varied from self-sufficient gang members to overindulged boys who seemed interested in nothing but pleasure.

A review of a representative sample of cases showed the following distribution of initial responses to the counselors' solicitation: [1]

1. Cordial acceptance of the counselors' offer by one or the other parent

[1] The last two categories combined constitute 9 percent of the total; this figure is sufficiently close to the proportion refusing the offer to indicate that the sample was probably adequate in size.

a. On basis of help being provided in a specific area mentioned by the counselor or requested by the parent, 34 percent

b. On basis of counselors' general description of the program, 40 percent

2. Parent either somewhat dubious, wanted further explanation, then accepted; or friendly but "not interested," acceptance won after one or a few interviews, 17 percent

3. Parent dubiously agreed, set limitations or otherwise indicated lack of interest, 7 percent

4. Definitely opposed, 2 percent

That so large a proportion of parents seemed pleased to have their sons receive the organization's services would appear, at first thought, to testify to the validity of the plan of going out and offering assistance rather than waiting for the parents of maladjusted boys to request help. Before we come to that conclusion, however, we have to consider what the offer was that these parents were accepting, and whether they and their sons accepted equally well all the kinds of help the counselors tried to give.

The initial offer made by the counselors was the provision of the kind of "advantages" that most parents want their children to have (health services, wholesome recreation, help with school difficulties, and the like) and that financially, culturally, or emotionally handicapped parents often cannot secure. That most of the parents accepted such an offer seemingly testifies to their interest in their children's welfare, in spite of the poor showing many of them made when their emotional relations with their children were examined. This kind of offer, it will be noted, is not the one that most case-work agencies make and to which they refer when they say that it is usually best to wait for parents to request service. The case-work agencies' offer is one that primarily has to do with help in overcoming behavior disorders, poor methods of child rearing, difficulties in parent-child relations, and other problems of somewhat similar nature. The Study, of course, also hoped to work in that area; in fact, to a considerable extent its original offer was regarded as a kind of entering wedge, a means rather than an end. To make the comparison of the Study with other case-work agencies meaningful, then, we must ask whether its clients accepted the implicit rather than the explicit aspect of its offer of service.

The above analysis of the kinds of boys who were helped and the methods by which help was given shows that the Study was most frequently successful when the work was carried on within the original frame of reference; when, in other words, the counselors did not attempt to improve parents' ways of handling the boys or to rectify unwholesome family situations but operated as parent-supplements, providing the services the parents could not or would not supply. Not all these services were of a "concrete" nature nor were all of them envisioned by the parents when they accepted the agency's offer. Nevertheless, most of them can be summed up under the heading of providing the kind of help (advice, encouragement, backing, ethical precepts, scientific information, as well as access to good recreational, educational, and medical facilities) that competent, affectionate parents themselves usually give.

We conclude, therefore, that the widespread acceptance of the counselors' offer had reference to its explicit rather than its implicit aim. For the most part, the counselors' attempts to direct the work to the parents rather than to the boys was usually unsuccessful. Accordingly, it cannot be deduced from this demonstration that most case-work agencies would do well to go out and solicit clients. Agencies that work directly with boys and girls (school social workers, for example; "Big Brothers," perhaps probation officers) might, however, take a cue from the findings: that disadvantaged parents are usually willing to let their children have the services the Study successfully afforded and that the children can benefit from such services if they have the traits described above.

The second Study principle to be considered is that which stated that contact with the boys should be maintained throughout adolescence [2] rather than being ended, in the usual case-work fashion, after needed services were rendered. Review of the data from this angle suggests that this principle need be followed only in exceptional cases. About a third of the boys who were significantly benefited were among those dropped when the program had to be contracted; obviously in these cases the long-continued contact was not required. In many other cases improvement in the boy's behavior occurred long before the termination of contact. In some

---

[2] The war interfered with carrying out this principle; otherwise, the Study would not have terminated contact when the boys became seventeen years old.

cases this took place after brief service of a material nature; in others there was a fairly slow working-out of environmental difficulties or emotional conflicts. Once the service was rendered, however, the boys continued at a rather even pace; they probably would have done so even if the counselors had no longer been in contact with them. The cases that appear to contradict this—those in which the work was said to have failed because the counselors did not sustain their original efforts—were those in which the needed service was not really completed or in which the boy was especially maladjusted. For some of these latter boys a long-continued relationship was clearly necessary. This was most clearly demonstrated in the cases of the few very maladjusted boys from very poor homes who were of a dependent, affection-seeking make-up (Sub-group 2, cases of Lawrence and Terrence), but it may also have been true of the much less handicapped boys who used their counselors as "ego ideals" (see Sub-group 2). Testimony to the effectiveness of this kind of work in such cases was given in some of the follow-up interviews.[3]

These facts suggest that a service program conducted along the lines of the Study can profitably follow the principle of soliciting clients instead of waiting for them to apply for its services but that it need not provide for most clients the long-time contact envisioned in the original plan.

The administrators of any such program—if they would use their time and money efficiently—must pay close attention to choice of clients and to the manner in which help is given to them. They cannot hope to accomplish much by way of prevention of chronic delinquency or of alleviation of other serious neurotic disorders. Their services will most frequently prove beneficial to children whose parents are fond of their children and interested in their welfare, even though they are emotionally immature, financially disadvantaged, or in some way or other unable to make good use of the complicated facilities than an American metropolis provides. To such children the organization should provide services carefully attuned to their needs, as defined chiefly by what they are not receiving from their parents. There will be a wide range in such lacks, of course. Occasionally a parent can be helped to express his affec-

[3] See Chap. XIII.

tion for his child more adequately or to give him wiser guidance than in the past; occasionally a broken home can be reconstituted or arrangements made for a child to leave a very poor home. For the most part, however, the parental lacks that the counselors can remedy will be less basic in nature, and the counselors will be well advised to attempt to effect changes in the boys rather than in their parents. This form of service is probably what Dr. Cabot had in mind when he set up the Study. If so, what the Study demonstrates is that such service is useful to certain boys, but that these are not the boys (the true delinquents) that Dr. Cabot was chiefly concerned about.

These prescriptions for successful work on the part of an organization modeled along the Study's lines call for much diagnostic skill, both in selecting boys and in determining the areas in which help is to be afforded them. How this can be developed—whether it can be developed—in an organization that does not have a staff of trained case workers is an open question. Perhaps such an organization should function as supplementary to other organizations' services, its "intake" being largely determined by some central diagnostic agency. Perhaps it can provide (as the Study did in its later years) its own diagnostic and supervisory service. However this is done, such an organization—like other community agencies —should clearly envision its function, its role in relation to other community services and to its clients, for the chief lesson of this experiment is that there is no one answer, no one form of service by which all manner of boys can be helped to deal with the difficulties that stand in the way of their healthy incorporation of social norms, which is the essence of good social adjustment.

RICHARD CLARKE CABOT

NOTE ON THE LIFE AND
SERVICES OF
RICHARD CLARKE CABOT

THE FOLLOWING NOTE ON THE LIFE AND SERVICES OF PROFESSOR RICHARD Clarke Cabot, Professor of Social Ethics and of Clinical Medicine, *Emeritus,* was placed on the records of the Faculty of Arts and Sciences of Harvard University at the meeting of October 3, 1939.

Richard Clarke Cabot was born in Brookline, Massachusetts, May 21st, 1868, and died May 7th, 1939, within two weeks of his seventy-first birthday. He was the fifth son of James Elliot and Elizabeth (Dwight) Cabot. After preparing for college at Noble and Greenough, he entered Harvard University, from which he received his A.B. degree, summa cum laude, in 1889 and his M.D. in 1892. Three honorary degrees were conferred in recognition of his attainments, an LL.D. by the University of Rochester in 1930, an L.H.D. by the University of Syracuse in 1934, and a D.D. by Colby College in 1938.

In 1894 he married Ella Lyman of Waltham, and until her death forty years later their happiness and devotion were a source of joy to their many friends and undoubtedly an important inspiration for much of his philosophical writing.

It is not possible to divide Cabot's life into clear-cut periods of activity, for one interest merged into another so naturally that his personality was one of almost complete unity. His interest in philosophy was not, as some have thought, a late interest. Rather it began early and continued until his death. In 1902–03 he was appointed Lecturer on Philosophy in Royce's seminar course in logic. In 1905, when he was 37 years old, he made his famous venture into applied ethics, inaugurating medical social service at the Massachusetts General Hospital. It is true, however, that the earlier half of his professional life was concerned primarily with medicine and the later half with social ethics. In 1903 he was appointed Instructor and in 1908 Assistant Professor in Clinical Medicine; in 1913 Assistant Professor of Medicine, and in 1918 Professor of Clinical Medicine. While holding this appointment he became in 1920 Professor of Social Ethics, thus filling twice as many chairs as it is possible for most mortals to occupy at Harvard in our generation. In 1933 he became Professor of Clinical Medicine *Emeritus,* and in 1934 Professor of Social Ethics *Emeritus.*

The reason for Cabot's early fame in medicine was his ability in pioneer lines of work and his indefatigable industry. At the age of 28 he published his first book, *Clinical Examination of the Blood,* which went into five editions in eight years. At the age of 31 he published *Serum Diagnosis of Disease.* His service in the Spanish-American War on the Hospital Ship *Bay State* as lieutenant in the Medical Corps was a great stimulant to his interest in the blood and in infectious diseases. In the ten years from 1901–11 he wrote three medical books of wide interest: the first, *Physical Diagnosis,* used the world over as a textbook, went through twelve editions between 1901 and 1938. *Case Histories in Medicine* appeared in 1906 and the first volume of *Differential Diagnosis* in 1911, the second in 1915, both volumes running into several editions.

Of great significance was his introduction of autopsy teaching in 1910, when he held the first of the long and continuous series of his famous Clinicopathological Conferences, the principal features of which have spread from the Massachusetts General Hospital all over the world. From 1902 to 1929 he conducted post-graduate courses in internal medicine which grew in size, as so many of his classes did, until they were almost unmanageable. He was an incomparable teacher, rugged and fiery in his exposition, yet distinguished most of all for his willingness to commit himself to the most rigid tests of his own diagnostic acumen. His courage and honesty inspired his students and his colleagues to learn through their errors as he did through his.

It was in 1905 during the intensive period of his medical work as private practitioner, instructor, author and out-patient physician that he established medical social work, a singularly inspired contribution to human welfare that has spread into all corners of the earth, and is everywhere associated with his name.

In 1914 at the beginning of the World War, in a short but vital paper, a landmark in medical history, Cabot made what is undoubtedly his most important contribution to technical medicine. The paper entitled "The Four Common Types of Heart Diseases" places him among the greatest contributors to cardiology in our generation. Its significance lies in its emphasis upon the etiological diagnosis of heart diseases in contrast to the over-emphasis on structural defects that had prevailed for more than two hundred years.

Richard Cabot was a reformer in the sense that he could never rest when he felt that something should be done and that he himself might be instrumental in the doing. In 1916 he and his wife went West on a vigorous speaking tour to help rouse the country to the cause of the Allies. During the war itself he gave his utmost energies as lieutenant colonel in the Medical Corps, serving as Chief of the Medical Staff at the Base Hospital in Bordeaux, and helping organize the dispensaries for refugees set up under the American Red Cross.

After the stirring days of the war he returned to take charge of the Department of Social Ethics. Now his life became relatively more peaceful, though ever richer and riper. To some who did not sense the change it seemed almost as if he had retired. True, he gradually relaxed his medical activities, but only that he might give increased time and effort to man's spiritual needs. He had become impatient with the mere healing of wounds and illness, and he had become impatient as well with the stereotyped education to be found in most schools and universities. Morons, he pointed out, can be superbly healthy and criminals can be highly educated. He threw himself, therefore, into the study and teaching of ethics. His courses on human relations and biography were conducted with all the gusto and rugged honesty of his famous clinics. With signal success he employed the case-method of teaching. Bare knowledge, unapplied to human welfare, untested by the single case, and unenlivened by artistic feeling, never won his allegiance nor his admiration. His style of speaking as of writing was lively and graceful, an expression of his remarkable ability to combine the values of science with the values of art.

The reformist tradition of his native New England was congenial to him. In the community he became a symbol of rugged integrity and public service. Some even thought him austere and self-righteous like the Puritan fathers. Certainly it took conviction for him to pursue his course; for his efforts, like those of other reformers, were not infrequently greeted with derision and disdain. But he never flinched, and lived to see many of his ideas accepted by those who at first were among the scornful.

For him the test of every course of action was its capacity to add to human stature. Will it make for growth? Through growing, each in his individual way, man expresses his reverence for God. By helping one another to grow, man shows reverence for God's creatures. In education, in work, in play, in love, in worship, in art, one grows, and perhaps especially in music. Much could be written of his devotion to his violin and to the choruses that he led. Famous were his bands of carolers who every Christmas Eve followed him into hospitals and through the lanes of Beacon Hill. Ascetic discipline too is required for growth; Cabot had as little use for self-indulgence as did the New England Puritans of old. But if growth requires self-discipline, it likewise requires liberty. Never reflecting on the logic of his position, he served both as President of the Anti-Saloon League of Massachusetts and as advisor to the American Civil Liberties Union. Like the elder Puritans, he wanted morality and freedom, and he fought for both.

Regarded almost as a patriarch by legions of social workers and elected President of the National Conference of Social Work in 1931, he kept always before the profession the need for severe tests by which to judge the value of social service. Fearful lest his preachment seem hollow, he devised in 1935 an experimental test, a project now known as The Cambridge-Somerville Youth Study, which will run ten years after his death and provide, he hoped, conclusive evidence as to whether or not social service may actually make for growth of personality.

As a lover of moral philosophy, of great and humane ideas, Richard Cabot had intense enthusiasm for individuals who could create and implement moral ideas. He admired Jane Addams, Ghandi, Tolstoy, Norman Thomas, and lesser persons as well, often his own students in whom he saw the spark of moral idealism. He had the gift of strengthening their self-confidence and of sending them forth with courage to pursue their own vision. It was always individuals who won his support; never barren causes nor lifeless institutions. He deplored the complacency of institutionalized interests, most of all perhaps vested educational and medical interests. To the end of his life he was actively concerned with new methods of teaching and with furthering the cause of group medicine, deterred not at all by the scorn nor even by the reprimands of his prosaic colleagues. Though by no means a radical, Cabot was often found in the vanguard of progressive thought simply because provocative moral ideas so readily fired his imagination.

His ethical writings, famous for their directness and charm, include *Social Service and the Art of Healing, The Christian Approach to Social Morality, What Men Live By, Social Work, Adventures on the Borderlands of Ethics, The Meaning of Right and Wrong, The Art of Ministering to the Sick* (with R. L. Dicks), *Christianity and Sex,* and *Honesty.* At the time of his death he was working on a final volume, *Creation,* which was to draw together the many threads of his interest and give mature expression to his deep religious faith.

Cabot's sturdy individualism was tempered by his disinterestedness and by his generous appreciation of others. Self-assured and tenacious as he was, he could suddenly yield in the course of battle and say, "I was wrong, you were right." When he admitted his errors of judgment, he admitted them whole-heartedly. This Faculty perhaps recalls the consternation he caused when he asked that a student's final grade be changed after it had been officially recorded, because he felt that he himself had made an error of judgment. When he won a combat, he was generous to the loser; when he lost, he congratulated the victor.

His colleagues will remember his magnanimity when in 1931 the present Department of Sociology was established to replace the Department of Social Ethics of which Cabot had for so long been Chairman. His generosity, so often commented upon by friend and opponent alike, stemmed from his deep desire to champion the right of each man to the fullest and freest opportunity for self-expression and for growth. His respect for individuality was deep-rooted in his religious creed.

His final illness lasted nearly a year. Uncomplaining and brave he followed the course of his own heart failure with great interest, challenging his physicians' diagnoses if he thought they were in error, but hastening to concede the value of their treatment. He demanded to know the truth and did not flinch from pain or from the grave prognosis. He persuaded his physicians to allow him for his mind's sake to work on his book and to teach. What he did seemed to help him physically, as he predicted it would. For months his classes from the Andover-Newton Theological School, where he taught after his retirement from Harvard, came to his bedroom twice a week and cherished their privilege as he cherished his.

His death ends a life of great service to mankind. Had he accomplished what he did in any one of his three chosen fields of endeavor—medicine, social service, ethics—it would have been more than enough. Though his last will and testament his spirit will continue to be active for many years to come. He bequeathed in his wife's name a fund to be used for fostering the work of individuals who show exceptional promise of making important contributions to humanity in any field of activity, in music, literature, philosophy, theology, education, or science. Thus in his legacy as in the noble example of his life he leaves a great heritage to posterity.

PAUL DUDLEY WHITE
RALPH BARTON PERRY
GORDON WILLARD ALLPORT, *Committee*

THE STAFF

CO-DIRECTORS
 Dr. Richard C. Cabot and
 Dr. P. Sidney de Q. Cabot   1935-1939

DIRECTORS
 Dr. P. Sidney de Q. Cabot   1939-1941
 Mr. Edwin Powers   1941-1948

HOME VISITORS
 Miss Margaret G. Reilly   1936-1938
 Miss Jean M. Kellock   1937-1938
 Mrs. Edwin Powers   1937-1938
 Miss Margaret E. Walker   1938
 Mrs. Douglas McGregor   1938

COUNSELORS
 Miss Margaret G. Reilly   1937-1945
 Miss Jean M. Kellock   1937-1943
 Mrs. Edwin Powers   1937-1941
 Mr. Edwin Powers   1937-1945
 Mr. Francis J. Daly   1937-1944
 Miss Margaret E. Walker   1938-1941
 Mr. Herbert J. Booth   1938-1941
 Mr. C. Wilson Anderson   1938-1941
 Mr. Francis T. Eaton   1939-1941
 Mr. Richard C. Raymond   1939-1942
 Mr. Charles W. Gaughan   1941-1945
 Mr. John W. Nichols   1941-1943
 Mr. James E. Daly   1942
 Mr. Lloyd W. Miller   1942-1945
 Mr. Carl H. Saxe   1942-1943
 Mr. Donald D. Dowling   1942-1945
 Mr. Hans-Lukas Teuber   1943
 Mr. Ashton M. Tenney   1943-1945
 Mr. Fred J. Murphy   1943-1945

RESEARCH

Mr. Henry C. Patey	1936–1939
Miss Madeleine Hale	1937–1939
Mr. Edwin Powers	1937–1947
Mr. J. C. Loring	1938
Miss Helen L. Hoff	1938–1939
Mrs. Burton A. Miller	1938–1939
Dr. William D. Turner	1939–1943
Dr. Donald W. Taylor	1941
Mrs. Douglas McGregor	1941
Mr. Emanuel Borenstein	1941–1942
Dr. George W. Hartmann	1942–1944
Dr. Hans-Lukas Teuber	1942–1944
Dr. Hans-Lukas Teuber	1946–1947
Mr. Francis J. Daly	1943
Mr. Walter Grossmann	1943
Miss Marianne L. Simmel	1944–1945
Mr. Robert Kagen	1944
Mrs. Joseph Bower	1945
Dr. Mary M. Shirley	1945–1946
Dr. Helen L. Witmer	1945–1948
Miss Margaret G. Reilly	1946–1947
Mr. Donald D. Dowling	1946–1947
Mrs. John K. Griffin	1946–1948
Mrs. E. Merle Adams Jr.	1946–1948

PSYCHOLOGISTS

Mr. Henry C. Patey	1936–1939
Mrs. Robert A. Young	1936–1945
Dr. Edward A. Lincoln	1937–1941
Dr. Alice M. Patterson	1938

TUTORS

Miss Marion F. Stevens	1939–1940
*Miss Ruth Borovoy	1940
*Miss Mary McGrath	1940
Mrs. Richard A. Montague	1940–1943
*Miss Deborah Calkins	1941
*Miss Laura Pettingill	1941
Mrs. George S. Wood	1941–1945
Miss Mary Buckley	1945

SECRETARIES OF THE STUDY

Mrs. John Volkmann	1936
Mrs. Reynald A. Jensen	1937–1938

* Volunteers.

Miss Dorothy D. Dolan	1938–1939
Miss Mildred A. Eck	1939–1943
Miss Alice O'Connor	1943–1945
Miss Louise E. Fouhy	1945–1950

SECRETARIAL ASSISTANTS

Miss Alice O'Gorman	1935–1939
Miss Rose E. Meade	1937–1944
Mrs. Burton A. Miller	1938–1948
Mrs. Raymond L. Newton	1938
Miss Evelyn Havey	1938
Miss Eleanor T. Daly	1938–1941
Miss Alice D. Doggett	1939–1941
Miss Alice G. O'Connor	1939–1941
Mrs. Lawrence J. Fitzpatrick	1943
Mrs. William M. Vogel	1943–1944
Miss Louise E. Fouhy	1944–1945
Mrs. Wayne V. Schell	1944
Mrs. Mario Gambardello	1944–1948
Mrs. John A. Bryant	1945–1946

SPECIAL INVESTIGATORS

Mr. Philip H. Meltzer	1938
Mr. Frederick H. Downs Jr.	1939
Mr. Burchill T. Sweeney	1939
Mr. Harry W. Green	1943
Mr. Irving Lazarus	1943
Mr. Henry Weinberg	1946–1947
Mr. E. Merle Adams Jr.	1946–1947
Mr. George P. Fanning	1947
Mr. Walter I. Wardwell	1947
Mr. Charles H. Anderson	1947
Mrs. Charles H. Anderson	1947

MEDICAL CONSULTANTS

Dr. Edward L. Tuohy	1941
Dr. Edward P. Cutter	1941–1942
Dr. Richard Wagner	1942–1945

EXAMINING PHYSICIANS

Dr. Richard C. Cabot	1936–1938
Dr. Donald Gates	1938–1939

PSYCHIATRIC CONSULTANTS

Dr. William L. Woods	1941–1942
Dr. Bryant E. Moulton	1943–1945

SELECTION COMMITTEE

Dr. Bryant E. Moulton	1937–1939
Mr. William C. Irving	1937–1939
Mr. Richard S. Winslow	1937–1939

CONSULTANT AND RESEARCH ASSOCIATE

Dr. P. Sidney de Q. Cabot	1941–1944

SUPERVISOR OF TREATMENT

Dr. Robert A. Young	1941–1945

CASE WORK CONSULTANT

Miss Elizabeth E. Bissell	1939–1940

SHOP INSTRUCTOR

Mr. Otto Chapman	1939–1942

REPRESENTING THE SCHOOL DEPARTMENT OF CAMBRIDGE

Miss Gertrude B. Duffy

REPRESENTING THE SCHOOL DEPARTMENT OF SOMERVILLE

Mr. Everett W. Ireland

RECORD FORMS
AND QUESTIONNAIRES

1. THE HOME VISITOR'S SCHEDULE

H. V. Schedule (B)

CAMBRIDGE-SOMERVILLE YOUTH STUDY

Date

Code: (✓) Presence   (0) Absence   (-) No information

IDENTIFYING SUMMARY

Name   Age   School grade
Referred by   Ordinal position
Descriptive summary of S.

HISTORY OF SUBJECT

Birthplace   D. of B.   Color
Birth wt.   Home   Hosp.   M.D.
Illnesses

Healthy baby

Fussy baby

HABITS (duration and intensity)

Thumbsucking

Nailbiting   Tics

Enuresis

   Attitude (Parents)

   Attitude (Subject)

Eating:

   Good habits

   Poor habits

Sleeping: Time to bed   Arises

    Attitude (Parents)

    Attitude (Subject)

RECREATION

Supervised activities

Unsupervised activities

SCHOOL

Name   Name of teacher

Truancy

    Attitude

STATUS

    Adopted   Boarded   State minor ward

RELIGION

ATTITUDE TOWARD DISCIPLINE

ATTITUDE TOWARD PARENTS

PERSONALITY OF S.

ATTITUDE OF NEIGHBORS TOWARD S.

HOME: No. of rooms   Bathroom   Tub   Toilet   Use

INCOME: Marginal   Relief   Adequate

FAMILY

Identifying data:

Interviewer   Interviewee   Telephone
Surname
Present address
Change of address
Former addresses
Agencies

Heredity

Father's History

First name   Age   Date of birth   Color
Birthplace
Res. in U.S.   Ctzn.

Occupational history

Education: Grammar   High   College

    Other

Literacy   Language

Health

Personality
Methods of discipline
Attitude toward S.

Mother's History

Maiden name	Age	Date of birth	Color

Birthplace

Res. in U.S.	Ctzn.

Occupational history

Education: Grammar   High   College

  Other

Literacy   Language

Health

Personality

Methods of discipline

Attitude toward S.

Marriage: Date	Separated	Reconciliation	Divorce

Rel., cult. & rec. int.

History of Siblings

Name	Age or d. of br.	Birthplace	Problems
1.			
2.			
3.			
4.			
5.			
6.			

Attitude of neighbors toward sibs.

	Name	D. of B.

STEP PARENTS or FOSTER PARENTS

NEIGHBORHOOD

HOME CONDITIONS

TOTAL SITUATION

1 -- continued

RATING SHEET FOR HOME VISITORS

Name of S.

Check (√) where appropriate

	Least able									Most able	
Standard of Living: (Ability to maintain health and decency)	'	'	'	'	'	'	'	'	'	'	'
	-5	-4	-3	-2	-1	0	+1	+2	+3	+4	+5

	Most likely									Least likely	
Rating of Home: (As place likely to produce delinquency)	'	'	'	'	'	'	'	'	'	'	'
	-5	-4	-3	-2	-1	0	+1	+2	+3	+4	+5

	Opposes discipline					Inert		Well balanced		Severe	
Discipline of S.: (By dominant parent)	'	'	'	'	'	'	'	'	'	'	'
	-5	-4	-3	-2	-1	0	+1	+2	+3	+4	+5

Comments: _____

_____

_____

Cooperativeness
(Approximately 1 in 20 families should fall in each extreme)

Least cooperative ____
Slightly uncooperative ____
Actively cooperative ____
Slightly more than aver. co-
operative ____
Most cooperative ____

Personality of Mother (underline)

Conscientious, anxious to do best for chn.
Talkative, jolly, colorful
Excitable, unpredictable
Domineering, set in ideas
Lacking in confidence, colorless
Straightforward, honest, fair in judgment
Vulgar, uncouth, shiftless

Comment or cross reference: _____

_____

_____

_____

Personality Traits of S.

Extremely quiet ____
Fresh ____
Over-talkative ____
Talkative ____
Rather quiet but responsive ____

Very lethargic ____
Slightly lethargic ____
Very restless ____
Restless ____
Average mobility ____

Suspicious ____
Inadequate ____

Immature ____
Mature response to others ____

Seclusive ____
Selfish ____
Jealous ____
Generous ____
Daydreams ____

Other outstanding traits: _____

_____

_____

2. DIRECTION FOR USE OF HOME VISITOR'S SCHEDULE

With the exception of the summary of "Total Family Situation," "Agencies," and statements in parentheses, the data are recorded in the words of the informant. When two or more informants are present, the identity of the informant will be indicated.

New data or corrections of old data secured after the case has been submitted to the Selection Committee shall be recorded on the schedule in red ink.

When there are two or more brothers in the Study, information regarding parents, siblings, neighborhood, home conditions and the Total Situation is to be recorded on the schedule of one S. with a cross reference to this specified on the schedules of the other Ss. concerned. Brothers are indicated in the master file by a silver star.

(It is suggested that in tracing the developmental history of S. the interviewer might use the method of comparing S. with other siblings to secure more precise descriptions from the interviewee.)

Where possible write (*v*) in red ink to indicate statements verified from records, and (*unv*) to indicate those unverified.

The interviewer shall be guided by the following explanations concerning the meanings of the terms used in the schedule.

Symbols used: (√) Present   (0) Not present   (-) No information

HISTORY OF SUBJECT

Ordinal position: Expressed in fractions; e.g., 3/4 showing third of four *own* brothers and sisters. Include all children, living and dead, but exclude pregnancies and stillbirths, which will be specially indicated under "Sibs."

Descriptive summary: This shall include where S. lives and with whom, as "At home with parents," and also any outstanding handicap, problem, or asset. Note general character of neighborhood area. A *short predictive statement* is desired.

Birthplace: Restricted area within country. (Where possible, give name of town, state and country.) State residence of fa. if it differs from birthplace of S.

Illnesses: Include deformities (birth injuries if possible), nutritional difficulties, convulsions in infancy, and any childhood diseases the interviewee mentions spontaneously.

Healthy baby: Unusual nursing difficulties, weight progress (normal range is doubling birth-weight at six months, tripling birth-weight at one year); unusual resistance to routine.

Fussy baby: May include outstanding difficulties about weaning, frequent crying spells, resistance to habit training, attention-getting habits.

Tics: Involuntary twitching of muscles of face or body.

Enuresis: Note if diurnal or nocturnal. Also any relationship to disease or emotional difficulties. *Attitude toward* enuresis: Includes expressions on part of mother which indicate a wish to keep child dependent or indifference toward establishing a training routine.

Eating habits -- Good: Refers to good appetite, regular meals, adequate foods. *Poor* refers to poor appetite, eats between meals, diet poor, fussy. State unusual likes and dislikes, emotional upsets.

Sleeping habits: Mention if irregular, insufficient, poor, giving probable reasons. Also mention dreams and fear of dark. Mention whether S. goes to bed or gets up readily; where difficulty exists, who prevails.

Recreation: Type of play activities. Special aptitudes and interests, such as music lessons (what instrument), dancing lessons, reading. Note interest in gambling games (specify details where possible). State whether interest is active or passive. How much and what kind of reading? Companions, mentioning age and age preferences, sex, stability of relationships, and if friendly with problem children. Note in parentheses if interviewer has directly observed S. at play. *Supervised activity* includes clubs, settlements, playgrounds. *Unsupervised activity* includes any group-play in streets, and lots, railroad yards, etc., without adult leadership. Note especially information gained about S.'s group behavior. (Very important with young children.) Note *Employment of S.,* which means employment outside the home on a job. Note what he does, and whether he turns the money over to the family or is allowed to use his own discretion in spending it. Household chores should *not* be considered employment, but they should be noted, and whether they are rewarded with a regular allowance, or constitute part of home responsibilities without monetary reward.

School -- Truancy: Unexcused absences from school; frequency. *Attitude* -- feeling toward teacher and school. Include retardation -- grades and times repeated with reasons.

Status -- Adopted. Legally adopted. *Boarded:* S. placed out. *State Minor Ward:* S. under guardianship of state. Note length of placements, age of S. when placed, whether paid for, S's. contact with own parents. Specify illegitimacy if suspected.

Religion: Indicate child's attitude and participation in church activities.

Personality of S.: Include such comments as the mother may make about S.'s affection, aggression, irritability, cooperation, ambition in school, leadership, seclusiveness, selfishness, jealousy, daydreaming, generosity, or any other outstanding traits. Secure information regarding marked changes in personality traits of S. as seen by mother, especially those following S.'s accidents or illnesses. What is S.'s sex knowledge? Where was it obtained? Attitude? Mother's attitude? Note whether S. is dependent on parents or siblings for direction or help, and if so, to what extent. Does he resent such help if forced upon him? Is he dependent on praise?

Income -- Marginal. No outside assistance except from relatives. Family managing with difficulty. Often considerable indebtedness. No savings. *Relief:* Receiving outside aid, other than from relatives. *Adequate:* Family income covering expenses for necessities, including recreation. Possible savings. See page — for Standard of Living rating, and make these ratings on separate mimeographed sheet.

FAMILY -- Identifying Data

Former addresses: Secure dates re most recent addresses as "places where family lived longest in past 15 years."
Agencies: List in red ink those learned from central clearing system, in addition to those given by family.
Heredity: Note informant's observations about outstanding physical or mental characteristics of relatives. Note any evidence of crime or delinquency in family history. Note birthplace of mgm., mgf., pgm., and pgf.
Father's history:
Citizenship: Note when naturalized or first papers applied for; or if a native born citizen.
Occupational history: Note present occupation, previous occupations, whether skilled or not, satisfaction with work. Where possible, indicate length of time in various occupations, including present one. Also night or day work and approximate hours.
Education: State grade left school. *Other:* Night school, trade school, etc. Differentiate between education in foreign countries and in U.S.
Literacy: State if able to read or write, and facility with each skill both in own and other languages, including English.
Health: Note present condition and energy level, abnormalities and illnesses.
Personality: Informant's comments. Also evidence towards emotional instability or mental abnormalities, including alcoholic tendencies, drug addictions, neuroses, psychoses, etc. Mention any evidence of unusual demands upon child set by father.
Methods of discipline: Rate according to scale on page — of this Manual and put on separate mimeographed rating sheet.
Attitude toward S.: Stress getting this important information.
Mother's history: Same as that of father.
Check on separate mimeographed rating sheet for personality traits of mo. in addition to general personality sketch. Substitute separately for fa. or other guardian when necessary; e.g., if mo. is dead or not living at home.
Marriage: Elaborate any significant facts when parents were married; when and why they have been separated, and for how long, and where S. lived during the separation of the parents.
Rel., cult., and rec. int. (Religious, cultural, and recreational interest): Note family activities and interest in religion, recrea-

tion, and family pattern. Note specific denomination and whether
attendance is regular or occasional (occasional church attendance
to be construed as active).

History of siblings: Include all children adopted, illegitimate
or half-sibs., alive or dead, at home or away, or who share in the
family life. Note any school, home, or community problems, and any
physical or emotional handicaps. Include history of pregnancies
and stillbirths.

Step Parents or Foster Parents: Follow outline on Parents in recording information.

NEIGHBORHOOD

Note: This is the recording of the facts gained from the interviewer's observations and other sources, and the interviewer's
interpretation of same.

Neighborhood: Note the type of character of the houses; whether
they are substantially or poorly built, owned or rented, well kept
or shabby and neglected; whether the area is open country or purely residential containing houses with yards, or congested containing business establishments, factories, railroad yards, and similar
features; whether sanitary conditions are good or bad, the streets
and premises clean or dirty, well kept or shabby and neglected;
whether there are opportunities for wholesome recreation available,
such as private yards, supervised playgrounds, athletic fields, and
parks; type of commercial recreation in the area, as motion picture
theatres, dance halls, and pool halls; also the neighborhood attitude toward law-breaking; the presence of bootleggers, gamblers,
prostitutes, and criminals, the existence of adult and juvenile
gangs, and their general character and reputation; whether the
neighborhood is quiet and restful, or noisy and characterized by
frequent quarrels and fights.

HOME CONDITIONS

Excellent home: Comfortable, roomy, well lighted and ventilated,
clean and orderly, adequately furnished, modern conveniences,
especially bathtub, some place in yard for outdoor play, and evidence of cultural opportunities within the home. *Good home:* Comfortable, moderately well-furnished, well lighted, clean and orderly, not crowded; recreation facilities provided for children. *Poor
home:* Badly crowded, dark, poorly ventilated, dirty, disorderly,
neglected appearance; no facilities for recreation for the children
Rate home on separate mimeographed rating sheet.

Note re TOTAL FAMILY SITUATION: This material includes the observations and interpretations of the interviewer. The points to be
covered are not all stated on the card, as this will be a running
summary and spacing will vary, but the material will be under the

following headings. (*Note:* It is important to record *interpreta-tions* as they affect S. Consensation is desired.)

Description of interview and interviewee: Give an account of how the interview proceeded with notes on individual's attitude toward the interview.

Summary of cultural aspects of home: Indicate the values, customs, tensions, in the family life as they apply to religion, education, recreation, nationality. Indicate reading interests. Note any evidence or suspicion of dissension, and whether any existing tensions might lead to eventual dissension. Alcoholism, immorality, marginal finances or opposing viewpoints on discipline of siblings should not be *assumed* to denote *dissension* in the home, though their existence might cause *tension* which if unresolved may ultimately lead to dissension.

Emotional atmosphere: Your observation concerning relationships between members of the family, any particular source of strain, and outstanding behavior.

Discipline: A summary of the use of authority on the part of the parents and the reaction on the part of the children. In addition to rating discipline of "dominant" parent, note opposing viewpoints, if any, maintained by other parent.

Willingness to cooperate with Study: Indicate what your opinion is of the likelihood that family will cooperate with the Study in a treatment program for S. Give reasons. Make ratings on separate mimeographed rating sheet.

Personality sketch: Synthesize previously noted data about S., including H.V.'s interpretations.

Disciplinary Rating

Discipline of S. by parent (or surrogate) taking major responsibility in terms of requiring him to meet the consequences of his own acts. Indicate attributes that enter into disciplinary relationships.

-5 Uses any issues as opportunity for disturbance.
     Uses any issue as opportunity for complaining about and interfering with disciplinary functions of other parent, school, or any group having responsibilities for S.

-4 Very self-defensive.
     Considers all disciplinary acts as reflecting on himself or herself. Actively opposes any such discipline.

-3 Self-defensive.
     Is defensive but motivation is less clear than in -4. Probably feels a personal stigma or stigma on family when son undergoes school, Sunday school, etc., discipline.

-2 Is apt to protect S.
     Too absorbed in S. Feels too much for him.

-1 Hinders discipline.
   Hinders but does not actively oppose school and other
   reasonable disciplinary measures. Possibly results from
   confused motivations; or lack of sufficient understanding
   to make possible intelligent co-operation.
 0 "Passes the buck."
   Simply passes responsibility to school, recreational resources, relatives or others.
+1 Agrees but does nothing.
   Agrees with other responsible persons, and even promises
   to take action, but attention dwindles and nothing is done.
+2 Responds to reason.
   Follows recommendations when teacher or school officials
   or other persons take the initiative; otherwise, methods
   are hit or miss.
+3 Is fair minded and definite.
   Take a very positive but fair attitude in assuring that
   his son meet social requirements and that he feel the consequences of his own acts.
+4 Somewhat too severe.
   Goes out of way to make sure that son "gets all that is
   coming to him." There is an element of fairness in his
   attitude.
+5 Unjustly severe.
   Takes delight in observing son suffer from disciplinary
   measure.

Standard of Living Rating

Let -5 represent the homes least able to maintain health and
decency; let +5 represent the homes able to maintain the highest
standard from this point of view.

The rating is a question of the domestic economy which a family
is able to keep, and depends both on income and the family's good
sense in using the income toward health and decency. This should
mean actual level of health and decency maintained, rather than
ability to maintain a particular standard. We want to know how the
family is living at present and on what level of decency.

Personality of Mother or Mother Substitute

Conscientious, anxious to do best for children
Talkative, jolly, colorful
Excitable, unpredictable
Domineering, set in ideas
Lacking in confidence, colorless
Straightforward, honest, fair in judgment
Vulgar, uncouth, shiftless

Cooperative Rating

Least cooperative
Slightly uncooperative   (Approximately 1 in 20
Actively cooperative   families should fall
Slightly more than average cooperative   in each extreme.)
Most cooperative

Rating of Home

Worker's rating of home as place likely to produce delinquents.
-5 Extremely high percentage of children from this type apt to be
   delinquent.
+5 Chances very low of boy from this type becoming delinquent.

3. TRAIT RECORD CARD

Date

Name in full
Home address
School
Teacher

Date of birth

Grade   Home Room No.

Check (√) any characteristics you have noticed. Double check (√√) the most outstanding characteristics. Please record your own personal observations. Where there are spaces in Section I below you are invited to add items. On the back of this card please write a paragraph describing this boy's personality and character. This information will be considered confidential.

A

( ) Blames others for his difficulties
( ) Resents criticism
( ) Makes excuses
( ) Is secretive, crafty, sly
( ) Is suspicious, distrustful
( ) Is rude, saucy, impudent
( ) Disobeys
( ) Refuses to cooperate
( ) Has temper tantrums
( ) Is cruel
( ) Tattles
( ) Meddles
( ) Is irritable
( ) Cheats

B

( ) Is extremely self-critical
( ) Worries
( ) Is moody
( ) Is unsuspecting
( ) Is easily hurt
( ) Is sullen
( ) Is easily moved to tears
( ) Has fears
( ) Is jealous
( ) Is easily imposed upon
( ) Is restless, nervous

C

( ) Seeks limelight
( ) Seeks attention

( ) Boasts
( ) Is a "show off"
( ) Is cocksure
( ) Acts silly
( ) Has "slap-dash" habits

D

( ) Is seclusive
( ) Is shy
( ) Is self-effacing
( ) Is easily embarrassed
( ) Lacks self-confidence
( ) Is apathetic
( ) Daydreams
( ) Tells imaginative lies
( ) Is forgetful
( ) Is meticulous
( ) Is punctilious
( ) Is sleepy
( ) Dawdles
( ) Procrastinates

E

( ) Vituperates
( ) Swears
( ) Argues
( ) Bosses
( ) Teases
( ) Bullies
( ) Is leader of a gang
( ) Quarrels
( ) Is irresponsible
( ) Fights

( ) Is stubborn
( ) Domineers
( ) Passes notes or pictures
( ) Has undesirable companions
( ) Does not conform
( ) Lies

F

( ) Stutters
( ) Retracts easily in argument
( ) Depends on constant direction
( ) Is "picked on"
( ) Has few friends
( ) Is dominated by others
( ) Lacks ambition
( ) Is indifferent
( ) Is cowardly
( ) Is easily led
( ) Holds himself apart
( ) Conforms scrupulously
( ) Is easily fooled

G

( ) Plays truant
( ) Steals

( ) Destroys property
( ) Gambles
( ) Smokes
( ) Talks obscenely
( ) Talks of toilet habits

H

( ) Is dull, slow, retarded
( ) Has poor work habits
( ) Has effeminate interests
( ) Wets clothes
( ) Sucks thumb
( ) Bites nails
( ) Masturbates
( ) Blushes
( ) Is a poor sport
( ) Is careless, slovenly, untidy
( ) Is tardy

I

( )
( )
( )
( )
( )

Date:
Personality and Character Sketch:

4. DESCRIPTIVE RATING SCALE

Name of boy   Grade   Date
                                    School

INSTRUCTIONS FOR USING THIS RATING SCALE

1. Please do not consult anyone in making your judgments.
2. When rating this boy on a particular question, disregard every other question but that one. Do not be disturbed if your ratings appear to contradict one another. There are contradic·tions in many boys.
3. When you have formed a judgment concerning this boy in respect to a particular question, indicate your rating by placing a check in the parenthesis (√) above the most appropriate descriptive phrase.
4. When rating a boy, try to compare him with other boys *of his own age.*
5. If because of insufficient evidence you feel you cannot rate this boy at all in respect to any particular question, you may omit it.
6. It is not necessary to sign this rating scale.

1. Is he interested in *manual activities?*

a	b	c	d	e
( )	( )	( )	( )	( )
Impatient with the necessity for any use of his hands	Rarely interested or loses interest quickly	Actively interested in manual activities	Definitely interested in developing several skills	Has a consuming exclusive interest in manual activities

2. Is he interested in *developing skill in athletics and physical play?*

a	b	c	d	e
( )	( )	( )	( )	( )
Actively opposes deliberate stimulation	Not interested but responds to suggestion	Some interest in physical skills	Wholehearted interest in learning how to do physical stunts	Consumed with interest in physical activity and play; no time for other activities

3. Is he *anxious to become more proficient in his school work?*

a	b	c	d	e
( )	( )	( )	( )	( )
Negativistic toward learning	Amenable but negligent	Moderately interested	Gives enthusiastic response	Completely absorbed

4. Is he *self-confident*?

a	b	c	d	e
( )	( )	( )	( )	( )
Usually depressed or feels inferior	Too easily discouraged; generally yields	Holds his own; yields when necessary	Quite self-confident	"Cocksure"

5. Is he *emotionally expressive*?

a	b	c	d	e
( )	( )	( )	( )	( )
Markedly inhibits emotional expression	Usually unresponsive	Ordinarily enthusiastic	Appears to enjoy expressing his emotions	Unrestrained in his emotional expression

6. Is he *courageous*?

a	b	c	d	e
( )	( )	( )	( )	( )
Fearful	Gets "cold feet"	Will take reasonable chances	Resolute	Daredevil

7. Is he *shy*?

a	b	c	d	e
( )	( )	( )	( )	( )
Painfully self-conscious	Timid; frequently embarrassed	Occasionally self-conscious	Well poised	Presumptuous and insensitive to social feelings

8. Is he *sensitive to the needs of others*?

a	b	c	d	e
( )	( )	( )	( )	( )
Cruel; spiteful; sarcastic; "hard-boiled"	Insensitive; inconsiderate	Reasonably considerate; warmhearted	Highly sensitive to emotional attitudes of others	Sentimental or demonstrative or overwhelmed by feelings of others

9. Is he *flexible*?

a	b	c	d	e
( )	( )	( )	( )	( )
Stubborn; hidebound; nonconformist	Slow to accept new ideas, customs or methods	Conforms willingly as necessity arises	Quick to adopt new customs and methods	Easily persuaded; suggestible

10. Is he *easily fatigued*?

a	b	c	d	e
( )	( )	( )	( )	( )
Is exhausted quickly	Does not appear to have ordinary endurance	Endures satisfactorily	Rarely shows fatigue	Usually vigorous and robust

11. Is he *slovenly or neat in personal appearance?*

a	b	c	d	e
( )	( )	( )	( )	( )
Very slovenly; unkempt	Rather negligent	Inconspicuous	Is concerned about dress; fairly neat	Fastidious; foppish

12. Is he *abstracted or wide-awake?*

a	b	c	d	e
( )	( )	( )	( )	( )
Continually absorbed in himself; daydreams	Frequently becomes abstracted	Usually aware of immediate surroundings	Keenly alive and alert; realistic	Excessively stimulated by immediate environment

13. Is his *attention sustained?*

a	b	c	d	e
( )	( )	( )	( )	( )
Distractible; jumps rapidly from one thing to another	Difficult to keep at task until completed	Attends adequately	Able to maintain attention for long periods	Is preoccupied in what he does

14. Does he *take an interest in things?*

a	b	c	d	e
( )	( )	( )	( )	( )
Is indifferent and unconcerned	Uninquisitive; rarely interested	Displays usual curiosity and interest	Interests are easily aroused	Has consuming interest in almost everything

15. Is he *physically energetic?*

a	b	c	d	e
( )	( )	( )	( )	( )
Extremely sluggish	Slow in action	Has satisfactory supply of physical energy	Energetic	Overactive; hyperkinetic

16. Is he *effeminate?*

a	b	c	d	e
( )	( )	( )	( )	( )
Is a "sissy"	Slightly effeminate	Has average masculine qualities	Very masculine	Entirely masculine; "a buck"

17. Is he *talkative?*

a	b	c	d	e
( )	( )	( )	( )	( )
Speaks very rarely	Generally quiet	Upholds his end of talk	Talks more than his share	Jabbers; very loquacious

18. Is he *sociable*?

a	b	c	d	e
( )	( )	( )	( )	( )
Lives almost entirely to himself	Follows few social and group activities	Pursues usual social and group activities	Actively seeks companionship of others	Exclusively prefers companionship of others to all else

19. Is he *amenable to authority*?

a	b	c	d	e
( )	( )	( )	( )	( )
Defiant	Critical of authority	Ordinarily obedient	Respectful and compliant	Entirely resigned and accepts all authority

20. Is he *assertive*?

a	b	c	d	e
( )	( )	( )	( )	( )
Never asserts self; servile	Generally yields	Holds his own; yields when necessary	Assertive	Insistent; obstinate

21. Is he *moody*?

a	b	c	d	e
( )	( )	( )	( )	( )
Stolid; impassive	Generally inexpressive	Responds appropriately	Has strong and frequent changes of mood	Has periods of extreme elation or depression

22. Is he *good humored*?

a	b	c	d	e
( )	( )	( )	( )	( )
Dejected; melancholic; in the dumps	Frequently dispirited	Usually in good humor	Cheerful; animated; chirping	Hilarious

23. Is he *easygoing*?

a	b	c	d	e
( )	( )	( )	( )	( )
Constantly worrying about something; has many anxieties	Apprehensive; often worries unduly	Does not worry without cause	Easygoing and lighthearted	Irresponsible and entirely carefree

24. Is he *suggestible*?

a	b	c	d	e
( )	( )	( )	( )	( )
Very suspicious; distrustful	Is convinced with difficulty	Generally open-minded	Considers and weighs evidence	Gullible; highly suggestible

25. Is he *impulsive*?

a	b	c	d	e
( )	( )	( )	( )	( )
Impulsive; bolts; acts on the spur of the moment	Frequently unreflective and imprudent	Acts with reasonable care	Deliberate and cautious	Excessively and scrupulously careful about details

26. Is he *restless*?

a	b	c	d	e
( )	( )	( )	( )	( )
Constantly on the move; irritable; fussing with hands; impatient	Quite restless at times; tires easily	Has short periods of some restlessness	Calm and composed most of the time	Extremely passive; lethargic

5. PHYSICIAN S REPORT

Directions: Check (√) indicates presence of characteristic
               Zero (0) indicates absence of characteristic
               Minus (-) indicates no information available

Name   School   Date

Teacher   Grade   Height standing

Weight   Age given   Age actual

Date of birth, given   Date of birth, actual

Lips: Good   Pale   Cyanotic

Conjunctiva: Normal   Pale

Skin: Disease   Clean   Dirty   B.O.

Head: Nits

Pupils: R.   L.
   Reacting
   Nonreacting

Vision: R.   L.   Both eyes

Ears: Discharge   Overlarge   Stigmata

Hearing: R.   L.

Nose: Discharge

Jaw: Normal   Underdeveloped

Teeth: Clean   Dirty   Hutchinsonian   Malocclusion
        Decay   Sl. carious   Mod. carious   Badly carious

Palate: Normal   Arched

Tonsils: Markedly enlarged   Infected   Lobulated

Glands: Normal   Enlarged   Speech: Lisping   Stuttering

Voice: Normal   Feeble   Loud   Thyroid: Normal   Bruit   Thrill

Shoulders: Normal   Stooping   Auxiliary hair

Chest: Normal   Rachitic   Asymmetrical   Lungs: Normal   Diseased

Heart: Normal   Diseased   Abdomen: Normal   Protuberant

Spine: Normal   Stiff   Curved   Knee jerks: Present

Bones of extremities: Normal   Thickening   Other abnormalities

Hands: Clammy   Nails: Normal   Diseased   Bitten

Summary: Estimate of general health: Good   Fair   Poor
           Structural development: Normal   Precocious   Deficient

TEMPORARY PROGNOSIS:

	-5 ...
Markedly "Difficult"	-4 ...
	-3 ...
	-2 ...
	-1 ...
	0 ...
	+1 ...
	+2 ...
	+3 ...
Markedly Not "Difficult"	+4 ...
	+5 ...
Unclassified	... _____

614

GENERAL IMPRESSION OF PHYSICIAN AND NURSE DURING PHYSICAL EXAMINATION
(To Accompany Each Report of Physician)

1. Health: Recent illnesses   Operations
      Sore throat   Earache   Toothache
      (Attitude)
2. Appetite: Good   Fussy
3. Sleep: Time to bed   Rising time
      (Attitude)
4. School: (Attitude)   Nickname
5. Family: Occupation of fa.
      (Attitude toward fa.)
      Occupation of mo.
      (Attitude toward mo.)
      Children
      (Attitude)
      Relatives living with family
      (Attitude)
6. Playmates: Age and names
      (Attitude)
      Gang or club
      Leader   Follower   Fighting
      (Attitude)
7. Activities after school
8. Activities on Saturdays
9. Activities on Sundays
10. Activities on rainy days
11. Movies: How often   Type of picture
12. Radio   Regular listener   Programs
13. Ambitions:
14. Three wishes:
15. Responsibilities: Home (chores, etc.)
      (Attitude)
      Paid work outside home
      (Attitude)
16. Fears   Dreams
17. Religion: Active   Nonactive
      (Attitude)
18. General behavior: Average   Hyperactive   Hypoactive
      Tense   Calm   Shy   Nervous   Anxious   Inert   Lively
      Responsive   Unresponsive   Talkative   Gentle   Effusive
      Surly
19. Bodily movement: Gait
                    Tics
20. Personality sketch (R.C.C.):

615

6. PROGNOSIS SHEET WITH PERSONALITY SKETCHES

Boy	Date of Birth	1937-38 Grade	1937-38 Teacher
School		City	

Description: Markedly "Difficult"

```
-5  . . .
-4  . . .
-3  . . .
-2  . . .
-1  . . .
 0  . . .
+1  . . .
+2  . . .
+3  . . .
```
Markedly Not "Difficult"
```
+4  . . .
+5  . . .
```

Writer: R.C.C.   Date of examination   S's age

Description: Markedly "Difficult"

```
-5  . . .
-4  . . .
-3  . . .
-2  . . .
-1  . . .
 0  . . .
+1  . . .
+2  . . .
+3  . . .
```
Markedly Not "Difficult"
```
+4  . . .
+5  . . .
```

Writer: Nurse   Date

Description: Markedly "Difficult"

```
-5  . . .
-4  . . .
-3  . . .
-2  . . .
-1  . . .
 0  . . .
+1  . . .
+2  . . .
+3  . . .
```
Markedly Not "Difficult"
```
+4  . . .
+5  . . .
```

Writer: Date of interview   S's age

616

Description: Markedly "Difficult"   -5 . . .
                                                              -4 . . .
                                                              -3 . . .
                                                              -2 . . .
                                                              -1 . . .
                                                               0 . . .
                                                              +1 . . .
                                                              +2 . . .
                                                              +3 . . .
                            Markedly Not "Difficult" +4 . . .
                                                              +5 . . .

Writer: Psychlgst.   Date of examination   S's age

Description: Markedly "Difficult"   -5 . . .
                                                              -4 . . .
                                                              -3 . . .
                                                              -2 . . .
                                                              -1 . . .
                                                               0 . . .
                                                              +1 . . .
                                                              +2 . . .
                                                              +3 . . .
                            Markedly Not "Difficult" +4 . . .
                                                              +5 . . .

Writer: H.V.   Date

Description: Markedly "Difficult"   -5 . . .
                                                              -4 . . .
                                                              -3 . . .
                                                              -2 . . .
                                                              -1 . . .
                                                               0 . . .
                                                              +1 . . .
                                                              +2 . . .
                                                              +3 . . .
                            Markedly Not "Difficult" +4 . . .
                                                              +5 . . .

Writer: A.B.C. (combined)   Date

7. TYPICAL PRE-TREATMENT SUMMARY[1]

Date of Summary: April 24, 1939. I have not seen either boy or fam.

Health and physical habits: RCC, 38-2-21: "Poor eyesight. Healthy. Badly carious teeth. Good coordination." ABC, 38-2-21: "Needs glasses. Had mumps in 1938." DRS, 38-2-23: "Usually vigorous and robust; energetic, entirely masculine." HV, 38-3-2: "Healthy baby except for colds and stomach upset. Good eating but casual sleeping habits. Sometimes picks nose." Parental health: Fa. in "fairly good" health; mo. bothered by bad teeth, colds, headaches.

Academic abilities and accomplishments: AMP, 38-3-10, reports, K.A. gives T.Q. as 88; S.A. gives T.Q. of 73. In second grade when tested. AMP remarks: "It is difficult to give a good word for boy. Poor study habits. Unwilling to do as told; noisy, thoughtless, irresponsible. In sch. work is not using all his ability because of instability and a poor attitude toward world in general. Cheats and copies; a poor influence. Academically unable to read and can not do good first grade work. Has almost no idea of numbers and their early combinations." FJD, 38-3-17, told by tr.: "You could not ask for a nicer boy in the classroom." DRS, 38-2-23: "Amenable but negligent about sch. Attends adequately. Irresponsible, restless." TRC, 37-5-27: Boy bosses, tattles, is sullen, and seeks attention. ABC, 38-2-21, told by boy he likes sch. HV, 38-3-2, told by mo. "not too crazy about sch. Only absent because of illness."

Interests: ABC, 38-2-21: "Likes movies. Collects copper for fa. to sell. Spends a lot of time 'walking around.' Goes out every evening." DRS, 38-2-23: "Actively interested in manual activities. Some interest in physical skills." HV, 38-3-2: "Boy has many un-satisfied wishes. Always wants to be outside. Plays on r.r. yards. Wants to go to Settlement and do things with his hands. Wants to play ball and to learn to swim. Prefers chn. of his own age. R.C. Attends S.S. regularly." FJD, 38-3-17, told by tr. boy was on the street day and night. "Great leader among boys, good athlete. Wants to be a gangster. Considers bro. Louis in special class a hero and chums mostly with him."

Personality: RCC, 38-2-21: "Affectionate, good-humored, conserva-tive, docile but adventurous. Nice kid. Bad environment." ABC, 38-2-21: "Suspicious, tough. Has an air of 'I'm not scared.' Scared by ghost stories. Dreams about spooks. Quarrels frequently. Friendly, appealing, naïve." PSC, 38-3-17, told by tr. boy was "as likeable

[1] *Abbreviations:*

ABC -- the nurse	mo. -- mother
DRS -- Descriptive Rating Scale	PGF -- paternal grandfather
HV -- home visitor	sib. -- sibling
AMP -- the psychologist	S.A. -- Stanford Achievement
K.A. -- Kuhlman-Anderson Test	FJD -- teacher interviewer
T.Q. -- test quotient	TRC -- Trait Record Card
S.P.C.C. -- Society for the Preven-	B. of P. -- Board of Probation
tion of Cruelty to Children	B. & E. -- breaking and entering
tr. -- teacher	D.P.W. -- Department of Public Welfare

as can be. Quick-tempered, but loses grudges easily. Would not let anything past him on the street. Would talk all day long." HV, 38-3-2, says boy is hard to manage and fairly able to look after himself. AMP, 38-3-10: "Rude, discourteous, tantalizing, noisy, thoughtless, irresponsible. Cheats and copies." All these remarks give a picture of a street gamin; noisy, rough, irresponsible, and unstable, but possessing friendly, responsive traits.

CIRCUMSTANCES

Fam. and home: HV, 38-3-2, reports the following. Boy is last ch. of 6, native-born of foreign-born peasant stock. Parents were born in old Poland. Fa. came to U.S. in 1907; has first papers. Mo. came about 1911 -- no papers. Parents speak little English, and fam. members talk in Polish, although chn. use English themselves. Fa. is a rather surly man on first impression. Became courteous and friendly after understanding HV, and then talked rapidly and a great deal. Probably dominates fam. Mo. likewise suspicious at first, but later became outgoing and friendly and almost eagerly expansive. Seems sturdy, hard-working, and vigorous. Both parents have very negative attitudes towards boy's present sch., feeling he is not given a chance there. No recreational activities other than church, except for fa. who attends monthly Polish society meetings. *Discipline:* Fa. "licks" boy fairly often. Considers him as one who may get out of hand if not watched. Mo. slaps boy. Fond of him, but a little distrustful about what he might be up to when out of her sight. Boy gets mad when punished: cries if it is too severe. HV rates discipline as +4 "?" *Social Agencies:* Delinquency Squad (38-12-29): "Walter a braggart, boaster, and bully, but not really such a bad kid. Complaints against him for assaulting boys and girls. Walter is now on probation. Has a cellar club with rumored bad behavior; has bad companions." B. of P., 38-3-12, gives the following record: Fa.: 6-1-37, arrested for being drunk, released. Bro. Herbard, 2-26-37, arrested for non-support and given 1 month in the House of Correction. Bro. Alec had 2 arrests for drunkenness with 1 probation. Sis. Alice, 15, given a suspended sentence to the Industrial Sch., 10-26-36, for lewdness, and placed on probation. Sis.-in-law Mildred arrested 7-28-36 for disturbing peace and the charge was dismissed. On 12-6-37 she was arrested for failure to report to the D.C.G. with infant ward -- on file. Bro. Louis (12) placed on probation 10-20-34 for B. and E.; on 9-18-37 given suspended sentence to Lyman Sch. and placed on probation for larceny. Camb. DPW, 38-3-18: Fa. applied for relief there on 27-5-5 as both parents had lost jobs through injuries. State temporary aid, 38-3-9, reports fam. applied for relief on 25-1-10 due to unemployment. Aid was continued '25 to '26. SPCC, 38-3-9, received a complaint made on 16-4-24 that PGF had punished 2 sons (one: boy's fa.) by putting their hands in stoves. No evidence of neglect on investigation and fam. seemed fond of chn. Believed punishment proper. PSC, 38-3-17, told

by tr. that the patrol wagon draws up to the boy's home every night
because of drinking. Boy once stole fa.'s wine and got sick from it
in sch. HV rates home as "-2."

Standard of living: HV, 38-3-2, says fam. lives on the second
floor of a large wooden house badly in need of repair. The rooms
are small with low ceilings, cluttered, and untidy. Furniture
broken and forlorn. Marginal income, quite inadequate, and HV rates
the standard of living as -2.

Occupational history of fa. and mo.: HV, 38-3-2, reports the following: fa. out of work for weeks prior to HV's. Had done farming
in Poland. Was boiler-maker in U.S. Then worked six years in a
machine shop, until he lost his job. Mo. has worked in brush factory and then employed in candy factory. Now scrubs floors and sup-
ports fam. with her earnings. Boy wants to do iron and foundry work
like his fa. No information on boy's attitude toward fa., so it is
difficult to interpret this, apart from the boy's own interest in
mechanical work.

Neighborhood: HV, 38-3-2, reports fam. lives in a very poor
neighborhood that has many run-down dilapidated homes with a few
stores nearby. There is no play space other than the cluttered yard
in front of house. FJD, 38-5-1, reports that the Baker home is back
of the Camb. Neighborhood House. The particular area is a mixture
of Portuguese, Lithuanian, Negroes, and whites. Population is said
to be residual from the group that has passed through it. FJD rates
the home as -1.

GENERAL INTERPRETATION OF DATA

A 10-year-old boy of foreign-born, Polish parentage. Fa. came to
U.S. with his parents when about 19 years and was brought up under
strict discipline, the like of which he maintains in his own home.
Parents are inclined to suspiciousness, but possess reasonably warm
and friendly traits. Income is inadequate, giving very little opportunity to members of the fam., if any. Fa. and all but one sib.
(Patricia) of boy have been in conflict with the law one or more
times. Boy likewise has been in trouble and is now on probation.
Complaints made against his stealing and assaulting other chn. Boy
is in good general health, except for poor eyesight. Has been retarded in sch., and is low in intelligence. Has made a poor sch.
adjustment, because of poor work habits and irresponsible attitude,
aided, no doubt, by his parents' negativistic attitude towards the
sch. Has several interests along constructive lines, such as handi-
crafts, but is denied the opportunity to develop or follow them.
Spends a lot of his time on the street. Although tough, suspicious,
and thoughtless, is capable of being friendly, responsive, and
likeable.

Staff ratings: RCC, +2; ABC, -2; PSC, -3; AMP, -4; HV, -2. It
seems quite possible that this irresponsible, aggressive ch. from a
poverty-level home of strict discipline, who is already delinquent

and is denied opportunities for constructive play, and with continued poor sch. adjustment, will engage in a delinquent career. Accordingly I would rate him if he were a control as -4.

TREATMENT OBJECTIVES

To obtain glasses for boy, the lack of which may contribute to his restlessness in sch. He needs to make a better and more satisfactory adjustment in sch. He likewise should have an opportunity for organized play to develop his native skills and interests already mentioned. It is doubtful if he will ever achieve much in sch., but a better adjustment and a renewed interest will do much to help him to gain self-confidence and to settle down. What responsibilities he gains will probably have to come through his life experiences, which, therefore, should be reasonably well ordered, allowing him opportunities to develop within his limited native ability.

PLANS

It will be difficult to get to this fam. despite HV's optimism, and I may need her help on follow-up visits. Once a friendly, comfortable relationship with the parents has been established, the task will be to build a similar one with the boy if it cannot be achieved simultaneously. The boy's need for glasses will be dependent, I presume, on the financial resources of the fam., should it prove to be impossible for the clinic to get him some. Likewise, I feel that it might be possible to work out some arrangement at the Neighborhood House for the boy's membership. He seems anxious and certainly should be given the opportunity, which, in my opinion, will mean a great deal to the ch. He needs a little more individualized attention in sch. in terms of his work. Perhaps he would benefit from special coaching and regular lesson plans. Primarily I plan to use my relationship as a basis of helping this boy to achieve something for himself that is meaningful and constructive.

8. QUESTIONS FOR INTERVIEWERS IN
POST-TREATMENT INTERVIEWS

1. *How did the program start? When? Why were you chosen?*

   [Specifically: Was boy initially bewildered? What explanations did he formulate for himself? What explanations were given to him? Were his earlier apprehensions or misconceptions (if any) alleviated later on? If so, how? *Or* -- is he still at a loss to explain "how it all came about," *why* he was "picked" etc.?]

2. *Did the relationship with counsellor stop? When? Why?*

   [Most of the intensive treatment cases were "terminated" whenever they reached their seventeenth birthdays or at the date of general termination of treatment, December 31, 1945 -- whichever was sooner.]

3. *What was the worker's (or workers') purpose?*

   [Regardless whether purpose was stated by worker or merely implied: What does the *boy* consider to be the purpose? Did the boy change his conceptions about the worker's purpose as time went on? How *adequate* or how *vague* does the boy's conception of the worker's purpose seem to us? Are there indications that the relationship fulfilled *one* purpose to the boy, *another* to the worker? If such discrepancies exist does the boy seem to be *aware* of them, and in *which terms* is such awareness expressed? Is such awareness a product of retrospective insight on the part of the boy, or did it arise during the course of the relationship? If the latter -- how soon? Why?]

4. *Is the boy able to give a designation to the worker's job?*

   [If so, does he do so spontaneously? What terms are used, exactly; e.g., does boy call worker a "counsellor," "social worker," or does he rather call them "helpers," "friends"? Does his choice of terms seem to be an adequate reflection of his own conception of worker's job? E.g., if boy calls worker a "friend" does he do so because he is not at all familiar with the term "social worker" -- or does he know the latter term, but deliberately chooses "friend" as the (to him) more appropriate designation?

   If boy does not seem to know any appropriate designation for the worker's job does he simply state, he doesn't know? If he uses circumlocutions, is he aware of their inadequacy or does he seem to be simply mistaken (e.g., "they are detectives")? If boy calls worker "social worker" or the like -- what kind of generalized attitudes (if any) does he seem to have toward social workers?]

5. *Are the worker's personal circumstances known to the boy?*

[Does boy know full name -- (first and last)? Which name did he use to address worker? What does he know about worker's family, etc., address, telephone number, present job (after close of treatment program)? How did he acquire more intimate knowledge -- especially was he introduced to worker's house?]

6. *.Are there indications of agency awareness?*

[Does the boy know relationship of individual worker to CSYS: Does he know name of agency? What does he think CSYS represents as an institution -- (what would he compare with it)? If he doesn't know much of agency -- what are his conceptions about worker's financial resources, etc.? Did boy, originally, or at any time during the course of the relationship, know less about the agency? What did he think then? How did he come to know about it? What are the boy's generalized (stereotyped) attitudes toward social agencies -- (if boy has any attitudes on this point)?]

7. *What direct descriptions and/or evaluations of the relationship are proferred by the boy?*

[Does the boy refer to the relationship as such, and, if so, in what terms -- (e.g., does he say "we were close," "he was like an older brother," or "I never liked his air'? To what other relationship is CSYS relationship compared (priest-parishioner, physician-patient, parole officer-parolee, pals, or what)?

Are there positive or negative comparisons in evaluation? E.g., "It's not as good as talking to a priest" or "It ain't social work 'cause it really helps."

What reasons are given, if any, for any kind of evaluation? (Do boys say, e.g., "I liked her because she'd give me hell," etc.?) Do the reasons that are given seem to have more than *ad hoc* value in explaining attachment or hostility? What signs of ambivalent relationship can be derived? Consider also anything bearing on boy's reaction to the presence of other boys in worker's caseload -- ("he had many other kids to take care of; I didn't fit with them") -- and to a worker's interest in other members of boy's family -- (" they only came to see my mother").]

8. *What is the boy's estimate of the frequency of contacts with his worker (or workers) at different times?*

[Is the boy able to specify? Does he over- or underestimate frequency of contacts (as checked against running records), and at what periods, and with which workers?

Did boy desire to see worker more often, less often, or just as often as he did see him (bears on #7 above).]

9. *What are the activities which the boy mentions* ("content" of
Y. S. relationship)?

[Note every activity which is spontaneously mentioned (e.g.,
"physical exams," "just talk," "advice," "camping," "buying me
ice cream cones," etc.). Note order in which items are mentioned,
repetitions, relative emphasis. Which activities seem to impress
the boy as central; which seem to him only incidental? Does boy
distinguish between activities which were central to him and
other activities which he thinks were central to the worker?]

10. *What reasons does boy give for active participation (or lack of
active participation) in Y. S. activities?*

[Cf. also ##3, 7, 9.]

[Does boy seem to be able to articulate such reasons? E.g., if
context indicates that boy merely acquiesced -- or that he exploited worker and agency -- is he able and/or willing to articulate this? (Cf. "I didn't go as often as Mr. X would like, but
only when there was something going on. The only reason I went
to the CSYS was to get some of the physical examinations, go on
picnics and do things like that." How genuine or specious do
such reasons seem to the interviewer? What reasons are given for
resisting part or all of CSYS? (E.g., "I didn't like those personal questions. I didn't answer them anyway if they were too
personal.") What comments (if any) are made on the research aspects of the Study; testing, special interviewing, etc.?]

11. *What was accomplished in the boy's opinion?*

[Does boy indicate that he was aware of an "instrumental" character of Y. S. activities (e.g., improvement, encouragement, advice, reform, medical treatment, etc.; see ##3, 9, 10)? If so,
what are his impressions concerning the outcome: does he feel
it was successful, indifferent, harmful? Does he intimate it was
indifferent in his case, but "might be a fine idea for other
kids"? If he feels Y. S. activity was a success (in his case or
in that of other boys) or a failure -- what are his criteria?
(Cf. "I would have been in reform school, were it not for Mr. X.")]

12. *What aspects of Y. S. activity would boy have liked to have
changed while Y. S. program was still going on? What suggestions
does boy have for changes in program in case Y. S. or similar
agency should be reopened?*

[Note whether boy spontaneously expresses concern about termination of program -- speculates on possibilities for reopening;
what are his ideas about financing the Study in such event? Relate to #2.]

13. *Does the boy give indications of an especial awareness of the delinquency-prevention motive?*

   [Cf. also ##3, 9, 10, 11.]
   [If so, in which terms? Does he think delinquency prevention was paramount or merely incidental? Does he think it was pertinent in his case or only for other treatment boys? Did he always know of delinquency-prevention motive or did he become aware of it only at a certain time and when, how? E.g., did a new worker tell him? Did he himself get into trouble just then; etc.? How does he feel about delinquency prevention in his case -- now -- and earlier?]

14. *What are the boy's general opinions on the causes and possible remedies of juvenile delinquency?*

   [Try to get both boy's "private" attitudes and his stereotyped opinions.]

15. *What are the boy's attitudes towards courts (especially juvenile courts) police, parole and probation officers, reform schools, etc.?*

   [Same specifications as for #14.]

9. POST-TREATMENT QUESTIONNAIRE

Name   Date

1. How did you first happen to get acquainted with the Study and when?

2. How did they happen to choose you?

3. Do you remember the names of any of the people you used to see during the years the Study was going on? (Underline the one you saw *most* often.)

4. How often did you see this person?

5. What did you think was the most important part of the program?

6. What did you do with the men or women that you saw? -- Swimming, tutoring, hiking, etc.?

7. What would you say their job was? How would you call it?

8. Did you ever talk to them about personal things? -- School, home, girls, etc.?

9. Did you ever get in trouble when you were younger? (Maybe in school, neighborhood, etc.) Did the men from the Study ever help you out? How?

10. What are some of the reasons why fellows get in trouble when they are young? I'm interested in personal experiences as well as what you think are the causes in general. Being in the service, meeting so many fellows, you must have some pretty good ideas on this.

11. How can delinquency be prevented?

12. Did you ever feel that there was anything that they could have done for you, but didn't -- (something you wanted them to do at the time you were in the program, or now)?

13. What was the Study all about? What do you think they were trying to do? Do you think they succeeded?

14. Did it help your home life in any way?

15. What was the worst thing about the Study?

16. What was the best thing about the Study?

17. Do you care who reads this?

18. What is your correct address today?

10. SCHEDULES USED IN INTERIM EVALUATIONS

a. TEACHERS' RATING BOOKLET

DIRECTIONS TO RATER: This material is part of the Cambridge-Somerville Youth Study. It is designed to see what changes, beneficial or otherwise, have occurred in a selected group of boys whose characters and personalities we are seeking to improve with the means at our command.

You represent an important source of information about the boy in question. We come to you because there is no other way of getting some highly important data required for our investigation.

Please rate the individual as carefully and as completely as you can with respect to all the features represented on the accompanying scales. If you do not believe yourself capable of a reasonably founded opinion on certain of these "traits," please say so specifically as we do not wish to force any judgments. Unhurried ratings, made tentatively on one occasion and then confirmed or corrected by reflective re-examination later, are probably the best.

Your ratings will be treated as confidential records and used for therapeutic and research purposes only with boys whose careers we are following.

From your class records about the boy, will you please supply this information:

1. How many times up to this date has he been *tardy* since the current school year opened last September, 1942? ......
2. How many times has he been *absent* since the current school year opened last September, 1942? ......
3. In your judgment, how many of these absences are:
   a. Actual instances of *truancy*? ......
   b. Due to family necessity or exceptional but legitimate instances of non-attendance for reasons other than personal illness? ......

POSTURE -- Check that point anywhere along the line which for you most nearly describes the boy's *normal carriage* under most circumstances. Remember, you may check *between* the descriptive phrases as well as at them, should that seem the most accurate location for the person in question.

| Badly slumped, suggestive of some gross bodily defects | Slouchy or drooped, as though chronically tired | Noticeable "rounding" of shoulders | Indistinguishable from the the multitude | Minor deviation from a good line in head, neck and hip region, but marked ease of movement | Carries himself "straight and tall" | Walks with easy erectness like a veteran Army officer |

SKIN CONDITION -- Check the quality of the skin of the face and neck *at the time of observation*. This is one of the weakest of the physical aspects of adolescence but do not let that disturb your appraisal of the boy's relative standing.

Severely scarred; active red or white pustulant eruptions over most of face	Badly "broken out" in *many* areas	Mild pimply condition in *several* places	Few pimples in one *limited* area	Roughened surface, with faint traces of earlier pimple scars	Free from blemishes, but oily, tough or sallow in texture	Skin is smooth, pink, and fresh in tone

CLEANLINESS -- Consider here the general and *usual* condition of the boy's *body* and *clothing*. Avoid overemphasizing minor details of appearance, but do not neglect them either if they really seem significant.

Filthy in appearance and repugnant smelling	Shabby, dirty, unkempt	Often fails to wash himself	Hard to tell apart from most other boys	Displays evidence of some care	Keeps himself clean constantly	Absolutely immaculate in every detail

GENERAL HEALTH -- Consider the definiteness of impression this boy makes upon you with respect to his physical condition and functioning as an animal organism. How much *energy* and *vitality* does he seem to have? What *reserves* of power for emergencies does he appear to possess? Does he strike you as one who has adhered to a *hygienic* and *sanitary* regime of living?

Pathetically feeble; chronic invalid	Sickly	Definitely on the weak side	Apparently normal throughout	Somewhat more than ordinary strength indicated	Strong, vigorous and energetic	Exceptionally robust, -- a "biological millionaire"

CONVERSATIONALIST -- Consider how *effectively* the boy communicates with others in ordinary social discourse. Can he express himself? Is he articulate? Does he respond freely to questions? Does he monopolize the discussion? Can he get others to talk?

A mummy or "wooden Indian"; says nothing	Needs lots of coaxing before participating	A trifle inhibited in exchanging ideas	Gets along like most youngsters in this respect	Babbles freely but disposed to disregard "partner's" interests or the value of what he says	Good form and content to remarks	Superb talker; one enjoys listening to him

QUALITY OF VOICE -- This refers to the "speaking" voice only since we are not concerned with singing ability. Consider the strictly physical or esthetic attributes of the boy's voice as a tool of social communication, disengaged from your feelings about the rest of him. Rate only the *present* voice; make no attempt to predict its quality after current pubertal changes are over.

Disagree-able tone	Mildly un-pleasant features predominate	Weak or "lazy" voice	Ordinary sound ef-fects	Clearly and easily heard but a bit too loud	Agreeable to listen to	Extraordi-narily fine voice for his age

COURTESY -- Consider chiefly the *habits of politeness* revealed by the boy. Avoid applying rigid or mechanically exact codes of the Emily Post variety, and try instead to detect overlooked evidences of a disposition toward gentlemanly conduct.

Deliberate-ly rude and offensive	Coarse and crude man-ner	Awkward	Indistin-guishable from his group in this respect	Somewhat on the "pol-ished" side	Good com-mand of social graces	Invariably considerate of others' feelings

ABILITY TO GET ALONG WITH OTHERS

A. Relation of Boy to *Superiors*

Consider how he *handles his various contacts* with older adult personages. Is he respectful or reasonably deferential without being a sycophant? Does he accept gracefully the normal exercise of "duly constituted" authority? Does he obey orders willingly and correctly? Does he make ordinary requests with the confident expectation that they will be fairly considered and granted?

Utterly awkward and incapable of managing even neces-sary asso-ciations	Clumsy; avoids contacts	Disposed to be faintly hostile or suspicious	Makes com-mon adjust-ments with-out trouble	Moderate skill in "managing" adults	Marked capacity for manipu-lating situations	Splendid voluntary relation-ships; grown-ups uniformly very fond of him

B. Relation of Boy to *Equals*

The term "equal" here means any other boy of approximately the same age who is physically and intellectually similar to the subject being rated. Presumably most of his *friends* will be drawn from such contemporaries. Focus your attention upon the nature of his ties with individuals construed as "colleagues."

Despised and re-jected by his fellows	Considered "queer" by his com-panions	Slightly marginal participant in boy group ac-tivities	A "run-of-mine" lad in this regard	Accepted with more than ordi-nary enthu-siasm by his "bunch"	Superior type of give-and-take inter-course	Gets along famously with his own kind

C. Relation of Boy to *Inferiors*

This refers to his practices in dealing with subordinates or "juniors" in age, strength, ability, etc. How does he deal with younger boys who stand below him in some important and easily recognizable respect?

Disliked or feared by smaller youngsters	Often acts the petty despot	Disposed to exploit his inferiors	Feels and acts a bit superior to them; patronizing	Inclined to be benevolent and helpful	Noticeably protective and fostering	Smaller boys look up to him confidently as a real friend

RECOGNITION AND PRAISE BY OTHERS -- Some individuals are starving for approval. The craving for status and prestige is far from being uniformly satisfied. Ask yourself: In how much *esteem* is this boy held by the "community" of which he is a member?

An object of pity, hostility, or contempt; quite wretched	Often jeered or scolded; feels humiliated	Occasionally "taken down a peg" with resulting ego-deflation	"Social" rewards and punishments evenly balanced	Usually given a "pat-on-the-back" as encouragement	Rarely criticized or blamed	Greatly admired, lauded and envied by people generally

SENSE OF HUMOR -- Consider the boy's capacity and readiness to see the *amusing* aspects of disturbing or threatening situations.

Wholly devoid of any sense of the comic	Expresses only grim or sardonic humor	May occasionally introduce a satirical note	Like most youngsters in this respect	Contains a noticeable "funny streak" or quietly appreciative of laughable matters; chuckles inwardly	A good punster or jokesmith	Frequently evokes smiles or laughter by witty remarks

TIMIDITY -- Consider various signs of fear and anxiety and the degree of freedom therefrom. How "secure" does this boy seem to be?

A pathetic and chronically frightened creature	Needs frequent reassurance	Lacks confidence in self	Subject to common fears and embarrassment	Good self-possession	Courageous	Absolutely fearless; supremely confident

IRRITABILITY -- How readily does this boy express anger and annoyance? You may think of this as a scale of grouchiness.

Known for his violent temper	Chronically irritated	Often fretful; a "crosspatch"	Ordinary "touchiness" or impatience	Good self-control	Generally displays equanimity	Always calm and placid

DEPENDABILITY -- Consider how "conscientious" this boy is in performing various duties. Is he as good as his word? Does he keep agreements faithfully? Is he reliable in executing written, oral, or implied "contracts" of all kinds?

Completely untrust- worthy	Sneaky and irresponsi- ble	Negligent in smaller matters	Not out- standing one way or the other	Usually "delivers the goods"	Good repu- tation in this regard	A model of fidelity

HELPFULNESS -- Consider the boy's disposition to assist others spontaneously. Whenever he sees an opportunity to make himself use- ful, does he do so? Is he benevolently and cooperatively inclined?

Looks after himself exclusively	"Can't be bothered"	Might aid a close friend	Mixed com- petitive and cooper- ative spirit	Slight dominance of "social service" impulses	Unusually generous of time and effort	Never misses a chance to do some kind deed

INDUSTRIOUSNESS -- Consider the boy's diligence, his willingness to work, and his stick-to-itiveness. Is he ready to put forth ef- fort? Does the necessity for strenuous labor upset him? Is he men- tally or physically "lazy"? Can he carry a job through to completion without prodding?

Lethargic; almost pur- poseless career	Evades work whenever possible	Weak per- formance	Does what is demanded but no more	Fairly per- sistent doer	Strong willed ad- herence to self-imposed schedule	Exception- ally am- bitious for his years

INITIATIVE -- How many things does this boy start "on his own hook"? Is he *resourceful* in getting much done with little in the way of equipment? Does he display *originality*? Is he a fountain of suggestions, orders, or requests by which others are energized or "managed"?

Never takes the lead in anything	Markedly deficient in origi- nality; prefers routine	Usually watches others for his "cues"	Occasional- ly offers a "bright idea" of his own	A fair "self- starter" and originator	Inventive and "dif- ferent"	A dynamo in launching varied enterprises

HAPPINESS -- If you compare him with others of the same age, how would you rate this boy's *general happiness*? Use this definition as a guide: "A relatively permanent state of well-being characterized by dominantly agreeable emotions ranging in value from mere con- tentment to positive felicity." Give due weight to all its manifes- tations. We assume that "the essence of *unhappiness* consists in longing to escape from the state of mind one is in" and that happi- ness itself is a condition which the person involved seeks to attain or maintain.

Place a cross (X) or check on the line below to show where he belongs. This mark may be placed *between* as well as *at* the descriptive phrases. Think of his *average feeling or condition over several months* and try to view him as objectively as possible.

Most un-happy of all	The *great* majority of persons are happier than he is	A *slight* majority of other people are happier than he is	About average	Somewhat happier than the general run of mankind	Far happier than the great majority of human beings	Happiest of all

EFFICIENCY -- Place a cross or check on the line below that best represents your estimate of the subject's possession of the trait of efficiency. Be as fair and impartial as you can, and ask: Can he perform (and does he!) promptly, smoothly, and adequately a great many tasks, originating either with himself or with others? Remember that the mark may be placed at *any* point on the scale.

Utterly in-competent to discharge any obligation	Very lax and irre-sponsible	Not as re-liable as one would like	Average capacity for manag-ing affairs properly	Handles matters with more than ordi-nary com-petence	Responsible and relia-ble in exe-cuting assignments	Extremely efficient in all duties

SYMPATHY -- Place a cross or check on the line below which best represents your estimate of the boy's possession of the trait of *sympathy*. Ask yourself: To what extent does he participate in the emotional experiences of others, i.e., how much *compassion* and *genuine kindliness* does he exhibit in his human relations?

Wholly de-void of sympathy; brutal	Callous and definitely unkind	Indifferent	Ordinary interest in others' problems	Distress of others understood and appre-ciated	Marked feeling of kinship with the "under-privileged"	Borders on the saintly in word and act

In which category does   belong?
Insert the *number* of the paragraph which best describes him in the *blank parentheses* provided after each attribute listed below.

A. *Intellectual Curiosity and Drive* ( )

1. Habitually wonders about information which is new to him. Recognizes that much of knowledge is as yet (by him) unexplored. Goes to some trouble to find what lies under the surface. Not content to cease seeking information when the class hour ends or a chapter is finished. Wants to know how things work, what others have thought, which means cause which results.
2. Prefers to know a great deal about a few subjects rather than a little bit about a great many. Tenacious in seeking all information available about a specialized field.
3. Ordinarily content to do his work in routine fashion, but on occasion (because of a personal interest, stimulus of a provocative idea, etc.) will explore a subject further.

4. Becomes enthusiastic over a new idea, thinks how satisfying it would be to know more about it, intends to, but never gets around to it.
5. Apathetic, no intellectual interest, indifferent, incurious, not responsive to intellectual stimulus.

B. *Scientific Approach* ( )

1. Precise, systematic, skeptical of "obvious" answers, scrupulous in weighing evidence, generally free from preconceived ideas. In most situations sifts evidence with discrimination and examines data objectively; but in certain areas bases his conclusions on personal bias.
2. So skeptical that he is unwilling to accept any solution not arrived at by him personally. Hypercritical.
3. Only occasionally seems to have arrived at a conclusion independently. Usually content to accept the opinion of his group. Indifferent to or impatient with arguments. Prefers to rest content with his own opinions rather than to find and weigh facts.
4. Believes everything he hears or reads. Not interested in proof. Antagonistic to evidence which runs counter to his belief.

C. *Practical Competence* ( )

1. Resourceful; considers all relevant factors before making decisions; logical and objective; knows how and where to obtain assistance if needed; alert, efficient.
2. Usually knows how to go about things; no great concern about how or why; occasional mistakes in some areas.
3. Gets along, but rather badly; frequent mistakes in many areas.
4. Fumbling, confused, illogical, unrealistic, capricious; unable to single out relevant facts.

D. *Group Leadership* ( )

1. Tends to be a leader, sought by others to manage them.
2. Likes others and is liked by them; upon occasion may be a leader.
3. Generally content to be a follower with limited contacts. Not much interested in and not sought by others.
4. Gets on poorly with and avoided by others. May be fearful, antagonistic, or excessively domineering, or seclusive, unfriendly, absorbed in self, or lacks fundamental social graces.

Be sure that you have skipped no pages. Look over each item again and see if you have been as OBJECTIVE as possible.

As soon as you have finished the ENTIRE booklet, please place it in the accompanying self-addressed envelope and mail to Cambridge-Somerville Youth Study, 21 Washington Avenue, Cambridge.

b. BELIEFS [SUPERSTITIONS]

Here is a list of things people believe in. Some people believe in most of them, others in only a very few. Read them now, and tell me the ones you *really* believe in *yourself* by putting a check mark in the blank spaces.

__ 1) Whenever one talks about a person, this person usually turns up.

__ 2) One should never give a knife to a friend -- it means trouble.

__ 3) One had better cross his fingers when telling something that is not true.

__ 4) Of all the days of the week there is an especially lucky one for each person.

__ 5) If one gets a high mark on a test in school one should keep the pen and always use it in tests.

__ 6) If the right person puts a curse on a fellow, it's pretty bad for him.

__ 7) Anything can happen in a family if you break a mirror.

__ 8) One should keep horseshoes -- they bring good luck.

__ 9) If one dreams of the same thing three nights in a row, it always comes true.

__ 10) It's a sign of coming misfortune to walk under a ladder.

__ 11) If you want to get a good grade on an examination, just keep thinking all the time that you will get a poor one.

__ 12) It's much better to have nothing to do with the number 13.

__ 13) If one finds a penny on the street, one should keep it in his wallet for luck.

__ 14) There is reason to feel uneasy when a black cat crosses one's path.

__ 15) A person's future is revealed by the lines and markings in the palms of his hands.

__ 16) It certainly means bad luck to light three cigarettes with one match.

__ 17) One should make a wish on seeing the first star in the evening.

__ 18) It means misfortune when a bird flutters at one's window.

__ 19) Your right ear itches or burns if somebody is saying nice things about you.

__ 20) It's good luck to find a four-leaf clover.

__ 21) One should never count the cars in a funeral procession.

__ 22) You can make a person turn and look by staring at his back.

__ 23) If you have tough luck when playing cards, it's a good thing to walk around the table three times.

__ 24) Success in life is just a matter of luck.

__ 25) If one talks about things going well, one had better knock on wood.

__ 26) It's lucky to find a pin with the point lying toward oneself.

__ 27) When friends are walking together, they should never let a post come between them.

-- 28) It's a good thing to carry a rabbit foot with you all the time.

-- 29) It's much better not to step on the cracks in the pavement of the sidewalk if you wish to have something you care for very much.

-- 30) If salt is spilled on the table, one should throw some of it over one's left shoulder; otherwise a quarrel will follow.

-- 31) By looking over your right shoulder into the new moon you can wish all kinds of evil on a person.

-- 32) If somebody drops a fork at the table, a lady will come to the house; if somebody drops a knife, a man will come.

-- 33) A cat washing himself in the house means that somebody very hungry is going to come to see you very soon.

-- 34) It brings bad luck to put shoes on a table, or a hat on the bed.

-- 35) I think I believe in a lot of things most other people do not believe in.

-- 36) Many people are just too superstitious.

c. A GAME OF THREES

1. Name 3 things you do that you *like* most.

2. Name 3 things you do that you *dislike* most.

3. If you had only 3 *wishes* and they could come true, what would they be?

4. If you could not be yourself, what 3 *persons* would you rather be?

5. What 3 things *annoy* you most or make you angriest?

6. Of what 3 things are you *most afraid*?

7. Name your 3 *favorite* movie actors (men).

8. Who are your 3 favorite *movie* actresses (ladies)?

9. What 3 *famous people* now alive do you *admire* most?

10. Name the 3 *persons in history* who died either a long or a short time ago that you most *admire*.

11. Tell here the names of the 3 *historical characters* you *dislike* most of all.

12. What 3 *important people now living* do you most *hate*?

13. If you had to live like Robinson Crusoe on an *uninhabited island* for 10 years, the 3 people you would want to have along are:

14. The 3 things I would like to do first if I ever had a *million dollars* are:

15. If I were *President* of the U.S., the first 3 things I would try to do for this country are:

16. If I were *Mayor* of the city in which I live, the 3 things I would try to do for this neighborhood are:

17. If I were my present *classroom teacher*, the 3 things I would try to do for the school pupils are:

18. If I were my *father*, the 3 things I would try to do for the family are:

19. If I were my *mother*, the 3 things I would try to do for the family are:

20. *Ten* years from now, I would like to be:

    Twenty-five years from now, I would like to be:

    Before I die, I would like to be:

21. If you could swiftly *change yourself* for the better, what 3 things would you first want to change?

22. What are the 3 *finest books* you have ever read?

23. If you could *live* wherever you wished, what *place* would you choose?

24. The ideal *number of children* in an American family today is:

25. If you were allowed only 3 funnies to read, or had just enough money to buy 3, which ones would you choose?

26. Name your 3 favorite radio programs to which you listen regularly.

THE CAMPING PROGRAM: STATISTICS

SCHEDULE I

Year	Cost to the Study	Parents' Contribution	Boys Sent
1939	$ 133.44		98
1940	400.50	$ 88.00	53
1941	952.20	206.50	90
1942	1,023.64	166.00	65
1943	562.71	106.00	18
1944	476.90	165.50	30
1945	932.46	122.00	32
	$4,481.85	$854.00	386 periods

Seasons at Camp	Number of Boys
1	96
2	57
3	31
4	11
5	9
	204 different boys

SCHEDULE II: CAMPS AND FARMS USED

Sponsoring Agency	Name of Camp	Location
Boston YMCA	Camp Dorchester	Ponkapoag, Mass.
Boys' Camp, Inc.	Camp Wing	Duxbury, Mass.
	Caddy Camp	Osterville, Mass.
Burroughs Foundation	Agassiz Village	West Poland, Maine
Cambridge Country Week	Lumawaki	Brattleboro, Vermong
Cambridge YMCA	Camp Massapoag	Dunstable, Mass.
	Stay-at-Home	Cambridge, Mass.
Camp Collyer	Camp Collyer	Amherst, N.H.
Catholic Charities	Vacation House	Nantucket, Mass.
City Missionary Society	Camp Waldron	Meredith, N.H.
Episcopal Church	Camp Dennen	Buzzards Bay, Mass.
Fellsland Council, BSA	Fellsland	Winchester, Mass.
Knights of Columbus	Camp K of C	Hawkey, Mass.
Morgan Memorial	Hayden Goodwill Village	South Athol, Mass.
Nippinickett Camp	Nippinickett	Bridgewater, Mass.
North Bennet Industrial Sch.	Caddy Camp	Maplewood, N.H.
Robert Gould Shaw House	Breezy Meadows	Holliston, Mass.
Sacred Heart Brothers	Sacred Heart Camp	Sharon Heights, Mass.
Scoutland, Inc.	Scoutland Reservation	Westwood, Mass.
Somerville Lions Club	Copithorne	Freedom, N.H.
Salvation Army	Wonderland	Sharon, Mass.
South End House	Caddy Camp	Poland Springs, Maine
Southern Middlesex TB Assn.	Camp Merriland	Sharon, Mass.
The Study	Sakukiak	Brownville, Maine

Farms

Robert MacKenzie	Norwich, Vermont
Oliver Whitcomb	Littleton, Mass.
Trescott Abele	Townsend Harbor, Mass.

PUBLISHED ARTICLES
BASED ON THE STUDY

1. Cabot, P. S. de Q. "A Long-term Study of Children: The Cambridge-Somerville Youth Study." *Child Development*, XI (1940), 143-151.
2. Murphy, Fred J., Mary M. Shirley and Helen L. Witmer. "The Incidence of Hidden Delinquency." *American Journal of Orthopsychiatry*, XVI (1946), 686-696.
3. Reilly, Margaret G., and Robert A. Young. "Agency-Initiated Treatment of a Potentially Delinquent Boy." *American Journal of Orthopsychiatry*, XVI (1946), 697-706.
4. Taylor, Donald W. "An Analysis of Predictions of Delinquency Based on Case Studies." *Journal of Abnormal and Social Psychology*, XLII (1947), 45-56.
5. Turner, William D. "Altruism and Its Measurement in Children." *Journal of Abnormal and Social Psychology*, XLIII (1948), 502-516.
6. Powers, Edwin. "An Experiment in Prevention of Delinquency." *Annals of the American Academy of Political and Social Science*, 261 (1949), 77-88.
7. Powers, Edwin. "The School's Reponsibility for the Early Detection of Delinquency-prone Children." *Harvard Educational Review*, XIX (1949), 80-86.
8. Powers, Edwin. "Some Reflections on Juvenile Delinquency." *Federal Probation*, XIV, No. 4 (1950), 21-26.

INDEX

(T and C refer to treated and control boys, respectively)

Accuracy test, in evaluation of character development during treatment, 315, 317

Activities schedule, in evaluation of character development during treatment, 301-2, 350

Adjustment, in evaluation, vii, xxi, 344; as variable in matching, 69, 81; ratio of, to social aggressiveness, as variable in matching, 71; and delinquency, 270; degree of, and success or failure of Study program, 556-61, 572-76; *see also under* Evaluation

Age, optimum, in delinquency-prevention program, xxv, 322-23; limits of, in original plan, 3-4; distribution of delinquents by, 25; as constant in matching, 75; differences in, of Ts and Cs, at time of assignment, 75; distribution of, at time of matching, 76, 79-80; distribution of, in case loads, 86; at beginning of treatment, 88-89; at terminal adjustment rating of Ts, 386, 394; insignificance of, in success of treatment, 546-47

Aggressiveness, ratio of, to social adjustment, as variable in matching, 71

Alcoholism among parents of Ts, 91

Allen, R. M., 273

Altruism Scale, in evaluation of character development during treatment, 298, 304

Assignment of boys to counselors, 7, 83-87; *see also under* Counselors

Authority, acceptance of, as variable in matching, 69, 81; attitude toward, as criterion of delinquency, 181-82

"Average" boy, inclusion of, in Study, 6, 30-31; meaning of, in Study, 55-56

Behavior Rating Schedules, *see* Haggerty-

Olson-Wickham Behavior Rating Schedules

Behavior ratings of delinquent and nondelinquent boys, 258-59, 267-68

Belief questionnaire, in evaluation of character development during treatment, 313, 316, 632

Big-brother approach, ix-x, 382

Bissell, Elizabeth E., 136

Board of Probation, referrals from 35; records of, in initial study, 47

Broken homes, and delinquency, xxiv; among Ts, 91; in relation to delinquency groups among Ts, 234-35

Bronner, Augusta F., 177, 238, 254, 270, 291

Cabot, Richard Clarke, v, vi, viii-x, xiv-xvii, xxv, 3-5, 46, 94-96, 99, 112, 129, 323, 343, 567, 571, 573, 583, 585-89

Cabot, P. Sidney de Q., 5, 52, 83, 129, 136, 179, 264

California Personality Test, in evaluation of character development during treatment, 297-98, 302, 305

Cambridge, Mass., social setting of the Study, 9-12; school system of, 14-16; delinquency in, 16-28

Cambridge-Somerville Youth Study, origin, v-vii, 3; objectives, vi, xvi, 3, 135, 385; plan, vii, 3-4; organization, 4-6; steps in development of, 6-8; Somerville schools included, 32; function and policies, 93-100; story of the first few years (to 1941), 111-26; change of headquarters (1939), 126-27; program reviewed, 129; new emphasis of, 129-31; new services added, 131-34; reformulation of objectives, 135; supervision of counselors provided, 136; retirement of cases, 136-38; effects of World War II

Emotional aspects of homes of delinquency groups, 237-38
Emotional inadequacy of home as cause of delinquency, xxiv, 237-38
Emotional outlets and tensions, as variable in matching, 65, 80; plotting of ratio of, 67
Emotional ratings of Ts' homes, 363-70; and terminal adjustment, 399-400
Enuresis, among Ts, 91
Environmental changes, policy of Study on, 98-99
Environmental pattern in matching, 71
Ethical Discrimination Test, in evaluation of character development during treatment, 312, 316
Ethics in social science, xxix
Euphorimeter, use of, in evaluation of character development during treatment, 314, 317
Evaluation, *general:* optimum time for, xiii, 322-23; problems of xv-xviii, 320-23, 341-46
— *"most delinquent" boys compared with "least delinquent" (or non-delinquent),* see under "Most delinquent" boys
— *predictions of delinquency of Ts and Cs compared with delinquency judgments,* see under Prediction of delinquency
— *character development tested during treatment (interim surveys):* samples used, 293-94, 308-9; method used, 295; measuring instruments used in, 295-303, 309-16, 625-34; scores of Ts and Cs compared, 303-6, 316-17
— *statistical analysis of delinquency-prevention:* usefulness of control group in, 320-21; time factor in, 321-22; optimum time for evaluation, 322-23; police statistics of Ts and Cs compared, 323-25; frequency of court appearances of Ts and Cs compared, 326-28; seriousness of offenses of Ts and Cs compared, 328-34; commitments to correctional institutions of Ts and Cs compared, 334-37; conclusions, 337-38
— *clinical and statistical analysis of adjustment* (with case illustrations): initial adjustment of Ts, 348-54; delinquent tendencies of Ts, 354-56; social conditions of Ts' homes, 356-62; emotional conditions of Ts' homes, 363-70; social-emotional conditions of Ts' homes, 370-73; initial adjustment rat-

ings compared with social-emotional ratings, 373-75; terminal adjustment of Ts, 386-93; age at terminal adjustment rating of Ts, 386, 394; terminal adjustment ratings compared with delinquency judgments of Ts, 394-96; terminal adjustment ratings compared with initial adjustment ratings of Ts, 396-98; factors related to terminal adjustment of Ts, 397-402; terminal adjustment ratings compared with social-emotional ratings of homes of Ts, 399-400; terminal adjustment ratings compared with predictive ratings of Ts, 400-2; follow-up of Cs, 402-6; rating terminal adjustment of Cs, 410-12; terminal adjustment ratings of Ts and Cs compared, 414-17; terminal adjustment ratings and predictive ratings of Ts and Cs compared, 417-18; conclusions, 419-20
— *clinical and statistical analysis of value of service to individuals* (with case illustrations): to supersede control-group comparisons, 419-20; meaning of value of service, 421-23; rating of value of service, 423-40; testing validity of ratings, 440-49; distribution of boys by value-of-service ratings and duration of service, 440-41; value-of-service ratings compared with terminal adjustment ratings, 441-42; value-of-service ratings compared with change from initial to terminal adjustment ratings, 442-43; boys' opinions of value of service, 443-48; value-of-service ratings compared with boys' opinions, 447-48; implications of findings, 449-53; value-of-service ratings compared with terminal adjustment ratings of Ts and Cs, 453-55; value-of-service ratings in relation to age and intelligence, 546-47; emotional maladjustment and value of service, 547-50; value-of-service ratings compared with initial adjustment ratings, 548; delinquent tendency ratings compared with value-of-service ratings, 549-50; extent of delinquency compared with value-of-service ratings, 550-51; delinquency judgments compared with value-of-service ratings, 551; emotional ratings of homes compared with value-of-service ratings, 552-53; value-of-service ratings of boys treated by Counselor A compared with those of

Treated boys (*Continued*)
justment of, as area of treatment, 116-17; physical condition of, as area of treatment, 117; opinions of, as to purpose of Study, 118-24; retirement of non-difficult, 136-38; dropping of cases, 142-44; termination of treatment of, 144; summary of disposition of all cases, 152; judgment of treatment by, 155-73; delinquency judgments made, 182-86; opinions of, as to causes of delinquency, 243-52; sample used in testing the validity of predictions, 274; sample used in evaluation of character development during treatment, 293-94; sample used in clinical evaluation, 346; behavior disorders of, at beginning of treatment, 347-56; degree of maladjustment in, 348-54; delinquent tendencies in, 354-56; *see also* Evaluation; "Most delinquent" boys; Treated-control comparisons

Treated-Control (T-C) comparisons, predictive ratings, 78-79; age, 79-80; ratings on variables used in matching, 80-82; age at time of predictive ratings, 275; predictive ratings of sample used to test validity of predictions, 275; age at time of delinquency judgment, 278; predictive ratings and delinquency judgments, 279-80; teachers' predictions and delinquency judgments, 282-83; Haggerty-Olson-Wickman Behavior Rating Schedule scores and delinquency judgments, 288; number appearing before Crime Prevention Bureau, 324; frequency of appearance before Crime Prevention Bureau, 324; court appearances, 326, 328; number appearing and number of offenses charged against them, 327; index of offenses arranged in order of seriousness, 331-32; offenses arranged in seriousness categories, 333, 335; offenses arranged by seriousness index in step intervals of two points, 334; commitments to correctional institutions for juvenile offenders, 336; commitments to correctional institutions for older offenders, 336; terminal adjustment ratings, 414-16; age at terminal adjustment rating, 415; terminal adjustment ratings and predictive ratings, 418; relative adjustment ratings by value-of-service ratings, 453-55

Treatment, concept of, in Study, 4; as step in Study, 7; length of period of, 8, 321-22

Treatment boys, *see* Treated boys

Treatment program, nature of, 88-101; summary of boys to be treated (Ts), 88-92; the staff, 92-93; policy and functions of, 93-101; friendly relationship in, 93-96; problem of offering unsolicited help in, 96-98; problem of group work in, 98-99; problem of environmental changes in, 98-99; case load of counselors, 99; frequency of contact of boy and counselor, 99-100; problem of financial aid, 100-1; problem of foster-home placement in, 101; relation of, to work of other agencies, 101; planning of, 111; problem of diagnosis in, 112-14; aims of counselors in, 114-15; treatment emphasis of counselors, 115-16; specific areas of help in, 116-18; recreational facilities provided, 129-30; medical and psychiatric services provided, 131; tutorial services provided, 132-34; supervision of counselors provided, 136; intensive work with fewer cases during war, 144-45; summary of, 152-54; boys' judgments of, 155-73; duration of, 321-22; possible harmful effects of, 509-18; inadequacy of friendly relationship in, 553-55; appropriateness to needs of boys as important factor in, 555-72, 582-83; *see also* Counseling; Counselors

Truancy of delinquents and non-delinquents, 264-65

Tuohy, Edward L., 131

Turner, William D., 145, 146, 295, 298

Tutorial services provided, 132-34

TZF and TZV (delinquency-proneness), as variables in matching, 68, 81

Unsolicited aid, ix, 96-98, 102-10; validity of principle of, 579-81, 582

U.S. Children's Bureau, 17, 25

Use of leisure time, boys' opinions of, as related to delinquency, 245-46

Value of service to individuals, *see under* Evaluation

Van Voorhis, Walter R., 281

Variables in matching, selection of, 63-65; starred (most important), 65-67; the twenty used, 67-69; ratios and patterns as, 70-71; plotting values of, 71-72, 73;

PATTERSON SMITH REPRINT SERIES IN
CRIMINOLOGY, LAW ENFORCEMENT, AND SOCIAL PROBLEMS

* new material added

PATTERSON SMITH REPRINT SERIES IN
CRIMINOLOGY, LAW ENFORCEMENT, AND SOCIAL PROBLEMS

* new material added   † new edition, revised or enlarged